NTC's
Dictionary
of
AMERICAN
ENGLISH
PHRASES

NTC's
Dictionary
of
AMERICAN
ENGLISH
PHRASES

Richard A. Spears, Ph.D.

Printed on recyclable paper

NTC *Publishing Group*
Lincolnwood, Illinois USA

CONTENTS

TO THE USER

The English language draws on a large set of core phrases that are used frequently in daily conversation and writing. These phrases include idioms, clichés, phrasal verbs, proverbs, greetings, and good-byes. This dictionary is a collection of the frequently used phrases in American English. It contains more than 15,000 complete sentence examples for approximately 7,000 common and useful phrases.

How to Use This Dictionary

1. First, try looking up the complete phrase that you are seeking in the dictionary. Each expression is alphabetized under the first word of the phrase. For example, **everything from soup to nuts** will be found in the section dealing with the letter "e." Entry phrases are never inverted or reordered like **from soup to nuts, everything** or **soup to nuts, everything from**. Initial articles — *a, an, the* — are not part of the entry except in the case of proverbs or other complete sentences, where the article never varies. In the entry heads, the words *someone* and *one* stand for persons, and *something* stands for things.

2. If you do not find the phrase you want, or if you cannot decide exactly what the phrase is, look up any major word in the phrase in the **Phrase-Finder Index**, which begins on page 462. There you will find all the phrases that contain the key word you have looked up. Pick out the phrase you want and find it in the dictionary.

3. An entry head may have one or more alternate forms. The entry head and its alternates are printed in **boldface type**, and the alternate forms are preceded by "AND." Two or more alternate forms are separated by a semicolon. For example:

> **as I see it** AND **in my opinion; in my view** the way I think about it. □ TOM: *This matter is not the same as some would make it out to be.* ALICE: *Yes. This whole affair has been overblown, as I see it.* □ BOB: *You're as*

wrong as can be. JOHN: *In my view, you are wrong.*

4. Many of the entry phrases have more than one major sense or meaning. These senses or meanings are numbered with boldface numerals. For example:

> **get over someone or something 1.** to move or climb over someone or something. □ *Fred was slumped ahead of me in the trench. I managed to get over him and moved on toward the big gun at the other end.* □ *I couldn't get over the huge rock in the path, so I went around it.* **2.** to recover from difficulties regarding someone or something. □ *I almost never got over the shock.* □ *Sharon finally got over Tom. He had been such a pest.* **3.** [with *something*] to recover from a disease. □ *It took a long time to get over the flu.* □ *I thought I would never get over the mumps.*

5. Individual numbered senses may have additional forms that appear in boldface type, in which case the AND and the additional form(s) follow the numeral. For example:

> **hold someone or something off 1.** to make someone or something wait. □ *I know a lot of people are waiting to see me. Hold them off for a while longer.* ⊤ *See what you can do to hold off the reporters.* **2.** AND **keep someone or something off** to stave someone or something off. □ *Tom was trying to rob us, but we managed to hold him off.* ⊤ *We held off the attackers.* ⊤ *I couldn't keep off the reporters any longer.*

6. The boldface entry head (together with any alternate forms) is followed by a definition or explanation. Alternate definitions are separated by a semicolon (;). These additional definitions are usually given to show slight differences in meaning or interpretation. For example:

> **jump to conclusions** to move too quickly to a conclusion; to form a

conclusion from too little evidence. □ *Please don't jump to any conclusions because of what you have seen.* □ *There is no need to jump to conclusions!*

7. Some entries are followed by instructions to look up another phrase. For example:

> **scarcer than hens' teeth** See *(as) scarce as hens' teeth.*

8. A definition may be followed by comments in parentheses. These comments tell about some of the variations of the phrase, explain what it alludes to, give other useful information, or indicate cross-referencing. For example:

> **desert a sinking ship** AND **leave a sinking ship** to leave a place, a person, or a situation when things become difficult or unpleasant. (Rats are said to be the first to leave a ship that is sinking.) □ *I hate to be the one to desert a sinking ship, but I can't stand it around here anymore.* □ *There goes Tom. Wouldn't you know he'd leave a sinking ship rather than stay around and try to help?*

9. Some definitions are preceded by additional information in square brackets. This makes the definition clearer by supplying information about the typical grammatical context in which the phrase is found. For example:

> **serve someone right** [for an act or event] to punish someone fairly (for doing something). □ *John copied off my test paper. It would serve him right if he fails the test.* □ *It'd serve John right if he got arrested.*

10. Sometimes the numbered senses refer only to people or things, but not both, even though the entry head indicates both *someone or something*. In such cases, the numeral is followed by "[with *someone*]" or "[with *something*]." For example:

> **burn someone or something out 1.** [with *someone*] to wear someone

out; to make someone ineffective through overuse. (*Someone* includes *oneself*.) □ *Facing all these problems at once will burn Tom out.* ⊤ *The continuous problems burned out the office staff in a few months.* □ *She burned herself out as a volunteer in the state prison.* **2.** [with *something*] to burn away the inside of something, getting rid of excess deposits. □ *The mechanic burned the carbon out of the manifold.* ⊤ *He burned out the carbon.* **3.** [with *something*] to wear out an electrical or electronic device through overuse. (More at *burn (itself) out.*) □ *Turn it off. You're going to burn it out!* ⊤ *He burned out the motor.*

11. Examples are introduced by a □ or a ⊤ and are in *italic type*. The ⊤ introduces an example containing two elements that have been transposed, such as a particle and the object of a verb. This is typically found with phrasal verbs. For example:

> **grade someone or something down**
> to lower the ranking, rating, or score on someone or something. □ *I had to grade you down because your paper was late.* ⊤ *I graded down the paper because it was late.*

12. *Slanted type* is used to show that a phrase being cited occurs as an entry head. For example: (See *jump to conclusions.*)

13. Some entry heads stand for two or more expressions. Parentheses are used to show which parts of the phrase that may not always be used. For example: **(as) flat as a pancake** stands for **as flat as a pancake** and **flat as a pancake**.

TERMS AND SYMBOLS

□   (a box) marks the beginning of an example.

Ⓣ   (a box containing a "T") marks the beginning of an example in which two elements of the phrase, usually a particle and an object, are transposed.

AND   indicates that an *entry head* has variant forms that are the same or similar in meaning as the *entry head*.

compare to   means to consult the *entry head* indicated and try to determine the degree to which it differs from the *entry block* in which the *compare to* instruction is found.

entry block   is the body of an entry starting with a boldface word or phrase and running to the next boldface word or phrase. *Entry blocks* are separated by white space.

entry head   is the first phrase or word, in boldface type, of an *entry block;* the phrase or word that the definition explains.

more at   means to consult the indicated *entry head* for syntactic variants of the *entry head* beginning the *entry block* containing the *more at* instruction.

see   means to turn to the *entry head* indicated.

see also   means to consult the *entry head* indicated for additional information or to find expressions similar in form or meaning to the *entry head* containing the *see also* instruction.

NTC's
Dictionary
of
AMERICAN
ENGLISH
PHRASES

A

A bird in the hand is worth two in the bush. Something you already have is better than something you might get. (Proverb.) □ *Bill has offered to buy my car for $3,000. Someone else might pay more, but Bill made a good offer, and a bird in the hand is worth two in the bush.* □ *I might be able to find a better offer, but a bird in the hand is worth two in the bush.*

a chip off the old block a person (usually a male) who behaves in the same way as or resembles his father. (The father is the *old block*.) □ *John looks like his father—a real chip off the old block.* □ *Bill Jones, Jr., is a chip off the old block. He's a banker just like his father.*

A fool and his money are soon parted. A person who acts unwisely with money soon loses it. (Proverb. Often said about a person who has just lost a sum of money because of poor judgment.) □ *When Bill lost a $400 bet on a horse race, Mary said, "A fool and his money are soon parted."* □ *When John bought a cheap used car that fell apart the next day, he said, "Oh, well, a fool and his money are soon parted."*

A friend in need is a friend indeed. A true friend is a person who will help you when you really need some help. (Proverb.) □ *When Bill helped me with geometry, I really learned the meaning of "A friend in need is a friend indeed."* □ *"A friend in need is a friend indeed" sounds silly until you need someone very badly.*

a little bird told me learned from a mysterious or secret source. (Often given as an evasive answer to someone who asks how you learned something. Rude in some circumstances.) □ *"All right," said Mary, "where did you get that information?" John replied, "A little bird told me."* □ *A little bird told me where I might find you.*

A little knowledge is a dangerous thing. Incomplete knowledge can embarrass or harm someone or something. (Proverb.) □ *The doctor said, "Even though you've had a course in first aid, you shouldn't have treated your own illness. A little knowledge is a dangerous thing."* □ *John thought he knew how to take care of the garden, but he killed all the flowers. A little knowledge is a dangerous thing.*

A penny saved is a penny earned. Money saved through thrift is the same as money earned by employment. (Proverb. Sometimes used to explain stinginess.) □ *"I didn't want to pay that much for the book," said Mary. "After all, a penny saved is a penny earned."* □ *Bob put his money in* *a new bank that pays more interest than his old bank, saying, "A penny saved is a penny earned."*

A rolling stone gathers no moss. an expression used to describe a person who keeps changing jobs or residences and, therefore, accumulates no possessions or responsibilities. (Proverb. Usually meant as a criticism but could also be praise.) □ *"John just can't seem to stay in one place," said Sally. "Oh, well, a rolling stone gathers no moss."* □ *Bill has no furniture to bother with because he keeps on the move. He keeps saying that a rolling stone gathers no moss.*

a stone's throw away a short distance; a relatively short distance. (May refer to distances in feet or miles.) □ *John saw Mary across the street, just a stone's throw away.* □ *Philadelphia is just a stone's throw away from New York City.*

A watched pot never boils. Concentration on a problem will not help solve it. (Proverb. Refers to the seemingly long time it takes water to boil when you are waiting for it. Said about a problem that a person is watching very closely.) □ *John was looking out the window, waiting eagerly for the mail to be delivered. Ann said, "Be patient. A watched pot never boils."* □ *Billy weighed himself four times a day while he was trying to lose weight. His mother said, "Relax. A watched pot never boils."*

Absolutely not! a strong denial or refusal. (Similar to *Definitely not!*) □ BOB: *Will you please slip this bottle into your pocket?* BILL: *Absolutely not!* □ BOB: *Can I please have the car again tonight?* FATHER: *Absolutely not! You can't have the car every night!*

according to Hoyle according to the rules; in keeping with the way it is normally done. (Refers to the rules for playing games. Edmond Hoyle wrote a book about games. This expression is usually used for something other than games.) □ *That's wrong. According to Hoyle, this is the way to do it.* □ *The carpenter said, "This is the way to drive a nail, according to Hoyle."*

ace in (to something) to happen onto something good; to manage to get into something. (Slang.) □ *I hope I can ace into the afternoon physics class.* □ *I don't know how I aced in. I guess I was just lucky.*

ace out to be fortunate or lucky. (Slang. More at *ace someone out.*) □ *I really aced out on that test in English.* □ *Freddy aced out at the dentist's office with only one cavity.*

ace someone out to outmaneuver someone; to win out over someone. (Slang. More at *ace out.*) □ *I plan to ace you out in the first lap.* T *Martha aced out Rebecca to win the first-place trophy.*

act high-and-mighty to act proud and powerful; to act haughty. □ *Why does the doctor always have to act so high-and-mighty?* □ *If Sally wouldn't act so high-and-mighty, she'd have more friends.*

act of God an occurrence (usually an accident) for which no human is responsible; an act of nature such as a storm, an earthquake, or a windstorm. □ *My insurance company wouldn't pay for the damage because it was an act of God.* □ *The thief tried to convince the judge that the diamonds were in his pocket due to an act of God.*

act one's age to behave more maturely; to act as grown-up as one really is. (This is frequently said to a child or a teenager.) □ *Come on, John, act your age. Stop throwing rocks.* □ *Mary! Stop picking on your little brother. Act your age!*

act something out 1. to perform in real life a role that one has imagined in a fantasy. □ *When I was onstage, I was really acting an old fantasy out.* T *Todd acted out his dreams.* **2.** to convert one's bad feelings into action rather than words. □ *Don't act your aggressions out on me!* T *Don't act out your aggressions on me!* **3.** to demonstrate or communicate something through action rather than words. T *Act out your request, if you can't say it.* □ *Fred, who had lost his voice, had to act his requests out.*

act up [for a thing or a person] to behave badly. □ *This car is acting up again.* □ *Andy, stop acting up!*

act (up)on something 1. to take action on a particular problem. (*Upon* is formal and less commonly used than *on*.) □ *You should act upon this problem at once.* □ *I will act on this immediately.* **2.** to take action because of some special information. □ *The police refused to act upon the information they were given.* □ *They will act on your suggestion today.*

Act your age! Behave more maturely! (A rebuke for someone who is acting childish. Often said to a child who is acting like an even younger child.) □ *Johnny was squirming around and pinching his sister. His mother finally said, "Johnny, act your age!"* □ CHILD: *Aw, come on! Let me see your book!* MARY: *Be quiet and act your age. Don't be such a baby.*

Actions speak louder than words. It is better to do something about a problem than just talk about it. (Proverb.) □ *Mary kept promising to get a job. John finally looked her in the eye and said, "Actions speak louder than words!"* □ *After listening to the senator promising to cut federal spending, Ann wrote a simple note saying, "Actions speak louder than words."*

add fuel to the fire AND **add fuel to the flame** to make a problem worse; to say or do something that makes a bad situation worse; to make an angry person get even more angry. □ *To spank a crying child just adds fuel to the fire.* □ *Bill was shouting angrily, and Bob tried to get him to stop by laughing at him. Of course, that was just adding fuel to the flame.*

add fuel to the flame See the previous entry.

add insult to injury to make a bad situation worse; to hurt the feelings of a person who has already been hurt. □ *First, the basement flooded, and then, to add insult to injury, a pipe burst in the kitchen.* □ *My car barely started this morning, and to add insult to injury, I got a flat tire in the driveway.*

admit something into something to allow something to be introduced into something else. □ *You cannot admit this document into the body of evidence.* □ *The attorney admitted questionable evidence into the record.*

advance (up)on someone or something to move toward someone or something. (Typically in military maneuvers or in team sports, for example in American football. *Upon* is formal and less commonly used than *on*.) □ *The troops advanced on the opposing army.* □ *They advanced upon the town.*

advise someone against someone or something to give someone advice about something or about choosing someone for some purpose. □ *I must advise you against trying that again.* □ *I advised them against Wally.*

afraid of one's own shadow easily frightened; always frightened, timid, or suspicious. (Never used literally.) □ *After Tom was robbed, he was even afraid of his own shadow.* □ *Jane has always been a shy child. She has been afraid of her own shadow since she was three.*

After while(, crocodile). Good-bye till later.; *See you later.* (The word *crocodile* is used only for the sake of the rhyme. It is the response to *See you later, alligator.*) □ MARY: *See you later.* BILL: *After while, crocodile.* □ JANE: *After while.* MARY: *Toodle-oo.*

After you. a polite way of encouraging someone to go ahead of oneself; a polite way of indicating that someone else should or can go first. □ *Bob stepped back and made a motion with his hand indicating that Mary should go first. "After you," smiled Bob.* □ BOB: *It's time to get in the food line. Who's going to go first?* BILL: *After you.* BOB: *Thanks.*

Again(, please). Say it one more time, please. □ *The play director said, "Again, please. And speak more clearly this time."* □ TOM: *I need some money. I'll pay you back.* BILL (pretending not to hear): *Again, please.* TOM: *I said I need some money. How many times do I have to say it?*

against the clock in a race with time; in a great hurry to get something done before a particular time. □ *Bill set a new track record, running against the clock. He lost the actual race, however.* □ *In a race against the clock, they rushed the special medicine to the hospital.*

Age before beauty. a comical and slightly rude way of encouraging someone to go ahead of oneself; a comical, teasing, and slightly grudging way of indicating that someone else should or can go first. □ *As they approached the door, Bob laughed and said to Bill, "Age before beauty."* □ *"No, no. Please, you take the next available seat," smiled Tom. "Age before beauty, you know."*

agree to something to consent to something; to allow something to be done; to approve something. □ *I wish you would agree to my request.* □ *I will not agree to it.*

agree (up)on someone or something to agree to the choice of someone or something. □ *Couldn't we just agree on John rather than going over the whole list of candidates?* □ *Let's try to agree upon a date.*

agree with someone (about someone or something) AND **agree with someone (on someone or something)** to hold the same opinion as someone else about someone or something; to be of the same mind as someone else about someone or something. □ *I agree with you on that point.* □ *We do not agree with you about Tom.*

agree with someone (on someone or something) See the previous entry.

agree with someone or something 1.
[with *someone*] [for something] to be
acceptable to someone as food. (Idiomatic. Usually negative.) ☐ *Onions
do not agree with me.* ☐ *Some foods do
not agree with people.* **2.** [with *something*] [for something] to look good or
go well with something else. ☐ *This
dress does not agree with these shoes,
does it?* ☐ *Your dress agrees with your
bag.* **3.** [with *something*] [for something] to be in accord with something
else. ☐ *The texture of the flooring agrees
with the straight lines of the wall covering.* ☐ *Your analysis agrees with mine.*

aim something at someone or something to point or direct something at
someone or something. ☐ *Wally
aimed the hose at Sarah.* ☐ *He aimed
the hose at the base of the bush.*

air someone's dirty linen in public to
discuss private or embarrassing matters in public, especially when quarreling. (This *linen* refers to problems
as if they were sheets and tablecloths
or other soiled cloth.) ☐ *John's
mother had asked him repeatedly not to
air the family's dirty linen in public.* ☐
*Mr. and Mrs. Johnson are arguing
again. Why must they always air their
dirty linen in public?*

air something out to allow fresh air
to freshen something, such as clothing, a stale-smelling room, etc. ☐
Should I air my jacket out? ⊤ *Please
air out your woolen jacket.*

all in a day's work part of what is
expected; typical or normal. ☐ *I
don't particularly like to cook, but it's
all in a day's work.* ☐ *Putting up with
rude customers isn't pleasant, but it's all
in a day's work.* ☐ *Cleaning up after
other people is all in a day's work for a
chambermaid.*

all in all AND **all things considered;
on balance** a transition indicating a
summary, a generalization, or the announcement of a conclusion. ☐
BILL: *All in all, this was a fine evening.*
ALICE: *I think so too.* ☐ *"Our time at
the conference was well spent, all in
all,"* thought Fred. ☐ BILL: *How did it
go?* ALICE: *On balance, it went quite
well.* ☐ BOB: *Did the play turn a
profit?* FRED: *I suppose that we made a
nice profit, all things considered.*

all over but the shouting decided
and concluded; finished except for a
celebration. (An elaboration of *all
over,* which means "finished.") ☐
*The last goal was made just as the final
whistle sounded. Tom said, "Well, it's
all over but the shouting."* ☐ *Tom
worked hard in college and graduated
last month. When he got his diploma, he
said, "It's all over but the shouting."*

All right. 1. an indication of
agreement or acquiescence. (Often
pronounced "aright" in familiar conversation.) ☐ FATHER: *Do it now, before you forget.* BILL: *All right.* ☐
TOM: *Please remember to bring me
back a pizza.* SALLY: *All right, but I get
some of it.* **2.** a shout of agreement or
encouragement. (Usually **All right!**)
☐ ALICE: *Come on, let's give Sally
some encouragement.* FRED: *All right,
Sally! Keep it up! You can do it!* ☐
"That's the way to go! All right!"
shouted various members of the audience.

All right(y) already! an impatient
way of indicating agreement or
acquiescence. (The second version is
more comical than rude. Dated but
still used.) ☐ ALICE: *All right
already! Stop pushing me!* MARY: *I
didn't do anything!* ☐ BILL: *Come on!*

Get over here! BOB: *All righty already! Don't rush me!*

All roads lead to Rome. There are many different routes to the same goal. (Proverb.) □ *Mary was criticizing the way Jane was planting the flowers. John said, "Never mind, Mary. All roads lead to Rome."* □ *Some people learn by doing. Others have to be taught. In the long run, all roads lead to Rome.*

all skin and bones See *nothing but skin and bones.*

All systems are go. an indication that everything is ready or that things are going along as planned. (Borrowed from the jargon used during America's early space exploration.) □ BILL: *Can we leave now? Is the car gassed up and ready?* TOM: *All systems are go. Let's get going.* □ SALLY: *Are you all rested up for the track meet?* MARY: *Yes. All systems are go.*

All that glitters is not gold. Many attractive and alluring things have no value. (Proverb.) □ *The used car looked fine but didn't run well at all. "Ah, yes," thought Bill, "all that glitters is not gold."* □ *When Mary was disappointed about losing Tom, Jane reminded her, "All that glitters is not gold."*

All the best to someone. See *Give my best to someone.*

All the more reason for doing something. AND **All the more reason to do something.** With even better reason or cause for doing something. (Can be included in a number of grammatical constructions.) □ BILL: *I don't do well in calculus because I don't like the stuff.* FATHER: *All the*

more reason for working harder at it. □ BOB: *I'm tired of painting this fence. It's so old it's rotting!* SALLY: *All the more reason to paint it.*

All the more reason to do something. See the previous entry.

all things considered See *all in all.*

all thumbs very awkward and clumsy, especially with one's hands. (Figurative. As if one's hands had only thumbs.) □ *Poor Bob can't play the piano at all. He's all thumbs.* □ *Mary is all thumbs when it comes to gardening.*

all walks of life all social, economic, and ethnic groups. (A fixed phrase. Does not occur in the singular or without *all.*) □ *We saw people there from all walks of life.* □ *The people who came to the art exhibit represented all walks of life.*

all wet completely wrong. (Slang.) □ *Wrong again! You're really all wet.* □ *If you think I'm going to take that kind of talk from you, you're all wet.*

All work and no play makes Jack a dull boy. One should have recreation as well as work. (Proverb. Jack does not refer to anyone in particular, and the phrase can be used for persons of either sex.) □ *Stop reading that book and go out and play! All work and no play makes Jack a dull boy.* □ *The doctor told Mr. Jones to stop working on weekends and start playing golf, because all work and no play makes Jack a dull boy.*

allow for someone or something to provide for someone or something. □ *Be sure to allow for a large number of sick people.* □ *Please allow for Liz also.*

Allow me. AND **Permit me.** a polite way of announcing that one is going to assist someone, unasked. (Typically said by a man assisting a woman by opening a door, lighting a cigarette, or providing support or aid in moving about. In *Allow me*, the stress is usually on *me*. In *Permit me*, the stress is usually on *mit*.) □ *Tom and Jane approached the door. "Allow me," said Tom, grabbing the doorknob.* □ *"Permit me," said Fred, pulling out a gold-plated lighter and lighting Jane's cigarette.*

allow someone or something in (something) to permit someone or something to enter something or some place. □ *Will they allow you in the restaurant without a tie?* □ *They won't allow your dog in the grocery store.*

All's well that ends well. An event that has a good ending is good even if some things went wrong along the way. (Proverb. This is the name of a play by Shakespeare. It is now used as a cliché.) □ *I'm glad you finally got here, even though your car had a flat tire on the way. Oh, well. All's well that ends well.* □ *The groom was late for the wedding, but everything worked out all right. All's well that ends well.*

Am I glad to see you! I am very glad to see you! (Not a question. There is a stress on *I* and another on *you*.) □ BILL: *Well, I finally got here!* JOHN: *Boy howdy! Am I glad to see you!* □ TOM (as Bill opens the door): *Here I am, Bill. What's wrong?* BILL: *Boy, am I glad to see you! Come on in. The hot water heater exploded.*

Am I right? Isn't that so?; Right? (A way of demanding a response and stimulating further conversation.) □

JOHN: *Now, this is the kind of thing we should be doing. Am I right?* SUE: *Well, sure. I guess.* □ FRED: *You don't want to do this for the rest of your life. Am I right?* BOB: *Yeah.* FRED: *You want to make something of yourself. Am I right?* BOB: *I suppose.*

amount to something 1. [for someone or something] to become worthwhile or valuable. □ *I hope Charles amounts to something some day.* □ *I doubt that this whole business will ever amount to a hill of beans.* **2.** [for something] to be the equivalent of something. □ *Why, this amounts to cheating!* □ *Your comments amount to treason.*

amount to the same thing (as something) to be the same (as something); to be the equivalent of something. □ *Whether it's red or blue, it amounts to the same thing.* □ *It all amounts to the same thing.*

An eye for an eye, a tooth for a tooth. The punishment should equal the offense. (Now used as a proverb. Biblical. Not literal.) □ *Little John pulled Jane's hair, so the teacher pulled John's hair as punishment, saying, "An eye for an eye, a tooth for a tooth."* □ *He kicked me in the leg, so I kicked him in the leg. After all, an eye for an eye, a tooth for a tooth.*

An ounce of prevention is worth a pound of cure. It is easier and better to prevent something bad than to deal with the results. (Proverb.) □ *When you ride in a car, you should buckle your seat belt. An ounce of prevention is worth a pound of cure.* □ *Every child should be vaccinated against polio. An ounce of prevention is worth a pound of cure.*

And how! an enthusiastic indication of agreement. □ MARY: *Wasn't that a great game? Didn't you like it?* SALLY: *And how!* □ BOB: *Hey, man! Don't you just love this pizza?* TOM: *And how!*

And you? AND **Yourself?** a way of redirecting a previously asked question to the asker or someone else. □ BILL: *Do you want some more cake?* MARY: *Yes, thanks. Yourself?* BILL: *I've had enough.* □ JANE: *Are you enjoying yourself?* BILL: *Oh, yes, and you?*

answer for someone [for someone] to speak for someone else. □ *I can't answer for Chuck, but I do have my own opinion.* □ *I will answer for him.*

Any friend of someone('s) (is a friend of mine). I am pleased to meet a friend of someone. (A response when meeting or being introduced to a friend of a friend.) □ FRED: *Well, nice to meet you Tom. Any friend of my brother is a friend of mine.* TOM: *Thanks, Fred. Nice to meet you too.* □ JOHN: *Thank you so much for helping me.* SALLY: *You're welcome. Any friend of Sue's.*

Anybody I know? See *Anyone I know?*

anyhow See *anyway.*

Anyone I know? AND **Anybody I know?** a coy way of asking *who?* □ SALLY: *Where were you last night?* JANE: *I had a date.* SALLY: *Anyone I know?* □ BILL: *I've got a date for the formal next month.* HENRY: *Anybody I know?*

Anything new down your way? Has any interesting event happened where you live? (Rural and familiar.) □ BILL: *Anything new down your way?* BOB: *Nothing worth talking about.* □ MARY: *Hi, Sally. Anything new down your way?* SALLY: *No, what's new with you?* MARY: *Nothing.*

Anything you say. Yes.; I agree. □ MARY: *Will you please take this over to the cleaners?* BILL: *Sure, anything you say.* □ SALLY: *You're going to finish this before you leave tonight, aren't you?* MARY: *Anything you say.*

Anytime. 1. an indication that one is available to be called upon, visited, or invited at any time in the future. □ MARY: *I'm so glad you invited me for tea.* JANE: *Anytime. Delighted to have you.* □ SALLY: *We really enjoyed our visit. Hope to see you again.* BILL: *Anytime. Please feel free to come back.* 2. a polite but casual way of saying *You're welcome.* □ MARY: *Thanks for driving me home.* BOB: *Anytime.* □ SALLY: *We were grateful for your help after the fire last week.* JANE: *Anytime.* 3. See also *Anytime you are ready.*

Anytime you are ready. an indication that the speaker is waiting for the person spoken to to make the appropriate move. □ MARY: *I think it's about time to go.* BILL: *Anytime you're ready.* □ DOCTOR: *Shall we begin the operation?* TOM: *Anytime you're ready.*

anyway AND **anyhow** in spite of all this; regardless. (Words such as this often use intonation to convey the connotation of the sentence that is to follow. The brief intonation pattern accompanying the word may indicate sarcasm, disagreement, caution, consolation, sternness, etc.) □ JOHN: *I just don't know what's going to happen.* MARY: *Things look very bleak.* JOHN: *Anyway, we'll all end up dead in the long run.* □ BOB: *Let's stop this silly argument.* FRED: *I agree. Anyhow, it's time to go home, so none of this* *argument really matters, does it?* BOB: *Not a bit.*

appear before someone 1. to show up in the presence of someone, suddenly. □ *The butler appeared before us with no sound or other warning.* □ *A frightful spector appeared before me.* **2.** to stand up in front of a particular judge in court. □ *You have to appear before Judge Cahill tomorrow.* □ *Have you ever appeared before him?*

apple of someone's eye someone's favorite person or thing; a boyfriend or a girlfriend; a person or a thing that someone wants. (A person or a thing that has caught someone's eye or attracted someone's attention.) □ *Tom is the apple of Mary's eye. She thinks he's great.* □ *John's new stereo is the apple of his eye.*

apply something to something 1. to put something onto something. □ *Apply the decal to the surface of the glass.* □ *A decal has been applied to the glass.* **2.** to use something, such as force, effort, etc., on something or in the performance of some task. □ *Apply more effort to the job.* □ *An even greater effort has been applied to the task.*

appoint someone to something to select or assign someone to serve in a particular role. (Usually focusing on the role of the person or on a group of persons with similar roles. *Someone* includes *oneself*.) □ *I am going to appoint you to the position of treasurer.* □ *Fred appointed himself to the board of directors, but was sued for doing it.*

arch over someone or something to bend or curve over someone or something; to stand or remain bent or curved over someone or some-

thing. □ *The trees arched gracefully over the walkway.* □ *A lovely bower of roses arched over the bride.*

(Are) things getting you down? Are things bothering you? □ JANE: *Gee, Mary, you look sad. Are things getting you down?* MARY: *Yeah.* JANE: *Cheer up!* MARY: *Sure.* □ TOM: *What's the matter, Bob? Things getting you down?* BOB: *No, I'm just a little tired.*

(Are you) doing okay? AND **You doing okay? 1.** How are you? □ MARY: *Doing okay?* BILL: *You bet! How are you?* □ BILL: *Hey, man! Are you doing okay?* TOM: *Sure thing! And you?* **2.** How are you surviving this situation or ordeal? □ MARY: *You doing okay?* BILL: *Sure. What about you?* MARY: *I'm cool.* □ TOM: *Wow, that was some gust of wind! Are you doing okay?* MARY: *I'm still a little frightened, but alive.*

(Are you) feeling okay? Do you feel well? (More than a greeting inquiry.) □ TOM: *Are you feeling okay?* BILL: *Oh, fair to middling.* □ MARY: *Are you feeling okay?* SUE: *I'm still a little dizzy, but it will pass.*

(Are you) going my way? If you are traveling in the direction of my destination, could I please go with you or can I have a ride in your car? □ MARY: *Are you going my way?* SALLY: *Sure. Get in.* □ *"Going my way?" said Tom as he saw Mary get into her car.*

(Are you) leaving so soon? AND **You leaving so soon?** a polite inquiry made to a guest who has announced a departure. (Appropriate only for the first few guests to leave. It would seem sarcastic to say this to the last guest to leave or one who is leaving very late at night.) □ SUE: *We really* must go. SALLY: *Leaving so soon?* SUE: *Fred has to catch a plane at five in the morning.* □ JOHN (seeing Tom at the door): *You leaving so soon?* TOM: *Yes, thanks for inviting me. I really have to go.* JOHN: *Well, good night, then.*

(Are you) ready for this? a way of presenting a piece of news or information that is expected to excite or surprise the person spoken to. □ TOM: *Boy, do I have something to tell you! Are you ready for this?* MARY: *Sure. Let me have it!* □ TOM: *Now, here's a great joke! Are you ready for this? It is so funny!* ALICE: *I can hardly wait.*

(Are you) ready to order? Would you care to tell me what you want to order to eat? (A standard phrase used in eating establishments to find out what one wants to eat.) □ *The waitress came over and asked, "Are you ready to order?"* □ TOM: *I know what I want. What about you, Sally? Are you ready to order?* SALLY: *Don't rush me!*

(Are you) sorry you asked? Now that you have heard (the unpleasant answer), do you regret having asked the question? (Compare to *You'll be sorry you asked.*) □ FATHER: *How are you doing in school?* BILL: *I'm flunking out. Sorry you asked?* □ MOTHER: *You've been looking a little down lately. Is there anything wrong?* BILL: *I probably have mono. Are you sorry you asked?*

argue against someone or something 1. [for someone] to make a case against someone or something; to oppose the choice of someone or something in an argument. □ *I am preparing myself to argue against the case.* □ *Liz argued against Tom, but*

we chose him anyway. **2.** [for something, such as facts] to support a case against someone or something in an argument; [for something, such as facts] to support a case against the choice of someone or something in an argument. □ *I have uncovered something that argues against continuing this discussion.* □ *His own remarks argue against the candidate, but he probably will be elected anyway.*

argue one's way out (of something) to talk and argue oneself free of a problem. □ *You can't argue your way out of this!* □ *It's a problem, and there is no way that you can argue your way out.*

argue someone or something down 1. [with *someone*] to defeat someone in a debate. □ *Sally could always argue him down if she had to.* ⊤ *She tries to argue down everyone she meets.* **2.** [with *something*] to defeat a proposal or a motion in a meeting through discussion. □ *I am prepared to argue the proposal down in court.* ⊤ *She will argue down the proposal in the council meeting.* **3.** [with *something*] to reduce something, such as a bill or a price, by arguing. □ *I tried to argue the price down, but it did no good.* ⊤ *Tom could not argue down the bill.*

arise from something AND **arise out of something 1.** to get up from something. □ *What time did you arise from bed?* □ *I arose out of bed at dawn.* **2.** to result from something; to be caused by something. □ *This whole problem arose from your stubbornness.* □ *The problem arose out of mismanagement.*

arise out of something See the previous entry.

arm in arm a phrase used to describe people linked or hooked together by the arms. □ *The two lovers walked arm in arm down the street.* □ *Arm in arm, the line of dancers kicked high, and the audience roared its approval.*

armed to the teeth heavily armed with deadly weapons. (As if all types of armaments were used, up to and including the teeth.) □ *The bank robber was armed to the teeth when he was caught.* □ *There are too many guns around. The entire country is armed to the teeth.*

arouse someone from something to activate a person out of a state of rest, sleep, or inaction. (*Someone* includes *oneself*.) □ *I could not arouse her from her sleep.* □ *She aroused herself from a deep sleep.*

arrange something with someone or something to prepare or plan something that will include someone or something. □ *I will arrange a fancy dinner with wine and cloth napkins.* □ *Paul arranged a meeting with his boss.*

arrive at something 1. to reach a place. □ *When will we arrive at the resort?* □ *We will arrive at home soon.* **2.** to reach a conclusion; to make a decision. □ *Have you arrived at a decision yet?* □ *We will arrive at an answer tomorrow.*

arrive (up)on the scene (of something) to reach the location of an event in progress. (*Upon* is formal and less commonly used than *on*.) □ *The police arrived on the scene of the crime.* □ *What did they do when they arrived upon the scene?*

as a duck takes to water easily and naturally. (Refers to baby ducks, who seem to be able to swim the first time they enter the water.) □ *She took to singing, just as a duck takes to water.* □ *The baby adapted to bottle-feeding as a duck takes to water.*

as an aside as a comment; as a comment that is not supposed to be heard by everyone. □ *At the wedding, Tom said as an aside, "The bride doesn't look well."* □ *At the ballet, Billy said as an aside to his mother, "I hope the dancers fall off the stage!"*

as bad as all that as bad as reported; as bad as it seems. (Usually expressed in the negative.) □ *Come on! Nothing could be as bad as all that.* □ *Stop crying. It can't be as bad as all that.*

(as) blind as a bat with imperfect sight; blind. (Bats, however, are typically not blind. Survives because of the alliteration.) □ *My grandmother is as blind as a bat.* □ *I'm getting blind as a bat. I can hardly read this page.*

(as) busy as a beaver AND **(as) busy as a bee** very busy. (This survives because of the alliteration.) □ *I don't have time to talk to you. I'm as busy as a beaver.* □ *You don't look busy as a beaver to me.* □ *Whenever there is a holiday, we are all as busy as bees.*

(as) busy as a bee See the previous entry.

(as) busy as Grand Central Station very busy; crowded with customers or other people. (This refers to Grand Central Station in New York City.) □ *This house is as busy as Grand Central Station.* □ *When the tourist season starts, this store is busy as Grand Central Station.*

(as) clear as mud not understandable. (Informal or joking.) □ *Your* *explanation is as clear as mud.* □ *This doesn't make sense. It's clear as mud.*

(as) comfortable as an old shoe very comfortable; very comforting and familiar. (Refers to a shoe that has been worn awhile and is comfortable.) □ *This old house is fine. It's as comfortable as an old shoe.* □ *That's a great tradition — comfortable as an old shoe.*

(as) cool as a cucumber calm and not agitated; with one's wits about one. (Cucumbers are not necessarily cool, however. Survives because of the alliteration.) □ *The captain remained as cool as a cucumber as the passengers boarded the lifeboats.* □ *During the fire the homeowner was cool as a cucumber.*

(as) crazy as a loon very silly; completely insane. (A *loon* is a waterfowl whose call sounds like a silly laugh.) □ *If you think you can get away with that, you're as crazy as a loon.* □ *Poor old John is crazy as a loon.*

(as) dead as a dodo dead; no longer in existence. (The *dodo* — an ancient bird of Mauritius — is extinct. The phrase survives because of the alliteration.) □ *Yes, Adolf Hitler is really dead — as dead as a dodo.* □ *That silly old idea is dead as a dodo.*

(as) dead as a doornail dead. (Of course, doornails were never alive. Survives because of the alliteration.) □ *This fish is as dead as a doornail.* □ *John kept twisting the chicken's neck even though it was dead as a doornail.*

as different as night and day completely different. □ *Although Bobby and Billy are twins, they are as different as night and day.* □ *Birds and bats appear to be similar, but they are different as night and day.*

(as) easy as (apple) pie very easy. (Making pies is assumed to be easy.) □ *Mountain climbing is as easy as pie.* □ *Making a simple dress out of cotton cloth is easy as pie.*

(as) easy as duck soup very easy; requiring no effort. (When a duck is cooked, it releases a lot of fat and juices, making a soup without effort.) □ *Finding your way to the shopping center is easy as duck soup.* □ *Getting Bob to eat fried chicken is as easy as duck soup.*

(as) far as I know AND **to the best of my knowledge** a signal of basic but not well-informed agreement. (Indicates that the speaker's knowledge may not be adequate.) □ TOM: *Is this brand of computer any good?* CLERK: *This is the very best one there is as far as I know.* □ FRED: *Are the trains on time?* CLERK: *To the best of my knowledge, all the trains are on time today.* □ BILL: *Are we just about there?* TOM: *Far as I know.* BILL: *I thought you'd been there before.* TOM: *Never.*

(as) far as I'm concerned 1. *from my point of view;* as it concerns my interests. □ BOB: *Isn't this cake good?* ALICE: *Yes, indeed. This is the best cake I have ever eaten as far as I'm concerned.* □ TOM: *I think I'd better go.* BOB: *As far as I'm concerned, you all can leave now.* **2.** *Okay,* as it concerns my interests. □ ALICE: *Can I send this package on to your sister?* JOHN: *As far as I'm concerned.* □ JANE: *Do you mind if I put this coat in the closet?* JOHN: *Far as I'm concerned. It's not mine.*

as far as it goes as much as something does, covers, or accomplishes. (Usually said of something that is inadequate.) □ *Your plan is fine as far as it goes. It doesn't seem to take care of everything, though.* □ *As far as it goes, this law is a good one. It should require stiffer penalties, however.*

(as) fit as a fiddle healthy and physically fit. (This survives because of the alliteration.) □ *Mary is as fit as a fiddle.* □ *Tom used to be fit as a fiddle. Look at him now!*

(as) flat as a pancake very flat. □ *The punctured tire was as flat as a pancake.* □ *Bobby squashed the ant flat as a pancake.*

(as) free as a bird carefree; completely free. □ *Jane is always happy and free as a bird.* □ *The convict escaped from jail and was as free as a bird for two days.* □ *In the summer I feel free as a bird.*

(as) full as a tick AND **(as) tight as a tick** very full of food or drink. (Refers to a tick that has filled itself full of blood.) □ *Little Billy ate and ate until he was as full as a tick.* □ *Our cat drank the cream until he became full as a tick.*

(as) funny as a crutch not funny at all. □ *Your trick is about as funny as a crutch. Nobody thought it was funny.* □ *The well-dressed lady slipped and fell in the gutter, which was funny as a crutch.*

(as) good as done the same as being done; almost done. (Many different past participles can replace *done* in this phrase: *cooked, dead, finished, painted, typed,* etc.) □ *This job is as good as done. It'll just take another second.* □ *Yes, sir, if you hire me to paint your house, it's as good as painted.* □ *When I hand my secretary a letter to be typed, I know that it's as good as typed right then and there.*

(as) good as gold genuine; authentic. (This survives because of the alliteration.) □ *Mary's promise is as good as gold.* □ *Yes, this diamond is genuine — good as gold.*

(as) happy as a clam happy and content. (Note the variations in the examples. Clams are not necessarily happy or sad.) □ *Tom sat there smiling, as happy as a clam.* □ *There they all sat, eating corn on the cob and looking happy as clams.*

(as) happy as a lark visibly happy and cheerful. (Note the variations in the examples.) □ *Sally walked along whistling, as happy as a lark.* □ *The children danced and sang, happy as larks.*

(as) hard as nails very hard; cold and cruel. (Refers to the nails that are used with a hammer.) □ *The old loaf of bread was dried out and became as hard as nails.* □ *Ann was unpleasant and hard as nails.*

(as) high as a kite AND **(as) high as the sky** **1.** very high. □ *The tree grew as high as a kite.* □ *Our pet bird got outside and flew up high as the sky.* **2.** drunk or drugged. □ *Bill drank beer until he got as high as a kite.* □ *The thieves were high as the sky on drugs.*

(as) high as the sky See the previous entry.

(as) hungry as a bear very hungry. □ *I'm as hungry as a bear. I could eat anything!* □ *Whenever I jog, I get hungry as a bear.*

as I see it AND **in my opinion; in my view** the way I think about it.

□ TOM: *This matter is not as bad as some would make it out to be.* ALICE: *Yes. This whole affair has been overblown, as I see it.* □ BOB: *You're as wrong as can be.* JOHN: *In my view, you are wrong.*

as I was saying AND **like I was saying** to repeat what I've been saying; to continue with what I was saying. (The first form is appropriate in any conversation. The second form is colloquial, informal, and familiar. In addition, this use of *like* for *as*, as in the second form, is objected to by many people.) □ BILL: *Now, Mary, this is one of the round ones that attaches to the wire here.* BOB (passing through the room): *Hello, you two! Catch you later.* BILL: *Yeah, see you around. Now, as I was saying, this goes here on this wire.* □ TOM: *I hate to interrupt, but someone's car is being broken into down on the street.* FRED: *As I was saying, these illegal practices must stop.*

(as) innocent as a lamb guiltless; naive. □ *"Hey! You can't throw me in jail," cried the robber. "I'm innocent as a lamb."* □ *Look at the baby, as innocent as a lamb.*

as it is the way things are; the way it is now. □ *"I wish I could get a better job," remarked Tom. "I'm just getting by as it is."* □ MARY: *Can we afford a new refrigerator?* FRED: *As it is, it would have to be a very small one.*

as it were as one might say. (Sometimes used to qualify an assertion that may not sound reasonable.) □ *He carefully constructed, as it were, a huge sandwich.* □ *The Franklins live in a small, as it were, exquisite house.*

(as) light as a feather of little weight. □ *Sally dieted until she was as light as a feather.* □ *Of course I can lift the box. It's light as a feather.*

as likely as not probably; with an even chance either way. □ *He will as likely as not arrive without warning.* □ *Likely as not, the game will be cancelled.*

as luck would have it by good or bad luck; as it turned out; by chance. (A fixed phrase; there are no other forms.) □ *As luck would have it, we had a flat tire.* □ *As luck would have it, the check came in the mail today.*

(as) mad as a hatter 1. crazy. (From the character called the Mad Hatter in Lewis Carroll's *Alice's Adventures in Wonderland*.) □ *Poor old John is as mad as a hatter.* □ *All these screaming children are driving me mad as a hatter.* 2. angry. (This is a misunderstanding of *mad* in the first sense.) □ *You make me so angry! I'm as mad as a hatter.* □ *John can't control his temper. He's always mad as a hatter.*

(as) mad as a hornet angry. (Hornets are known to have terrible tempers.) □ *You make me so angry. I'm as mad as a hornet.* □ *Jane can get mad as a hornet when somebody criticizes her.*

(as) mad as a March hare crazy. (From the name of a character in Lewis Carroll's *Alice's Adventures in Wonderland*.) □ *Sally is getting as mad as a March hare.* □ *My Uncle Bill is mad as a March hare.*

(as) mad as a wet hen angry. (One can assume that a fussy hen would become angry if wet.) □ *Bob was screaming and shouting—as mad as a wet hen.* □ *What you said made Mary mad as a wet hen.*

as one as if a group were one person. (Especially with *act*, *move*, or *speak*.)

□ *All the dancers moved as one.* □ *The chorus spoke as one.*

(as) plain as day 1. very plain and simple. □ *Although his face was as plain as day, his smile made him look interesting and friendly.* □ *Our house is plain as day, but it's comfortable.* **2.** clear and understandable. (As transparent as daylight.) □ *The lecture was as plain as day. No one had to ask questions.* □ *His statement was plain as day.*

(as) plain as the nose on one's face obvious; clearly evident. □ *What do you mean you don't understand? It's as plain as the nose on your face.* □ *Your guilt is plain as the nose on your face.*

(as) poor as a church mouse very poor. (Assuming that those associated with churches are impoverished, the lowly mouse would be the poorest creature in a church.) □ *My aunt is as poor as a church mouse.* □ *The Browns are poor as church mice.*

(as) pretty as a picture very pretty. (This survives because of the alliteration.) □ *Sweet little Mary is as pretty as a picture.* □ *Their new house is pretty as a picture.*

(as) proud as a peacock very proud; haughty. (This refers to the beautiful tail feathers that the peacock displays. Survives because of the alliteration.) □ *John is so arrogant. He's as proud as a peacock.* □ *The new father was proud as a peacock.*

(as) quick as a wink very quickly. (This refers to the wink of an eye.) □ *As quick as a wink, the thief took the lady's purse.* □ *I'll finish this work quick as a wink.*

(as) quiet as a mouse very quiet; shy and silent. (Often used with children.) □ *Don't yell; whisper. Be as quiet as a mouse.* □ *Mary hardly ever says anything. She's quiet as a mouse.*

(as) regular as clockwork dependably regular. □ *She comes into this store every day, as regular as clockwork.* □ *Our tulips come up every year, regular as clockwork.*

(as) scarce as hens' teeth AND **scarcer than hens' teeth** very scarce or nonexistent. (Chickens don't have teeth.) □ *I've never seen one of those. They're as scarce as hens' teeth.* □ *I was told that the part needed for my car is scarcer than hens' teeth, and it would take a long time to find one.*

(as) sick as a dog very sick; sick and vomiting. (This refers to the agonized retching of a dog.) □ *We've never been so ill. The whole family was sick as dogs.* □ *Sally was as sick as a dog and couldn't go to the party.*

(as) slippery as an eel devious; undependable. □ *Tom can't be trusted. He's as slippery as an eel.* □ *It's hard to catch Joe in his office because he's slippery as an eel.*

(as) sly as a fox smart and clever. □ *My nephew is as sly as a fox.* □ *You have to be sly as a fox to outwit me.*

(as) snug as a bug in a rug cozy and snug. (The kind of thing said when putting a child to bed. This survives because of the rhyme.) □ *Let's pull up the covers. There you are, Bobby, as snug as a bug in a rug.* □ *What a lovely little house! I know I'll be snug as a bug in a rug.*

(as) sober as a judge 1. very formal, somber, or stuffy. □ *You certainly look gloomy, Bill. You're sober as a judge.* □ *Tom's as sober as a judge. I think he's angry.* **2.** not drunk; alert and completely sober. (This is a misunderstanding of the first sense.) □ *John's drunk? No, he's as sober as a judge.* □ *You should be sober as a judge when you drive a car.*

(as) soft as a baby's bottom very soft and smooth to the touch. □ *This cloth is as soft as a baby's bottom.* □ *No, Bob doesn't shave yet. His cheeks are soft as a baby's bottom.*

(as) soon as possible at the earliest time. □ *I'm leaving now. I'll be there as soon as possible.* □ *Please pay me soon as possible.*

(as) strong as an ox very strong. □ *Tom lifts weights and is as strong as an ox.* □ *Now that Ann has recovered from her illness, she's strong as an ox.*

(as) stubborn as a mule very stubborn. □ *My husband is as stubborn as a mule.* □ *Our cat is stubborn as a mule.*

as such authentic; in the way just mentioned; as one would expect. □ ALICE: *Did you have a good vacation?* JOHN: *Well, sort of. It wasn't a vacation, as such. We just went and visited Mary's parents.* ALICE: *That sounds nice.* JOHN: *Doesn't it.* □ ANDREW: *Someone said you bought a beach house.* HENRY: *Well, it's certainly not a beach house, as such. More like a duck blind, in fact.*

as the crow flies straight across the land, as opposed to distances measured on a road, river, etc. (This assumes that crows fly in a straight line.) □ *It's twenty miles to town on the highway, but only ten miles as the crow flies.* □ *Our house is only a few miles from the lake as the crow flies.*

(as) thick as pea soup very thick. (Usually used in reference to fog.) □ *This fog is as thick as pea soup.* □ *Wow, this coffee is strong! It's thick as pea soup.*

(as) thick as thieves very close-knit; friendly; allied. (This survives because of the alliteration.) □ *Mary, Tom, and Sally are as thick as thieves. They go everywhere together.* □ *Those two families are thick as thieves.*

(as) tight as a tick See *(as) full as a tick.*

(as) tight as Dick's hatband very tight. (Very old.) □ *I've got to lose some weight. My belt is as tight as Dick's hatband.* □ *This window is stuck tight as Dick's hatband.*

as we speak just now; at this very moment. (This has almost reached cliché status.) □ *"I'm sorry, sir,"* consoled the agent at the gate, *"the plane is taking off as we speak."* □ TOM: *Waiter, where is my steak? It's taking a long time.* WAITER: *It is being grilled as we speak, sir—just as you requested.*

(as) weak as a kitten weak; weak and sickly. (This refers to a newborn kitten.) □ *John is as weak as a kitten because he doesn't eat well.* □ *Oh! Suddenly I feel weak as a kitten.*

(as) white as the driven snow very white. □ *I like my bed sheets to be as white as the driven snow.* □ *We have a new kitten whose fur is white as the driven snow.*

(as) wise as an owl very wise. □ *Grandfather is as wise as an owl.* □ *My goal is to be wise as an owl.*

as you say 1. AND **like you say** a phrase indicating [patronizing] agreement with someone. (The *like* is used colloquially only.) □ JOHN: *Things* *are not going well for me today. What should I do?* BOB: *Some days are like that. As you say, it's just not going well for you, that's all.* □ JOHN: *This arrangement is not really good. There's not enough room for both of us.* MARY: *I guess you're right. It is crowded, and, like you say, there's not enough room.* **2.** a polite and formal way of indicating agreement or acquiescence. (Usually **As you say.** Literally, I will do as you say.) □ JOHN: *Please take this to the post office.* BUTLER: *As you say, sir.* □ BUTLER: *There is a Mr. Franklin at the door.* MARY: *Thank you, James. Tell him I've gone to Egypt for the winter.* BUTLER: *As you say, madam.*

ask after someone to inquire about the health and well-being of someone. □ *Molly asked after you.* □ *I asked after Molly and her family.*

ask for the moon to ask for too much; to make great demands; to ask for something that is difficult or impossible to obtain. (Not literal.) □ *When you're trying to get a job, it's unwise to ask for the moon.* □ *Please lend me the money. I'm not asking for the moon!*

ask for trouble to do or say something that will cause trouble. □ *Stop talking to me that way, John. You're just asking for trouble.* □ *Anybody who threatens a police officer is just asking for trouble.*

ask someone in((to) some place) to invite someone inside some place. □ *We asked them into the house.* □ *We asked them in.*

ask someone out (for something) See the following entry.

ask someone out (to something) AND **ask someone out (for something)** to invite someone to go out to something or some place [on a date]. □ *He asked her out to dinner, but she had other plans.* T *She couldn't go, so he asked out someone else.* □ *Liz asked Carl out for dinner.*

ask someone over to invite someone who lives close by to come to one's home [for a visit]. (Maybe to a house or apartment.) □ *Can we ask Tom over?* □ *He has been asked over a number of times.*

ask someone up to ask someone to come to one's home for a visit. (Usually said when someone must travel north, up a hill, or to an upper-level apartment for the visit.) □ *Let's ask Judy up for the weekend.* □ *She has been asked up before.*

asleep at the switch not attending to one's job; failing to do one's duty at the proper time. (Need not have anything to do with a real switch.) □ *The guard was asleep at the switch when the robber broke in.* □ *If I hadn't been asleep at the switch, I'd have seen the stolen car.*

assign someone or something to someone or something to designate someone or something as belonging to someone or something. (*Someone* includes *oneself.*) □ *They assigned the new car to Roger.* □ *They assigned the new worker to the mail room.* □ *Fred assigned himself to the busiest committee.* □ *I assigned the three new clerks to Mrs. Brown.*

assign something to someone to attribute something to someone; to blame something on someone. □ *We* were forced to assign the blame to Robert. □ *Is the blame assigned to Robert now?*

at a premium at a high price; priced high because of something special. □ *Sally bought the shoes at a premium because they were of very high quality.* □ *This car model is selling at a premium because so many people want to buy it.*

at a snail's pace very slowly. □ *When you watch a clock, time seems to move at a snail's pace.* □ *You always eat at a snail's pace. I'm tired of waiting for you.*

at death's door near death. (Euphemistic and literary.) □ *I was so ill that I was at death's door.* □ *The family dog was at death's door for three days, and then it finally died.*

at half-mast halfway up or down. (Primarily referring to flags. Can be used for things other than flags as a joke.) □ *The flag was flying at half-mast because the general had died.* □ *Americans fly flags at half-mast on Memorial Day.* □ *The little boy ran out of the house with his pants at half-mast.*

at loggerheads in opposition; at an impasse; in a quarrel. □ *Mr. and Mrs. Franklin have been at loggerheads for years.* □ *The two political parties were at loggerheads during the entire legislative session.*

at loose ends 1. restless and unsettled. □ *Just before school starts, all the children are at loose ends.* □ *When Tom is home on the weekends, he's always at loose ends.* **2.** unemployed. □ *Jane has been at loose ends ever since she lost her job.*

at one fell swoop AND **in one fell swoop** in a single incident; as a single event. (This phrase preserves the old word *fell*, meaning "terrible" or "deadly." Now a cliché, sometimes with humorous overtones.) □ *The party guests ate up all the snacks at one fell swoop.* □ *When the stock market crashed, many large fortunes were wiped out in one fell swoop.*

at one's wit's end at the limits of one's mental resources. □ *I'm at my wit's end with this problem. I cannot figure it out.* □ *Tom could do no more. He was at his wit's end.*

at sea (about something) confused; lost and bewildered. (As if one were lost at sea.) □ *Mary is all at sea about getting married.* □ *When it comes to higher math, John is totally at sea.*

at sixes and sevens disorderly; lost and bewildered. (Borrowed from gambling with dice.) □ *Mrs. Smith is at sixes and sevens since the death of her husband.* □ *Bill is always at sixes and sevens when he's home by himself.*

at someone's doorstep AND **on someone's doorstep** in someone's care; as someone's responsibility. (Not literal.) □ *Why do you always have to lay your problems at my doorstep?* □ *I shall put this issue on someone else's doorstep.* □ *I don't want it on my doorstep.*

at the bottom of the ladder at the lowest level of pay and status. □ *Most people start work at the bottom of the ladder.* □ *When Ann got fired, she had to start all over again at the bottom of the ladder.*

at the drop of a hat immediately and without urging. □ *John was always ready to go fishing at the drop of a hat.* □ *If you need help, just call on me. I can come at the drop of a hat.*

at the eleventh hour at the last possible moment. □ *She always turned her term papers in at the eleventh hour.* □ *We don't worry about death until the eleventh hour.*

at the end of one's rope AND **at the end of one's tether** at the limits of one's endurance. □ *I'm at the end of my rope! I just can't go on this way!* □ *These kids are driving me out of my mind. I'm at the end of my tether.*

at the end of one's tether See the previous entry.

at the last minute at the last possible chance. □ *Please don't make reservations at the last minute.* □ *Why do you ask all your questions at the last minute?*

at the outside at the very most. □ *The car repairs will cost $300 at the outside.* □ *I'll be there in three weeks at the outside.*

at the present time now. □ *"We are very sorry to report that we are unable to fill your order at the present time," stated the little note on the order form.* □ MARY: *How long will it be until we can be seated?* WAITER: *There are no tables available at the present time, madam.* MARY: *But, how long?*

at the top of one's lungs See the following entry.

at the top of one's voice AND **at the top of one's lungs** with a very loud voice; as loudly as is possible to speak or yell. □ *Bill called to Mary at the top of his voice.* □ *How can I work when you're all talking at the top of your lungs?*

at this stage (of the game) at the current point in some event; currently. □ *We'll have to wait and see. There isn't much we can do at this stage of the*

game. □ *At this stage, we are better off not calling the doctor.*

attach oneself to someone or something 1. [with *someone*] to become emotionally attached to someone. □ *Fred seems to have attached himself to a much older woman, who has captured his attention.* □ *Somehow, Fred has attached himself emotionally to Susan, and neither of them has any idea of what to do about it.* 2. [with *someone*] to follow after someone; to become a constant companion to someone. □ *Andy's little brother attached himself to Andy and his friends — much to Andy's distress.* □ *John attached himself to his older brother and drove him crazy.* 3. [with *something*] to choose to associate with a particular thing, group, or organization. □ *Todd attached himself to a volleyball team that practices at the school.* □ *The manager attached himself to the luncheon club and became a regular fixture there.* 4. [with *something*] to connect or secure oneself to something. □ *Tony attached himself to the helm and proceeded to steer the boat.* □ *Susan attached herself to the seat with the belt provided for that purpose.*

auction something off to sell something [to the highest bidder] at an auction. □ *He auctioned his home off.* Ⓣ *He auctioned off his home.* Ⓣ *The duke was required to auction off his ancestral home.*

audition for something to try out for a part in something. (One's singing, speaking, or playing is heard and judged.) □ *I plan to audition for the play.* □ *Liz auditioned for The Mikado.*

audition someone for something to allow someone to try out for a part in a performance; to judge someone's singing, speaking, or playing potentiality for a part in a performance. □ *Will you audition anyone else for the part?* □ *Have you been auditioned for the part?*

average out to even out ultimately; to be fair over the long term. □ *Everything will average out in the end.* □ *Yes, it will all average out.*

aw **1.** an interjection indicating dissent. □ BILL: *Put the film in the fridge.* BOB: *Aw, that's stupid! It'll just get cold!* □ TOM: *The new cars are all unsafe.* BILL: *Aw, you don't know what you're talking about!* **2.** an interjection indicating pleading. □ TOM: *No!* FRED: *Aw, come on! Please!* □

MARY: *Get away from my door!* JOHN: *Aw, come on! Let me in!* □ FRED: *You hurt my feelings.* BOB: *Aw, I didn't mean it.*

away from one's desk not available for a telephone conversation; not available to be seen. (Sometimes said by the person who answers a telephone in an office. It means that the person whom the caller wants is not immediately available due to personal or business reasons. Typically, the person has gone to the rest room.) □ *I'm sorry, but Ann is away from her desk just now. Can you come back later?* □ *Tom is away from his desk, but if you leave your number, he will call you right back.*

B

babe in the woods a naive or innocent person; an inexperienced person. □ *Bill is a babe in the woods when it comes to dealing with plumbers.* □ *As a painter, Mary is fine, but she's a babe in the woods as a musician.*

back away (from someone or something) AND **back off (from someone or something)** **1.** to move backwards from a person or thing; to withdraw physically from someone or something. □ *You should back away from the fire.* □ *Please back off from the man who is threatening you.* □ *You should back off.* □ *Jane backed away.* **2.** to begin to appear uninterested in someone or something; to withdraw one's interest from someone or something. □ *The board of directors began to back away from the idea of taking over the other company.* □ *They backed off from the whole idea.*

back in circulation **1.** [for something to be] available to the public again. (Said especially of things that circulate, such as money, library books, and magazines.) □ *I've heard that gold coins are back in circulation in Europe.* □ *I would like to read* War and Peace. *Is it back in circulation, or is it still checked out?* **2.** [for a person to be] socially active again; dating again after a divorce or breakup with one's lover. □ *Now that Bill is a free man, he's back in circulation.* □ *Tom was in the hospital for a month, but now he's back in circulation.*

back off (from someone or something) See *back away (from someone or something).*

back out (of something) **1.** [for someone or something] to move out of something backwards. □ *The rabbit tried to back out of its burrow.* □ *The rabbit backed out.* **2.** [for someone] to withdraw from something. □ *Are you going to try to back out of our agreement?* □ *You won't back out, will you?*

back someone up to provide someone with help in reserve; to support someone. □ *Don't worry. I will back you up when you need me.* T *Will you please back up Nancy over the weekend?*

back-to-back **1.** adjacent and touching backs. □ *They started the duel by standing back-to-back.* □ *Two people who stand back-to-back can manage to see in all directions.* **2.** following immediately. (Said of things or events. In this case, the events are figuratively back-to-front.) □ *The doctor had appointments set up back-to-back all day long.* □ *I have three lecture courses back-to-back every day of the week.*

back to the drawing board it is time to start over again; it is time to plan something over again. (Note the variations in the examples. Refers to the drafting board, where buildings or machines are designed.) □ *It didn't work. Back to the drawing board.* □ *I flunked English this semester. Well, back to the old drawing board.*

back to the salt mines time to return to work, school, or something else that might be unpleasant. (The phrase implies that the speaker is a slave who works in the salt mines.) □ *It's eight o'clock. Time to go to work! Back to the salt mines.* □ *School starts again in the fall, and then it's back to the salt mines again.*

bag and baggage AND **part and parcel** with one's luggage; with all one's possessions. (A fixed phrase.) □ *Sally showed up at our door bag and baggage one Sunday morning.* □ *All right, if you won't pay the rent, out with you, bag and baggage!* □ *Get all your stuff — part and parcel — out of here!*

Bag it! AND **Bag your face!** *Be quiet!; Shut up* and go away! (Rude and youthful slang.) □ MARY: *Sally, you look just terrible! What happened?* SALLY: *Bag it!* MARY: *Sorry I asked!* □ BILL: *Did I ever tell you about the time I went to Germany?* SUE: *Give it a rest, Bill. Can it! Bag it!* □ SUE: *Can I borrow your car again?* MARY: *Bag your face, Sue!* SUE: *Well, I never!*

bag of tricks a collection of special techniques or methods. □ *What have you got in your bag of tricks that could help me with this problem?* □ *Here comes Mother with her bag of tricks. I'm sure she can help us.*

Bag your face! See *Bag it!*

bail out (of something) 1. to parachute out of an airplane. □ *The pilot bailed out of the plane at the last moment.* □ *At the last moment, he bailed out.* 2. to escape from or abandon something. □ *I had to bail out of the company because I decided it was failing.* □ *I bailed out before it was too late.*

bail someone or something out (of something) 1. to get someone or something out of trouble or difficulty. □ *I'm really late on this deadline and I need help. Can you bail me out?* ⊤ *The government will not bail out the failing banks.* □ *No one will bail us out of our difficulties.* 2. [with *someone*] to pay bail or bond money to get a person out of jail. (*Someone* includes oneself.) □ *Try to get someone to bail me out of jail.* ⊤ *Can you bail out your friend?* □ *I don't want to bail him out.* □ *She bailed herself out of jail with her last fifty dollars.* 3. [with *something*] to remove water from something. □ *Bail the water out of the boat before we sink!* ⊤ *My dad bailed out the water as fast as he could, but it still kept rushing in.*

band together (against someone or something) to unite in opposition to someone or something; to unite against someone or something. □ *We must band together against the enemy.* □ *Everyone banded together.*

bang into someone or something to knock or bump into someone or something. □ *Why did you bang into me with your car?* □ *I banged into the door by accident.*

bang one's head against a brick wall See *beat one's head against the wall.*

bank on something to count on something; to rely on something. (To trust in something the way one might trust in a bank.) □ *The weather service said it wouldn't rain, but I wouldn't bank on that prediction.* □ *My word is to be trusted. You can bank on it.*

bargain for something to expect or anticipate something; to foresee something. □ *I didn't bargain for this.*

barge in on someone or something to go or come rudely into a place and interrupt people or their activities. □ *Albert barged in on Ted without knocking.* □ *I didn't mean to barge in on your meeting.*

barge into someone or something to bump or crash into someone or something, possibly on purpose. □ *She just barged into me and nearly knocked me over.* □ *Tom barged into the watercooler and hurt his knee.*

bark up the wrong tree to make the wrong choice; to ask the wrong person; to follow the wrong course. (Refers to a hunting dog that has chased a creature up a tree, but stands barking or howling at the wrong tree.) □ *If you think I'm the guilty person, you're barking up the wrong tree.* □ *The baseball players blamed their bad record on the pitcher, but they were barking up the wrong tree.*

bawl someone out to scold someone. □ *Then Maggie proceeded to bawl Tony out.* ⊤ *You can't bawl out everyone who was involved. There are too many.*

be a copycat to be a person who copies or mimics what someone else does. (Usually juvenile.) □ *Sally wore a pink dress just like Mary's. Mary called Sally a copycat.* □ *Bill is such a copycat. He bought a coat just like mine.*

be a fan of someone to be a follower of someone; to idolize someone. (This word *fan* is from *fanatic* meaning "follower.") □ *My mother is still a fan of the Beatles.* □ *I'm a great fan of the mayor of the town.*

be a thorn in someone's side to be a constant bother or annoyance to someone. □ *This problem is a thorn in my side. I wish I had a solution to it.* □ *John was a thorn in my side for years before I finally got rid of him.*

be at someone to be argumentative or contentious with someone. □ *She is always at him about something.* □ *I wish you weren't at me all the time.*

be behind (in something) to have failed to do one's work on time; to have failed to keep up with one's work. □ *I can't go out tonight. I'm behind in my work.* □ *I don't like to be behind.*

Be careful. 1. an instruction to take care in a particular situation. □ BILL: *I'm going to the beach tomorrow.* SALLY: *Be careful. Use lots of sunscreen!* □ JANE: *Well, we're off to the Amazon.* MARY: *Heavens! Be careful!* **2.** a way of saying *good-bye* while cautioning someone to take care. □ JOHN: *See you around, Fred.* FRED: *Be careful.* □ ALICE: *Well, I'm off.* JOHN: *Bye, Alice, be careful.*

be death on someone or something to be very harmful to someone or something. □ *The salt they put on the roads in the winter is death on cars.* □ *That teacher is death on slow learners.*

be down 1. to be depressed or melancholy. □ *Ann's down a little. I think it's just the weather.* □ *I'm always down after a performance.* **2.** to be inoperable; to be not working.

(Typically and originally said of a computer.) □ *The computer is down again.* □ *My television set was down, and I couldn't watch the football game.*

be down (from some place) to have come down from some higher place. □ *Billy's down from his tree house.* □ *Is Billy down yet?*

be down with something to be sick with some disease. □ *She's down with the flu.* □ *Lily is down with a sore throat.*

be from Missouri to require proof; to have to be shown (something). (From the nickname of the state of Missouri, the Show Me State.) □ *You'll have to prove it to me. I'm from Missouri.* □ *She's from Missouri and has to be shown.*

Be good. a departure response meaning "Good-bye and behave yourself." □ JANE: *Well, we're off. Be back in a week.* MARY: *Okay, have fun. Be good.* JANE: *Do I have to?* □ TOM: *Bye. Be good.* BILL: *See ya.*

be halfhearted (about someone or something) to be unenthusiastic about someone or something. □ *Ann was halfhearted about the choice of Sally for president.* □ *She didn't look halfhearted to me. She looked angry.*

Be happy to (do something). See *(I'd be) happy to (do something).*

be in to be in attendance; to be available; to be in one's office. □ *Is the doctor in?* □ *Mr. Franklin is not in.*

be in on something to share in something; to be involved in something. □ *I want to be in on the planning of the party.* □ *I wasn't in on it.*

be into something 1. to interfere or meddle with something. □ *She is* always into other people's business. □ *I'm sorry I'm into your affairs so much.* **2.** to be interested or involved in something. (Slang.) □ *I'm into model planes right now.* □ *Are you into Chinese food?*

Be my guest. *Help yourself.; After you.* (A polite way of indicating that one should go first, help oneself, or take the last one of something.) □ MARY: *I would just love to have some more cake, but there is only one piece left.* SALLY: *Be my guest.* MARY: *Wow! Thanks!* □ JANE: *Here's the door. Who should go in first?* BILL: *Be my guest. I'll wait out here.* JANE: *Why don't you go first?*

be off 1. [for one's plans or predictions] to be incorrect or inexact. (See also *be off on someone or something, be off (on something)*.) □ *My estimate was off a little bit.* □ *Your idea of the plane's arrival time was off, but it did land safely two hours later.* **2.** to be not turned on. (As with electric switches or the things they control.) □ *These switches are now off.* □ *Is the fan off?* **3.** to have started. (As with runners in a race or any similar contest.) □ *They're off!* □ *Are the horses off yet?*

be off on someone or something to be in a rage about someone or something; to be on a tirade about someone or something. □ *Are you off on Sally again? Why can't you leave her alone?* □ *I'm off on my diet again.*

be off (on something) 1. to be incorrect in one's planning or prediction. □ *I was off on my estimates a little bit.* □ *I guess I was off too much.* **2.** to have started on something, such as a task or a journey. □ *What time* *should we be off on our trip?* □ *We should be off by dawn.*

be old hat to be old-fashioned; to be outmoded. (Refers to anything—except a hat—that is like a hat that is out of style.) □ *That's a silly idea. It's old hat.* □ *Nobody does that anymore. That's just old hat.*

be on 1. to be turned on. (As with electric switches or the things they control.) □ *Is the motor on?* □ *It's not on now.* **2.** [for some agreement or plan] to be confirmed and in effect. (Often used with a *for* phrase.) □ *Is everything still on for Friday night?* □ *Yes, the party is on.*

be on something 1. to be resting on something. □ *Karen is on that rock over there.* □ *People were on anything that would hold them, resting after the long climb.* **2.** to be taking medication. □ *I am on an antibiotic for my chest cold.* □ *I want you to be on this drug for another week.* **3.** taking an illegal drug or controlled substance and acting strangely. □ *What is the matter with that kid? Is he on something?* □ *She acted as if she were on barbiturates or something.*

be onto someone or something 1. [with *someone*] to have figured out what someone is doing; to have figured out that someone is being dishonest. □ *No more cheating. I think they are onto us.* □ *I'm onto you!* **2.** [with *something*] to have found something useful or promising; to be on the verge of discovering something. □ *I think we are really onto something this time.* □ *I am onto a new discovery.*

be out from under someone or something 1. to be clear of and no longer beneath someone or something. □ *I*

was glad to be out from under the bed where I had been hiding. □ *The football player could not get out from under the stack of other players.* **2.** to be free from the control of someone or something. □ *It's good to be out from under the dictator.* □ *I was very glad to be out from under my daily work pressure.*

be (out) in the open 1. to be visible in an open space; to be exposed in an open area. □ *The trucks are out in the open where we can see them.* □ *They're in the open.* **2.** [for something] to be public knowledge. □ *Is this matter out in the open, or is it still secret?* □ *Let's get this in the open and discuss it.*

be out (of something) 1. to be gone; to have left some place; to be absent from a place. □ *The monkey is out of its cage.* □ *Sam is out of the building at present.* □ *Sam's out right now.* **2.** to have no more of something. □ *Sorry, we are fresh out of cucumbers.* □ *Sorry, we're out.*

be out (on strike) to be away from one's job in a strike or protest. □ *The workers are out on strike.* □ *We can't do anything while the workers are out.*

be out something to lack something; to have lost or wasted something. □ *I'm out ten bucks because of your miscalculation.* □ *I'm out the price of a meal.*

be poles apart to be very different; to be far from coming to an agreement. (Refers to the North and South poles of the earth, which are thought to be as far apart as any two points on earth.) □ *Mr. and Mrs. Jones have never gotten along well. They are poles* *apart.* □ *They'll never sign the contract because they are poles apart.*

Be quiet! Stop talking or making noise. (Made polite with *please*.) □ BILL (entering the room): *Hey, Tom!* TOM: *Please be quiet! I'm on the phone.* □ TOM: *Hey, Bill!* BILL: *Be quiet! You're too noisy.* TOM: *Sorry.*

be that as it may even though that may be true. □ SUE: *I'm sorry that I am late for the test. I overslept.* RACHEL: *Be that as it may, you have missed the test and will have to petition for a make-up examination.* □ HENRY: *I lost my job, so I couldn't make the car payment on time.* RACHEL: *Be that as it may, the payment is overdue, and we'll have to take the car back.*

be the spit and image of someone AND **be the spitting image of someone** to look very much like someone; to resemble someone very closely. □ *John is the spit and image of his father.* □ *I'm not the spit and image of anyone.* □ *At first, I thought you were saying spitting image.*

be the spitting image of someone See the previous entry.

be the teacher's pet to be the teacher's favorite student. (To be treated like a pet, such as a cat or a dog.) □ *Sally is the teacher's pet. She always gets special treatment.* □ *The other students don't like the teacher's pet.*

be through with someone or something to be finished with someone or something. □ *I'm all through with course requirements. Now I can learn something.* □ *Lily is through with Max.*

be up for something 1. [for someone] to be mentally ready for something. □ *The team is up for the game tonight.* □ *We are all up for the contest.* **2.** [for something] to be available for something, such as auction, grabs, sale, etc. □ *The outcome of the game is up for grabs.* □ *The car is up for sale.*

be (up)on someone to be someone's obligation or responsibility. □ *The obligation is upon you to settle this.* □ *The major part of the responsibility is on you.*

be with it to be up-to-date; to be knowledgeable about contemporary matters. □ *You're just not with it.* □ *I will never be with it!*

bear down (on someone or something) to press down on someone or something. □ *Bear down on the pen. You have to make a lot of copies.* □ *Don't bear down too hard on your employees.*

bear one's cross AND **carry one's cross** to endure one's burdens or difficulties. (This is a biblical theme. It is always used figuratively except in the biblical context.) □ *It's a very bad disease, but I'll bear my cross.* □ *I can't help you with it. You'll just have to carry your cross.*

bear someone or something in mind See *keep someone or something in mind*.

bear someone or something up 1. to hold someone or something up; to support someone or something. (*Someone* includes *oneself*.) □ *Will this bench bear me up?* ⊤ *This bench would bear up an elephant.* **2.** [with *someone*] to sustain or encourage someone. (*Someone* includes *oneself*.) □ *Your encouragement bore me up through a very hard time.* ⊤ *I will bear up the widow through the funeral* *service as well as I can.* □ *He bore himself up with thoughts of a brighter future.*

bear the brunt (of something) to withstand or endure the worst part or the strongest part of something, such as an attack. □ *I had to bear the brunt of her screaming and yelling.* □ *Why don't you talk with her the next time? I'm tired of bearing the brunt.*

bear up (under something) **1.** to hold up under something; to sustain the weight of something. □ *How is the new beam bearing up under the weight of the floor?* □ *It isn't bearing up. It broke.* **2.** to remain brave under a mental or emotional burden. □ *Jill did not bear up well under problems in her home.* □ *Jill bore up quite well.*

bear (up)on something [for information or facts] to concern something or be relevant to something. (*Upon* is formal and less commonly used than *on.*) □ *How do those facts bear on this matter?* □ *They do not bear upon this matter at all.*

bear watching to need watching; to deserve observation or monitoring. (This is the verb *to bear.*) □ *This problem will bear watching.* □ *This is a very serious disease, and it will bear watching for further developments.*

bear with someone or something to be patient with someone or something; to wait upon someone or something. (Especially through difficulties.) □ *Please bear with me for a moment while I try to get this straightened out.* □ *Can you bear with the committee until it reaches a decision?*

beard the lion in his den to face an adversary on the adversary's home ground. (To tease or frighten—as if grabbing the beard of something frightening, such as a lion.) □ *I went to the tax collector's office to beard the lion in his den.* □ *He said he hadn't wanted to come to my home, but it was better to beard the lion in his den.*

beat a dead horse to continue fighting a battle that has been won; to continue to argue a point that is settled. (A phrase meaning that a dead horse will not run no matter how hard it is beaten.) □ *Stop arguing! You have won your point. You are just beating a dead horse.* □ *Oh, be quiet. Stop beating a dead horse.*

beat a path to someone's door [for people] to come to someone in great numbers. (A phrase meaning that so many people will wish to come and see you that they will wear down a pathway to your door.) □ *I have a product so good that everyone is beating a path to my door.* □ *If you really become famous, people will beat a path to your door.*

beat about the bush See the following entry.

beat around the bush AND **beat about the bush** to avoid answering a question; to stall; to waste time. □ *Stop beating around the bush and answer my question.* □ *Let's stop beating about the bush and discuss this matter.*

beat down on someone or something to fall on someone or something. □ *The rain beat down on us for an hour.* □ *The rock slide beat down on the car and totally ruined the body.*

Beat it! *Go away!; Get out!* (Slang.) □ BILL: *Sorry I broke your radio.* BOB: *Get out of here! Beat it!* □ *"Beat it, you kids! Go play somewhere else!" yelled the storekeeper.*

beat one's head against the wall AND **bang one's head against a brick wall** to waste one's time trying to accomplish something that is completely hopeless. (Not literal.) □ *You're wasting your time trying to fix up this house. You're just beating your head against the wall.* □ *You're banging your head against a brick wall trying to get that dog to behave properly.*

beat someone or something down 1. [with *someone*] to defeat or demoralize someone. (*Someone* includes oneself.) □ *The constant bombing finally beat them down.* ⊤ *The attackers beat down the defenders.* □ *She beat herself down with self-doubt and guilt.* **2.** [with *something*] to break something in; to break through something. □ *Don't beat the door down! I'm coming!* ⊤ *Please don't beat down the door!* **3.** [with *something*] to flatten something. □ *Sam beat the veal down to the thickness of a piece of paper.* ⊤ *First you have to beat down the meat to a very thin layer.*

beat something into something to beat or whip something with a utensil until it changes into something else. □ *Beat the white of the egg into stiff peaks.* □ *Beat the batter into a satiny paste.*

beat something up 1. to whip up something, such as an egg. □ *Beat the egg up and pour it in the skillet.* ⊤ *Beat up another egg and do the same.* **2.** to ruin something; to damage something. □ *The banging of the door has really beat this wall up.* ⊤ *The door handle beat up the wall.*

beat the gun to manage to do something before the ending signal. (Originally from sports. Refers to making a goal in the last seconds of a game.) □ *The ball beat the gun and dropped through the hoop just in time.* □ *Tom tried to beat the gun, but he was one second too slow.*

Beauty is only skin deep. Looks are only superficial. (Proverb. Often implies that a beautiful person may be very cruel inside.) □ BOB: *Isn't Jane lovely?* TOM: *Yes, but beauty is only skin deep.* □ *I know that she looks like a million dollars, but beauty is only skin deep.*

bed down (for something) to lie down to sleep for a period of time. □ *After she had bedded down for the night, the telephone rang.* □ *All the chickens bedded down hours ago.*

beef something up to strengthen or fortify something. □ *Can we beef the last act up a little bit? It's really weak.* ⊤ *Try to beef up the defensive plays of the team.*

been through the mill been badly treated; exhausted. (Like grain that has been pulverized in a mill.) □ *This has been a rough day. I've really been through the mill.* □ *This old car is banged up, and it hardly runs. It's been through the mill.*

before you can say Jack Robinson almost immediately. (Often found in children's stories.) □ *And before you could say Jack Robinson, the bird flew away.* □ *I'll catch a plane and be there before you can say Jack Robinson.*

beg off ((on) something) to make excuses for not doing something. (Compare to *beg something off.*) □ *I'm going to have to beg off on our date.* □ *I'm sorry, I have to beg off.*

Beg pardon. See *(I) beg your pardon.*

beg something off to decline an invitation politely. (Compare to *beg off* *((on) something).)* □ *She begged the trip to the zoo off.* T *We all begged off the dinner invitation.*

Beggars can't be choosers. One should not criticize something one gets for free.; If one asks or begs for something, one does not get a choice of things. (Proverb.) □ *I don't like the old hat that you gave me, but beggars can't be choosers.* □ *It doesn't matter whether people like the free food or not. Beggars can't be choosers.*

Begging your pardon, but See *(I) beg your pardon, but.*

begin to see daylight to begin to see the end of a long task. (As if facing dawn at the end of a long night of work.) □ *I've been working on my thesis for two years, and at last I'm beginning to see daylight.* □ *I've been so busy. Only in the last week have I begun to see daylight.*

begin to see the light to begin to understand (something). □ *My algebra class is hard for me, but I'm beginning to see the light.* □ *I was totally confused, but I began to see the light after your explanation.*

Behind you! Look behind you!; There is danger behind you! □ *"Behind you!" shouted Tom just as a car raced past and nearly knocked Mary over.* □ *Alice shouted, "Behind you!" just as the pickpocket made off with Fred's wallet.*

belch out to burst, billow, or gush out. □ *Smoke belched out of the chimney.*

believe it or not an expression asserting the truth of something that the speaker has said, indicating that the statement is true whether or not the hearer believes it. □ TOM: *Well,*

Fred really saved the day. SUE: *Believe it or not, I'm the one who saved the day.* □ BILL: *How good is this one?* CLERK: *This is the best one we have, believe it or not.*

Believe you me! You really should believe me!; You'd better take my word for it! □ ALICE: *Is it hot in that room?* FRED: *It really is. Believe you me!* □ SUE: *How do you like my cake?* JOHN: *Believe you me, this is the best cake I've ever eaten!*

belt up to secure oneself with a belt, usually a seat belt. (Also a slogan encouraging people to use their seat belts.) □ *Please belt up. Safety first!*

bend down to curve downward; [for someone] to lean down. □ *Please bend down and pick up the little bits of paper you just dropped.* □ *The snow-laden bushes bent down.*

bend over [for someone] to bend down at the waist. □ *I bent over and picked up the coin.* □ *When he bent over, something ripped.*

bend someone's ear to talk to someone, perhaps annoyingly. (Not literal. The person's ear is not touched.) □ *Tom is over there, bending Jane's ear about something.* □ *I'm sorry. I didn't mean to bend your ear for an hour.*

Better late than never. A catch phrase said when someone arrives late or when something happens or is done late. □ MARY: *Hi, Tom. Sorry I'm late.* BILL: *Fret not! Better late than never.* □ *When Fred showed up at the doctor's office three days after his appointment, the receptionist said, "Well, better late than never."*

better left unsaid [refers to a topic that] should not be discussed; [refers to a thought that] everyone is thinking, but would cause difficulty if talked about in public. (A typical beginning for this phrase might be *It is, That is, The details are,* or even *Some things are.*) □ MARY: *I really don't know how to tell you this.* BOB: *Then don't. Maybe it's better left unsaid.* □ BILL: *I had such a terrible fight with Sally last night. I can't believe what I said.* BOB: *I don't need to hear all about it. Some things are better left unsaid.*

Better luck next time. **1.** an expression that comforts someone for a minor failure. (Said with a pleasant tone of voice.) □ BILL: *That does it! I can't run any farther. I lose!* BOB: *Too bad. Better luck next time.* □ MARY: *Well, that's the end of my brand new weight-lifting career.* JANE: *Better luck next time.* **2.** an expression that ridicules someone for a failure. (Said with rudeness or sarcasm. The tone of voice distinguishes sense 2 from sense 1.) □ SALLY: *I lost out to Sue, but I think she cheated.* MARY: *Better luck next time.* □ SUE: *You thought you could get ahead of me, you twit! Better luck next time!* SALLY: *I still think you cheated.*

between a rock and a hard place AND **between the devil and the deep blue sea** in a very difficult position; facing a hard decision. □ *I couldn't make up my mind. I was caught between a rock and a hard place.* □ *He had a dilemma on his hands. He was clearly between the devil and the deep blue sea.*

between the devil and the deep blue sea See the previous entry.

beyond one's depth **1.** in water that is too deep. (Literal.) □ *Sally swam out until she was beyond her depth.* □ *Jane swam out to get her even though it was beyond her depth, too.* **2.** beyond one's understanding or capabilities. □ *I'm beyond my depth in algebra class.* □ *Poor John was involved in a problem that was really beyond his depth.*

beyond one's means more than one can afford. □ *I'm sorry, but this house is beyond our means. Please show us a cheaper one.* □ *Mr. and Mrs. Brown are living beyond their means.*

beyond the pale unacceptable; outlawed. □ *Your behavior is simply beyond the pale.* □ *Because of Tom's rudeness, he's considered beyond the pale and is never asked to parties anymore.*

big frog in a small pond to be an important person in the midst of less important people. □ *I'd rather be a big frog in a small pond than the opposite.* □ *The trouble with Tom is that he's a big frog in a small pond. He needs more competition.*

bind someone or something up (with something) to tie someone or something with string or rope. □ *We bound her up with the drapery cords.* T *Please bind up both of them with twine.* T *Could you bind up the newspapers with twine?*

bind someone over (to someone or something) to deliver someone to some legal authority. (Legal.) □ *They bound the suspect over to the sheriff.* T *The sheriff will bind over the suspect to the police chief.* □ *When will you bind the prisoner over?*

Bingo! That's it, just what I've been waiting for! (From the game Bingo, where the word "Bingo!" is shouted by the first person to succeed in the game.) □ *Bob was looking in the button box for an old button to match the* ones on his shirt. "Bingo!" he cried. "Here it is!" □ BILL: I've found it! Bingo! MARY: I guess you found your contact lens?

birds and the bees human reproduction. (A euphemistic way of referring to human sex and reproduction.) □ My father tried to teach me about the birds and the bees. □ He's twenty years old and doesn't understand about the birds and the bees.

Birds of a feather flock together. People of the same type seem to gather together. (Proverb.) □ Bob and Tom are just alike. They like each other's company because birds of a feather flock together. □ When Mary joined a club for redheaded people, she said, "Birds of a feather flock together."

bite off more than one can chew to take (on) more than one can deal with; to be overconfident. (This is used literally for food and figuratively for other things, especially difficult projects.) □ Billy, stopping biting off more than you can chew. You're going to choke on your food someday. □ Ann is exhausted again. She's always biting off more than she can chew.

bite on something 1. to chew on something; to grasp something with the teeth. □ The injured cowboy bit on his wallet while they probed for the bullet. □ Don't bite on your collar. 2. to respond to a lure. □ Do you think the fish will bite on this? □ No one would bite on that bait. Try another approach.

bite one's nails to be nervous or anxious; to bite one's nails from nervousness or anxiety. (Used both literally and figuratively.) □ I spent all afternoon biting my nails, worrying about you. □ We've all been biting our nails from worry.

bite one's tongue to struggle not to say something that you really want to say. (Used literally only to refer to an accidental biting of one's tongue.) □ I had to bite my tongue to keep from telling her what I really thought. □ I sat through that whole conversation biting my tongue.

bite the dust to fall to defeat; to die. (Typically heard in movies about the old western frontier.) □ A bullet hit the sheriff in the chest, and he bit the dust. □ Poor old Bill bit the dust while mowing the lawn. They buried him yesterday.

bite the hand that feeds one to do harm to someone who does good things for you. (Not literal. Refers to the act of a thankless dog.) □ I'm your mother! How can you bite the hand that feeds you? □ She can hardly expect much when she bites the hand that feeds her.

Bite your tongue! an expression said to someone who has just stated an unpleasant supposition that unfortunately may be true. □ MARY: I'm afraid that we've missed the plane already. JANE: Bite your tongue! We still have time. □ MARY: Marry him? But you're older than he is! SALLY: Bite your tongue!

black out 1. to pass out; to become unconscious. □ After I fell, I must have blacked out. □ I think I am going to black out. 2. [for lights] to go out. (See also black something out.) □ Suddenly the lights blacked out.

black sheep of the family the worst member of the family. (A black sheep is an unwanted offspring in a herd of otherwise white sheep.) □ *Mary is the black sheep of the family. She's always in trouble with the police.* □ *He keeps making a nuisance of himself. What do you expect from the black sheep of the family?*

black something out 1. to cut or turn out the lights or electric power. (See also *black out*.) □ *The lightning strike blacked the entire town out.* ⊤ *The manager blacked out the whole building during the emergency to prevent an explosion.* **2.** to prevent the broadcast of a specific television or radio program in a specific area. (Usually refers to a sporting event.) □ *Will they black the game out around here?* ⊤ *They blacked out the basketball game in this area.*

blame someone for something to hold someone responsible for something; to name someone as the cause of something. (*Someone* includes *oneself*.) □ *Please don't blame Jill for it.* □ *She blamed herself for everything that went wrong.*

blame something on someone to say that something is someone's fault; to place the guilt for something on someone. □ *Don't blame it on me.* □ *I blamed it all on someone else.*

blank something out 1. to forget something, perhaps on purpose; to blot something out of memory. □ *I'm sorry, I just blanked your question out.* ⊤ *I blanked out your question. What did you say?* **2.** to erase something, as on a computer screen. ⊤ *Who blanked out the information that was on my screen?* □ *Please blank your password out as soon as you type it.*

blast off (for some place) 1. [for a rocket ship] to take off and head toward a destination. □ *The rocket*

blasted off for the moon. □ *Will it blast off on time?* **2.** [for someone] to leave for a destination. (Jocular.) □ *Ann blasted off for the library, so she could study.* □ *I've got to blast off. It's late.*

blaze down (on someone or something) [for the sun or other hot light] to burn down on someone or something. □ *The sun blazed down on the people on the beach.* □ *The stage lights blazed down on the set while the actors rehearsed.*

blaze up 1. [for flames] to expand upward suddenly. □ *The fire blazed up and warmed all of us.* □ *As the fire blazed up, we moved away from the fireplace.* **2.** [for trouble, especially violent trouble] to erupt suddenly. □ *The battle blazed up again, and the fighting started to become fierce.* □ *As the battle blazed up, the cowards fled into the hills.*

blend in (with someone or something) to mix well with someone or something; to combine with someone or something. □ *Everyone there blended in with our group.* □ *This color doesn't blend in with the upholstery fabric I have chosen.*

blend in (to something) to combine nicely with something; to mix well with something. □ *The oil won't blend into the water very well.* □ *It simply won't blend in.*

blend something in (to something) AND **blend something together (with something)** to mix something evenly into or with something else. □ *We should blend the strawberry jam into the peanut butter slowly.* ⊤ *You should blend in some more jam.* □ *Blend the egg together with the cream.* □ *Blend the ingredients together and pour them into a baking pan.*

blend something together (with something) See the previous entry.

blind leading the blind a phrase used to describe a situation where people who don't know how to do something try to explain it to other people. □ *Tom doesn't know anything about cars, but he's trying to teach Sally how to change the oil. It's a case of the blind leading the blind.* □ *When I tried to show Mary how to use a computer, it was the blind leading the blind.*

blink back one's tears to fight back tears; to try to keep from crying. □ *She blinked back her tears and went on.* T *He blinked his tears back.*

block something off to prevent movement through something by putting up a barrier; to close a passageway. □ *Sam blocked the corridor off with a row of chairs.* T *He used some chairs to block off the hallway.*

block something out 1. to lay something out carefully; to map out the details of something. □ *She blocked it out for us, so we could understand.* T *Let me block out this project for you right now.* **2.** to obscure a clear view of something. □ *The trees blocked the sun out.* T *The bushes blocked out my view of the car that was approaching.*

block something up to obstruct something; to stop the flow within a channel. □ *The heaps of debris blocked the channel up.* T *It blocked up the channel.*

blot someone or something out 1. to forget someone or something by covering up memories or by trying to forget. □ *I try to blot those bad thoughts out.* T *I tried to blot out those unhappy thoughts.* □ *I blotted David out and tried to keep him out of my mind.* **2.** [with *something*] to make something invisible by covering it with a spot or smudge. □ *Don't blot the name out on the application form.* T *Who blotted out the name on this form?*

blow away [for something light] to be carried away by the wind. □ *The leaves blew away on the autumn winds.* □ *My papers blew away!*

blow in [for something] to cave in to the pressure of moving air. □ *The door blew in during the storm.* □ *The window blew in.*

blow itself out [for a storm or a tantrum] to lose strength and stop; to subside. □ *The storm blew itself out.*

blow off 1. [for something] to be carried off of something by moving air. □ *The leaves of the trees blew off in the strong wind.* □ *My papers blew off the table.* **2.** [for a valve or pressure-maintaining device] to be forced off or away by high pressure. □ *The safety valve blew off and all the pressure escaped.* □ *The valve blew off, making a loud pop.*

blow off steam See *let off steam*.

blow one's own horn See *toot one's own horn*.

blow over [for something] to diminish; to subside. (As with a storm or a temper tantrum.) □ *Her display of temper finally blew over.* □ *The storm will blow over soon, I hope.*

blow someone or something away [for the wind] to carry someone or something away. □ *The wind almost blew her away.* T *The high wind blew away the entire barn.* T *It nearly blew away all of us.*

blow someone or something down [for a rush of air] to knock someone or something over. □ *The wind blew Chuck down.* T *It blew down many people.* □ *It almost blew the barn down.*

blow someone or something over [for the wind] to move strongly and upset someone or something. □ *The wind almost blew us over.* T *The wind blew over the shed.*

blow someone or something up 1. to destroy someone or something by explosion. (*Someone* includes *oneself.* More at *blow up.*) □ *The terrorists blew the family up as they slept.* T *They blew up the bridge.* □ *He blew himself up with the bomb he was making.* **2.** to exaggerate something [good or bad] about someone or something. (*Someone* includes *oneself.*) □ *I hope no one blows the story up.* T *The press always blows up reports of bad behavior.* □ *She blows herself up whenever she gives an interview.* **3.** [with *something*] to inflate something. □ *He didn't have enough breath to blow the balloon up.* T *They all blew up their own balloons.* **4.** [with *something*] to enlarge a photograph. □ *How big can you blow this picture up?* T *I will blow up this snapshot and frame it.*

blow someone's cover to reveal someone's true identity or purpose. (Informal or slang.) □ *The spy was very careful not to blow her cover.* □ *I tried to disguise myself, but my dog recognized me and blew my cover.*

blow something out to extinguish a flame by blowing air on it. □ *I blew the candle out.* T *I blew out the candle.*

blow something out of all proportion to cause something to be unrealistically proportioned relative to something else. (The *all* can be left out.) □ *The press has blown this issue out of all proportion.* □ *Let's be reasonable. Don't blow this thing out of proportion.*

blow the whistle (on someone) to report someone's wrongdoing to someone (such as the police) who can stop the wrongdoing. (As if one were blowing a police whistle.) □ *The citizens' group blew the whistle on the street gangs by calling the police.* □ *The gangs were getting very bad. It was definitely time to blow the whistle.*

blow up 1. [for something] to explode. (More at *blow someone or something up.*) □ *The bomb might have blown up if the children had tried to move it.* □ *The firecracker blew up.* **2.** [for someone] to have an outburst of anger. □ *She got mad and blew up.*

bog down to become encumbered and slow down; to slow down. (As if one were walking through a bog and getting stuck in the mud.) □ *The process bogged down and almost stopped.* □ *The whole thing bogged down soon after it started.*

boggle someone's mind to overwhelm someone; to mix up someone's thinking; to astound someone. □ *The size of the house boggles my mind.* □ *She said that his arrogance boggled her mind.*

boil down to something 1. [for a liquid] to be condensed to something by boiling. □ *Boil this mixture down to about half of what it was.* **2.** [for a complex situation] to be reduced to its essentials. □ *It boils down to the question of who is going to win.* □ *It boils down to a very minor matter.*

boil over [for a liquid] to overflow while being boiled. □ *The pudding boiled over and stuck to the stove.* □ *Don't let the stew boil over!*

boil something out (of something) to remove something from something by boiling. □ *I boiled the cleaning fluid out of the cloths.* Ⓣ *I boiled out the cleaning fluid.* □ *We boiled the oily stuff out.*

bone of contention the subject or point of an argument; an unsettled point of disagreement. (Like a bone that dogs fight over.) □ *We've fought for so long that we've forgotten what the bone of contention is.* □ *The question of a fence between the houses has become quite a bone of contention.*

book someone through (to some place) to make transportation arrangements for someone that involve a number of changes and transfers. (*Someone* includes *oneself*.) □ *The travel agent booked me through to Basra.* □ *I would be happy to book you through if you would like.* □ *She booked herself through to Budapest.*

boom out [for a loud sound] to sound out like thunder. □ *His voice boomed out so everyone could hear.* □ *An explosion boomed out and frightened us all.*

boot someone out (of something) to force someone to leave something or some place. □ *The board booted Greg out of the job.* Ⓣ *After a unanimous vote, they booted out all the old guard.*

boot something up to start up a computer. (More at *boot up*.) □ *She booted her computer up and went to work.* Ⓣ *Please go boot up your computer so we can get started.*

boot up to start up one's computer. (More at *boot something up*.) □ *He*

turned on the computer and booted up. □ *Try to boot up again and see what happens.*

border (up)on something 1. [for something] to touch upon a boundary. (*Upon* is formal and less commonly used than *on*.) □ *Our property borders on the lakeshore.* □ *The farm borders upon the railroad right-of-way.* **2.** [for some activity or idea] to be very similar to something else. (Not usually physical objects. *Upon* is formal and less commonly used than *on*.) □ *This notion of yours borders upon mutiny!* □ *It borders on insanity.*

born with a silver spoon in one's mouth born with many advantages; born to a wealthy family; already showing the signs of great wealth at birth. □ *Sally was born with a silver spoon in her mouth.* □ *I'm glad I was not born with a silver spoon in my mouth.*

boss someone around to order someone around. □ *Please don't boss me around so much.* Ⓣ *You boss around everybody!*

botch something up to mess something up; to do a bad job of something. □ *You really botched this up.* Ⓣ *I did not botch up your project.*

bottle something up (inside (someone)) [for someone] to keep serious emotions within and not express them. □ *Don't bottle it up inside you.* Ⓣ *Don't bottle up all your feelings.* □ *You can't just bottle it up.*

bottom out finally to reach the lowest or worst point. □ *The prices on the stock market finally bottomed out.* □ *When the market bottoms out, I'll buy some stock.*

Bottoms up. AND **Down the hatch!; Here's looking at you.; Here's mud**

in your eye.; Here's to you.; Skoal! an expression said as a toast when people are drinking together. (The *bottoms* refers to the bottoms of the drinking glasses.) □ BILL: *Bottoms up.* TOM: *Here's mud in your eye.* BILL: *Care for another?* □ *"Well, down the hatch," said Fred, pouring the smooth and ancient brandy slowly across his tongue.*

bounce for something See *spring for something.*

bounce off ((of) something) to rebound from something. (The *of* is colloquial.) □ *The ball bounced off of the wall and struck a lamp.* □ *It hit the wall and bounced off.*

bounce out (of something) to rebound out of or away from something. □ *The ball bounced out of the corner into my hands.* □ *The window was open and the ball bounced out.*

bounce something off (of) someone or something 1. to make something rebound off someone or something. (The *of* is colloquial.) □ *She bounced the ball off the wall, turned, and tossed it to Wally.* □ *She bounced the ball off of Harry and into the wastebasket.* **2.** to try an idea or concept out on someone or a group. (Figurative. The *of* is colloquial.) □ *Let me bounce this off of the committee, if I may.* □ *Can I bounce something off you people, while you're here?*

bound hand and foot with hands and feet tied up. □ *The robbers left us bound hand and foot.* □ *We remained bound hand and foot until the maid found us and untied us.*

bow and scrape to be very humble and subservient. (To bow low and touch the ground. Not usually lit-eral.) □ *Please don't bow and scrape. We are all equal here.* □ *The sales-clerk came in, bowing and scraping, and asked if he could help us.*

bow out (of something) to withdraw from something. □ *I decided to bow out of the organization.* □ *The time had come for me to bow out.*

bowl someone over 1. to knock someone over. □ *The huge dog ran by and bowled me over.* Ⓣ *The wind bowled over all the pedestrians.* **2.** to astound someone. (Figurative.) □ *His statement just bowled me over.* Ⓣ *The announcement bowled over every-one.*

box someone or something in to trap or confine someone or something. (Literal and figurative uses. *Someone* includes *oneself.*) □ *He boxed her in so she could not get away from him.* Ⓣ *They tried to box in the animals, but they needed more space.* □ *Don't try to box me in.*

Boy howdy! an exclamation of excited surprise. (Colloquial and folksy.) □ BOB: *Well, I finally got here.* FRED: *Boy howdy! Am I glad to see you!* □ BILL: *How do you like my horse?* FRED: *That's one fine-looking filly! Boy howdy!*

boy (oh boy) a sentence opener expressing surprise or emphasis. (This is not a term of address and can be used with either sex, although it is quite informal. The alternate form is more informal and more emphatic. Words such as this often use into-nation to convey the connotation of the sentence that is to follow. The brief intonation pattern accompany-ing the word may indicate sarcasm, disagreement, caution, consolation,

sternness, etc.) □ JOHN: *Hi, Bill.*
BILL: *Boy, am I glad to see you!* □
BOB: *What happened here?* FRED: *I
don't know.* BOB: *Boy, this place is a
mess!* □ *"Boy, I'm tired!"* moaned
Henry. □ *"Boy oh boy, this cake looks
good," thought Jack.*

brace someone or something up to
prop up or add support to someone
or something. (*Someone* includes *oneself.*) □ *They braced the tree up for the
expected windstorm.* ⊤ *They braced up
the tree again after the storm.* □ *John
had to brace himself up with a splint before he could walk.*

branch off (from something) to separate off from something; to divide
away from something. □ *A small
stream branched off from the main
channel.* □ *An irrigation ditch branched off here and there.*

branch out (from something) 1. for
a branch or limb to grow out of
another plant or tree. □ *A twig
branched out of the main limb and grew
straight up.* □ *The bush branched out
from the base.* **2.** to expand away from
something; to diversify away from
narrower interests. □ *The speaker
branched out from her prepared
remarks.* □ *The topic was very broad,
and she was free to branch out.*

branch out (into something) 1. to
diversify and go into new areas. □ *I
have decided to branch out into some
new projects.* □ *Business was very
good, so I decided to branch out.* **2.** to
develop many branches, tributaries,
or interests. □ *I got tired of sales and
branched out.* □ *The river branches
out near its mouth.*

Bravo! a cheer of praise for someone
who has done something very well.

□ *"Keep it up! Bravo!" cheered the
audience.* □ *At the end of the tenor's
aria, the members of the audience leapt
to their feet and with one voice shouted,
"Bravo!"*

bread and butter someone's liveli-
hood or income. (The source of
money that puts bread and butter, or
other food, on the table.) □ *Selling
cars is a lot of hard work, but it's my
bread and butter.* □ *It was hard to give
up my bread and butter, but I felt it was
time to retire.*

Break a leg! a parting word of encouragement given to a performer
before a performance. (It is tradi-
tionally viewed as bad luck to wish a
performer good luck, so the performer is wished bad luck in hopes of
causing good luck.) □ BILL: *The big
show is tonight. I hope I don't forget my
lines.* JANE: *Break a leg, Bill!* □
MARY: *I'm nervous about my solo.*
BOB: *You'll do great. Don't worry.
Break a leg!*

break away (from someone) AND
**break free (from someone); break
loose (from someone) 1.** to get free
of the physical hold of someone. □ *I
tried to break away from him, but he
was holding me too tight.* □ *She broke
free from him, at last.* □ *I broke free
from the intruder.* □ *I could not break
loose from my captors.* □ *At last, I
broke free.* **2.** to sever a relationship
with another person, especially the
parent-child relationship. □ *He
found it hard to break away from his
mother.* □ *She was almost thirty before
she finally broke free.* □ *I found it hard
to break loose from my parents.*

break camp to close down a camp-
site; to pack up and move on. □ *Early*

this morning we broke camp and moved on northward. □ Okay, everyone. It's time to break camp. Take those tents down and fold them neatly.

break down 1. [for a mechanical device] to cease working. □ The car broke down in the middle of the expressway. **2.** [for someone] to have an emotional or mental collapse. □ Finally, after many sleepless nights, he broke down totally.

break down (and do something) to surrender to demands or emotions and do something. □ Max finally broke down and confessed. □ I knew he would break down. □ I had to stop and break down and cry. I was so depressed. □ I was afraid I would break down and cry.

break free (from someone) See break away (from someone).

break in (on someone or something) 1. [with someone] to burst into a place and violate someone's privacy. □ The police broke in on him at his home and arrested him. □ They needed a warrant to break in. **2.** [with someone] to interrupt someone's conversation. □ If you need to talk to me, just break in on me. □ Feel free to break in if it's an emergency. **3.** [with something] to interrupt something; to intrude upon something. □ I didn't mean to break in on your discussion. □ Please don't break in on the meeting just now. This is important.

break into something See break up (into something).

break in(to something or some place) to force entry into a place criminally; to enter some place forcibly for the purpose of robbery or other illegal acts. □ The thugs broke into the liquor store. □ They broke in and took all the money.

Break it up! Stop fighting!; Stop arguing! □ TOM: Then I'm going to break your neck! BILL: I'm going to mash in your face! BOB: All right, you two, break it up! □ When the police officer saw the boys fighting, he came over and hollered, "Break it up! You want me to arrest you?"

break loose (from someone) See break away (from someone).

break new ground to begin to do something that no one else has done; to pioneer (in an enterprise). □ Dr. Anderson was breaking new ground in cancer research. □ They were breaking new ground in consumer electronics.

break off (from something) [for a piece of something] to become separated from the whole. □ This broke off from the lamp. What shall I do with it? □ This piece broke off.

break one's back (to do something) See the following entry.

break one's neck (to do something) AND **break one's back (to do something)** to work very hard to do something. (Never used in its literal sense.) □ I broke my neck to get here on time. □ That's the last time I'll break my neck to help you. □ There is no point in breaking your back. Take your time.

break out 1. [for widespread fighting] to emerge, erupt, or begin. □ Fighting broke out again in the streets. **2.** [for a disease] to erupt and become epidemic. □ Chicken pox broke out in Tony's school.

break out in a cold sweat to perspire from fever, fear, or anxiety; to begin to sweat suddenly and profusely. □ *I was so frightened I broke out in a cold sweat.* □ *The patient broke out in a cold sweat.*

break out into tears See the following entry.

break (out) into tears AND **break out into tears** to start crying suddenly. □ *I was so sad that I broke out into tears.* □ *I always break into tears at a funeral.* □ *It's hard not to break out in tears under those circumstances.* □ *Every single child broke out into tears in the movie.* □ *The child broke into tears and started howling.*

break out of something to get out of a confining place or situation; to escape from something or some place. □ *He couldn't break out of a paper bag!*

break out (with something) [for the skin] to erupt with a specific disease such as measles, chicken pox, rubella, etc. □ *Nick and Dan broke out with chicken pox.* □ *They both broke out at the same time.*

break someone down to cause a person to submit; to pressure a person to submit to something. □ *The police broke her down, and she confessed.* T *They found it easy to break down the suspect.*

break someone in to train someone to do a new job; to supervise someone who is learning to do a new job. (*Someone* includes *oneself.*) □ *Who will break the new employee in?* T *I have to break in a new typist.* □ *She broke herself in on the new job by practicing at home.*

break someone up to cause someone to begin laughing very hard. (*Someone* includes *oneself.*) □ *Everything*

she says just breaks me up. T *The joke broke up the audience.* □ *He broke himself up with the realization of what a silly mistake he had made.*

break someone's fall to cushion a falling person; to lessen the impact of a falling person. □ *When the little boy fell out of the window, the bushes broke his fall.* □ *The old lady slipped on the ice, but a snowbank broke her fall.*

break someone's heart to cause someone emotional pain. (Not literal.) □ *It just broke my heart when Tom ran away from home.* □ *Sally broke John's heart when she refused to marry him.*

break something down to destroy a barrier. □ *The court broke a number of legal barriers down this week.* T *I did not break down your door!*

break something in 1. to crush or batter something to pieces. □ *Why are you breaking the door in? Here's the key!* T *Who broke in the door?* 2. to use a new device until it runs well and smoothly; to wear shoes, perhaps a little at a time, until they feel comfortable. □ *I can't travel on the highway until I break this car in.* T *I want to go out this weekend and break in the car.* T *I hate to break in new shoes.*

break something off ((of) something) to fracture or dislodge a piece off something. (The *of* is colloquial.) □ *He broke a piece of the decorative stone off of the side of the church.* T *He didn't mean to break off anything.* □ *He didn't mean to break it off.*

break something up to put an end to some kind of fighting or arguing. (See also *break something up (into something)*, *break up*.) □ *Okay, you*

39

guys, break it up! □ Break it up and leave the area! ⊤ The teacher broke up the fight in the school yard.

break something up (into something) to break something into smaller pieces. □ We broke the crackers up into much smaller pieces. ⊤ Please break up the crackers into smaller pieces if you want to feed the ducks. □ They broke the crackers up.

break the ice to initiate social interchanges and conversation; to get something started. (The *ice* sometimes refers to social coldness. Also used literally.) □ Tom is so outgoing. He's always the first one to break the ice at parties. □ It's hard to break the ice at formal events. □ Sally broke the ice by bidding $20,000 for the painting.

break the news (to someone) to tell someone some important news, usually bad news. □ The doctor had to break the news to Jane about her husband's cancer. □ I hope that the doctor broke the news gently.

break through (something) to force [one's way] through an obstruction. □ The fire fighters broke through the wall easily. □ They broke through with no difficulty.

break up 1. [for something] to fall apart; to be broken to pieces. (Typically said of a ship breaking up on rocks. See also *break up (into something), break something up.*) □ In the greatest storm of the century, the ship broke up on the reef. □ It broke up and sank. **2.** [for two people] to end a romance; [for lovers] to separate permanently. □ Terry and Albert broke up. Did you hear? **3.** [for married persons] to divorce. □ After many years of bickering, they finally broke up.

4. [for a marriage] to dissolve in divorce. □ The marriage finally broke up. □ It broke up almost immediately. **5.** to begin laughing very hard. □ The comedian told a particularly good joke, and the audience broke up. □ I always break up when I hear her sing. She is so bad!

break up (into something) AND **break into something** to divide into smaller parts. (More at *break something up (into something)*. See also *break up*.) □ The glass broke up into a thousand pieces. □ It hit the floor and broke up, flinging bits everywhere.

break up (with someone) to end a romantic relationship with someone. □ Jill broke up with Albert. □ I just knew they would break up.

breathe down someone's neck 1. to keep close watch on someone; to watch someone's activities. (Refers to standing very close behind a person. Can be used literally.) □ I can't work with you breathing down my neck all the time. Go away. □ I will get through my life without your help. Stop breathing down my neck. **2.** to try to hurry someone along; to make someone get something done on time. (The subject does not have to be a person. See the second example.) □ I have to finish my taxes today. The tax collector is breathing down my neck. □ I have a deadline breathing down my neck.

breathe one's last to die; to breathe one's last breath. □ Mrs. Smith breathed her last this morning. □ I'll keep running every day until I breathe my last.

breathe something in to take something into the lungs, such as air, medicinal vapors, gas, etc. □ Breathe

the vapor in slowly. It will help your cold. T *Breathe in that fresh air!*

breathe something out to exhale something. □ *At last, he breathed his last breath out, and that was the end.* T *Breathe out your breath slowly.*

breeze along to travel along casually, rapidly, and happily; to go through life in a casual and carefree manner. □ *Kristine was just breezing along the road when she ran off onto the shoulder.* □ *We just breezed along the highway, barely paying attention to what we were doing.* □ *Don't just breeze along through life!*

breeze in (to some place) to enter a place quickly, in a happy and carefree manner. □ *She breezed into the conference room and sat down at the head of the table.* □ *Jerry breezed in and said hello.*

breeze through (something) 1. to complete some task rapidly and easily. □ *I breezed through my calculus assignment in no time at all.* □ *It was not hard. I just breezed through.* **2.** to travel through a place rapidly. □ *They breezed through every little town without stopping.* □ *We didn't stop. We just breezed through.*

brew something up 1. to brew something, as in making coffee or tea. □ *Can somebody brew some coffee up?* T *Let me brew up a pot of coffee, and then we'll talk.* **2.** to cause something to happen; to foment something. (Figurative. More at *brew up.*) □ *I could see that they were brewing some kind of trouble up.* T *Don't brew up any trouble!*

brew up to build up; [for something] to begin to build and grow. (Typically said of a storm. See also

brew something up.) □ *A bad storm is brewing up in the west.* □ *Something serious is brewing up in the western sky.*

bring a verdict in [for a jury] to deliver its decision to the court. □ *Do you think they will bring a verdict in today?* T *The jury brought in their verdict around midnight.* □ *A verdict was finally brought in by the jury.*

bring someone down 1. to assist or accompany someone from a higher place to a lower place. □ *Please bring your friends down so I can meet them.* T *She brought down her cousin, who had been taking a nap upstairs.* □ *Aunt Mattie was brought down for supper.* **2.** to bring someone to a place for a visit. □ *Let's bring Tom and Terri down for a visit this weekend.* T *We brought down Tom just last month.* □ *They were brought down at our expense for a weekend visit.* **3.** to restore someone to a normal mood or attitude. (After a period of elation or, perhaps, drug use.) □ *The bad news brought me down quickly.* T *I was afraid that the change of plans would bring down the entire group.*

bring someone in (on something) to include someone in some deed or activity. □ *I'm going to have to bring a specialist in on this.* T *Please bring in several specialists on this.* □ *Let's bring Dave in before we go any further.* □ *Dave was brought in at the last minute.*

bring someone or something up 1. to cause someone or something to go up with one from a lower place to a higher place. □ *We brought them up and let them view the city from the balcony.* T *I brought up some binoculars so you can enjoy the view from up here.* □ *They were brought up from below.* **2.** to mention someone or

41

something. (*Someone* includes *oneself*.) □ *Why did you have to bring that up?* T *Must you bring up bad memories?* T *Why did you bring up Walter?* □ *He brought himself up again and again. What a self-centered person!* **3.** to raise someone or something; to care for someone or something up to adulthood. □ *We brought the dog up from a pup.* T *We brought up the dog carefully and sold it for a good profit.* □ *I brought Sammy up the best I could.* □ *Sammy was brought up with the best child-raising methods.*

bring someone to to help someone return to consciousness. □ *We worked to bring him to before he went into shock.* □ *He was finally brought to with the smelling salts.*

bring someone up for something 1. to suggest someone's name for something. (*Someone* includes *oneself*.) □ *I would like to bring Beth up for vice president.* T *I will bring up Beth for this office if you don't.* □ *Tom always brings himself up for head of the department.* **2.** to put someone's name up for promotion, review, discipline, etc. (*Someone* includes *oneself*.) □ *We brought Tom up for promotion.* T *The boss brought up Tom too.* □ *I had to bring myself up for promotion.*

bring someone up on something to provide something while raising a child to adulthood. □ *She brought her children up on fast food.* T *You shouldn't bring up your children on that kind of entertainment!*

bring something about to make something happen. □ *I am unable to bring the desired result about.* T *He claimed he could bring about a miracle.*

bring something back to restore an earlier style or practice. □ *Please*

bring the good old days back. T *Bring back good times for all of us.* □ *Those days cannot be brought back.*

bring something back (to someone) to remind someone of something. □ *The funeral brought memories back.* T *The warm winds brought back the old feeling of loneliness that I had experienced so many times in the tropics.*

bring something down 1. to move something from a higher place to a lower place. □ *Bring that box down, please.* T *And while you're up there, please bring down the box marked winter clothing.* **2.** to lower something, such as prices, profits, taxes, etc. □ *The governor pledged to bring taxes down.* T *I hope they bring down taxes.* **3.** to defeat or overcome something, such as an enemy, a government, etc. □ *The events of the last week will probably bring the government down.* T *The scandal will bring down the government, I hope.* □ *The government was brought down by the scandal.*

bring something in to earn an amount of money; to draw or attract something, especially an amount of money. □ *My part-time job brings thirty dollars in every month.* T *She brings in a lot of money.* □ *A lot of money was brought in by Lily's parents.* T *Their appeal for donations brought in a lot of contributions.*

bring something on 1. to cause something to happen; to cause a situation to occur. □ *What brought this event on?* T *What brought on the event?* □ *My comments were brought on by something I read last night.* **2.** to cause a case or an attack of a disease. □ *What brought your coughing fit on?* □ *Something brought it on.* □ *The attack was brought on by an allergy.*

bring something on someone to cause something to go wrong for someone. (*Someone* includes *oneself*.) □ *You brought it on yourself. Don't complain.* □ *Max brought this problem on all of us.*

bring something out to issue something; to publish something; to present something [to the public]. □ *I am bringing a new book out.* T *I hear you have brought out a new edition of your book.* □ *A new edition has been brought out.*

bring something out (in someone) to cause a particular quality to be displayed by a person, such as virtue, courage, a mean streak, selfishness, etc. □ *You bring the best out in me.* T *This kind of thing brings out the worst in me.* □ *This brings the worst out.*

bring something to light to make something known; to discover something. (As if someone were bringing some hidden thing out into the light of day.) □ *The scientists brought their findings to light.* □ *We must bring this new evidence to light.*

bring the house down to excite a theatrical audience to laughter or applause or both. (Not literal.) □ *This is a great joke. The last time I told it, it brought the house down.* T *It didn't bring down the house; it emptied it.*

bring up the rear to move along behind everyone else; to be at the end of the line. (Originally referred to marching soldiers.) □ *Here comes John, bringing up the rear.* □ *Hurry up, Tom! Why are you always bringing up the rear?*

brown out [for the electricity] to decrease in power. (Causing electric lights to dim. Not quite a blackout.)

□ *The lights browned out and almost went out altogether.* □ *After the lights browned out, they stayed on for an hour.*

brush by someone or something AND **brush past someone or something** to push quickly past someone or something. □ *She brushed by the little group of people standing there talking.* □ *I brushed by the plant, knocking it over.* □ *You just brushed past me!*

brush past someone or something See the previous entry.

brush someone off 1. to remove something, such as dust or lint, from someone by brushing. □ *The porter brushed Mr. Harris off and was rewarded with a very small tip.* T *The porter had never brushed off such a miserly man before.* 2. to reject someone; to dismiss someone. □ *He brushed her off, telling her she had no appointment.* T *He brushed off Mrs. Franklin, who was only trying to be nice to him.* □ *Mr. Franklin should not be brushed off.*

brush something away (from something) to remove something from something by brushing; to get dirt or crumbs off something by brushing. □ *He brushed a bit of lint away from Tom's collar.* T *She brushed away the crumbs from the table.* □ *Liz brushed the crumbs away.* □ *The dust was brushed away from his shoes.*

brush something down to clean and neaten fur or fabric by brushing. □ *Why don't you brush your coat down? It's very linty.* T *I brushed down my trousers, and they looked much better.* □ *My coat was brushed down before I left home.*

brush something off ((of) someone or something) to remove something from someone or something by brushing. □ *I brushed a little lint off her collar.* T *I brushed off the lint that was on her collar.* □ *Liz brushed it off.*

brush (up) against someone or something to move past and touch someone or something. □ *I brushed up against the freshly painted wall as I passed.* □ *I guess I brushed against Walter as I walked by.* □ *The houseplant was brushed up against so much that it finally lost all its leaves.*

brush up (on something) to improve one's knowledge of something or one's ability to do something. □ *I need to brush up on my German.* □ *My German is weak. I had better brush up.*

bubble over 1. [for boiling or effervescent liquid] to spill or splatter over the edge of its container. □ *The pot bubbled over and put out the cooking fire.* □ *The stew bubbled over.* **2.** [for someone] to be so happy and merry that it spills over onto other people. □ *She was just bubbling over, she was so happy.* □ *Lily bubbled over with joy.*

buckle someone in to attach someone securely with a vehicle's seat belt. (This includes airplane seat belts. *Someone* includes *oneself.*) □ *Don't forget to buckle the children in.* T *Did you buckle in the children?* □ *The children are all buckled in.* □ *Please buckle yourself in.*

buckle someone or something up to attach someone or something securely with straps that buckle together. (This emphasizes the completeness and security of the act.

Someone includes *oneself.* More at *buckle up.*) □ *Buckle the children up before we leave.* T *Buckle up your shoes.* T *I will buckle up Jimmy.* □ *Buckle yourself up, if you please.*

buckle up to buckle one's seat belt, as in a car or plane. (More at *buckle someone or something up.*) □ *Please buckle up!* □ *I wish you would obey the law and buckle up.*

buddy up (to someone) to become overly familiar or friendly with someone. □ *Don't try to buddy up to me now. It won't do any good.* □ *He always tries to buddy up, no matter how badly you treat him.*

buddy up (with someone) to join with another person to form a pair that will do something together or share something. □ *I buddied up with Carl, and we shared the canoe.* □ *Carl and I buddied up, and we shared the canoe.* □ *Let's buddy up, okay?* □ *They buddied up with each other.*

build castles in Spain See the following entry.

build castles in the air AND **build castles in Spain** to daydream; to make plans that can never come true. (Neither phrase is used literally.) □ *Ann spends most of her time building castles in Spain.* □ *I really like to sit on the porch in the evening, just building castles in the air.*

build on((to) something) to add to something by constructing an extension. □ *Do you plan to build onto this house?* □ *Yes, we are going to build on.*

build someone in(to something) to make a person an integral part of an organization or a plan. □ *We built the mayor's nephew into the organizational structure of the town.* T *He* built in his relatives from the very beginning. □ He built them in while he was president.

build someone or something up 1. to praise or exalt someone or something; to exaggerate the virtues of someone or something. (*Someone* includes *oneself*.) □ *Clare liked to build Tom up because she was in love with him.* T *The master of ceremonies built up the act too much.* **2.** [with *someone*] to strengthen someone; to make someone healthier or stronger. (*Someone* includes *oneself*.) □ *You need more exercise and better food to build yourself up again.* T *The coach wanted to build up Roger into a stronger player.* □ *I need to do some exercises to build myself up.* **3.** [with *something*] to add buildings to an area of land or a neighborhood. □ *They are really building this area up. There is no more open space.* T *They built up the area over the years.* **4.** [with *something*] to develop, accumulate, or increase something, such as wealth, business, goodwill, etc. (More at *build up.*) □ *I built this business up through hard work and hope.* T *She built up a good business over the years.*

build someone up (for something) to prepare someone for something; to lead a person into a proper state of mind to receive some information. (*Someone* includes *oneself*.) □ *We built them up for what was about to happen.* T *We had to build up the woman for what we were going to tell her.* □ *They built John up carefully and then told him the bad news.* □ *She built herself up for a wonderful evening.*

build something in(to something) 1. to make a piece of furniture or an appliance a part of a building's con-struction. □ *We will build this chest into the wall about here.* T *We are going to build in a second chest.* □ *Then we will build another one in.* **2.** to make a particular characteristic a basic part of something. □ *We build quality into our cars before we put our name on them.* □ *We build compassion into our approach to therapy.* T *We build in quality.* **3.** to make a special restriction or specification a part of the plan of something. □ *I built the restriction into our agreement.* T *I built in the rule.* □ *We built the rule in.*

build something out of something to construct something from parts or materials. □ *She built a tower out of the blocks.* □ *They will build the tower out of cast concrete.*

build up to increase; to develop. (More at *build someone or something up.*) □ *The storm clouds are building up. Better close the windows.* □ *The bad weather has been building up for days.*

bull in a china shop a very clumsy person around breakable things; a thoughtless or tactless person. (*China* is fine crockery.) □ *Look at Bill, as awkward as a bull in a china shop.* □ *Get that big dog out of my garden. It's like a bull in a china shop.* □ *Bob is so rude, a regular bull in a china shop.*

Bully for you! 1. an expression that praises someone or someone's courage. (Dated, but still heard.) □ *The audience shouted, "Bravo! Bully for you!"* □ BOB: *I quit my job today.* SALLY: *Bully for you! Now what are you going to do?* BOB: *Well, I need a little loan to tide me over.* **2.** a sarcastic phrase ridiculing someone's statement or accomplishment. □ BOB: *I* *managed to save three dollars last week.* BILL: *Well, bully for you!* □ MARY: *I won a certificate good for a free meal!* SALLY: *Bully for you!*

bump (up) against someone or something to strike someone or something accidentally, usually relatively gently. □ *The car bumped up against the curb.* □ *This wall has been bumped against a lot. It needs painting.*

bunch someone or something up to pack or cluster things or people together. (More at *bunch up.*) □ *Bunch them up so you can squeeze them into the sack.* T *Kelly bunched up the roses and put them in a vase.* □ *Bunch the people up so more will fit in.*

bunch up to pack together or cluster. (More at *bunch someone or something up.*) □ *Spread out. Don't bunch up!* □ *The cars are bunching up at the expressway entrance.*

bundle off to leave in a hurry; to take all one's parcels and leave in a hurry. □ *She got ready and bundled off after her bus.* □ *Lily bundled off just in time.*

bundle (oneself) up (against something) to wrap oneself up in protective clothing or bedding as protection against the cold. □ *Please bundle the children up against the frigid wind.* □ *Bundle yourself up.* □ *Better bundle up.* □ *Be sure and bundle yourself up against the cold. It's freezing out there.*

bundle someone in(to something) 1. to put someone, usually a child, into heavy outdoor clothing. (*Someone* includes *oneself.*) □ *Bill bundled Billy into his parka.* □ *He was hard to bundle in because he wouldn't stand still.* □ *Tom bundled himself into his parka and opened the door to go out.* **2.**

to put someone, usually a child, into bed. □ *She bundled Sarah into bed just in time.* □ *June pulled back the sheets and bundled Sarah in.*

bundle someone up (in something) to wrap someone up in protective clothing or bedding. (*Someone* includes *oneself.*) □ *Bill bundled Billy up in his parka.* T *Bill bundled up Mary in her parka.* □ *He bundled her up.* □ *The child bundled himself up into the covers and went to sleep.*

bundle something off (to someone or some place) to send something off in a bundle to someone or some place. □ *He bundled his laundry off to his mother, who would wash it for him.* T *Mary bundled off the package to her brother.* □ *She put stamps on the package and bundled it off.*

buoy someone or something up 1. to keep someone or something afloat. (*Someone* includes *oneself.*) □ *Use this cushion to buoy yourself up.* T *The log buoyed up the swimmer until help came.* □ *The air trapped in the hull buoyed the boat up.* **2.** [with *someone*] to support, encourage, or sustain someone. (*Someone* includes *oneself.*) □ *The good news buoyed her up considerably.* T *Her good humor buoyed up the entire party.* □ *She buoyed herself up by keeping in touch with friends.*

burn away 1. [for something] to burn until there is no more of it. (More at *burn something away.*) □ *All the oil burned away.* □ *The fuel burned away and things are cooling down.* **2.** for something to keep on burning rapidly. □ *The little fire burned away brightly, warming the tiny room.* □ *The candle burned away, giving a tiny bit of light to the huge room.*

burn down **1.** [for a building] to be destroyed by fire. (More at *burn something down.*) □ *The barn burned down.* □ *There was a fire, and the barn was burned down.* **2.** [for a fire] to burn and dwindle away. □ *The flame burned down and then went out.* □ *As the fire burned down, it began to get cold.*

burn (itself) out **1.** [for a flame or fire] to run out of fuel and go out. □ *Finally, the fires burned themselves out.* □ *The fire finally burned out.* □ *The flame burned itself out.* **2.** [for an electrical part] to fail and cease working or make a larger unit cease working. (More at *burn someone or something out.*) □ *The motor finally burned itself out.* □ *The motor burned out.*

burn off [for some excess volatile or flammable substance] to burn away or burn up. (More at *burn something off ((of) something).*) □ *A film of oil on the surface of the water was burning off, making dense black smoke.* □ *The alcohol burned off and left a delicious flavor in the cherries jubilee.*

burn one's bridges (behind one) **1.** to make decisions that cannot be changed in the future. □ *If you drop out of school now, you'll be burning your bridges behind you.* □ *You're too young to burn your bridges that way.* **2.** to be unpleasant in a situation that you are leaving, ensuring that you'll never be welcome to return. □ *If you get mad and quit your job, you'll be burning your bridges behind you.* □ *No sense burning your bridges. Be polite and leave quietly.* **3.** to cut off the way back to where you came from, making it impossible to retreat. □ *The army, which had burned its bridges behind it, couldn't go back.* □ *By blowing up the road, the spies had burned their bridges behind them.*

burn someone at the stake **1.** to set fire to a person tied to a post (as a form of execution). □ *They used to burn witches at the stake.* □ *Look, officer, I only ran a stop sign. What are you going to do, burn me at the stake?* **2.** to chastise or denounce someone severely, but without violence. □ *Stop yelling. I made a simple mistake, and you're burning me at the stake for it.* □ *Sally only spilled her milk. There is no need to shout. Don't burn her at the stake for it.*

burn someone or something out **1.** [with *someone*] to wear someone out; to make someone ineffective through overuse. (*Someone* includes *oneself.*) □ *Facing all these problems at once will burn Tom out.* ⊤ *The continuous problems burned out the office staff in a few months.* □ *She burned herself out as a volunteer in the state prison.* **2.** [with *something*] to burn away the inside of something, getting rid of excess deposits. □ *The mechanic burned the carbon out of the manifold.* ⊤ *He burned out the carbon.* **3.** [with *something*] to wear out an electrical or electronic device through overuse. (More at *burn (itself) out.*) □ *Turn it off. You're going to burn it out!* ⊤ *He burned out the motor.*

burn someone or something to a crisp to burn someone or something totally or very badly. □ *The flames burned him to a crisp.* □ *The cook burned the meat to a crisp.*

burn someone or something up **1.** to destroy someone or something by fire. (More at *burn up.*) □ *The barn fire burned Walter up.* ⊤ *The fire burned up both of them.* □ *The fire*

burned the papers up and left no trace.
2. [with *someone*] to make someone
very angry. (Figurative.) □ *You really
burn me up! I'm very angry at you!* T
The whole mess burned up everyone.

burn something away to remove or
destroy something by burning. (More
at *burn away*.) □ *The doctor burned
the wart away.* T *The doctor burned
away the wart.*

burn something down [for a fire] to
destroy a building completely. (More
at *burn down*.) □ *The fire burned the
barn down.* T *It burned down the
barn.*

burn something off ((of) something)
to cause excess volatile or flammable
substance to burn until there is no
more of it. (The *of* is colloquial.
More at *burn off*.) □ *We burnt the
gasoline off the water's surface.* T *Why
did you burn off the gasoline?* □ *I
burned the vapors off.*

burn the candle at both ends to work
very hard and stay up very late at
night. (A way of getting the most out
of a candle, or figuratively, of oneself.) □ *No wonder Mary is ill. She
has been burning the candle at both
ends for a long time.* □ *You can't keep
on burning the candle at both ends.*

burn the midnight oil to stay up
working, especially studying, late at
night. (Refers to working by the light
of an oil lamp before electricity.) □ *I
have to go home and burn the midnight
oil tonight.* □ *If you burn the midnight
oil night after night, you'll probably become ill.*

burn up 1. to become destroyed or
consumed by fire. □ *The wood
burned up and left only ashes.* □ *The
deed burned up in the fire.* **2.** to have a

fever. □ *The cranky child was burning
up, and we raced her to the hospital.* □
*I was burning up until the nurse gave
me some aspirin.*

burn with a low blue flame to be
very angry. (Refers to the imaginary
heat caused by extreme anger. A *low
blue flame* is very hot despite its
smallness and calmness.) □ *By the
time she showed up three hours late, I
was burning with a low blue flame.* □
*Whenever Ann gets mad, she just
presses her lips together and burns with
a low blue flame.*

burst at the seams 1. [for someone]
to explode with pride or laughter.
(Figurative.) □ *Tom nearly burst at
the seams with pride.* □ *We laughed so
hard we just about burst at the seams.*
2. to explode from fullness. (Figurative.) □ *The room was so crowded
that it almost burst at the seams.* □ *I
ate so much I almost burst at the seams.*

**burst in ((up)on someone or some-
thing)** to intrude or come in
thoughtlessly and suddenly and interrupt someone or something. (*Upon* is formal and less commonly used
than *on*.) □ *I didn't mean to burst in
on you.* □ *She feared that someone
would burst in upon her.* □ *He just
burst in!*

burst in (with something) to interrupt with some comment. □ *Ted
burst in with his opinion.* □ *He burst in
to tell us the news.*

burst in(to some place) to intrude or
come into a place thoughtlessly and
suddenly. □ *Ted burst into the room
and sat down right in the middle of the
meeting.* □ *Why did you just burst in?*

burst out to explode outward; to
break open under force. □ *The door*

burst out and released the trapped people. □ When the glass burst out, Gerald was injured.

burst out doing something to begin to do something suddenly, such as cry, laugh, shout, etc. □ Suddenly, she burst out singing. □ Ted burst out smiling.

burst (out) into something 1. [for plants or trees] to open their flowers seemingly suddenly and simultaneously. □ The flowers burst out into blossom very early. □ They burst into blossom during the first warm day. 2. [for someone] to begin suddenly doing a particular activity, such as crying, laughing, chattering; or to begin producing the evidence of such activities as laughter, chatter, tears, etc. □ Suddenly, she burst out into laughter. □ The child burst into tears.

burst out (of some place) [for people] to come out of a place rapidly. □ Everyone burst out of the burning building. □ Suddenly, they all burst out.

burst out of something to explode out of something; to become [suddenly] too big for something, such as clothes, a house, etc. □ She is bursting out of her dress. □ The butterfly burst out of the chrysalis.

burst out with something to utter something loudly and suddenly. □ The child burst out with a scream. □ Lily burst out with song.

burst through something to break through or penetrate something with force. □ The tank burst through the barrier easily. □ The workers burst through the wall after a lot of hard work.

burst (up)on someone [for an idea] to strike someone suddenly. (Upon is formal and less commonly used than on.) □ Then, this really tremendous idea burst upon me. □ It burst on me like a bolt of lightning.

burst (up)on the scene to appear suddenly somewhere; to enter or arrive suddenly some place. (Upon is formal and less commonly used than on.) □ The police suddenly burst upon the scene. □ They burst on the scene and took over.

burst with joy to be full to the bursting point with happiness. □ When I got my grades, I could have burst with joy. □ Joe was not exactly bursting with joy when he got the news.

bury one's head in the sand AND **hide one's head in the sand** to ignore or hide from obvious signs of danger. (Refers to an ostrich, which sticks head into the sand or the ground when frightened.) □ Stop burying your head in the sand. Look at the statistics on smoking and cancer. □ And stop hiding your head in the sand. All of us will die somehow, whether we smoke or not.

bury someone or something away (some place) to put or hide someone or something some place. (Someone includes oneself.) □ The dog buried the bone away under a bush. □ They buried her uncle away in the cemetery. □ They buried him away. □ Don't bury yourself away. Get out and have some fun.

bury the hatchet to stop fighting or arguing; to end old resentments. (Burying a hatchet is symbolic of ending a war or a battle.) □ All right, *you two. Calm down and bury the hatchet.* □ *I wish Mr. and Mrs. Franklin would bury the hatchet. They argue all the time.*

bush out [for something] to develop many small branches or hairs. (Said of a plant, bush, beard, head of hair, etc.) □ *His beard bushed out and really needed trimming.* □ *I hope the hedge bushes out nicely this year.*

butt in (on someone or something) to interrupt or intrude on someone or something. (More at *butt into something.*) □ *I didn't mean to butt in on your conversation.* □ *Please don't butt in.* □ *How can we talk when you keep butting in on us?*

butt into something to intrude upon something; to break into a conversation. (More at *butt in (on someone or something).*) □ *Please don't butt into my conversation.* □ *I don't like my conversations being butted into by perfect strangers!*

Butt out! Go away and mind your own business! (Rude. Said to someone who has "butted in.") □ *Jane and Mary were talking when Bill came over and interrupted. "Butt out!" said Jane.* □ TOM: *Look, Mary, we've been going together for nearly a year.* JANE (approaching): *Hi, you guys!* TOM: *Butt out, Jane, we're talking.*

butt (up) against someone or something to press against someone or something firmly. □ *This board is supposed to butt up against the one over there.* □ *The goat butted against Fred, but didn't hurt him.*

butter someone up AND **butter up to someone** to flatter someone; to treat someone especially nicely in hopes of receiving special favors. □

A student tried to butter the teacher up. T *She buttered up the teacher again.* □ *She is always buttering up to the teacher.*

butter up to someone See the previous entry.

button one's lip to get quiet and stay quiet. (Often used with children.) □ *All right now, let's button our lips and listen to the story.* □ *Button your lip, Tom! I'll tell you when you can talk.*

button something up to fasten the edges of something with buttons. (More at *button up.*) □ *Button your shirt up, please.* T *I will button up my shirt.*

button up to fasten one's buttons. (More at *button something up.*) □ *Your jacket is open. You'd better button up. It's cold.* □ *I'll button up in the car.*

buttress something up 1. to brace something; to provide architectural support for something. □ *We have to buttress this part of the wall up while we work on it.* T *The workers buttressed up the wall.* 2. to provide extra support, often financial support, for something. (Figurative.) □ *We rounded up some money to buttress the company up through the crisis.* T *The loan buttressed up the company for a few minutes.*

buy a pig in a poke to purchase or accept something without having seen or examined it. (A *poke* is a bag or sack.) □ *Buying a car without test-driving it is like buying a pig in a poke.* □ *He bought a pig in a poke when he ordered a diamond ring by mail.*

buy in(to something) to purchase shares of something; to buy a part of something, sharing the ownership with other owners. □ *I bought into a company that makes dog food.* □ *Sounds like a good company. I would like to buy in.*

buy one's way out (of something) to get out of trouble by bribing someone to ignore what one has done wrong. □ *You can't buy your way out of this mess, buster!* □ *You made this mess and you can't buy your way out!*

buy someone off to bribe someone to ignore what one is doing wrong. □ *Do you think you can buy her off?* T *Max tried to buy off the cops.*

buy someone or something out 1. to purchase full ownership of something from someone or a group. □ *We liked the company, so we borrowed a lot of money and bought it out.* T *Carl bought out the owners of the company.* □ *He bought the company out.* **2.** [with *something*] to buy all of a particular item. □ *The kids came in and bought all our bubble gum out.* T *They bought out the bubble gum.*

buy something to believe someone; to accept something to be a fact. (Also used literally.) □ *It may be true, but I don't buy it.* □ *I just don't buy the idea that you can swim that far.*

buy something back (from someone) to repurchase something that one has previously sold from the person who bought it. □ *Can I buy it back from you? I have decided I need it.* T *He bought back his book from George.* □ *I sold it too cheap. I want to buy it back.*

buy something for a song to buy something cheaply. □ *No one else wanted it, so I bought it for a song.* □ *I could buy this house for a song, because it's so ugly.*

buy something sight unseen to buy something without seeing it first. □ *I bought this land sight unseen. I didn't know it was so rocky.* □ *It isn't usually safe to buy something sight unseen.*

buy something up to buy all of something; to buy the entire supply of something. □ *He bought the oranges up.* T *He bought up all the oranges and drove up the price.*

buzz in (to some place) to come into a place rapidly or unexpectedly. □ *The child buzzed into the shop and bought a nickel's worth of candy.* □ *I just buzzed in to say hello.*

by a hair's breadth AND **by a whisker** just barely; by a very small distance. □ *I just missed getting on the plane by a hair's breadth.* □ *The arrow missed the deer by a whisker.*

by a whisker See the previous entry.

by leaps and bounds rapidly; by large movements forward. (Not often used literally, but it could be.) □ *Our garden is growing by leaps and bounds.* □ *The profits of my company are increasing by leaps and bounds.*

by return mail by a subsequent mailing (back to the sender). (A phrase indicating that an answer is expected soon, by mail.) □ *Since this bill is overdue, would you kindly send us your check by return mail?* □ *I answered your request by return mail over a year ago. Please check your records.*

by the nape of the neck by the back of the neck. (Mostly found in real or mock threats. Grabbing in the way that one picks up a puppy.) □ *He grabbed me by the nape of the neck and told me not to turn around if I valued* *my life. I stood very still.* □ *If you do that again, I'll pick you up by the nape of the neck and throw you out the door.*

by the same token in the same way; reciprocally. □ *Tom must be good when he comes here, and, by the same token, I expect you to behave properly when you go to his house.* □ *The mayor votes for his friend's causes. By the same token, the friend votes for the mayor's causes.* □ TOM: *I really got cheated!* BOB: *You think they've cheated you, but, by the same token, they believe that you've cheated them.* □ *"By the same token, most people really want to be told what to do," counseled Henry.*

by the seat of one's pants by sheer luck and very little skill; just barely. (Especially with *to fly*.) □ *I got through school by the seat of my pants.* □ *The jungle pilot spent most of his days flying by the seat of his pants.*

by the skin of one's teeth just barely; by an amount equal to the thickness of the (imaginary) skin on one's teeth. □ *I got through that class by the skin of my teeth.* □ *I got to the airport late and missed the plane by the skin of my teeth.* □ HENRY: *I almost didn't make it.* ANDREW: *What happened?* HENRY: *I had to flag down a taxi. I just made it by the skin of my teeth.* □ *"Well, Bob, you passed the test by the skin of your teeth," said the teacher.*

by the sweat of one's brow by one's efforts; by one's hard work. □ *Tom raised these vegetables by the sweat of*

his brow. □ *Sally polished the car by the sweat of her brow.*

by the way AND **incidentally** **1.** a phrase indicating that the speaker is adding information. □ TOM: *Is this one any good?* CLERK: *This is the largest and, by the way, the most expensive one we have in stock.* □ BILL: *I'm a realtor. Is your house for sale?* ALICE: *My house is not for sale, and, by the way, I too am a realtor.* **2.** a phrase indicating that the speaker is casually opening a new subject. □ BILL: *Oh, by the way, Fred, do you still have that hammer you borrowed from me?* FRED: *I'll check. I thought I gave it back.* □ JANE: *By the way, don't you owe me some money?* SUE: *Who, me?*

by virtue of something because of something; due to something. □ *She's permitted to vote by virtue of her age.* □ *They are members of the club by virtue of their great wealth.*

by word of mouth by speaking rather than writing. (A fixed phrase.) □ *I learned about it by word of mouth.* □ *I need it in writing. I don't trust things I hear about by word of mouth.*

Bye. *Good-bye.* (Friendly and familiar.) □ TOM: *Bye.* MARY: *Take care. Bye.* □ SALLY: *See you later. Bye.* TOM: *Bye.*

Bye-bye. *Good-bye.* (Very familiar.) □ MARY: *Bye-bye.* ALICE: *See you later. Bye-bye.* □ TOM: *Bye-bye. Remember me to your brother.* BILL: *I will. Bye.*

C

call a spade a spade to call something by its right name; to speak frankly about something, even if it is unpleasant. □ *Well, I believe it's time to call a spade a spade. We are just avoiding the issue.* □ *Let's call a spade a spade. The man is a liar.*

Call again. Please visit this shop again sometime. (Said by shopkeepers and clerks.) □ *"Thank you," said the clerk, smiling, "call again."* □ CLERK: *Is that everything?* JOHN: *Yes.* CLERK: *That's ten dollars even.* JOHN: *Here you are.* CLERK: *Thanks. Call again.*

call in (to some place) to telephone to some central place, such as one's place of work. □ *I have to call in to the office at noon.* □ *I will call in whenever I have a chance.*

call it a day to quit work and go home; to say that a day's work has been completed. □ *I'm tired. Let's call it a day.* □ *The boss was mad because Tom called it a day at noon and went home.*

call it quits to quit; to resign from something; to announce that one is quitting. □ *Okay! I've had enough! I'm calling it quits.* □ *Time to go home, John. Let's call it quits.*

call out (to someone) to call or shout to someone. □ *She called out to Mike, but he didn't hear her.* □ *Sue called out to her friends.*

call someone down to criticize or scold someone; to ask someone to behave better; to challenge someone's bad behavior. □ *The teacher called Todd down for being late.* T *The teacher called down all the students who were late.*

call someone in (for something) 1. to request that someone come to have a talk. □ *The manager called Karen in for a talk.* T *The manager called in Gary for questioning.* □ *She called Gary in.* 2. to request a consultation with a specialist in some field. □ *We will have to call a specialist in for a consultation.* T *We called in another specialist for an opinion.* □ *We called someone else in.*

call someone on the carpet to reprimand a person. (The phrase presents images of a person called into the boss's carpeted office for a reprimand.) □ *One more error like that and the boss will call you on the carpet.* □ *I'm sorry it went wrong. I really hope he doesn't call me on the carpet again.*

call someone or something back 1. to call out that someone or something should come back. □ *As she left, the clerk called her back.* T *The clerk called back the customer.* □ *They had to call the order back because it was incomplete.* 2. [with someone] to call someone again on the telephone. □ *Since she is not there, I will call her back in half an hour.* Ⓣ *Carl called back the person who called earlier.* **3.** [with *someone*] to return a telephone call to a person who had called earlier. □ *I have to call Judy back now.* □ *I will call him back tomorrow.*

√ **call someone or something out 1.** to request the services of someone or a group. □ *Things got bad enough that the governor called the militia out.* Ⓣ *The governor called out the militia.* Ⓣ *The governor called out his hatchet man for the job.* **2.** [with *something*] to draw on something, such as a particular quality or talent. □ *It's times like these that call the best out in us.* Ⓣ *These times call out our best.* **3.** [with *something*] to shout out something. □ *Who called the warning out?* Ⓣ *You should call out a warning to those behind you on the trail.*

call someone or something up 1. to request that someone or a group report for active military service. □ *The government called the fourth battalion up for active service.* Ⓣ *They called up another battalion.* **2.** to call someone, a group, or a company on the telephone. □ *I will call them up and see what they have to say.* Ⓣ *Please call up the supplier.*

call someone over (to some place) to request that someone come to where one is. □ *I will call her over to us, and you can ask her what you want to know.* Ⓣ *Call over the waitress so we can order.* □ *I called Ted over.*

call something (back) in to order that something be returned. □ *The car company called many cars back in for repairs.* □ *They called a lot of cars*

in. Ⓣ *They called in a lot of defective cars.*

call something off to cancel something. □ *We had to call the picnic off because of rain.* Ⓣ *Who called off the picnic?*

call the dogs off to stop threatening, chasing, or hounding (a person); to order dogs away from the chase. (Both literal and figurative.) □ *All right, I surrender. You can call your dogs off.* Ⓣ *Tell the sheriff to call off the dogs. We caught the robber.* Ⓣ *Please call off your dogs!*

call (up)on someone 1. to visit someone. (*Upon* is formal and less commonly used than *on*.) □ *My mother's friends call upon her every Wednesday.* □ *Let's call on Mrs. Franklin this afternoon.* **2.** to choose someone to respond, as in a classroom. □ *The teacher called upon me, but I was not ready to recite.* □ *Please don't call on me. I can't remember a thing.*

call (up)on someone (for something) 1. to choose someone to do or to help with some particular task. (*Upon* is formal and less commonly used than *on*.) □ *Can I call upon you for help?* □ *You can call on me at any time.* **2.** to choose someone to respond, as in a classroom. □ *The teacher called upon me to recite, but I was not ready.* □ *Please don't call on me. I can't remember a thing.*

calm down to relax; to become less busy or active. (More at *calm someone or something down*.) □ *Now, now, calm down. Take it easy.* □ *Please calm down. Nothing bad is going to happen.*

calm someone or something down to cause someone or some creature to be less active, upset, or unsettled. (*Someone* includes *oneself.* More at *calm down.*) □ *Please try to calm yourself down!* Ⓣ *Can you calm down your dog?* □ *Please calm your horse down.* □ *Can you calm yourself down?*

camp out to live out of doors temporarily in a tent or camping vehicle, as on a vacation or special camping trip. □ *I love to camp out in the winter.* □ *We plan to camp out again next month.*

Can do. I can do it. (The opposite of *No can do.*) □ JANE: *Will you be able to get this finished by quitting time today?* ALICE: *Can do. Leave it to me.* □ BOB: *Can you get this pack of papers over to the lawyer's office by noon?* BILL: *Can do. I'm leaving now. Bye.*

Can I join you? See *Could I join you?*

Can I speak to someone? See *Could I speak to someone?*

Can it! *Be quiet!*; *Stop talking!*; *Drop the subject!* (Slang and fairly rude.) □ BOB: *I'm tired of this place. Let's go.* FRED: *That's enough out of you! Can it!* □ JOHN: *Hey, Tom! What are you doing, man?* TOM: *Can it! I'm studying.*

Can you handle it? **1.** Are you able to deal with this problem? (May be a personal problem or a work assignment.) □ BILL: *This file is a mess. Can you handle it?* □ FATHER: *This is a difficult situation, son. Can you handle it?* BOB: *Yeah, dad. Don't worry.* **2.** AND **Could you handle it?** Will you agree to deal with what I have described?; Would you do it? □ MARY: *I need someone to work on the Jones account. Can you handle it?* JANE: *Sure.* □ BILL: *Someone is on the*

phone about the car payments. Could you handle it? FATHER: *Yes.*

Can you hold? See *Could you hold?*

cancel out (of something) to withdraw from something. □ *I hate to cancel out of the event at the last minute, but this is an emergency.* □ *It's too late to cancel out.*

can't carry a tune unable to sing a simple melody; lacking musical ability. (Almost always negative. Also with *cannot.*) □ *I wish that Tom wouldn't try to sing. He can't carry a tune.* □ *Listen to poor old John. He really cannot carry a tune.*

can't hold a candle to someone not equal to someone; not worthy to associate with someone; unable to measure up to someone. (Refers to not being worthy enough even to hold a candle to light someone's way. Also with *cannot.*) □ *Mary can't hold a candle to Ann when it comes to auto racing.* □ *As for singing, John can't hold a candle to Jane.*

can't make heads or tails (out) of someone or something unable to understand someone or something; unable to tell one end of someone or something from the other. (Because the thing or person is obscured or confusing. Also with *cannot.*) □ *John is so strange. I can't make heads or tails of him.* □ *Do this report again. I can't make heads or tails out of it.*

can't see beyond the end of one's nose unaware of the things that might happen in the future; not farsighted; self-centered. (Also with *cannot.*) □ *John is a very poor planner. He can't see beyond the end of his nose.* □ *Ann can't see beyond the end of her nose. She is very self-centered.*

can't see one's hand in front of one's face unable to see very far, usually due to darkness or fog. (Also with *cannot*.) □ *It was so dark that I couldn't see my hand in front of my face.* □ *Bob said that the fog was so thick he couldn't see his hand in front of his face.*

Capeesh? Do you understand? (Italian.) □ TOM: *Do I have to stay here?* FRED: *That's the way it's going to be. Capeesh?* TOM: *Yeah.* □ MARY: *I will not tolerate any of this anymore. Capeesh?* BILL: *Sure. Gotcha!*

carry a torch (for someone) AND **carry the torch** to be in love with someone who is not in love with you; to brood over a hopeless love affair. □ *John is carrying a torch for Jane.* □ *Is John still carrying a torch?* □ *Yes, he'll carry the torch for months.*

carry coals to Newcastle to do something unnecessary; to do something that is redundant or duplicative. (An old proverb from England. Newcastle was a town from which coal was shipped to other parts of England. It would be senseless to bring coal into this town.) □ *Taking food to a farmer is like carrying coals to Newcastle.* □ *Mr. Smith is so rich he doesn't need any more money. To give him money is like carrying coals to Newcastle.*

carry on (about someone or something) 1. to talk excitedly or at length about someone or something. □ *She was carrying on about the new governor.* □ *Jane was carrying on about her job.* □ *Stop carrying on, Jane.* 2. to have an emotional display of distress about someone or something; to behave badly or wildly about someone or something. □ *Must you carry on so about virtually nothing?* □ *Jane carried on about her husband.* □ *Jane is carrying on again.*

carry on (with someone or something) 1. [with *someone*] to flirt with someone; to have a love affair with someone. □ *It looks like Heather is carrying on with James.* □ *Heather, stop carrying on!* 2. [with *something*] to continue doing something. □ *Please carry on with your singing.* □ *Oh, do carry on!*

carry one's cross See *bear one's cross.*

carry over (to something) 1. [for a sum or other figure] to be taken to another column of figures. □ *This amount carries over into the next column.* □ *Yes, this number carries over.* 2. to last or continue until another time. □ *Will this enthusiasm carry over to the following week?* □ *Of course, it will carry over.*

carry someone or something about to carry someone or something with one; to carry someone or something from place to place. □ *Do I have to carry these books about all over campus?* □ *You are too heavy, sweetie. I don't want to carry you about all day.*

carry someone or something away to take or steal someone or something. □ *Someone carried our lawn furniture away.* ⊤ *The kidnappers carried away the child.* □ *They carried the child away.*

carry someone or something off 1. to take or steal someone or something. □ *The kidnappers carried the child off.* ⊤ *They carried off the child.* □ *Someone carried the patio chairs off.* 2. [with *something*] to make something happen; to accomplish something; to make some sort of deception believable and successful.

□ *Do you think you can carry the deal off?* T *Sure, I can carry off the deal.* □ *It sounds like a great trick. Can you carry it off?* T *I can carry off the entire scheme perfectly.*

carry something on 1. to do something over a period of time. □ *Do you think you can carry this on for a year?* T *I will carry on this activity for three years if you want.* 2. to continue to do something as a tradition. □ *We intend to carry this celebration on as long as the family can gather for the holidays.* T *We will carry on this tradition for decades, in fact.*

carry something on (to something) to take something onto a vehicle. □ *Do you plan to carry this bag onto the plane?* T *I'd like to carry on two bags.* □ *Can I carry them on?*

carry the ball 1. to be the player holding the ball, especially in football when a goal is made. □ *It was the fullback carrying the ball.* □ *Yes, Tom always carries the ball.* 2. to be in charge; to make sure that a job gets done. □ *We need someone who knows how to get the job done. Hey, Sally! Why don't you carry the ball for us?* □ *John can't carry the ball. He isn't organized enough.*

carry the torch 1. to uphold a set of goals; to lead or participate in a figurative crusade. □ *The battle was over, but John continued to carry the torch.* □ *If Jane hadn't carried the torch, no one would have followed, and the whole thing would have failed.* 2. See also *carry a torch (for someone).*

carry the weight of the world on one's shoulders to appear to be burdened by all the problems in the whole world. □ *Look at Tom. He appears to be carrying the weight of the world on his shoulders.* □ *Cheer up, Tom! You don't need to carry the weight of the world on your shoulders.*

carry through (on something) to carry something out satisfactorily; to complete some act as promised. □ *I hope you will carry through on this project.* □ *Yes, I'll carry through.*

carry weight (with someone) [for someone] to have influence with someone; [for something] to have significance for someone. (Often in the negative.) □ *Everything Mary says carries weight with me.* □ *Don't pay any attention to John. What he says carries no weight around here.* □ *Your proposal is quite good, but since you're not a member of the club, it carries no weight.*

cart someone or something off to take or haul someone or something away. (When used with *someone* the person is treated like an object.) □ *The police came and carted her off.* T *Let's cart off these boxes.* □ *They carted the trash off.*

carve something in (to something) to cut letters or symbols into something. □ *He carved his initials into a tree.* T *He carved in the letters.* □ *He carved them in.*

carve something into something to create a carved object by sculpturing raw material. □ *She carved the soap into a little elephant.* □ *Ken carved the apple into a tiny snowman.*

carve something out to hollow something out by carving; to make something hollow by carving. □ *Did the Boy Scout learn to carve a bowl out?* T *He carved out the bowl of the pipe and then began to sand it.*

carve something out (of something) to remove something from the inside of something else by carving or cutting. □ *She carved the insides out of the pumpkin.* T *She carved out the insides of the pumpkin.* □ *John carved the insides out.*

carve something up to divide something up, perhaps carelessly. □ *You can't carve the country up!* T *You can't just carve up one country and give the pieces away.*

case in point an example of what one is talking about. □ *Now, as a case in point, let's look at nineteenth-century England.* □ *Fireworks can be dangerous. For a case in point, look what happened to Bob Smith last week.*

cash-and-carry having to do with a sale of goods or a way of selling that requires payment at the time of sale and requires that you take the goods with you. □ *I'm sorry. We don't deliver. It's strictly cash-and-carry.* □ *You cannot get credit at that drugstore. They only sell cash-and-carry.*

cash in (on something) to earn a lot of money at something; to make a profit at something; to take advantage of something. □ *This is a good year for farming, and you can cash in on it if you're smart.* □ *It's too late to cash in.* □ *Everyone was trying to cash in on the current interest in the military.*

cash (one's chips) in 1. to turn in one's gaming tokens or poker chips when one quits playing. □ *When you leave the game, you should cash your chips in.* T *Cash in your chips before you go.* □ *I'm going to cash in.* 2. to quit [anything]. (As if one were cashing in gaming tokens.) □ *I guess I'll cash my chips in and then go home.*

T *Well, it's time to cash in my chips and go home.* □ *I've eaten enough. I'm going to cash in.* 3. to die. (Slang. Using the same metaphor as sense 2.) □ *There's a funeral procession. Who cashed his chips in?* T *Poor Fred cashed in his chips last week.* □ *He took a slug in the gut and cashed in.*

Cash or credit (card)? Do you wish to pay for your purchases with cash or a credit card? □ *Mary put all her packages on the counter. Then the clerk said, "Cash or credit card?"* □ CLERK: *Is that everything?* RACHEL: *Yes. That's all.* CLERK: *Cash or credit?*

cast off (from something) [for the crew of a boat or ship] to push away from the dock or pier; to begin the process of undocking a boat or ship. □ *The crew cast off from the dock.* □ *It's time to cast off.*

cast (one's) pearls before swine to waste something good on someone who doesn't care about it. (Biblical. As if throwing something of great value under the feet of pigs. It is considered insulting to refer to people as swine.) □ *To sing for them is to cast pearls before swine.* □ *To serve them French cuisine is like casting one's pearls before swine.*

cast someone or something off to dispose of someone or something; to throw someone or something aside or away. □ *You can't just cast me off like an old coat!* T *She cast off her husband of three months.* T *Lee cast off his coat.*

cast someone or something out to throw someone or something out. (Stilted.) □ *You are not going to cast me out on a night like this!* T *Jane cast out the cat and slammed the door.* □ *I cast the offensive child out.*

cast someone or something up [for the waves] to bring up and deposit someone or something on the shore. □ *The waves cast the body of the sailor up, and it was found on the shore.* T *The waves cast up the body of a sailor.* □ *The action of the waves cast a lot of driftwood up.*

cast the first stone to make the first criticism; to be the first to attack. (Biblical.) □ *Well, I don't want to be the one to cast the first stone, but she sang horribly.* □ *John always casts the first stone. Does he think he's perfect?*

catch cold AND **take cold** to contract a cold (the disease). □ *Please close the window, or we'll all catch cold.* □ *I take cold every year at this time.*

Catch me later. AND **Catch me some other time.** Please try to talk to me later. □ BILL (angry): *Tom, look at this phone bill!* TOM: *Catch me later.* □ *"Catch me some other time,"* hollered Mr. Franklin over his shoulder. *"I've got to go to the airport."*

Catch me some other time. See the previous entry.

catch on (to someone or something) to figure out someone or something. □ *I finally caught on to what she was talking about.* □ *It takes a while for me to catch on.*

catch on (with someone) [for something] to become popular with someone. □ *I hope our new product catches on with children.* □ *I'm sure it will catch on.*

catch one's death (of cold) AND **take one's death of cold** to contract a cold; to catch a serious cold. □ *If I go out in this weather, I'll catch my death of cold.* □ *Dress up warm or you'll take your death of cold.* □ *Put on your raincoat or you'll catch your death.*

catch someone off-balance to catch a person who is not prepared; to surprise someone. (Also used literally.) □ *Sorry I acted so flustered. You caught me off-balance.* □ *The robbers caught Ann off-balance and stole her purse.*

catch someone up in something [for excitement or interest] to extend to and engross someone. □ *The happenings caught everyone up in the excitement.* □ *The accident caught us all up in the resultant confusion.*

catch someone up (on someone or something) to tell someone the news of someone or something. (Someone includes oneself.) □ *Oh, please catch me up on what your family is doing.* □ *Yes, do catch us up!* □ *I have to take some time to catch myself up on the news.*

catch someone's eye AND **get someone's eye** to establish eye contact with someone; to attract someone's attention. (Also with *have*, as in the examples.) □ *The shiny red car caught Mary's eye.* □ *Tom got Mary's eye and waved to her.* □ *When Tom had her eye, he smiled at her.*

catch up (on someone or something) **1.** to learn the news of someone or something. □ *I need a little time to catch up on the news.* □ *We all need to catch up on Tony.* □ *I need some time to catch up.* **2.** [with *something*] to bring one's efforts with something up to date; to do the work that one should have done. □ *I need a quiet time so I can catch up on my work.* □ *I have to catch up and become more productive.*

catch up (to someone or something) to get even with or equal to someone or something. □ *I finally caught up to Fred, who was way ahead of me in the race.* □ *Jane caught up to the bus that had almost left her behind.* □ *Don't worry, I'll catch up.*

catch up (with someone or something) to increase the rate of movement or growth in order to become even with or equal to someone or something. □ *Martin is finally catching up with his taller brother.* □ *This puppy will never catch up with the others.* □ *The competing companies will never catch up with this one.* □ *I'm smaller than the others. Will I ever catch up?*

caught in the cross fire caught between two fighting people or groups. (As if one were stranded between two opposing armies who are firing bullets at each other.) □ *In western movies, innocent people are always getting caught in the cross fire.* □ *In the war, Corporal Smith was killed when he got caught in the cross fire.*

caught short to be without something you need, especially money. □ *I needed eggs for my cake, but I was caught short.* □ *Bob had to borrow money from John to pay for the meal. Bob is caught short quite often.*

cause (some) eyebrows to raise to shock people; to surprise and dismay people. □ *John caused eyebrows to raise when he married a poor girl from Toledo.* □ *If you want to cause some eyebrows to raise, just start singing as you walk down the street.*

cause (some) tongues to wag to cause people to gossip; to give people something to gossip about. □ *The way John was looking at Mary will surely cause some tongues to wag.* □ *The way Mary was dressed will also cause tongues to wag.*

cave in (on someone or something) [for a roof or ceiling] to collapse on someone or something. □ *The roof caved in on the miners.* □ *The roof caved in.*

cave in (to someone or something) to give in to someone or something. □ *Finally, the manager caved in to the customer's demands.* □ *I refuse to cave in.*

center something on someone or something to base something on someone or something. □ *Let us center the discussion on Walter.* □ *We centered our whole meeting on the conservation question.*

Certainly! See *Definitely!*

Certainly not! See *Definitely not!*

chalk something out **1.** to draw a picture of something in chalk, especially to illustrate a plan of some type. □ *The coach chalked the play out so the players could understand what they were to do.* Ⓣ *She chalked out the play.* **2.** to explain something carefully to someone, as if one were talking about a chalk drawing. (Often figurative.) □ *Here, let me chalk it out for you. Listen carefully.* Ⓣ *She chalked out the details of the plan.*

chalk something up 1. to write something on a chalkboard. □ *Let me chalk this formula up so you all can see it.* Ⓣ *I'll chalk up the formula.* **2.** to add a mark or point to one's score. □ *Chalk another goal up.* Ⓣ *Chalk up another basket for the other side.*

chalk something up to something to account for something with something else; to blame something on something else. □ *You can chalk her mistake up to ignorance.* □ *Chalk Ted's success up to preparedness.* T *I will chalk up this defeat to his youth.*

champ at the bit to be ready and anxious to do something. (Originally said about horses.) □ *The kids were champing at the bit to get into the swimming pool.* □ *The dogs were champing at the bit to begin the hunt.*

chance (up)on someone or something to find someone or something by accident; to happen on someone or something. (*Upon* is formal and less commonly used than *on*.) □ *I chanced upon a nice little restaurant on my walk today. The prices looked good too.* □ *I chanced on an old friend of yours in town today.*

change horses in midstream to make major changes in an activity that has already begun; to choose someone or something else after it is too late. (Usually regarded as a bad idea.) □ *I'm already baking a cherry pie. I can't bake an apple pie. It's too late to change horses in midstream.* □ *The house is half-built. It's too late to hire a different architect. You can't change horses in midstream.*

change out of something to take off a set of clothing and put on another. □ *I have to change out of these wet clothes.* □ *You should change out of your casual clothes and put on something more formal for dinner.*

charge in(to some place) to bolt or run wildly into a place. □ *The people charged into the store on the day of the sale.* □ *They all charged in like thirsty camels.*

charge off to bolt or run away. □ *He got angry and charged off.* □ *Juan charged off to talk to the boss.*

charge out of some place to bolt or stomp out of some place. □ *Carol charged out of the house, trying to catch Sally before she got on the bus.* □ *Juan got mad and charged out of the office.*

charge someone or something up 1. [with *someone*] to excite someone; to make a person enthusiastic about something. (*Someone* includes oneself.) □ *The excitement of the day charged them up so they could not sleep.* T *The speaker charged up the crowd.* □ *He reread the report, hoping to charge himself up enough to make some sensible comments.* **2.** [with *something*] to apply an electrical charge to a battery. □ *How long will it take to charge this battery up?* T *It takes an hour to charge up your battery.* **3.** [with *something*] to load or fill something, such as a fire extinguisher. □ *We had to send the extinguishers back to the factory, where they charged them up.* T *How much does it cost to charge up an extinguisher?* **4.** to reinvigorate something. □ *What can we do to charge this play up?* T *A murder in the first act would charge up the play.*

√ **charge something (up) to someone or something** to place the cost of something on the account of someone or a group. □ *I will have to charge this up to your account.* □ *Do you have to charge this to my account?* □ *Is this order charged to anyone yet?*

Charity begins at home. One should be kind to one's own family, friends, or fellow citizens before trying to help others. (Proverb.) □ *"Mother, may I please have some pie?" asked Mary. "Remember, charity begins at* home." □ At church, the minister reminded us that charity begins at home, but we must remember others also.

Charmed(, I'm sure). an expression said after being introduced to someone. (Almost a parody. Would not be used in most everyday situations.) □ MARY: *I want you to meet my great-aunt Sarah.* SALLY: *Charmed, I'm sure.* □ MARY: *Bill, meet Sally. Sally, this is Bill.* BILL: *My pleasure.* SALLY: *Charmed.*

chart something out (for someone or something) to lay out a plan or course for someone or something. □ *The first mate charted the course out for the skipper.* ⊤ *The first mate charted out the course for us.* □ *Shall I chart it out?* ⊤ *I will chart out the course for our journey.*

chase someone or something down to track down and seize someone or something. □ *Larry set out to chase Betsy down.* ⊤ *The police chased down the suspect.* □ *They chased her down.*

cheat someone out of something to get something from someone by deception. (*Someone* includes *oneself.*) □ *Are you trying to cheat me out of what is rightfully mine?* □ *She cheated herself out of an invitation because she lied about her affiliation.*

Check. That is correct.; That is accounted for. □ SUE: *Is the coffee ready yet?* JOHN: *Check.* □ MARY: *Let's go over the list. Flashlight?* JOHN: *Check.* MARY: *Band-Aids?* JOHN: *Check.* MARY: *Pencils?* JOHN: *Check.* MARY: *Matches?* JOHN: *Check.* MARY: *Great!*

check back (on someone or something) to look into the state of

someone or something again at a later time. □ *I'll have to check back on you later.* □ *I'll check back later.*

check back (with someone) to inquire of someone again at a later time. □ *Please check back with me later.* □ *Okay. I'll check back.*

check in (at something) to go to a place and record one's arrival. □ *When you get there, check in at the front office.* □ *All right. I'll check in when I arrive.*

check in on someone or something to go into a place and look in on someone or something there. □ *I think I will go check in on Timmy.* □ *Let me check in on how things are going in the kitchen.*

check into something 1. to investigate a matter. □ *I asked the manager to check into it.* □ *Something is wrong, and I will check into it.* **2.** to sign oneself into a place to stay, such as a hotel, hospital, motel, etc. □ *She checked into a private hospital for some kind of treatment.* □ *They checked into the first motel they came to on the highway.*

check on someone or something to look into the legitimacy or condition of someone or something. □ *Sarah will check on the matter and report to us.* □ *I will check on Jeff.* □ *While you're upstairs, would you check on the baby?*

check out [for someone or something] to prove to be correctly represented. (See also *check someone or something out.*) □ *Everything you told me checks out.* □ *Your story checks out, Max.*

check out (from something) to do the paperwork necessary to leave a place and then leave. □ *I will check out from the office and come right to where you are.* □ *I'll be there as soon as I check out.*

check out (of something) to do the paperwork necessary to leave a place, such as a hotel. □ *I will check out of the hotel at about noon.* □ *I check out at noon.*

Check, please. AND **Could I have the bill?; Could I have the check?** Could I please have the bill for this food or drink? □ *When they both had finished their dessert and coffee, Tom said, "Check, please."* □ BILL: *That meal was really good. This is a fine place to eat.* TOM: *Waiter! Check, please.* WAITER: *Right away, sir.*

check someone or something in 1. [with *someone*] to record the arrival of someone. (*Someone* includes *oneself.*) □ *Ask the guard to check you in when you get there.* □ *She checked herself in and went on to the dressing room.* 2. [with *something*] to record that someone has returned something. □ *I asked the librarian to check the book in for me.* T *Did the librarian check in the book?* 3. [with *something*] to take something to a place, return it, and make sure that its return has been recorded. □ *I checked the video in on time.* T *Did you really check in the book on time?* 4. to examine a shipment or an order received and make certain that everything ordered was received. □ *I checked the order in and sent a report to the manager.* T *Tim checked in the order from the supplier to make sure that everything was there.*

check someone or something off to mark or cross out the name of a person or thing on a list. (*Someone* includes *oneself.*) □ *I am glad to see that you were able to come. I will check you off.* T *I checked off the recent arrivals.* □ *I checked the items off.* □ *Mary checked herself off and proceeded to start the day's work.*

check someone or something out to evaluate someone or something. (*Someone* includes *oneself.* See also *check out.*) □ *It sounds good. I'll check it out.* T *I'll check out everyone else.* □ *The doctor will check you out.* □ *She checked herself out, but found no broken bones.*

check someone or something over to examine someone or something closely. (*Someone* includes *oneself.*) □ *You should have the doctor check you over before you go back to work.* T *The doctor checked over the children who had shown the worst symptoms.* □ *The mechanic checked the car over.* □ *After checking herself over, Sally picked up her parcels, got up, and continued to walk down the street.*

check up (on someone or something) to determine the state of someone or something. □ *Please don't check up on me. I can be trusted.* □ *I see no need to check up.*

cheer someone up to make a sad person happy. (*Someone* includes *oneself.* More at *cheer up.*) □ *Let's try to cheer Karen up.* T *Yes, let's cheer up Karen.* □ *Usually I can cheer myself up on days like this, but not today.*

cheer up 1. [for a sad person] to become happy. (More at *cheer someone up.*) □ *After a while, she began to cheer up.* □ *Cheer up! Things could be worse.* 2. *Don't worry. Try to be happy!* (Usually **Cheer up!**) □ TOM: *Things are really looking bad for me* *financially.* MARY: *Cheer up! Things'll work out for the best.* □ SUE: *Cheer up! In no time at all, things will be peachy keen.* BOB: *In no time at all, they'll be a lot worse.*

Cheerio. *Good-bye.* (Chiefly British.) □ BOB: *Bye.* TOM: *Cheerio.* □ *"Cheerio," said Mary, skipping out of the room like a schoolgirl.*

chew something off ((of) something) to bite or gnaw something off something. (The *of* is colloquial.) □ *The puppy chewed the heel off of my shoe.* □ *The puppy chewed the heel off.*

chew something up to grind food with the teeth until it can be swallowed. □ *You had better chew that stuff up well.* ⊤ *Please chew up your food well.*

chime in (with something) to add a comment to the discussion. □ *Little Billy chimed in with a suggestion.* □ *He chimed in too late.*

chip away [for something] to break off or break away in small chips. □ *The edges of the marble step chipped away over the years.* □ *Some of the stone figures had chipped away so badly that we couldn't see what they were.*

chip in (on something) (for someone) to contribute money toward something for someone. □ *Would you please chip in on the present for Richard?* □ *Will you chip in for Randy?* □ *I would like to chip in on the gift.* □ *I won't chip in.*

choke on something to begin to gag and cough on something stuck in the throat. □ *The dog choked on the meat.* □ *The restaurant patron began to choke on a fish bone.*

choke someone up to cause someone to feel like sobbing. (More at *choke up.*) □ *Sad stories like that always choke me up.* □ *Your complaints choke me up considerably.*

choke something back to fight hard to keep something from coming out of one's mouth, such as sobs, tears, angry words, vomit, etc. □ *I tried to choke the unpleasant words back, but I could not.* ⊤ *She choked back her grief, but it came forth nonetheless.* □ *I could hardly choke my tears back.*

choke something down to work hard to swallow something, usually because it tastes bad. □ *The medicine was terrible, but I managed to choke it down.* ⊤ *She choked down the horrible medicine.*

choke something up 1. to clog something up; to fill up and block something. □ *Branches and leaves choked the sewer up.* ⊤ *Rust choked up the pipes.* 2. to cough or choke until something that has blocked one's windpipe is brought up. □ *The old man was unable to choke the candy up that was stuck in his windpipe.* ⊤ *He choked up the chunk of meat and could breathe again.*

choke up 1. to feel like sobbing. (More at *choke someone up.*) □ *I choked up when I heard the news.* □ *He was beginning to choke up as he talked.* 2. to become frightened or saddened so that one cannot speak. □ *I choked up when he came in.* □ *I was choking up, and I knew I would not be able to go on.* □ *Henry was so choked up he couldn't speak.*

choke up (about someone or something) to become very emotional about someone or something. □ *I choke up about Tom every time I think about his illness.* □ *I choked up at the thought.*

choose up sides to select opposing sides for a debate, fight, or game. □ *Let's choose up sides and play basketball.* □ *The children chose up sides and began the game.*

chop someone off to stop someone in the middle of a sentence or speech. □ *I'm not finished. Don't chop me off!* Ⓣ *The moderator chopped off the speaker.*

chop something down to fell a tree or a pole; to fell a person by cutting with a sword or something similar. □ *George chopped the tree down for some unknown reason.* Ⓣ *He chopped down the cherry tree.* Ⓣ *The knight chopped down the peasant.*

chop something off to cut something off, perhaps with an axe. □ *Chop this branch off, please.* Ⓣ *I'll chop off the branch.*

Chow. See the following entry.

Ciao. AND **Chow.** *Good-bye.* (Italian. *Chow* is not an Italian spelling.) □ JOHN: *Ciao.* MARY: *Ciao, baby.* □ *"Ciao," said Mary Francine as she swept from the room.*

circulate something through something to route something through something; to make something travel through something. □ *Walter circulated the memo from the boss through the department.* □ *I would like for you to circulate this through the members of the club.* □ *This pump circulates the hot water through the heating pipes.*

circulate through something 1. [for a fluid in a closed system of pipes or tubes] to flow through the various pathways of pipes and tubes. □ *Cold water circulates through the entire building and keeps it cool.* □ *Blood circulates through the veins and arteries,* carrying food to, and wastes away from, all parts of the body. **2.** to travel through something; to make the rounds through something. □ *Rumors circulated through the department about Tom's retirement.* □ *Please circulate through the room and hand out these papers to each person over thirty.*

clamp down (on someone or something) to restrain or limit someone or someone's actions. □ *The police clamped down on the gang.* □ *They had to clamp down to keep the streets safe.*

claw something off ((of) someone or something) to rip or tear something off from someone or something. □ *We saw a guy clawing his burning clothes off himself.* Ⓣ *He clawed off his burning clothes.* □ *He clawed them off.*

clean one's act up to start behaving better. □ *You had better clean your act up and be a better citizen.* Ⓣ *Clean up your act!*

clean someone or something down to clean someone or something by brushing or with flowing water. (*Someone* includes oneself.) □ *He was covered with mud, and we used the garden hose to clean him down* Ⓣ *Please clean down the sidewalk.* □ *He cleaned himself down with water from the hose.*

clean someone or something out (of something) to remove people or things from something or some place. □ *Someone should clean those bums out of political office.* Ⓣ *Yes! Clean out those bums.* □ *Clean the dust out of the cupboards.* □ *Clean them out!*

clean someone or something up to get someone or something clean.

65

(*Someone* includes *oneself.*) □ *Please go into the bathroom and clean yourself up.* T *I'll clean up the kids a little bit before we leave for dinner.* □ *Can you clean this place up a little?* □ *Oh, go clean yourself up. You're a mess.*

clean something off to take something off something; to remove something such as dirt or dirty dishes. □ *Please clean the table off and put the dishes in the kitchen.* T *I'll clean off the table.*

clean something off ((of) something) to remove something from something. □ *Judy cleaned the writing off the wall.* T *I'm glad she cleaned off the writing.* □ *Sam cleaned it off.*

clean something out to remove dirt or unwanted things from the inside of something. □ *Someone has to clean the garage out.* T *I'll clean out the garage.*

clean up (on someone or something) to make a large profit from someone or some business activity. □ *We are really going to clean up on this product.* □ *We will clean up on Tom. He is buying everything we have.* □ *We are really going to clean up.*

clear out (of some place) to get out of some place. □ *Will you all clear out of here?* □ *Please clear out!*

clear something away to take something away. □ *Please clear the tea things away.* T *Would you clear away the dishes?*

clear something off ((of) something) to take something off something. (The *of* is colloquial.) □ *Please clear the dishes off the table.* T *I'll clear off the dishes.* □ *Please clear them off.*

clear something up 1. to clarify something; to take away the con-

fusion about something. □ *Let me take a few minutes to clear things up.* T *I would like to clear up this confusion for you.* 2. to cure a disease. □ *I think I can clear this up with a salve.* T *Will this salve clear up the rash?*

clear the table to remove the dishes and other eating utensils from the table after a meal. □ *Will you please help clear the table?* □ *After you clear the table, we'll play cards.*

Clear the way! Please get out of the way because someone or something is coming through and needs room. □ *The movers were shouting "Clear the way!" because they needed room to take the piano out of the house.* □ TOM: *Clear the way! Clear the way!* MARY: *Who does he think he is?* BOB: *I don't know, but I'm getting out of the way.*

clear up 1. [for something] to become more understandable. □ *At about the middle of the very confusing lecture, things began to clear up.* □ *I was having trouble, but things are beginning to clear up.* 2. [for a disease] to improve or become cured. □ *His cold cleared up after a couple of weeks.* □ *I'm sure your rash will clear up soon.* 3. [for the sky] to become more clear. □ *Suddenly, the sky cleared up.* □ *When the sky cleared up, the breeze began to blow.*

climb on the bandwagon to join others in supporting someone or something. □ *Come join us! Climb on the bandwagon and support Senator Smith!* □ *Look at all those people climbing on the bandwagon! They don't know what they are getting into!*

clip someone's wings to restrain someone; to reduce or put an end to a teenager's privileges. (As with birds or fowl whose wings are clipped to keep them at home.) □ *You had better learn to get home on time, or I will clip your wings.* □ *My mother clipped my wings. I can't go out tonight.*

clip something on((to) someone or something) to attach something to someone or something with a clip. □ *I clipped a little name tag onto him before I put him on the plane.* T *I clipped on a name tag.* □ *Liz clipped it on.*

clip something out (of something) to remove something from something by clipping or cutting. □ *Please clip the article out of the magazine.* T *Could you clip out the article?* □ *Sam clipped it out.*

clock in to record one's time of arrival. □ *What time did she clock in?* □ *She forgot to clock in today.*

clock out to record one's time of departure. □ *I will clock out just before I go home.* □ *Juan clocked out before the official closing time.*

clock someone in to observe and record someone's time of arrival. (*Someone* includes *oneself.*) □ *The manager says he clocked you in at noon. That's a bit late, isn't it?* T *Does she clock in everyone?* □ *Henry clocked himself in and went straight to work.*

clock someone out to observe and record someone's time of departure. (*Someone* includes *oneself.*) □ *The manager clocked him out at about midnight.* T *Does the manager clock out everyone?* □ *Jane clocked herself out and went home.*

clog something up [for something] to obstruct a channel or conduit. (More at *clog up.*) □ *The leaves clogged the*

gutters up. T *They clogged up the gutter.*

clog up [for a channel or conduit] to become blocked. (More at *clog something up.*) □ *The canal clogged up with leaves and mud.*

close at hand within reach; handy. □ *I'm sorry, but your letter isn't close at hand. Please remind me what you said in it.* □ *When you're cooking, you should keep all the ingredients close at hand.*

close down [for a business, office, shop, etc.] to close permanently or temporarily. (More at *close someone or something down.*) □ *This shop will have to close down if they raise taxes.* □ *I am afraid that you will have to close down for a while because of the gas leak.*

close in (on someone or something) to move in on someone or something. □ *The cops were closing in on the thugs.* □ *They closed in quietly.*

close ranks **1.** to move closer together in a military formation. □ *The soldiers closed ranks and marched on the enemy.* □ *All right! Stop that talking and close ranks.* **2.** to join (with someone). □ *We can fight this menace only if we close ranks.* □ *Let's all close ranks behind Ann and get her elected.*

close someone or something down to force someone or someone's business, office, shop, etc., to close permanently or temporarily. (More at *close down.*) □ *The police closed the bookstore down.* T *They closed down the shop.* □ *The recession closed down Tom, whose shop could just barely make it in good times.*

close someone or something up 1. to close someone or someone's business, office, shop, etc., temporarily or permanently. □ *Tom's restaurant nearly went out of business when the health department closed him up.* ⊤ *The health department closed up the restaurant.* □ *Dave's shop was failing. The bank closed him up.* **2.** to close someone or something completely. (Said of a person being stitched up at the end of a surgical procedure.) □ *Fred, would you close her up for me?* ⊤ *Fred closed up the patient.* ⊤ *I closed up the box and put it on the shelf.*

close someone out of something to prevent someone from getting into something, such as a class, a room, a waiting list, etc. □ *They closed me out of the class I wanted.*

close something out 1. to sell off a particular kind of merchandise with the intention of not selling it in the future. □ *These are not selling. Let's close them out.* ⊤ *They closed out the merchandise that wouldn't sell.* **2.** to prevent further registration in something. □ *We are going to have to close this class out.* ⊤ *The registrar closed out the class.*

close up [for an opening] to close completely. □ *The door closed up and would not open again.* □ *The shop closed up and did not open until the next day.*

cloud up [for the sky] to fill with clouds. □ *By midmorning, the sky had clouded up.* □ *I hope it doesn't cloud up today.*

clown around (with someone) to join with someone in acting silly; [for two or more people] to act silly together. □ *The boys were clowning* around with each other. □ *The kids are having fun clowning around.*

clue someone in (on something) to inform someone about something. □ *Would you please clue me in on what you are talking about?* ⊤ *I will clue in everyone on this matter if you want.* □ *Please clue me in.*

clutter something up to mess something up; to fill something or some place up with too many things. □ *Heaps of newspapers cluttered the room up and made it a fire hazard.* ⊤ *Who cluttered up this house?*

coast-to-coast from the Atlantic to the Pacific oceans (in the U.S.A.); all the land between the Atlantic and Pacific oceans. □ *My voice was once heard on a coast-to-coast radio broadcast.* □ *Our car made the coast-to-coast trip in eighty hours.*

cock-and-bull story a silly, made-up story; a story that is a lie. □ *Don't give me that cock-and-bull story.* □ *I asked for an explanation, and all I got was your ridiculous cock-and-bull story!*

coil something up to roll or twist something into a coil. □ *Maria coiled the strip of stamps up and put them in the little dispenser.* ⊤ *Please coil up the rope.*

collapse into something 1. to fall down into something. □ *She was so tired, she collapsed into the chair.* □ *Juan collapsed into a chair and fell fast asleep.* **2.** [for someone] to fall into a particular kind of despair. □ *The poor man collapsed into a deep depression.* □ *Scott collapsed into his own personal brand of grieving.*

collapse under someone or something to cave in under the weight of someone or something. □ *The* framework collapsed under the weight of the spectators. □ The bridge collapsed under the heavy traffic.

comb something out to comb something and make it straight or neat. □ She combed her hair out. T She combed out her hair every morning.

comb something out (of something) to remove knots and snarls from something by combing. □ I had to comb the gum out of her hair. T I had to comb out the gum. □ Maria combed it out.

come a cropper to have a misfortune; to fail. (Literally, to fall off one's horse.) □ Bob invested all his money in the stock market just before it fell. Boy, did he come a cropper. □ Jane was out all night before she took her tests. She really came a cropper.

come about [for a boat] to change its angle against the wind; [for a boat] to change tack. □ The boat will have to come about. The wind shifted. □ We came about and went back to shore.

Come again. 1. Please come back again sometime. □ MARY: I had a lovely time. Thank you for asking me. SALLY: You're quite welcome. Come again. □ "Come again," said Mrs. Martin as she let Jimmy out the door. 2. I didn't hear what you said. Please repeat it. (Usually **Come again?** A little dated and folksy.) □ SALLY: Do you want some more carrots? MARY: Come again? SALLY: Carrots. Do you want some more carrots? □ Uncle Henry turned his good ear toward the clerk and said, "Come again?"

Come and get it! Dinner's ready. Come eat! (Folksy and familiar.) □ The camp cook shouted, "Soup's on! Come and get it!" □ TOM: Come and get it! Time to eat! MARY: What is it this time? More bean soup? TOM: Certainly not! Lentils.

come apart at the seams to lose one's emotional self-control suddenly. (From the literal sense, referring to a garment falling apart.) □ Bill was so upset that he almost came apart at the seams. □ I couldn't take any more. I just came apart at the seams.

come around 1. to agree in the end; to agree finally. □ I knew you would come around in the end. □ Finally, she came around and agreed to our terms. 2. to return to consciousness. □ After we threw cold water in his face, he came around. □ Ken came around almost immediately after he had fainted.

come away empty-handed to leave or return without anything. □ All right, go gambling. Don't come away empty-handed, though. □ Go to the bank and ask for the loan again. This time don't come away empty-handed.

come away (from someone or something) to move away from someone or something. □ Please come away from the fire. You will get burned if you don't. □ Come away from that filthy person! □ Come away!

come back to return to an advantageous or favorable state or condition. □ Walter practiced his singing every day, hoping to come back in a wave of glory. □ When will the good old days come back?

Come back and see me. See the following entry.

Come back and see us. AND **Come back and see me.** Come visit us [or me] again. (Often said by a host or hostess to departing guests.) □ BILL: Good night. Thanks for having me.

SALLY: *Oh, you're quite welcome. Come back and see us.* □ BOB: *I enjoyed my visit. Good-bye.* MARY: *It was very nice of you to pay me a visit. Come back and see me.*

Come back anytime. Please come and visit us again. You're always welcome. (Often said by a host or hostess to departing guests.) □ MARY: *So glad you could come.* BILL: *Thank you. I had a wonderful time.* MARY: *Come back anytime.* □ BOB: *Thanks for the coffee and cake. Bye.* MARY: *We're glad to have you. Please come back anytime.*

come back (to someone or something) to return to someone or something. □ *Please come back to me. I'm lonely.* □ *Come back to your home!* □ *Please come back!*

Come back when you can stay longer. Come back again sometime when your visit can be longer. (Often said by a host or hostess to departing guests.) □ JOHN: *I really must go.* SUE: *So glad you could come. Please come back when you can stay longer.* □ BILL: *Well, I hate to eat and run, but I have to get up early tomorrow.* MARY: *Well, come back when you can stay longer.*

come by something 1. to travel by a specific carrier, such as a plane, a boat, or a car. (Literal.) □ *We came by train. It's more relaxing.* □ *Next time, we'll come by plane. It's faster.* **2.** to find or get something. □ *How did you come by that haircut?* □ *Where did you come by that new shirt?*

come down in the world to lose one's social position or financial standing. □ *Mr. Jones has really come down in the world since he lost his job.* □ *If I*

were unemployed, I'm sure I'd come down in the world, too.

come down with something to catch a disease. □ *Dan came down with chicken pox.* □ *I don't want to come down with the flu again.*

come home (to roost) to return to cause trouble (for someone). (As chickens or other birds return home to roost.) □ *As I feared, all my problems came home to roost.* □ *Yes, problems all come home eventually.*

come in 1. to enter. (Often a command or polite request.) □ *Please come in.* □ *If you will come in and have a seat, I will tell Betty that you are here.* **2.** to arrive; [for a shipment of something] to arrive. □ *New models come in almost every week.* □ *When do you expect a new batch to come in?* □ *The tomatoes will come in at the end of July.* □ *The election results came in early in the evening.*

Come in and make yourself at home. Please come into my home and make yourself comfortable. □ SUE: *Oh, hello, Tom. Come in and make yourself at home.* TOM: *Thanks. I will.* (entering) *Oh, it's nice and warm in here.* □ *"Come in and make yourself at home,"* invited Bob.

Come in and set a spell. See the following entry.

Come in and sit a spell. AND **Come in and set a spell.; Come in and sit down.; Come in and take a load off your feet.** Please come in and have a seat and a visit. (Colloquial and folksy. *Set* is especially folksy.) □ *"Hi, Fred,"* smiled Tom. *"Come in and sit a spell."* □ TOM: *I hope I'm not intruding.* BILL: *Not at all. Come in and set a spell.*

Come in and sit down. See the previous entry.

Come in and take a load off your feet. See *Come in and sit a spell.*

come in out of the rain to become alert and sensible. (Also used literally.) □ *Pay attention, Sally! Come in out of the rain!* □ *Bill will fail if he doesn't come in out of the rain and study.*

come into one's or its own 1. [for one] to achieve one's proper recognition. □ *Sally finally came into her own.* □ *After years of trying, she finally came into her own.* **2.** [for something] to achieve its proper recognition. □ *The idea of an electric car finally came into its own.* □ *Film as an art medium finally came into its own.*

come of age to reach an age when one is old enough to own property, get married, and sign legal contracts. □ *When Jane comes of age, she will buy her own car.* □ *Sally, who came of age last month, entered into an agreement to purchase a house.*

come off to happen as planned; to come to fruition; to succeed. (Colloquial.) □ *When is this party going to come off?* □ *Did the concert come off okay?*

Come off it! Don't act so haughty!; Stop acting that way! □ TOM: *This stuff just doesn't meet my requirements.* BILL: *Come off it, Tom! This is exactly what you've always bought.* TOM: *That doesn't mean I like it.* □ MARY: *We are not amused by your childish antics.* SUE: *Come off it, Mary. Who do you think you're talking to?*

come off ((of) something) [for something] to become detached from something else. (The *of* is colloqui-al.) □ *This piece came off of the top, not the bottom.* □ *There is a broken place here. I think something came off.*

come off second-best to win second place or worse; to lose out to someone else. □ *John came off second-best in the race.* □ *Why do I always come off second-best in an argument with you?*

come on 1. Stop it!; Stop doing that. (Usually **Come on!**) □ *Sally was tickling Tom, and he was laughing like mad. Finally, he sputtered, "Come on!"* □ MARY: *Are you really going to sell your new car?* SALLY: *Come on! How dumb do you think I am?* **2.** please oblige me. □ MOTHER: *Sorry. You can't go!* BILL: *Come on, let me go to the picnic!* □ *"Come on," whined Jimmy, "I want some more!"* **3.** to hurry along after someone. (Usually a command.) □ *Come on! We'll be late.* □ *Don't linger behind. Come on!* **4.** [for electricity or some other device] to start operating. □ *After a while, the lights came on again.* □ *I hope the heat comes on soon.* **5.** to walk out and appear on stage. □ *You are to come on when you hear your cue.* □ *Juan did not come on when he was supposed to.* **6.** [for a pain] to begin hurting; [for a disease] to attack someone. □ *The pain began to come on again, and Sally had to lie down.* □ *As a fainting spell came on, Gerald headed for a chair.* **7.** to yield; to agree. (Usually a command.) □ *Come on! Do it!* □ *Come on, now! Be a sport!* **8.** [for a program] to be broadcast on radio or television. □ *When does the news come on?* □ *The news didn't come on until an hour later.*

Come (on) in. Enter.; Come into this place. (A polite invitation to enter someone's home, office, room, etc. It is more emphatic with *on*.) □ BOB: *Hello, you guys. Come on in. We're just about to start the music.* MARY: *Great! Um! Something smells good!* TOM: *Yeah. When do we eat?* BOB: *Just hold your horses. All in good time.* □ BILL: *Come in. Nice to see you.* MARY: *I hope we're not too early.* BILL: *Not at all.*

come on((to) someone or something) to find someone or something by accident; to happen onto someone or something. □ *When I was out on my walk, I came on a little shop that sells leather goods.* □ *I came on an old friend of yours downtown today.*

come out 1. to exit; to leave the inside of a place. □ *Please come out. We have to leave.* □ *When do you think they will all come out?* **2.** to result; to succeed; to happen. □ *I hope everything comes out okay.* □ *It will come out okay. Don't worry.* **3.** to come before the public; to be published; to be made public. □ *A new magazine has just come out.* □ *When will your next book come out?* **4.** to become visible or evident. □ *His pride came out in his refusal to accept help.* □ *The real reason finally came out, and it was not flattering.*

come out ahead to end up with a profit; to improve one's situation. □ *I hope you come out ahead with your investments.* □ *It took a lot of money to buy the house, but I think I'll come out ahead.*

come out in the wash to work out all right. (This means that problems or difficulties will go away as dirt goes away in the process of washing.) □ *Don't worry about that problem. It'll all come out in the wash.* □ *This trouble will go away. It'll come out in the wash.*

come out of the closet 1. to reveal one's secret interests. □ *Tom Brown came out of the closet and admitted that he likes to knit.* □ *It's time that all of you lovers of chamber music came out of the closet and attended our concerts.* **2.** to reveal that one is a homosexual. □ *Tom surprised his parents when he came out of the closet.* □ *It was difficult for him to come out of the closet.*

come out with something 1. to publish something. □ *When are you going to come out with a new edition?* □ *The publisher decided not to come out with the book.* **2.** to express or utter something. □ *It was over an hour before the president came out with an explanation.* □ *My nephew comes out with the cleverest remarks.* □ *Who came out with that rude remark?*

come over to come for a visit. □ *Why don't you come over next week?* □ *I would love to come over.*

come over someone or something 1. [for something] to move over and above someone or something. □ *A cloud came over us and rained like fury.* □ *A storm came over the city and did what it had to.* **2.** [for something] to affect someone or something, perhaps suddenly. □ *I just don't know what came over me.* □ *A shocked silence came over the audience.*

come over (to our side) to join up with our side; to become one of our group, party, etc. □ *Seven of the other team came over to our side.* □ *I hope that Lynn comes over.*

come over to something to change to something; to convert to something. □ *We are going to come over to gas* next year. □ *Why don't you come over to a diesel-powered car?*

Come right in. Come in, please, you are very welcome here. □ *"Come right in and make yourself at home!" said the host.* □ FRED (opening door): *Well, hi, Bill.* BILL: *Hello, Fred. Good to see you.* FRED: *Come right in.* BILL: *Thanks.*

come through to be approved; to be sanctioned. □ *The mortgage came through.* □ *If the loan comes through, the car is yours.*

come through (for someone or something) to produce or perform as promised for someone or a group. □ *You knew I would come through for you, didn't you?* □ *The team came through for the college again.* □ *I knew they would come through.*

come through (something) 1. to survive something. □ *We were never sure we would come through the ordeal.* □ *I knew I would come through all right.* **2.** to pass through something. □ *Please chain the gate up again when you come through.* □ *Please come through now.*

come through (with something) to produce or deliver something as promised. □ *Finally, Bob came through with the money he had promised.* □ *I knew he would come through.*

come to to become conscious; to return to consciousness. □ *After just a few seconds, she came to.* □ *He came to just after fainting.*

come to a bad end to have a disaster, perhaps one that is deserved or expected; to die an unfortunate death. □ *My old car came to a bad end. Its engine burned up.* □ *The evil merchant came to a bad end.*

come to a dead end to come to an absolute stopping point. □ *The building project came to a dead end.* □ *The street came to a dead end.* □ *We were driving along and came to a dead end.*

come to a head to come to a crucial point; to come to a point when a problem must be solved. □ *Remember my problem with my neighbors? Well, last night the whole thing came to a head.* □ *The battle between the two factions of the city council came to a head yesterday.*

come to a standstill to stop, temporarily or permanently. □ *The building project came to a standstill because the workers went on strike.* □ *The party came to a standstill until the lights were turned on again.*

come to an end to stop; to finish. □ *The party came to an end at midnight.* □ *Her life came to an end late yesterday.*

come to an untimely end to come to an early death. □ *Poor Mr. Jones came to an untimely end in a car accident.* □ *Cancer caused Mrs. Smith to come to an untimely end.*

come to grief to fail; to have trouble or grief. □ *The artist wept when her canvas came to grief.* □ *The wedding party came to grief when the bride passed out.*

come to grips with something to face something; to comprehend something. □ *He found it difficult to come to grips with his grandmother's death.* □ *Many students have a hard time coming to grips with algebra.*

come to light to become known. □ *Some interesting facts about your past have just come to light.* □ *If too many* *bad things come to light, you may lose your job.*

come to one's senses to wake up; to become conscious; to start thinking clearly. □ *John, come to your senses. You're being quite stupid.* □ *In the morning I don't come to my senses until I have had two cups of coffee.*

come to pass to happen. (Literary.) □ *When did all of this come to pass?* □ *When will this event come to pass?*

come to the point AND **get to the point** to get to the important part (of something). □ *He has been talking a long time. I wish he would come to the point.* □ *Quit wasting time! Get to the point!* □ *We are talking about money, Bob! Come on, get to the point.*

come to think of it I just remembered ...; now that I think of it ... □ *Come to think of it, I know someone who can help.* □ *I have a screwdriver in the trunk of my car, come to think of it.*

come true to become real; [for a dream or a wish] actually to happen. □ *When I got married, all my dreams came true.* □ *Coming to the big city was like having my wish come true.*

come up 1. to come from a lower place to a higher one. □ *You can come up now. They are gone.* □ *Come up and enjoy the view from the tallest rooftop in the county.* 2. to come near; to approach. □ *He came up and began to talk to us.* □ *A heron came up while we were fishing, but it just ignored us.* 3. to come to someone's attention. □ *The question of what time to be there never came up.* □ *The matter came up, but it was never dealt with.*

come up against someone or something to reach an obstacle in the form of someone or something. □ *I have come up against something I cannot handle.* □ *I have never come up against anyone like him before.*

come up in the world to improve one's status or situation in life. □ *Since Mary got her new job, she has really come up in the world.* □ *A good education helped my brother come up in the world.*

come up something [for a tossed coin] to turn out to be either heads or tails. □ *We tossed a coin, and it came up heads.* □ *The coin came up tails.*

come what may no matter what might happen. □ *I'll be home for the holidays, come what may.* □ *Come what may, the mail will get delivered.*

Coming through(, please). Please let me pass through. (Often said by someone trying to get through a crowd of people, as in a passageway or an elevator. Similar to *Out, please.*) □ TOM: *Coming through, please.* SUE: *Give him some room. He wants to get by.* □ MARY (as the elevator stops): *Well, this is my floor. Coming through, please. I've got to get off.* JOHN: *Bye, Mary. It's been good talking to you.*

connect (up) to something to attach to something; to attach something to some electrical device. □ *When we finish the house, we will connect up to the utilities.* □ *We have to connect to the outside telephone lines ourselves.*

conspicuous by one's absence to have one's absence (from an event) noticed. □ *We missed you last night. You were conspicuous by your absence.*

☐ How could the bride's father miss the wedding party? He was certainly conspicuous by his absence.

contract something out to make an agreement with someone to do a specific amount of work. (Rather than doing it oneself or in one's own place of business.) ☐ I will contract this out and have it done by experts. T I contracted out this kind of job the last time.

control the purse strings to be in charge of the money in a business or a household. ☐ I control the purse strings at our house. ☐ Mr. Williams is the treasurer. He controls the purse strings.

cook out to prepare food out of doors. (More at cook something out.) | | Shall we cook out tomorrow? ☐ Yes, let's cook out.

cook someone's goose to damage or ruin someone. (To do something that cannot be undone.) ☐ I cooked my own goose by not showing up on time. ☐ Sally cooked Bob's goose for treating her the way he did.

cook something out to prepare food out of doors. (More at cook out.) ☐ I will cook this out. It's too hot in the kitchen to cook there. T Shall we cook out chicken tonight?

cook something up (with someone) to arrange or plan to do something with someone. (The something is usually the word something.) ☐ I tried to cook something up with Karen for Tuesday. T I want to cook up something with John. ☐ Let's see if we can cook something up.

cook the accounts to cheat in bookkeeping; to make the accounts appear to balance when they do not. ☐

Jane was sent to jail for cooking the accounts of her mother's store. ☐ It's hard to tell whether she really cooked the accounts or just didn't know how to add.

cool down AND **cool off** 1. to become cooler. (More at cool someone or something down.) ☐ After the sun set, things began to cool down a bit. ☐ The evening began to cool off. 2. [for someone] to become less angry. (More at cool someone or something down.) ☐ They were very angry at first, but then they cooled down. ☐ Cool off, you guys!

cool off See the previous entry.

cool one's heels to wait (for someone). ☐ I spent all afternoon cooling my heels in the waiting room while the doctor talked on the telephone. ☐ All right. If you can't behave properly, just sit down here and cool your heels until I call you.

cool someone or something down AND **cool someone or something off** 1. to make someone or something less hot. (Someone includes oneself. More at cool down.) ☐ Use ice to cool him down and reduce his fever. ☐ The refrigerator cooled the pudding off in a hurry. ☐ Here, have a cold drink. Cool yourself down. T The ice cooled down the feverish child. T We need to cool off the pudding in a hurry. 2. [with someone] to make someone less angry. (Someone includes oneself. More at cool down.) ☐ Things are less threatening now. That ought to cool him off. ☐ Time cooled them off a little. ☐ She meditated for a while to cool herself down.

cool someone or something off See the previous entry.

cost a pretty penny to cost a lot of money. □ *I'll bet that diamond cost a pretty penny.* □ *You can be sure that house cost a pretty penny. It has seven bathrooms.*

cost an arm and a leg to cost too much. □ *It cost an arm and a leg, so I didn't buy it.*

Could I be excused? Would you give me permission to leave?; Would you give me permission to leave the table? (Also used with *can* or *may* in place of *could.*) □ BILL: *I'm finished, Mom. Could I be excused?* MOTHER: *Yes, of course, when you use good manners like that.* □ *"Can I be excused?" said Bill, with a big grin on his face and his broccoli hidden in his napkin.*

(Could I) buy you a drink? 1. Could I purchase a drink for you? (An offer by one person — usually in a bar — to buy a drink for another. Then the two will drink together. Also used with *can* or *may* in place of *could.*) □ *When Sally and Mary met at the agreed time in the hotel bar, Sally said to Mary, "Could I buy you a drink?"* □ *Then this strange man sat down and said, "Buy you a drink?" Well, I could have just died!* **2.** Could I make you a drink? (A slightly humorous way of offering to prepare and serve someone a drink, as in one's home. Also used with *can* or *may* in place of *could.*) □ BILL: *Come in, Fred. Can I buy you a drink?* FRED: *Sure. What are you having?* BILL: *I've got wine and beer.* □ MARY: *Can I buy you a drink? What do you have there now?* BOB: *Oh, sure. It's just gin and tonic.* MARY: *Great! I'll be right back with it.*

Could I call you? 1. I am too busy to talk to you now. Do you mind if I

telephone you later on? (Usually in a business context. Also used with *can* in place of *could. May* is too polite here.) □ SALLY: *I can't talk to you right now. Could I call you?* TOM: *Sure, no problem.* □ BILL: *I've got to run. Sorry. Can I call you?* BOB: *No, I'm leaving town. I'll try to get in touch next week.* **2.** Do you mind if I call you and ask for another date sometime?; Do you mind if I call you sometime (in order to further our relationship)? (Usually in a romantic context. Also used with *can* or *may* in place of *could.*) □ MARY: *I had a marvelous time, Bob.* BOB: *Me too. Can I call you?* MARY: *Sure.* □ BOB: *I had a marvelous time, Mary. May I call you?* MARY: *Maybe in a week or two. I have a very busy week ahead. I'll call you, in fact.*

Could I come in? Do you mind if I enter? (Also used with *can* or *may* in place of *could.*) □ TOM (standing in the doorway): *Hello, I'm with the Internal Revenue Service. Could I come in?* MARY: *Go ahead, make my day!* □ BILL: *Hi, Tom. What are you doing here?* TOM: *Could I come in? I have to talk to you.* BILL: *Sure. Come on in.*

Could I get by, please? Would you please allow me space to pass by? (Also used with *can* or *may* in place of *could. May* is almost too polite.) □ *Poor Bill, trapped at the back of the elevator behind a huge man, kept saying, "Could I get by, please?" But nobody moved.* □ *"Can I get by, please?" Jane said, squeezing between the wall and a wheelchair.*

(Could I) get you something (to drink)? an expression offering a drink, usually an alcoholic drink. (Also used with *can* or *may* in place of *could*. Compare to *(Could I) buy you a drink?*) □ BILL: *Hi, Alice! Come on in! Can I get you something to drink?* ALICE: *Just a little soda, if you don't mind.* □ WAITER: *Get you something to drink?* JOHN: *No, thanks. I'll just order now.*

(Could I) give you a lift? Can I offer you a ride to some place? (Also used with *can* or *may* in place of *could*.) □ *Bill stopped his car at the side of the road where Tom stood. "Can I give you a lift?" asked Bill.* □ JOHN: *Well, I've got to leave.* ALICE: *Me too.* JOHN: *Give you a lift?* ALICE: *Sure. Thanks.*

Could I have a lift? AND **How about a lift?** Would you please give me a ride (in your car)? (This usually refers to a destination that is the same as the driver's or on the way to the driver's destination. Also used with *can* or *may* in place of *could*.) □ BOB: *Going north? Could I have a lift?* BILL: *Sure. Hop in.* BOB: *Thanks. That's such a long walk to the north end of campus.* □ SUE: *Can I have a lift? I'm late.* MARY: *Sure, if you're going somewhere on Maple Street.*

Could I have a word with you? See *I'd like (to have) a word with you.*

Could I have someone call you? a question asked by a telephone answerer when the person the caller is seeking is not available. (The *someone* can be a person's name or a pronoun, or even the word *someone*. Also used with *can* or *may* in place of *could*.) □ TOM: *Bill's not here now. Could I have him call you?* BOB: *Yeah. Ask him to leave a message on my machine.* TOM: *Sure.* □ *"Could I have her call you?" asked Mrs. Wilson's secretary.*

Could I have the bill? See *Check, please.*

Could I have the check? See *Check, please.*

Could I help you? Could I assist you? (Said by shopkeepers, clerks, food service workers, and telephone answerers. Also used with *can* or *may* in place of *could*.) □ *The clerk came over and said, "Could I help you?"* □ CLERK: *May I help you?* MARY: *No thanks, I'm just looking.*

Could I join you? AND **Can I join you?; (Do you) care if I join you?; (Do you) mind if I join you?** Will you permit me to sit with you? (An inquiry seeking permission to sit at someone's table or join someone else in some activity. Also used with *can* or *may* in place of *could*.) □ *Tom came into the cafe and saw Fred and Sally sitting in a booth by the window. Coming up to them, Tom said, "Could I join you?"* □ *"Do you mind if I join you?" asked the lady. "There are no other seats."*

Could I leave a message? the phrase used on the telephone to request that a message be written down for a person who is not available to come to the telephone. (Can be said with *can* or *may*.) □ BILL: *Can I talk to Fred?* MARY: *He's not here.* BILL: *Could I leave a message?* MARY: *Sure. What is it?* □ *"May I leave a message?" asked Mary politely.*

Could I see you again? Could we go out on another date sometime? (Also with *can* or *may*.) □ TOM: *I had a wonderful time, Mary. Can I see you again?* MARY: *Call me tomorrow, Tom. Good night.* □ *"Could I see you again?" muttered Tom, dizzy with the magic of her kiss.*

Could I see you in my office? I want to talk to you in the privacy of my office. (Typically said by the boss to an employee. Also used with *can* or *may* in place of *could*.) □ *"Mr. Franklin,"* said Bill's boss sort of sternly, *"could I see you in my office for a minute? We need to talk about something."* □ SUE: *Could I see you in my office?* JOHN: *Sure. What's cooking?*

Could I speak to someone? AND **Can I speak to someone?; May I speak to someone?** the phrase used to request to talk to a particular person, usually on the telephone. (The *someone* stands for someone's name. Also used with *talk* in place of *speak*.) □ TOM (answering the phone): *Good morning, Acme Air Products. With whom do you wish to speak?* BILL: *Can I speak to Mr. Wilson?* TOM: *One moment.* □ SALLY: *May I speak to the manager, please?* CLERK: *Certainly, madam. I'm the manager.*

Could I take a message? the phrase used on the telephone to offer to take a message and give it to the person the caller is seeking. (Can be used with *can* or *may*.) □ BILL: *Can I talk to Fred?* MARY: *He's not here. Could I take a message?* □ *"May I take a message?"* asked Mary politely.

Could I take your order (now)? an expression used by food service personnel to determine if the customer is ready to order food. (Also used with *can* or *may* in place of *could*.) □ WAITER: *May I take your order now?* MARY: *Of course. Jane, what are you going to have?* JANE: *I'm having what you're having.* MARY: *Oh.* WAITER: *I'll be back in a minute.* □ MARY: *This is a nice place.* BILL: *Yes, it is.*

WAITER: *Can I take your order?* MARY: *Yes, we're ready.*

Could I tell someone who's calling? a question asked by telephone answerers to find out politely who is asking for someone. (*Someone* is replaced by a person's name or by a pronoun. Also used with *can* or *may* in place of *could*.) □ MARY (on the phone): *Hello. Could I speak to Bill Franklin?* SALLY: *Could I tell him who's calling?* □ BILL (on the phone): *Is Tom there?* MARY: *May I tell him who's calling?* BILL: *It's Bill.* MARY: *Just a minute.*

Could I use your powder room? AND **Where is your powder room?** a polite way to ask to use the bathroom in someone's home. (Refers to powdering one's nose. Also used with *can* or *may* in place of *could*.) □ MARY: *Oh, Sally, could I use your powder room?* SALLY: *Of course. It's just off the kitchen, on the left.* □ TOM: *Nice place you've got here. Uh, where is your powder room?* BETH: *At the top of the stairs.*

Could we continue this later? Could we go on with this conversation at a later time? (Also used with *can* or *may* in place of *could*.) □ BOB: *After that we both ended up going out for a pizza.* SUE: *Could we continue this later? I have some work I have to get done.* BOB: *Sure. No problem.* □ As Mary and John were discussing something private, Bob entered the room. *"Could we continue this later?"* whispered John. *"Yes, of course,"* answered Mary.

Could you excuse us, please? AND **Would you excuse us, please?; Will you excuse us, please?** We must leave. I hope you will forgive us. (A polite way of announcing a departure. Also with *can* in place of *could*.) □ BILL: *Will you excuse us, please? We really must leave now.* BOB: *Oh, sure. Nice to see you.* □ BILL: *Could you excuse us, please? We simply must rush off.* ALICE: *So sorry you have to go. Come back when you can stay longer.*

Could you handle it? See *Can you handle it?*

Could you hold? AND **Will you hold?; Can you hold?** Do you mind if I put your telephone call on hold? (Also with *can* in place of *could*.) □ *"Could you hold?" asked the operator.* □ SUE: *Hello. Acme Motors. Can you hold?* BOB: *I guess.* SUE (after a while): *Hello. Thank you for holding. Can I help you?*

Could you keep a secret? I am going to tell you something that I hope you will keep a secret. (Also used with *can* in place of *could*.) □ TOM: *Could you keep a secret?* MARY: *Sure.* TOM: *Don't tell anybody, but I'm going to be a daddy.* □ SUE: *Can you keep a secret?* ALICE: *Of course.* SUE: *We're moving to Atlanta.*

count down to count backwards to an event that will start when zero is reached. □ *The project manager was counting down — getting ready for the launch of the rocket.* □ *I can still hear the captain counting down: "Five, four, three, two, one, zero, blastoff!"*

count heads See the following entry.

count noses AND **count heads** to count people. (Because there is only one head or nose per person.) □ *I'll tell you how many people are here after I count noses.* □ *Everyone is here. Let's*

count heads so we can order hamburgers.

count off [for a series of people, one by one] to say aloud the next number in a fixed sequence. (More at *count someone or something off*.) □ *The soldiers counted off by threes.* □ *The sergeant told them to count off.*

count one's chickens before they hatch to plan how to utilize good results of something before those results have occurred. (Frequently used in the negative.) □ *You're way ahead of yourself. Don't count your chickens before they hatch.* □ *You may be disappointed if you count your chickens before they hatch.*

count someone or something off to count people or things, to see if they are all there. (More at *count off*.) □ *Let's count them off to see who's missing.* □ *Count off each person, one by one.* □ *I counted each one off.*

count someone out (for something) to exclude someone from something. (*Someone* includes *oneself*.) □ *We are going to count you out for the party unless you pay in advance.* □ *Please don't count me out yet!* □ *I must count myself out for the nomination.*

count something in to include something in a count of something. □ *Did you count the tall ones in?* □ *Did you count in the tall ones in the corner?*

count something out to give out things, counting them, one by one. □ *She counted the cookies out, one by one.* □ *She counted out the cookies to each child.*

count (up)on someone or something to rely on someone or something. (*Upon* is formal and less commonly used than *on*.) □ *Can I count upon* *you to do the job?* □ *You can count on me.* □ *Can I count on the court to rule fairly?*

couple up (with someone) [for one person] to join another person. □ *I decided to couple up with Larry.* □ *Larry and I coupled up with each other.* □ *Larry and I coupled up.* □ *By midnight, they all had coupled up and were dancing.*

cover a lot of ground 1. to travel over a great distance; to investigate a wide expanse of land. □ *The prospectors covered a lot of ground, looking for gold.* □ *My car can cover a lot of ground in one day.* **2.** to deal with much information and many facts. □ *The history lecture covered a lot of ground today.* □ *Mr. and Mrs. Franklin always cover a lot of ground when they argue.*

cover for someone 1. to make excuses for someone; to conceal someone's errors. □ *If I miss class, please cover for me.* □ *If you're late, I'll cover for you.* **2.** to handle someone else's work. □ *Dr. Johnson's partner agreed to cover for him during his vacation.* □ *I'm on duty this afternoon. Will you please cover for me? I have a doctor's appointment.*

cover someone or something up 1. to place something on someone or something for protection or concealment. (*Someone* includes *oneself.*) □ *Cover the pie up, so Terry won't see it.* Ⓣ *Cover up the money, so they won't know we were gambling.* Ⓣ *Cover up Jimmy so he doesn't get cold.* □ *Tom — hiding in the leaves — covered himself up so no one could see any part of him.* **2.** [with *something*] to conceal a wrongdoing; to conceal evidence.

□ *They tried to cover the crime up, but the broken lock gave them away.* Ⓣ *She could not cover up her misdeeds.*

cover (up) for someone to conceal someone's wrongdoing by lying or working in someone's place. □ *Are you covering up for the person who committed the crime?* □ *I wouldn't cover for anyone.*

crack a joke to tell a joke. □ *She's never serious. She's always cracking jokes.* □ *As long as she's cracking jokes, she's okay.*

crack a smile to smile a little, perhaps reluctantly. □ *She cracked a smile, so I knew she was kidding.* □ *The soldier cracked a smile at the wrong time and had to march for an hour as punishment.*

crack down (on someone or something) to put limits on someone or something; to become strict about enforcing rules on someone or something. □ *The police cracked down on the kids.* □ *They cracked down once last year too.*

crack someone or something up 1. to damage someone or something. (*Someone* includes *oneself.* More at *crack up.*) □ *Who cracked my car up?* Ⓣ *Who cracked up my car? Who was driving?* □ *The accident cracked him up a little.* □ *She cracked herself up pretty badly in the accident.* **2.** [with *someone*] to make someone laugh. (More at *crack up.*) □ *The professor's witty joke cracked the students up.* Ⓣ *The toddler's innocent question cracked up the adults.*

crack up 1. to have a crash; to have a wreck. (More at *crack someone or something up.*) □ *The car ran off the road and cracked up.* □ *Who cracked* *up my car?* **2.** to break out laughing. (More at *crack someone or something up.*) □ *The audience cracked up at the actor's incompetence.* □ *We all cracked up at the clown's situation.* **3.** to go crazy. □ *Things were so hectic that I was going to crack up.* □ *Some students actually crack up near the end of the semester.*

cramp someone's style to limit someone in some way. □ *I hope this doesn't cramp your style, but could you please not hum while you work?* □ *To ask him to keep regular hours would really be cramping his style.*

crash into someone or something to bump or ram into someone or something. □ *The student crashed into the teacher.* □ *The car crashed into a bus.*

crash through something to break through something. □ *The cows crashed right through the fence.* □ *Don't crash through the door. I'll open it as soon as I get it unlocked.*

cream of the crop the best of all. □ *This particular car is the cream of the crop.* □ *The kids are very bright. They are the cream of the crop.*

creep by [for time] to pass slowly. □ *The minutes crept by as I awaited Mrs. Barron's telephone call.* □ *I know the days will creep by until we finally move into the new house.*

Crime doesn't pay. Crime will not benefit a person. (Proverb.) □ *At the end of the radio program, a voice said, "Remember, crime doesn't pay."* □ *No matter how tempting it may appear, crime doesn't pay.*

crop out to appear on the surface; [for something] to reveal itself in the open; to begin to show above the surface. □ *A layer of rock cropped out at the edges of the desert.* □ *A little anger began to crop out.*

crop up to appear without warning; to happen suddenly; [for something] to begin to reveal itself in the open. □ *A new crisis has cropped up.* □ *Some new problems cropped up at the last minute.*

cross a bridge before one comes to it to worry excessively about something before it happens. (Note the variations in the examples.) □ *There is no sense in crossing that bridge before you come to it.* □ *She's always crossing bridges before coming to them. She needs to learn to relax.*

cross a bridge when one comes to it to deal with a problem only when one is faced with the problem. (Note the variations in the examples.) □ *Please wait and cross that bridge when you come to it.* □ *He shouldn't worry about it now. He can cross that bridge when he comes to it.*

cross-examine someone to ask someone questions in great detail; to question a suspect or a witness at great length. □ *The police cross-examined the suspect for three hours.* □ *The lawyer plans to cross-examine the witness tomorrow morning.*

cross one's heart (and hope to die) to pledge or vow that the truth is being told. □ *It's true, cross my heart and hope to die.* □ *It's really true — cross my heart.*

cross someone or something off ((of) something) to eliminate a name from a list or record. (*Someone* includes *oneself.* The *of* is colloquial.) □ *We will have to cross her off our list.* Ⓣ *We crossed off Sarah.* □ *I crossed the sweater off of the list and gave it* *away.* □ *Looking at the length of the list, Alice was willing to cross herself off.*

cross someone or something out to draw a line through the name of someone or something on a list or record. (*Someone* includes *oneself.*) □ *You can cross me out. I'm not going.* ⊤ *Please cross out Sarah.* □ *I crossed the sweater out. It was an error.* □ *Alice crossed herself out without any argument.*

cross swords (with someone) to enter into an argument with someone. (Not literal.) □ *I don't want to cross swords with Tom.* □ *The last time we crossed swords, we had a terrible time.*

crouch down to stoop or huddle down. □ *Crouch down here, next to me.* □ *Suddenly, Tex crouched down and reached for his pistol.*

crowd in (on someone or something) to press or crush around someone or something. □ *Please don't crowd in on the guest of honor.* □ *Can you keep them back from me? I don't like it when they crowd in.* □ *The people crowded in on us and frightened us a little bit.* □ *Don't crowd in on the display case. It is an antique.*

crowd in (to some place) to push or squeeze into some place. □ *Please don't try to crowd into this place.* □ *Too many people are trying to crowd in.*

crowd together to pack tightly together. □ *The tenants crowded together in the lobby.* □ *All the kittens crowded together to keep warm.*

crumble something (up) (into something) to crunch up or break up something into pieces. □ *Now, crumble the dried bread up into crumbs.* ⊤ *Crumble up the bread into crumbs.*

□ *Ed crumbled the soil up to make planting easier.*

crumple someone or something up to fold up or crush someone or something. □ *Walter crumpled the paper up.* ⊤ *He crumpled up the paper.* □ *The accident crumpled the poor dog up, but it recovered.*

crunch someone or something up to break someone or something up into pieces. (Also without *up*, but not eligible as an entry.) □ *That machine will crunch you up. Stay away from it!* ⊤ *A number of blows with the hammer crunched up the rocks into pebbles.* □ *Try to crunch the larger chunks up.*

crush something out to put out a fire or flame by crushing. □ *She crushed her cigarette out and put the butt into the sink.* ⊤ *Please crush out your cigarette.*

crush something up (into something) **1.** to press something with great force until it is reduced to something smaller. □ *The chef crushed the almonds up into a powder and sprinkled them on the dessert.* ⊤ *Please crush up the almonds into a powder.* □ *I will crush them up.* **2.** to break something up into small pieces. □ *The machine crushed the glass up into chunks and sent them on to be recycled.* ⊤ *It crushed up all the glass into tiny bits.* □ *The machine crushed it up.*

crush (up) against someone or something to press hard against someone or something. □ *The crowd crushed up against the people standing in line.* □ *The eager theatergoers crushed against the lobby doors.*

crux of the matter the central issue of the matter. (*Crux* is an old word meaning "cross.") □ *All right, this is the crux of the matter.* □ *It's about time that we looked at the crux of the matter.*

cry before one is hurt to cry or complain before one is injured. □ *Bill always cries before he's hurt.* □ *There is no point in crying before one is hurt.*

cry bloody murder AND **scream bloody murder** to scream as if something very serious has happened. (To scream as if one had found the result of a bloody act of murder.) □ *Now that Bill is really hurt, he's screaming bloody murder.* □ *There is no point in crying bloody murder about the bill if you aren't going to pay it.*

cry one's eyes out to cry very hard. (Not literal.) □ *When we heard the news, we cried our eyes out with joy.* □ *She cried her eyes out after his death.*

cry over spilled milk to be unhappy about having done something that cannot be undone. (Usually viewed as a childish action. *Spilled* can also be spelled *spilt*.) □ *I'm sorry that you broke your bicycle, Tom. But there is nothing that can be done now. Don't cry over spilled milk.* □ *Ann is always crying over spilt milk.*

cry wolf to cry or complain about something when nothing is really wrong. □ *Pay no attention. She's just crying wolf again.* □ *Don't cry wolf too often. No one will come.*

cuddle up (to someone or something) to nestle or snuggle close to someone or something to get warm or to be intimate. □ *She cuddled up to him and went to sleep.* □ *Let's cuddle up to the warm wall, near the fireplace.*

cue someone in to give a signal or cue to someone at the right time, usually in a performance of some kind. □ *Be sure to cue me in when you want me to talk.* T *Cue in the lighting technician at the right time.*

Curiosity killed the cat. It is dangerous to be curious. (Proverb.) □ *Don't ask so many questions, Billy. Curiosity killed the cat.* □ *Curiosity killed the cat. Mind your own business.*

curl someone's hair to frighten or alarm someone severely; to shock someone with sight, sound, or taste. (Also used literally.) □ *Don't ever sneak up on me like that again. You really curled my hair.* □ *The horror film curled my hair.*

curl something up to roll something up into a coil. □ *She curled the edges of the paper up while she spoke.* T *Why did she curl up the paper?*

curl up and die to retreat and die. □ *When I heard you say that, I could have curled up and died.* □ *No, it wasn't an illness. She just curled up and died.*

curl up (in(to) something) 1. to roll into a coil. □ *The snake curled up into a neat coil.* □ *It curled up so we couldn't get at it.* 2. to roll into a coil in a resting place, such as a chair or a bed. □ *Colleen curled up in the chair and took a nap.* □ *She curled up and took a nap.*

cut back (on something) to reduce the use, amount, or cost of something. □ *You are all going to have to cut back on water usage.* □ *You simply must cut back.*

cut class to skip going to class. (Refers to high school or college classes.) □ *If Mary keeps cutting classes, she'll fail the course.* □ *I can't* *cut that class. I've missed too many already.*

cut down (on something) to reduce the amount of something or the amount of time spent doing something; to use or buy less of something. □ *You will have to cut down on your use of water.* □ *They told us to cut down.* □ *The doctor told him to cut down on his drinking.* □ *It was hard for him to cut down.*

cut in (on someone or something) 1. to interrupt someone or something. □ *While Gloria was telling us her story, Tom kept cutting in on her.* □ *I'm talking. Please don't cut in!* **2.** to participate in something even when not invited, particularly a dancing couple. □ *Can I cut in on this little party?* □ *Yes, do cut in.* □ *Excuse me, may I cut in?* □ *Please don't cut in on our dance.* **3.** to interrupt something, especially some sort of electronic transmission. □ *I didn't mean to cut in on your announcement.* □ *Who cut in on my telephone call?*

cut in (with something) to interrupt [someone] with a comment; to speak abruptly, interrupting what someone else is saying. □ *Jimmy cut in with a particularly witty remark.* □ *Must you always cut in while others are talking?*

Cut it out! Stop doing that!; Stop saying that! (Colloquial and familiar.) □ SUE: *Why, I think you have a crush on Mary!* TOM: *Cut it out!* □ *"Cut it out!" yelled Tommy as Billy hit him again.*

cut off to turn off of a road, path, highway, etc. □ *This is the place where you are supposed to cut off.* □ *Cut off right here.*

cut off one's nose to spite one's face a phrase meaning that one harms oneself in trying to punish another person. (The phrase is variable in form.) □ *Billy loves the zoo, but he refused to go with his mother because he was mad at her. He cut off his nose to spite his face.* □ *Find a better way to be angry. It is silly to cut your nose off to spite your face.*

cut one's (own) throat [for someone] to experience certain failure; to do damage to someone. (Also used literally.) □ *If I were to run for office, I'd just be cutting my throat.* □ *Judges who take bribes are cutting their own throats.*

cut someone or something off from something to isolate someone or something from some place or something. □ *They cut the cattle off from the wheat field.* □ *The road construction cut Jane off from her office.* ⊤ *The tanks cut off the troops from their camp.*

cut someone or something (off) short to end something before it is finished; to end one's speaking before one is finished. □ *We cut the picnic short because of the storm.* □ *I'm sorry to cut you off short, but I must go now.*

cut someone or something to the bone 1. to slice deep to a bone. (Literal.) □ *The knife cut John to the bone. He had to be sewed up.* □ *Cut each slice of ham to the bone. Then each slice will be as big as possible.* **2.** [with *something*] to cut down severely on something. (Not literal.) □ *We cut our expenses to the bone and are still losing money.* □ *Congress had to cut the budget to the bone in order to balance it.*

cut someone to the quick to hurt someone's feelings very badly. (Can be used literally when *quick* refers to the tender flesh at the base of fingernails and toenails.) □ *Your criticism cut me to the quick.* □ *Tom's sharp words to Mary cut her to the quick.*

cut someone's losses to reduce someone's losses of money, goods, or other things of value. □ *I sold the stock as it went down, thus cutting my losses.* □ *He cut his losses by putting better locks on the doors. There were fewer robberies.* □ *The mayor's reputation suffered because of the scandal. He finally resigned to cut his losses.*

cut something away (from something) to separate something from something else by cutting. □ *The doctor cut the wart away from the patient's foot.* ⊤ *She cut away the wart.* □ *Eric cut the bushes away from the front door.* □ *He cut the old surface roots away so no one would trip.*

cut something back to prune plants; to reduce the size of plants, bushes, etc. □ *Let's cut these bushes back. They're getting in the way.* ⊤ *Don't cut back my roses!* □ *They have been cut back already.*

cut something down 1. to chop something down; to saw or cut at something until it is felled. □ *Stop cutting the trees down!* ⊤ *Don't cut down that tree!* 2. to destroy someone's argument; to destroy someone's position or standing. □ *The lawyer cut the testimony down quickly.* ⊤ *The lawyer cut down the witness's story.* 3. to reduce the price of something. (Also without *down*, but not eligible as an entry.) □ *They cut the prices down to sell the goods off quickly.* ⊤ *I wish they would cut down the prices in this store.*

cut something in(to something) to mix something into something else. (Colloquial.) □ *Carefully cut the butter into the flour mixture.* ⊤ *Now, cut in some more butter.* □ *Cut some more butter in.*

cut something off 1. to shorten something. □ *Cut this board off a bit, would you?* ⊤ *Cut off this board a little, please.* 2. to turn something off, such as power, electricity, water, the engine, etc. □ *Would you please cut that engine off?* ⊤ *Cut off the engine, Chuck.*

cut something out to stop doing something. (Colloquial. Usually **Cut that out!**) □ *Cut that noise out!* ⊤ *Cut out that noise!* □ *Now, cut that out!*

cut something out (from something) See the following entry.

cut something out (of something) AND **cut something out (from something)** to cut a pattern or shape from cloth, paper, sheet metal, etc.; to remove something from something by cutting; to excise something from something. (When both *out* and *of* are used, no direct object can intervene.) □ *Sam cut a pig out from the paper.* □ *I cut the picture out of a magazine.* ⊤ *I cut out the shape of the moon from the paper.* □ *Cut the pictures out and pin them up.* □ *The doctor cut the tumor out.* ⊤ *She cut out the tumor.*

Cut the comedy! AND **Cut the funny stuff!** Stop acting silly and telling jokes!; Be serious! □ JOHN: *All right, you guys! Cut the comedy and get to work!* BILL: *Can't we ever have any fun?* JOHN: *No.* □ BILL: *Come on, Mary, let's throw Tom in the pool!*

MARY: *Yeah, let's drag him over and give him a good dunking!* TOM: *Okay, you clowns, cut the funny stuff! I'll throw both of you in!* BILL: *You and what army?*

Cut the funny stuff! See the previous entry.

cut the ground out from under someone to destroy the foundation of someone's plans or someone's argument. □ *The politician cut the ground out from under his opponent.* Ⓣ *Congress cut out the ground from under the president.*

D

dab something on((to) something) to pat or paint carefully something onto something else. □ *Dab some medicine onto the scratch.* T *Dab on some medicine.* □ *Just dab some on.*

dam something up to erect a barrier in a river, stream, brook, etc. □ *We are going to have to dam this stream up to make a pond for the cattle.* T *Let's dam up this stream.* □ *Why is this river dammed up?*

dance to another tune to shift quickly to different behavior; to change one's behavior or attitude. □ *After being yelled at, Ann danced to another tune.* □ *A stern talking-to will make her dance to another tune.*

dash cold water on something See *pour cold water on something.*

dash off [for someone] to leave in a hurry. □ *I have to dash off. Good-bye.* □ *Ken dashed off and left me behind to deal with the angry customer.*

dash out (for something) [for someone] to leave a place in a hurry to get something. □ *Harry dashed out for some cigarettes.* □ *Excuse me. I just have to dash out.*

dash something off 1. to make or do something quickly. □ *I will dash this off now and try to take more time with the rest of them.* T *I will see if I can dash off a cherry pie before dinner.* **2.**

to write a note or letter quickly and send it off. □ *I have to dash this note off, then I will be with you.* T *I'll dash off a note to her.*

date back (to someone or something) to have origins that extend back to the time of someone or something. □ *This part of the palace dates back to Catherine the Great.* □ *This is old! It really must date back.* □ *Carl had an old rifle that dates back to the Civil War.*

date back (to sometime) to extend back to a particular time; to have been alive at a particular time in the past. □ *My late grandmother dated back to the Civil War.* □ *This record dates back to the sixties.* □ *How far do you date back?*

dawn (up)on someone [for a fact] to become apparent to someone; [for something] to be realized by someone. (*Upon* is formal and less commonly used than *on.*) □ *Then it dawned upon me that I was actually going to have the job.* □ *It never dawned on me that this might be the case.*

dead and buried gone forever. (Refers literally to persons and figuratively to ideas and other things.) □ *Now that Uncle Bill is dead and buried, we can read his will.* □ *That kind of thinking is dead and buried.*

dead to the world tired; exhausted; sleeping soundly. (Asleep and oblivious to what is going on in the rest of the world.) □ *I've had such a hard day. I'm really dead to the world.* □ *Look at her sleep. She's dead to the world.*

deal something out to pass something out piece by piece, giving everyone equal shares. □ *The manager dealt the proposals out, giving each person an equal number to read.* ⊤ *I'll deal out some more proposals.*

Dear me! an expression of mild dismay or regret. □ SUE: *Dear me, is this all there is?* MARY: *There's more in the kitchen.* □ *"Oh, dear me!" fretted John. "I'm late again."*

death on someone or something 1. very effective in acting against someone or something. □ *This road is terribly bumpy. It's death on tires.* □ *The sergeant is death on lazy soldiers.* **2.** [with *something*] accurate or deadly at doing something requiring skill or great effort. □ *John is death on curve balls. He's our best pitcher.* □ *The boxing champ is really death on those fast punches.*

decide (up)on someone or something to choose someone or something; to make a judgment about some aspect of someone or something. (*Upon* is formal and less commonly used than *on.*) □ *Will you please hurry up and decide upon someone?* □ *I decided on chocolate.*

deck someone or something out (in something) AND **deck someone or something out (with something)** to decorate someone or something with something. (*Someone* includes oneself.*) □ *Sally decked all her children out for the holiday party.* ⊤ *She decked out her children in Halloween costumes.* □ *Tom decked the room out with garlands of flowers.* □ *He decked the hall out.* □ *She decked herself out in her finest clothes.*

deck someone or something out (with something) See the previous entry.

Definitely! AND **Certainly!** Yes, I agree! □ BILL: *Will you be there Saturday?* MARY: *Definitely!* □ SUE: *Would you be so kind as to carry this up the stairs?* BILL: *Certainly!*

Definitely not! AND **Certainly not!** No, without any doubt at all. (Similar to *Absolutely not!*) □ BILL: *Will you lend me some money?* BOB: *No way! Definitely not!* □ BOB: *Have you ever stolen anything?* FRED: *Certainly not!*

dent something up to mar or make depressions in something. □ *I don't want to dent my car up. It's still new.* ⊤ *He dented up my car!* □ *Wow, is this dented up!*

deposit something in(to) something to put something into something. □ *Please deposit your chewing gum into the wastebasket.* □ *You should deposit your money in the bank.*

desert a sinking ship AND **leave a sinking ship** to leave a place, a person, or a situation when things become difficult or unpleasant. (Rats are said to be the first to leave a ship that is sinking.) □ *I hate to be the one to desert a sinking ship, but I can't stand it around here anymore.* □ *There goes Tom. Wouldn't you know he'd leave a sinking ship rather than stay around and try to help?*

diamond in the rough a valuable or potentially excellent person or thing hidden by an unpolished or rough exterior. □ *Ann looks like a stupid woman, but she's a fine person — a real diamond in the rough.* □ *That piece of property is a diamond in the rough. Some day it will be valuable.*

did you hear? See *have you heard?*

die away to fade away. □ *The sound of the waterfall finally died away.* □ *When the applause died away, the tenor sang an encore.*

die back [for vegetation] to die part way back to the roots. □ *The hedge died back in the winter and had to be replaced in the spring.* □ *This kind of grass dies back every year.*

die down to fade to almost nothing; to decrease gradually. □ *The fire died down and went out.* □ *As the applause died down, a child came on stage with an armload of roses for the singer.*

die of a broken heart 1. to die of emotional distress. □ *I was not surprised to hear of her death. They say she died of a broken heart.* □ *In the movie, the heroine appeared to die of a broken heart, but the audience knew she was poisoned.* 2. to suffer from emotional distress, especially from a failed romance. (Figurative.) □ *Tom and Mary broke off their romance and both died of broken hearts.* □ *Please don't leave me. I know I'll die of a broken heart.*

die of boredom to suffer from boredom; to be very bored. □ *No one has ever really died of boredom.* □ *We sat there and listened politely, even though we almost died of boredom.*

die off [for living things] to perish one by one until there are no more. (Very similar to *die out.*) □ *Most of the larger lizards died off eons ago.* □ *It*

would be really bad if all the owls died off. □ *The cucumber blossoms all died off.*

die on someone to perish while in someone's care. □ *"Don't die on me!" cried the emergency room nurse.* □ *We don't like it when patients die on us.*

die on the vine See *wither on the vine.*

die out 1. [for a species or family] to perish totally because of the failure to produce offspring. (Very similar to *die off.*) □ *I am the last one in the family, so I guess it will die out.* □ *The owls might die out if you ruin their nesting area.* 2. [for an idea, practice, style, etc.] to fade away through time. □ *That way of doing things died out a long time ago.* □ *It died out like the horse and buggy.*

dig down 1. to excavate deeply. □ *They are really having to dig down to reach bedrock.* □ *We are not to the buried cable yet. We will have to dig down some more.* 2. to be generous; to dig deep into one's pockets and come up with as much money as possible to donate to something. □ *Please dig down. We need every penny you can spare.* □ *Dig down deep. Give all you can.*

Dig in! Please start eating your meal (heartily). □ *When we were all seated at the table, Grandfather said, "Dig in!" and we all did.* □ SUE: *Sit down, everybody.* BOB: *Wow, this stuff looks good!* ALICE: *It sure does.* SUE: *Dig in!*

dig in(to something) 1. to use a shovel to penetrate a mass of something. □ *He dug into the soft soil and made a deep hole for the roots of the bush.* □ *He grabbed a shovel and dug in where he thought the tree ought to* go. **2.** to begin to process something; to go to work on something. □ *I have to dig into all these applications today and process at least half of them.* □ *Jed got out the stack of applications and dug in.* **3.** to begin to eat food. (Slang.) □ *We dug into the huge pile of fried chicken.* □ *I stuck the corner of my napkin in my collar and dug in.*

dig out (of something) to channel one's way out of something. (More at *dig someone or something out (of something)*.) □ *The miner had to dig out of the cave-in.* □ *They were too exhausted to dig out.*

dig some dirt up on someone to find out something bad about someone. (The *dirt* is gossip.) □ *If you don't stop trying to dig some dirt up on me, I'll get a lawyer and sue you.* T *The citizens' group dug up some dirt on the mayor and used it against her at election time.*

dig someone or something out (of something) to excavate in order to get someone or something out of something; to dig about in order to get someone or something out of something. (*Someone* includes *oneself.* Also figurative uses. More at *dig out (of something)*.) □ *Let's dig the bones out of the sand and send them to the museum.* T *She dug out the bones.* □ *Jimmy found Tim and dug him out of the pile of leaves in which he had been hiding.* □ *The dog dug itself out of the rubble of the fallen building.*

dig something in(to something) to stab or jab something into something. □ *Dig your fork into that heavenly cake!* T *He dug in his fork.* □ *Jed dug his fork in and took a huge bite.*

Dig up! Listen carefully. (Slang.) □ JOHN: *All right, you guys! Dig up! You're going to hear this one time and one time only!* BILL: *Get quiet, you guys!* □ BILL: *Dig up! I'm only going to say this once.* BOB: *What was that?* BILL: *I said listen!*

dim out [for a light] to grow dim and go out altogether. □ *The lights dimmed out twice during the storm.* □ *I was afraid that the lights would dim out, leaving us in the dark.*

dim something down to make lights dim; to use a dimmer to lower the lights. (A *dimmer* is a rheostat, variable transformer, or something similar. Compare to *dim something up*.) □ *Why don't you dim the lights down and put on some music?* T *Let me dim down the lights and put on some music.*

dim something up to use a dimmer to make the lights brighter. (Theatrical. The expression, a seeming contradiction, is the opposite of *dim something down*.) □ *As the curtain rose, the electrician dimmed the lights up to reveal a beautiful scene.* T *You dimmed up the lights too fast.*

din something in(to someone) to repeat something over and over to someone. (Figurative. As if one could "hammer" words into someone.) □ *The teacher dinned it into her constantly, but it did no good.* T *He dinned in the same message over and over.* □ *He needed to learn Spanish, so he bought a tape recorder and dinned it in day and night.*

dine in to eat at home rather than at a restaurant. □ *I think we will dine in tonight.* □ *I am tired of dining in. Let's go out.*

dine off something to make a meal of something; to make many meals of something. (Formal.) □ *Do you think we can dine off the leg of lamb for more than one meal?* □ *I hope we dine off the turkey only one more time.*

dine out to eat away from home. □ *I love to dine out so I don't have to cook.* □ *We both want to dine out tonight.*

Dinner is served. It is time to eat dinner. Please come to the table. (Formal, as if announced by a butler.) □ SUE: *Dinner is served.* MARY (aside): *Aren't we fancy tonight?* □ *"Dinner is served," said Bob, rather formally for a barbecue.*

dip in((to) something) **1.** to reach into a liquid. □ *I dipped into the dishwater, looking for the missing spoon.* □ *I dipped in and there it was.* **2.** to reach into a substance, usually to remove some of the substance. □ *I dipped into the sour cream with a potato chip and brought out an enormous glob.* □ *He grabbed the jar of peanut butter and dipped in.* **3.** to take out part of something one has been saving. (Figurative.) □ *I had to dip into my savings in order to pay for my vacation.* □ *I went to the bank and dipped in. There wasn't much left.*

dip something in((to) something) to put something into a substance in order to take some of it. □ *Tom dipped some of the bread into the cheese sauce.* T *Dip in the bread again and get some more cheese on it.* □ *I dipped the soap in to get it wet enough to work up a lather.*

dirty one's hands See *get one's hands dirty.*

dirty something up to get something dirty. □ *Those pants are brand-new!*

Don't dirty them up! T *Don't dirty up your brand-new pants!*

dish something out (to someone) **1.** AND **dish something up (for someone)** to place food onto dishes for someone. □ *Please dish the lasagna out to everyone.* T *Todd dished out the lasagna to everyone.* □ *He dished it out.* □ *He dished some up for everyone.* □ *He dished some up.* **2.** to give out criticism or punishment to someone. □ *He really knows how to dish the punishment out, doesn't he?* □ *He can really dish it out, but can he take it?* T *The boys dished out too much criticism of the meal. They were sent from the room.*

dish something up (for someone) See the previous entry.

dive in(to something) **1.** to plunge into something; to jump into something head first. □ *Don't dive into that water! It's too shallow.* □ *Donna dived into the pool.* □ *David walked to the edge of the pool and dived in.* **2.** to plunge into some business or activity. (Figurative.) □ *I can't wait to dive into the next project.* □ *Clara dives into her work eagerly every morning.*

divide something in something See the following entry.

divide something into something **1.** AND **divide something in something** to separate something into parts. □ *I will divide it into two parts.* □ *I will divide the cake in half.* □ *If you divide the pie in fourths, the pieces will be too big.* **2.** to do mathematical division so that the divisor goes into the number that is to be divided. □ *Divide seven into forty-nine and what do you get?* □ *If seven is divided into forty-nine, what do you get?*

do a land-office business to do a large amount of business in a short period of time. (As if selling land during a land rush.) □ *The ice-cream shop always does a land-office business on a hot day.* □ *The tax collector's office did a land-office business on the day that taxes were due.*

(Do) have some more. an invitation to take more of something, usually food or drink. □ BILL: *Wow, Mrs. Franklin, this scampi is great!* SALLY: *Thank you, Bill. Do have some more.* □ JANE: *What a lovely, light cake.* MARY: *Oh, have some more. Otherwise the boys will just wolf it down.*

Do I have to paint (you) a picture? See the following entry.

Do I have to spell it out (for you)? AND **Do I have to paint (you) a picture?** What do I have to do to make this clear enough for you to understand? (Shows impatience.) □ MARY: *I don't think I understand what you're trying to tell me, Fred.* FRED: *Do I have to spell it out for you?* MARY: *I guess so.* FRED: *We're through, Mary.* □ SALLY: *Would you please go over the part about the square root again?* MARY: *Do I have to paint you a picture? Pay attention!*

Do I make myself (perfectly) clear? Do you understand exactly what I mean? (Very stern.) □ MOTHER: *You're going to sit right here and finish that homework. Do I make myself perfectly clear?* CHILD: *Yes, ma'am.* □ SUE: *No, the answer is no! Do I make myself clear?* BILL: *Are you sure?*

Do sit down. *Don't stand on ceremony.; please sit down.* (A polite phrase encouraging people to resume their seats after rising for an intro-

duction or out of deference.) □ *Tom rose when Mary approached the table, but she said graciously, "Do sit down. I just wanted to thank you again for the lovely gift."* □ TOM: *Hello, Bill.* BILL (rising): *Hi, Tom.* TOM (standing): *Do sit down. I just wanted to say hello.*

do someone or something in 1. to wear someone or some creature out. (*Someone* includes *oneself.*) □ *All this walking will do me in.* Ⓣ *The walking did in most of the hikers.* □ *The climbing did them in.* □ *I did myself in running the race.* **2.** to destroy or ruin someone or something. □ *Who did my car in?* Ⓣ *Who did in my car?* **3.** to kill someone or some creature. (*Someone* includes *oneself.*) □ *Max tried to do Lefty in.* Ⓣ *Max tried to do in Lefty.* □ *The speeding car did my cat in.* □ *He lost all his money on the horses and did himself in.*

do someone or something over to remodel or redecorate something; to redo someone's appearance. □ *I am going to have to do this room over. It is beginning to look drab.* Ⓣ *Yes, you should do over this room.* □ *There's no need to do it over.* □ *The beauty consultant did Janet over, and now she looks like a model.*

do someone or something up 1. to make someone or something attractive; to decorate or ornament someone or something. (*Someone* includes *oneself.*) □ *Sally did Jane up for the party.* Ⓣ *She did up Jane nicely.* Ⓣ *Would you do up this present for Jane? It's her birthday.* □ *She did herself up just beautifully.* **2.** [with *something*] to fasten, zip, hook, or button some item of clothing. □ *Would you do my buttons up in back?* Ⓣ *Please do up my buttons.* **3.** [with *something*] to arrange, fix, repair, cook, or clean something. □ *I have to do the kitchen up before the guests get here.* T *Do up the kitchen now, please.*

do someone's heart good to make someone feel good emotionally. (Also used literally.) □ *It does my heart good to hear you talk that way.* □ *When she sent me a get-well card, it really did my heart good.*

do something by hand to do something with one's hands rather than with a machine. □ *The computer was broken so I had to do the calculations by hand.* □ *All this tiny stitching was done by hand. Machines cannot do this kind of work.*

do something hands down to do something easily and without opposition. (Without anyone raising a hand in opposition.) □ *The mayor won the election hands down.* □ *She was the choice of the people hands down.*

Do tell. a response to one of a series of statements by another person. (The expression can indicate disinterest. Each word has equal stress. See also *You don't say.*) □ BILL: *The Amazon basin is about ten times the size of France.* MARY: *Do tell.* □ FRED: *Most large ships produce their own fresh water.* SUE: *Do tell. Say, Fred, has anyone ever told you how interesting you are?* FRED: *No.* SUE: *I suspected as much.*

do the dishes to wash the dishes; to wash and dry the dishes. □ *Bill, you cannot go out and play until you've done the dishes.* □ *Why am I always the one who has to do the dishes?*

do the honors to act as host or hostess and serve one's guests by pouring drinks, slicing meat, making (drinking) toasts, etc. □ *All the guests were seated, and a huge juicy turkey sat on the table. Jane Thomas turned to her husband and said, "Bob, will you do the honors?" Mr. Thomas smiled and began slicing thick slices of meat from the turkey.* □ *The mayor stood up and addressed the people who were still eating their salads. "I'm delighted to do the honors this evening and propose a toast to your friend and mine, Bill Jones. Bill, good luck and best wishes in your new job in Washington." And everyone sipped a bit of wine.*

Do we have to go through all that again? Do we have to discuss that matter again? (Compare to *Let's not go through all that again.*) □ BILL: *Now, I still have more to say about what happened last night.* SALLY: *Do we have to go through all that again?* □ SALLY: *I can't get over the way you treated me at our own dinner table.* FRED: *I was irritated at something else. I said I was sorry. Do we have to go through all that again?*

do without (someone or something) to manage or get along without someone or something that is needed. □ *I guess I will have to do without dinner.* □ *Yes, you'll do without.*

(Do you) care if I join you? See *Could I join you?*

Do you expect me to believe that? That is so unbelievable that you do not expect me to believe it, do you? (A bit impatient. Similar to *You can't expect me to believe that.*) □ BILL: *I'm going to quit my job and open a restaurant.* MARY: *That's silly. Do* you expect me to believe that? BILL: I guess not. □ MARY: *Wow! I just got selected to be an astronaut!* SALLY: *Do you expect me to believe that?* MARY: *Here's the letter! Now do you believe me?*

Do you follow? Do you understand what I am saying?; Do you understand my explanation? □ MARY: *Keep to the right past the fork in the road, then turn right at the crossroads. Do you follow?* JANE: *No. Run it by me again.* □ JOHN: *Take a large bowl and break two eggs into it and beat them. Do you follow?* SUE: *Sure.*

(Do you) get my drift? AND **(Do you) get the message?** Do you understand what I mean?; Do you understand what I am getting at? (Slang.) □ FATHER: *I want you to settle down and start studying. Get my drift?* BOB: *Sure, Pop. Whatever you say.* □ MARY: *Get out of my way and stop following me around. Get the message?* JOHN: *I guess so.*

(Do you) get the message? See the previous entry.

(Do you) get the picture? Do you understand the situation?; Do you know what this means you have to do? □ BILL: *I want to get this project wrapped up before midnight. Do you get the picture?* TOM: *I'm afraid I do.* BILL: *Well, then, get to work.* □ FRED: *I'm really tired of all this. Get the picture? I want you to straighten up and get moving. Get the picture?* BILL: *I got it.*

(Do) you hear? Do you hear and understand what I said? (Typically southern.) □ JOHN: *I want you to clean up this room this instant! Do you hear?* SUE: *Okay. I'll get right on it.* □ BOB: *Come over here, Sue. I want to*

show you something, you hear? SUE: *Sure. What is it?*

(Do you) know what? AND **You know what?** an expression used to open a conversation or switch to a new topic. □ BOB: *You know what?* MARY: *No, what?* BOB: *I think this milk is spoiled.* □ BOB: *Know what?* BILL: *Tell me.* BOB: *Your hair needs cutting.* BILL: *So what?*

(Do you) know what I mean? See the following entry.

(Do you) know what I'm saying? AND **You know (what I'm saying)?; (Do you) know what I mean?; You know what I mean?** Do you understand me?; Do you agree? (The *You know?* is frowned on by many people.) □ JOHN: *This is really great for me and the whole group. You know?* SUE: *Yes, I know.* □ SUE: *This is, like, really great! Do you know what I'm saying?* MARY: *Yeah, I've been there. It's great.*

(Do) you mean to say something? AND **(Do) you mean to tell me something?** Are you really saying something? (A way of giving someone an opportunity to alter a comment. The *something* represents a quote or a paraphrase.) □ MARY: *I'm leaving tomorrow.* SALLY: *Do you mean to say you're leaving school for good?* MARY: *Yes.* □ BOB: *Do you mean to tell me that this is all you've accomplished in two weeks?* BILL: *I guess so.* BOB: *I expected more.*

(Do) you mean to tell me something? See the previous entry.

Do you mind? **1.** You are intruding on my space!; You are offending me! (Impatient or incensed. Essentially, "Do you mind stopping what you are doing?") □ *The lady behind her in line kept pushing against her every time the line moved. Finally, Sue turned and said sternly, "Do you mind?"* □ *All through the first part of the movie, two people in the row behind John kept up a running conversation. Finally, as the din grew loud enough to cause a number of people to say "shhh," John rose and turned, leaned over into their faces, and shouted, "Do you mind?"* **2.** Do you object to what I am poised to do? □ *Mary had her hand on the lovely silver cake knife that would carry the very last piece of cake to her plate. She looked at Tom, who stood next to her, eyeing the cake. "Do you mind?" she asked coyly.* □ *"Do you mind?" asked John as he raced by Sally through the door.*

(do you) mind if? a polite way of seeking someone's permission or agreement. □ MARY: *Do you mind if I sit here?* JANE: *No, help yourself.* □ TOM: *Mind if I smoke?* BILL: *I certainly do.* TOM: *Then I'll go outside.*

(Do you) mind if I join you? See *Could I join you?*

Do you read me? 1. an expression used by someone communicating by radio, asking if the hearer understands the transmission clearly. □ CONTROLLER: *This is Aurora Center, do you read me?* PILOT: *Yes, I read you loud and clear.* □ CONTROLLER: *Left two degrees. Do you read me?* PILOT: *Roger.* **2.** Do you understand what I am telling you? (Used in general conversation, not in radio communication.) □ MARY: *I want you to pull yourself together and go out and get a job. Do you read me?* BILL: *Sure. Anything you say.* □ MOTHER: *Get this place picked up immediately. Do you read me?* CHILD: *Yes, ma'am.*

(Do you) want to know something? AND **(You want to) know something?** an expression used to open a conversation or switch to a new topic. □ JOHN: *Want to know something?* SUE: *What?* JOHN: *Your hem is torn.* □ BILL: *Hey, Tom! Know something?* TOM: *What is it?* BILL: *It's really hot today.* TOM: *Don't I know it!*

(Do you) want to make something of it? AND **You want to make something of it?** Do you want to start a fight about it? (Rude and contentious.) □ TOM: *You're really bugging me. It's not fair to pick on me all the time.* BILL: *You want to make something of it?* □ BOB: *Please be quiet. You're making too much noise.* FRED: *Do you want to make something of it?* BOB: *Just be quiet.*

(Do) you want to step outside? an expression inviting someone to go out-of-doors to settle an argument by fighting. □ JOHN: *Drop dead!* BOB: *All right, I've had enough out of you. You want to step outside?* □ BILL: *So you're mad at me! What else is new? You've been building up to this for a long time.* BOB: *Do you want to step outside and settle this once and for all?* BILL: *Why not?*

Does it work for you? Is this all right with you?; Do you agree? (Colloquial. Can be answered by *(It) works for me.*) □ BILL: *I'll be there at noon. Does it work for you?* BOB: *Works for me.* □ MARY: *We're having dinner at eight. Does it work for you?* JANE: *Sounds just fine.*

dole something out (to someone) to distribute something to someone. □ *The cook doled the oatmeal out to each camper who held out a bowl.* T *Please* dole out the candy bars, one to a customer. □ She doled it out fairly.

doll someone up to dress someone up in fancy clothes. (*Someone* includes oneself.) □ *She dolled her children up for church each Sunday.* T *She dolls up all her kids once a week.* □ *I just love it when you doll yourself up like that.*

dollar for dollar considering the amount of money involved; considering the cost. (Often seen in advertising.) □ *Dollar for dollar, you cannot buy a better car.* □ *Dollar for dollar, this laundry detergent washes cleaner and brighter than any other product on the market.*

Don't ask. You would not like the answer you would get, so do not ask.; It is so bad, I do not wish to be reminded about it, so do not ask about it. □ JOHN: *How was your class reunion?* ALICE: *Oh, heavens! Don't ask.* □ TOM: *What was your calculus final exam like?* MARY: *Don't ask.* □ SUE: *How old were you on your last birthday?* FRED: *Don't ask.*

Don't ask me. See *How should I know?*

Don't be gone (too) long. *Good-bye.;* Hurry back here. □ TOM: *I've got to go to the drugstore to get some medicine.* SUE: *Don't be gone too long.* TOM: *I'll be right back.* □ *"Don't be gone long,"* said Bill's uncle. *"It's about time to eat."*

Don't be too sure. I think you are wrong, so do not sound so certain.; You may be wrong, you know. (Similar to *Don't speak too soon.*) □ BILL: *Ah, it's sure great being home and safe — secure in one's castle.* MARY: *Don't be too sure. I just heard glass breaking*

downstairs. □ BILL: *I think I've finally saved up enough money to retire.* JOHN: *Don't be too sure. Inflation can ruin your savings.*

Don't bother. Please don't do it. It is not necessary, and it is too much trouble. □ MARY: *Should I put these in the box with the others?* BILL: *No, don't bother.* □ SUE: *Do you want me to save this spoonful of mashed potatoes?* JANE: *No, don't bother. It isn't worth it.* SUE: *I hate to waste it.*

Don't bother me! Go away!; *Leave me alone!* □ TOM: *Hey, Bill!* BILL: *Don't bother me! I'm busy. Can't you see?* □ *"Don't bother me! Leave me alone!"* the child shouted at the dog.

Don't breathe a word of this to anyone. This is a secret or secret gossip. Do not tell it to anyone. □ MARY: *Can you keep a secret?* JOHN: *Sure.* MARY: *Don't breathe a word of this to anyone, but Tom is in jail.* □ BILL: *Have you heard about Mary and her friends?* SALLY: *No. Tell me! Tell me!* BILL: *Well, they all went secretly to Mexico for the weekend. Everyone thinks they are at Mary's, except Mary's mother, who thinks they are at Sue's. Now, don't breathe a word of this to anyone.* SALLY: *Of course not! You know me!*

Don't call us, we'll call you. We will let you know if we wish to talk to you further.; We will let you know if you got the job, so don't bother calling and asking. (Often a dismissal.) □ SALLY: *Thank you for coming by for the interview. We'll let you know.* BILL: *How soon do you think Mr. Franklin will decide?* SALLY: *Don't call us, we'll call you.* □ *"Don't call us, we'll call you,"* said the assistant director, as if he *had said it a hundred times already today, which he probably had.*

Don't do anything I wouldn't do. an expression said when two friends are parting. (Familiar and colloquial.) □ BILL: *See you tomorrow, Tom.* TOM: *Yeah, man. Don't do anything I wouldn't do.* BILL: *What wouldn't you do?* □ MARY: *Where are you going, Bill?* BILL: *Oh, just around.* MARY: *Sure, you're spinning. Well, don't do anything I wouldn't do.* BILL: *Okay, but what wouldn't you do?* MARY: *Beat it, you clown!* BILL: *I'm off.*

Don't even look like something! Do not even appear to be doing something! (The *something* can be thinking about something or actually doing something.) □ MARY: *Are you thinking about taking that last piece of cake?* BOB: *Of course not.* MARY: *Well, don't even look like you're doing it!* □ JOHN: *You weren't going to try to sneak into the theater, were you?* BOB: *No.* JOHN: *Well, don't even look like it, if you know what's good for you.*

Don't even think about (doing) it. Do not do it, and do not even think about doing it. □ *John reached into his jacket for his wallet. The cop, thinking John was about to draw a gun, said, "Don't even think about it."* □ MARY: *Look at that diver! It must be forty feet down to the water.* BOB: *Don't even think about doing it yourself.*

Don't even think about it (happening). Do not even think about something like that happening. (Compare to *Don't even think about (doing) it.*) □ MARY: *Oh, those cars almost crashed! How horrible!* FRED: *Don't even think about it.* □ SALLY: *If the banks fail, we'll lose everything we have.* SUE: *Don't even think about it!*

Don't forget to write. See *Remember to write.*

Don't get up. Please, there is no need to rise to greet me or in deference to me. (Often with *please*.) □ *Mary approached the table to speak to Bill. Bill started to push his chair back as if to rise. Mary said, "Don't get up. I just want to say hello."* □ TOM (rising): *Hello, Fred. Good to see you.* FRED (standing): *Don't get up. How are you?*

Don't get your bowels in an uproar! Do not get so excited! (Slang.) □ BILL: *What have you done to my car? Where's the bumper? The side window is cracked!* BOB: *Calm down! Don't get your bowels in an uproar!* □ FATHER: *Now, son, we need to talk a little bit about you and your pet snake. Where is it?* JOHN: *I don't know.* FATHER (outraged): *What!* JOHN: *Don't get your bowels in an uproar! It always turns up.*

Don't give it a (second) thought. See *Think nothing of it.*

Don't give it another thought. See *Think nothing of it.*

Don't give up! Do not stop trying!; Keep trying! □ JOHN: *Get in there and give it another try. Don't give up!* BILL: *Okay. Okay. But it's hopeless.* □ JANE: *I asked the boss for a raise, but he said no.* TOM: *Don't give up. Try again later.*

Don't give up the ship! Do not give up yet!; Do not yield the entire enterprise! (From a naval expression.) □ BILL: *I'm having a devil of a time with calculus. I think I want to drop the course.* SALLY: *Keep trying. Don't give up the ship!* □ BILL: *Every time we get enough money saved up to* make a down payment on a house, the price of houses skyrockets. I'm about ready to stop trying. SUE: *We'll manage. Don't give up the ship!*

Don't give up too eas(il)y! AND **Don't give up without a fight!** Do not yield so easily.; Keep struggling and you may win.; Do not give up too soon. □ SUE: *She says no every time I ask her for a raise.* MARY: *Well, don't give up too easily. Keep after her.* □ JOHN: *I know it's my discovery, not hers, but she won't admit it.* SALLY: *Don't give up without a fight.*

Don't give up without a fight! See the previous entry.

Don't hold your breath. Do not stop breathing while you are waiting for something to happen. (Meaning that it will take longer for it to happen than you can possibly hold your breath.) □ TOM: *The front yard is such a mess.* BOB: *Bill is supposed to rake the leaves.* TOM: *Don't hold your breath. He never does his share of the work.* □ SALLY: *Someone said that gasoline prices would go down.* BOB: *Oh, yeah? Don't hold your breath.*

Don't I know it! I know that very well! □ MARY: *Goodness gracious! It's hot today.* BOB: *Don't I know it!* □ SUE: *You seem to be putting on a little weight.* JOHN: *Don't I know it!*

Don't I know you from somewhere? a way of striking up a conversation with a stranger, probably at a party or other gathering. □ BILL: *Don't I know you from somewhere?* MARY: *I don't think so. Where did you go to school?* □ HENRY: *Don't I know you from somewhere?* ALICE: *No, and let's keep it that way.*

Don't let someone or something get you down. Don't let someone or something bother you. □ TOM: *I'm so mad at her I could scream!* SUE: *Don't let her get you down.* □ JOHN: *This project at work is getting to be a real mess.* JANE: *Don't let it get you down. It will be over with soon.*

Don't let the bastards wear you down. Don't let those people get the best of you. (Use caution with *bastard*.) □ BILL: *The place I work at is really rough. Everybody is rude and jealous of each other.* TOM: *Don't let the bastards wear you down.* □ JANE: *I have to go down to the county clerk's office and figure out what this silly bureaucratic letter means.* SUE: *You might call them on the phone. In any case, don't let the bastards wear you down.*

Don't look a gift horse in the mouth. One should not expect perfect gifts. (Proverb. Usually stated in the negative. Note the variation in the examples. The age of a horse and, therefore, its usefulness can be determined by looking at its teeth. It would be greedy to inspect the teeth of a horse given as a gift to make sure the horse is of the best quality.) □ *Don't complain. You shouldn't look a gift horse in the mouth.* □ *John complained that the television set he got for his birthday was black and white rather than color. He was told, "Don't look a gift horse in the mouth."*

Don't make me laugh! Do not make such ridiculous statements; they only make me laugh. (Compare to *You make me laugh!*) □ MARY: *I'll be a millionaire by the time I'm thirty.* TOM: *Don't make me laugh!* MARY: *I will! I will!* □ MARY: *I'm trying out for* *cheerleader.* SUE: *You, a cheerleader? Don't make me laugh!*

Don't make me say it again! AND **Don't make me tell you again!** I have told you once, and now I'm mad, and I'll be madder if I have to tell you again. (Typically said to a child who will not mind.) □ MOTHER: *I told you thirty minutes ago to clean up this room! Don't make me tell you again!* CHILD: *Okay. I'll do it.* □ BILL: *No, Sue, I will not buy you a beach house. Don't make me say it again!* SUE: *Are you sure?*

Don't make me tell you again! See the previous entry.

Don't mind me. Don't pay any attention to me.; Just ignore me. (Sometimes sarcastic.) □ *Bill and Jane were watching television when Jane's mother walked through the room, grabbing the newspaper on the way. "Don't mind me," she said.* □ *Bob was sitting at the table and Mary and Bill started up this sort of quiet and personal conversation. Bob stared off into space and said, "Don't mind me." Bill and Mary didn't even notice.*

Don't push (me)! Don't put pressure on me to do something! (Also a literal meaning.) □ SUE: *You really must go to the dentist, you know.* JOHN: *Don't push me. I'll go when I'm good and ready.* □ BOB: *Come on! You can finish. Keep trying.* BILL: *Don't push me! I have to do it under my own steam!*

Don't quit trying. See *Keep (on) trying.*

Don't rush me! Don't try to hurry me! □ BILL: *Hurry up! Make up your mind!* BOB: *Don't rush me!* BILL: *I want to get out of here before midnight.*

□ BILL: *The waiter wants to take your order. What do you want?* JANE: *Don't rush me! I can't make up my mind.* WAITER: *I'll come back in a minute.*

Don't say it! I don't want to hear it!; I know, so you don't have to say it. □ JOHN (joking): *What is that huge pile of stuff on your head?* BILL: *Don't say it! I know I need a haircut.* □ FRED: *And then I'll trade that car in on a bigger one, and then I'll buy a bigger house.* BOB: *Fred!* FRED: *Oh, don't say it!* BOB: *You're a dreamer, Fred.* FRED: *I had hoped you wouldn't say that.*

Don't speak too soon. I think you may be wrong. Don't speak before you know the facts. (Compare to *Don't be too sure.*) □ BILL: *It looks like it'll be a nice day.* MARY: *Don't speak too soon. I just felt a raindrop.* □ TOM: *It looks like we made it home without any problems.* BILL: *Don't speak too soon, there's a cop behind us in the driveway.*

Don't spend it all in one place. a catch phrase said after giving someone some money, especially a small amount of money. □ FRED: *Dad, can I have a dollar?* FATHER: *Sure. Here. Don't spend it all in one place.* □ *"Here's a quarter, kid," said Tom, flipping Fred a quarter. "Don't spend it all in one place."* □ ALICE: *Here's the five hundred dollars I owe you.* TOM: *Oh, thanks. I need this.* ALICE: *Thank you. Don't spend it all in one place.* TOM: *I have to or they'll take my car back.*

Don't stand on ceremony. Do not wait for a formal invitation.; Please be at ease and make yourself at home. (Some people read this as "Don't remain standing because of ceremony," and others read it "Don't be totally obedient to the

99

requirements of ceremony.") □
JOHN: *Come in, Tom. Don't stand on
ceremony. Get yourself a drink and
something to eat and mingle with the
other guests.* TOM: *Okay, but I can
only stay for a few minutes.* □ *"Don't
stand on ceremony, Fred," urged Sally.
"Go around and introduce yourself to
everyone."*

Don't stay away so long. Please visit
more often. (Said upon the arrival or
departure of a guest.) □ JOHN: *Hi,
Bill! Long time no see. Don't stay away
so long!* BILL: *Thanks, John. Good to
see you.* □ MARY: *I had a nice time.
Thanks for inviting me.* SALLY: *Good
to see you, Mary. Next time, don't stay
away so long.*

Don't sweat it! Don't worry about it.
(Slang.) □ BILL: *I think I'm flunking
algebra!* BOB: *Don't sweat it! Everybody's having a rough time.* □ MARY:
*Good grief! I just stepped on the cat's
tail, but I guess you heard.* SUE: *Don't
sweat it! The cat has got to learn to
keep out of the way.*

Don't tell a soul. Please do not tell
anyone this gossip. □ BILL: *Is your
brother getting married?* SALLY: *Yes,
but don't tell a soul. It's a secret.* □
MARY: *Can you keep a secret?* JOHN:
Sure. MARY: *Don't tell a soul, but Tom
is in jail.*

Don't tell me what to do! Do not
give me orders. □ BOB: *Get over
there and pick up those papers before
they blow away.* SALLY: *Don't tell me
what to do!* BOB: *Better hurry. One of
those papers is your paycheck. But it's
no skin off my nose if you don't.* □
SUE: *Next, you should get a haircut,
then get some new clothes. You really
need to fix yourself up.* SALLY: *Don't*

*tell me what to do! Maybe I like me the
way I am!*

Don't waste my time. Do not take up
my valuable time with a poor presentation.; Do not waste my time trying
to get me to do something. □ BOB:
*I'd like to show you our new line of in-
dustrial strength vacuum cleaners.* BILL:
Beat it! Don't waste my time. □
*"Don't waste my time!" said the man-
ager when Jane made her fourth appeal
for a raise.*

Don't waste your breath. You will
not get a positive response to what
you have to say, so don't even say it.;
Talking will get you nowhere. □
ALICE: *I'll go in there and try to convince her otherwise.* FRED: *Don't waste
your breath. I already tried it.* □
SALLY: *No, I won't agree! Don't waste
your breath.* BILL: *Aw, come on.*

Don't waste your time. You will not
get anywhere with it, so don't waste
time trying. □ MARY: *Should I ask
Tom if he wants to go to the convention,
or is he still in a bad mood?* SALLY:
Don't waste your time. MARY: *Bad
mood, huh?* □ JANE: *I'm having
trouble fixing this doorknob.* MARY:
*Don't waste your time. I've ordered a
new one.*

Don't work too hard. an expression
said at the end of a conversation
after or in place of *good-bye.* □
MARY: *Bye, Tom.* TOM: *Bye, Mary.
Don't work too hard.* □ SUE: *Don't
work too hard!* MARY: *I never do.*

Don't worry. Do not become anxious, everything will be all right. □
*"Don't worry, Fred," comforted Bill,
"everything will be all right."* □ BILL: *I
think I left the car windows open.* SUE:
Don't worry, I closed them.

Don't worry about a thing. Everything will be taken care of. Do not be anxious. □ MARY: *This has been such an ordeal.* SUE: *I'll help. Don't worry about a thing.* □ *"Don't worry about a thing," the tax collector had said. "We'll take care of everything." Or was it "We'll take everything?"*

Don't you know? **1.** Don't you know the answer?; I don't know, I thought you did. □ MARY: *How do I get to the Morris Building? Where do I turn?* JANE: *Don't you know? I have no idea!* □ SUE: *We're supposed to either sign these contracts or rewrite them. Which is it?* JOHN: *Don't you know?* **2.** AND **Don't you see?** Do you understand?; Do you see? (Usually pronounced "doan-cha know," often without rising question intonation. Typically, nothing more than a call for some quick response from the person being talked to.) □ JOHN: *This whole thing can be straightened out with hardly any trouble at all, don't you know?* SUE: *What makes you so sure?* JOHN: *I've had this same problem before.* □ BILL: *Why are you stopping the car?* JOHN: *We usually stop here for the night, don't you know?* BILL: *I know a better place down the road.*

Don't you know it! You can be absolutely sure about that!; You're exactly right, and I agree with you. (This is not a question.) □ ALICE: *Man, is it hot!* FRED: *Don't you know it!* □ BOB: *This is the best cake I have ever eaten. The cook is the best in the world!* BILL: *Don't you know it!*

Don't you see? See *Don't you know?*

(Don't) you wish! Don't you wish that what you have just said were really true? □ MARY: *I'm going to get a job that lets me travel a lot.* SALLY:

Don't you wish! □ SALLY: *Sorry you lost the chess game. It was close, but your opponent was top-notch.* BOB: *Next time, I'll do it! I'll win the next round.* SALLY: *Don't you wish!*

dose of one's own medicine the same kind of treatment that one gives to other people. (Often with *get* or *have*.) □ *Sally never is very friendly. Someone is going to give her a dose of her own medicine someday.* □ *He didn't like getting a dose of his own medicine.*

double back (on something) to follow one's own pathway back toward where one started. □ *I doubled back on my own trail.* □ *The horse doubled back.*

double over to bend in the middle. (More at *double someone or something over*.) □ *Suddenly, he doubled over and collapsed.* □ *The people in the audience doubled over with laughter.*

double someone or something over to cause someone or something to bend in the middle or fold over. (More at *double over*.) □ *The blow to the back of the head doubled Steve over.* □ *The wind almost doubled Debbie over.* ⊤ *Double over the paper twice, then press it flat.* □ *Double the cloth over a few times before you pack it away.*

double up (on someone or something) [for people] to deal with someone or something in pairs. □ *We are going to have to double up in this job.* □ *We will double up and get it done.* □ *The doctors doubled up on Fred and got him to breath again.*

double up (with someone or something) **1.** [with *someone*] to share something with someone. □ *We* don't have enough. You will have to double up with Sam. □ Let's double up and use the book together. **2.** [with something] to bend in the middle with something such as laughter, howls, pain, etc. (Sometimes figurative or an exaggeration.) □ The man doubled up with laughter when he heard why we were there. □ He laughed so hard that he doubled up.

down in the dumps sad or depressed. □ I've been down in the dumps for the past few days. □ Try to cheer Jane up. She's down in the dumps for some reason.

down in the mouth sad-faced; depressed and unsmiling. (Refers to a frown or sagging mouth.) □ Since her dog died, Barbara has been down in the mouth. □ Bob has been down in the mouth since the car wreck.

down the drain lost forever; wasted. (Also used literally.) □ I just hate to see all that money go down the drain. □ Well, there goes the whole project, right down the drain.

Down the hatch! See *Bottoms up.*

down to the wire at the very last minute; up to the very last instant. (Refers to a wire that marks the end of a horse race.) □ I have to turn this in tomorrow, and I'll be working down to the wire. □ When we get down to the wire, we'll know better what to do.

doze off (to sleep) to slip away into sleep. □ I dozed off to sleep during the second act of the opera. □ I was so comfortable that I just dozed off.

drag behind to follow along behind someone. □ His little brother came along, dragging behind. □ Stop dragging along behind!

drag on to go on slowly for a very long time; to last a very long time. □ The lecture dragged on and on. □ Why do these things have to drag on so?

drag out to last for a long time. □ The lecture dragged out for nearly an hour. □ How much longer do you think this thing will drag out?

drag someone or something in(to something) 1. to haul or pull someone or something into something or some place. (*Someone* includes *oneself.*) □ The child's mother dragged him into store after store, looking for new shoes. Ⓣ She dragged in the child to get some shoes. □ Despite his broken leg, he dragged himself into the shelter. **2.** to involve someone or a group in something. □ Please don't drag me into your argument. □ Don't drag the committee into this argument. □ It is a mess, and please don't drag me into it.

drag someone or something off (to someone or something) to haul someone or something away to someone, something, or some place. □ The cops dragged her off to jail. Ⓣ They dragged off the criminal to the judge. □ We dragged him off.

drag someone up to force someone to come up or to come and stand nearby. (*Someone* includes *oneself.*) □ He wouldn't come on his own, so I dragged him up. □ You will have to drag him up. He is too tired to walk by himself. □ I had to drag myself up to bed.

drag something behind one to pull something that is behind one. □ The child dragged the wooden toy behind him. □ What is that you are dragging behind you?

drag something out to make something last for a long time. □ *Why does the chairman have to drag the meeting out so long?* T *Don't drag out the meetings so long!*

drag something out of someone to force someone to reveal something; to pull an answer or information out of someone laboriously. □ *Why don't you just tell me? Do I have to drag it out of you?* T *We had to drag out the information, but she finally told us.*

drain away [for something] to flow away. (More at *drain something away (from something)*.) □ *All the water drained away, and the fish lay dead on the bottom of the pond.* □ *When the water drained away, we found three snapping turtles in the bottom of the pond.*

drain out to flow out or empty. (More at *drain something out of something*.) □ *All the milk drained out of the container onto the bottom of the refrigerator.* □ *All the oil drained out of the crankcase.*

drain something away (from something) to channel some liquid away from something. (More at *drain away.*) □ *Drain all of the standing water away from the foundation of the house.* T *Drain away the water from the foundation.* □ *Please drain it away.*

drain something off (from something) AND **drain something off ((of) something)** to cause or permit something to flow out of something or from the surface of something. □ *Drain some of the fat off the gravy before you serve it.* T *Please drain off the fat!* □ *Oh, yes! Drain it off, please!* □ *Drain some of the broth off the chicken.* T *Drain off the broth.* □ *Drain the fat off.*

drain something off ((of) something) See the previous entry.

drain something out of something to cause something to flow from something; to empty all of some liquid out of something. (More at *drain out.*) □ *She drained the last drop out of the bottle.* T *She drained out the last drop.*

draw a blank 1. to get no response; to find nothing. □ *I asked him about Tom's financial problems, and I just drew a blank.* □ *We looked in the files for an hour, but we drew a blank.* **2.** to fail to remember (something). □ *I tried to remember her telephone number, but I could only draw a blank.* □ *It was a very hard test with just one question to answer, and I drew a blank.*

draw a line between something and something else to separate two things; to distinguish or differentiate between two things. (The *a* can be replaced with *the*. Also used literally.) □ *It's necessary to draw a line between bumping into people and striking them.* □ *It's very hard to draw the line between slamming a door and just closing it loudly.*

draw away (from someone or something) to pull back or away from someone or something. □ *Please don't draw away from me. I won't bite.* □ *She drew away.*

draw back (from someone or something) to pull back from someone or something; to recoil from someone or something. □ *The timid puppy drew back from my hand.* □ *She drew back from me, shocked.* □ *The cat drew back as the snake hissed at it.*

draw blood 1. to hit or bite (a person or an animal) and make a wound that bleeds. □ *The dog chased me and* bit me hard, but it didn't draw blood. □ The boxer landed just one punch and drew blood immediately. **2.** to anger or insult a person. □ Sally screamed out a terrible insult at Tom. Judging by the look on his face, she really drew blood. □ Tom started yelling and cursing, trying to insult Sally. He wouldn't be satisfied until he had drawn blood, too.

draw near [for a particular time] to approach. □ The time to depart is drawing near. □ As the time drew near, Ann became more and more nervous.

draw near (to someone or something) to come near to someone or something. □ Draw near to me, and let me look at you. □ Draw near to the table and look at this.

draw on someone or something to use someone or something in some beneficial way. □ I may have to draw on your advice in order to complete this project. □ If there is some way you can draw on me to your advantage, let me know.

draw oneself up (to something) to stand up straight and reach a certain height. □ Walter drew himself up to his six-foot height and walked away. □ She drew herself up and walked away. □ Tom drew himself up to his full height.

draw people together to make people seek one another for emotional support. □ The accident drew them all together. □ Do you think the meeting will draw us together better?

draw someone or something in(to something) **1.** to pull someone or something into something; to attract someone or something. □ She drew the child into the shoe store and plunked

her down. T Liz opened the door and drew in the child. □ The advertisement drew a lot of people in. **2.** to sketch a picture, adding someone or something into the picture. (Someone includes oneself.) □ She drew a little dog into the lower corner of the picture. □ I drew the man in. □ She drew herself into the scene. **3.** to involve someone or something in something. □ Don't draw me into this argument. □ This is not the time to draw that argument into the discussion.

draw someone or something out (of something) **1.** to lure someone or some creature out of something or some place. □ I thought the smell of breakfast would draw him out of his reverie. T The good smells drew out the rest of the family. □ The warm sunlight drew the snake out of its lair. **2.** to pull someone or something out of something or some place. □ We drew him out of the slot in the wall where he lay hiding. T We drew out the concealed microphone. □ Tom drew the stowaway out of the locker.

draw someone or something to(ward) someone or something to pull someone or something to someone or something. □ She drew him toward her and kissed him. □ Todd drew the child toward the light. □ Kelly tried to draw the chair to the window.

draw someone out (about someone or something) See the following entry.

draw someone out (on someone or something) AND **draw someone out (about someone or something)** to find out someone's private thoughts about someone or something. □ I tried to draw him out on this matter, but he would not say any more. T I tried to *draw out the speaker, but she was very careful about what she said.* T *Fred wanted to draw out information about the company's plans, but the controller had nothing to say.* □ *We were not able to draw her out as hard as we tried.*

draw something off (from something) to remove a portion of a liquid from something; to cause something to flow from something. □ *The steward drew some wine off from the cask.* T *He drew off some wine.* □ *We drew some more off.*

draw something out **1.** to extend something in time. □ *Do we have to draw this thing out? Let's get it over with.* T *Stop drawing out the proceedings.* **2.** to lengthen something. □ *She drew the bubble gum out and made a long pink string.* T *Look at her drawing out that gum. What a mess!*

draw something out (of someone) to get some kind of information from someone. □ *He kept his mouth closed, and we couldn't draw anything out of him.* T *We were able to draw out the information we wanted.*

draw something up **1.** to pull something close by, such as a chair, stool, etc. (Compare to *draw up.*) □ *Draw a chair up and sit down.* T *She drew up a chair and sat down.* **2.** to draft a document; to prepare a document. □ *Who will draw a contract up?* T *I will draw up a contract for the work.*

draw up to pull up; to shrink up. (Compare to *draw something up.*) □ *When they got wet, his trunks drew up and became very tight.* □ *This cheap underwear has a tendency to draw up.*

draw (up) alongside ((of) someone or something) to move up even with someone or something in motion. □ *The police officer drew up alongside us and ordered us to pull over.* □ *A car drew up alongside of us.* □ *Draw up alongside that car.*

dream about someone or something AND **dream of someone or something** to have mental pictures about someone or something, especially in one's sleep. □ *I dreamed about you all night last night.* □ *I dreamed of a huge chocolate cake.*

dream come true a wish or a dream that has become real. □ *Going to Hawaii is like having a dream come true.* □ *Having you for a friend is a dream come true.*

dream of someone or something See *dream about someone or something.*

dream something up to invent something; to fabricate something. (The *something* can be the word *something.*) □ *I don't know what to do, but I'll dream something up.* T *Please dream up a solution for this problem.*

dredge someone or something up **1.** to scoop something up from underwater. □ *The workers dredged the lifeless body up from the cold black water.* T *They dredged up the lifeless body.* T *They were amazed to dredge up an equally surprised scuba diver.* **2.** to seek and find someone or something. (Slang.) □ *I will see if I can dredge a date up for Friday.* T *Can you dredge up a date for me?* □ *I don't have a wrench here, but I'll see if I can dredge one up.*

dress someone down to scold someone. □ *His mother dressed him down* *but good.* T *I hate to have to get mad and dress down some helpless kid.*

dress someone or something (up) (in something) to clothe, decorate, or ornament someone or something in something. (*Someone* includes oneself.) □ *She dressed her dolls up in special clothing.* T *She dressed up her dolls in tiny outfits.* T *She dressed up all of them.* □ *Roger dressed his nephew up for the service.* □ *Dress yourself up in your finest.*

dress (up) as someone or something to dress in the manner of someone or something or to look like someone or something. □ *I am going to dress up as a ghost for Halloween.* □ *Larry will dress up as the pumpkin from Cinderella.* □ *Sam will dress as himself.*

drift back (to someone or something) to move back to someone or something slowly, on the surface of water. (Considerable metaphorical use.) □ *The canoe drifted back to shore.* □ *Finally he drifted back to her and they made up.*

drift in(to something) to move slowly and gradually into something, as if on the surface of water. (Both figurative and literal uses.) □ *The people drifted slowly into the hall.* □ *The boats drifted into the masses of pondweed.*

drift off to move slowly away, as if on the surface of water. (Both figurative and literal uses.) □ *The boat slowly drifted off and was gone.* □ *The clouds drifted off and were soon gone.*

drift out to move out of a place slowly, as if on the surface of water. (Both figurative and literal uses.) □

After there was no more food, the people drifted out, one by one. □ *The boat drifted out and almost got away.*

drift to(ward) someone or something to move slowly and gradually toward someone or something, as if on the surface of water. (Both figurative and literal uses.) □ *The clouds drifted toward us, and we could see that a storm was coming.* □ *As the clouds drifted to us, we could feel the humidity increase.*

drill into something to bore into or penetrate something. □ *The worker drilled into the wall in three places.* □ *Please don't drill into the wall here, where it shows.*

drill something in(to someone or something) to force knowledge into someone or something. (Figurative.) □ *Learn this stuff! Drill it into your brain.* T *Drill in this information so you know it by heart!* □ *Yes, I will drill it in.*

drink something down to drink something; to consume all of something by drinking it. □ *Here, drink this down, and see if it makes you feel better.* T *Drink down this medicine.*

drink something in to absorb something; to take in information, sights, a story, etc. (Figurative.) □ *Terry and Amy drove up to the top of the hill to drink the sights in.* T *They drank in the beautiful view.*

drink something up to drink all of something. (More at *drink up*.) □ *Who drank all the root beer up?* T *I drank up the root beer.*

drink to excess to drink too much alcohol; to drink alcoholic beverages continually. □ *Mr. Franklin drinks to excess.* □ *Some people drink to excess only at parties.*

drink up to drink all of something. (More at *drink something up.*) □ *Drink up, and let's get going.* □ *Let's drink up and be on our way.*

drip something in(to something) to make something fall into something drop by drop. □ *Alice dripped a little candle wax into the base of the candlestick.* ⊤ *Don't pour it all into the jar. Drip in a little at a time.* □ *Don't just drip it in. Pour it all in at once.*

drive a hard bargain to work hard to negotiate prices or agreements in one's own favor. □ *I saved $200 by driving a hard bargain when I bought my new car.* □ *All right, sir, you drive a hard bargain. I'll sell you this car for $12,450.* □ *You drive a hard bargain, Jane, but I'll sign the contract.*

drive away to leave some place driving a vehicle. □ *They got in the car and drove away.* □ *They drove away and left us here.*

drive down (to some place) to run a vehicle to a relatively lower place or to a place in the south. (More at *drive someone down (to some place).*) □ *We are going to drive down to Houston for the weekend.* □ *We were going to fly, but it will be nice to drive down.*

drive off to leave somewhere, driving a vehicle. □ *She got in her car and drove off.* □ *Please don't drive off and leave me!*

drive on to continue driving; to continue with one's journey. □ *We drove on for a little while.* □ *The traffic jam is breaking up, so we can drive on.*

drive out (to some place) to propel a vehicle to a place that is away from the center of things. □ *We drove out to a little place in the country for a picnic.* □ *Why don't you drive out this weekend? We would love to have you here.*

drive over (to some place) to motor to some place that is neither close by nor far away. □ *Let's drive over to Larry's place.* □ *Yes, let's drive over. It's too far to walk.*

Drive safely. an expression used to advise a departing person to be careful while driving. □ MARY: Goodbye, Sally. Drive safely. SALLY: Good-bye. I will. □ *"Drive safely!" everyone shouted as we left on our trip.*

drive someone down (to some place) to transport someone to a relatively lower place or to a place in the south. (*Someone* includes *oneself.* More at *drive down (to some place).*) □ *We have to drive Andrew down to school in the fall.* □ *She drove herself down to the hospital.* □ *Would you drive Sally down when you come this weekend?*

drive someone on (to something) to make someone move onward toward some kind of success. (*Someone* includes *oneself.*) □ *She said her parents drove her on to her great success.* ⊤ *They drove on their daughter to great things.* □ *The thought of earning a large salary drove him on.* □ *He drove himself on, even when he was exhausted.*

drive someone or something (away) (from some place) to repel someone or some creature from some place. □ *We drove the monkeys away from the pineapples.* ⊤ *We drove away the monkeys from the fruit.* □ *Get out there and drive those deer out of my flowers!* □ *The gang's activity drove a* lot of people away from the neighborhood. ⊤ His drinking drove away his family and his friends.

drive someone or something back 1. to force someone or something away; to force someone or something to retreat. □ The infantry drove the attackers back into the desert. ⊤ They drove back the invading army. □ We drove them back. **2.** [with something] to propel a vehicle back to where it started. □ Mary drove back and parked the car where it had been when she started. □ You drive us there, and I'll drive back.

drive someone or something off to repel or chase away someone or something. □ The campers drove the cows off before the animals trampled the tents. ⊤ They drove off the cows. □ They drove them off.

drive someone or something out (of something) to force or chase someone or some creature out of something or some place. □ We drove them all out of the country. ⊤ We drove out the troublesome kids.

drive someone to the wall See force someone to the wall.

drive someone up (to some place) to transport someone to a place on a higher level or to a place in the north. □ Ralph drove Sally up to the cabin. □ He was going to drive her up last week, but could not.

drive something down to force the price of something down. □ The lack of buyers drove the price down. ⊤ The lack of buyers drove down the price.

drive something down (to some place) to transport a vehicle to a place by driving it there. □ I will drive the car down to the college and leave it

there for you. ⊤ I'll drive down the car and meet you. □ Do I have to drive the car down? Can't you fly up here and get it?

drive something up AND **force something up** to force the price of something upwards. □ Someone is buying a lot of this stuff and driving the price up. ⊤ They are driving up the price. ⊤ They forced up the price by cornering the market on these goods.

drive through (something) to motor from one side of something to the other; to pass through something while driving. □ We drove through some nice little towns on the way here. □ We didn't stop. We just drove through.

drive up to something to motor up close to something; to pull a car up to something. □ The car drove up to the curb and stopped. □ If you want to order fried chicken here, you drive up to the window and place your order.

drizzle down (on someone or something) to lightly rain on someone or something. □ The light rain drizzled down on the garden. □ The rain drizzled down and soaked us because we had no umbrella. □ A light rain drizzled down all day.

drone on (about someone or something) to lecture or narrate in a low-pitched, dull, and boring manner. □ The dull old professor droned on about Byron—or was it Keats? □ It was Shelley and, yes, he did drone on. □ The professor droned on for what seemed like hours. □ Why does he drone on so? Is he asleep too?

drop away 1. to fall off; to fall away. □ The leaves were still dropping away from the trees in November. □ The *dead branches dropped away from the tree.* **2.** to reduce in number over time. □ *His friends gradually dropped away.* □ *As the other contenders dropped away, Mary's chances improved.*

drop back 1. to fall back to an original position. □ *His arm raised up and then dropped back.* □ *The lid dropped back to its original position as soon as we let go of it.* **2.** to go slowly and lose one's position in a march or procession. □ *He dropped back a bit and evened up the spacing in the line of marchers.* □ *He got tired and dropped back a little.*

drop behind (in something) to fail to keep up with a schedule. □ *I don't want to drop behind in my work.* □ *She is dropping behind and needs someone to help her.*

drop behind (someone or something) 1. to reduce speed and end up after someone or a group, at the back of a moving line. □ *I dropped behind the rest of the people, because I couldn't walk that fast.* □ *I dropped behind the speeding pack of cars and drove a little slower.* **2.** to fail to keep up with the schedule being followed by someone or a group. □ *My production output dropped behind what it should have been.* □ *I stayed later at work to keep from dropping behind.*

drop below someone or something to fall to a point lower than someone or something. □ *The gunman dropped below the cowboy's hiding place and got ready to take a shot.* □ *The temperature dropped below the freezing point.*

Drop by for a drink (sometime). AND **Drop by sometime.; Drop over sometime.** a casual invitation for

someone to pay a visit. (This probably is not meant literally. It leaves an opening for invitations from either party.) □ BOB: *Good to see you, Mary. Drop by for a drink sometime.* MARY: *Love to. Bye.* □ *"Drop by sometime, stranger," said Bill to his old friend, Sally.*

drop by (some place) AND **go by (some place)** to stop for a casual visit. (Go by means to stop at, not to pass by, in this expression.) □ *I hope you can drop by our house sometime.* □ *We really want you to drop by.* □ *We went by the house, but there was no one home.*

Drop by sometime. See *Drop by for a drink (sometime).*

drop by the wayside AND **fall by the wayside 1.** to leave a march or procession to rest beside the pathway. (The origin of the figurative usage in sense 2.) □ *A few of the marchers dropped by the wayside in the intense heat.* □ *They fell by the wayside, one by one.* **2.** to fail to keep up with others. (Figurative.) □ *Many of the students will drop by the wayside and never finish.* □ *Those who fall by the wayside will find it hard to catch up.*

drop down 1. [for someone] to fall down or stoop down. □ *Suddenly, Ted dropped down, trying not to be seen by someone in a passing car.* □ *I dropped down as soon as I heard the loud sounds.* **2.** [for something] to fall from above. □ *The tiles on the ceiling dropped down, one by one, over the years.* □ *The raindrops dropped down and gave the thirsty plants a drink.*

drop in (on someone) to come for an unexpected, casual visit. □ *Guess who dropped in on us last night?* □ *I* *never thought Wally Wilson would drop in without calling first.* □ *Please drop in when you get a chance.* □ *I hope you don't mind if I drop in for a while.*

drop in one's tracks to stop or collapse from exhaustion; to die suddenly. □ *If I keep working this way, I'll drop in my tracks.* □ *Uncle Bob was working in the garden and dropped in his tracks. We are all sorry that he's dead.*

Drop in sometime. Visit my home or office sometime when you are nearby. □ BOB: *Bye, Bill, nice seeing you.* BILL: *Hey, drop in sometime.* BOB: *Okay.* BILL: *Great! Bye.* □ *"Drop in sometime," said Bob to his uncle.*

drop in (to say hello) to come for a brief, friendly visit. □ *We just dropped in to say hello. How are you all?* □ *We just wanted to drop in and see you.*

Drop it! See *Drop the subject!*

Drop me a line. Communicate with me in writing or by mail and tell me your news. (The *lines* refer to lines of writing.) □ JOHN: *If you get into our area, drop me a line.* FRED: *I sure will, John.* JOHN: *Bye.* □ MARY: *I'm going to Cleveland for a few days.* SUE: *Drop me a line when you get there.* MARY: *I will. Bye.*

Drop me a note. Communicate with me by mail, and let me know what is going on with you. □ MARY: *I'm off for Brazil. Good-bye.* SALLY: *Have a good time. Drop me a note.* □ *"Drop me a note from France," said Bill, waving good-bye.*

drop off 1. [for someone or something] to fall off something. □ *The leaves finally dropped off about the middle of November.* □ *When do the*

leaves normally drop off in Vermont? **2.** [for a part of something] to break away and fall off. □ *The car's bumper just dropped off — honest.* □ *I lifted boxes until I thought my arms would drop off.* **3.** to decline. (Figurative.) □ *Attendance at the meetings dropped off after Martin became president.* □ *Spending dropped off as the recession became worse.*

drop out (of something) 1. [for someone] to resign from or cease participation in something, especially school. □ *Sally dropped out of school for some unknown reason.* □ *But why did she drop out?* **2.** to fall out of something. □ *One by one, the divers dropped out of the plane.* □ *The marshmallows dropped out of the bag.* **3.** [for the bottom of something] to break loose and drop. (Both literal and figurative.) □ *The bottom dropped out of the box, spilling everything everywhere.* □ *The bottom dropped out of the market, and we lost a lot of money.*

drop over to come for a casual visit. □ *We would love for you to drop over.* □ *I would really like to drop over soon.*

Drop over sometime. See *Drop by for a drink (sometime).*

drop someone a few lines See the following entry.

drop someone a line AND **drop someone a few lines** to write a letter or a note to someone. (The *lines* refer to lines of writing.) □ *I dropped Aunt Jane a line last Thanksgiving.* □ *She usually drops me a few lines around the first of the year.*

drop someone or something down to let someone or something fall. □ *He dropped his pants down, revealing the* swimming trunks beneath. ⊤ *The rescuer dropped down the baby to the doctor a few feet below.* □ *Sam went to the well and dropped a rock down.*

drop someone or something in(to something) to let someone or something fall into something. □ *He dropped a quarter into the slot and waited for something to happen.* ⊤ *He dropped in a quarter.* □ *Johnny Green dropped a cat into a well.* □ *He went to the well and dropped a cat in.* □ *The murderer dropped the corpse into the lake.*

drop someone or something off ((at) some place) 1. to let someone or a group out of a vehicle at a particular place; to deliver someone or something some place. □ *Let's drop these shirts off at the cleaners.* ⊤ *Let's drop off Tom and Jerry at the hamburger joint.* ⊤ *Please drop off my shirts too.* □ *I'd be happy to drop them off.* **2.** to give someone or a group a ride to some place. □ *Can I drop you off somewhere in town?* ⊤ *I dropped off the kids at the party.* □ *I can't drop you off there because I'm not going there.*

drop someone or something off (of something) to let someone or something fall from something; to make someone or something fall from something. □ *They dropped the feather off the top of the building.* ⊤ *Jake dropped off a feather and it fell to the ground.* □ *Max took Lefty to the top of the building and threatened to drop him off.*

drop the ball to make a blunder; to fail in some way. (Also literally, in sports: to drop a ball in error.) □ *Everything was going fine in the election until my campaign manager dropped the ball.* □ *You can't trust John to do the job right. He's always dropping the ball.*

drop the other shoe to do the deed that completes something; to do the expected remaining part of something. (Refers to the removal of shoes at bedtime. One shoe is dropped, and then the process is completed when the second shoe drops.) □ *Mr. Franklin has left his wife. Soon he'll drop the other shoe and divorce her.* □ *Tommy has just failed three classes in school. We expect him to drop the other shoe and quit altogether any day now.*

Drop the subject! AND **Drop it!** Do not discuss it further! □ BILL: *Yes, you're gaining a little weight. I thought you were on a diet.* SALLY: *That's enough! Drop the subject!* □ BILL: *That house looks expensive. What do you think it's worth?* MARY: *That's my aunt's house. Just what did you want to know about it?* BILL: *Oh, drop it! Sorry I asked.*

drop up (some place) to come for a visit to a place that is relatively higher or in the north. □ *Drop up and see us sometime.* □ *Please drop up when you can.*

drown one's sorrows See the following entry.

drown one's troubles AND **drown one's sorrows** to try to forget one's problems by drinking a lot of alcohol. □ *Bill is in the bar, drowning his troubles.* □ *Jane is at home, drowning her sorrows.*

drown someone or something out 1. [for a flood] to drive someone or some creature away from home. □ *The high waters almost drowned the* farmers out last year. T *The water drowned out the fields.* □ *The flood almost drowned us out.* **2.** to make more noise than someone or something. □ *The noise of the passing train drowned our conversation out.* T *The noise of the passing train drowned out our conversation.* □ *The train drowned us out.*

drug on the market on the market in great abundance; a glut on the market. □ *Right now, small computers are a drug on the market.* □ *Ten years ago, small transistor radios were a drug on the market.*

drum some business up to stimulate people to buy what you are selling; to create business or commerce in some item. (As if someone were beating a drum to get the attention of customers.) □ *I need to do something to drum some business up.* T *A little bit of advertising would drum up some business.* □ *I'll go out and drum some business up.* T *Please go out and drum up some business.*

drum someone out of something to force someone to leave a position or an organization. □ *The citizens' group drummed the mayor out of office.* T *They drummed out the crooked politicians.*

drum something in(to someone) AND **drum something in(to someone's head)** to teach someone something intensely. (Figurative. As if one were pounding knowledge into someone's head.) □ *Her mother had drummed good manners into her.* T *She drummed in good manners day after day.* □ *The teacher drummed the multiplication tables into Tom's head.* □ *The teacher drummed them in.*

drum something in(to someone's head) See the previous entry.

drum something out to beat a rhythm, loudly and clearly, as if teaching it to someone. □ *Drum the rhythm out before you try to sing this song.* T *Drum out the rhythm first.*

dry behind the ears [not] mature; [not] experienced. (Always expressed as a negative. Compare to *wet behind the ears.*) □ *Tom is going into business by himself? Why, he's hardly dry behind the ears.* □ *That kid isn't dry behind the ears. He'll go broke in a month.*

dry out 1. to become dry. (More at *dry something out*). □ *The clothes finally dried out in the wet weather.* **2.** to allow alcohol and the effects of drunkenness to dissipate from one's body. □ *He required about three days to dry out completely.* □ *He dried out in three days.*

dry someone or something off to remove the moisture from someone or something. (*Someone* includes oneself.) □ *Please dry your feet off before coming in.* T *Dry off your feet before you come in here!* □ *Todd dried the baby off and dressed him.* □ *I have to dry myself off before I catch cold.*

dry something out to make something become dry. (More at *dry out.*) □ *Dry this out and put it on immediately.* T *Dry out your jacket in the clothes dryer.*

dry something up 1. to cause moisture to dry away to nothing. (More at *dry up.*) □ *Dry this spill up with the hair dryer.* T *Will the hair dryer dry up this mess?* **2.** to cure a skin rash by the use of medicine that dries. □ *Let's use some of this to try to dry that* *rash up.* ⊤ *This medicine will dry up your rash in a few days.*

dry up **1.** [for something] to become dry; [for something] to dry away to nothing. (More at *dry something up.*) □ *Finally, the water on the roads dried up, and we were able to continue.* □ *When will the fields dry up so we can plant?* **2.** [for someone] to be quiet or go away. (Slang.) □ *Dry up, you jerk!* □ *I wish you would dry up!*

dub something in to mix a new sound recording into an old one. □ *The actor messed up his lines, but they dubbed the correct words in later.* ⊤ *They dubbed in his lines.*

duck down to stoop down quickly, as if to avoid being hit. □ *The police officer ducked down when he heard the gunshot.* □ *Duck down and get out of the way.*

duck out (of some place) to sneak out of some place. □ *She ducked out of the theater during the intermission.* □ *When no one was looking, she ducked out.*

duck out of something to evade something; to escape doing something. □ *Are you trying to duck out of your responsibility?* □ *Fred tried to duck out of going to the dance.*

dust someone or something off to wipe or brush the dust off someone or something. (*Someone* includes *oneself.*) □ *Dust this vase off and put it on the shelf.* ⊤ *Please dust off this vase.* □ *Tom dusted Fred off and offered him a chair.* □ *He got up and dusted himself off.*

dust something out to brush the dust out of something. □ *Dust this cabinet out and put the china back in.* ⊤ *Please dust out this cabinet.*

E

Early to bed, early to rise(, makes a man healthy, wealthy, and wise). Going to bed early and getting up early is good for you. (Proverb. Sometimes said to explain why a person is going to bed early. The last part of the saying is sometimes left out.) □ *Tom left the party at ten o'clock, saying, "Early to bed, early to rise, makes a man healthy, wealthy, and wise." □ I always get up at six o'clock. After all, early to bed, early to rise.*

earn one's keep to help out with chores in return for food and a place to live; to earn one's pay by doing what is expected. □ *I earn my keep at college by shoveling snow in the winter.* □ *Tom hardly earns his keep around here. He should be fired.*

ease away (from someone or something) to pull away from someone or something slowly and carefully. □ *The great ship eased away from the pier.* □ *The ship eased away slowly.*

ease back on something to move something back slowly and carefully. (Usually refers to a throttle or some other control on an airplane or other vehicle.) □ *Ann eased back on the throttle and slowed down.* □ *Please ease back on the volume control a little. You will deafen us.*

ease off [for something] to diminish. □ *The rain began to ease off.* □ *The storm seems to have eased off a little.*

ease off (from someone or something) to move away from someone or something, slowly and carefully. □ *Ease off carefully from the deer, so you don't frighten it.* □ *Ease off quietly.*

ease off (on someone or something) to let up doing something to someone or something; to diminish one's pressure or demands on someone or something. □ *Ease off on him. He's only a kid!* □ *Ease off! He's just a kid!*

ease someone or something out (of something) 1. to get someone or something out of something carefully. (*Someone* includes *oneself.*) □ *The paramedics eased the injured man out of the wreckage.* □ *I eased myself out of the parking space with no trouble.* □ *The bystanders eased the injured child out of the wrecked car.* □ *I eased myself out of the chair and walked away.* **2.** [with *someone*] to get someone out of an office or position quietly and without much embarrassment. (*Someone* includes *oneself.*) □ *We eased the sheriff out of office without a fight.* □ *We eased him out just before the election.* □ *He eased himself out of office, and no one was suspicious.*

ease up (on someone or something) to treat someone or something more gently. □ *Ease up on the guy! He can only do so much.* □ *Ease up on the gas! You want to kill us all?* □ *Please ease up! I'm tired.*

easy come, easy go said to explain the loss of something that required only a small amount of effort to get in the first place. □ *Ann found twenty dollars in the morning and spent it foolishly at noon. "Easy come, easy go," she said.* □ *John spends his money as fast as he can earn it. With John it's easy come, easy go.*

Easy does it. 1. Move slowly and carefully. □ BILL (holding one end of a large crate): *It's really tight in this doorway.* BOB (holding the other end): *Easy does it. Take your time.* □ NURSE (holding Sue's arm): *Easy does it. These first few steps are the hardest.* SUE: *I didn't know I was so weak.* **2.** Calm down.; Don't lose your temper. □ JOHN: *I'm so mad I could scream.* BOB: *Easy does it, John. No need to get so worked up.* JOHN: *I'm still mad!* □ SUE (frantic): *Where is my camera? My passport is gone too!* FRED: *Easy does it, Sue. I think you have someone else's purse.*

eat (away) at someone or something 1. [with *someone*] [for a problem] to trouble someone constantly. (Figurative.) □ *The nasty situation at work began to eat away at me.* □ *Nagging worries ate at me day and night.* **2.** [with *something*] to eat something eagerly and rapidly. □ *They ate away at the turkey until it was all gone.* □ *We just ate at it little by little.* **3.** [with *something*] to erode something. □ *The acid ate away at the metal floor.* □ *Fingers have a mild acid that eats at the metal of the doorknob.*

eat humble pie 1. to act very humble when one is shown to be wrong. □ *I*

think I'm right, but if I'm wrong, I'll eat humble pie.* □ *You think you're so smart. I hope you have to eat humble pie.* **2.** to accept insults and humiliation. □ *John, stand up for your rights. You don't have to eat humble pie all the time.* □ *Beth seems quite happy to eat humble pie. She should stand up for her rights.*

eat in to eat a meal at home. □ *I really don't want to eat in tonight.* □ *Let's eat in. I'm tired.*

eat in(to something) to erode into something; to etch something. □ *The acidic water ate into the rocks on the shore.* □ *The acid ate in and weakened the structure.*

eat like a bird to eat only small amounts of food; to peck at one's food. □ *Jane is very slim because she eats like a bird.* □ *Bill is trying to lose weight by eating like a bird.*

eat like a horse to eat large amounts of food. □ *No wonder he's so fat. He eats like a horse.* □ *John works like a horse and eats like a horse, so he never gets fat.*

eat one's cake and have it too See *have one's cake and eat it too.*

eat one's hat a phrase telling the kind of thing that one would do if a very unlikely event really happens. (Always used with *if.* Never used literally.) □ *If we get there on time, I'll eat my hat.* □ *I'll eat my hat if you get a raise.* □ *He said he'd eat his hat if she got elected.*

eat one's heart out 1. to be very sad about someone or something. (Figurative.) □ *Bill spent a lot of time eating his heart out after his divorce.* □ *Sally ate her heart out when she had to sell her house.* **2.** to be envious of someone or something. (Figurative.) □ *Do you like my new watch? Well, eat your heart out. It was the last one in the store.* □ *Don't eat your heart out about my new car. Go get one of your own.*

eat one's words to have to take back one's statements; to confess that one's predictions were wrong. □ *You shouldn't say that to me. I'll make you eat your words.* □ *John was wrong about the election and had to eat his words.*

eat out to eat a meal away from home. □ *I just love to eat out every now and then.* □ *Let's eat out tonight. I'm tired.*

eat out of someone's hand(s) to do what someone else wants; to obey someone eagerly; to grovel to someone. (Often with *have*.) □ *Just wait! I'll have everyone eating out of my hands. They'll do whatever I ask.* □ *The president has Congress eating out of his hands.* □ *A lot of people are eating out of his hands.* □ *I've got her eating out of my hand. She'll do anything I ask.* □ *He will be eating out of your hand before you are finished with him.*

eat someone out of house and home to eat a lot of food (in someone's home); to eat all the food in the house. □ *Billy has a huge appetite. He almost eats us out of house and home.* □ *When the kids come home from college, they always eat us out of house and home.*

eat someone or something up **1.** [with *someone*] to consume a person. (Figurative.) □ *The whole idea of going to the South Pole was just eating her up.* □ *Juan's obsession almost ate him up.* **2.** [with *someone*] [for insects] to bite a person all over. (Figurative.) □ *These mosquitoes are just eating me up!* □ *Don't let the bugs eat you up.* **3.** [with *something*] to devour all of some food or some creature. □ *They ate the turkey up, and no one had to eat leftovers.* ⊤ *Please eat up the turkey.* **4.** [with *something*] [for someone] to believe something completely. □ *Your story was really good. Everybody just ate it up.* ⊤ *They will eat up almost any lie.*

eat something away to erode something; to consume something bit by bit. □ *The acid ate the finish away.* ⊤ *It ate away the finish.*

eat something off ((of) something) to erode something off a larger part. (The *of* is colloquial.) □ *The acidic rain ate the finish off the steeple.* ⊤ *The acid ate off the finish.* □ *It ate the chrome off.*

eat something out **1.** to eat a meal or a particular food away from home. □ *We eat fish out, but we don't cook it at home.* □ *We almost never eat breakfast out.* **2.** [for something or some creature] to consume the inside of something. □ *The ants ate the inside of the pumpkin out.* ⊤ *The ants ate out the pumpkin.*

eat (something) out of something to eat food directly from a container, such as a bag, box, can, etc. □ *You shouldn't eat out of the can.* □ *Maria was eating potato chips right out of the bag.*

eat up to eat everything; to eat eagerly. (Usually a command to begin eating.) □ *Come on, let's eat up and get going.* □ *Eat up, you guys, and get back to work!*

echo back to something [for something] to recall something similar in the past. □ *This idea echoes back to the end of the last century, when people thought this way.*

edge away (from someone or something) to move cautiously away from someone or something. □ *We edged away from the dirty man in the ragged clothes.* □ *As others saw the gun, they edged away.*

egg someone on to incite someone to do something; to encourage someone to do something. □ *I want Richard to stop making up those horrible puns. Please don't egg him on.* □ *She does not need any encouragement. Don't egg her on.*

eke something out to extend something; to add to something. □ *He worked at two jobs in order to eke his salary out.* T *He managed to eke out a living.*

elbow (one's way) through something to push or drive oneself through something, such as a crowd, perhaps using one's elbows or arms to move people out of the way. □ *She elbowed her way through the crowd.* ⊔ *Jerry elbowed through the people gathered at the door.*

elbow someone aside to push someone aside with one's arm. □ *She elbowed the other woman aside and there was almost a fight.* T *The rude woman elbowed aside all the other people.*

emblazon something on(to) something 1. to decorate something with something. □ *The workers emblazoned wild decorations on the door.* □ *They emblazoned their name on the side of the building.* **2.** to put some writing or symbols that proclaim something onto something. □ *The knight emblazoned his name onto his shield.* T *The craftsman emblazoned the knight's name on his shield.*

empty something out to remove or pour all of the contents from something. □ *Please empty this drawer out and clean it.* T *She emptied out the aquarium and cleaned it well.*

end in itself for its own sake; toward its own ends; toward no purpose but its own. □ *For Bob, art is an end in itself. He doesn't hope to make any money from it.* □ *Learning is an end in itself. Knowledge does not have to have a practical application.*

end of the line See the following entry.

end of the road AND **end of the line** the finish; the end of the whole process; death. (*Line* originally referred to railroad tracks.) □ *Our house is at the end of the road.* □ *We rode the train to the end of the line.* □ *When we reach the end of the road on this project, we'll get paid.* □ *You've come to the end of the line. I'll not lend you another penny.* □ *When I reach the end of the road, I wish to be buried in a quiet place, near some trees.*

end something up to terminate something; to bring something to an end. (More at *end up.*) □ *He ended his vacation up by going to the beach.* T *She ended up her speech with a poem.*

end up to come to an end. (More at *end something up.*) □ *When will all this end up?* □ *I think that the party will have to end up about midnight.*

end up at something to be at something or some place at the end. □ *The* plane ended up at Denver airport because of a storm in Colorado Springs. □ We ended up at home for the evening because the car broke down.

end up doing something to have to do something one has tried to get out of doing. □ I refused to do it, but I ended up doing it anyway. □ Juan didn't want to end up going home alone.

end up somehow to come to the end of something in a particular way. □ I really didn't want to end up this way. □ I ended up broke when my vacation was over.

end up something to become something at the end of everything. □ I always knew I would end up a doctor. □ If I don't get a job, I will end up a beggar.

end up with the short end of the stick See get the short end of the stick.

engrave something on(to) something See the following entry.

engrave something (up)on something AND **engrave something on(to) something 1.** to imprint something firmly on someone's mind. □ I engraved the combination to the safe upon my brain. □ The teacher engraved the definition of a noun on my consciousness. **2.** to cut letters, a design, or symbols into the surface of something. □ He asked them to engrave his initials upon the back of his watch. □ He engraved his name on the desktop.

Enjoy! I hope you enjoy what you are going to do.; I hope you enjoy what I have served you to eat.; I hope you enjoy life in general. □ "Here's your

coffee, dear," said Fred. "Enjoy!" □ SUE: What a beautiful day! Good-bye. TOM: Good-bye. Enjoy!

Enjoy your meal. an expression used by food service personnel after the food has been served. □ The waiter set the plates on the table, smiled, and said, "Enjoy your meal." □ WAITER: Here's your dinner. JANE: Oh, this lobster looks lovely! TOM: My steak looks just perfect. WAITER: Enjoy your meal.

enlarge (up)on something to add details to a report about something. □ Would you care to enlarge upon your remarks? □ I enlarged on my original comments.

enlist someone in something to recruit someone into something; to recruit someone into the armed services. □ They tried to enlist me in the army, but I decided against it. □ David enlisted his brother in an organization that gave assistance to peasants in South America.

Enough is enough! That is enough! I won't stand for any more! □ SUE: That color of lipstick is all wrong for you, Sally. SALLY: Enough is enough! Sue, get lost! SUE: I was just trying to help. □ BOB: Enough is enough! I'm leaving! BILL: What on earth did I do? BOB: Good-bye.

enter in something to enroll as a participant in something, such as a contest, competition, etc. □ She was not ready to enter in the competition. □ I can't enter in that contest. I'm not prepared.

enter into something 1. to get into something. □ She entered into the house and immediately went to work. □ As the people entered into the cathedral, they became quiet. **2.** to join in something. □ *I couldn't get him to enter into the spirit of the party.* □ *She just loves to enter into things and have a good time with people.*

enter one's mind to come to one's mind; [for an idea or memory] to come into one's consciousness; to be thought of. □ *Leave you behind? The thought never even entered my mind.* □ *A very interesting idea just entered my mind. What if I ran for Congress?*

enter someone or something in((to) something) to enroll someone or something in something; to make someone or something a competitor in something. (*Someone* includes *oneself.*) □ *I will enter you into the contest whether you like it or not.* □ *Ed entered his favorite horse in the race.* □ *She entered herself into the contest.*

enter (up)on something 1. to come in at a particular point as marked by something. □ *We entered the theater upon the most delicate point of the story.* □ *We entered on the tail end of a live scene.* **2.** to begin something. □ *Todd entered upon a new phase of his life.* □ *He entered on the management of a new project.*

entomb someone or something in something 1. to place someone or something in a tomb. (*Someone* includes *oneself.*) □ *In the opera, they entombed Aida and her lover in a dusty place where they sang themselves to death.* □ *They accidentally entombed the queen's jewels in the vault with her.* □ *She entombed herself in her final resting place and waited for death.* **2.** to imprison someone or some creature in a tomblike enclosure. □ *Please don't entomb me in that huge, cold office.* □ *Unknowingly, when they closed the door, they had entombed a tiny mouse within.*

erase something from something to delete or wipe something from something. □ *Please erase the writing from the blackboard.* □ *I will erase the incorrectly spelled word from my paper.*

erupt from something to burst out of something or some place. □ *A billow of smoke erupted from the chimney.* □ *A mass of ashes and gasses erupted from the volcano.*

erupt into something to become a serious problem suddenly; to blow up into something. (Figurative.) □ *The argument erupted into a terrible fight.* □ *They were afraid the fight would erupt into a riot.*

escalate into something to intensify into something; to increase gradually into something. □ *This argument is going to escalate into something serious very soon.* □ *These cases of the flu could escalate into a real epidemic.*

even something off to make something even or smooth. □ *Please even this surface off before you paint it.* T *You need to even off this surface.*

even something out to make something even or level. □ *Please even the road out.* T *They evened out the surface of the road.*

even something up to make something even, square, level, equal, balanced, etc. □ *I'll even the table up.* T *See if you can even up the legs of this table. It wobbles.*

Every cloud has a silver lining. There is something good in every bad thing. (Proverb.) □ *Jane was upset when she* *saw that all her flowers had died from the frost. But when she saw that the weeds had died too, she said, "Every cloud has a silver lining."* □ *Sally had a sore throat and had to stay home from school. When she learned she missed a math test, she said, "Every cloud has a silver lining."*

Every dog has his day. See the following entry.

Every dog has its day. AND **Every dog has his day.** Everyone will get a chance, even the lowliest. (Proverb.) □ *Don't worry, you'll get chosen for the team. Every dog has its day.* □ *You may become famous someday. Every dog has his day.*

every living soul every person. □ *I expect every living soul to be there and be there on time.* □ *This is the kind of problem that affects every living soul.*

every minute counts AND **every moment counts** Time is very important. □ *Doctor, please try to get here quickly. Every minute counts.* □ *When you take a test, you must work rapidly because every minute counts.* □ *When you're trying to meet a deadline, every moment counts.*

every moment counts See the previous entry.

everything but the kitchen sink almost everything one can think of. □ *When Sally went off to college, she took everything but the kitchen sink.* □ *John orders everything but the kitchen sink when he goes out to dinner, especially if someone else is paying for it.*

everything from A to Z See the following entry.

everything from soup to nuts AND **everything from A to Z** almost

everything one can think of. (The main entry is used especially when describing the many things served at a meal.) □ *For dinner we had everything from soup to nuts.* □ *In college I studied everything from soup to nuts.* □ *She mentioned everything from A to Z.*

Everything will be all right. See *Everything's going to be all right.*

Everything will work out (all right). See *Things will work out (all right).*

Everything will work out for the best. See *Things will work out (all right).*

Everything's going to be all right. AND **Everything will be all right.** Do not worry, everything will be okay. (A number of other expressions can be substituted for *all right,* such as *okay, just fine, great,* etc.) □ *"Don't worry, Fred," comforted Bill. "Everything will be all right."* □ MARY: *I just don't know if I can go on!* BOB: *Now, now. Everything will be just fine.*

exact something from someone to demand something from someone; to take something from someone. □ *The bill collector sought to exact payment from them for a debt that had been paid off long ago.* □ *You cannot exact a single cent from me.*

Excellent! Great!; Fine! □ BOB: *What's happening?* FRED: *Hi! I'm getting a new car.* BOB: *Excellent!* □ BOB: *All the players are here and ready to go.* SUE: *Excellent!* BOB: *When do we start the game?*

exclude someone or something from something to leave someone or something out of something; to leave someone or something off a list.

(*Someone* includes *oneself.*) □ *Did you mean to exclude me from the party?* □ *I excluded chocolate cake from the shopping list.* □ *I exclude myself from consideration for the nomination.*

Excuse me. AND **Excuse, please.; Pardon (me).; 'Scuse (me).; 'Scuse, please.** (*'Scuse* is colloquial, and the apostrophe is not always used.) **1.** an expression asking forgiveness for some minor social violation, such as belching or bumping into someone. □ JOHN: *Ouch!* BOB: *Excuse me. I didn't see you there.* □ MARY: *Oh! Ow!* SUE: *Pardon me. I didn't mean to bump into you.* □ TOM: *Ouch!* MARY: *Oh, dear! What happened?* TOM: *You stepped on my toe.* MARY: *Excuse me. I'm sorry.* **2.** Please let me through.; Please let me by. □ TOM: *Excuse me. I need to get past.* BOB: *Oh, sorry. I didn't know I was in the way.* □ MARY: *Pardon me.* SUE: *What?* MARY: *Pardon me. I want to get past you.*

Excuse me? AND **Pardon (me)?; 'Scuse me?** What do you mean by that last remark?; *I beg your pardon?* (Shows amazement at someone's rudeness.) □ MARY: *Your policies seem quite inflexible to me.* BILL: *Excuse me?* □ BOB: *These silly people are getting on my nerves.* MARY: *Pardon me?*

Excuse, please. See *Excuse me.*

exempt someone from something to release someone from the obligation to do something; to allow a person not to be affected by a rule or law. (*Someone* includes *oneself.*) □ *I cannot exempt anyone from this rule.* □ *The members of Congress exempted themselves from the wage freeze.*

expand into something to grow into something; to enlarge into something. □ *The little problem expanded into a big one in no time at all.* □ *In no time at all, the vegetable garden had expanded into a small farm.*

expand something into something to enlarge something into something; to make something grow into something. □ *She expanded her business into a national company.* □ *I would like to do something to expand this room into a more usable space.*

expand (up)on something to add detail to a report about something. □ *Would you please expand upon that last remark?* □ *May I expand on your remarks?*

expecting (a child) pregnant. (A euphemism.) □ *Tommy's mother is expecting a child.* □ *Oh, I didn't know she was expecting.*

experiment (up)on someone or something to use someone or something as the subject of an experiment. (*Upon* is formal and less commonly used than *on.*) □ *Mother always experimented on us with her new recipes.* □ *The researchers were experimenting on a new drug that might cure rabies.*

explain something away to explain something so that it is no longer a problem. □ *You can try to explain it away if you want, but that won't solve the problem.* T *You can't just explain away all your problems.*

extend across something to spread across something. □ *The shadows extended across the whole land.* □ *The fog extended across the low-lying land.*

F

face off 1. to begin a hockey game with two players facing one another. □ *They faced off and the match was on.* **2.** to prepare for a confrontation. (From sense 1.) □ *The opposing candidates faced off and the debate began.* □ *They faced off and I knew there was going to be a fight.*

face someone down to make a face-to-face stand with someone who eventually backs down. □ *Chuck succeeded in facing Tom down.* T *Facing down Tom wasn't difficult for Chuck.*

face the music to receive punishment; to accept the unpleasant results of one's actions. □ *Mary broke a dining-room window and had to face the music when her father got home.* □ *After failing a math test, Tom had to go home and face the music.*

face up (to someone or something) to confront with courage someone or something representing a threat or unpleasantness. □ *You are simply going to have to face up to Fred.* □ *You must face up to the authorities if you have done something wrong.* □ *You will simply have to face up.*

fade away into something to diminish into something. □ *The light faded away into nothing.* □ *The sound of the drums faded away into the distance.*

fade down [for sound] to diminish. □ *The roar of the train faded down as it passed and fled into the night.* □ *As the thunder faded down, the sun began to break through the clouds.*

Fair to middling. a response to a greeting inquiry into the state of one's health. (Colloquial and folksy.) □ JOHN: *How are you doing?* BOB: *Oh, fair to middling, I guess. And you?* JOHN: *Things could be worse.* □ BILL: *How are you feeling?* JANE: *Oh, fair to middling, thanks.* BILL: *Still a little under the weather, huh?* JANE: *Just a little.*

fair-weather friend someone who is your friend only when things are going well for you. (This person will desert you when things go badly for you.) □ *Bill wouldn't help me with my homework. He's just a fair-weather friend.* □ *A fair-weather friend isn't much help in an emergency.*

fall apart to break into pieces; to disassemble. (Both literal and figurative uses.) □ *The whole thing fell apart.* □ *Gerald's whole life began falling apart.*

fall back to move back from something; to retreat from something. □ *The gang members fell back, and I took that opportunity to get away.* □ *The troops fell back to regroup.*

fall back on(to) someone or something 1. to fall backwards onto someone or something. □ *She stumbled* *and fell back onto the lady behind her.* □ *She fell back on the couch.* **2.** to begin to use someone or something held in reserve. (Figurative.) □ *We fell back on our savings to get us through the hard times.* □ *We had to fall back on our emergency generator.*

fall behind (in something) AND **fall behind (on something); fall behind (with something); get behind (in something); get behind (on something); get behind (with something)** to lag behind schedule in some kind of work or some other scheduled activity. □ *You are falling behind in your car payments.* □ *I tried not to get behind on them.* □ *Please don't fall behind with your payments.* □ *I won't fall behind again.*

fall behind (on something) See the previous entry.

fall behind (with something) See *fall behind (in something)*.

fall by the wayside See *drop by the wayside*.

fall down to drop or topple. □ *The baby fell down.* □ *Walk carefully on this ice or you will fall down.*

fall down on the job to fail to do something properly; to fail to do one's job adequately. (Also used literally.) □ *The team kept losing because the coach was falling down on the job.* □ *Tom was fired because he fell down on the job.*

fall (down) to something to fall or drop to something below. □ *The coconut fell down to the people below.* □ *It fell to the people shaking the tree.*

fall flat (on its face) See *the following entry*.

fall flat (on one's face) AND **fall flat (on its face)** to be completely unsuccessful. □ *I fell flat on my face when I tried to give my speech.* □ *The play fell flat on its face.* □ *My jokes fall flat most of the time.*

fall in to get into line and stand at attention. (Military. Often a command.) □ *The commander ordered that the troops fall in.* □ *If you don't fall in now, you'll all have to do a hundred push-ups.*

fall in love [for two people] to become enamored of each other. □ *They fell in love.* □ *When they fell in love, they thought it was forever.*

fall in love (with someone or something) to become enamored of someone or something. □ *I simply fell in love with the dress. I had to have it.* □ *I fell in love with her.*

fall in(to) line (with someone or something) **1.** to get into a line with other people or a group. □ *I fell in line with the others and waited my turn.* □ *Please fall in line and stay there.* **2.** to behave in a manner similar to someone or something. (Figurative.) □ *You are expected to fall into line with the other people.* □ *We want you to fall in line and obey the rules.*

fall in(to) place to move into place; to fit into the correct place; to become organized. (Both literal and figurative.) □ *At last, things began to fall into place, and life became livable again.* □ *In the end, everything fell in place.* □ *After we heard the whole story, things began to fall in place.* □ *As the hours passed, the puzzle pieces fell into place.*

fall in(to step) to get into the same marching pattern as everyone else as regards which foot moves forward. (Everyone should be moving the same foot forward at the same time.) □ *I just can't seem to fall into step. I am very uncoordinated.* □ *Fall in! March with the others!*

fall off to decline. □ *At dawn, the horrible insect noises of the night began to fall off.* □ *As business began to fall off, so did my income.*

fall off ((of) something) to drop off something. (The *of* is colloquial.) □ *A button fell off my shirt.* □ *I fell off the log.* □ *The twigs fell off of him as he stood up.*

fall outside something to be beyond someone's power, responsibility, or jurisdiction. □ *This matter falls outside my bailiwick.* □ *Her offense fell outside of the manager's jurisdiction.*

fall over to topple over and fall down. □ *The fence fell over and dented the car.* □ *I felt faint and almost fell over.*

fall over backwards (to do something) to go to great extremes to do something; to endure all sorts of trouble to do something. (Figurative.) □ *She fell over backwards to make everyone comfortable.* □ *Just do your best. There is no need to fall over backwards.*

fall over someone or something to stumble over someone or something. □ *Sam came into the house and fell over a kitchen chair.* □ *Walter fell over Roger, who was napping on the floor.*

fall short (of something) 1. to lack something; to lack enough of something. □ *We fell short of money at the end of the month.* □ *When baking a cake, the cook fell short of eggs and had to go to the store for more.* **2.** to fail to achieve a goal. □ *We fell short of our*

goal of collecting a thousand dollars. □ *Ann ran a fast race, but fell short of the record.*

fall through [for something, such as plans] to fail. □ *Our party for next Saturday fell through.* □ *I hope our plans don't fall through.*

fall to to begin doing something. □ *She asked for help, and everyone fell to.* □ *Fall to, you guys!*

fall to pieces 1. to break into pieces. □ *The road was so rough the car almost fell to pieces.* □ *I was afraid that my bicycle would fall to pieces before I got there.* **2.** to become emotionally upset. (Figurative.) □ *I was so nervous, I fell to pieces and couldn't give my speech.* □ *Roger fell to pieces and couldn't attend the sales meeting.*

fall to someone or something to become the responsibility of someone or a group. □ *It falls to you to go and tell Mrs. Wilson that you broke her window.* □ *The responsibility falls to the board of directors.*

fall (up)on someone (to do something) to become someone's responsibility to do something. □ *It falls upon you to explain this matter to her.* □ *It falls on you to fix the window.*

Familiarity breeds contempt. Knowing a person closely for a long time leads to bad feelings. (Proverb.) □ *Bill and his brothers are always fighting. As they say: "Familiarity breeds contempt."* □ *Mary and John were good friends for many years. Finally they got into a big argument and became enemies. That just shows that familiarity breeds contempt.*

fan out (from some place) to spread or move outward from a particular area in the shape of a fan. □ *The* paths seem to fan out from the wide trail that starts at the house. □ The trails fanned out and soon we were all separated.

fan something out to spread something out so that all parts can be seen better. (As one opens a wood and paper fan.) □ *Todd fanned the cards out so we could see which ones he held.* T *He fanned out the cards.*

Fancy meeting you here! I am very surprised to meet you here! (A catch phrase.) □ TOM: *Hi, Sue! Fancy meeting you here!* SUE: *Hi, Tom. I was thinking the same thing about you.* □ *"Fancy meeting you here," said Mr. Franklin when he bumped into Mrs. Franklin at the racetrack.*

Fancy that! AND **Imagine that!** I am very surprised to hear that.; That is hard to imagine or believe. □ MARY: *My father was elected president of the board.* SALLY: *Fancy that!* □ SUE: *This computer is ten times faster than the one we had before.* JANE: *Imagine that! Is it easy to operate?* SUE: *Of course not.*

Farewell. Good-bye. □ MARY: *See you later, Bill.* BILL: *Farewell, my dear.* MARY: *Take care.* □ BOB: *Have a good trip.* SUE: *Farewell, Bob.* BOB: *Don't do anything I wouldn't do.*

farm someone or something out 1. [with *someone*] to send someone, particularly a child, somewhere for care or development. □ *When my mother died, they farmed me out to my aunt and uncle.* T *The team manager farmed out the baseball player to the minor leagues until he improved.* 2. [with *someone*] [for someone in control] to send someone to work for someone else. □ *I have farmed my electrician out for a week, so your work will have to wait.* T *We farmed out the office staff.* 3. [with *something*] to send something (elsewhere) to be dealt with. T *I farmed out various parts of the work to different people.* □ *Bill farmed his chores out to his brothers and sisters and went to a movie.* 4. [with *something*] to deplete the fertility of land by farming too intensely. □ *They farmed their land out through careless land management.* T *They farmed out their land.* 5. [with *something*] to make money by renting out land or buildings. □ *I farmed the pasture out.* T *I farmed out the west pasture to Bill Franklin, who will graze his cattle there.* 6. [with *something*] to send work to someone to be done away from one's normal place of business; to subcontract work. □ *We farmed the sewing out.* T *We always farm out the actual sewing together of the dresses.*

fasten something up to close something up, using buttons, a zipper, snaps, hooks, a clasp, or other things meant to hold something closed. □ *Please fasten this up for me. I can't reach the zipper.* T *Please fasten up my buttons in back.*

fasten (up)on someone or something 1. to take firm hold of someone or something. □ *She fastened upon me and would not let me go until she finished speaking.* □ *I don't like people who fasten on you.* 2. to fix one's attention on someone or something. (Figurative.) □ *He fastened upon the picture for a brief moment and then turned away.* □ *The baby fastened on the television screen and watched it for many minutes.*

fatten someone or something up (with something) to use something to make someone or some creature fat. (*Someone* includes *oneself.*) □ *We will fatten the calf up with corn.* T *I don't know why they keep fattening up their children with so much food.* □ *They keep fattening them up.* □ *I fattened myself up with lots of good food.*

feast one's eyes (on someone or something) to look at someone or something with pleasure, envy, or admiration. (As if such visions provided a feast of visual delight for one's eyes.) □ *Just feast your eyes on that beautiful juicy steak!* □ *Yes, feast your eyes. You won't see one like that again for a long time.*

feather in one's cap an honor; a reward for something. □ *Getting a new client was really a feather in my cap.* □ *John earned a feather in his cap by getting an A in physics.*

feather one's (own) nest **1.** to decorate and furnish one's home in style and comfort. (Birds line their nests with feathers to make them warm and comfortable.) □ *Mr. and Mrs. Simpson have feathered their nest quite comfortably.* □ *It costs a great deal of money to feather one's nest these days.* **2.** to use power and prestige to provide for oneself selfishly. (Said especially of politicians who use their offices to make money for themselves.) □ *The mayor seemed to be helping people, but she was really feathering her own nest.* □ *The building contractor used a lot of public money to feather his nest.*

feed off (of) something AND **feed (up)on someone or something 1.** to eat someone or something. (The *of* is colloquial. *Upon* is formal and less commonly used than *on.*) □ *This creature feeds off fallen fruit.* □ *Mosquitoes feed off of me!* □ *They say that some Bengal tigers feed upon people.* □ *They feed on anything that moves.* **2.** to thrive on something. (Figurative.) □ *Aunt Mary just feeds on gossip.* □ *My uncle feeds off old war movies.*

feed the kitty to contribute money. (The *kitty* is a name for a container into which money is put.) □ *Please feed the kitty. Make a contribution to help sick children.* □ *Come on, Bill. Feed the kitty. You can afford a dollar for a good cause.*

feed (up)on someone or something See *feed off (of) something.*

feel for someone to feel the emotional pain that someone else is feeling; to empathize or sympathize with someone. □ *I really feel for you. I'm so sorry it turned out this way.* □ *Fred felt for Dave, but there was nothing he could do for him.*

feel like a million (dollars) to feel well and healthy, both physically and mentally. (To feel like something unbelievably good.) □ *A quick swim in the morning makes me feel like a million dollars.* □ *What a beautiful day! It makes you feel like a million.*

feel like a new person to feel refreshed and renewed, especially after getting well or getting dressed up. □ *I bought a new suit, and now I feel like a new person.* □ *Bob felt like a new person when he got out of the hospital.*

feel out of place to feel that one does not belong in a place. □ *I feel out of place at formal dances.* □ *Bob and Ann felt out of place at the picnic, so they went home.*

feel out of something to feel alienated from something. □ *I feel out of things lately. Are people ignoring me?* □ *I feel a little out of it at this party, but I will try to join in the fun.*

feel someone out (about someone or something) to find out what someone thinks about someone or something. □ *I will feel him out about what he thinks about going to Florida.* T *Let me feel out the boss about this matter.* □ *I felt the boss out. The answer will be no, so don't ask.*

feel something in one's bones AND **know something in one's bones** to sense something; to have an intuition about something. □ *The train will be late. I feel it in my bones.* □ *I failed the test. I know it in my bones.*

feel up to something to feel like doing something; to feel well enough to do something. □ *I'm sorry, but I don't feel up to going out.* □ *Do you feel up to playing a game of cards?*

fence someone or something off (from something) to separate someone or something from something else with a fence or barrier. (*Someone* includes *oneself.*) □ *We fenced the children's play area off from the rest of the yard.* T *Dave fenced off the play area.* T *We fenced off the children from the rest of the yard.* □ *He fenced himself off from the rest of the crowd.*

fence something in to enclose some creature or something within a fence or barrier. □ *We fenced the yard in to keep the dogs at home.* T *We had to fence in the dog.* □ *We fenced the garden in.*

fend someone or something off to hold someone or something off; to fight someone or something off. □

We knew we could fend them off only a little while longer. T *They could not fend off the attackers.* □ *Max fended Lefty off.*

fiddle around (with someone or something) to play around with someone or something. □ *I will fiddle around with this for a while and maybe I can fix it.* □ *I wish you would stop fiddling around and hire someone to fix it.*

fight against someone or something to battle against someone or something. □ *The boxer refused to fight against the challenger, who was much stronger.* □ *He fought against the disease to the very end.*

fight back (at someone or something) to defend oneself against someone or something; to retaliate against someone or something. □ *You are going to have to fight back at them. You can't expect us to defend you.* □ *It's hard for me to fight back.*

fight (one's way) back to something to struggle to return to something or some place. □ *She fought her way back to the head of the line.* □ *Jan fought back to good health.*

fight one's way out of something to struggle to get out of something or some place. □ *He fought his way out of the crowded room and out through the door.* □ *He couldn't fight his way out of a paper bag.*

fight (one's way) through something 1. to struggle to get through something; to struggle to penetrate something. □ *I'll have to fight my way through all this crepe paper in order to reach the punch bowl.* □ *The room was filled with trash, and I had to fight through it to get to the other door.* **2.** to struggle to work through all of something. □ *I have to fight my way through this stack of papers by noon.* □ *I am tired of fighting through red tape.*

fight someone or something down 1. to fight against and defeat someone or something. □ *We fought the opposition down and got our bill through the committee.* T *We had to fight down Fred, who wanted something entirely different.* **2.** [with *something*] to struggle to hold something back; to struggle to keep from being overwhelmed by something. □ *She fought her anger down and managed to stay till the end.* T *She fought down the urge.* **3.** [with *something*] to struggle to swallow something; to fight to get something down one's throat. □ *It tasted terrible, but I managed to fight it down.* T *She fought down the medicine.*

fight someone or something hammer and tongs AND **fight someone or something tooth and nail; go at it hammer and tongs; go at it tooth and nail** to fight against someone or something energetically and with great determination. (These phrases are old and refer to fighting with and without weapons.) □ *They fought against the robber tooth and nail.* □ *The dogs were fighting each other hammer and tongs.* □ *The mayor fought the new law hammer and tongs.* □ *We'll fight this zoning ordinance tooth and nail.*

fight someone or something tooth and nail See the previous entry.

fight something through (something) to force something through some sort of procedure or process. □ *The governor fought the bill through the legislature successfully.* □ *Our committee fought it through.*

figure on something to plan on something; to count on doing something. □ *We figured on going down to the country next weekend.* □ *Did you figure on doing the repair work yourself?*

figure someone or something in((to) something) to reckon someone or something into the total. (*Someone* includes *oneself.*) □ *I will figure the electric bill into the total.* T *We can figure in one more person.* □ *Did you figure David in?* □ *Did you figure yourself into the final total?*

figure someone or something out to comprehend someone or something; to understand someone or something better. (*Someone* includes *oneself.*) □ *I just can't figure you out.* T *I can't figure out quiet people readily.* □ *It will take a while for me to figure the instructions out.* □ *Well, I can't figure myself out. I don't know how you could either.*

figure something up to add up the amount of something. □ *Please figure the bill up. We have to go now.* T *I will figure up the bill right away.* T *I will figure up how many yards of material I need.*

file in((to) something) [for a line of people] to move into something or some place. □ *The people filed into the hall quietly.* □ *Everyone filed in quietly.*

file out (of something) [for a line of people] to move out of something or some place. □ *The people filed quietly out of the theater.* □ *They filed out at the end.*

file something away to put something away, usually in a file folder or file cabinet; to keep something in one's memory. □ *She filed the letter away* for future reference. □ *Please file this away. You will need it some day.*

fill in (for someone or something) to substitute for someone or something; to take the place of someone or something. □ *I will have to fill in for Wally until he gets back.* □ *I don't mind filling in.*

Fill in the blanks. You can figure out the rest.; You can draw a conclusion from that. □ MARY: *What happened at Fred's house last night?* BILL: *There was a big fight, then the neighbors called the police.* MARY: *Then what happened?* BILL: *Fill in the blanks. What do you think?* □ JOHN: *They had been lost for two days, then the wolves came, and the rest is history.* JANE: *Yes, I think I can fill in the blanks.*

fill out to become full, to gain weight □ *About a month after her debilitating illness, Maggie began to fill out again.* □ *The fruit on the trees began to fill out, and we knew it was going to ripen soon.*

fill someone in (on someone or something) to tell someone the details about someone or something. □ *Please fill me in on what happened last night.* T *Please fill in the committee on the details.* □ *Please fill me in!*

fill someone's shoes to take the place of some other person and do that person's work satisfactorily. (As if you were wearing the other person's shoes, that is, filling the shoes with your feet.) □ *I don't know how we'll be able to do without you. No one can fill your shoes.* □ *It'll be difficult to fill Jane's shoes. She did her job very well.*

fill something in 1. to add material to an indentation, hole, etc., to make it full. □ *You had better fill the crack in with something before you paint the wall.* T *You should fill in the cracks first.* **2.** to write in the blank spaces on a paper; to write on a form. □ *Please fill this form in.* T *I will fill in the form for you.*

fill something out to complete a form by writing in the blank spaces. □ *Please fill this form out and send it back to us in the mail.* T *I will fill out the form as you asked.*

fill the bill to be exactly the thing that is needed. □ *Ah, this steak is great. It really fills the bill.* □ *This new pair of shoes fills the bill nicely.*

fill up 1. to become full. □ *The creek filled up after the heavy rain yesterday.* □ *The rain barrel began to fill up during the storm.* **2.** to fill one's gas tank. (Informal.) □ *I've got to stop and fill up. I'm running low.* □ *We will fill up at the next little town.*

find for someone or something [for a jury or a judge] to announce a decision in favor of one side of a lawsuit. □ *The judge found for Mrs. Franklin and that made everyone quite happy.* □ *The court found for the law firm and admonished the disgruntled client.*

find it in one's heart (to do something) to have the courage or compassion to do something. □ *She couldn't find it in her heart to refuse to come home to him.* □ *I can't do it! I can't find it in my heart.*

find one's or something's way somewhere 1. [with *one's*] to discover the route to a place. □ *Mr. Smith found his way to the museum.* □ *Can you find your way home?* **2.** [with *something's*] to end up in a place. (This expression avoids accusing someone of moving the thing to the place.) □ *The money found its way into the mayor's pocket.* □ *The secret plans found their way into the enemy's hands.*

Finders keepers(, losers weepers). Since I found it, it is mine. (A proverb meaning that the person who finds something gets to keep it. The person who loses it can only weep.) □ *John lost a quarter in the dining room yesterday. Ann found the quarter there today. Ann claimed that since she found it, it was hers. She said, "Finders keepers, losers weepers."* □ *John said, "I'll say finders keepers when I find something of yours!"*

fine kettle of fish a real mess; an unsatisfactory situation. (Not meaningful literally.) □ *The dog has eaten the steak we were going to have for dinner. This is a fine kettle of fish!* □ *This is a fine kettle of fish. It's below freezing outside, and the furnace won't work.*

finish someone or something up to finish doing something to someone or something. (More at *finish up.*) □ *The hairdresser had to work fast in order to finish Mrs. Wilson up by quitting time.* Ⓣ *She finished up Fred in a short time.* □ *I will finish this typing up in a few minutes.*

finish something off to eat or drink up all of something; to eat or drink up the last portion of something. □ *Let's finish the turkey off.* Ⓣ *You finish off the turkey. I've had enough.* Ⓣ *Let's finish off this pot of coffee and I'll make some more.*

finish up to complete the doing of something. (More at *finish someone or something up.*) □ *When do you think you will finish up?* □ *I will finish up next week sometime.*

fire (something) back at someone or something to shoot a gun back at someone or something. □ *We fired about ten rounds back at them.* □ *The soldiers in the fort did not fire back at the attackers.*

firm something up 1. to make something more stable or firm. (See also *firm up.*) □ *We need to firm this table up. It is very wobbly.* Ⓣ *You need to learn to firm up your meringues better.* 2. to make a monetary offer for something more appealing and definite. □ *You will have to firm the offer up with cash today, if you really want the house.* Ⓣ *Please firm up this offer if you still want the house.*

firm up 1. to become more stable or viable; to recover from or stop a decline. (Figurative. See also *firm something up.*) □ *The economy will probably firm up soon.* □ *I hope that cattle prices firm up next spring.* 2. to develop better muscle tone; to become less flabby. (See also *firm something up.*) □ *I need to do some exercises so I can firm up.* □ *You really ought to firm up.*

first and foremost first and most important. □ *First and foremost, I think you should work harder on your biology.* □ *Have this in mind first and foremost: Keep smiling!*

First come, first served. The first people to arrive will be served first. □ *They ran out of tickets before we got there. It was first come, first served, but we didn't know that.* □ *Please line up and take your turn. It's first come, first served.*

first of all the very first, and perhaps most important thing; before anything else. (Similar expressions, *second of all* or *third of all*, are said, but do not make a lot of sense.) □ *First of all, put your name on this piece of paper.* □ *First of all, we'll try to find a place to live.* □ *"First of all, let me say how happy I am to be here," said Fred, beginning his speech.* □ HENRY: *How much is all this going to cost, Doctor?* DOCTOR: *First of all, do you have any insurance?*

first thing (in the morning) before anything else in the morning. □ *Please call me first thing in the morning. I can't help you now.* □ *I'll do that first thing.*

first things first the most important things must be taken care of first. □ *It's more important to get a job than to buy new clothes. First things first!* □ *Do your homework now. Go out and play later. First things first*

fish for a compliment to try to get someone to pay you a compliment. (As if one were tempting someone to utter a compliment.) □ *When she showed me her new dress, I could tell that she was fishing for a compliment.* □ *Tom was certainly fishing for a compliment when he modeled his fancy haircut for his friends.*

Fish or cut bait. Either do the job you are supposed to be doing or quit and let someone else do it. (Attend to the job of fishing or move aside and prepare the bait for others more active in the task of fishing.) □ *Mary is doing much better on the job since her manager told her to fish or cut bait.* □ *The boss told Tom, "Quit wasting time! Fish or cut bait!"*

fish someone or something out (of something) to pull someone or something out of something or some place. □ *She is down at the riverbank,*

fishing driftwood out of the water. ⊤ *She fished out a lot of wood.* □ *We need more wood. Please fish it all out.*

fish something up (out of something) to pull or hoist something out of something. □ *The old shopkeeper fished a huge pickle up out of the barrel.* ⊤ *He fished up a huge pickle.* ⊤ *Please fish up another one.*

fit for a king totally suitable; suitable for royalty. □ *What a delicious meal. It was fit for a king.* □ *Our room at the hotel was fit for a king.*

fit in((to) something) [for something] to be a suitable size to go into something. □ *This peg does not fit into this hole.* □ *It simply doesn't fit in.*

fit like a glove to fit very well; to fit tightly or snugly. □ *My new shoes fit like a glove.* □ *My new coat is a little tight. It fits like a glove.*

fit someone or something in((to) something) to manage to place someone or something into something. □ *I think I can fit you into my schedule.* ⊤ *I have fit in three people already today.* □ *The shelf is tight, but I think I can fit one more book in.*

fit someone or something out (for something) to equip someone or something for something; to outfit someone or something for something. (*Someone* includes *oneself*.) □ *We are going to fit our boat out so we can live on it during a long cruise.* ⊤ *We fit out the children in funny costumes for Halloween.* □ *We fit them all out and sent them off to their costume party.* □ *Let's fit ourselves out for the expedition.*

fit someone to a T See *suit someone to a T*.

131

fit something on((to) something) to manage to place something onto something. □ *See if you can fit this lid onto that jar over there.* □ *Sorry, I can't fit it on.*

fix someone or something up to rehabilitate someone or something. □ *The doctor said he could fix me up with a few pills.* ⊤ *The doctor fixed up the hunter and sent him home.* □ *I fixed the car up so it was safe to travel in.* □ *Is the car fixed up yet?*

fix someone's wagon to punish someone; to get even with someone; to plot against someone. □ *If you ever do that again, I'll fix your wagon!* □ *Tommy! You clean up your room this instant, or I'll fix your wagon!* □ *He reported me to the boss, but I fixed his wagon. I knocked his lunch on the floor.*

fix something over to redo something; to redecorate something. □ *I want to fix this room over next spring.* ⊤ *I really want to fix over this room.*

flag someone or something down to show a signal or wave, indicating that someone should stop. □ *Please go out and flag a taxi down. I'll be right out.* ⊤ *She went to flag down a taxi.* □ *The hitchhiker tried to flag us down.*

flame up 1. [for something] to catch fire and burst into flames. □ *The trees flamed up one by one in the forest fire.* □ *Suddenly the car flamed up and exploded.* **2.** [for a fire] to expand and send out larger flames. □ *The raging fire flamed up and jumped to even more trees.* □ *As Bob opened the door and came in, the fire flamed up and brightened the room.*

flare up 1. [for something] to ignite and burn. □ *The flames flared up at last—four matches having been used.*

2. [for a fire] to expand rapidly. □ *After burning quietly for a while, the fire suddenly flared up and made the room very bright.* **3.** [for a disease] to get worse suddenly. □ *My arthritis flares up during the damp weather.* **4.** [for a dispute] to break out or escalate into a battle. □ *A war flared up in the Middle East.* □ *We can't send the whole army every time a dispute flares up.*

flare up (at someone or something) to lose one's temper at someone or something. □ *I could tell by the way he flared up at me that he was not happy with what I had done.* □ *I didn't mean to flare up.*

flash back (on someone or something) to provide a glimpse of someone or something in the past. (In films, literature, and television.) □ *The next scene flashed back on Fred's murder.* □ *The story then flashed back, giving us information out of the past.*

flash in the pan someone or something that draws a lot of attention for a very brief time. □ *I'm afraid that my success as a painter was just a flash in the pan.* □ *Tom had hoped to be a singer, but his career was only a flash in the pan.*

flat broke completely broke; with no money at all. □ *I spent my last dollar, and I'm flat broke.* □ *The bank closed its doors to the public. It was flat broke!*

flatten someone or something out to make someone or something flat. □ *If you fall under the steamroller, it will flatten you out.* ⊤ *Flatten out that dough a little more.* □ *Please flatten it out.*

flesh and blood 1. a living human body, especially with reference to its natural limitations; a human being. □ *This cold weather is more than flesh and blood can stand.* □ *Carrying 300 pounds is beyond mere flesh and blood.* **2.** the quality of being alive. □ *The paintings of this artist are lifeless. They lack flesh and blood.* □ *These ideas have no flesh and blood.* **3.** one's own relatives; one's own kin. □ *That's no way to treat one's own flesh and blood.* □ *I want to leave my money to my own flesh and blood.* □ *Grandmother was happier living with her flesh and blood.*

flesh out to become more fleshy. □ *She began to flesh out at the age of thirteen.* □ *After his illness, Tom fleshed out and regained his strength.*

flesh something out (with something) to make the frame or skeleton of something complete; to add detail to the basic framework of something. □ *I will flesh this out with more dialogue and music here and there. Then we'll have a fine play.* T *We will flesh out the outline with more details later.* □ *Give me the outline, and I will flesh it out.*

flick something off to turn something off, using a toggle switch. □ *Mary flicked the light off and went out of the room.* □ *Please flick the light off as you go out the door.* T *Please flick off the light.*

flick something off ((of) someone or something) to brush or knock a speck of something off of someone or something. (The *of* is colloquial.) □ *She flicked a speck of lint off his collar.* T *She flicked off the lint.* □ *Harriet flicked it off.*

flick something on to turn something on, using a toggle switch. □ *Mary came into the room and flicked the light*

on. □ *Please flick the light on as you go out the door.* T *Please flick on the light.*

flicker out [for a flame] to dwindle, little by little, until it goes out. □ *The candle flickered out, leaving us in total darkness.* □ *When the last flame flickered out, the room began to get cold.*

fling something off (of oneself) **1.** to yank something off of oneself hastily. □ *She flung the blanket off herself.* T *She flung off the blanket.* □ *Sarah flung the books off her lap when the phone rang.* **2.** to pull or take off an article of clothing. □ *Larry flung his jacket off and went straight to the kitchen.* T *He flung off his jacket.* □ *Todd flung his jacket off.*

flip through something to go quickly through the leaves of a book, etc., page by page. □ *She flipped through the book, looking at the pictures.* □ *Don't just flip through it. Read it.*

float a loan to get a loan; to arrange for a loan. □ *I couldn't afford to pay cash for the car, so I floated a loan.* □ *They needed money, so they had to float a loan.*

flock in((to) some place) to move into some place in crowds. □ *People were flocking into the store where everything was on sale.* □ *They flocked in in droves.*

flock together to gather together in great numbers. (Typically said of birds and sheep.) □ *A large number of blackbirds flocked together, making a lot of noise.* □ *Do sheep really flock together in a storm?*

flood in(to something) to pour into something. (Both literally, with water, and figuratively.) □ *The people flooded* *into the hall.* □ *We opened the door, and the people flooded in.* □ *The water flooded in under the door.*

flood out (of something) to pour out of something or some place. (Both literal and figurative uses.) □ *The people flooded out of the theater, totally disgusted with the performance.* □ *The water flooded out of the break in the dam.* □ *Jimmy tipped over the jug of milk and the contents flooded out.*

flood someone or something out (of something) [for too much water] to force someone or something to leave something or some place. □ *The high waters flooded them out of their home.* ⊤ *The high waters flooded out a lot of people.* □ *The water flooded many farms out.*

flow in (to something) to course into something; to pour into something. (Both literal and figurative.) □ *The strength flowed into my body, and I felt alive again.* □ *The water flowed in when I opened the door on the flood.*

flow out (of something) 1. to course or pour out of something. □ *The apple juice flowed out of the press as we turned the crank.* □ *It stopped flowing out when we had crushed the apples totally.* 2. to issue forth from something. □ *The people flowed out of the stadium exits.* □ *At the end of the game, the people flowed out in a steady stream.*

flush something away to wash something unwanted away. □ *Flush all this away and be done with it.* ⊤ *Fred flushed away all the leaves on the sidewalk.*

fly by 1. to soar past. □ *Three jet fighters flew by.* □ *A huge hawk flew by, frightening all the smaller birds.*

2. [for time] to go quickly. (Figurative.) □ *The hours just flew by, because we were having fun.* □ *Time flew by so fast that it was dark before we knew it.*

fly in the face of someone or something AND **fly in the teeth of someone or something** to disregard, defy, or show disrespect for someone or something. □ *John loves to fly in the face of tradition.* □ *Ann made it a practice to fly in the face of standard procedures.* □ *John finds great pleasure in flying in the teeth of his father.*

fly in the ointment a small, unpleasant matter that spoils something; a drawback. □ *We enjoyed the play, but the fly in the ointment was not being able to find our car afterward.* □ *It sounds like a good idea, but there must be a fly in the ointment somewhere.*

fly in the teeth of someone or something See *fly in the face of someone or something.*

fly in(to something) to arrive in an airplane at something or some place. □ *I flew into Denver on time.* □ *When did you fly in?*

fly off 1. to take to flight quickly. □ *The stork flew off before we got a good look at it.* □ *The little birds flew off and things were quiet again.* 2. to leave in a hurry. (Figurative.) □ *Well, it's late. I must fly off.* □ *She flew off a while ago.*

fly off the handle to lose one's temper. □ *Every time anyone mentions taxes, Mrs. Brown flies off the handle.* □ *If she keeps flying off the handle like that, she'll have a heart attack.*

foam at the mouth to be very angry. (Related to a "mad dog" — a dog with rabies — that foams at the mouth.)

□ Bob was raving—foaming at the mouth. I've never seen anyone so angry. □ Bill foamed at the mouth in anger.

fob someone or something off (on(to) someone) to get rid of someone or something by transferring that someone or something to someone else. □ Don't try to fob your girlfriend off on me! T She fobbed off her brother onto her friend. □ I took him to my grandmother's house and fobbed him off.

fog over [for something made of glass] to become covered over with water vapor. □ The windshield fogged over because I forgot to turn on the defroster. □ The mirror fogged over, and I couldn't see to shave.

fog something up to cause something made of glass to become covered with a film of water. □ The moisture fogged the windshield up, and we had to stop to clean it off. T The moisture fogged up the glass.

fog up [for something made of glass] to become partially or completely obscured by a film of water. □ The glass fogged up, and we couldn't see out.

fold something back to bend a sheet or flap of something back. □ She very carefully folded the page back to mark her place in the book. T She folded back the page to mark her place in the book. □ The surgeon folded the flap of skin back, revealing the torn ligament. T He folded back his shirt cuffs carefully.

fold something in(to something) to blend something, such as eggs, into batter. □ Carefully, the chef folded the eggs into the other ingredients. T The chef folded in the eggs. □ Now fold the egg whites in carefully.

fold something over to double something over; to make a crease in something. □ I folded the paper over twice to make something I could fan myself with. □ Fold the cloth over a few times before you put it away.

fold something up to double something over into its original folded position. □ Please fold the paper up when you are finished. T Please fold up the paper.

fold up 1. [for something] to close by folding. □ The table just folded up with no warning, trapping my leg. □ I would like to find a map that would fold up by itself. 2. [for a business] to cease operating. □ Our shop finally folded up because of the recession. □ Tom's little candy shop folded up. 3. [for someone] to faint. □ She folded up when she heard the news. □ I was so weak that I was afraid I was going to fold up.

follow one's heart to act according to one's feelings; to obey one's sympathetic or compassionate inclinations. □ I couldn't decide what to do, so I just followed my heart. □ I trust that you will follow your heart in this matter.

follow someone up AND **follow up (on someone)** to check on the work that someone has done. □ I have to follow Sally up and make sure she did everything right. T I follow up Sally, checking on her. □ I'll follow up on her. □ Someone has to follow up.

follow something through See *follow through (with something)*.

follow something up AND **follow up (on something)** 1. to check something out. □ Would you please follow this lead up? It might be important. T Please follow up this lead. □ I'll follow up on it. □ *Yes, please follow up.* **2.** to make sure that something was done the way it was intended. □ *Please follow this up. I want it done right.* T *Please follow up this business.* □ *I'll follow up on it.* □ *I'll follow up.*

follow through (on something) to supervise something to its completion; to oversee something to make sure it gets done properly. □ *I want someone to follow through on this project.* □ *It isn't enough to start a project; you've got to follow through.*

follow through (with something) AND **follow something through** to complete an activity, doing what was promised. □ *I wish you would follow through with the project we talked about.* □ *You never follow through!* □ *When you start a project, you should be prepared to follow it through.*

follow up (on someone) See *follow someone up.*

follow up (on something) See *follow something up.*

food for thought something to think about. □ *I don't like your idea very much, but it's food for thought.* □ *Your lecture was very good. It contained much food for thought.*

fool around to waste time doing something unnecessary or doing something amateurishly. □ *Stop fooling around.* □ *I wish you didn't spend so much time fooling around.*

foot the bill to pay the bill; to pay (for something). □ *Let's go out and eat. I'll foot the bill.* □ *If the bank goes broke, don't worry. The government will foot the bill.*

for all intents and purposes seeming as if; looking as if. □ *Tom stood there, looking, for all intents and purposes, as*

if he were going to strangle Sally, but, being the gentleman that he is, he just glowered. □ MARY: *Is this finished now?* JOHN: *For all intents and purposes, yes.*

For crying in a bucket! See the following entry.

For crying out loud! AND **For crying in a bucket!** an exclamation of shock, anger, or surprise. □ FRED: *For crying out loud! Answer the telephone!* BOB: *But it's always for you!* □ JOHN: *Good grief! What am I going to do? This is the end!* SUE: *For crying in a bucket! What's wrong?*

for fear of something out of fear for something; because of fear of something. □ *He doesn't drive for fear of an accident.* □ *They lock their doors for fear of being robbed.*

For Pete('s) sake(s)! See the following entry.

For pity('s) sake(s)! AND **For Pete('s) sake(s)!** a mild exclamation of surprise or shock. (The extra *(s)* is colloquial.) □ FRED: *For pity's sake! What on earth is this?* ALICE: *It's just a kitten.* □ JOHN: *Good grief! What am I going to do? This is the end!* SUE: *What is it now, for Pete's sake?*

For shame! That is shameful! □ SUE: *Did you hear that Tom was in jail?* FRED: *For shame! What did he do?* SUE: *Nobody knows.* □ MARY: *I've decided not to go to the conference.* JOHN: *For shame! Who will represent us?*

For sure. Yes.; *Certainly.* (Colloquial.) □ SALLY: *Are you ready to go?* BOB: *For sure.* SALLY: *Then, let's go.* □ JANE: *Are you coming with us?* JOHN: *For sure. I wouldn't miss this for the world.*

for the devil of it AND **for the heck of it; for the hell of it** just for fun; because it is slightly evil; for no good reason. (Some people may object to the word *hell*.) □ *We filled their garage with leaves just for the devil of it.* □ *Tom tripped Bill for the heck of it.* □ *John picked a fight with Tom just for the hell of it.*

for the heck of it See the previous entry.

for the hell of it See *for the devil of it.*

for the odds to be against one for things to be against one generally; for one's chances to be slim. □ *You can give it a try, but the odds are against you.* □ *I know the odds are against me, but I wish to run in the race anyway.*

for the record so that (one's own version of) the facts will be known; so there will be a record of a particular fact. (This often is said when there are reporters present.) □ *I'd like to say — for the record — that at no time have I ever accepted a bribe from anyone.* □ *For the record, I've never been able to get anything done around city hall without bribing someone.*

for what it's worth a phrase added to a piece of information. □ MARY: *What do you think about it, Fred?* FRED: *Well, let me tell you something, for what it's worth.* □ JOHN: *For what it's worth, you're doing great!* SUE: *Thanks! It's worth a lot!*

for your information a phrase that introduces or follows a piece of information. (Can be spoken with considerable impatience.) □ MARY: *What is this one?* SUE: *For your information, it is exactly the same as the one you just asked about.* □ BOB: *How long do I have to wait here?* BILL: *For your information, we will be here until the bus driver feels that it is safe to travel.*

force someone or something out (of something) to drive someone or something out of something or some place. □ *The citizens' group forced the governor out of office.* ⊤ *They forced out the governor.* □ *We forced him out.*

force someone to the wall AND **drive someone to the wall** to push someone to an extreme position; to put someone into an awkward position. □ *He wouldn't tell the truth until we forced him to the wall.* □ *They don't pay their bills until you drive them to the wall.*

force someone's hand to force a person to reveal plans, strategies, or secrets. (Refers to a handful of cards in card playing.) □ *We didn't know what she was doing until Tom forced her hand.* □ *We couldn't plan our game until we forced the other team's hand in the last play.*

force something down to force oneself to swallow something. □ *I can't stand sweet potatoes, but I manage to force them down just to keep from making a scene.* ⊤ *She forced down the sweet potatoes.*

force something through something to press or drive something through resistance. □ *They forced the bill through the legislature.* □ *We were not able to force the matter through the board of directors.*

force something up See *drive something up.*

Forget (about) it! **1.** *Drop the subject!; Never mind!;* Don't bother me with it. □ JANE: *Then, there's this matter of the unpaid bills.* BILL: *Forget it!* □ SALLY: *What's this I hear about you and Tom?* SUE: *Forget about it!* **2.** *Nothing.* □ SUE: *What did you say?* MARY: *Forget it!* □ TOM: *Now I'm ready to go.* SUE: *Excuse me?* TOM: *Oh, nothing. Just forget it.* **3.** *You're welcome.;* It was nothing. □ JOHN: *Thank you so much for helping me!* BILL: *Oh, forget it!* □ BOB: *We're all very grateful to you for coming into work today.* MARY: *Forget about it! No problem!*

forgive and forget to forgive someone (for something) and forget that it ever happened. □ *I'm sorry, John. Let's forgive and forget. What do you say?* □ *It was nothing. We'll just have to forgive and forget.*

fork money out (for something) to pay (perhaps unwillingly) for something. (Often mention is made about the amount of money.) □ *Do you think I'm going to fork twenty dollars out for that book?* □ *Forking money out to everyone is part of life in a busy economy.* T *I like that stereo, but I don't want to fork out a lot of money.* T *I hate having to fork out money day after day.*

fork something over (to someone) to give something to someone. (Slang. Usually refers to money.) □ *Come on! Fork the money over to me!* T *Fork over the money!* □ *Fork it over!*

form an opinion to think up or decide on an opinion. (Note the variations in the examples.) □ *I don't know enough about the issue to form an opinion.* □ *Don't tell me how to think! I can form my own opinion.* □ *I don't form opinions without careful consideration.*

foul play illegal activity; bad practices. □ *The police investigating the death suspect foul play.* □ *Each student got an A on the test, and the teacher imagined it was the result of foul play.*

'Fraid not. See *(I'm) afraid not.*

'Fraid so. See *(I'm) afraid so.*

frankly speaking See *(speaking) (quite) frankly.*

free and easy casual. □ *John is so free and easy. How can anyone be so relaxed?* □ *Now, take it easy. Just act free and easy. No one will know you're nervous.*

free-for-all a disorganized fight or contest involving everyone; a brawl. □ *The picnic turned into a free-for-all after midnight.* □ *The race started out in an organized manner, but ended up being a free-for-all.*

freeze over [for a body of water] to get cold and form a layer of ice on top. □ *The pond froze over, so we went skating.*

freeze up 1. [for something] to freeze and stop functioning. □ *The joint froze up and wouldn't move anymore.* **2.** [for someone] to become frightened and anxious, and be unable to continue with something. □ *I froze up and couldn't say anything more.*

freshen someone or something up to revive or restore the appearance or vitality of someone or something. (*Someone* includes *oneself.*) □ *What can we do to freshen this room up?* T *A cold shower freshened up the runner.* □ *Let me take a moment to freshen myself up before we go into the dining room.*

Fret not! *Don't worry!;* Do not fret about it! □ MARY: *Oh, look at the* clock! I'm going to be late for my appointment! BOB: *Fret not! I'll drive you.* □ *"Fret not!" said Sally. "We're almost there!"*

frighten someone or something away AND **frighten someone or something off** to scare someone or something away. □ *The noise frightened the burglar away.* Ⓣ *Something frightened away the prowlers.* □ *The high prices frightened the shoppers off.* □ *You frightened the deer off!*

frighten someone or something off See the previous entry.

from hand to hand from one person to a series of other persons; passed from one hand to another. □ *The book traveled from hand to hand until it got back to its owner.* □ *By the time the baby had been passed from hand to hand, it was crying.*

from my perspective AND **from where I stand; from my point of view; the way I see it** a phrase used to introduce one's own opinion. □ MARY: *What do you think of all this?* TOM: *From my perspective, it is just terrible.* □ BOB: *From my point of view, this looks like a very good deal.* BILL: *That's good for you. I stand to lose money on it.* □ ALICE: *From where I stand, it appears that you're going to have to pay a lot of money to get this matter settled.* SUE: *I'll pay anything. I just want to get all this behind me.*

from my point of view See the previous entry.

from pillar to post from one place to a series of other places; from person to person, as with gossip. (Figurative.) □ *My father was in the army, and we moved from pillar to post year after year.* □ *After I told one person my secret, it went quickly from pillar to post.*

from rags to riches from poverty to wealth; from modesty to elegance. □ *The princess used to be quite poor. She certainly moved from rags to riches.* □ *After I inherited the money, I went from rags to riches.*

from start to finish from the beginning to the end; throughout. □ *I disliked the whole business from start to finish.* □ *Mary caused problems from start to finish.*

from stem to stern from one end to another. (Refers to the front and back ends of a ship. Also used literally in reference to ships.) □ *Now, I have to clean the house from stem to stern.* □ *I polished my car carefully from stem to stern.*

from the bottom of one's heart sincerely. □ *When I returned the lost kitten to Mrs. Brown, she thanked me from the bottom of her heart.* □ *Oh, thank you! I'm grateful from the bottom of my heart.*

from the ground up from the beginning; from start to finish. (Used literally in reference to building a house or other building.) □ *We must plan our sales campaign carefully from the ground up.* □ *Sorry, but you'll have to start all over again from the ground up.*

from the word go from the beginning; from the very start of things. (Actually from the uttering of the word *go*.) □ *I knew about the problem from the word go.* □ *She was failing the class from the word go.*

from top to bottom from the highest point to the lowest point; throughout. □ *I have to clean the house from* top to bottom today. □ We need to replace our elected officials from top to bottom.

from where I stand See *from my perspective.*

fuel up to fill one's tank with fuel. □ *Let's stop here and fuel up.* □ *I need to fuel up at the next little town.*

fun and games playing around; doing worthless things; activities that are a waste of time. □ *All right, Bill, the* fun and games are over. It's time to get down to work. □ *This isn't a serious course. It's nothing but fun and games.*

fuss (around) with someone or something to keep bothering with someone or something; to fiddle, mess, or tinker with someone or something. □ *Don't fuss around with it. We'll have to get a new one.* □ *Don't fuss with your children. They will get along just fine without all that attention.*

G

gamble on someone or something 1.
to make a wager on something concerning someone or something. □ *I wouldn't gamble on it happening.* □ *Don't gamble on Betty. You'll be sorry.* **2.** to run a risk by choosing or depending on someone or something. □ *I wouldn't gamble on Ted's being able to come. I don't think he can.* □ *Don't gamble on Ted. I'm almost sure he won't come.*

gang up (on someone or something) [for a group] to make an assault on someone or something. □ *They ganged up on us!* □ *We can't do it alone. We will have to gang up.*

Gangway! *Clear the way!; Get out of the way!* □ *"Gangway!" cried Fred. "Here comes the band!"* □ TOM: *Please move so we can get by.* BOB: *You'll never get anywhere with that. Gangway! Gangway! Gangway!*

gather something in 1. to collect something and bring it in; to harvest something. □ *We gathered the pumpkins in just before Halloween.* T *We gathered in the pumpkins just in time.* **2.** to fold or bunch cloth together when sewing or fitting clothing. □ *Try gathering it in on each side to make it seem smaller.* T *I will have to gather in this skirt.*

gather something up to collect something; to pick something up. □ *Let's*

gather our things up and go. T *Please gather up your things.*

gaze out on something to look out on something, such as a lovely view, from inside a building. □ *She gazed out on the flowering trees and knew that life would go on.* □ *Henry sat for hours, gazing out on the lake.*

gee an exclamation expressing disappointment, disagreement, surprise, or other emotions. (Words such as this often use intonation to convey the connotation of the sentence that is to follow. The brief intonation pattern accompanying the word may indicate sarcasm, disagreement, caution, consolation, sternness, etc.) □ *"Gee, why not?" whined Billy.* □ BILL: *Gee, I really want to go.* JANE: *Well then, go ahead and go!* □ JOHN: *Gee, Tom, I'm sort of surprised.* TOM: *You shouldn't be.* □ ALICE: *Gee, I thought you were gone.* BOB: *No, I'm still here.*

get a black eye (Also with *have.* Note: *Get* can be replaced with *have.* Note variations in the examples. *Get* usually means to become, to acquire, or to cause. *Have* usually means to possess, to be, or to have resulted in.) **1.** to get a bruise near the eye from being struck. □ *I got a black eye from walking into a door.* □ *I have a black eye where John hit me.* **2.** to have one's character or reputation harmed. □ *Mary got a black eye because of her complaining.* □ *The whole group now has a black eye.*

get a clean bill of health [for someone] to be pronounced healthy by a physician. (Also with *have.* See the note at *get a black eye.*) □ *Sally got a clean bill of health from the doctor.* □ *Now that Sally has a clean bill of health, she can go back to work.*

get a load off one's feet AND **take a load off one's feet** to sit down; to enjoy the results of sitting down. □ *Come in, John. Sit down and take a load off your feet.* □ *Yes, I need to get a load off my feet. I'm really tired.*

get a load off one's mind to say what one is thinking. □ *He sure talked a long time. I guess he had to get a load off his mind.* □ *You aren't going to like what I'm going to say, but I have to get a load off my mind.*

get a lump in one's throat to have the feeling of something in one's throat — as if one were going to cry. (Also with *have.* See the note at *get a black eye.*) □ *Whenever they play the national anthem, I get a lump in my throat.* □ *I have a lump in my throat because I'm frightened.*

get a word in edgeways See the following entry.

get a word in edgewise AND **get a word in edgeways** to manage to say something when other people are talking and ignoring you. (Often in the negative. As if one were trying to fit in or squeeze in one's contribution to a conversation.) □ *It was such an exciting conversation that I could hardly get a word in edgewise.* □ *Mary talks so fast that nobody can get a word in edgeways.*

get about AND **get around** to move around freely. □ *I can hardly get about anymore.* □ *It's hard for Aunt Mattie to get around.*

get across (something) to manage to cross something. □ *We finally got across the river where it was very shallow.* □ *Where the water was low, it was easy to get across.*

get after someone 1. to bother or nag someone about doing something. □ *I will get after Fred about his behavior.* □ *Please don't get after me all the time.* **2.** to begin to chase someone. □ *The other boys got after him and almost caught him.* □ *Henry got after Bill and almost caught up with him.*

get (all) dolled up to dress (oneself) up. (Usually used for females, but not necessarily.) □ *I have to get all dolled up for the dance tonight.* □ *I just love to get dolled up in my best clothes.*

get along (on a shoestring) to be able to afford to live on very little money. □ *For the last two years, we have had to get along on a shoestring.* □ *With so little money, it's hard to get along.*

get along with someone or something to manage with someone or something; to manage with only something. □ *I can't get along with only one assistant.* □ *Mary said she could not get along with the old computer.*

get along without someone or something to manage without someone or something. □ *I don't think I can get along without you.* □ *Laura can't get along without her dictionary.*

get around See *get about.*

get at someone or something 1. to manage to lay hands on someone or something; to get someone or something. □ *Just wait till I get at Charlie*

J. Wilson! □ *I want to get at that chocolate cake.* **2.** to manage to attack
someone or something. □ *The dog
was chained up, so it couldn't get at us.*
□ *The army was unable to get at the
munitions storage area.* **3.** [with *something*] to arrive at a point of discussion; to work toward stating a
point of discussion or an accusation.
□ *What are you trying to get at?* □
*We were trying to get at the basis of the
problem.*

**get away (from someone or some-
thing) 1.** to go away from someone
or something. □ *Please get away from
me!* □ *Get away from that cake!* **2.** to
escape from someone, something, or
some place. □ *Max did get away from
the police but not away from Lefty.* □
*Mary couldn't get away from the tele-
phone all morning.*

get back (at someone) to get revenge
on someone. □ *I will get back at her
someday, somehow.* □ *I'll get back,
don't worry.*

get back on one's feet 1. to recover
from an illness and leave one's
sickbed. (Both literal and figurative.)
□ *I will go back to work as soon as I
get back on my feet.* □ *I want to get
back on my feet as soon as possible.* **2.**
to recover from anything, especially
financial problems. (Figurative.) □ *I
can't afford to buy a car until I get a job
and get back on my feet.* □ *I'll get back
on my feet and start living normally.*

get back (some place) to manage to
return to some place. □ *I can't wait
till we get back home.* □ *When will we
get back? Is it much farther?*

Get back to me (on this). Report
back to me. (Often a deadline is
added.) □ TOM: *Here's a contract for*
*you to go over. Get back to me on this
by Monday morning.* MARY: *Sure
thing, Tom.* □ ALICE: *When you have
this thing figured out, get back to me,
and we'll talk.* TOM: *Righto.*

get back to someone or something
to return to dealing with someone or
something. □ *I will have to get back to
you. I can't deal with this matter now.*
□ *I want to get back to my work.*

get behind (in something) See *fall
behind (in something).*

get behind (on something) See *fall
behind (in something).*

get behind someone or something to
back or support someone or something; to put oneself into a position
to push or promote someone or
something. □ *Let's all get behind
Andrew for president!* □ *I want all of
you to get behind the committee and
support their efforts.*

get behind (with something) See *fall
behind (in something).*

get by (on something) to survive
with only something; to survive by
relying on something. □ *I can't get by
on that much money.* □ *That is a very
small amount of money to live on. No
one could get by.*

**get by without someone or some-
thing** to survive without someone or
something. □ *I can't get by without
you.* □ *We can probably get by without
two cars.*

get cold feet to become timid or
frightened; to have one's feet seem
to freeze with fear. (Also with *have.*
See the note at *get a black eye.*) □ *I
usually get cold feet when I have to
speak in public.* □ *John got cold feet
and wouldn't run in the race.* □ *I can't
give my speech now. I have cold feet.*

get down to brass tacks to begin to talk about important things. □ *Let's get down to brass tacks. We've wasted too much time chatting.* □ *Don't you think that it's about time to get down to brass tacks?*

get down to something See the following entry.

get down to work AND **get down to something** to begin to get serious; to begin to negotiate or conduct business; to begin to work on something seriously. (Especially with *business*, *work*, and *cases*.) □ *All right, everyone. Let's get down to business. There has been enough playing around.* □ *When the president and vice president arrive, we can get down to business.* □ *They're here. Let's get down to work.* □ *Now, let's get down to business.*

get fresh (with someone) to become overly bold or impertinent. □ *When I tried to kiss Mary, she slapped me and shouted, "Don't get fresh with me!"* □ *I can't stand people who get fresh.*

get goose bumps AND **get goose pimples** [for someone's skin] to feel prickly or become bumpy due to fear or excitement. (Also with *have*. See the note at *get a black eye*. For one's flesh to become like the flesh of a plucked goose. Very few Americans have ever seen a plucked goose.) □ *When he sings, I get goose bumps.* □ *I never get goose pimples.* □ *That really scared her. Now she's got goose pimples.*

get goose pimples See the previous entry.

get in someone's hair to bother or irritate someone. (Not usually literal.) □ *Billy is always getting in his mother's hair while she is on the phone.* □ *I wish you'd stop getting in my hair.*

get into the swing of things to join into the routine or the activities. (Refers to the rhythm of routinized activity.) □ *Come on, Bill. Try to get into the swing of things.* □ *John just couldn't seem to get into the swing of things.*

Get lost! *Go away!;* Stop bothering me! □ BILL: *I'm still real mad at you.* TOM: *Bill! Bill! I'm sorry about it. Let's talk.* BILL: *Get lost!* □ *Fred kicked his foot at the dog behind him and said, "Get lost, you worthless mutt!"*

get off easy AND **get off lightly** to receive little or no punishment for doing something wrong. □ *She really got off easy, considering what she did.* □ *You got off lightly in court. She is a hard judge.*

get off lightly See the previous entry.

Get off my back! Stop harassing me!; Leave me alone about this matter! (Slang.) □ TOM: *You'd better get your paper written.* BILL: *I'll do it when I'm good and ready. Get off my back!* □ ALICE: *I'm tired of your constant criticism! Get off my back!* JANE: *I was just trying to help.*

Get off my tail! **1.** Stop following me!; Stop following me so closely! (Slang.) □ *There was a car following too close, and Tom shouted into the rearview mirror, "Get off my tail!"* □ TOM: *Look, Bill. Don't you have something else to do? Quit following me around! Get off my tail!* BILL: *Can I help it if we both go to the same places?* **2.** *Get off my back!* □ TOM: *You'd better get your laundry done.* BILL: *I'll do it when I'm good and ready. Get off my tail!* □ BILL: *Get off my tail! I don't need a watchdog!* JANE: *You certainly do.*

get off ((of) something) to stop discussing the topic that one is supposed to be discussing [and start discussing something else]; to stray from the topic at hand. (The *of* is colloquial.) □ *I wish you wouldn't get off the subject so much.* □ *This writer gets off his topic all the time.*

get off scot-free See *go scot-free.*

get on to get along; to thrive. □ *Well, how are you two getting on?* □ *We are getting on okay.*

get on someone's nerves to irritate someone. □ *Please stop whistling. It's getting on my nerves.* □ *All this arguing is getting on their nerves.*

get on the bandwagon AND **jump on the bandwagon** to join the popular side (of an issue); to take a popular position. □ *You really should get on the bandwagon. Everyone else is.* □ *Jane has always had her own ideas about things. She's not the kind of person to jump on the bandwagon.*

get on with someone to get along with someone. □ *How does Colleen get on with Tracy?* □ *I hear that Mary gets on with Henry quite well.*

get on with something to continue doing something. □ *Let's get on with the game!* □ *We need to get on with our lives.*

get on without someone or something to survive and carry on without someone or something. □ *I think we can get on without bread for a day or two.* □ *Can you get on without your secretary for a while?*

get one's ducks in a row to put one's affairs in order; to get things ready. (Informal or slang. As if one were lining up wooden ducks to shoot them one by one in a carnival game.) □ *You can't hope to go into a company and sell something until you get your ducks in a row.* □ *As soon as you people get your ducks in a row, we'll leave.*

get one's feet on the ground to get firmly established or reestablished. (Also with *have*. See the note at *get a black eye.*) □ *He's new at the job, but soon he'll get his feet on the ground.* □ *Her productivity will improve after she gets her feet on the ground again.* □ *Don't worry about Sally. She has her feet on the ground.*

get one's feet wet to begin something; to have one's first experience of something. (As if one were wading into water.) □ *Of course he can't do the job right. He's hardly got his feet wet yet.* □ *I'm looking forward to learning to drive. I can't wait to get behind the steering wheel and get my feet wet.*

get one's fill of someone or something to receive enough of someone or something. (Also with *have*. See the note at *get a black eye.*) □ *You'll soon get your fill of Tom. He can be quite a pest.* □ *I can never get my fill of shrimp. I love it.* □ *Three weeks of visiting grandchildren is enough. I've had my fill of them.*

get one's fingers burned to have a bad experience. (Also used literally.) □ *I tried that once before and got my fingers burned. I won't try it again.* □ *If you go swimming and get your fingers burned, you won't want to swim again.*

get one's foot in the door to achieve a favorable position (for further action); to take the first step in a process. (People selling things from door to door used to block the door with a

145

foot, so it could not be closed on them. Also with *have*. See the note at *get a black eye*.) □ *I think I could get the job if I could only get my foot in the door.* □ *It pays to get your foot in the door. Try to get an appointment with the boss.* □ *I have a better chance now that I have my foot in the door.*

get one's hands dirty AND **dirty one's hands; soil one's hands** to become involved with something illegal; to do a shameful thing; to do something that is beneath one. □ *The mayor would never get his hands dirty by giving away political favors.* □ *I will not dirty my hands by breaking the law.* □ *Sally felt that to talk to the hobo was to soil her hands.*

get one's head above water to get ahead of one's problems; to catch up with one's work or responsibilities. (Also used literally. Also with *have*. See the note at *get a black eye*.) □ *I can't seem to get my head above water. Work just keeps piling up.* □ *I'll be glad when I have my head above water.*

get one's just deserts to get what one deserves. □ *I feel better now that Jane got her just deserts. She really insulted me.* □ *Bill got back exactly the treatment that he gave out. He got his just deserts.*

get one's second wind **1.** [for someone] to achieve stability in breathing after brief exertion. (Also with *have*. See the note at *get a black eye*.) □ *John was having a hard time running until he got his second wind.* □ *Bill had to quit the race because he never got his second wind.* □ *"At last," thought Ann, "I have my second wind. Now I can really swim fast."* **2.** to become more active or productive (after starting off slowly). □ *I usually get my*

second wind early in the afternoon. □ *Mary is a better worker now that she has her second wind.*

get one's teeth into something to start on something seriously, especially a difficult task. (Also used literally in reference to eating.) □ *Come on, Bill. You have to get your teeth into your biology.* □ *I can't wait to get my teeth into this problem.*

get on(to) someone (about something) to remind someone about something. □ *I'll have to get onto Sarah about the deadline.* □ *I'll get on Gerald right away.*

get out [for something] to become publicly known. □ *We don't want the secret to get out.* □ *The word soon got out that he had a prison record.*

Get out of here! *Go away!*; Leave this place! □ JOHN: *I've heard enough of this! Get out of here!* BILL: *I'm going! I'm going!* □ BILL: *Where have you been? You smell like a sewer! Get out of here!* FRED: *I can't imagine what you smell.*

Get out of my face! Go away and stop bothering me!; Get yourself away from me! □ ALICE: *Beat it! Get out of my face! Go away and stop bothering me!* FRED: *What on earth did I do?* □ BILL: *You really think I'll buy something that has been copied?* BOB: *I want you to give my proposal some thought.* BILL: *Get out of my face! I'll never buy something that's stolen!*

get out (of something) 1. to escape from something. □ *I've got to get out of here.* □ *Max wanted to get out of jail, but didn't know how.* □ *He doubted that he would get out alive.* **2.** to get free of the responsibility of doing something. □ *Are you trying to* get out of this job? □ *You agreed to do it, and you can't get out of it!*

get out of the wrong side of the bed See *get up on the wrong side of the bed.*

get over someone or something 1. to move or climb over someone or something. □ *Fred was slumped ahead of me in the trench. I managed to get over him and moved on toward the big gun at the other end.* □ *I couldn't get over the huge rock in the path, so I went around it.* **2.** to recover from difficulties regarding someone or something. □ *I almost never got over the shock.* □ *Sharon finally got over Tom. He had been such a pest.* **3.** [with *something*] to recover from a disease. □ *It took a long time to get over the flu.* □ *I thought I would never get over the mumps.*

get second thoughts about someone or something to have doubts about someone or something. (Also with *have.* See the note at *get a black eye.*) □ *I'm beginning to get second thoughts about Tom.* □ *Tom is getting second thoughts about it, too.* □ *We now have second thoughts about going to Canada.*

get someone down to make someone depressed or sad. □ *Now, now, don't let this matter get you down.* □ *All of this is beginning to get me down.*

get someone in(to something) to manage to get someone enrolled into something; to manage to get someone accepted into something. (Someone includes *oneself.*) □ *Somehow, we managed to get Jody into a fine private school.* □ *We got her in at last!* □ *Well, I managed to get myself into the class I wanted.*

get (someone) off the hook to free someone from an obligation; to help someone out of an awkward situation. □ *Thanks for getting me off the hook. I didn't want to attend that meeting.* □ *I couldn't get off the hook by myself.*

get someone on(to) someone or something to assign someone to attend to someone or something. □ *Get someone onto the injured man in the hall right now.* □ *Get someone on the telephone switchboard at once!*

get someone over a barrel AND **get someone under one's thumb** to put someone at one's mercy; to get control over someone. (Also with *have.* See the note at *get a black eye.*) □ *He got me over a barrel, and I had to do what he said.* □ *Ann will do exactly what I say. I've got her over a barrel.* □ *All right, John. You've got me under your thumb. What do you want me to do?*

get someone under one's thumb See the previous entry.

get someone up (for something) to get someone into peak condition for something; to prepare someone for something. □ *I hope we can get Walter up for the race.* □ *Sharon was not quite prepared for the race, and the trainer did everything possible to get her up.*

get someone's back up See the following entry.

get someone's dander up AND **get someone's back up; get someone's hackles up; get someone's Irish up** to make someone angry. (Also with *have.* See the note at *get a black eye.*) □ *Now, don't get your dander up. Calm down.* □ *Bob had his Irish* up all day yesterday. I don't know what was wrong. □ She really got her back up when I asked her for money. □ Now, now, don't get your hackles up. I didn't mean any harm.

get someone's ear to get someone to listen (to you); to have someone's attention. (Also with *have*. See the note at *get a black eye*. Not literal.) □ He got my ear and talked for an hour. □ While I have your ear, I'd like to tell you about something I'm selling.

get someone's eye See *catch someone's eye*.

get someone's hackles up See *get someone's dander up*.

get someone's Irish up See *get someone's dander up*.

get something across (to someone) to make someone understand something. (Especially if the details are difficult to understand or if the person being explained to understands poorly.) □ I hope I can get this across to you once and for all. □ Try as I may, I just can't get this across. □ She doesn't pay any attention, and I don't think I am getting it across.

get something down (on paper) to write some information down on paper; to capture some information in writing. □ This is important. Please get it down on paper. □ Please speak slowly. I want to get this down.

get something into someone's thick head See *get something through someone's thick skull*.

get something off one's chest to tell something that has been bothering you. (Also with *have*. See the note at *get a black eye*.) □ I have to get this off my chest. I broke your window with

a stone. □ I knew I'd feel better when I had that off my chest.

get something off (the ground) to get something started. □ I can relax after I get this project off the ground. □ You'll have a lot of free time when you get the project off.

get something off (to someone or something) to send something to someone or something. □ I have to get a letter off to Aunt Mary. T Did you get off all your packages? □ I have to get this parcel off to the main office.

get something out 1. to remove or extricate something. □ Please help me get this splinter out. T Would you help me get out this splinter? □ The tooth was gotten out without much difficulty. 2. to manage to get something said. □ He tried to say it before he died, but he couldn't get it out. □ I had my mouth full and couldn't get the words out.

get something out of someone or something 1. to remove something from someone or something. □ He probably will be okay when they get the tumor out of him. □ Please get that dog out of the living room. 2. [with someone] to cause or force someone to give specific information. □ We will get the truth out of her yet. □ The detective couldn't get anything out of the suspect. □ They got a confession out of him by beating him.

get something over (to someone) 1. to deliver something to someone. □ Get these papers over to Mr. Wilson's office right away. □ He needs it now, so try to get it over as soon as you can. 2. to make someone understand something; to succeed in explaining something to someone. □ I finally got *it over to him.* □ *He tries to understand what I'm talking about, but I can't get it over.*

get something sewed up (Also with *have.* See the note at *get a black eye.*) **1.** to have something stitched together (by someone). (Literal.) □ *I want to get this tear sewed up now.* □ *I'll have this hole sewed up tomorrow.* **2.** AND **get something wrapped up** to have something settled or finished. (Also with *have.*) □ *I'll take the contract to the mayor tomorrow morning. I'll get the whole deal sewed up by noon.* □ *Don't worry about the car loan. I'll have it sewed up in time to make the purchase.* □ *I'll get the loan wrapped up, and you'll have the car this week.*

get something straight to understand something clearly. (Also with *have.* See the note at *get a black eye.*) □ *Now get this straight. You're going to fail history.* □ *Let me get this straight. I'm supposed to go there in the morning?* □ *Let me make sure I have this straight.*

get something through someone's thick skull AND **get something into someone's thick head** to make someone understand something; to get some information into someone's head. □ *He can't seem to get it through his thick skull.* □ *If I could get this into my thick head once, I'd remember it.*

get something under one's belt (Also with *have.* See the note at *get a black eye.*) **1.** to eat or drink something. (This means the food goes into one's stomach and is under one's belt.) □ *I'd feel a lot better if I had a cool drink under my belt.* □ *Come in out of the cold and get a nice warm meal under your belt.* **2.** to learn something well; to assimilate some information. (Not literal. The knowledge is in one's mind and nowhere near the belt.) □ *I have to study tonight. I have to get a lot of algebra under my belt.* □ *Now that I have my lessons under my belt, I can rest easy.*

get something under way to get something started. (Also with *have.* See the note at *get a black eye.* Originally nautical.) □ *The time has come to get this meeting under way.* □ *Now that the president has the meeting under way, I can relax.*

get something up to organize, plan, and assemble something. □ *Let's get a team up and enter the tournament.* [T] *I think we can get up a team quite easily.* [T] *She got up a party on very short notice.*

get something wrapped up See *get something sewed up.*

get stars in one's eyes to be obsessed with show business; to be stagestruck. (Also with *have.* See the note at *get a black eye.* Refers to stardom, as in the stars of Hollywood or New York.) □ *Many young people get stars in their eyes at this age.* □ *Ann has stars in her eyes. She wants to go to Hollywood.*

get the benefit of the doubt to receive a judgment in your favor when the evidence is neither for you nor against you. (Also with *have.* See the note at *get a black eye.*) □ *I was right between a B and an A. I got the benefit of the doubt — an A.* □ *I thought I should have had the benefit of the doubt, but the judge made me pay a fine.*

get the blues to become sad or depressed; to become melancholy. (Also with *have*. See the note at *get a black eye*.) □ *You'll have to excuse Bill. He has the blues tonight.* □ *I get the blues every time I hear that song.*

get the final word See *get the last word*.

get the hang of something to learn how to do something; to learn how something works. (Also with *have*. See the note at *get a black eye*.) □ *As soon as I get the hang of this computer, I'll be able to work faster.* □ *Now that I have the hang of starting the car in cold weather, I won't have to get up so early.*

get the inside track to get the advantage (over someone) because of special connections, special knowledge, or favoritism. (Also with *have*. See the note at *get a black eye*.) □ *If I could get the inside track, I could win the contract.* □ *The boss likes me. Since I have the inside track, I'll probably be the new office manager.*

get the jump on someone to do something before someone; to get ahead of someone. (Also with *have*. See the note at *get a black eye*.) □ *I got the jump on Tom and got a place in line ahead of him.* □ *We'll have to work hard to get the contract, because they have the jump on us.*

get the last laugh to laugh at or ridicule someone who has laughed at or ridiculed you; to put someone in the same bad position that you were once in. (Also with *have*. See the note at *get a black eye*.) □ *John laughed when I got a D on the final exam. I got the last laugh, though. He failed the course.* □ *Mr. Smith said I*

was foolish when I bought an old building. I had the last laugh when I sold it a month later for twice what I paid for it.

get the last word AND **get the final word** to get to make the final point (in an argument); to get to make the final decision (in some matter). (Also with *have*. See the note at *get a black eye*.) □ *The boss gets the last word in hiring.* □ *Why do you always have to have the final word in an argument?*

Get the lead out! AND **Shake the lead out!** *Hurry up!* (Slang. As if slowed down by lead in one's pockets or somewhere else.) □ *"Move it, you guys!" hollered the coach. "Shake the lead out!"* □ BOB: *Get the lead out, you loafer!* BILL: *Don't rush me!*

get the message See *get the word*.

get the nod to be chosen. (Also with *have*. See the note at *get a black eye*.) □ *The boss is going to pick the new sales manager. I think Ann will get the nod.* □ *I had the nod for captain of the team, but I decided not to do it.*

get the red-carpet treatment to receive very special treatment; to receive royal treatment. (This refers — sometimes literally — to the rolling out of a clean red carpet for someone to walk on.) □ *I love to go to fancy stores where I get the red-carpet treatment.* □ *The queen expects to get the red-carpet treatment wherever she goes.*

get the runaround to receive a series of excuses, delays, and referrals. □ *You'll get the runaround if you ask to see the manager.* □ *I hate it when I get the runaround.*

get the shock of one's life to receive a serious (emotional) shock. (Also with *have*. See the note at *get a black* eye.) □ *I opened the telegram and got the shock of my life.* □ *I had the shock of my life when I won $5,000.*

get the short end of the stick AND **end up with the short end of the stick** to end up with less (than someone else); to end up cheated or deceived. (Also with *have.* See the note at *get a black eye.*) □ *Why do I always get the short end of the stick? I want my fair share!* □ *She's unhappy because she has the short end of the stick again.* □ *I hate to end up with the short end of the stick.*

get the upper hand (on someone) to get into a position superior to someone; to get the advantage of someone. (Also with *have.* See the note at *get a black eye.*) □ *John is always trying to get the upper hand on someone.* □ *He never ends up having the upper hand, though.*

get the word AND **get the message** to receive an explanation; to receive the final and authoritative explanation. (Also with *have.* See the note at *get a black eye.*) □ *I'm sorry, I didn't get the word. I didn't know the matter had been settled.* □ *Now that I have the message, I can be more effective in answering questions.*

get through (something) 1. to complete something; to manage to finish something. □ *I can't wait till I get through school.* □ *I'll get through in five years instead of four.* 2. to penetrate something. □ *We couldn't get through the hard concrete with a drill, so we will have to blast.* □ *The hardest drill bit we have couldn't get through.*

get through to someone or something 1. to make contact, usually on the telephone, with someone or a group. □ *I could not get through to her until the end of the day.* □ *Harry couldn't get through to his office.* 2. to manage to get one's message, feelings, desires, etc., understood by someone or a group. □ *I am really angry! Am I getting through to you?* □ *Nancy really wanted to get through to the bank, but they just seemed to ignore her.*

get through with someone or something 1. to finish with someone or something. □ *I can't wait to get through with this lecture.* □ *Every student was anxious to get through with the professor.* 2. to manage to transport someone or something through difficulties or barriers. □ *Customs was a mess, but we got through with all our baggage in only twenty minutes.* □ *I got through with my aged father without any trouble.*

get time to catch one's breath to find enough time to relax or behave normally. (Also with *have.* See the note at *get a black eye.*) □ *When things slow down around here, I'll get time to catch my breath.* □ *Sally was so busy she didn't even have time to catch her breath.*

get to first base (with someone or something) AND **reach first base (with someone or something)** to make a major advance with someone or something. (*First base* refers to baseball.) □ *I wish I could get to first base with this business deal.* □ *John adores Sally, but he can't even reach first base with her. She won't even speak to him.* □ *He smiles and acts friendly, but he can't get to first base.*

get to one's feet to stand up. □ *On a signal from the director, the singers got* *to their feet.* □ *I was so weak, I could hardly get to my feet.*

get to the bottom of something to get an understanding of the causes of something. □ *We must get to the bottom of this problem immediately.* □ *There is clearly something wrong here, and I want to get to the bottom of it.*

get to the heart of the matter to get to the essentials of a matter. □ *We have to stop wasting time and get to the heart of the matter.* □ *You've been very helpful. You really seem to be able to get to the heart of the matter.*

get to the point See *come to the point.*

get two strikes against one to get several things against one; to be in a position where success is unlikely. (From baseball where one is "out" after three strikes. Also with *have.* See the note at *get a black eye.*) □ *Poor Bob got two strikes against him when he tried to explain where he was last night.* □ *I can't win. I've got two strikes against me before I start.*

get under someone's skin to bother or irritate someone. (Refers to an irritant such as an insect or chemical that penetrates the skin.) □ *John is so annoying. He really gets under my skin.* □ *I know he's bothersome, but don't let him get under your skin.* □ *This kind of problem gets under my skin.*

get up enough nerve (to do something) to get brave enough to do something. □ *I could never get up enough nerve to sing in public.* □ *I'd do it if I could get up enough nerve, but I'm shy.*

get up on the wrong side of the bed AND **get out of the wrong side of** the bed to get up in the morning in a bad mood. (As if the choice of the side of the bed makes a difference in one's humor.) □ *What's wrong with you? Did you get up on the wrong side of the bed today?* □ *Excuse me for being grouchy. I got out of the wrong side of the bed.*

get wind of something to hear about something; to receive information about something. (The *wind* may be someone's breath or words, but more likely it refers to catching the scent of something in the wind long in advance of its appearance.) □ *I just got wind of your marriage. Congratulations.* □ *Wait until the boss gets wind of this. Somebody is going to get in trouble.*

get worked up (about someone or something) See the following entry.

get worked up (over someone or something) AND **get worked up (about someone or something)** to get excited or emotionally distressed about something. □ *Please don't get worked up over this matter.* □ *They get worked up about these things very easily.* □ *I try not to get worked up.*

Get your nose out of my business. See *Mind your own business.*

gild the lily to add ornament or decoration to something that is pleasing in its original state; to attempt to improve something that is already fine the way it is. (Often refers to flattery or exaggeration. The lily is considered beautiful enough as it is. Gilding it — covering it with gold — is overdoing it.) □ *Your house has lovely brickwork. Don't paint it. That would be gilding the lily.* □ *Oh, Sally. You're beautiful the way you are. You* *don't need makeup. You would be gilding the lily.*

gird (up) one's loins to get ready; to prepare oneself (for something). (Means essentially to dress oneself in preparation for something. Biblical.) □ *Well, I guess I had better gird up my loins and go to work.* □ *Somebody has to do something about the problem. Why don't you gird your loins and do something?*

give a good account of oneself to do (something) well or thoroughly. □ *John gave a good account of himself when he gave his speech last night.* □ *Mary was not hungry, and she didn't give a good account of herself at dinner.*

give as good as one gets to give as much as one receives; to pay someone back in kind. (Usually in the present tense.) □ *John can take care of himself in a fight. He can give as good as he gets.* □ *Sally usually wins a formal debate. She gives as good as she gets.*

give credit where credit is due to give credit to someone who deserves it; to acknowledge or thank someone who deserves it. □ *We must give credit where credit is due. Thank you very much, Sally.* □ *Let's give credit where credit is due. Mary is the one who wrote the report, not Jane.*

give in to cave in; to push in. □ *The rotting door gave in when we pushed, and we went inside.* □ *The wall gave in where I kicked it.*

give in (to someone or something) to give up to someone or something; to capitulate to someone or something. □ *Why do I always have to give in to you?* □ *I'm the one who always gives in.*

Give it a rest! Stop talking so much. Give your mouth a rest. (Familiar or rude. Compare to *Give me a rest!*) □ MARY: *So, I really think we need to discuss things more and go over all our differences in detail. You never seem to want to talk. You just sit there, staring straight ahead.* BILL: *Okay, I've heard enough. Give it a rest!* MARY: *Oh, am I disturbing you?* □ TOM: *Now, I would also like to say something else.* ALICE: *Give it a rest, Tom. We're tired of listening to you.*

Give it up! Stop trying. You are wasting your time. (Informal.) □ BOB: *Today was too much! I just can't do calculus!* BILL: *Give it up! Get out of that course and get into something less cruel.* BOB: *I think I will.* □ TOM: *I'm just not a very good singer, I guess.* SUE: *It's no good, Tom. Give it up!* TOM: *Don't you think I'm doing better, though?* SUE: *Give it up, Tom!*

Give me a break! 1. Please *give me a chance!;* Please give me another chance! □ BOB: *I know I can do it. Let me try again.* MARY: *Well, I don't know.* BOB: *Give me a break!* MARY: *Well, okay.* □ *"Give me a break!" cried Mary to the assistant director. "I know I can handle the part."* 2. I have had enough! Drop this matter!; Stop bothering me! □ TOM: *Now I'm going to sing a song about the hill people in my country.* MARY: *Give me a break! Sing something I know!* □ *"Give me a break!" shouted Bob. "Go away and stop bothering me!"*

Give me a call. AND **Give me a ring.** Please call me (later) on the telephone. □ MARY: *See you later, Fred.* FRED: *Give me a call if you get a chance.* □ *"When you're in town again, Sue, give me a call," said John.*

□ BOB: *When should we talk about this again?* BILL: *Next week is soon enough. Give me a ring.*

Give me a chance! 1. Please give me an opportunity to do something! □ MARY: *I just know I can do it. Oh, please give me a chance!* SUE: *All right. Just one more chance.* □ BOB: *Do you think you can do it?* JANE: *Oh, I know I can. Just give me a chance!* **2.** Please give me a fair chance and enough time to complete the task. □ ALICE: *Come on! I need more time. Give me a chance!* JANE: *Would another ten minutes help?* □ BOB: *You missed that one!* BILL: *You moved it! There was no way I could hit it. Give me a chance! Hold it still!*

Give me a rest! Stop being such a pest!; Stop bothering me with this problem! (Compare to *Give it a rest!*) □ *"Go away and stop bothering me!" moaned Bob. "Give me a rest!"* □ BOB: *I need an answer to this right away!* BILL: *I just gave you an answer!* BOB: *That was something different. This is a new question.* BILL: *Give me a rest! Can't it wait?*

Give me a ring. See *Give me a call.*

Give me five! AND **Give me (some) skin!; Skin me!; Slip me five!; Slip me some skin!** Shake my hand!; Slap my hand in greeting! (Slang.) □ *"Yo, Tom! Give me five!" shouted Henry, raising his hand.* □ BOB: *Hey, man! Skin me!* BILL: *How you doing, Bob?*

Give me (some) skin! See the previous entry.

Give my best to someone. AND **All the best to someone.** Please convey my good wishes to a particular person. (The *someone* can be a person's name or a pronoun. See also *Say hello to someone (for me).*) □ ALICE: *Good-bye, Fred. Give my best to your mother.* FRED: *Sure, Alice. Good-bye.* □ TOM: *See you, Bob.* BOB: *Give my best to Jane.* TOM: *I sure will. Bye.* □ BILL: *Bye, Rachel. All the best to your family.* RACHEL: *Thanks. Bye.*

Give one an inch, and one will take a mile. AND **If you give one an inch, one will take a mile.** A person who is granted a little of something (such as a reprieve or some lenience) will want more. (Proverb.) □ *I told John he could turn in his paper one day late, but he turned it in three days late. Give him an inch, and he'll take a mile.* □ *First we let John borrow our car for a day. Now he wants to go on a two-week vacation. If you give him an inch, he'll take a mile.*

give one one's freedom to set someone free; to divorce someone. (Usually euphemistic for divorce.) □ *Mrs. Brown wanted to give her husband his freedom.* □ *Well, Tom, I hate to break it to you this way, but I have decided to give you your freedom.*

give one's right arm (for someone or something) to be willing to give something of great value for someone or something. (Never literal.) □ *I'd give my right arm for a nice cool drink.* □ *I'd give my right arm to be there.* □ *Tom really admired John. Tom would give his right arm for John.*

give oneself airs to act conceited or superior. □ *Sally is always giving herself airs. You'd think she had royal blood.* □ *Come on, John. Don't act so haughty. Stop giving yourself airs.*

give out 1. to wear out and stop; to quit operating. □ *My old bicycle finally gave out.* □ *I think that your shoes are about ready to give out.* **2.** to be depleted. □ *The paper napkins gave out, and we had to use paper towels.* □ *The eggs gave out, and we had to eat pancakes for breakfast for the rest of the camping trip.*

give someone a black eye 1. to hit someone near the eye so that a dark bruise appears. □ *John became angry and gave me a black eye.* **2.** to harm the character or reputation of someone. □ *The constant complaining gave the whole group a black eye.*

give someone a buzz See *give someone a ring.*

give someone a clean bill of health [for a doctor] to pronounce someone well and healthy. □ *The doctor gave Sally a clean bill of health.*

give someone a piece of one's mind to bawl someone out; to tell someone off. (Actually to give someone a helping of what one is thinking about.) □ *I've had enough from John. I'm going to give him a piece of my mind.* □ *Sally, stop it, or I'll give you a piece of my mind.*

give someone a ring AND **give someone a buzz** to call someone on the telephone. (*Ring* and *buzz* refer to the bell in a telephone.) □ *Nice talking to you. Give me a ring sometime.* □ *Give me a buzz when you're in town.*

give someone or something a wide berth to keep a reasonable distance from someone or something; to steer clear of someone or something. (Originally referred to sailing ships.) □ *The dog we are approaching is very mean. Better give it a wide berth.* □ *Give Mary a wide berth. She's in a very bad mood.*

give someone or something back (to someone or something) to return someone or something to someone or something. □ *Please give it back to me.* □ *You took Gloria away from me. You had better give her back.* □ *She gave the pencil back to the carpenter.*

give someone or something up (to someone) to hand someone or something over to someone; to relinquish claims on someone or something in favor of someone else. □ *We had to give the money we found up to the police.* ⊤ *We gave up the money to the police.* □ *Mary still wanted it, but she had to give it up.*

give someone the benefit of the doubt to make a judgment in someone's favor when the evidence is neither for nor against that person. □ *I'm glad the teacher gave me the benefit of the doubt.* □ *Please, judge. Give me the benefit of the doubt.*

give someone the eye to look at someone in a way that communicates romantic interest. (Not literal.) □ *Ann gave John the eye. It really surprised him.* □ *Tom kept giving Sally the eye. She finally left.*

give someone the red-carpet treatment to give someone very special treatment; to give someone royal treatment. □ *We always give the queen the red-carpet treatment when she comes to visit.*

give someone the runaround to give someone a series of excuses, delays, and referrals. □ *If you ask to see the manager, they'll give you the runaround.*

give someone the shirt off one's back to be very generous or solicitous to someone. □ *Tom really likes Bill. He'd give Bill the shirt off his back.* □ *John is so friendly that he'd give anyone the shirt off his back.*

give someone tit for tat to give someone something equal to what was given you; to exchange a series of things, one by one, with someone. □ *They gave me the same kind of difficulty that I gave them. They gave me tit for tat.* □ *He punched me, so I punched him. Every time he hit me, I hit him. I just gave him tit for tat.*

give something a lick and a promise to do something poorly or quickly and carelessly. □ *John! You didn't clean your room! You just gave it a lick and a promise.* □ *This time, Tom, comb your hair. It looks as if you just gave it a lick and a promise.*

give something away (to someone) 1. to donate to, or bestow something upon, someone. □ *I gave the old clothing away to Tom.* ⊤ *I gave away my coat to Tom.* □ *Don't just give it away!* **2.** to tell a secret to someone. □ *Please don't give the surprise away to anyone.* ⊤ *Don't give away my secret.* □ *I had planned a surprise party but Donna gave it away.* **3.** to reveal the answer to a question, riddle, or problem to someone. □ *Don't give the answer away to them!* ⊤ *Don't give away the answer!* □ *Carla would have figured it out, but the audience gave it away.*

give something out 1. to distribute something; to pass something out. □ *The teacher gave the test papers out.* ⊤ *The teacher gave out the papers.* **2.** to make something known to the public. □ *When will you give the*

announcement out? ⊤ *The president gave out the news that the hostages had been released.*

give something over (to someone or something) to hand something over to someone or something. □ *Please give the money over to Sherri, who handles the accounts.* □ *She is waiting at the front office. Just go there and give it over.*

give the bride away [for a bride's father] to accompany the bride to the groom in a wedding ceremony. □ *Mr. Brown is ill. Who'll give the bride away?* □ *In the traditional wedding ceremony, the bride's father gives the bride away.*

give the devil her due See the following entry.

give the devil his due AND **give the devil her due** to give your foe proper credit (for something). (This usually refers to a person who has acted evil —like the devil.) □ *She's generally impossible, but I have to give the devil her due. She cooks a terrific cherry pie.* □ *John may cheat on his taxes and yell at his wife, but he keeps his car polished. I'll give the devil his due.*

give up to quit; to quit trying. □ *I give up! I won't press this further.* □ *Are you going to give up or keep fighting?*

give up (on someone or something) to give up trying to do something with someone or something, such as being friendly, giving advice, managing, etc. □ *I gave up on jogging. My knees went bad.* □ *Gloria tried to be friendly with Kelly, but finally gave up.*

give up the ghost to die; to release one's spirit. (Considered literary or humorous.) □ *The old man sighed,* rolled over, and gave up the ghost. □ I'm too young to give up the ghost.

glance back (at someone) **1.** to look quickly again at someone. □ *He glanced back at Mary, so he could remember her smile.* □ *She saw him briefly but never even glanced back.* **2.** to look quickly at someone who is behind you. □ *Dan glanced back at the man chasing him and ran on even faster.* □ *He glanced back and ran faster.*

glance down (at something) to look quickly downward at something. □ *Sherri glanced down at her watch and then pressed on the accelerator.* □ *She glanced down and hurried off.*

glance off ((of) someone or something) to bounce off someone or something. (The *of* is colloquial.) □ *The bullet glanced off the huge boulder.* □ *The baseball glanced off of Tom and left a bruise on his side where it had touched.* □ *The stone glanced off the window glass without breaking it.*

glance over someone or something to examine someone or something very quickly. □ *I only glanced over the papers. They look okay to me.* □ *The doctor glanced over the injured woman and called for an ambulance.*

glance through something to look quickly at the contents of something. □ *I glanced through the manuscript, and I don't think it is ready yet.* □ *Would you glance through this when you have a moment?*

Glory be! an exclamation expressing surprise or shock. (A bit old-fashioned.) □ MARY: *Glory be! Is that what I think it is?* SUE: *Well, it's a kitten, if that's what you thought.* □ SALLY: *First a car just missed·hitting her, then she fell down on the ice.* MARY: *Glory be!*

gnaw (away) at someone or something **1.** to chew at someone or something. □ *I hear a mouse gnawing away at the wall.* □ *The mosquitoes are gnawing at me something awful.* **2.** [with *someone*] to worry someone; to create constant anxiety in someone. (Figurative.) □ *The thought of catching some horrible disease gnawed away at her.* □ *A lot of guilt gnawed at him day and night.*

gnaw on something to chew on something. (Usually said of an animal.) □ *The puppy has been gnawing on my slippers!* □ *This slipper has been gnawed on!*

go about one's business to mind one's business; to move elsewhere and mind one's own business. □ *Leave me alone! Just go about your business!* □ *I have no more to say. I would be pleased if you would go about your business.*

go after someone or something **1.** to pursue someone or something. □ *The dogs went after the burglar.* □ *I went after the gang that took my wallet.* **2.** to charge or attack someone or some creature. □ *The bear went after the hunters and scared them to death.* □ *Then the bear went after the hunting dogs and killed two.*

go against someone or something to disfavor someone or something; to turn against someone or something; to oppose someone or something. □ *When did the trial go against us?* □ *The weather went against the cruise on the second day out.*

go against the grain to go against the natural direction or inclination.

(Refers to the lay of the grain of wood. *Against the grain* means perpendicular to the lay of the grain.) □ *Don't expect me to help you cheat. That goes against the grain.* □ *Would it go against the grain for you to call in sick for me?*

Go ahead. Please do it.; You have my permission and encouragement to do it. □ ALICE: *I'm leaving.* JOHN: *Go ahead. See if I care.* □ JANE: *Can I put this one in the refrigerator?* JANE: *Sure. Go ahead.*

(Go ahead,) make my day! 1. Just try to do me harm or disobey me. I will enjoy punishing you. (From a phrase said in a movie where the person saying the phrase is holding a gun on a villain and would really like the villain to do something that would justify firing the gun. Now a cliché. Compare to *Keep it up!*) □ *The crook reached into his jacket for his wallet. The cop, thinking the crook was about to draw a gun, said, "Go ahead, make my day!"* □ *As Bill pulled back his clenched fist to strike Tom, who is much bigger and stronger than Bill, Tom said, "Make my day!"* 2. Go ahead, ruin my day!; Go ahead, give me the bad news. (A sarcastic version of sense 1.) □ TOM (standing in the doorway): *Hello, I'm with the Internal Revenue Service. Could I come in?* MARY: *Go ahead, make my day!* □ SALLY: *I've got some bad news for you.* JOHN: *Go ahead, make my day!*

go along for the ride to accompany (someone) for the pleasure of riding along; to accompany someone for no special reason. □ *Join us. You can go along for the ride.* □ *I don't really need to go to the grocery store, but I'll go along for the ride.* □ *We're having a little party next weekend. Nothing fancy. Why don't you come along for the ride?*

go along with someone or something 1. to agree with someone or agree to something. □ *I will go along with you on that matter.* □ *I will go along with Sharon's decision, of course.* 2. to consent on the choice of someone or something. □ *I go along with Jane. She would be a good treasurer.* □ *Sharon will probably go along with chocolate. Everyone likes chocolate!*

go and never darken my door again to go away and not come back. □ *The heroine of the drama told the villain never to darken her door again.* □ *She touched the back of her hand to her forehead and said, "Go and never darken my door again!"*

go around to serve a need; to serve all who have a need. □ *There's not enough coffee to go around.* □ *Will there be enough chocolates to go around?*

go around someone to avoid dealing with someone. (Figurative.) □ *I try to go around Steve. He can be very difficult.* □ *We will want to go around the boss. He will say no if asked.*

go (a)round the bend 1. to go around a turn or a curve; to make a turn or a curve. □ *You'll see the house you're looking for as you go round the bend.* □ *John waved to his father until the car went round the bend.* 2. to go crazy; to lose one's mind. □ *If I don't get some rest, I'll go round the bend.* □ *Poor Bob. He has been having trouble for a long time. He finally went around the bend.*

go at it hammer and tongs See *fight someone or something hammer and tongs.*

go at it tooth and nail See *fight someone or something hammer and tongs.*

Go away! Leave me!; Get away from me! □ MARY: *You're such a pest, Sue. Go away!* SUE: *I was just trying to help.* □ *"Go away!" yelled the child at the bee.*

go away empty-handed to depart with nothing. □ *I hate for you to go away empty-handed, but I cannot afford to contribute any money.* □ *They came hoping for some food, but they had to go away empty-handed.*

go away with someone or something 1. to leave in the company of someone or something. □ *I saw him go away with Margie.* □ *She went away with the others.* 2. to take someone, some creature, or a group away with one. □ *He went away with the baby in his arms.* □ *He went away with the package.*

go back to return to the place of origin. □ *That's where I came from, and I'll never go back.* □ *I don't want to go back.*

go back on one's word to break a promise that one has made. □ *I hate to go back on my word, but I won't pay you $100 after all.* □ *Going back on your word makes you a liar.*

go back on something to reverse one's position on something, especially one's word or a promise. □ *You went back on what you promised! Can't I trust you?* □ *I don't want to go back on my word, but there has been an emergency.* □ *I hope she doesn't go back on her word.*

go behind someone's back 1. to move behind someone; to locate oneself at someone's back. □ *The mugger went behind my back and put a gun to my spine.* □ *Bob went behind my back and pushed me through the opening.* 2. to do something that is kept a secret from someone. (Figurative.) □ *I hate to go behind her back, but she makes so much trouble about things like this.* □ *Please don't try to go behind my back again!*

go belly-up See *turn belly-up.*

go below to go beneath the main deck of a ship. (Nautical.) □ *I will have to go below and fiddle with the engine.* □ *The captain went below to escape the worst of the storm.*

go by (some place) See *drop by (some place).*

Go chase yourself! AND **Go climb a tree!; Go fly a kite!; Go jump in the lake!** Go away and stop bothering me! □ BOB: *Get out of here! You're driving me crazy! Go chase yourself!* BILL: *What did I do to you?* BOB: *You're just in the way. Go!* □ BILL: *Dad, can I have ten bucks?* FATHER: *Go climb a tree!* □ FRED: *Stop pestering me. Go jump in the lake!* JOHN: *What did I do?* □ BOB: *Well, Bill, don't you owe me some money?* BILL: *Go fly a kite!*

Go climb a tree! See the previous entry.

go down 1. to sink below a normal or expected level or height. □ *The plane went down in flames.* □ *The ship went down with all hands aboard.* 2. to descend to a lower measurement. □ *Her fever went down.* □ *The price of the stock went down yesterday.* 3. to be swallowed. □ *The medicine went down without any trouble at all.* □ *The food simply would not go down. The puppy was going to starve.* 4. to fall or drop down, as when struck or injured. □ *Sam went down when he was struck on the chin.* □ *The deer went down when it was hit with the arrow.*

go down in history to be remembered as historically important. □ *Bill is so great. I'm sure that he'll go down in history.* □ *This is the greatest party of the century. I bet it'll go down in history.*

go Dutch to share the cost of a meal or some other event. □ JANE: *Let's go out and eat.* MARY: *Okay, but let's go Dutch.* □ *It's getting expensive to have Sally for a friend. She never wants to go Dutch.*

Go fly a kite! See *Go chase yourself!*

Go for it! *Go ahead!* Give it a good try! □ SALLY: *I'm going to try out for the basketball team. Do you think I'm tall enough?* BOB: *Sure you are! Go for it!* □ BOB: *Mary can't quit now! She's almost at the finish line!* BILL: *Go for it, Mary!* ALICE: *Come on, Mary!*

go in for something to enjoy doing something; to be fond of something. □ *Laurie goes in for skating and skiing.* □ *We don't go in for that kind of thing.*

go in one ear and out the other [for something] to be heard and then forgotten. (Not literal.) □ *Everything I say to you seems to go in one ear and out the other. Why don't you pay attention?* □ *I can't concentrate. Things people say to me just go in one ear and out the other.*

go in with someone (on something) to join efforts with someone on a project; to pool financial resources with someone to buy something. □ *I would be happy to go in with you on the charity ball. I'll find a hall.* □ *Yes, we can pool our money. I'll go in with you.* □ *Let's go in with Sally on a gift for Walter.*

go into a nosedive AND **take a nosedive** **1.** [for an airplane] to dive suddenly toward the ground, nose first. □ *It was a bad day for flying, and I was afraid we'd go into a nosedive.* □ *The small plane took a nosedive. The pilot was able to bring it out at the last minute, so the plane didn't crash.* **2.** to go into a rapid emotional or financial decline, or a decline in health. □ *Our profits took a nosedive last year.* □ *After he broke his hip, Mr. Brown's health went into a nosedive, and he never recovered.*

go into a tailspin **1.** [for an airplane] to lose control and spin to the earth, nose first. □ *The plane shook and then suddenly went into a tailspin.* □ *The pilot was not able to bring the plane out of the tailspin, and it crashed into the sea.* **2.** [for someone] to become disoriented or panicked; [for someone's life] to fall apart. □ *Although John was a great success, his life went into a tailspin. It took him a year to get straightened out.* □ *After her father died, Mary's world fell apart, and she went into a tailspin.*

go into one's song and dance about something to start giving one's usual or typical explanations and excuses about something. (One's can be replaced by the same old. Does not involve singing or dancing.) □ *Please don't go into your song and dance about how you always tried to do what was right.* □ *John went into his song and dance about how he won the war all by himself.* □ *He always goes into the same old song and dance every time he makes a mistake.*

go in((to) something) to enter something; to penetrate something. □ *The needle went into the vein smoothly and painlessly.* □ *It went in with no trouble.*

Go jump in the lake! See *Go chase yourself!*

go like clockwork to progress with regularity and dependability. (Refers more to mechanical works in general than to clocks.) □ *The building project is progressing nicely. Everything is going like clockwork.* □ *The elaborate pageant was a great success. It went like clockwork from start to finish.*

go off 1. [for an explosive device] to explode. □ *The fireworks all went off as scheduled.* □ *The bomb went off and did a lot of damage.* 2. [for a sound-creating device] to make its noise. □ *The alarm went off at six o'clock.* □ *The siren goes off at noon every day.* 3. [for an event] to happen or take place. □ *The party went off as planned.* □ *Did your medical examination go off as well as you had hoped?*

go off (by oneself) to go into seclusion; to isolate oneself. □ *She went off by herself where no one could find her.* □ *I have to go off and think about this.*

go off the deep end AND **jump off the deep end** to become deeply involved (with someone or something) before one is ready; to follow one's emotions into a situation. (Refers to going into a swimming pool at the deep end — rather than the shallow end — and finding oneself in deep water. Applies especially to falling in love.) □ *Look at the way Bill is looking at Sally. I think he's about to go off the deep end.* □ *Now, John, I know you really want to go to Australia, but don't go jumping off the deep end. It isn't all perfect there.*

go off with someone to go away with someone. □ *Tom just now went off with Maggie.* □ *I think that Maria went off with Fred somewhere.*

go on 1. to continue. □ *Please go on.* □ *Can I go on now?* 2. to hush up; to stop acting silly. (Always a command. No tenses.) □ *Go on! You're crazy!* □ *Oh, go on! You don't know what you are talking about.* 3. to happen. □ *What went on here last night?* □ *The teacher asked what was going on.* 4. That's silly!; You don't mean that! (Usually **Go on!**) □ JOHN: *Go on! You're making that up!* BILL: *I am not. It's the truth!* □ BILL: *Gee, that looks like a snake there in the path.* BOB: *Go on! That isn't a snake. No snake is that big.*

go on a fishing expedition to attempt to discover information. (Also used literally. As if one were sending bait into the invisible depths of a body of water trying to catch something, but nothing in particular.) □ *We are going to have to go on a fishing expedition to try to find the facts.* □ *One lawyer went on a fishing expedition in court, and the other lawyer objected.*

go on (and on) about someone or something to talk endlessly about someone or something. □ *She just went on and on about her new car.* □ *Albert went on about the book for a long time.*

go on at someone to rave at someone. □ *He must have gone on at her for over an hour — screaming and waving his arms.* □ *I wish you would stop going on at me.*

go (on) before (someone) **1.** to precede someone. □ *Please go on before me. I will follow.* □ *She went on before.* **2.** to die before someone. (Euphemism.) □ *Uncle Herman went on before Aunt Margaret by a few years.* □ *He went before her, although we had all thought it would be the other way around.*

go out **1.** to leave one's house. □ *Call me later. I'm going out now.* □ *Sally told her father that she was going out.* **2.** to become extinguished. □ *The fire finally went out.* □ *The lights went out and left us in the dark.*

go out for someone or something to leave in order to bring back someone or something. □ *Albert just went out for a newspaper.* □ *Fran went out for Bob, who was on the back porch, smoking a cigarette.*

go out (for something) to try out for a sports team. □ *Walter went out for football in his junior year.* □ *Did you ever go out for any sports?*

go (out) on strike [for a group of people] to quit working at their jobs until certain demands are met by management. □ *If we don't have a contract by noon tomorrow, we'll go out on strike.* □ *The entire work force went on strike at noon today.*

go out with someone to go on a date with someone; to date someone on a regular basis. □ *Will you go out with me next Saturday?* □ *Do you want to go out with Alice and Ted tomorrow night?* □ *Mary's parents are upset because she's going out with someone they don't approve of.*

go over someone's head [for the intellectual content of something] to be too difficult for someone to understand. (As if it flew over one's head rather than entering into one's store of knowledge.) □ *All that talk about computers went over my head.* □ *I hope my lecture didn't go over the students' heads.*

go over something with a fine-tooth comb AND **search something with a fine-tooth comb** to search through something very carefully. (As if one were searching for something very tiny lost in some kind of fiber.) □ *I can't find my calculus book. I went over the whole place with a fine-tooth comb.* □ *I searched this place with a fine-tooth comb and didn't find my ring.*

go over with a bang [for something] to be funny or entertaining. (Refers chiefly to jokes or stage performances.) □ *The play was a success. It really went over with a bang.* □ *That's a great joke. It went over with a bang.*

go overboard **1.** to fall off or out of a boat or ship. □ *My fishing pole just went overboard. I'm afraid it's lost.* □ *That man just went overboard. I think he jumped.* **2.** to do too much; to be extravagant. □ *Look, Sally, let's have a nice party, but don't go overboard. It doesn't need to be fancy.* □ *Okay, you can buy a big comfortable car, but don't go overboard.*

go scot-free AND **get off scot-free** to go unpunished; to be acquitted of a crime. (This *scot* is an old word meaning "tax" or "tax burden.") □ *The thief went scot-free.* □ *Jane cheated on the test and got caught, but she got off scot-free.*

go stag to go to an event (which is meant for couples) without a member of the opposite sex. (Originally referred only to males.) □ *Is Tom* *going to take you, or are you going stag?* □ *Bob didn't want to go stag, so he took his sister to the party.*

go the distance to do the whole amount; to play the entire game; to run the whole race. (Originally sports use.) □ *That horse runs fast. I hope it can go the distance.* □ *This is going to be a long, hard project. I hope I can go the distance.*

go the limit to do as much as possible. □ *What do I want on my hamburger? Go the limit!* □ *Don't hold anything back. Go the limit.*

go through to be approved; to pass examination; to be ratified. □ *I hope the amendment goes through.* □ *The proposal failed to go through.*

go through channels to proceed by consulting the proper persons or offices. (*Channels* refers to the route a piece of business must take through a hierarchy or a bureaucracy.) □ *If you want an answer to your question, you'll have to go through channels.* □ *If you know the answers, why do I have to go through channels?*

go through someone to work through someone; to use someone as an intermediary. □ *I can't give you the permission you seek. You will have to go through our main office.* □ *I have to go through the treasurer for all expenditures.*

go through something 1. to search through something. □ *She went through his pants pockets, looking for his wallet.* □ *He spent quite a while going through his desk, looking for the papers.* 2. to use up all of something rapidly. □ *We have gone through all the aspirin again!* □ *How can you go through your allowance so fast?* 3. [for

something] to pass through an opening. □ *The piano wouldn't go through the door.* □ *Do you think that such a big truck can go through the tunnel under the river?* 4. to pass through various stages or processes. □ *The pickles went through a number of processes before they were packed.* □ *Johnny is going through a phase where he wants everything his way.* 5. to work through something, such as an explanation or story. □ *I went through my story again, carefully and in great detail.* □ *I would like to go through it again, so I can be sure to understand it.* 6. to experience or endure something. □ *You can't believe what I've gone through.* □ *Mary has gone through a lot lately.* 7. to rehearse something; to practice something for performance. □ *They went through the second act a number of times.* □ *We need to go through the whole play a few more times.*

go through the motions to make a feeble effort to do something; to do something insincerely. □ *Jane isn't doing her best. She's just going through the motions.* □ *Bill was supposed to be raking the yard, but he was just going through the motions.*

go through the roof to go very high; to reach a very high degree (of something). (Not literal in this sense.) □ *It's so hot! The temperature is going through the roof.* □ *Mr. Brown got so angry he almost went through the roof.*

go to bat for someone to support or help someone. (From the use of a substitute batter in baseball.) □ *I tried to go to bat for Bill, but he said he didn't want any help.* □ *I heard them gossiping about Sally, so I went to bat for her.*

go to Davy Jones's locker to go to the bottom of the sea. (Thought of as a nautical expression.) □ *My camera fell overboard and went to Davy Jones's locker.* □ *My uncle was a sailor. He went to Davy Jones's locker during a terrible storm.*

go to pot AND **go to the dogs** to go to ruin; to deteriorate. □ *My whole life seems to be going to pot.* □ *My lawn is going to pot. I had better weed it.* □ *The government is going to the dogs.*

go to rack and ruin AND **go to wrack and ruin** to become ruined. (The words *rack* and *wrack* mean "wreckage" and are found only in this expression.) □ *That lovely old house on the corner is going to go to rack and ruin.* □ *My lawn is going to wrack and ruin.*

go to seed See *run to seed.*

go to someone's head to make someone conceited; to make someone overly proud. □ *You did a fine job, but don't let it go to your head.* □ *He let his success go to his head, and soon he became a complete failure.*

go to the dogs See *go to pot.*

go to the wall to fail or be defeated after being pushed to the extreme. □ *We really went to the wall on that deal.* □ *The company went to the wall because of that contract. Now it's broke.*

go to town to work hard or fast. (Also used literally.) □ *Look at all those ants working. They are really going to town.* □ *Come on, you guys! Let's go to town. We have to finish this job before noon.*

go to wrack and ruin See *go to rack and ruin.*

go under 1. to sink beneath the surface of the water. □ *After capsizing, the ship went under very slowly.* □ *I was afraid that our canoe would go under in the rapidly moving water.* 2. [for something] to fail. □ *The company went under exactly one year after it opened.* □ *We tried to keep it from going under.* 3. to become unconscious from anesthesia. □ *After a few minutes, she went under and the surgeon began to work.* □ *Tom went under and the operation began.*

go up in flames AND **go up in smoke** to burn up; to be consumed in flames. □ *The whole museum went up in flames.* □ *My paintings — my whole life's work — went up in flames.* □ *What a shame for all that to go up in smoke.*

go up in smoke See the previous entry.

go without (someone or something) to manage without a particular type of person or thing. □ *I can't go without a doctor much longer.* □ *I need a doctor now. I simply can't go without.* □ *We can go without food for only so long.* □ *I simply can't go without.*

God forbid! a phrase expressing the desire that God would forbid the situation that the speaker has just mentioned from ever happening. □ TOM: *It looks like taxes are going up again.* BOB: *God forbid!* □ BOB: *Bill was in a car wreck. I hope he wasn't hurt!* SUE: *God forbid!*

God only knows! Only God knows.; No one knows but God. □ TOM: *How long is all this going to take?* ALICE: *God only knows!* □ BOB: *Where are we going to find one hundred thousand dollars?* MARY: *God only knows!*

God willing. an expression indicating that there is a high certainty that something will happen, so high that only God could prevent it. □ JOHN: *Please try to be on time.* ALICE: *I'll be there on time, God willing.* □ BOB: *Will I see you after your vacation?* MARY: *Of course, God willing.*

Golly! an expression of surprise or interest. □ ALICE: *Golly, is it real?* MARY: *Of course it's real!* □ JANE: *Look at the size of that fish!* SUE: *Golly!*

(Good) afternoon. 1. the appropriate greeting for use between noon and supper time. □ SALLY: *How are you today?* JANE: *Good afternoon. How are you?* SALLY: *Fine, thank you.* □ BOB: *Afternoon. Nice to see you.* BILL: *Good afternoon. How are you?* BOB: *Fine, thanks.* **2.** an expression used on departure or for dismissal between noon and supper time. □ SALLY: *See you later, Bill.* BILL: *Afternoon. See you later.* □ MARY: *Nice to see you.* TOM: *Good afternoon. Take care.*

Good-bye. the standard thing to say when departing. □ SALLY: *It's time to go. Good-bye.* MARY: *Good-bye. See you later.* □ JOHN: *We had a wonderful time. Good-bye.* MARY: *Good-bye, come again.*

good-bye and good riddance a phrase marking the departure of someone or something unwanted. □ FRED: *Supposing I was to walk out of here, just like that?* MARY: *I'd say good-bye and good riddance.* □ *As the garbage truck drove away, carrying the drab old chair that Mary hated so much, she said, "Good-bye and good riddance."*

Good-bye for now. AND **(Good-bye) until next time.; Till next time.;**

Till we meet again.; Until we meet again. Good-bye, I'll see you soon.; Good-bye, I'll see you next time. (Often said by the host at the end of a radio or television program.) □ ALICE: *See you later. Good-bye for now.* JOHN: *Bye, Alice.* □ MARY: *See you later.* BOB: *Good-bye for now.* □ *The host of the talk show always closed by saying, "Good-bye until next time. This is Wally Ott, signing off."*

(Good-bye) till later. See *(Good-bye) until then.*

(Good-bye) till then. See *(Good-bye) until then.*

(Good-bye) until later. See *(Good-bye) until then.*

(Good-bye) until next time. See *Good-bye for now.*

(Good-bye) until then. AND **(Good-bye) till then.; (Good-bye) till later.; (Good-bye) until later.** Good-bye until sometime in the future. □ SALLY: *See you tomorrow. Good-bye until then.* SUE: *Sure thing. See you.* □ MARY: *See you later.* BOB: *Until later.* □ *The announcer always ended by saying, "Be with us again next week at this time. Good-bye until then."*

Good enough. That's good.; That's adequate. □ BILL: *Well, now. How's that?* BOB: *Good enough.* □ BOB: *I'll be there about noon.* BOB: *Good enough. I'll see you then.*

(Good) evening. 1. the appropriate greeting for use between supper time and the time of taking leave for the night or by midnight. (Compare to *Good night.*) □ BOB: *Good evening, Mary. How are you?* MARY: *Evening, Bob. Nice to see you.* □ *"Good evening," said each of the guests as they passed by Mrs. Franklin.* **2.** the

165

appropriate phrase used for leave-taking between supper time and before the time of final leave-taking to go to bed. □ MARY: *Let's call it a day. See you tomorrow, Bill.* BILL: *Yes, it's been a long and productive day. Good evening, Mary.* □ BOB: *Nice seeing you, Mr. Wilson.* MR. WILSON: *Good evening, Bob.*

Good for you! a complimentary expression of encouragement for something that someone has done. □ SUE: *I just got a raise.* BILL: *Good for you!* □ JANE: *I really told him what I thought of his rotten behavior.* SUE: *Good for you! He needs it.*

Good grief! an exclamation of surprise, shock, or amazement. □ ALICE: *Good grief! I'm late!* MARY: *That clock's fast. You're probably okay on time.* □ BILL: *There are seven newborn kittens under the sofa!* JANE: *Good grief!*

(Good) heavens! an exclamation of surprise, shock, or amazement. (See also *(My) heavens!*) □ JOHN: *Good heavens! A diamond ring!* BILL: *I bet it's not real.* □ JANE: *Ouch!* JOHN: *Good heavens! What happened?* JANE: *I just stubbed my toe.*

Good job! See *Nice going!*

Good luck! **1.** a wish of good fortune to someone. □ MARY: *I have my recital tonight.* JANE: *I know you'll do well. Good luck!* □ SALLY: *I hear you're leaving for your new job tomorrow morning.* BOB: *That's right.* SALLY: *Well, good luck!* **2.** You will certainly need luck, but it probably will not work. (Sarcastic.) □ BILL: *I'm going to try to get this tax bill lowered.* SUE: *Good luck!* □ BILL: *I'm*

sure I can get this cheaper at another store. CLERK: *Good luck!*

(Good) morning. the standard greeting phrase used any time between midnight and noon. □ BOB: *Good morning.* BILL: *Good morning, Bob. You sure get up early!*

(Good) night. **1.** the appropriate departure phrase for leave-taking after dark. (This assumes that the speakers will not see one another until morning at the earliest. *Night* alone is familiar.) □ JOHN: *Bye, Alice.* ALICE: *Night. See you tomorrow.* □ BILL: *Good night, Mary.* MARY: *Night, Bill.* **2.** the appropriate phrase for wishing someone a good night's sleep. □ FATHER: *Good night Bill.* BILL: *Night, Pop.* □ FATHER: *Good night.* MOTHER: *Good night.* **3.** a mild exclamation. □ JANE: *Good night! It's dark! What time is it?* MARY: *It's two AM.* JANE: *In that case, good morning.* □ *"Good night!" cried Fred. "Look at this mess!"*

Gotcha! **1.** I understand what you said or what you want. □ JOHN: *I want this done now! Understand?* ALICE: *Gotcha!* □ BILL: *Now, this kind of thing can't continue. We must do anything to prevent it happening again. Do you understand what I'm saying to you?* BOB: *Gotcha!* **2.** I've caught you at your little game. □ *Mary was standing by the hall table, going through mail very slowly. Fred came through and saw her. "Gotcha!" said Fred to an embarrassed Mary.* □ BILL: *My flight was nearly six hours late.* BOB: *Gotcha! I just heard you tell Mary it was three hours late.*

grab on(to someone or something) to grasp someone or something; to hold on to someone or something.

☐ *Here, grab onto this rope!* ☐ *Grab on and hold tight.*

grade someone or something down to lower the ranking, rating, or score on someone or something. ☐ *I had to grade you down because your paper was late.* ⊤ *I graded down the paper because it was late.*

graduate from something to earn and receive a degree from an educational institution. ☐ *I graduated from a large midwestern university.* ☐ *Bill intends to graduate in the spring.*

graze on something 1. [for animals] to browse or forage in a particular location. ☐ *The cattle are grazing on the neighbor's land.* ☐ *I wish they wouldn't graze on other people's land.* **2.** [for animals] to browse or forage, eating something in particular. ☐ *The deer are grazing on my carrots!* ☐ *The cows were grazing on the meadow grasses for weeks.*

Great! That is wonderful!; I am pleased to hear it. ☐ JANE: *I'm getting a new job.* BILL: *Great!* ☐ MARY: *I'm done now.* SALLY: *Great! We can leave right away.*

Great Scott! an exclamation of shock or surprise. ☐ *"Great Scott! You bought a truck!" shrieked Mary.* ☐ FRED: *The water heater just exploded!* BILL: *Great Scott! What do we do now?* FRED: *Looks like cold showers for a while.*

green with envy envious; jealous. (Not literal.) ☐ *When Sally saw me with Tom, she turned green with envy. She likes him a lot.* ☐ *I feel green with envy whenever I see you in your new car.*

Greetings. Hello. ☐ SALLY: *Greetings, my friend.* BOB: *Hello, Sally.* ☐

MARY: *Hi, Tom.* TOM: *Greetings, Mary. How are things?* MARY: *Just great, thanks. What about you?* TOM: *I'm cool.*

Greetings and felicitations! AND **Greetings and salutations!** Hello and good wishes. (A bit stilted.) ☐ *"Greetings and felicitations! Welcome to our talent show!" said the master of ceremonies.* ☐ BILL: *Greetings and salutations, Bob!* BOB: *Come off it, Bill. Can't you just say "Hi" or something?*

Greetings and salutations! See the previous entry.

grin and bear it to endure something unpleasant in good humor. ☐ *There is nothing you can do but grin and bear it.* ☐ *I hate having to work for rude people. I guess I have to grin and bear it.*

grind someone down to wear someone down by constant requests; to wear someone down by constant nagging. ☐ *If you think you can grind me down by bothering me all the time, you are wrong.* ⊤ *The constant nagging ground down the employees at last.*

grind something away to remove something by grinding. ☐ *Grind the bumps away and make a smooth wall.* ⊤ *Please grind away the bumps.*

grind something down to make something smooth or even by grinding. ☐ *Grind this down to make it smooth.* ⊤ *Please grind down this rough spot.*

grind something out 1. to produce something by grinding. ☐ *Working hard, he ground the powder out, a cup at a time.* ⊤ *He ground out the powder, a cup at a time.* **2.** to produce something in a mechanical or perfunctory manner. □ *The factory just keeps grinding these toys out, day after day.* Ⓣ *The factory grinds out toys all day long.*

grind something up to pulverize or crush something by crushing, rubbing, or abrasion. □ *Please grind the fennel seeds up.* Ⓣ *Grind up the fennel seeds and sprinkle them on the top.*

grind to a halt to slow to a stop; to run down. □ *By the end of the day, the factory had ground to a halt.* □ *The car ground to a halt, and we got out to stretch our legs.*

grit one's teeth to grind one's teeth together in anger or determination. □ *I was so mad, all I could do was stand there and grit my teeth.* □ *All*

through the race, Sally was gritting her teeth. She was really determined.

Guess what! a way of starting a conversation; a way of forcing someone into a conversation. □ ALICE: *Guess what!* BOB: *I don't know. What?* ALICE: *I'm going to Europe this summer.* BOB: *That's very nice.* □ JOHN: *Guess what!* JANE: *What?* JOHN: *Mary is going to have a baby.* JANE: *Oh, that's great!*

gun for someone to be looking for someone, presumably to harm them with a gun. (Originally from western and gangster movies.) □ *The coach is gunning for you. I think he's going to bawl you out.* □ *I've heard that the sheriff is gunning for me, so I'm getting out of town.*

H

hack something down to chop something down. □ *Who hacked this cherry tree down?* ⊤ *Who hacked down this cherry tree?*

hack something up 1. to chop something up into pieces. □ *Hack all this old furniture up, and we'll burn it in the fireplace.* ⊤ *Hack up this stuff, and we'll burn it.* **2.** to damage or mangle something. □ *Who hacked my windowsill up?* ⊤ *Who hacked up my windowsill?*

hail-fellow-well-met friendly to everyone; falsely friendly to everyone. (Usually said of males.) □ *Yes, he's friendly, sort of hail-fellow-well-met.* □ *He's not a very sincere person. Hail-fellow-well-met—you know the type.* □ *What a pain he is! Good old Mr. Hail-fellow-well-met. What a phony!*

hair of the dog that bit one a drink of liquor taken when one has a hangover; a drink of liquor taken when one is recovering from drinking too much liquor. (This has nothing to do with dogs or hair.) □ *Oh, I'm miserable. I need some of the hair of the dog that bit me.* □ *That's some hangover you've got there, Bob. Here, drink this. It's some of the hair of the dog that bit you.*

hale and hearty well and healthy. □ *Doesn't Ann look hale and hearty?* □ *I*

don't feel hale and hearty. I'm really tired.

Half a loaf is better than none. Having part of something is better than having nothing. (Proverb.) □ *When my raise was smaller than I wanted, Sally said, "Half a loaf is better than none."* □ *People who keep saying "Half a loaf is better than none" usually have as much as they need.*

ham something up to perform in something in an exaggerated and exhibitionist manner. □ *Stop hamming it up! This is a serious drama.* ⊤ *She really hammed up her part in the play.*

hammer (away) at someone to interrogate someone; to ask questions endlessly of someone. (Figurative.) □ *The cops kept hammering away at Max until he told them everything they wanted to know.* □ *They hammered at Max for hours.*

hammer something down to pound something down, even with the surrounding area. □ *Hammer all the nails down so that none of them will catch on someone's shoe.* ⊤ *Hammer down all these nails!*

hammer something in(to someone) AND **pound something in(to someone)** to teach something to someone intensively, as if one were driving the information in by force. (Figurative.)

□ Her parents had hammered good manners into her head since she was a child. ⊤ They hammered in good manners every day. □ They pounded proper behavior into the children. □ The teacher held a review session on the material and really pounded the stuff in.

hammer something in (to something) AND **pound something in (to something)** to drive something into something as with a hammer. □ Todd hammered the spike into the beam. ⊤ He hammered in the spike. □ He hammered it in with two hard blows. □ The carpenter pounded the nail into the board. ⊤ The carpenter pounded in the nail.

hand in glove (with someone) very close to someone. □ John is really hand in glove with Sally. □ The teacher and the principal work hand in glove.

hand over fist [for money and merchandise to be exchanged] very rapidly. □ What a busy day. We took in money hand over fist. □ They were buying things hand over fist.

hand over hand [moving] one hand after the other (again and again). □ Sally pulled in the rope hand over hand. □ The man climbed the rope hand over hand.

hand something down [for a court] to issue a ruling. (Legal.) □ The appeals court handed down a negative opinion. □ The court has not yet handed down a ruling.

hand something down (to someone) to pass on something to a younger person, often a younger relative. □ I will hand this down to my grandson also. ⊤ I will hand down this dress to my niece. □ When I am finished with this, I will hand it down.

hand something off (to someone) to give a football directly to another player. (Football.) □ Roger handed the ball off to Jeff. ⊤ He handed off the ball. □ Tim handed it off.

hand something out (to someone) to pass something, usually papers, out to people. □ The teacher handed the tests out to the students. ⊤ Please hand out these papers. □ Hand them out, if you would.

handle someone with kid gloves to be very careful with a touchy person; to deal with someone who is very difficult. □ Bill has become so sensitive. You really have to handle him with kid gloves. □ You don't have to handle me with kid gloves. I can take it.

hang around (some place) to loiter some place; to be in a place or in an area, doing nothing in particular. □ Why are you hanging around my office? □ It's comfortable here. I think I'll hang around here for a while. □ Stop hanging around and get a job.

hang around with someone to spend time doing nothing in particular with someone. □ You spend most of your day hanging around with your friends. □ I like to hang around with people I know.

hang back (from someone or something) to lag back behind someone or something; to stay back from someone or something, perhaps in avoidance. □ Why are you hanging back from the rest of the group? □ Come on! Don't hang back!

hang by a hair AND **hang by a thread** to be in an uncertain position; to depend on something very insubstantial for support. (Also with *on*, as in the second example.) □ *Your whole argument is hanging by a thread.* □ *John isn't failing geometry, but he's just hanging on by a hair.*

hang by a thread See the previous entry.

hang in the balance to be in an undecided state; to be between two equal possibilities. □ *The prisoner stood before the judge with his life hanging in the balance.* □ *This whole issue will have to hang in the balance until Jane gets back from her vacation.*

Hang in there. Be patient, things will work out. □ BOB: *Everything is in such a mess. I can't seem to get things done right.* JANE: *Hang in there, Bob. Things will work out.* □ MARY: *Sometimes I just don't think I can go on.* SUE: *Hang in there, Mary. Things will work out.*

hang on 1. to survive for a while. (Figurative. See also *Hang on (a minute).*) □ *I think we can hang on without electricity for a little while longer.* □ *We can't hang on much longer.* 2. to linger or persist. □ *This cold has been hanging on for a month.* □ *This is the kind of flu that hangs on for weeks.* 3. to be prepared for fast or rough movement. (Usually **Hang on!**) □ *Hang on! Here we go!* □ *The airplane passengers suddenly seemed weightless. Someone shouted, "Hang on!"*

Hang on (a minute). AND **Hang on a moment.; Hang on a second.** Please wait a while. □ MARY: *Hang on a minute.* TOM: *What do you want?* MARY: *I want to ask you something.* □ JANE (entering the room): *Oh, Bill.*

BILL (covering the telephone receiver): *Hang on a second. I'm on the phone.* □ *Hang on a minute. I need to talk to you.* □ *Hang on. Let me catch up with you.* □ *Please hang on. I'll call her to the phone.*

Hang on a moment. See the previous entry.

Hang on a second. See *Hang on (a minute).*

hang on someone's every word to listen carefully to everything someone says. □ *He gave a great lecture. We hung on his every word.* □ *Look at the way John hangs on Mary's every word. He must be in love with her.*

hang on (to someone or something) AND **hold on (to someone or something)** 1. to grasp someone or something. □ *She hung on to her husband to keep warm.* □ *She sat there and hung on, trying to keep warm.* □ *Jane hung on to Jeff to keep from slipping on the ice.* 2. to keep someone or something. □ *Please hang on to Tom. I need to talk to him.* □ *If you have Ted there, hang on. I need to talk to him.* □ *Hang on to your money. You will need it later.*

Hang on to your hat! AND **Hold on to your hat!** Grasp your hat.; Prepare for a sudden surprise or shock. □ *What a windy day. Hang on to your hat!* □ *Here we go! Hold on to your hat!* □ *Are you ready to hear the final score? Hang on to your hat! We won ten to nothing!*

hang out (with someone or something) to associate with someone or a group on a regular basis. □ *She hangs out with Alice too much.* □ *I wish you would stop hanging out with* that crowd of boys. □ Kids hang out too much these days.

hang someone in effigy to hang a dummy or some other figure of a hated person. □ They hanged the dictator in effigy. □ The angry mob hanged the president in effigy.

hang together 1. [for something or a group of people] to hold together; to remain intact. □ I hope our bridge group hangs together until we are old and gray. □ I don't think that this car will hang together for another minute. **2.** [for a story] to flow from element to element and make sense. □ This story simply does not hang together. □ Your novel hangs together quite nicely. **3.** [for people] to spend time together. □ We hung together for a few hours and then went our separate ways. □ The boys hung together throughout the evening.

hang up 1. [for a machine or a computer] to grind to a halt; to stop because of some internal complication. □ Our computer hung up right in the middle of the job. □ I was afraid that my computer would hang up permanently. **2.** to replace the telephone receiver after a call. □ I said good-bye and hung up. □ Please hang up and place your call again.

happen (up)on someone or something to find someone or something, as if by accident. □ I just happened upon a strange little man in the street who offered to sell me a watch. □ Andrew happened on a book that interested him, so he bought it.

hard-and-fast rule a strict rule. □ It's a hard-and-fast rule that you must be home by midnight. □ You should have

your project completed by the end of the month, but it's not a hard-and-fast rule.

hard on someone's heels following someone very closely; following very closely to someone's heels. □ I ran as fast as I could, but the dog was still hard on my heels. □ Here comes Sally, and John is hard on her heels.

hardly have time to breathe to be very busy. □ This was such a busy day. I hardly had time to breathe. □ They made him work so hard that he hardly had time to breathe.

harp on someone or something to criticize someone or something constantly. □ I wish you would quit harping on Jeff all the time. He couldn't be all that bad. □ Stop harping on my mistakes and work on your own.

hash something over (with someone) to discuss something with someone. □ I need to hash this matter over with you. ⊤ I've hashed over this business enough. □ We need to get together with Rachel and hash this over.

Haste makes waste. Time gained in doing something rapidly and carelessly will be lost when one has to do the thing over again correctly. (Proverb.) □ Now, take your time. Haste makes waste. □ Haste makes waste, so be careful as you work.

hate someone's guts to hate someone very much. (Informal and rude.) □ Oh, Bob is terrible. I hate his guts! □ You may hate my guts for saying so, but I think you're getting gray hair.

haul someone in [for an officer of the law] to take someone to the police station. □ The officer hauled the boys in and booked every one of them. ⊤ He hauled in the young boys.

haul someone over the coals See *rake someone over the coals.*

Have a ball! Enjoy yourself! (Informal.) □ BILL: *Well, we're off to the party.* JANE: *Okay. Have a ball!* □ *"Have a ball!" said Mary as her roommate went out the door.*

have a bee in one's bonnet to have an idea or a thought remain in one's mind; to have an obsession. (The *bee* is a thought that is inside one's head, which is inside a bonnet.) □ *I have a bee in my bonnet that you'd be a good manager.* □ *I had a bee in my bonnet about swimming. I couldn't stop wanting to go swimming.*

have a big mouth to be a gossiper; to be a person who tells secrets. (The *mouth* is too loud or is heard by too many people.) □ *Mary has a big mouth. She told Bob what I was getting him for his birthday.* □ *You shouldn't say things like that about people all the time. Everyone will say you have a big mouth.*

have a bone to pick (with someone) to have a matter to discuss with someone; to have something to argue about with someone. □ *Hey, Bill. I've got a bone to pick with you. Where is the money you owe me?* □ *I had a bone to pick with her, but she was so sweet that I forgot about it.* □ *You always have a bone to pick.*

have a brush with something to have a brief contact with something; to have an experience with something. (Especially with the law. Sometimes a close brush.) □ *Ann had a close brush with the law. She was nearly arrested for speeding.* □ *When I was younger, I had a brush with scarlet fever, but I got over it.*

have a buzz on to be tipsy or alcohol intoxicated. (Slang. *Have got* can replace *have.*) □ *Todd has a buzz on and is giggling a lot.* □ *Both of them had a buzz on by the end of the celebration.*

have a chip on one's shoulder to be tempting someone to have an argument or a fight. (An invitation to a fight can be expressed as an invitation to knock a chip off someone's shoulder, which would be sufficient provocation for a fight. A person who goes about seeming to have such a chip is always daring someone to fight or argue.) □ *Who are you mad at? You always seem to have a chip on your shoulder.* □ *John has had a chip on his shoulder ever since he got his speeding ticket.*

have a close call See the following entry.

have a close shave AND **have a close call** to have a narrow escape from something dangerous. □ *What a close shave I had! I nearly fell off the roof when I was working there.* □ *I almost got struck by a speeding car. It was a close shave.*

have a familiar ring [for a story or an explanation] to sound familiar. □ *Your excuse has a familiar ring. Have you done this before?* □ *This term paper has a familiar ring. I think it has been copied.*

Have a go at it. Give it a try.; Try your hand at it. □ ALICE: *Wow! This is fun!* BOB: *Can I have a go at it?* □ TOM: *I am having a good time painting this fence. It takes a lot of skill.* HENRY: *It does look challenging.* TOM: *Here, have a go at it.* HENRY: *Thanks!*

Have a good day. See *Have a nice day.*

have a good head on one's shoulders to have common sense; to be sensible and intelligent. □ *Mary doesn't do well in school, but she's got a good head on her shoulders.* □ *John has a good head on his shoulders and can be depended on to give good advice.*

Have a good one. See *Have a nice day.*

Have a good time. Enjoy yourself in what you are about to do. □ BILL: *I'm leaving for the party now.* FATHER: *Have a good time.* □ SUE: *Tonight is the formal dance at the Palmer House, and I'm going.* MARY: *Have a good time. I'm watching television right here.*

Have a good trip. AND **Have a nice trip.** Have a pleasant journey. (Compare to *Have a safe trip.* This phrase avoids references to safety.) □ *As Sue stepped onto the plane, someone in a uniform said, "Have a nice trip."* □ *"Have a good trip," said Bill, waving his good-byes.*

have a green thumb to have the ability to grow plants well. (Not literal.) □ *Just look at Mr. Simpson's garden. He has a green thumb.* □ *My mother has a green thumb when it comes to houseplants.*

have a heart **1.** to be compassionate; to be generous and forgiving; to have an especially compassionate heart. □ *Oh, have a heart! Give me some help!* □ *If Ann had a heart, she'd have made us feel more welcome.* **2.** Please be kind and compassionate. (Usually **Have a heart!**) □ TEACHER: *Things are looking bad for your grade in this class, Bill.* BILL: *Gee, have a heart! I*

work hard. □ *"Have a heart, officer. I wasn't going all that fast," pleaded Alice.*

have a heart of gold to be generous, sincere, and friendly. (Not literal. To have a wonderful character and personality.) □ *Mary is such a lovely person. She has a heart of gold.* □ *You think Tom stole your watch? Impossible! He has a heart of gold.*

have a heart of stone to be cold, unfeeling, and unfriendly. (Not literal.) □ *Sally has a heart of stone. She never even smiles.* □ *The villain in the play had a heart of stone. He was an ideal villain.*

have a lot going (for one) to have many things working to one's benefit. □ *Jane is so lucky. She has a lot going for her.* □ *She has a good job and a nice family. She has a lot going.*

have a low boiling point to anger easily. □ *Be nice to John. He's upset and has a low boiling point.* □ *Mr. Jones sure has a low boiling point. I hardly said anything, and he got angry.*

Have a nice day. AND **Have a good day.; Have a good one.** an expression said when parting or saying good-bye. (This is now quite hackneyed, and many people do not like to hear it.) □ CLERK: *Thank you.* TOM: *Thank you.* CLERK: *Have a nice day.* □ BOB: *See you, man!* JOHN: *Bye, Bob. Have a good one!*

Have a nice flight. Please enjoy your flight. (Said when wishing someone well on an airplane trip. Often said by airline personnel to their passengers.) □ CLERK: *Here's your ticket, sir. Have a nice flight.* FRED: *Thanks.* □ *As Mary boarded the* *plane, almost everyone said, "Have a nice flight."*

Have a nice trip. See *Have a good trip.*

have a price on one's head to be wanted by the authorities, who have offered a reward for one's capture. (Not literal. Usually limited to western and gangster movies. As if the presentation of one's head would produce payment or reward.) □ *We captured a thief who had a price on his head, and the sheriff gave us the reward.* □ *The crook was so mean, he turned in his own brother, who had a price on his head.*

Have a safe journey. See the following entry.

Have a safe trip. AND **Have a safe journey.** I hope that your journey is safe.; Be careful and assure that your journey is safe. □ BILL: *Well, we're off for London.* SALLY: *Have a safe trip.* □ BILL: *You're driving all the way to San Francisco?* BOB: *Yes, indeed.* BILL: *Well, have a safe trip.*

have a scrape (with someone or something) to come into contact with someone or something; to have a small battle with someone or something. □ *I had a scrape with the county sheriff.* □ *John and Bill had a scrape, but they are friends again now.*

have a soft spot in one's heart for someone or something to be fond of someone or something. □ *John has a soft spot in his heart for Mary.* □ *I have soft spot in my heart for chocolate cake.*

have a spaz to get angry or hysterical. (Slang. Teens and collegiate.) □ *If my dad hears about this, he'll have a spaz.* □ *The teacher had a spaz when I came in so late.*

have a sweet tooth to desire to eat many sweet foods—especially candy and pastries. (As if a certain tooth had a craving for sweets.) □ *I have a sweet tooth, and if I don't watch it, I'll really get fat.* □ *John eats candy all the time. He must have a sweet tooth.*

have a weakness for someone or something to be unable to resist someone or something; to be fond of someone or something; to be (figuratively) powerless against someone or something. □ *I have a weakness for chocolate.* □ *John has a weakness for Mary. I think he's in love.*

have an ax to grind to have something to complain about. □ *Tom, I need to talk to you. I have an ax to grind.* □ *Bill and Bob went into the other room to argue. They had an ax to grind.*

have an eye out (for someone or something) AND **keep an eye out (for someone or something)** to watch for the arrival or appearance of someone or something. (The *an* can be replaced by *one's*.) □ *Please try to have an eye out for the bus.* □ *Keep an eye out for rain.* □ *Have your eye out for a raincoat on sale.* □ *Okay. I'll keep my eye out.*

have an in (with someone) to have a way to request a special favor from someone; to have influence with someone. (The *in* is a noun.) □ *Do you have an in with the mayor? I have to ask him a favor.* □ *Sorry, I don't have an in, but I know someone who does.*

have an itching palm See the following entry.

175

have an itchy palm AND **have an itching palm** to be in need of a tip; to tend to ask for tips; to crave money. (As if placing money in the palm would stop the itching.) □ *All the waiters at that restaurant have itchy palms.* □ *The cab driver was troubled by an itching palm. Since he refused to carry my bags, I gave him nothing.*

Have at it. Start doing it.; Start eating it. □ JOHN: *Here's your hamburger. Have at it.* JANE: *Thanks. Where's the mustard?* □ JOHN: *Did you notice? The driveway needs sweeping.* JANE: *Here's the broom. Have at it.*

have bats in one's belfry to be slightly crazy. (The *belfry*—a bell tower—represents one's head or brains. The *bats* represent an infestation of confusion.) □ *Poor old Tom has bats in his belfry.* □ *Don't act so silly, John. People will think you have bats in your belfry.*

have clean hands to be guiltless. (As if the guilty person would have bloody hands.) □ *Don't look at me. I have clean hands.* □ *The police took him in, but let him go again because he had clean hands.*

have dibs on something AND **put one's dibs on something** to reserve something for oneself; to claim something for oneself. □ *I have dibs on the last piece of cake.* □ *John put his dibs on the last piece again. It isn't fair.*

have egg on one's face to be embarrassed because of an error that is obvious to everyone. (Rarely literal.) □ *Bob has egg on his face because he wore jeans to the party and everyone else wore formal clothing.* □ *John was completely wrong about the weather for the picnic. It snowed! Now he has egg on his face.*

have eyes bigger than one's stomach to have a desire for more food than one could possibly eat. □ *I know I have eyes bigger than my stomach, so I won't take a lot of food.*

have eyes in the back of one's head to seem to be able to sense what is going on outside of one's vision. (Not literal.) □ *My teacher seems to have eyes in the back of her head.* □ *My teacher doesn't need to have eyes in the back of his head. He watches us very carefully.*

have feet of clay [for a strong person] to have a defect of character. □ *All human beings have feet of clay. No one is perfect.* □ *Sally was popular and successful. She was nearly fifty before she learned that she, too, had feet of clay.*

have foot-in-mouth disease to embarrass oneself through a silly blunder. (This is a parody on *foot-and-mouth disease* or *hoof-and-mouth disease*, which affects cattle and deer.) □ *I'm sorry I keep saying stupid things. I guess I have foot-in-mouth disease.* □ *Yes, you really have foot-in-mouth disease tonight.*

Have fun. Have a good time.; Have an enjoyable time. □ BILL: *I'm leaving for the picnic now.* MOTHER: *Have fun.* □ BILL: *Good-bye.* BOB: *Good-bye, Bill.* FRED: *Bye, Bill. Have fun.*

have good vibes to have good feelings (about someone or something). (Slang. *Have got* can replace *have.*) □ *I've got good vibes about Alice.* □ *I know everything will go all right. I have good vibes.*

have it all together to be mentally and physically organized; to be of sound mind. (Slang. *Have got* can replace *have*.) □ *I don't have it all together today.* □ *Try me again later when I have it all together.*

have it out (with someone) to settle something with someone by fighting or arguing. □ *Finally, John had it out with Carl, and now they are speaking to one another again.* □ *Elaine had been at odds with Sam for a long time. She finally decided to have it out.*

Have it your way. It will be done your way.; You will get your way. (Usually shows irritation on the part of the speaker.) □ TOM: *I would like to do this room in blue.* SUE: *I prefer yellow. I really do.* TOM: *Okay. Have it your way.* □ JANE: *Let's get a pie. Apple would be good.* BOB: *No, if we are going to buy a whole pie, I want a cherry pie, not apple.* JANE: *Oh, have it your way!*

have mixed feelings (about someone or something) to be uncertain about someone or something. □ *I have mixed feelings about Bob. Sometimes I think he likes me; other times I don't.* □ *I have mixed feelings about my trip to England. I love the people, but the climate upsets me.* □ *Yes, I also have mixed feelings.*

have money to burn to have lots of money; to have more money than one needs; to have enough money that some can be wasted. □ *Look at the way Tom buys things. You'd think he had money to burn.* □ *If I had money to burn, I'd just put it in the bank.*

have one's back to the wall to be in a defensive position. □ *He'll have to*

give in. He has his back to the wall. □ *How can I bargain when I've got my back to the wall?*

have one's cake and eat it too AND **eat one's cake and have it too** to enjoy both having something and using it up. (Usually stated in the negative.) □ *Tom wants to have his cake and eat it too. It can't be done.* □ *Don't buy a car if you want to walk and stay healthy. You can't eat your cake and have it too.*

have one's ear to the ground AND **keep one's ear to the ground** to listen carefully, hoping to get advance warning of something. (Not literal. As if one were listening for the sound of distant horses' hoofs pounding on the ground.) □ *John had his ear to the ground, hoping to find out about new ideas in computers.* □ *His boss told him to keep his ear to the ground so that he'd be the first to know of a new idea.*

have one's finger in the pie to be involved in something. (Not literal.) □ *I like to have my finger in the pie so I can make sure things go my way.* □ *As long as John has his finger in the pie, things will happen slowly.*

have one's hand in the till to be stealing money from a company or an organization. (The *till* is a cash box or drawer.) □ *Mr. Jones had his hand in the till for years before he was caught.* □ *I think that the new clerk has her hand in the till. There is cash missing every morning.*

have one's hands full (with someone or something) to be busy or totally occupied with someone or something. □ *I have my hands full with my three children.* □ *You have your hands* full with the store. □ We both have our hands full.

have one's hands tied to be prevented from doing something. □ I can't help you. I was told not to, so I have my hands tied. □ John can help. He doesn't have his hands tied.

have one's head in the clouds to be unaware of what is going on. □ "Bob, do you have your head in the clouds?" said the teacher. □ She walks around all day with her head in the clouds. She must be in love.

have one's heart in one's mouth to feel strongly emotional about someone or something. □ "Gosh, Mary," said John, "I have my heart in my mouth whenever I see you." □ My heart is in my mouth whenever I hear the national anthem.

have one's heart set on something to be desiring and expecting something. □ Jane has her heart set on going to London. □ Bob will be disappointed. He had his heart set on going to college this year. □ His heart is set on it.

have one's nose in a book to be reading a book; to read books all the time. □ Bob has his nose in a book every time I see him. □ His nose is always in a book. He never gets any exercise.

have one's tail between one's legs to be frightened or cowed. (Refers to a frightened dog. Also used literally with dogs.) □ John seems to lack courage. Whenever there is an argument, he has his tail between his legs. □ You can tell that the dog is frightened because it has its tail between its legs.

have one's words stick in one's throat to be so overcome by emotion that one can hardly speak. □ I sometimes have my words stick in my throat. □ John said that he never had his words stick in his throat.

have other fish to fry to have other things to do; to have more important things to do. (Other can be replaced by bigger, better, more important, etc. Not used literally.) □ I can't take time for your problem. I have other fish to fry. □ I won't waste time on your question. I have bigger fish to fry.

have someone dead to rights to have proven someone unquestionably guilty. □ The police burst in on the robbers while they were at work. They had the robbers dead to rights. □ All right, Tom! I've got you dead to rights! Get your hands out of the cookie jar.

have someone in one's pocket to have control over someone. □ Don't worry about the mayor. She'll cooperate. I've got her in my pocket. □ John will do just what I tell him. I've got him and his brother in my pocket.

have someone or something in one's hands to have control of or responsibility for someone or something. (Have can be replaced with leave or put.) □ You have the whole project in your hands. □ The boss put the whole project in your hands. □ I have to leave the baby in your hands while I go to the doctor.

have something at hand See the following entry.

have something at one's fingertips AND **have something at hand** to have something within (one's) reach. (Have can be replaced with keep.) □ I have a dictionary at my fingertips. □ I try to have everything I need at hand. □ I keep my medicine at my fingertips.

have something hanging over one's head to have something bothering or worrying one; to have a deadline worrying one. (Also used literally.) □ *I keep worrying about getting drafted. I hate to have something like that hanging over my head.* □ *I have a history paper that is hanging over my head.*

have something in stock to have merchandise available and ready for sale. □ *Do you have extra large sizes in stock?* □ *Of course, we have all sizes and colors in stock.*

have something out to have something, such as a tooth, stone, tumor, removed surgically. □ *You are going to have to have that tumor out.* □ *I don't want to have my tooth out!*

have something to spare to have more than enough of something. □ *Ask John for some firewood. He has firewood to spare.* □ *Do you have any candy to spare?*

have the right-of-way to possess the legal right to occupy a particular space on a public roadway. □ *I had a traffic accident yesterday, but it wasn't my fault. I had the right-of-way.* □ *Don't pull out onto a highway if you don't have the right-of-way.*

have the shoe on the other foot to experience the opposite situation (from a previous situation). (Also with *be* instead of *have*.) □ *I used to be a student, and now I'm the teacher. Now I have the shoe on the other foot.* □ *You were mean to me when you thought I was cheating. Now that I have caught you cheating, the shoe is on the other foot.*

have the time of one's life to have a very good time; to have the most ex-citing time in one's life. □ *What a great party! I had the time of my life.* □ *We went to Florida last winter and had the time of our lives.*

have too many irons in the fire to be doing too many things at once. (As if a blacksmith had allowed more things to get hot in the fire than could possibly be dealt with.) □ *Tom had too many irons in the fire and missed some important deadlines.* □ *It's better if you don't have too many irons in the fire.*

(Have you) been keeping busy? AND **(Have you been) keeping busy?; You been keeping busy?** a vague greeting asking about how someone has been occupied. □ TOM: *Been keeping busy?* BILL: *Yeah. Too busy.* □ SUE: *Hi, Fred. Have you been keeping busy?* FRED: *Not really. Just doing what I have to.*

(Have you been) keeping busy? See the previous entry.

(Have you) been keeping cool? AND **(Have you been) keeping cool?; You been keeping cool?** an inquiry about how someone is surviving very hot weather. □ TOM: *What do you think of this hot weather? Been keeping cool?* SUE: *No, I like this weather just as it is.* □ MARY: *Keeping cool?* BILL: *Yup. Run the air-conditioning all the time.*

(Have you) been keeping out of trouble? AND **(Have you been) keeping out of trouble?; You been keeping out of trouble?** a vague greeting asking one what one has been doing. □ BOB: *Hi, Mary. Have you been keeping out of trouble?* MARY: *Yeah. And you?* BOB: *Oh, I'm getting by.* □ TOM: *Hey, man! Been keeping* *out of trouble?* BOB: *Hell, no! What are you up to?* TOM: *Nothing.*

(Have you been) keeping out of trouble? See the previous entry.

(Have you) been okay? AND **You been okay?** a vague greeting asking if one has been well. □ TOM: *Hey, man. How you doing?* BOB: *I'm okay. You been okay?* TOM: *Sure. See you!* □ MARY: *I heard you were sick.* SALLY: *Yes, but I'm better. Have you been okay?* MARY: *Oh, sure. Healthy as an ox.*

(Have you) changed your mind? AND **You changed your mind?** Have you decided to alter your decision? □ SALLY: *As of last week, they said you are leaving. Changed your mind?* BILL: *No. I'm leaving for sure.* □ TOM: *Well, have you changed your mind?* SALLY: *Absolutely not!*

have you heard? AND **did you hear?** a question used to introduce a piece of news or gossip. □ SALLY: *Hi, Mary.* MARY: *Hi. Have you heard about Tom and Sue?* SALLY: *No, what happened?* MARY: *I'll let one of them tell you.* SALLY: *Oh, come on! Tell me!* □ BOB: *Hi, Tom. What's new?* TOM: *Did you hear that they're raising taxes again?* BOB: *That's not new.*

Have you met someone? a question asked when introducing someone to someone else. (The question need not be answered. The *someone* is usually a person's name.) □ TOM: *Hello, Mary. Have you met Fred?* MARY: *Hello, Fred. Glad to meet you.* FRED: *Glad to meet you, Mary.* □ TOM: *Hey, Mary! Good to see you. Have you met Fred?* MARY: *No, I don't believe I have. Hello, Fred. Glad to meet you.* FRED: *Hello, Mary.*

Haven't I seen you somewhere before? AND **Haven't we met before?** a polite way of trying to meet someone. □ BOB: *Hi. Haven't I seen you somewhere before?* MARY: *I hardly think so.* □ BILL (moving toward Jane): *Haven't we met before?* JANE (moving away from Bill): *No way!*

Haven't we met before? See the previous entry.

He laughs best who laughs last. See the following entry.

He who laughs last, laughs longest. AND **He laughs best who laughs last.** Whoever succeeds in making the last move or pulling the last trick has the most enjoyment. (Proverb.) □ *Bill had pulled many silly tricks on Tom. Finally Tom pulled a very funny trick on Bill and said, "He who laughs last, laughs longest." □ Bill pulled another, even bigger trick on Tom, and said, laughing, "He laughs best who laughs last."*

head and shoulders above someone or something [to be] clearly superior to someone or something. (Often with *stand,* as in the examples.) □ *This wine is head and shoulders above that one.* □ *John stands head and shoulders above Bob.*

head back (some place) to start moving back to some place. □ *I walked to the end of the street and then headed back home.* □ *This is far enough. Let's head back.*

head someone or something off to intercept and divert someone or something. □ *I think I can head her off before she reaches the police station.* T *I hope we can head off trouble.* □ *We can head it off. Have no fear.*

head something up 1. to get something pointed in the right direction. (Especially a herd of cattle or a group of covered wagons.) □ *Head those wagons up—we're moving out.* ⊤ *Sheep dogs often head up the herds.* 2. to be in charge of something; to be the head of some organization. □ *I was asked to head the new committee up for the first year.* ⊤ *Will you head up the committee for me?*

Heads up! Look around! There is danger! □ *The load the crane was lifting swung over near the foreman. "Heads up!" shouted one of the workers, and the foreman just missed getting bonked on the head.* □ *Boxes were falling everywhere as the boat rolled back and forth in the storm. "Heads up!" called a sailor, and a big case of marmalade just missed my left shoulder.*

heal over [for the surface of a wound] to heal. □ *The wound healed over very quickly, and there was very little scarring.* □ *I hope it will heal over without having to be stitched.*

heal up [for an injury] to heal. □ *The cut healed up in no time.* □ *My pulled muscle took two weeks to heal up.*

heap something up to make something into a pile. □ *He heaped the mashed potatoes up on my plate, because he thought I wanted lots.* ⊤ *Heap up the leaves in the corner of the yard.*

heap something (up)on someone or something 1. to pile something up on someone or something. (*Upon* is formal and less commonly used than *on*.) □ *Please don't heap so much trouble upon me!* □ *Wally heaped leaves on the flower bed.* 2. to give someone too much of something, such as homework, praise, criticism, etc. (Figurative. *Upon* is formal and less commonly used than *on*.) □ *Don't heap too much praise on her. She will get conceited.* □ *The manager heaped criticism on the workers.*

hear someone out 1. to hear all of what someone has to say. □ *Please hear me out. I have more to say.* □ *Hear him out. Don't jump to conclusions.* 2. to hear someone's side of the story. □ *Let him talk! Hear him out! Listen to his side!* ⊤ *We have to hear out everyone in this matter.*

heat up 1. to get warmer or hot. □ *It really heats up in the afternoon around here.* □ *How soon will dinner be heated up?* 2. to grow more animated or combative. □ *The debate began to heat up near the end.* □ *Their argument was heating up, and I was afraid there would be fighting.*

heavy into someone or something much concerned with someone or something; obsessed with someone or something. (Slang. Black.) □ *Freddie was heavy into auto racing and always went to the races.* □ *Sam is heavy into Mary.*

Hello. the standard, general word of greeting and the standard way to answer a telephone. (The answer to a telephone call is usually spoken with rising question intonation and written with a question mark.) □ TOM: *Hello.* SUE: *Hello, how are you?* TOM: *Fine. How are you?* □ JANE: *Hello.* ALICE: *What's up, Jane?* JANE: *Nothing much.* □ RACHEL: *Hello?* TOM: *Is Andrew there?* RACHEL: *Just a minute.* (calling loudly) *Andrew! It's for you!*

Hell's bells (and buckets of blood)! an exclamation of anger or surprise. □ ALICE: *Your pants are torn in back.*

JOHN: *Oh, hell's bells! What will happen next?* □ BILL: *Congratulations, you just flunked calculus.* JANE: *Hell's bells and buckets of blood! What do I do now?*

help out some place to help [with the chores] in a particular place. □ *Would you be able to help out in the kitchen?* □ *Sally is downtown, helping out at the shop.*

help out (with something) to help with a particular chore. □ *Would you please help out with the dishes?* □ *I have to help out at home on the weekends.* □ *I'll come over and help out before the party.*

help someone back (to something) to help someone return to something or some place. □ *The ushers helped him back to his seat.* □ *When she returned, I helped her back.*

help someone off with something to help someone take off an article of clothing. □ *Would you please help me off with my coat?* □ *We helped the children off with their boots and put their coats in the hall.*

help (someone) out to help someone do something; to help someone with a problem. □ *I am trying to raise this window. Can you help me out?* ⊤ *I'm always happy to help out a friend.* □ *This calculus assignment is impossible. Can you help out?*

Help yourself. Please take what you want without asking permission. □ SALLY: *Can I have one of these doughnuts?* BILL: *Help yourself.* □ *Mother led the little troop of my friends to the kitchen table, which was covered with cups of juice and plates of cookies. "Help yourself," she said.*

Here! Stop that!; No more of that! □ BOB: *You say that again and I'll bash you one.* BILL: *You and what army?* FATHER: *Here! That's enough!* □ *"Here! Stop that fighting, you two," shouted the school principal.*

Here we go again. We are going to experience the same thing again.; We are going to hear about or discuss the same thing again. □ JOHN: *Now, I would like to discuss your behavior in class yesterday.* BILL (to himself): *Here we go again.* □ FRED: *We must continue our discussion of the Wilson project.* SUE: *Here we go again.* FRED: *What's that?* SUE: *Nothing.*

Here's looking at you. See *Bottoms up.*

Here's mud in your eye. See *Bottoms up.*

Here's to you. See *Bottoms up.*

hey 1. a word used to get someone's attention; a sentence opener that catches someone's attention. (Informal. Often **Hey!** Words such as this often use intonation to convey the connotation of the sentence that is to follow. The brief intonation pattern accompanying the word may indicate sarcasm, disagreement, caution, consolation, sternness, etc. See also *say.*) □ BILL: *Hey, Tom. Over here. I'm over here by the tree.* TOM: *Hi, Bill. What's up?* □ TOM: *Hey, who are you?* MARY: *Who do you think, Tom?* □ *"Hey, let's go for a ride!" cried little Billy.* □ BOB: *Hey, stop that!* ALICE: *Gee! What did I do?* □ *"Hey, look out!" warned Henry.* □ FRED: *Hey, come over here.* BOB: *What do you want?* □ FRED: *Hey, come here, Bob!* BOB: *What's up?* **2.** Hello! (A southern U.S. greeting.) □ MARY: *Hey, Bill.* BILL: *Hey, Mary.*

What's up? □ JANE: *Hey!* MARY: *Hey!* JANE: *You okay?* MARY: *Wonderful!*

Hi! *Hello!* (Very common.) □ *"Hi! What's cooking?" asked Tom.* □ BILL: *Hi, Tom. How are you?* TOM: *Fine. How are you doing?* □ FRED: *Hi, old buddy. Give me some skin.* TOM: *Good to see you, man.*

hide one's head in the sand See *bury one's head in the sand.*

hide one's light under a bushel to conceal one's good ideas or talents. (Biblical.) □ *Jane has some good ideas, but she doesn't speak very often. She hides her light under a bushel.* □ *Don't hide your light under a bushel. Share your gifts with other people.*

hide out (from someone or something) to hide oneself so that one cannot be found by someone or something. □ *Max was hiding out from the police in Detroit.* □ *Lefty is hiding out too.*

hide someone or something away (some place) to conceal someone or something somewhere. (*Someone* includes *oneself.*) □ *Please hide Randy away where no one can find him.* □ *Rachel hid the cake away, hoping to save it for dessert.* ⊤ *Mary hid away the candy so the kids wouldn't eat it all.* □ *He hid himself away in his study until Mrs. Bracknell had gone.*

high man on the totem pole the person at the top of the hierarchy; the person in charge of an organization. (See also *low man on the totem pole.*) □ *I don't want to talk to a secretary. I demand to talk to the high man on the totem pole.* □ *Who's in charge around here? Who's high man on the totem pole?*

hike something up to raise something, such as prices, interest rates, a skirt, pants legs, etc. □ *The grocery store is always hiking prices up.* ⊤ *She hiked up her skirt so she could wade across the creek.*

hinge (up)on someone or something to depend on someone or something; to depend on what someone or something does. (*Upon* is formal and less commonly used than *on.*) □ *The success of the project hinges upon you and how well you do your job.* □ *It all hinges on the weather.*

hire someone away (from someone or something) [for one] to get someone to quit working for someone or something and begin working for one. □ *We hired Elaine away from her previous employer, and now she wants to go back.* ⊤ *The new bank hired away all the tellers from the old bank.* □ *They tried to hire them all away.*

hit a happy medium See *strike a happy medium.*

hit a snag to run into a problem. □ *We've hit a snag with the building project.* □ *I stopped working on the roof when I hit a snag.*

hit a sour note See *strike a sour note.*

hit back (at someone or something) to strike someone or something back. □ *Tom hit Fred, and Fred hit back at Tom.* □ *I have to hit back when someone hits me.*

hit bottom to reach the lowest or worst point. □ *Our profits have hit bottom. This is our worst year ever.* □ *When my life hit bottom, I began to feel much better. I knew that if there was going to be any change, it would be for the better.*

hit it off (with someone) to start a good and friendly relationship with someone from the first meeting. □ *I really hit it off with my new boss.* □ *From the moment I met her, we really hit it off.* □ *They hit it off with each other from the start.*

hit someone between the eyes to become completely apparent; to surprise or impress someone. (Also with *right.* Also used literally.) □ *Suddenly, it hit me right between the eyes. John and Mary were in love.* □ *Then — as he was talking — the exact nature of the evil plan hit me between the eyes.*

hit (someone) like a ton of bricks to surprise, startle, or shock someone. □ *Suddenly, the truth hit me like a ton of bricks.* □ *The sudden tax increase hit like a ton of bricks. Everyone became angry.*

hit someone (up) for something to ask someone for the loan of money or for some other favor. (Colloquial.) □ *The tramp hit me up for a dollar.* □ *My brother hit me for a couple of hundred bucks.*

hit something off to begin something; to launch an event. □ *The mayor hit the fair off by giving a brief address.* ⊤ *She hit off the fair with a speech.*

hit the books AND **pound the books** to study hard. (Slang.) □ *I spent the weekend pounding the books.* □ *I gotta go home and hit the books.*

hit the bricks AND **hit the pavement** **1.** to start walking; to go into the streets. (Slang.) □ *I have a long way to go. I'd better hit the bricks.* □ *Go on! Hit the pavement! Get going!* **2.** to go out on strike. □ *The workers hit the pavement on Friday and haven't*

been back on the job since. □ *Agree to our demands, or we hit the bricks.*

hit the bull's-eye **1.** to hit the center area of a circular target. (Literal.) □ *The archer hit the bull's-eye three times in a row.* □ *I didn't hit the bull's-eye even once.* **2.** to achieve the goal perfectly. □ *Your idea really hit the bull's-eye. Thank you!* □ *Jill has a lot of insight. She knows how to hit the bull's-eye.*

hit the fan to become publicly known; to become a scandal. (Slang. From the phrase "when the shit hit the fan.") □ *I wasn't even in the country when it hit the fan.* □ *It hit the fan, and within ten minutes the press had spread it all over the world.*

hit the nail (right) on the head to do exactly the right thing; to do something in the most effective and efficient way. □ *You've spotted the flaw, Sally. You hit the nail on the head.* □ *Bob doesn't say much, but every now and then he hits the nail right on the head.*

hit the pavement See *hit the bricks.*

hit the spot to be exactly right; to be refreshing. □ *This cool drink really hits the spot.* □ *That was a delicious meal, dear. It hit the spot.*

hit (up)on someone or something **1.** to discover someone or something. □ *I think I have hit upon something. There is a lever you have to press in order to open this cabinet.* □ *I hit on Tom in an amateur play production. I offered him a job in my nightclub immediately.* **2.** to strike or pound on someone or something. (Colloquial. *Upon* is formal and less commonly used than *on.*) □ *Jeff hit upon the* *mugger over and over.* □ *I hit on the radio until it started working again.*

hitch a ride See *thumb a ride.*

Hiya! *Hello!* (Very informal. From *Hi to you.*) □ HENRY: *Hiya, chum. What are you doing?* BILL: *Nothing.* □ JOHN: *Hey, man! How's by you?* BOB: *Hiya! Nothing much.*

hold back (on something) to withhold something; to give only a limited amount. □ *Hold back on the gravy. I'm on a diet.* □ *That's enough. Hold back. Save some for the others.*

Hold everything! Stop everything!; Everyone, stop! □ *"Hold everything!" cried Mary. "There's a squirrel loose in the kitchen!"* □ BILL: *Hold everything! Let's try this part again.* BOB: *But we've already rehearsed it four times.*

hold forth (on someone or something) to speak at great length about someone or something. □ *Sadie held forth on the virtues of home cooking.* □ *Sharon is holding forth, and everyone is paying close attention.*

Hold it! Stop right there. □ TOM: *Hold it!* MARY: *What's wrong?* TOM: *You almost stepped on my contact lens.* □ BILL: *Hold it!* BOB: *What is it?* BILL: *Sorry. For a minute, that stick looked like a snake.*

hold off ((from) doing something) to avoid doing something; to postpone doing something. □ *Can you hold off from buying a new car for another few months?* □ *I will hold off firing him until next week.*

hold on 1. to wait. □ *Hold on a minute! Let me catch up!* □ *Hold on and wait till I get there.* □ *Hold on. I'll call her to the phone.* **2.** to be patient. □ *Just hold on. Everything will work out*

in good time. □ *If you will just hold on, everything will probably be all right.* **3.** Stop right there!; Wait a minute! (Usually **Hold on (a minute)!** or **Hold on for a minute!** *Minute* can be replaced by *moment, second,* or other time periods.) □ BOB: *Hold on, Tom.* TOM: *What?* BOB: *I want to talk to you.* □ *"Hold on!" hollered Tom. "You're running off with my shopping cart!"*

hold on (to someone or something) See *hang on (to someone or something).*

Hold on to your hat! See *Hang on to your hat!*

hold one's end (of the bargain) up AND **hold up one's end (of the bargain)** to do one's part as agreed; to attend to one's responsibilities as agreed. □ *Tom has to learn to cooperate. He must hold up his end of the bargain.* □ *If you don't hold your end up, the whole project will fail.*

hold one's ground See *stand one's ground.*

hold one's head up AND **hold up one's head** to have one's self-respect; to retain or display one's dignity. □ *I've done nothing wrong. I can hold my head up in public.* □ *I'm so embarrassed and ashamed. I'll never be able to hold up my head again.*

hold one's own to do as well as anyone else. □ *I can hold my own in a footrace any day.* □ *She was unable to hold her own, and she had to quit.*

hold one's peace to remain silent. □ *Bill was unable to hold his peace any longer. "Don't do it!" he cried.* □ *Quiet, John. Hold your peace for a little while longer.*

hold one's temper See *keep one's temper.*

hold one's tongue to refrain from speaking; to refrain from saying something unpleasant. (Not literal.) ☐ *I felt like scolding her, but I held my tongue.* ☐ *Hold your tongue, John. You can't talk to me that way.*

hold out to survive; to last. ☐ *I don't know how long we can hold out.* ☐ *They can probably hold out for another day or two.*

hold out (against someone or something) to continue one's defense against someone or something. ☐ *We can hold out against them only a little while longer.* ☐ *Dave can hold out forever.*

hold out (for someone or something) to strive to wait for someone or something. ☐ *I will hold out for someone who can do the job better than your last suggestion.* ☐ *I want to hold out for a better offer.*

hold out the olive branch to offer to end a dispute and be friendly; to offer reconciliation. (The *olive branch* is a symbol of peace and reconciliation. Biblical.) ☐ *Jill was the first to hold out the olive branch after our argument.* ☐ *I always try to hold out the olive branch to someone I have hurt. Life is too short for a person to bear grudges for very long.*

Hold, please. See *Hold the wire(, please).*

hold someone or something down 1. to keep someone, something, or some creature down. ☐ *The heavy beam held him down, and he could not rise.* ☐ *The hunter held the animal down until the porters arrived.* ☐ *Hold him down until I get out my handcuffs.*

2. to prevent someone or something from advancing. ☐ *I had a disability that held me down in life.* ☐ *The company had a lot of debt that held it down, even in prosperous times.*

hold someone or something off 1. to make someone or something wait. ☐ *I know a lot of people are waiting to see me. Hold them off for a while longer.* ⊤ *See what you can do to hold off the reporters.* **2.** AND **keep someone or something off** to stave someone or something off. ☐ *Tom was trying to rob us, but we managed to hold him off.* ⊤ *We held off the attackers.* ⊤ *I couldn't keep off the reporters any longer.*

hold someone or something out (of something) 1. to keep someone or something out of something. ☐ *We held the kids out of the party room as long as we could.* ☐ *We couldn't hold them out any longer.* **2.** to set someone or something aside from the rest; to prevent someone or a group from participating. ☐ *Her parents held her out of sports because of her health.* ☐ *The school board held the team out of competition as punishment for something.* ⊤ *They held out every player.*

hold someone or something over to keep a performer or performance for more performances. (Because the performer or performance is a success.) ☐ *The manager held Julie over for a week because she was so well received.* ☐ *They held our act over too.*

hold someone or something up 1. to keep someone or something upright. ☐ *Johnny is falling asleep. Please hold him up until I prepare the bed.* ☐ *Hold the window up while I prop it open.* **2.** to rob someone or a group. ☐ *Some punk tried to hold me up.* ⊤ *The* *mild-looking man held up the bank and shot a teller.* **3.** to delay someone or something. □ *Driving the kids to school held me up.* □ *We were stuck in traffic, and I couldn't see what was holding us up.* T *An accident on Main Street held up traffic for thirty minutes.*

hold something out (to someone) to offer something to someone. □ *I held an offer of immunity out to her.* T *I held out an offer of immunity from prosecution to her, but she would not cooperate.* T *The court held out an offer of leniency, but the defendant turned it down.*

hold the fort to take care of a place, such as a store or one's home. (From western movies.) □ *I'm going next door to visit Mrs. Jones. You stay here and hold the fort.* □ *You should open the store at eight o'clock and hold the fort until I get there at ten o'clock.*

Hold the line(, please). See the following entry.

Hold the wire(, please). AND **Hold, please.; Hold the line(, please).; Please hold.** Please wait on the telephone and do not hang up. (A phrase in use before telephone "hold" circuitry was in wide use.) □ BILL: *Hold the wire, please.* (turning to Tom) *Tom, the phone's for you.* TOM: *Be right there.* □ RACHEL: *Do you wish to speak to Mr. Jones or Mr. Franklin?* HENRY: *Jones.* RACHEL: *Thank you. Hold the line, please.* □ SUE: *Good afternoon, Acme Motors, hold please.* (click) BILL (hanging up): *That makes me so mad!*

hold true [for something] to be true; [for something] to remain true. □ *Does this rule hold true all the time?* □ *Yes, it holds true no matter what.*

hold up (for someone or something) to wait; to stop and wait for someone or something. □ *Hold up for Wallace. He's running hard to catch up to us.* □ *Hold up a minute. There may be someone better.*

hold up (on someone or something) to delay or postpone further action on someone or something. □ *Hold up on the project, would you?* □ *We need to hold up for a while longer.*

hold up one's end (of the bargain) See *hold one's end (of the bargain) up.*

hold up one's head See *hold one's head up.*

Hold your horses! Slow down! Don't be so eager! □ MARY: *Come on, Sally, let's get going!* SALLY: *Oh, hold your horses! Don't be in such a rush!* □ *"Hold your horses!" said Fred to the herd of small boys trying to get into the station wagon.*

Hold your tongue! You have said enough!; You have said enough rude things. □ BILL: *You're seeing Tom a lot, aren't you? You must be in love.* JANE: *Hold your tongue, Bill Franklin!* □ *After listening to the tirade against him for nearly four minutes, Tom cried out, "Hold your tongue!"*

hole in one 1. an instance of hitting a golf ball into a hole in only one try. (From the game of golf.) □ *John made a hole in one yesterday.* □ *I've never gotten a hole in one.* **2.** an instance of succeeding the first time. (Figurative. From sense 1.) □ *It worked the first time I tried it — a hole in one.* □ *Bob got a hole in one on that sale. A lady walked in the door, and he sold her a car in five minutes.*

hole up to hide (somewhere). (Slang.)
□ *Lefty wanted to hole up some-where till things cooled down.* □ *I just want to hole up until the whole matter is settled.*

hollow something out to make the inside of something hollow. □ *Martha hollowed the book out and put her money inside.* T *She hollowed out a book.*

home in (on someone or something) to aim directly at someone or something. □ *She came into the room and homed in on the chocolate cake.* □ *She saw the cake and homed in.*

honor someone's check to accept someone's personal check. □ *The clerk at the store wouldn't honor my check. I had to pay cash.* □ *The bank didn't honor your check when I tried to deposit it. Please give me cash.*

hook in(to something) to connect into something. □ *We will hook into the water main tomorrow morning.* □ *We dug the pipes up and hooked in.*

hook someone or something up (to someone or something) AND **hook someone or something up (with someone or something)** to attach someone or something to someone or something. (*Someone* includes one-self.*) □ *The nurse hooked the patient up to the oxygen tubes.* T *They hooked up the patient with the tubes.* □ *Let's hook the dog up to the post.* □ *We hooked the dog up.* □ *She hooked her-self up to the machine and began her biofeedback session.*

hook someone or something up (with someone or something) See the previous entry.

hook something into something to connect something to something. □ *I want to hook another communication line into the system.* □ *Is it possible to hook my computer into your network?*

hook something up to set something up and get it working. (The object is to be connected to electricity, gas, water, telephone lines, etc.) □ *Will it take long to hook the telephone up?* T *As soon as they hook up the telephone, I can call my friends.*

hop in(to something) to jump into something; to get into something. □ *Hop into your car and drive over to my house.* □ *I hopped in and drove off.*

Hop to it! Get started right now! □ BILL: *I have to get these things stacked up before I go home.* BOB: *Then hop to it! You won't get it done standing around here talking.* □ *"Hurry up! Hop to it!" urged Bill. "We've got to get this done!"*

hope against all hope to have hope even when the situation appears to be hopeless. □ *We hope against all hope that she'll see the right thing to do and do it.* □ *There is little point in hoping against all hope, except that it makes you feel better.*

hopefully it is to be hoped that. (Many people object to this usage.) □ HENRY: *Hopefully, this plane will get in on time so I can make my connec-tion.* RACHEL: *I hope so, too.* □ RACHEL: *Hopefully, all the problems are solved.* HENRY: *Don't be too sure.*

horn in (on someone) to attempt to displace someone. □ *I'm going to ask Sally to the party. Don't you dare try to horn in on me!* □ *I wouldn't think of horning in.*

horse of a different color See the following entry.

horse of another color AND **horse of a different color** another matter altogether. □ *I was talking about the tree, not the bush. That's a horse of another color.* □ *Gambling is not the same as investing in the stock market. It's a horse of a different color.*

Horsefeathers! Nonsense! □ FRED: *I'm too old to walk that far.* SUE: *Horsefeathers!* □ *"Horsefeathers!" said Jane. "You're totally wrong!"*

Hot diggety (dog)! AND **Hot dog!**; **Hot ziggety!** an expression of excitement and delight. (These expressions have no meaning and no relationship to dogs.) □ RACHEL: *I got an A! Hot diggety dog!* HENRY: *Good for you!* □ BILL: *Look, here's the check! We're rich!* JANE: *Hot dog!* BILL: *What'll we spend it on?* JANE: *How about saving it?* □ TOM: *You won first place!* MARY: *Hot ziggety!*

Hot dog! See the previous entry.

hot under the collar very angry. □ *The boss was really hot under the collar when you told him you lost the contract.* □ *I get hot under the collar every time I think about it.*

Hot ziggety! See *Hot diggety (dog)!*

How about a lift? See *Could I have a lift?*

How about you? What do you think?; What is your choice?; *What about you?* □ BOB: *How are you, Bill?* BILL: *I'm okay. How about you?* BOB: *Fine, fine. Let's do lunch sometime.* □ WAITER: *Can I take your order?* BILL: *I'll have the chef's salad and*

ice tea. WAITER (turning to Sue): *How about you?* SUE: *I'll have the same.*

How (are) you doing? a standard greeting inquiry. (The entry without *are* is informal and usually pronounced "How ya doin'?") □ JANE: *How are you doing?* MARY: *I'm okay. What about you?* JANE: *Likewise.* □ SALLY: *Sue, this is my little brother, Bill.* SUE: *How are you, Bill?* BILL: *Okay. How you doing?*

How (are) you feeling? an inquiry into the state of someone's health. □ SALLY: *How are you feeling?* BILL: *Oh, better, thanks.* SALLY: *That's good.* □ BILL: *Hey, Jane! You been sick?* JANE: *Yeah.* BILL: *How you feeling?* JANE: *Not very well.*

How are you getting on? How are you managing?; How are you doing? □ JANE: *Well, Mary, how are you getting on?* MARY: *Things couldn't be better.* □ SUE: *Hey, John! How are you getting on? What's it like with all the kids out of the house?* JOHN: *Things are great, Sue!*

How can I help you? See *How may I help you?*

How can I serve you? See *How may I help you?*

How come? How did that come about?; Why? □ SALLY: *I have to go to the doctor.* MARY: *How come?* SALLY: *I'm sick, silly.* □ JOHN: *I have to leave now.* BILL: *How come?* JOHN: *I just have to, that's all.* □ HENRY: *How come you always put your right shoe on first?* RACHEL: *Do I have to have a reason for something like that?*

How could you (do something)? How could you bring yourself to do a thing like that? (No answer is expected.) □ *Looking first at the broken lamp and then at the cat, Mary shouted, "How could you do that?"* □ TOM: *Then I punched him in the nose.* RACHEL: *Oh, how could you?*

How-de-do. AND **Howdy(-do).** a greeting inquiry meaning "How do you do." (These forms never have rising question intonation, but the first instance of either one calls for a response. Familiar and folksy.) □ BILL: *Well, here's my old pal, Tom. How-de-do Tom.* TOM: *How-de-do. How you been?* □ SALLY: *How do you do, Mr. Johnson.* TOM: *Howdy, ma'am.* SALLY: *Charmed, I'm sure.*

How do you do. a standard greeting inquiry and response. (This expression never has rising question intonation, but the first instance of its use calls for a response. Sometimes the response does, in fact, explain how one is.) □ SALLY: *Hello. How do you do.* BOB: *How do you do.* □ MARY: *How do you do. So glad to meet you, Tom.* TOM: *Thank you. How are you?* MARY: *Just fine. Your brother tells me you like camping.* TOM: *Yes. Are you a camper?* MARY: *Sort of.*

How do you know? 1. How did you get that information? (A straightforward question. The stress is on *know*.) □ BILL: *The train is about to pull into the station.* SUE: *How do you know?* BILL: *I hear it.* □ FRED: *I have to apologize for the coffee. It probably isn't very good.* JANE: *How do you know?* FRED: *Well, I made it.* 2. What makes you think you are correct?; Why do you think you have enough information to make this judgment? (Contentious. The heaviest stress is on *you*.) □ BILL: *This is the best recording made all year.* BOB: *How do you know?* BILL: *Well, I guess it's just my opinion.* □ TOM: *Having a baby can be quite an ordeal.* MARY: *How do you know?* TOM: *I read a lot.*

How do you like school? a phrase used to start a conversation with a school-age person. □ BOB: *Well, Billy, how do you like school?* BILL: *I hate it.* BOB: *Too bad.* □ MARY: *How do you like school?* BOB: *It's okay. Almost everything else is better, though.*

How do you like that? 1. Do you like that?; Is that to your liking? □ TOM: *There's a bigger one over there. How do you like that?* BILL: *It's better, but not quite what I want.* □ CLERK: *Here's one without pleats. How do you like that?* FRED: *That's perfect!* 2. an expression said when administering punishment. □ *"How do you like that?" growled Tom as he punched John in the stomach.* □ BILL (being spanked): *Ouch! Ow! No!* MOTHER (spanking): *How do you like that?* BILL: *Not much.* MOTHER: *It hurts me more than it hurts you.* 3. an expression said to show surprise at someone's bad or strange behavior or at some surprising event. □ TOM (shouting at Sue): *Can it! Go away!* SUE (looking at Mary, aghast): *Well, how do you like that!* MARY: *Let's get out of here!* □ FRED: *How do you like that?* SUE: *What's the matter?* FRED: *My wallet is gone.*

How do you like this weather? a greeting inquiry. (A direct answer is expected.) □ HENRY: *Hi, Bill. How do you like this weather?* BILL: *Lovely weather for ducks. Not too good for me, though.* □ ALICE: *Gee, it's hot! How do you like this weather?* RACHEL: *You can have it!*

How dumb do you think I am? Your question is insulting. I am not stupid. (Shows agitation. An answer is not expected or desired.) □ MARY: *Are you really going to sell your new car?* SALLY: *Come on! How dumb do you think I am?* □ TOM: *Do you think you could sneak into that theater without paying?* BOB: *Good grief! How dumb do you think I am?*

How goes it (with you)? How are things going with you? □ TOM: *How goes it?* JANE: *Great! How goes it with you?* TOM: *Couldn't be better.* □ SALLY: *Greetings, Sue. How goes it?* SUE: *Okay, I guess. And you?* SALLY: *The same.*

How (have) you been? one of the standard greeting inquiries. (See also *How you is?*) □ BOB: *Hi, Fred! How have you been?* FRED: *Great! What about you?* BOB: *Fine.* □ BOB: *How you been?* SUE: *Okay, I guess. You okay?* BOB: *Yup.*

How many times do I have to tell you? a phrase admonishing someone who has forgotten instructions. □ MOTHER: *How many times do I have to tell you? Do your homework!* BILL: *Mom! I hate school!* □ MARY: *Clean this place up! How many times do I have to tell you?* BILL: *I'll do it! I'll do it!*

How may I help you? AND **How can I help you?; How can I serve you?; May I help you?; What can I do for you?** In what way can I serve you? (Usually said by shopkeepers and food service personnel. The first question is the most polite, and the last is the least polite.) □ WAITER: *How can I help you?* SUE: *I'm not ready to order yet.* □ CLERK: *May I help you?* JANE: *I'm looking for a gift for my aunt.*

How should I know? AND **Don't ask me.** I do not know. Why should I be expected to know? (Shows impatience or rudeness.) □ BILL: *Why is the orca called the killer whale?* MARY: *How should I know?* □ SALLY: *Where did I leave my glasses?* TOM: *Don't ask me.*

How will I know you? See the following entry.

How will I recognize you? AND **How will I know you?** a question asked by one of two people who have agreed to meet for the first time in a large busy place. □ TOM: *Okay, I'll meet you at the west door of the station.* MARY: *Fine. How will I recognize you?* TOM: *I'll be wearing dark glasses.* □ BILL: *I'll meet you at six. How will I recognize you?* MARY: *I'll be carrying a brown umbrella.*

How you be? See the following entry.

How you is? AND **How you be?; How you was?** *How are you?* (Usually a jocular version of *How are you?*) □ BOB: *Hey, man! How you is?* JOHN: *Great!* □ FRED: *How you was?* JOHN: *Okay. Yourself?* FRED: *I'm cool, man.*

How you was? See the previous entry.

Howdy(-do). See *How-de-do.*

How're things going? one of the standard greeting inquiries. □ BOB: *Hi, Fred! How're things going?* FRED: *Could be better. How's by you?* □ BILL: *How are things going?* MARY: *Fine, but I need to talk to you.*

How're things (with you)? a greeting inquiry. □ SALLY: *How are you?* BILL: *Fine. How are things?* □ BILL:

How are things going? MARY: *Fine. How are things with you?*

How's business? a question asked in a conversation about the state of someone's business or job. □ TOM: *Hello, Sally. How's business?* SALLY: *Okay, I suppose.* □ BOB: *Good to see you, Fred.* FRED: *Hello, Bob. How's business?* BOB: *Just okay.*

How's by you? a greeting inquiry. (Informal.) □ FRED: *Hey, man! How's by you?* JOHN: *Groovy, Fred. Tsup?* □ BOB: *Hello. What's cooking?* BILL: *Nothing. How's by you?*

How's every little thing? How are things with you? (Informal and familiar.) □ BILL: *Hello, Tom.* TOM: *Hi, Bill. How's every little thing?* BILL: *Couldn't be better.* □ BILL: *Hi, Mary. How's every little thing?* MARY: *Things are fine. How are you?* BILL: *Fine, thanks.*

How's it going? one of the standard informal greeting inquiries. □ SUE: *How's it going?* BILL: *Just great! How are you?* SUE: *Fine, thanks.* □ MARY: *How are you, Sue?* SUE: *Things just couldn't be better! I'm gloriously in love!* MARY: *Anybody I know?*

How's (it) with you? a greeting inquiry. (Slang.) □ TOM: *Hey, man. How's with you?* BOB: *Great! And you?* TOM: *Okay.* □ BILL: *How's with you, old buddy?* JOHN: *Can't complain. And you?* BILL: *Couldn't be better.*

How's my boy? AND **How's the boy?** How are you? (Male to male and familiar. The speaker may outrank the person addressed.) □ BOB: *How's my boy?* BILL: *Hi, Tom. How are you?* □ FRED: *Hello, old buddy. How's the boy?* BOB: *Hi, there! What's cooking?* FRED: *Nothing much.*

How's that again? Please say that again. I did not hear it all. □ SUE: *Would you like some coffee?* MARY: *How's that again?* SUE: *I said, would you like some coffee?* □ TOM: *The car door is frozen closed.* BOB: *How's that again?* TOM: *The car door is frozen closed.*

How's the boy? See *How's my boy?*

How's the family? AND **How's your family?** an expression that carries the greeting inquiries beyond the speakers present. □ BOB: *Hello, Fred. How are you?* FRED: *Fine, thanks.* BOB: *How's the family?* FRED: *Great! How's yours?* BOB: *Couldn't be better.* □ *"How's the family?" asked Bill, greeting his boss.*

How's the wife? a phrase inquiring about one's wife. (Usually male to male.) □ TOM: *Hi, Fred, how are you?* FRED: *Good. And you?* TOM: *Great! How's the wife?* FRED: *Okay, and yours?* TOM: *Couldn't be better.* □ BILL: *Hi, Bill. How's the wife?* BOB: *Doing fine. How's every little thing?* BILL: *Great!*

How's the world (been) treating you? How are things going for you? □ SUE: *Hello there, Bob. How's the world treating you?* BOB: *I can't complain. How are you?* SUE: *Doing just fine, thanks.* □ MARY: *Morning, Bill.* BILL: *Good morning, Mary. How's the world been treating you?* MARY: *Okay, I guess.*

How's tricks? a greeting inquiry. (Slang.) □ BOB: *Fred! How's tricks?* FRED: *How are you doing, Bob?* BOB: *Doing great!* □ BILL: *What's up? How's tricks?* BOB: *I can't complain. How are things going for you?* BILL: *Can't complain.*

How's your family? See *How's the family?*

huddle (up) (together) to bunch up together. □ *The children huddled up together to keep warm.* □ *They huddled up to keep warm.* □ *The newborn rabbits huddled together and squirmed hungrily.*

hunch up to squeeze or pull the parts of one's body together. □ *He hunched up in a corner to keep warm.* □ *Why is that child hunched up in the corner?*

hunt someone or something down 1. to chase and catch someone or something. □ *I don't know where Amy is, but I'll hunt her down. I'll find her.* ⊤ *I will hunt down the villain.* **2.** to locate someone or something. □ *I don't have a big enough gasket. I'll have to hunt one down.* ⊤ *I have to hunt down a good dentist.*

hunt someone or something out to find someone or something even if concealed. □ *We will hunt them all out and find every last one of those guys.* ⊤ *We will hunt out all of them.* ⊤ *They hunted out the murderer.*

hunt someone or something up to seek someone or something. □ *I don't know where Jane is. I'll hunt her up for you, though.* ⊤ *I'll help you hunt up Jane.* ⊤ *Will someone please hunt up a screwdriver?*

hunt through something to search through the contents of something; to search among things. □ *Joel hunted through his wallet for a dollar bill.* □ *I will have to hunt through my drawers for a pair of socks that match.*

hurl someone or something down to throw or push someone or something downward to the ground. (*Someone* includes *oneself.*) □ *Roger hurled the football down and it bounced away wildly.* ⊤ *He hurled down the football in anger.* □ *The angry player hurled the ball down.* □ *Fred hurled himself down and wept at the feet of the queen.*

hurry away AND **hurry off** to leave in a hurry. □ *I have to hurry away. Excuse me, please. It's an emergency.* □ *Don't hurry off. I need to talk to you.*

hurry back (to someone or something) to return to someone or something immediately or as fast as possible. □ *Oh, please hurry back to me as soon as you can.* □ *Hurry back!*

hurry off See *hurry away.*

hurry on AND **hurry up** to move faster. □ *Hurry up! You're going to be late.* □ *Please hurry on. We have a lot to do today.* □ TOM: *Get going! Hurry on!* SUE: *I'm hurrying as fast as I can.* □ MARY: *Hurry on!* CHILD: *I can't go any faster!*

hurry someone or something in(to something) to make someone or something go into something fast. □ *She hurried the chickens into the coop and closed the door on them for the night.* □ *It was beginning to rain, so Jerry hurried the children in.* □ *Please don't hurry me into a decision.*

hurry someone or something up to make someone or something go or work faster. □ *Please hurry them all up. We are expecting them very soon.* □ *See if you can hurry this project up a little.*

hurry up See *hurry on.*

hush someone or something up 1. to make someone or something be quiet or stop talking. (More at *hush up.*)

□ *Please hush the children up. I have a telephone call.* □ *Can you hush that radio up, please?* **2.** [with *something*] to keep something from public knowledge. □ *The company moved quickly to hush the bad news up.* T *They wanted to hush up the bad financial report.*

hush up to be quiet; to get quiet; to stop talking. (More at *hush someone or something up.*) □ *You talk too much. Hush up!* □ *I want you to hush up and sit down.*

hyped (up) 1. excited; stimulated. (Slang.) □ *They were all hyped up before the game.* □ *She said she had to get hyped before the tennis match.* **2.** contrived; heavily promoted; falsely advertised. □ *I just won't pay good money to see these hyped-up movies.* □ *If it has to be hyped so much, it probably isn't very good.*

I

(I) beg your pardon 1. AND **Beg pardon.** a phrase said to excuse oneself for interrupting or committing some very minor social offence. □ *As Sue brushed by the old man, she turned and said, "Beg pardon."* □ JANE: *Ouch! That's my toe you stepped on!* SUE: *I beg your pardon. I'm so sorry.* **2.** a phrase that indicates the speaker's need to pass by another person. □ *The hallway was filled with people. Bob said, "I beg your pardon," and then he said it again and again.* □ FRED: *Beg pardon. Need to get by.* SUE: *I'm sorry.* **3.** an exclamation that shows, as politely as possible, one's indignation at something that someone has said. (In a way, this signals the offender of the magnitude of the offence and invites a revision of the original offending statement.) □ BILL: *I think you've really made a poor choice this time.* MARY: *I beg your pardon!* BILL: *I mean, you normally do better.* MARY: *Well, I never!* □ SUE: *Your spaghetti sauce is too sweet.* SALLY: *I beg your pardon!* SUE: *Maybe not.*

(I) beg your pardon, but AND **Begging your pardon, but** Please excuse me, but. (A very polite and formal way of interrupting, bringing something to someone's attention, or asking a question of a stranger.) □ RACHEL: *Beg your pardon, but I think your right front tire is a little low.* HENRY: *Well, I guess it is. Thank you.* □ JOHN: *Begging your pardon, ma'am, but weren't we on the same cruise ship in Alaska last July?* RACHEL: *Couldn't have been me.*

I believe so. See *I guess (so).*

I believe we've met. a phrase indicating that one has already met a person to whom one is being introduced. □ JOHN: *Alice, have you met Fred?* ALICE: *Oh, yes, I believe we've met. How are you, Fred?* FRED: *Hello, Alice. Good to see you again.* □ ALICE: *Tom, this is my cousin, Mary.* TOM: *I believe we've met. Nice to see you again, Mary.* MARY: *Hello, Tom. Good to see you again.*

I can accept that. I accept your evaluation as valid. □ BOB: *Now, you'll probably like doing the other job much better. It doesn't call for you to do the things you don't do well.* TOM: *I can accept that.* □ SUE: *On your evaluation this time, I noted that you need to work on telephone manners a little bit.* BILL: *I can accept that.*

I can live with that. That is something I can get used to.; That is all right *as far as I'm concerned.* □ SUE: *I want to do this room in green.* BILL: *I can live with that.* □ CLERK: *This one will cost twelve dollars more.* BOB: *I can live with that. I'll take it.*

(I) can too. You are wrong, I can.; Don't say I can't, because I can! (The response to *(You) can't!*) □ SUE: *I'm going to the party.* MOTHER: *You can't.* SUE: *I can too.* MOTHER: *Cannot!* SUE: *Can too!* □ *"Can too!" protested Fred. "I can, if you can!"*

I can't accept that. I do not believe what you said.; I reject what you said. □ SUE: *The mechanic says we need a whole new engine.* JOHN: *What? I can't accept that!* □ TOM: *You're now going to work on the night shift. You don't seem to be able to get along with some of the people on the day shift.* BOB: *I can't accept that. It's them, not me.*

(I) can't argue with that. I agree with what you said.; It sounds like a good idea. □ TOM: *This sure is good cake.* BOB: *Can't argue with that.* □ SUE: *What do you say we go for a swim?* FRED: *I can't argue with that.*

(I) can't beat that. AND **(I) can't top that.** I cannot do better than that.; I cannot exceed that. □ HENRY: *That was really great. I can't beat that.* RACHEL: *Yes, that was really good.* □ *"What a great joke! I can't top that," said Kate, still laughing.*

I can't believe (that)! That is unbelievable! □ TOM: *What a terrible earthquake! All the houses collapsed, one by one.* JANE: *I can't believe that!* □ BILL: *This lake is nearly two hundred feet deep.* SUE: *I can't believe that!* BILL: *Take my word for it.*

(I) can't complain. AND **(I have) nothing to complain about.** a response to a greeting inquiry asking how one is or how things are going for one. □ SUE: *How are things going?* MARY: *I can't complain.* □ MARY: *Hi, Fred! How are you doing?* FRED: *Nothing to complain about.*

I can't get over something! I am just so amazed! (The *something* can be a fact or a pronoun, such as *that* or *it.* Also with *just.*) □ *"I just can't get over the way everybody pitched in and helped," said Alice.* □ BOB: *The very idea, Sue and Tom doing something like that!* BILL: *I can't get over it!*

(I) can't help it. There is nothing I can do to help the situation.; That is the way it is; there is nothing I can do. (Often in answer to a criticism.) □ MARY: *Your hair is a mess.* SUE: *It's windy. I can't help it.* □ FRED: *I wish you'd quit coughing all the time.* SALLY: *I can't help it. I wish I could too.*

(I) can't rightly say. I do not know with any certainty. (Colloquial and a little folksy.) □ FRED: *When do you think we'll get there?* BILL: *Can't rightly say.* □ BOB: *Okay, how does this look to you?* BILL: *I can't rightly say. I've never seen anything like it before.*

(I) can't say (as) I do. See *(I) can't say that I do.*

(I) can't say (as) I have. See *(I) can't say that I have.*

(I) can't say for sure. I do not know with any certainty. □ TOM: *When will the next train come through?* JANE: *I can't say for sure.* □ BOB: *How can the driver hit so many potholes?* BILL: *Can't say for sure. I know he doesn't see too well, though.*

(I) can't say that I do. AND **(I) can't say's I do.; (I) can't say (as) I do.** a vague response to a question about whether one remembers, knows about, likes, etc., something or someone. (A polite way of saying no. Colloquial and folksy. The *say as* and *say's* are not standard English.) □ JANE: *You remember Fred, don't you?* JOHN: *Can't say as I do.* □ BOB: *This is a fine looking car. Do you like it?* BILL: *I can't say I do.*

(I) can't say that I have. AND **(I) can't say's I have.; (I) can't say (as) I have.** a vague response to a question about whether one has ever done something or been somewhere. (A polite way of saying no. Colloquial and folksy. The *say as* and *say's* are not standard English.) □ BILL: *Have you ever been to a real opera?* BOB: *I can't say as I have.* □ MARY: *Well, have you thought about going with me to Fairbanks?* FRED: *I can't say I have, actually.*

(I) can't say's I do. See *(I) can't say that I do.*

(I) can't say's I have. See *(I) can't say that I have.*

(I) can't thank you enough. a polite expression of gratitude. □ BILL: *Here's the book I promised you.* SUE: *Oh, good. I can't thank you enough.* □ TOM: *Well, here we are.* BILL: *Well, Tom. I can't thank you enough. I really appreciate the ride.*

(I) can't top that. See *(I) can't beat that.*

I can't understand (it). See *I don't understand (it).*

(I) changed my mind. I have reversed my previous decision or statement. □ TOM: *I thought you were going to Atlanta today.* BILL: *I changed my mind. I'm leaving tomorrow.* □ MARY: *I thought that this room was going to be done in red.* SUE: *I changed my mind.*

(I) could be better. See *(Things) could be better.*

(I) could be worse. See *(Things) could be worse.*

(I) couldn't ask for more. Everything is fine, and there is no more that I could want. □ BILL: *Are you happy?* SUE: *Oh, Bill. I couldn't ask for more.* □ WAITER: *Is everything all right?* BILL: *Oh, yes, indeed. Couldn't ask for more.*

I couldn't ask you to do that. That is a very kind offer, but I would not ask you to do it. (This is not a refusal of the offer.) □ SALLY: *Look, if you want, I'll drive you to the airport.* MARY: *Oh, Sally. I couldn't ask you to do that.* □ BILL: *I'll lend you enough money to get you through the week.* SALLY: *I couldn't ask you to do that.*

(I) couldn't be better. I am fine. □ JOHN: *How are you?* JANE: *Couldn't be better.* □ BILL: *I hope you're completely well now.* MARY: *I couldn't be better.*

(I) could(n't) care less. It doesn't matter to me. (The *less* bears the heaviest stress in both versions. Both versions are idiomatic. Despite the apparent contradiction, either reading of this—both the affirmative and negative—usually have the same meaning. The exception would be in a sentence where the *could* bears the heaviest stress: I COULD *care less [,but I don't].*) □ TOM: *It's raining in! The carpet will get wet!* MARY: *I couldn't care less.* □ BILL: *I'm going to go in there and tell him off!* JOHN: *I could care less.*

(I) couldn't help it. There was no way I could prevent it.; I was unable to prevent something from happening.; I was unable to control myself. □ SALLY: *You let the paint dry with brush marks in it.* MARY: *I couldn't help it. The telephone rang.* □ FRED: *You got fingerprints all over the window.* MARY: *Sorry. Couldn't help it.*

I didn't catch the name. AND **I didn't catch your name.** I don't remember your name.; I didn't hear your name when we were introduced. □ BILL: *How do you like this weather?* BOB: *It's not too good. By the way, I didn't catch your name. I'm Bob Wilson.* BILL: *I'm Bill Franklin.* BOB: *Nice to meet you, Bill.* □ BOB: *Sorry, I didn't catch the name.* BILL: *It's Bill, Bill Franklin. And you?* BOB: *I'm Bob Wilson.*

I didn't catch your name. See the previous entry.

I didn't get that. See *I didn't (quite) catch that (last) remark.*

I didn't hear you. See the following entry.

I didn't (quite) catch that (last) re-mark. AND **I didn't get that.; I didn't hear you.** I didn't hear what you said, so would you please repeat it. □ JOHN: *What did you say? I didn't quite catch that last remark.* JANE: *I said it's really a hot day.* □ BILL: *Have a nice time, if you can.* SALLY: *I didn't get that.* BILL: *Have a nice time! Enjoy!*

I (do) declare! I am surprised to hear that! (Old-fashioned.) □ MARY: *I'm the new president of my sorority!* GRANDMOTHER: *I declare! That's very nice.* □ *A plane had landed right in the middle of the cornfield. The old farmer shook his head in disbelief. "I do de-clare!" he said over and over as he walked toward the plane.*

I don't believe it! an expression of amazement and disbelief. □ BOB: *Tom was just elected president of the trade association!* MARY: *I don't believe it!* □ BOB: *They're going to build a Disney World in Moscow.* SALLY: *I don't believe it!*

(I) don't believe I've had the pleasure. an expression meaning "I haven't met you yet." □ TOM: *I'm Tom Thomas. I don't believe I've had the pleasure.* BILL: *Hello. I'm Bill Franklin.* TOM: *Nice to meet you, Bill.* BILL: *Likewise.* □ BOB: *Looks like rain.* FRED: *Sure does. Oh, I don't be-lieve I've had the pleasure.* BOB: *I'm Bob, Bob Jones.* FRED: *My name is Fred Wilson. Glad to meet you.*

I don't believe this! This is very strange!; I do not believe that this is happening. □ *"I don't believe this!" muttered Sally as all the doors in the house slammed at the same time.* □ SALLY: *You're expected to get here early and make my coffee every morning.* JOHN: *I don't believe this.*

I don't care. It doesn't matter to me. □ MARY: *Can I take these papers away?* TOM: *I don't care. Do what you want.* □ BILL: *Should this room be white or yellow?* SALLY: *I don't care.*

I don't have time to breathe. See the following entry.

I don't have time to catch my breath. AND **I don't have time to breathe.** I am very busy.; I have been very busy. □ HENRY: *I'm so busy these days. I don't have time to catch my breath.* RACHEL: *Oh, I know what you mean.* □ SUE: *Would you mind finishing this for me?* BILL: *Sorry, Sue. I'm busy. I don't have time to breathe.*

I don't know. a common expression of ignorance. □ FATHER: *Why can't you do better in school?* BILL: *I don't know.* □ BILL: *Well, what are we going to do now?* SUE: *I don't know.*

I don't mean maybe! I am very serious about my demand or order. □ BOB: *Do I have to do this?* SUE: *Do it now, and I don't mean maybe!* □ FATHER: *Get this place cleaned up! And I don't mean maybe!* JOHN: *All right! I'll do it!*

(I) don't mind if I do. Yes, I would like to. □ SALLY: *Have some more coffee?* BOB: *Don't mind if I do.* □ JANE: *Here are some lovely roses. Would you like to take a few blossoms with you?* JOHN: *I don't mind if I do.*

(I) don't think so. See *I guess not.*

I don't understand (it). AND **I can't understand (it).** I am confused and bewildered (by what has happened). □ BILL: *Everyone is leaving the party.* MARY: *I don't understand. It's still so early.* □ BOB: *The very idea, Sue and Tom doing something like that!* ALICE: *It's very strange. I can't understand it.*

I don't want to alarm you, but AND **I don't want to upset you, but** an expression used to introduce bad or shocking news or gossip. ⊔ BILL: *I don't want to alarm you, but I see someone prowling around your car.* MARY: *Oh, goodness! I'll call the police!* □ BOB: *I don't want to upset you, but I have some bad news.* TOM: *Let me have it.*

I don't want to sound like a busybody, but an expression used to introduce an opinion or suggestion. □ BOB: *I don't want to sound like a busybody, but didn't you intend to have your house painted?* BILL: *Well, I guess I did.*

□ BOB: *I don't want to sound like a busybody, but some of your neighbors wonder if you could stop parking your car on your lawn.* SALLY: *I'll thank you to mind your own business!*

I don't want to upset you, but See *I don't want to alarm you, but.*

I don't want to wear out my welcome. a phrase said by a guest who doesn't want to be a burden to the host or hostess or to visit too often. □ MARY: *Good night, Tom. You must come back again soon.* TOM: *Thank you. I'd love to. I don't want to wear out my welcome, though.* □ BOB: *We had a fine time. Glad you could come to our little gathering. Hope you can come again next week.* FRED: *I don't want to wear out my welcome, but I'd like to come again.* BOB: *Good. See you next week. Bye.* FRED: *Bye.*

I don't wonder. See *I'm not surprised.*

I doubt it. I do not think so. □ TOM: *Think it will rain today?* SUE: *I doubt it.* □ SALLY: *Think you'll go to New York?* MARY: *I doubt it.*

I doubt that. I do not believe that something is so. □ BOB: *I'll be there exactly on time.* SUE: *I doubt that.* □ JOHN: *Fred says he can't come to work because he's sick.* JANE: *I doubt that.*

I expect. See *I guess.*

I expect not. See *I guess not.*

I expect (so). See *I guess (so).*

I guess. AND **I expect.; I suppose.; I suspect.** 1. a phrase that introduces a supposition. (Frequently, in speech, *suppose* is reduced to *'spose*, and *expect* and *suspect* are reduced to *'spect.* The apostrophe is not always used.) □ BOB: *I guess it's going to rain.* BILL:

Oh, I don't know. Maybe so, maybe not. □ ALICE: *I expect you'll be wanting to leave pretty soon.* JOHN: *Why? It's early yet.* **2.** a vague way of answering yes. □ JOHN: *You want some more coffee?* JANE: *I 'spose.* □ ALICE: *Ready to go?* JOHN: *I spect.*

I guess not. AND **(I) don't think so.; I expect not.; I suppose not.; I suspect not.; I think not.** a vague statement of negation. (More polite or gentle than no. Frequently, in speech, *suppose* is reduced to *'spose*, and *expect* and *suspect* are reduced to *'spect*. The apostrophe is not always used.) □ BILL: *It's almost too late to go to the movie. Shall we try anyway?* MARY: *I guess not.* □ TOM: *Will it rain?* MARY: *I 'spect not.*

I guess (so). AND **I believe so.; I expect (so).; I suppose (so).; I suspect (so).; I think so.** a vague expression of assent. (Frequently, in speech, *suppose* is reduced to *'spose*, and *expect* and *suspect* are reduced to *'spect*. The apostrophe is not always used.) □ TOM: *Will it rain today?* BOB: *I suppose so.* □ SUE: *Happy?* BILL: *I 'spect.* SUE: *You don't sound happy.* BILL: *I guess not.*

I had a lovely time. AND **We had a lovely time.** a polite expression of thanks to the host or hostess. □ FRED: *Good-bye. I had a lovely time.* BILL: *Nice to have you. Do come again.* □ JANE: *We had a lovely time.* MARY: *Thank you and thanks for coming.*

(I) had a nice time. the standard "good-bye and thank you" said to a host or hostess by a departing guest. □ JOHN: *Thank you. I had a nice time.* SALLY: *Don't stay away so long next time. Bye.* □ MARY: *Had a nice*

time. Bye. Got to run. SUE: *Bye. Drive safely.*

(I) hate to eat and run. an apology made by someone who must leave a social event soon after eating. □ BILL: *Well, I hate to eat and run, but it's getting late.* SUE: *Oh, you don't have to leave, do you?* BILL: *I think I really must.* □ MARY: *Oh, my goodness! I hate to eat and run, but I have to catch an early plane tomorrow.* BOB: *Do you have to go?* MARY: *Afraid so.*

(I have) no problem with that. That is okay with me. (See also *No problem.*) □ BOB: *Is it okay if I sign us up for the party?* SALLY: *I have no problem with that.* □ BILL: *It looks as though we will have to come back later. They're not open yet. Is that all right?* JANE: *No problem with that. When do they open?*

(I have) nothing to complain about. See *(I) can't complain.*

(I) have to be moving along. AND **(I) have to move along.** It is time for me to leave. □ BILL: *Bye, now. Have to be moving along.* SALLY: *See you later.* □ RACHEL: *I have to be moving along. See you later.* ANDREW: *Bye, now.* □ SALLY: *It's late. I have to move along.* MARY: *If you must. Good-bye. See you tomorrow.*

(I) have to go now. an expression announcing the need to leave. □ FRED: *Bye, have to go now.* MARY: *See you later. Take it easy.* □ SUE: *Would you help me with this box?* JOHN: *Sorry. I have to go now.*

(I) have to move along. See *(I) have to be moving along.*

(I) have to push off. See *(I) have to shove off.*

(I) have to run along. an expression announcing the need to leave. □ JANE: *It's late. I have to run along.* TOM: *Okay, Jane. Bye. Take care.* □ JOHN: *Leaving so soon?* SALLY: *Yes, I have to run along.*

(I) have to shove off. AND **(I've) got to be shoving off.; (I've) got to shove off.; (I) have to push off.; (It's) time to shove off.** a phrase announcing one's need to depart. □ JOHN: *Look at the time! I have to shove off!* JANE: *Bye, John.* □ JANE: *Time to shove off. I have to feed the cats.* JOHN: *Bye, Jane.* □ FRED: *I have to push off. Bye.* JANE: *See you around. Bye.*

I have to wash a few things out. an excuse for not going out or for going home early. (Of course, it can be used literally.) □ JANE: *Time to shove off. I have to wash a few things out.* JOHN: *Bye, Jane.* □ BILL: *I have to wash out a few things.* BOB: *Why don't you use a machine?* BILL: *Oh, I'll see you later.*

(I) haven't got all day. Please hurry. I'm in a hurry. □ RACHEL: *Make it snappy! I haven't got all day.* ALICE: *Just take it easy. There's no rush.* □ HENRY: *I haven't got all day. When are you going to finish with my car?* BOB: *As soon as I can.*

(I) haven't seen you in a long time. an expression said as part of the greeting series. □ MARY: *Hi, Fred! Haven't seen you in a long time.* FRED: *Yeah. Long time no see.* □ TOM: *Well, John. Is that you? I haven't seen you in a long time.* JOHN: *Good to see you, Tom!*

(I) haven't seen you in a month of Sundays. I haven't seen you in a long time. (Colloquial and folksy.) □

TOM: *Hi, Bill. Haven't seen you in a month of Sundays!* BILL: *Hi, Tom. Long time no see.* □ BOB: *Well, Fred! Come right in! Haven't seen you in a month of Sundays!* FRED: *Good to see you, Uncle Bob.*

I hear what you're saying. AND **I hear you.** **1.** I know exactly what you mean! □ JOHN: *The prices in this place are a bit steep.* JANE: *Man, I hear you!* □ BILL: *I think it's about time for a small revolution!* ANDREW: *I hear what you're saying.* **2.** an expression indicating that the speaker has been heard, but implying that there is no agreement. □ TOM: *Time has come to do something about that ailing dog of yours.* MARY: *I hear what you're saying.* □ JANE: *It would be a good idea to have the house painted.* JOHN: *I hear what you're saying.*

I hear you. See the previous entry.

(I) hope not. a phrase expressing the desire and wish that something is not so. □ JOHN: *It looks like it's going to rain.* JANE: *Hope not.* □ JOHN: *The Wilsons said they might come over this evening.* JANE: *I hope not. I've got things to do.*

(I) hope so. a phrase expressing the desire and wish that something is so. □ BILL: *Is this the right house?* BOB: *Hope so.* □ JOHN: *Will you be coming to dinner Friday?* SUE: *Yes, I hope so.*

(I) hope to see you again (sometime). an expression said when taking leave of a person one has just met. □ BILL: *Nice to meet you, Tom.* TOM: *Bye, Bill. Nice to meet you. Hope to see you again sometime.* □ BILL: *Good talking to you. See you around.* BOB: *Yes, I hope to see you again. Good-bye.*

(I) just want(ed) to a sentence opener that eases into a statement or question. (Can be followed by words like *say, ask, tell you, be,* and *come.*) □ RACHEL: *I just wanted to say that we all loved your letter. Thank you so much.* ANDREW: *Thanks. Glad you liked it.* □ RACHEL: *I just wanted to tell you how sorry I am about your sister.* ALICE: *Thanks. I appreciate it.* □ ANDREW: *Just wanted to come by for a minute and say hello.* TOM: *Well, hello. Glad you dropped by.*

I kid you not. I am not kidding you.; I am not trying to fool you. □ BILL: *Whose car is this?* SALLY: *It's mine. It really is. I kid you not.* □ *"I kid you not," said Tom, glowing. "I outran the whole lot of them."*

I know (just) what you mean. I know exactly what you are talking about, and I feel the same way about it. □ JOHN: *These final exams are just terrible.* BOB: *I know just what you mean.* JOHN: *Why do we have to go through this?* □ MARY: *What a pain! I hate annual inventories.* JOHN: *I know what you mean. It's really boring.*

(I) love it! It is just wonderful. (Colloquial. This is just a common, idiomatic variant of *I love it.*) □ MARY: *What do you think of this car?* BILL: *Love it! It's really cool!* □ BOB: *What a joke, Tom!* JANE: *Yes, love it!* TOM: *Gee, thanks.*

I must be off. an expression announcing the speaker's intention of leaving. □ BILL: *It's late. I must be off.* BOB: *Me, too. I'm out of here.* □ SUE: *I must be off.* JOHN: *The game's not over yet.* SUE: *I've seen enough.*

I must say good night. an expression announcing the speaker's intention

of leaving for the night. □ JANE: *It's late. I must say good night.* BOB: *Can I see you again?* JANE: *Call me. Good night, Bob.* BOB: *Good night, Jane.* □ SUE: *I must say good night.* MARY: *Good night, then. See you tomorrow.*

I need it yesterday. an answer to the question "When do you need this?" (Indicates that the need is urgent.) □ BOB: *When do you need that urgent survey?* BILL: *I need it yesterday.* □ MARY: *Where's the Wilson contract?* SUE: *Do you need it now?* MARY: *I need it yesterday! Where is it?*

(I) never heard of such a thing. an expression of amazement and disbelief. (Compare to *Well, I never!*) □ BILL: *The company sent out a representative to our very house to examine the new sofa and see what the problem was with the wobbly leg.* JANE: *I've never heard of such a thing! That's very unusual.* □ BILL: *The tax office is now open on Sunday!* SUE: *Never heard of such a thing!*

(I) never thought I'd see you here! I am surprised to see you here. □ TOM: *Hi, Sue! I never thought I'd see you here!* SUE: *Hi, Tom. I was thinking the same thing about you.* □ BILL: *Well, Tom Thomas. I never thought I'd see you here!* TOM: *Likewise. I didn't know you liked opera.*

I owe you one. Thank you, now I owe you a favor. □ BOB: *I put the extra copy of the book on your desk.* SUE: *Thanks, I owe you one.* □ BILL: *Let me pay for it.* BOB: *Thanks a lot, I owe you one.*

I promise you! I am telling you the truth! (Similar to *Trust me!*) □ JOHN: *Things will work out, I promise you!* JANE: *Okay, but when?* □ SUE:

I'll be there exactly when I said. BOB: *Are you sure?* SUE: *I promise you, I'm telling the truth!*

(I) read you loud and clear. 1. a response used by someone communicating by radio stating that the hearer understands the transmission clearly. (See also *Do you read me?*) □ CONTROLLER: *This is Aurora Center, do you read me?* PILOT: *Yes, I read you loud and clear.* □ CONTROLLER: *Left two degrees. Do you read me?* PILOT: *Roger. Read you loud and clear.* **2.** I understand what you are telling me. (Used in general conversation, not in radio communication.) □ BOB: *Okay. Now, do you understand exactly what I said?* MARY: *I read you loud and clear.* □ MOTHER: *I don't want to have to tell you again. Do you understand?* BILL: *I read you loud and clear.*

(I) really must go. an expression announcing or repeating one's intention to depart. □ BOB: *It's getting late. I really must go.* JANE: *Good night, then. See you tomorrow.* □ SALLY: *I really must go.* JOHN: *Do you really have to? It's early yet.*

I spoke out of turn. I said the wrong thing.; I should not have said what I did. (An apology.) □ BILL: *You said I was the one who did it.* MARY: *I'm sorry. I spoke out of turn. I was mistaken.* □ BILL: *I seem to have said the wrong thing.* BOB: *You certainly did.* BILL: *I spoke out of turn, and I'm sorry.*

I spoke too soon. 1. I am wrong.; I spoke before I knew the facts. □ BILL: *I know I said I would, but I spoke too soon.* SUE: *I thought so.* □ JOHN: *You said that everything would be all right.* JANE: *I spoke too soon. That was before I learned that you had been ar-*

rested. **2.** What I had said was just now contradicted. □ BOB: *It's beginning to brighten up. I guess it won't rain after all.* JOHN: *I'm glad to hear that.* BOB: *Whoops! I spoke too soon. I just felt a raindrop on my cheek.* □ BILL: *Thank heavens! Here's John now.* BOB: *No, that's Fred.* BILL: *I spoke too soon. He sure looked like John.*

I suppose. See *I guess.*

I suppose not. See *I guess not.*

I suppose (so). See *I guess (so).*

I suspect. See *I guess.*

I suspect not. See *I guess not.*

I suspect (so). See *I guess (so).*

I think not. See *I guess not.*

I think so. See *I guess (so).*

(I was) just wondering. a comment made after hearing a response to a previous question. (See the examples for typical patterns.) □ JOHN: *Do you always keep your film in the refrigerator?* MARY: *Yes, why?* JOHN: *I was just wondering.* □ BOB: *Did this cost a lot?* SUE: *I really don't think you need to know that.* BOB: *Sorry. Just wondering.*

I was up (all night) with a sick friend. an unlikely, but popular excuse for not being where one was supposed to be the night before. □ BILL: *Where in the world were you last night?* MARY: *Well, I was up all night with a sick friend.* □ Mr. Franklin said rather sheepishly, *"Would you believe I was up with a sick friend?"*

I wish I'd said that. a comment of praise or admiration for someone's clever remark. □ MARY: *The weed of crime bears bitter fruit.* SUE: *I wish I'd said that.* MARY: *I wish I'd said it first.*

☐ JOHN: *Tom is simply not able to see through the airy persiflage of Mary's prolix declamation.* JANE: *I wish I'd said that.* JOHN: *I'm sorry I did.*

(I) wonder if a phrase introducing a hypothesis. ☐ HENRY: *I wonder if I could have another piece of cake.* SUE: *Sure. Help yourself.* ☐ ANDREW: *Wonder if it's stopped raining yet.* RACHEL: *Why don't you look out the window?* ☐ ANDREW: *I wonder if I'll pass algebra.* FATHER: *That thought is on all our minds.*

(I) won't breathe a word (of it). AND **(I) won't tell a soul.** I will not tell anyone your secret. ☐ BILL: *Don't tell anybody, but Sally is getting married.* MARY: *I won't breathe a word of it.* ☐ ALICE: *The Jacksons are going to have to sell their house. Don't spread it around.* MARY: *I won't tell a soul.*

I won't give up without a fight. I will not give in easily. (Compare to *Don't give up too eas(il)y.*) ☐ SUE: *Stick by your principles, Fred.* FRED: *Don't worry, I won't give up without a fight.* ☐ BOB: *The boss wants me to turn the Wilson project over to Tom.* SUE: *How can he do that?* BOB: *I don't know. All I know is that I won't give up without a fight.*

(I) won't tell a soul. See *(I) won't breathe a word (of it).*

(I) would if I could(, but I can't). I simply can't do it. ☐ JANE: *Can't you fix this yourself?* JOHN: *I would if I could, but I can't.* ☐ BOB: *Can you go to the dance? Hardly anyone is going.* ALICE: *Would if I could.*

I would like to introduce you to someone. See the following entry.

I would like you to meet someone. AND **I would like to introduce you**

to someone. an expression used to introduce one person to another. ☐ MARY: *I would like you to meet my Uncle Bill.* SALLY: *Hello, Uncle Bill. Nice to meet you.* ☐ TOM: *I would like to introduce you to Bill Franklin.* JOHN: *Hello, Bill. Glad to meet you.* BILL: *Glad to meet you, John.*

(I) wouldn't bet on it. AND **(I) wouldn't count on it.** I do not believe that something will happen. (Also with *that* or some specific happening.) ☐ JOHN: *I'll be a vice president in a year or two.* MARY: *I wouldn't bet on that.* ☐ JOHN: *I'll pick up a turkey on the day before Thanksgiving.* MARY: *Did you order one ahead of time?* JOHN: *No.* MARY: *Then I wouldn't count on it.*

(I) wouldn't count on it. See the previous entry.

(I) wouldn't if I were you. a polite way to advise someone not to do something. ☐ MARY: *Do you think I should trade this car in on a new one?* SALLY: *I wouldn't if I were you.* ☐ BOB: *I'm going to plant nothing but corn this year.* SUE: *I wouldn't if I were you.* BOB: *Why?* SUE: *It's better to diversify.*

(I) wouldn't know. There is no way that I would know the answer to that question. ☐ JOHN: *When will the flight from Miami get in?* JANE: *Sorry, I wouldn't know.* ☐ BOB: *Are there many fish in the Amazon River?* MARY: *Gee, I wouldn't know.*

ice over [for water] to freeze and develop a covering of ice. ☐ *I can't wait for the river to ice over so we can do some ice fishing.*

ice something down to cool something with ice. ☐ *They are icing the* *champagne down now.* T *They are icing down the champagne now.*

ice up to become icy. □ *Are the roads icing up?*

(I'd be) happy to (do something). AND **Be happy to (do something).** I would do it with pleasure. (The *something* is replaced with a description of an activity.) □ JOHN: *I tried to get the book you wanted, but they didn't have it. Shall I try another store?* MARY: *No, never mind.* JOHN: *I'd be happy to give it a try.* □ ALICE: *Would you fix this, please?* JOHN: *Be happy to.*

(I'd) better be going. AND **(I'd) better be off.** an expression announcing the need to depart. □ BOB: *Better be going. Got to get home.* BILL: *Well, if you must, you must. Bye.* □ FRED: *It's midnight. I'd better be off.* HENRY: *Okay. Bye, Fred.* □ HENRY: *Better be off. It's starting to snow.* JOHN: *Yes, it looks bad out.*

(I'd) better be off. See the previous entry.

(I'd) better get moving. an expression announcing the need to depart. □ JANE: *It's nearly dark. Better get moving.* MARY: *Okay. See you later.* □ BOB: *I'm off. Good night* BILL: *Look at the time! I'd better get moving too.*

(I'd) better get on my horse. an expression indicating that it is time that one departed. (Casual and folksy.) □ JOHN: *It's getting late. Better get on my horse.* RACHEL: *Have a safe trip. See you tomorrow.* □ *"I'd better get on my horse. The sun'll be down in an hour," said Sue, sounding like a cowboy.*

(I'd) better hit the road. See *(It's) time to hit the road.*

I'd like (for) you to meet someone. an expression used to introduce someone to someone else. (The *someone* can be a person's name, the name of a relationship, or the word *someone*.) □ TOM: *Sue, I'd like you to meet my brother, Bill.* SUE: *Hi, Bill. How are you?* BILL: *Great! How are you?* □ BOB: *Hello, Fred. I'd like for you to meet Bill.* FRED: *Hello, Bill. I'm glad to meet you.* BILL: *Hello, Fred. My pleasure.*

I'd like (to have) a word with you. AND **Could I have a word with you?** I need to speak to you briefly in private. (The alternate entry is also used with *can* or *may* in place of *could.*) □ BOB: *Can I have a word with you?* SALLY: *Sure. I'll be with you in a minute.* □ SALLY: *Tom?* TOM: *Yes.* SALLY: *I'd like to have a word with you.* TOM: *Okay. What's it about?*

I'd like to speak to someone(, please). the standard way of requesting to speak with a specific person on the telephone or in an office. □ SUE (answering the phone): *Hello?* BILL: *Hello, this is Bill Franklin. I'd like to speak to Mary Gray, please.* SUE: *I'll see if she's in.* □ *"I'd like to speak to Tom," said the voice at the other end of the line.*

identify someone or something with someone or something to associate people and things, in any combination. (*Someone* includes *oneself.*) □ *I tend to identify Wally with big cars.* □ *We usually identify green with grass.* □ *We tend to identify big cars with greedy people.* □ *We always identify Tom with the other kids from Toledo.*

idle something away to waste one's time in idleness; to waste a period of time, such as an afternoon, evening, or one's life. □ *She idled the afternoon away and then went to a party.* T *Don't idle away the afternoon.*

if I were you an expression introducing a piece of advice. □ JOHN: *If I were you, I'd get rid of that old car.* ALICE: *Gee, I was just getting to like it.* □ HENRY: *I'd keep my thoughts to myself, if I were you.* BOB: *I guess I should be careful about what I say.*

if I've told you once, I've told you a thousand times an expression that introduces a scolding, usually to a child. □ MOTHER: *If I've told you once, I've told you a thousand times, don't leave your clothes in a pile on the floor!* BILL: *Sorry.* □ *"If I've told you once, I've told you a thousand times, keep out of my study!" yelled Bob.*

If that don't beat all! AND **That beats everything!** That surpasses everything!; That is amazing!; *That takes the cake!* (The grammar error, *that don't* is built into this catch phrase.) □ TOM: *The mayor is kicking the baseball team out of the city.* BILL: *If that don't beat all!* □ JOHN: *Now, here's a funny thing. South America used to be attached to Africa.* FRED: *That beats everything!* JOHN: *Yeah.*

If the shoe fits, wear it. You should pay attention to something if it applies to you. (Proverb.) □ *Some people here need to be quiet. If the shoe fits, wear it.* □ *This doesn't apply to everyone. If the shoe fits, wear it.*

If there's anything you need, don't hesitate to ask. a polite phrase offering help in finding something or by providing something. (Often said by a host or by someone helping someone settle into something.) □

MARY: *This looks very nice. I'll be quite comfortable here.* JANE: *If there's anything you need, don't hesitate to ask.* □ *"If there is anything you need, don't hesitate to ask," said the room clerk.*

if worst comes to worst in the worst possible situation; if things really get bad. □ *If worst comes to worst, we'll hire someone to help you.* □ *If worst comes to worst, I'll have to borrow some money.*

if you don't mind 1. an expression that rebukes someone for some minor social violation. (Usually **If you don't mind!**) □ *When Bill accidently sat on Mary's purse, which she had placed in the seat next to her, she said, somewhat angrily, "If you don't mind!"* □ BILL (pushing his way in front of Mary in the checkout line): *Excuse me.* MARY: *If you don't mind! I was here first!* BILL: *I'm in a hurry.* MARY: *So am I!* 2. a polite way of introducing a request. □ BILL: *If you don't mind, could you move a little to the left?* SALLY: *No problem.* (moving) *Is that all right?* BILL: *Yeah. Great! Thanks!* □ JANE: *If you don't mind, could I have your broccoli?* JOHN: *Help yourself.* 3. a vague phrase answering yes to a question that asks whether one should do something. □ TOM: *Do you want me to take these dirty dishes away?* MARY: *If you don't mind.* □ BILL: *Shall I close the door?* SALLY: *If you don't mind.*

If you don't see what you want, just ask (for it). See the following entry.

If you don't see what you want, please ask (for it). AND **If you don't see what you want, just ask (for it).** a polite phrase intended to help people get what they want. □ CLERK: *May I help you?* SUE: *I'm just* *looking.* CLERK: *If you don't see what you want, please ask.* □ CLERK: *I hope you enjoy your stay at our resort. If you don't see what you want, just ask for it.* SALLY: *Great! Thanks.*

If you give one an inch, one will take a mile. See *Give one an inch, and one will take a mile.*

if you know what's good for you if you know what will work to your benefit; if you know what will keep you out of trouble. □ MARY: *I see that Mary has put a big dent in her car.* SUE: *You'll keep quiet about that if you know what's good for you.* □ SALLY: *My boss told me I had better improve my spelling.* BILL: *If you know what's good for you, you'd better do it too.*

if you must All right, if you have to. □ SALLY: *It's late. I have to move along.* MARY: *If you must. Good-bye. See you tomorrow.* □ ALICE: *I'm taking these things with me.* JANE: *If you must, all right. They can stay here, though.*

if you please AND **if you would(, please)** **1.** a polite phrase indicating assent to a suggestion. □ BILL: *Shall I unload the car?* JANE: *If you please.* □ SUE: *Do you want me to take you to the station?* BOB: *If you would, please.* **2.** a polite phrase introducing or following a request. □ JOHN: *If you please, the driveway needs sweeping.* JANE: *Here's the broom. Have at it.* □ JANE: *Take these down to the basement, if you would, please.* JOHN: *Can't think of anything I'd rather do, sweetie.*

if you would(, please) See the previous entry.

(I'll) be right there. I'm coming. □ BILL: *Tom! Come here.* TOM: *Be right*

there. □ MOTHER: *Can you come down here a minute?* CHILD: *I'll be right there, Mom.*

(I'll) be right with you. Please be patient, I will attend to you soon. (Often said by someone attending a sales counter or by an office receptionist.) □ MARY: *Oh, Miss?* CLERK: *I'll be right with you.* □ BOB: *Sally, can you come here for a minute?* SALLY: *Be right with you.*

(I'll) be seeing you. Good-bye, I will see you sometime in the near future. □ BOB: *Bye. Be seeing you.* SALLY: *Yeah. See you later.* □ JOHN: *Have a good time on your vacation. I'll be seeing you.* SALLY: *See you next week. Bye.*

I('ll) bet **1.** I'm pretty sure that something is so or that something will happen. □ BOB: *I bet you miss your plane.* RACHEL: *No, I won't.* □ SUE: *I'll bet it rains today.* ALICE: *No way! There's not a cloud in the sky.* **2.** I agree. (Often sarcastic.) □ TOM: *They're probably going to raise taxes again next year.* HENRY: *I bet.* □ FRED: *If we do that again, we'll really be in trouble.* ANDREW: *I'll bet.*

I'll bite. Okay, I will answer your question.; Okay, I will listen to your joke or play your little guessing game. □ BOB: *Guess what is in this box.* BILL: *I'll bite.* BOB: *A new toaster!* □ JOHN: *Did you hear the joke about the used car salesman?* JANE: *No, I'll bite.*

I'll call back later. a standard phrase indicating that a telephone caller will call again at a later time. □ SALLY: *Is Bill there?* MARY (speaking into the telephone): *Sorry, he's not here right now.* SALLY: *I'll call back later.* □ JOHN (speaking into the telephone):

Hello. Is Fred there? JANE: *No. Can I take a message?* JOHN: *No, thanks. I'll call back later.*

(I'll) catch you later. I will talk to you later. □ MARY: *Got to fly. See you around.* SALLY: *Bye. Catch you later.* □ JOHN: *I have to go to class now.* BILL: *Okay, catch you later.*

I'll drink to that! I agree with that totally, and I salute it with a drink. (The phrase is used even when no drinking is involved.) □ JOHN: *Hey, Tom! You did a great job!* MARY: *I'll drink to that!* TOM: *Thanks!* □ JANE: *I think I'll take everybody out to dinner.* SALLY: *I'll drink to that!*

I'll get back to you (on that). AND **Let me get back to you (on that).** I will report back later with my decision. (More likely said by a boss to an employee than vice versa.) □ BOB: *I have a question about the Wilson project.* MARY: *I have to go to a meeting now. I'll get back to you on that.* BOB: *It's sort of urgent.* MARY: *It can wait. It will wait.* □ SUE: *Shall I close the Wilson account?* JANE: *Let me get back to you on that.*

I'll get right on it. I will begin work on that immediately. □ BOB: *Please do this report immediately.* FRED: *I'll get right on it.* □ JANE: *Please call Tom and ask him to rethink this proposal.* JOHN: *I'll get right on it.*

I'll have the same. AND **The same for me.** I would like the same thing that the last person chose. □ WAITRESS: *What would you like?* TOM: *Hamburger, fries, and coffee.* JANE: *I'll have the same.* □ JOHN: *For dessert, I'll have strawberry ice cream.* BILL: *I'll have the same.*

I'll have to beg off. a polite expression used to turn down an informal invitation. □ ANDREW: *Thank you for inviting me, but I'll have to beg off. I have a conflict.* HENRY: *I'm sorry to hear that. Maybe some other time.* □ BILL: *Do you think you can come to the party?* BOB: *I'll have to beg off. I have another engagement.* BILL: *Maybe some other time.*

I'll look you up when I'm in town. I will try to visit you the next time I am in town. □ BILL: *I hope to see you again sometime.* MARY: *I'll look you up when I'm in town.* □ ANDREW: *Good-bye, Fred. It's been nice talking to you. I'll look you up when I'm in town.* FRED: *See you around, dude.*

I'll put a stop to that. I'll see that the undesirable activity is stopped. □ FRED: *There are two boys fighting in the hall.* BOB: *I'll put a stop to that.* □ SUE: *The sales force is ignoring almost every customer in the older neighborhoods.* MARY: *I'll put a stop to that!*

(I'll) see you in a little while. a phrase indicating that the speaker will see the person spoken to within a few hours at the most. □ JOHN: *I'll see you in a little while.* JANE: *Okay. Bye till later.* □ SALLY: *I have to get dressed for tonight.* FRED: *I'll pick you up about nine. See you in a little while.* SALLY: *See you.*

I'll see you later. AND **(See you) later.** Good-bye until I see you again. □ JOHN: *Good-bye, Sally. I'll see you later.* SALLY: *Until later, then.* □ BOB: *Time to go. Later.* MARY: *Later.*

(I'll) see you next year. a good-bye expression said toward the end of one year. □ BOB: *Happy New Year!*

SUE: *You, too! See you next year.* □ JOHN: *Bye. See you tomorrow.* MARY: *It's New Year's Eve. See you next year!* JOHN: *Right! I'll see you next year!*

(I'll) see you (real) soon. *Good-bye. I will meet you again soon.* □ BILL: *Bye, Sue. See you.* SUE: *See you real soon, Bill.* □ JOHN: *Bye, you two.* SALLY: *See you soon.* JANE: *See you, John.*

(I'll) see you then. I will see you at the time we've just agreed upon. □ JOHN: *Can we meet at noon?* BILL: *Sure. See you then. Bye.* JOHN: *Bye.* □ JOHN: *I'll pick you up just after midnight.* SALLY: *See you then.*

(I'll) see you tomorrow. I will see you when we meet again tomorrow. (Typically said to someone whose daily schedule is the same as one's own.) □ BOB: *Bye, Jane.* JANE: *Good night, Bob. See you tomorrow.* □ SUE: *See you tomorrow.* JANE: *Until tomorrow. Bye.*

(I'll) talk to you soon. I will talk to you on the telephone again soon. □ SALLY: *Bye now. Talk to you soon.* JOHN: *Bye now.* □ BILL: *Nice talking to you. Bye.* MARY: *Talk to you soon. Bye.*

I'll thank you to keep your opinions to yourself. I do not care about your opinion of this matter. □ JANE: *This place is sort of drab.* JOHN: *I'll thank you to keep your opinions to yourself.* □ BILL: *Your whole family is sort of long-legged.* JOHN: *I'll thank you to keep your opinions to yourself.*

I'll thank you to mind your own business. a polite version of *Mind your own business.* (Shows a little anger.) □ TOM: *How much did this cost?* JANE: *I'll thank you to mind your*

own business. □ BOB: *Is your house in your name or your brother's?* JOHN: *I'll thank you to mind your own business.*

(I'll) try to catch you later. See the following entry.

(I'll) try to catch you some other time. AND **(I'll) try to catch you later.; I'll try to see you later.** We do not have time to talk now, so we'll try to talk later. (An expression said when it is inconvenient for one or both parties to meet or converse.) □ BILL: *I need to get your signature on this contract.* SUE: *I really don't have a second to spare right now.* BILL: *Okay, I'll try to catch you some other time.* SUE: *Later this afternoon would be fine.* □ BILL: *I'm sorry for the interruptions, Tom. Things are very busy right now.* TOM: *I'll try to see you later.*

I'll try to see you later. See the previous entry.

(I'm) afraid not. AND **'Fraid not.** I believe, regrettably, that the answer is no. (The apostrophe is not always used.) □ RACHEL: *Can I expect any help with this problem?* HENRY: *I'm afraid not.* □ ANDREW: *Will you be there when I get there?* BILL: *Afraid not.*

(I'm) afraid so. AND **'Fraid so.** I believe, regrettably, that the answer is yes. (The apostrophe is not always used.) □ ALICE: *Do you have to go?* JOHN: *Afraid so.* □ RACHEL: *Can I expect some difficulty with Mr. Franklin?* BOB: *I'm afraid so.*

I'm all ears. See *I'm listening.*

I'm busy. Do not bother me now.; I cannot attend to your needs now. □ BOB: *Can I talk to you?* BILL: *I'm busy.* BOB: *It's important.* BILL: *Sorry, I'm* *busy!* □ FRED: *Can you help me with this?* BILL: *I'm busy. Can it wait a minute?* FRED: *Sure. No rush.*

I'm cool. I'm fine. (Slang.) □ BOB: *How you been?* FRED: *I'm cool, man. Yourself?* BOB: *The same.* □ FATHER: *How are you, son?* BILL: *I'm cool, Dad.* FATHER (misunderstanding): *I'll turn up the heat.*

(I'm) delighted to have you (here). AND **(We're) delighted to have you (here).** You're welcome here any time.; *Glad you could come.* (See also *(It's) good to have you here.*) □ BILL: *Thank you for inviting me for dinner, Mr. Franklin.* MR. FRANKLIN: *I'm delighted to have you.* □ *"We're delighted to see you," said Tom's grandparents. "It's so nice to have you here for a visit."*

(I'm) delighted to make your acquaintance. I am very glad to meet you. □ TOM: *My name is Tom. I work in the advertising department.* MARY: *I'm Mary. I work in accounting. Delighted to make your acquaintance.* TOM: *Yeah. Good to meet you.* □ FRED: *Sue, this is Bob. He'll be working with us on the Wilson project.* SUE: *I'm delighted to make your acquaintance, Bob.* BOB: *My pleasure.*

(I'm) doing okay. 1. I'm just fine. □ BOB: *How you doing?* BILL: *Doing okay. And you?* BOB: *Things could be worse.* □ MARY: *How are things going?* SUE: *I'm doing fine, thanks. And you?* MARY: *Doing okay.* **2.** I'm doing as well as can be expected.; I'm feeling better. □ MARY: *How are you feeling?* SUE: *I'm doing okay — as well as can be expected.* □ TOM: *I hope you're feeling better.* SALLY: *I'm doing okay, thanks.*

I'm easy (to please). I accept that.; I am not particular. □ TOM: *Hey, man! Do you care if we get a sausage pizza rather than mushroom?* BOB: *Fine with me. I'm easy.* □ MARY: *How do you like this music?* BOB: *It's great, but I'm easy to please.*

(I'm) feeling okay. I am doing well.; I am feeling well. □ ALICE: *How are you feeling?* JANE: *I'm feeling okay.* □ JOHN: *How are things going?* FRED: *Feeling okay.*

(I'm) glad to hear it. a phrase expressing pleasure at what the speaker has just said. □ SALLY: *We have a new car, finally.* MARY: *I'm glad to hear it.* □ TOM: *Is your sister feeling better?* BILL: *Oh, yes, thanks.* TOM: *Glad to hear it.*

(I'm) glad you could come. AND **(We're) glad you could come.** a phrase said by the host or hostess to a guest. □ TOM: *Thank you so much for having me.* SALLY: *We're glad you could come.* JOHN: *Yes, we are. Bye.* □ BILL: *Bye.* SALLY: *Bye, Bill. Glad you could come.*

(I'm) glad you could drop by. AND **(We're) glad you could drop by.; (I'm) glad you could stop by.; (We're) glad you could stop by.** a phrase said by the host or hostess to a guest who has appeared suddenly or has come for only a short visit. □ TOM: *Good-bye. Had a nice time.* MARY: *Thank you for coming, Tom. Glad you could drop by.* □ TOM: *Thank you so much for having me.* SALLY: *We're glad you could drop by.*

(I'm) glad you could stop by. See the previous entry.

I'm gone. an expression said just before leaving. (Slang. See also *I'm out* *of here.*) □ BOB: *Well, that's all. I'm gone.* BILL: *See ya!* □ JANE: *I'm gone. See you guys.* JOHN: *See you, Jane.* FRED: *Bye, Jane.*

(I'm) having a wonderful time; wish you were here. a catch phrase that is thought to be written onto postcards by people who are away on vacation. □ *John wrote on all his cards, "Having a wonderful time; wish you were here." And he really meant it too.* □ *"I'm having a wonderful time; wish you were here," said Tom, speaking on the phone to Mary, suddenly feeling very insincere.*

I'm having quite a time. 1. I am having a very enjoyable time. □ JOHN: *Having fun?* JANE: *Oh, yes. I'm having quite a time.* □ BOB: *Do you like the seashore?* SALLY: *Yes, I'm having quite a time.* **2.** I am having a very difficult time. □ DOCTOR: *Well, what seems to be the problem?* MARY: *I'm having quite a time. It's my back.* DOCTOR: *Let's take a look at it.* □ FATHER: *How's school?* BILL: *Pretty tough. I'm having quite a time. Calculus is killing me.*

(I'm) having the time of my life. I am having the best time ever. □ BILL: *Are you having a good time, Mary?* MARY: *Don't worry about me. I'm having the time of my life.* □ MARY: *What do you think about this theme park?* BILL: *Having the time of my life. I don't want to leave.*

(I'm) just getting by. an expression indicating that one is just surviving, financially or otherwise. □ BOB: *How you doing, Tom?* TOM: *Just getting by, Bob.* □ *"I wish I could get a better job," remarked Tom. "I'm just getting by as it is."*

I'm just looking. See *I'm only looking.*

(I'm just) minding my own business. an answer to a greeting inquiry asking what one is doing. (This answer also can carry the implication "Since I am minding my own business, why aren't you minding your own business?") □ TOM: *Hey, man, what are you doing?* BILL: *Minding my own business. See you around.* □ SUE: *Hi, Mary. What have you been doing?* MARY: *I'm just minding my own business and trying to keep out of trouble.*

(I'm) (just) plugging along. I am doing satisfactorily.; I am just managing to function. □ BILL: *How are things going?* BOB: *I'm just plugging along.* □ SUE: *How are you doing, Fred?* FRED: *Just plugging along, thanks. And you?* SUE: *About the same.*

(I'm) (just) thinking out loud. I'm saying things that might better remain as private thoughts. (A way of characterizing or introducing one's opinions or thoughts. Also past tense.) □ SUE: *What are you saying, anyway? Sounds like you're scolding someone.* BOB: *Oh, sorry. I was just thinking out loud.* □ BOB: *Now, this goes over here.* BILL: *You want me to move that?* BOB: *Oh, no. Just thinking out loud.*

I'm like you an expression introducing a statement of a similarity that the speaker shares with the person spoken to. □ MARY: *And what do you think about this pair?* JANE: *I'm like you, I like the ones with lower heels.* □ *"I'm like you," confided Fred. "I think everyone ought to pay the same amount."*

I'm listening. AND **I'm all ears.** You have my attention, so you should talk. □ BOB: *Look, old pal. I want to talk to you about something.* TOM: *I'm listening.* □ BILL: *I guess I owe you an apology.* JANE: *I'm all ears.*

I'm not finished with you. I still have more to say to you. □ *Bill started to turn away when he thought the scolding was finished. "I'm not finished with you," bellowed his father.* □ *When the angry teacher paused briefly to catch his breath, Bob turned as if to go. "I'm not finished with you," screamed the teacher, filled anew with breath and invective.*

I'm not kidding. I am telling the truth.; I am not trying to fool you. □ MARY: *Those guys are all suspects in the robbery.* SUE: *No! They can't be!* MARY: *I'm not kidding!* □ JOHN (gesturing): *The fish I caught was this big!* JANE: *I don't believe it!* JOHN: *I'm not kidding!*

I'm not surprised. AND **I don't wonder.** It is not surprising.; It should not surprise anyone. □ MARY: *All this talk about war has my cousin very worried.* SUE: *No doubt. At his age, I don't wonder.* □ JOHN: *All of the better-looking ones sold out right away.* JANE: *I'm not surprised.*

I'm off. an expression said by someone who is just leaving. (Slang.) □ BOB: *Time to go. I'm off.* MARY: *Bye.* □ SUE: *Well, it's been fun. Good-bye. Got to go.* MARY: *I'm off too. Bye.*

I'm only looking. AND **I'm just looking.** I am not a buyer, I am only examining your merchandise. (A phrase said to a shopkeeper or clerk who asks, "May I help you?") □ CLERK: *May I help you?* MARY: *No, thanks. I'm only looking.* □ CLERK: *May I help you?* JANE: *I'm just looking, thank you.*

I'm out of here. AND **I'm outa here.** I am leaving this minute. (Slang.) □ *In three minutes I'm outa here.* □ *I'm out of here. Bye.*

I'm outa here. See the previous entry.

(I'm) pleased to meet you. an expression said when introduced to someone. □ TOM: *I'm Tom Thomas.* BILL: *Pleased to meet you. I'm Bill Franklin.* □ JOHN: *Have you met Sally Hill?* BILL: *I don't believe I've had the pleasure. I'm pleased to meet you, Sally.* SALLY: *My pleasure, Bill.*

I'm (really) fed up (with someone or something). I have had enough of someone or something. Something must be done. □ TOM: *This place is really dull.* JOHN: *Yeah. I'm fed up with it. I'm out of here!* □ SALLY: *Can't you do anything right?* BILL: *I'm really fed up with you! You're always picking on me!*

(I'm) sorry. the phrase used for a simple apology. □ BILL: *Oh! You stepped on my toe!* BOB: *I'm sorry.* □ JOHN: *You made me miss my bus!* SUE: *Sorry.*

(I'm) sorry to hear that. an expression of consolation. □ JOHN: *My cat died last week.* JANE: *I'm sorry to hear that.* □ BILL: *I'm afraid I won't be able to continue here as head teller.* MARY: *Sorry to hear that.*

(I'm) sorry you asked (that). I regret that you asked about something I wanted to forget. □ TOM: *What on earth is this hole in your suit jacket?* BILL: *I'm sorry you asked. I was feeding a squirrel and it bit through my pocket where the food was.* □ SALLY: *Why is there only canned soup in the cupboard?*

JOHN: *Sorry you asked that. We're broke. We have no money for food.* SALLY: *Want some soup?*

I'm speechless. I am so surprised that I cannot think of anything to say. □ MARY: *Fred and I were married last week.* SALLY: *I'm speechless.* □ TOM: *The mayor just died!* JANE: *What? I'm speechless!*

(I'm) (very) glad to meet you. a polite expression said to a person to whom one has just been introduced. □ MARY: *I'd like you to meet my brother, Tom.* BILL: *I'm very glad to meet you, Tom.* □ JANE: *Hi! I'm Jane.* BOB: *Glad to meet you. I'm Bob.*

I'm with you. I agree with you.; I will join with you in doing what you suggest. (With a stress on both *I* and *you*.) □ SALLY: *I think this old bridge is sort of dangerous.* JANE: *I'm with you. Let's go back another way.* □ BOB: *This place is horrible.* BILL: *I'm with you. Want to go somewhere else?*

Imagine that! See *Fancy that!*

immunize someone against something to vaccinate someone against some disease; to do a medical procedure that causes a resistance or immunity to a disease to develop in a person. □ *They wanted to immunize all the children against the measles.* □ *Have you been immunized against polio?*

implant something in(to) someone or something to embed something into someone or something. □ *The surgeon implanted a pacemaker into Fred.* □ *They implanted the device in Fred's chest.*

implicate someone in something to say that someone is involved in something. (*Someone* includes one-

self.) □ *Dan implicated Ann in the crime.* □ *Ted refused to implicate himself in the affair.*

impose something (up)on someone to force something on someone. (*Upon* is formal and less commonly used than *on*.) □ *Don't try to impose your ideas upon me!* □ *The colonists tried to impose their values on the indigenous peoples.*

impose (up)on someone to make a bothersome request of someone. (*Upon* is formal and less commonly used than *on*.) □ *I don't mean to impose upon you, but could you put me up for the night?* □ *Don't worry, I won't let you impose on me.*

impress someone with someone or something to awe someone with someone or something. □ *Are you trying to impress me with your wisdom?* □ *She impressed him with her friend, who was very tall.*

impress something (up)on someone to make someone fully aware of something. (*Upon* is formal and less commonly used than *on*.) □ *You must impress these facts upon everyone you meet.* □ *She impressed its importance on me.*

imprint something on(to) something 1. to print something onto something. □ *We imprinted your name onto your stationery and your business cards.* □ *Please imprint my initials on this watch.* **2.** AND **imprint something into something** to record something firmly in the memory of someone. □ *The severe accident imprinted a sense of fear onto Lucy's mind.* □ *Imprint the numbers into your brain and never forget them!* **3.** AND **imprint something into something**

to make a permanent record of something in an animal's brain. (As with newly hatched fowl, which imprint the image of the first moving creature into their brains.) □ *The sight of its mother imprinted itself on the little gosling's brain.* □ *Nature imprints this information into the bird's memory.*

imprint something into something See the previous entry.

imprison someone in something to lock someone up in something. □ *The authorities imprisoned him in a separate cell.* □ *Bob imprisoned Timmy in the closet for an hour.*

improve (up)on something to make something better. (*Upon* is formal and less commonly used than *on*.) □ *Do you really think you can improve upon this song?* □ *No one can improve on my favorite melody.*

improvise on something [for a musician] to create a new piece of music on an existing musical theme. □ *For an encore, the organist improvised on "Mary Had a Little Lamb."* □ *She chose to improvise on an old folk theme.*

in a bad way See *in bad shape.*

in a dead heat finishing a race at exactly the same time; tied. (Here, *dead* means "exact" or "total.") □ *The two horses finished the race in a dead heat.* □ *They ended the contest in a dead heat.*

in a flash quickly; immediately. □ *I'll be there in a flash.* □ *It happened in a flash. Suddenly my wallet was gone.*

in a huff in an angry or offended manner. (*In* can be replaced with *into.*) □ *He heard what we had to say, then left in a huff.* □ *She came in a huff and ordered us to bring her some-*thing to eat. □ *She gets into a huff very easily.*

in a mad rush in a hurry; in a busy rush. □ *I ran around all day today in a mad rush, looking for a present for Bill.* □ *Why are you always in a mad rush?*

in a snit in a fit of anger or irritation. (Slang.) □ *Don't get in a snit. It was an accident.* □ *Mary is in a snit because they didn't ask her to come to the shindig.*

in a (tight) spot caught in a problem; in a difficult position. (*In* can be replaced with *into.*) □ *Look, John, I'm in a tight spot. Can you lend me twenty dollars?* □ *I'm in a spot too. I need $300.* □ *I have never gotten into a tight spot.*

in a twit upset; frantic. (Slang.) □ *She's all in a twit because she lost her keys.* □ *Todd was in a twit and was quite rude to us.*

in a vicious circle in a situation in which the solution of one problem leads to a second problem, and the solution of the second problem brings back the first problem, etc. (*In* can be replaced with *into.*) □ *Life is so strange. I seem to be in a vicious circle most of the time.* □ *I put lemon in my tea to make it sour, then sugar to make it sweet. I'm in a vicious circle.* □ *Don't let your life get into a vicious circle.*

in a world of one's own aloof; detached; self-centered. (*In* can be replaced with *into.*) □ *John lives in a world of his own. He has very few friends.* □ *Mary walks around in a world of her own, but she's very intelligent.* □ *When she's thinking, she drifts into a world of her own.*

in any case a phrase that introduces or follows a conclusion. □ JANE: *In any case, I want you to do this.* JOHN: *All right. I'll do it.* □ MARY: *This one may or may not work out.* SUE: *In any case, I can do it if necessary.*

in bad faith without sincerity; with bad or dishonest intent; with duplicity. □ *It appears that you acted in bad faith and didn't live up to the terms of our agreement.* □ *If you do things in bad faith, you'll get a bad reputation.*

in bad shape AND **in a bad way** 1. injured or debilitated in any manner. (Slang.) □ *Fred had a little accident, and he's in bad shape.* □ *Tom needs exercise. He's in bad shape.* 2. pregnant. □ *Molly's in bad shape again, I hear.* □ *Yup, she's in bad shape all right — about four months in bad shape.*

in bad sorts in a bad humor. □ *Bill is in bad sorts today. He's very grouchy.* □ *I try to be extra nice to people when I'm in bad sorts.*

in bad taste AND **in poor taste** rude; vulgar; obscene. □ *Mrs. Franklin felt that your joke was in bad taste.* □ *We found the play to be in poor taste, so we walked out in the middle of the second act.*

in black and white official, in writing or printing. (Said of something, such as an agreement or a statement, that has been recorded in writing. *In* can be replaced with *into*.) □ *I have it in black and white that I'm entitled to three weeks of vacation each year.* □ *It says right here in black and white that oak trees make acorns.* □ *Please put the agreement into black and white.*

in broad daylight publicly visible in the daytime. □ *The thief stole the car in broad daylight.* □ *There they were, selling drugs in broad daylight.*

in creation See *on earth*.

in deep 1. deeply involved (with someone or something). (Slang.) □ *Mary and Sam are in deep.* □ *Carl is in deep with the mob.* 2. deeply in debt. (Often with *with* or *to*.) □ *Reggie is in deep with his bookie.* □ *I'm in deep to the department store.*

in deep water in a dangerous or vulnerable situation; in a serious situation; in trouble. (As if one were swimming in or fell into water that is over one's head. *In* can be replaced with *into*.) □ *John is having trouble with his taxes. He's in deep water.* □ *Bill is in deep water in algebra class. He's almost failing.* □ *He really got himself into deep water.*

in due time after the appropriate amount of time has expired; in a while. □ MARY: *When do you think the plane will arrive?* BILL: *In due time, my dear, in due time.* □ JOHN: *All these things will straighten out in due time.* JANE: *I just can't wait that long.*

in fine feather in good humor; in good health. (Refers to a healthy, and therefore beautiful, bird. *In* can be replaced with *into*.) □ *Hello, John. You appear to be in fine feather.* □ *Of course I'm in fine feather. I get lots of sleep.* □ *Good food and lots of sleep put me into fine feather.*

in full swing in progress; operating or running without restraint. (*In* can be replaced with *into*.) □ *We can't leave now! The party is in full swing.* □ *Our program to help the starving people is in full swing. You should see results soon.* □ *Just wait until our project gets into full swing.*

in good condition See the following entry.

in good shape AND **in good condition** physically and functionally sound and sturdy. (Used for both people and things. *In* can be replaced with *into*.) □ *This car isn't in good shape.* □ *I'd like to have one that's in better condition.* □ *Mary is in good condition. She works hard to keep healthy.* □ *You have to make an effort to get into good shape.*

in heat in a period of sexual excitement; in estrus. (Estrus is the period of time in which females are most willing to breed. This expression is usually used for animals. It has been used for humans in a joking sense. *In* can be replaced with *into*. See also *in season*.) □ *Our dog is in heat.* □ *She goes into heat every year at this time.* □ *When my dog is in heat, I have to keep her locked in the house.*

in less than no time very quickly. □ *I'll be there in less than no time.* □ *Don't worry. This won't take long. It'll be over with in less than no time.*

in mint condition in perfect condition. (Refers to the perfect state of a coin that has just been minted. *In* can be replaced with *into*.) □ *This is a fine car. It runs well and is in mint condition.* □ *We went through a house in mint condition and decided to buy it.* □ *We put our house into mint condition before we sold it.*

in my humble opinion a phrase introducing the speaker's opinion. □ *"In my humble opinion," began Fred, arrogantly, "I have achieved what no one else ever could."* □ BOB: *What are we going to do about the poor condition of the house next door?* BILL: *In my humble opinion, we will mind our own business.*

in my opinion See *as I see it*.

in my view See *as I see it*.

in name only nominally; not actual, only by terminology. □ *The president is head of the country in name only. Congress makes the laws.* □ *Mr. Smith is the boss of the Smith Company in name only. Mrs. Smith handles all the business affairs.*

in no mood to do something not to feel like doing something; to wish not to do something. □ *I'm in no mood to cook dinner tonight.* □ *Mother is in no mood to put up with our arguing.*

in nothing flat in exactly no time at all. □ *Of course I can get there in a hurry. I'll be there in nothing flat.* □ *We covered the distance between New York and Philadelphia in nothing flat.*

in one ear and out the other [for something to be] ignored; [for something to be] unheard or unheeded. (*In* can be replaced with *into*.) □ *Everything I say to you goes into one ear and out the other!* □ *Bill just doesn't pay attention. Everything is in one ear and out the other.*

in one fell swoop See *at one fell swoop*.

in one's birthday suit naked; nude. (In the "clothes" in which one was born. *In* can be replaced with *into*.) □ *I've heard that John sleeps in his birthday suit.* □ *We used to go down to the river and swim in our birthday suits.* □ *You have to get into your birthday suit to bathe.*

in one's blood See *in the blood*.

in one's mind's eye in one's mind. (Refers to visualizing something in one's mind.) □ *In my mind's eye, I can see trouble ahead.* □ *In her mind's eye, she could see a beautiful building beside the river. She decided to design such a building.*

in one's or its prime at one's or its peak or best time. □ *Our dog — that is in its prime — is very active.* □ *The program ended in its prime when we ran out of money.* □ *I could work long hours when I was in my prime.*

in one's right mind sane; rational and sensible. (Often in the negative.) □ *That was a stupid thing to do. You're not in your right mind.* □ *You can't be in your right mind! That sounds crazy!*

in one's second childhood being interested in things or people that normally interest children. □ *My father bought himself a toy train, and my mother said he was in his second childhood.* □ *Whenever I go to the river and throw stones, I feel as though I'm in my second childhood.*

in one's spare time in one's extra time; in the time not reserved for doing something else. □ *I write novels in my spare time.* □ *I'll try to paint the house in my spare time.*

in other words a phrase introducing a restatement of what has just been said. □ HENRY: *Sure I want to do it, but how much do I get paid?* ANDREW: *In other words, you're just doing it for the money.* □ BILL: *Well, I suppose I really should prepare my entourage for departure.* BOB: *In other words, you're leaving?* BILL: *One could say that, I suppose.* BOB: *Why didn't one?*

in over one's head with more difficulties than one can manage. □ *Cal-*culus is very hard for me. I'm in over my head.* □ *Ann is too busy. She's really in over her head.*

in play 1. being played. (Slang. Said of a ball in a game.) □ *The ball's in play, so you made the wrong move.* □ *No, it wasn't in play, you twit!* **2.** having to do with a company (or its stock) that is a candidate for acquisition by another company. (Financial markets.) □ *The company was in play, but nobody was buying it.* □ *The deal stocks that are in play right now offer excellent buying opportunities.*

in poor taste See *in bad taste.*

in print [for a book] to be available for sale. (Compare to *out of print.*) □ *I think I can get that book for you. It's still in print.* □ *This is the only book in print on this subject.*

in rags in worn-out and torn clothing. □ *Oh, look at my clothing. I can't go to the party in rags!* □ *I think the new casual fashions make you look as if you're in rags.*

in round figures See the following entry.

in round numbers AND **in round figures** as an estimated number; a figure that has been rounded off to the closest whole number. (*In* can be replaced with *into.*) □ *Please tell me in round numbers what it'll cost.* □ *I don't need the exact amount. Just give it to me in round figures.*

in season 1. currently available for selling. (Some foods and other things are available only at certain seasons. *In* can be replaced with *into,* especially when used with *come.*) □ *Oysters are available in season.* □ *Strawberries aren't in season in*

January. □ *When do strawberries come into season?* **2.** legally able to be caught or hunted. □ *Catfish are in season all year round.* □ *When are salmon in season?* **3.** [of a dog] in estrus; in heat. □ *My dog is in season every year at this time.* □ *When my dog is in season, I have to keep her locked in the house.*

in seventh heaven in a very happy state. (This is the highest heaven, where God exists.) □ *Ann was really in seventh heaven when she got a car of her own.* □ *I'd be in seventh heaven if I had a million dollars.*

in short order very quickly. □ *I can straighten out this mess in short order.* □ *The people came in and cleaned the place up in short order.*

in short supply scarce. (*In* can be replaced with *into*.) □ *Fresh vegetables are in short supply in the winter.* □ *Yellow cars are in short supply because everyone likes them and buys them.* □ *At this time of the year, fresh vegetables go into short supply.*

in stock readily available, as with goods in a store. □ *I'm sorry, I don't have that in stock. I'll have to order it for you.* □ *We have all our Christmas merchandise in stock now.*

in the air everywhere; all about. (Also used literally.) □ *There is such a feeling of joy in the air.* □ *We felt a sense of tension in the air.*

in the bag achieved; settled. (Slang.) □ *It's in the bag — as good as done.* □ *The election is in the bag unless the voters find out about my past.*

in the bargain in addition to what was agreed on. (*In* can be replaced with *into*.) □ *I bought a car, and they threw an air conditioner into the bar-*gain. □ *When I bought a house, I asked the seller to include the furniture in the bargain.*

in the black not in debt; in a financially profitable condition. (Refers to writing figures in black ink rather than in red ink, which would indicate a debit. *In* can be replaced with *into*. Compare to *in the red*.) □ *I wish my accounts were in the black.* □ *Sally moved the company into the black.*

in the blood AND **in one's blood** built into one's personality or character. (Actually in the genes, not the blood.) □ *John's a great runner. It's in his blood.* □ *The whole family is very athletic. It's in the blood.*

in the bullpen [for a baseball pitcher to be] in a special place near a baseball playing field, warming up to pitch. (*In* can be replaced with *into*.) □ *You can tell who is pitching next by seeing who is in the bullpen.* □ *Our best pitcher just went into the bullpen. He'll be pitching soon.*

in the cards in the future. □ *Well, what do you think is in the cards for tomorrow?* □ *I asked the boss if there was a raise in the cards for me.*

in the doghouse in trouble; in (someone's) disfavor. (As if a person would be sent outside for misbehavior — as one might send a dog from the comforts of the house to the discomforts of the yard. *In* can be replaced with *into*.) □ *I'm really in the doghouse. I was late for an appointment.* □ *I hate being in the doghouse all the time. I don't know why I can't stay out of trouble.*

in the doldrums sluggish; inactive; in low spirits. (*In* can be replaced with into.) □ He's usually in the doldrums in the winter. □ I had some bad news yesterday, which put me into the doldrums.

in the first place originally; basically; for openers. (This can run through **in the second place, in the third place**, but not much higher.) □ BILL: What did I do? BOB: In the first place, you had no business being there at all. In the second place, you were acting rude. □ BILL: Why on earth did you do it in the first place? SUE: I don't know.

in the flesh really present; in person. □ I've heard that the queen is coming here in the flesh. □ Is she really here? In the flesh? □ I've wanted a color television for years, and now I've got one right here in the flesh.

in the gutter [for a person to be] in a low state; depraved. (In can be replaced with into.) □ You had better straighten out your life, or you'll end up in the gutter. □ His bad habits put him into the gutter.

in the hole in debt. (In can be replaced with into. Also used literally.) □ I'm $200 in the hole. □ Our finances end up in the hole every month.

in the interest of saving time I can hurry things along. □ MARY: In the interest of saving time, I'd like to save questions for the end of my talk. BILL: But I have an important question now! □ "In the interest of saving time," said Jane, "I'll give you the first three answers."

in the know knowledgeable. (In can be replaced with into.) □ Let's ask Bob. He's in the know. □ I have no knowledge of how to work this machine.

I think I can get into the know very quickly though.

in the lap of luxury in luxurious surroundings. (In can be replaced with into.) □ John lives in the lap of luxury because his family is very wealthy. □ When I retire, I'd like to live in the lap of luxury.

in the limelight AND **in the spotlight** at the center of attention. (In can be replaced with into. The literal sense is also used. Limelight is an obsolete type of spotlight, and the word occurs only in this phrase.) □ John will do almost anything to get himself into the limelight. □ I love being in the spotlight. □ All elected officials spend a lot of time in the limelight.

in the line of duty as part of the expected (military or police) duties □ When soldiers fight people in a war, it's in the line of duty. □ Police officers have to do things they may not like in the line of duty.

in the long run over a long period of time; ultimately. □ We'd be better off in the long run buying one instead of renting one. □ In the long run, we'd be happier in the South.

in the main basically; generally. □ MARY: Everything looks all right — in the main. SALLY: What details need attention? MARY: Just a few things here and there. Like on the next page. □ JOHN: Are you all ready? SUE: I think we're ready, in the main. JOHN: Then, we shall go.

in the money 1. wealthy. □ John is really in the money. He's worth millions. □ If I am ever in the money, I'll be generous. 2. in a winning position in a race or contest. (As if one had won the prize money.) □ *I knew when Jane came around the final turn that she was in the money.* □ *The horses coming in first, second, and third are said to be in the money.*

in the nick of time just in time; at the last possible instant; just before it's too late. □ *The doctor arrived in the nick of time. The patient's life was saved.* □ *I reached the airport in the nick of time.*

in the pink (of condition) in very good health; in very good condition, physically and emotionally. (*In* can be replaced with *into*.) □ *The garden is lovely. All the flowers are in the pink of condition.* □ *Jane has to exercise hard to get into the pink of condition.* □ *I'd like to be in the pink, but I don't have the time.*

in the prime of life in the best and most productive period of one's life. (*In* can be replaced with *into*.) □ *The good health of one's youth can carry over into the prime of life.* □ *He was struck down by a heart attack in the prime of life.*

in the public eye publicly; visible to all; conspicuous. (*In* can be replaced with *into*.) □ *Elected officials find themselves constantly in the public eye.* □ *The mayor made it a practice to get into the public eye as much as possible.*

in the red in debt. (Refers to writing debit figures in red ink rather than in black ink. *In* can be replaced with *into*. Compare to *in the black*.) □ *My accounts are in the red at the end of every month.* □ *It's easy to get into the red if you don't pay close attention to the amount of money you spend.*

in the right on the moral or legal side of an issue; on the right side of an issue. □ *I felt I was in the right, but the judge ruled against me.* □ *It's hard to argue with Jane. She always believes that she's in the right.*

in the same boat in the same situation; having the same problem. (*In* can be replaced with *into*.) □ TOM: *I'm broke. Can you lend me twenty dollars?* BILL: *Sorry. I'm in the same boat.* □ *Jane and Mary are in the same boat. They both have been called for jury duty.*

in the same breath [stated or said] almost at the same time; as part of the same thought or conversation. □ *He told me I was lazy, but then in the same breath he said I was doing a good job.* □ *The teacher said that the students were working hard and, in the same breath, that they were not working hard enough.*

in the spotlight See *in the limelight*.

in the suds alcohol intoxicated. (Slang.) □ *Fred is in the suds and can't see.* □ *When Bob is in the suds, he's mean.*

in the tube **1.** in the arched underside of the leading edge of a large wave. (Surfing slang.) □ *Todd is in the tube and looks great.* □ *On a day like today, I want to be out there in the tube.* **2.** at risk. □ *He's in the tube now, but things should straighten out soon.* □ *If you find yourself in the tube in this matter, just give me a ring.*

in the twinkling of an eye very quickly. (Biblical.) □ *In the twinkling of an eye, the deer had disappeared into the forest.* □ *I gave Bill ten dollars and, in the twinkling of an eye, he spent it.*

in the wind about to happen. (Also used literally.) □ *There are some major changes in the wind. Expect these* *changes to happen soon.* □ *There is something in the wind. We'll find out what it is soon.*

in the world See *on earth.*

in the wrong on the wrong or illegal side of an issue; guilty or in error. □ *I felt she was in the wrong, but the judge ruled in her favor.* □ *It's hard to argue with Jane. She always believes that everyone else is in the wrong.*

in there sincere; likable. (Slang.) □ *Martha is really in there. Everybody likes her.* □ *I like a guy who's in there — who thinks about other people.*

in this day and age now; in these modern times. □ BILL: *Ted flunked out of school.* MOTHER: *Imagine that! Especially in this day and age.* □ BILL: *Taxes keep going up and up.* BOB: *What do you expect in this day and age?*

in two shakes of a lamb's tail very quickly. □ *I'll be there in two shakes of a lamb's tail.* □ *In two shakes of a lamb's tail, the bird flew away.*

in view of due to; because of. □ *"In view of the bad weather," began Tom, "the trip has been canceled."* □ ANDREW: *Can we hurry? We'll be late.* MARY: *In view of your attitude about going in the first place, I'm surprised you even care.*

incarcerate someone in something to imprison someone in something. □ *The sheriff incarcerated Lefty in the town jail.* □ *He had wanted to incarcerate Max in the jail too.*

inch by inch one inch at a time; little by little. □ *Traffic moved along inch by inch.* □ *Inch by inch, the snail moved across the stone.*

incidentally See *by the way.*

incline toward someone or something 1. to lean or slant toward someone or something. □ *The piece of scenery inclined toward Roger very slowly and stopped its fall just in time.* □ *The tree inclined toward the flow of the wind.* **2.** to favor or lean toward choosing someone or something. □ *I don't know who to choose. I incline toward Terri but I also favor Amy.* □ *I'm inclining toward chocolate.*

include someone in (something) to invite someone to participate in something. (*Someone* includes *oneself.*) □ *Let's include Terri in the planning session.* □ *I will include her in.* □ *Without asking, Henry included himself in the group going on a picnic.*

incorporate someone or something in(to) something to build someone or something into something; to combine someone or something into something. (*Someone* includes *oneself.*) □ *We want to incorporate you into our sales force very soon.* □ *The prince had incorporated himself into the main governing body.*

inoculate someone against something to immunize someone against a disease. □ *We need to inoculate all the children against whooping cough.* □ *Have you been inoculated against measles?*

ins and outs of something the correct and successful way to do something; the special things that one needs to know to do something. □ *I don't understand the ins and outs of politics.* □ *Jane knows the ins and outs of working with computers.*

inscribe something on(to) something AND **inscribe something with something** to write or engrave certain information on something. (Emphasis is on the message that is inscribed.) □ *The jeweler inscribed Amy's good wishes onto the watch.* □ *I inscribed my name on my tools.* □ *Could you please inscribe this trophy with the information on this sheet of paper?* □ *I inscribed the bracelet with her name.*

inscribe something with something See the previous entry.

insist (up)on something to demand something. (*Upon* is formal and less commonly used than *on*.) □ *I want you here now! We all insist upon it!* □ *I insist on it too.*

instill something in(to) something to add something to a situation. □ *The presence of the mayor instilled a legitimacy into the proceedings.* □ *Sharon sought to instill a little levity in the meeting.*

intervene in something to get involved in something. □ *I will have to intervene in this matter. It's getting out of hand.* □ *I want to intervene in this before it gets out of hand.*

introduce someone to someone to make someone acquainted with someone else. (*Someone* includes *oneself*.) □ *I would like to introduce you to my cousin, Rudolph.* □ *Allow me to introduce myself to you.*

intrude (up)on someone or something to encroach on someone or something or matters that concern only someone or something. (*Upon* is formal and less commonly used than *on*.) □ *I didn't mean to intrude upon you.* □ *Please don't intrude on our meeting. Please wait outside.*

invest in someone or something to put resources into someone or some-

thing in hopes of increasing the value of the person or thing. (The emphasis is on the act of investing.) □ *We invested in Tom, and we have every right to expect a lot from him.* □ *She invested in junk bonds heavily.*

invite someone in(to some place) to bid or request someone to enter a place. (*Someone* includes *oneself*.) □ *Don't leave Dan out there in the rain. Invite him into the house!* ⊤ *Oh, do invite in the visitors!* □ *Yes, invite them in.* □ *To my horror, he invited himself in.*

invite someone out to ask someone out on a date. □ *I would love to invite you out sometime. If I did, would you go?* □ *Have you been invited out this week?*

invite someone over (for something) to bid or request someone to come to one's house for something, such as a meal, party, chat, cards, etc. □ *Let's invite Tony and Nick over for dinner.* ⊤ *Let's invite over some new people.* □ *I will invite Amy over for a talk.*

iron something out **1.** to use a flatiron to make cloth flat or smooth. □ *I will iron the drapes out, so they will stay flat.* ⊤ *I ironed out the drapes.* **2.** to ease a problem; to smooth out a problem. (Figurative. Here *problem* is synonymous with *wrinkle*.) □ *It's only a little problem. I can iron it out very quickly.* ⊤ *We will iron out all these little matters first.*

(Is) anything going on? Is there anything exciting or interesting happening here? □ ANDREW: *Hey, Man! Anything going on?* HENRY: *No. This place is dull as can be.* □ BOB: *Come in, Tom.* TOM: *Is anything going* on? BOB: *No. You've come on a very ordinary day.*

(Is) everything okay? How are you?; How are things? □ JOHN: *Hi, Mary. Is everything okay?* MARY: *Sure. What about you?* JOHN: *I'm okay.* □ WAITER: *Is everything okay?* BILL: *Yes, it's fine.*

(Is it) cold enough for you? a greeting inquiry made during very cold weather. □ BOB: *Hi, Bill! Is it cold enough for you?* BILL: *It's unbelievable!* □ JOHN: *Glad to see you. Is it cold enough for you?* BILL: *Oh, yes! This is awful!*

(Is it) hot enough for you? a greeting inquiry made during very hot weather. □ BOB: *Hi, Bill! Is it hot enough for you?* BILL: *Yup.* □ JOHN: *Nice to see you here! Is it hot enough for you?* BILL: *Good grief, yes! This is awful!*

Is someone there? a way of requesting to talk to someone in particular over the telephone. (This is not just a request to find out where *someone* is. The *someone* is usually a person's name.) □ TOM: *Hello?* MARY: *Hello. Is Bill there?* TOM: *No. Can I take a message?* □ TOM: *Hello?* MARY: *Hello. Is Tom there?* TOM: *Speaking.*

Is that everything? See *(Will there be) anything else?*

Is that right? See the following entry.

Is that so? AND **Is that right? 1.** Is what you said correct? (With rising question intonation.) □ HENRY: *These are the ones we need.* ANDREW: *Is that right? They don't look so good to me.* □ FRED: *Tom is the one who came in late.* RACHEL: *Is that so? It looked like Bill to me.* **2.** That is what you

say, but I do not believe you. (No rising question intonation. Slightly rude.) □ MARY: *You are making a mess of this.* ALICE: *Is that so? And I suppose that you're perfect?* □ BOB: *I found your performance to be weak in a number of places.* HENRY: *Is that right? Why don't you tell me about those weaknesses.*

Is there anything else? See *(Will there be) anything else?*

Is there some place I can wash up? See *Where can I wash up?*

(Is) this (seat) taken? an inquiry made by a person in a theater, auditorium, etc., asking someone already seated whether an adjacent seat is available or already taken. □ *Finally, Bill came to a row where there was an empty seat. Bill leaned over to the person sitting beside the empty seat and whispered, "Is this seat taken?"* □ FRED: *'Scuse me. This taken?* ALICE: *No. Help yourself.*

(It) beats me. AND **(It's) got me beat.; You got me beat.** I do not know the answer.; I cannot figure it out.; The question has me stumped. (The stress is on *me*.) □ BILL: *When are we supposed to go over to Tom's?* BOB: *Beats me.* □ SALLY: *What's the largest river in the world?* BOB: *You got me beat.*

It blows my mind! It really amazes and shocks me. (Slang.) □ BILL: *Did you hear about Tom's winning the lottery?* SUE: *Yes, it blows my mind!* □ JOHN: *Look at all that paper! What a waste of trees!* JANE: *It blows my mind!*

(It) can't be helped. Nothing can be done to help the situation.; It isn't anyone's fault. □ JOHN: *The accident has blocked traffic in two directions.*

JANE: *It can't be helped. They have to get the people out of the cars and send them to the hospital.* □ BILL: *My goodness, the lawn looks dead!* SUE: *It can't be helped. There's no rain and water is rationed.* □ JOHN: *I'm sorry I broke your figurine.* SUE: *It couldn't be helped.* JOHN: *I'll replace it.* SUE: *That would be nice.* □ BILL: *I'm sorry I'm late. I hope it didn't mess things up.* BOB: *It can't be helped.*

(It) couldn't be better. AND **(Things) couldn't be better.** Everything is fine. □ JOHN: *How are things going?* JANE: *Couldn't be better.* □ BILL: *I hope everything is okay with your new job.* MARY: *Things couldn't be better.*

(It) doesn't bother me any. AND **(It) doesn't bother me at all.** It does not trouble me at all.; I have no objection. (Not very polite or cordial. Compare to *(It) don't bother me none.*; *(It) won't bother me any.*) □ JOHN: *Do you mind if I sit here?* JANE: *Doesn't bother me any.* □ SALLY (smoking a cigarette): *Do you mind if I smoke?* BILL: *It doesn't bother me any.*

(It) doesn't bother me at all. See the previous entry.

(It) doesn't hurt to ask. AND **(It) never hurts to ask.** a phrase said when one asks a question, even when the answer is known to be no. □ JOHN: *Can I take some of these papers home with me?* JANE: *No, you can't. You know that.* JOHN: *Well, it doesn't hurt to ask.* □ SUE: *Can I have two of these?* SALLY: *Certainly not!* SUE: *Well, it never hurts to ask.* SALLY: *Well, it just may!*

It doesn't quite suit me. See *This doesn't quite suit me.*

(It) don't bother me none. AND **(It) don't make me no nevermind.** It does not affect me one way or the other.; *It doesn't bother me any.* (Familiar and ungrammatical. Sometimes used for effect.) □ JOHN: *Mind if I sit here?* BOB: *It don't bother me none.* □ MARY: *Can I smoke?* BILL: *Don't bother me none.*

(It) don't make me no nevermind. See the previous entry.

(It) hasn't been easy. AND **Things haven't been easy.** Things have been difficult, but I have survived. □ BILL: *I'm so sorry about all your troubles. I hope things are all right now.* BOB: *It hasn't been easy, but things are okay now.* □ JOHN: *How are you getting on after your dog died?* BILL: *Things haven't been easy.*

It isn't worth it. **1.** Its value does not justify the action you propose. □ MARY: *Should I write a letter in support of your request?* SUE: *No, don't bother. It isn't worth it.* □ JOHN: *Do you suppose we should report that man to the police?* JANE: *No, it isn't worth it.* **2.** Its importance does not justify the concern you are showing. □ TOM: *I'm so sorry about your roses all dying.* MARY: *Not to worry. It isn't worth it. They were sort of sickly anyway.* □ JOHN: *Should I have this coat cleaned? The stain isn't coming out.* SUE: *It isn't worth it. I only wear it when I shovel snow anyway.*

It isn't worth the trouble. *Don't bother. It isn't worth it.* □ TOM: *Shall I wrap all this stuff back up?* MARY: *No. It's not worth the trouble. Just stuff it in a paper bag.* □ JANE: *Do you want me to try to save this little bit of cake?* JOHN: *Oh, no! It's not worth the trouble. I'll just eat it.*

(It) just goes to show (you) (something). That incident or story has an important moral or message. □ TOM: *The tax people finally caught up with Henry.* SALLY: *See! It just goes to show.* □ *Indignant over the treatment she received at the grocery and angry at the youthful clerk, Sally muttered, "Young people. They expect too much. It just goes to show you how society has broken down."*

(It) makes me no difference. See *(It) makes no difference to me.*

(It) makes me no nevermind. See *(It) makes no difference to me.*

(It) makes no difference to me. AND **(It) makes me no difference.; (It) makes me no nevermind.** I really do not care, one way or the other. (The first one is standard, the others are colloquial.) □ BILL: *Mind if I sit here?* TOM: *Makes no difference to me.* □ BILL: *What would you say if I ate the last piece of cake?* BOB: *Makes me no difference.*

(It) never hurts to ask. See *(It) doesn't hurt to ask.*

It never rains but it pours. a lot of bad things tend to happen at the same time. (Proverb.) □ *The car won't start, the stairs broke, and the dog died. It never rains but it pours.*

(It) (really) doesn't matter to me. I do not care. □ ANDREW: *What shall I do? What shall I do?* ALICE: *Do whatever you like. Jump off a bridge. Go live in the jungle. It really doesn't matter to me.* □ TOM: *I'm leaving you. Mary and I have decided that we're in love.* SUE: *So, go ahead. It doesn't matter to me. I don't care what you do.*

it strikes me that it seems to me that. □ HENRY: *It strikes me that you are losing a little weight.* MARY: *Oh, I love you!* □ *"It strikes me that all this money we are spending is accomplishing very little," said Bill.*

(It) suits me (fine). It is fine with me. □ JOHN: *Is this one okay?* MARY: *Suits me.* □ JOHN: *I'd like to sit up front where I can hear better.* MARY: *Suits me fine.*

(It) won't bother me any. AND **(It) won't bother me at all.** It will not trouble me at all.; I have no objection if you wish to do that. (Not very polite or cordial. Compare to *(It) doesn't bother me any.*) □ JOHN: *Will you mind if I sit here?* JANE: *Won't bother me any.* □ SALLY (lighting a cigarette): *Do you mind if I smoke?* BILL: *It won't bother me at all.*

(It) won't bother me at all. See the previous entry.

(It) works for me. It is fine with me. (Slang. With stress on *works* and *me.* The answer to *Does it work for you?*) □ BOB: *Is it okay if I sign us up for the party?* SALLY: *It works for me.* □ TOM: *Is Friday all right for the party?* BILL: *Works for me.* BOB: *It works for me too.*

It's all someone needs. See *That's all someone needs.*

It's been. a phrase said on leaving a party or other gathering. (Slang or familiar colloquial. A shortening of *It's been lovely* or some similar expression.) □ MARY: *Well, it's been. We really have to go, though.* ANDREW: *So glad you could come over. Bye.* □ FRED: *Bye, you guys. See you.* SALLY: *It's been. Really it has. Toodle-oo.*

(It's been) good talking to you. AND **(It's) been good to talk to you.; (It's**

been) **nice talking to you.** a polite phrase said upon departure, at the end of a conversation. □ MARY (as the elevator stops): *Well, this is my floor. I've got to get off.* JOHN: *Bye, Mary. It's been good talking to you.* □ JOHN: *It's been good talking to you, Fred. See you around.* FRED: *Yeah. See you.*

(It's) been good to talk to you. See the previous entry.

(It's been) nice talking to you. See *(It's been) good talking to you.*

(It's) better than nothing. Having something that is not satisfactory is better than having nothing at all. □ JOHN: *How do you like your dinner?* JANE: *It's better than nothing.* JOHN: *That bad, huh?* □ JOHN: *Did you see your room? How do you like it?* JANE: *Well, I guess it's better than nothing.*

It's for you. This telephone call is for you. □ HENRY: *Hello?* FRED: *Hello. Is Bill there?* HENRY: *Hey, Bill! It's for you.* BILL: *Thanks. Hello?* □ *"It's for you,"* said Mary, handing the telephone receiver to Sally.

(It's) good to be here. AND **(It's) nice to be here.** I feel welcome in this place.; It is good to be here. □ JOHN: *I'm so glad you could come.* JANE: *Thank you. It's good to be here.* □ ALICE: *Welcome to our house!* JOHN: *Thank you, it's nice to be here.*

(It's) good to have you here. AND **(It's) nice to have you here.** Welcome to this place.; It is good that you are here. □ JOHN: *It's good to have you here.* JANE: *Thank you for asking me.* □ ALICE: *Oh, I'm so glad I came!* FRED: *Nice to have you here.*

(It's) good to hear your voice. a polite phrase said upon beginning or

ending a telephone conversation. □ BOB: *Hello?* BILL: *Hello, it's Bill.* BOB: *Hello, Bill. It's good to hear your voice.* □ BILL: *Hello, Tom. This is Bill.* TOM: *Hi, Bill. It's good to hear your voice. What's cooking?*

(It's) good to see you (again). a polite phrase said when greeting someone whom one has met before. □ BILL: *Hi, Bob. Remember me? I met you last week at the Wilsons'.* BOB: *Oh, hello, Bill. Good to see you again.* □ FRED: *Hi. Good to see you again!* BOB: *Nice to see you, Fred.*

(It's) got me beat. See *(It) beats me.*

(It's) just what you need. See *That's all someone needs.*

(It's) nice to be here. See *(It's) good to be here.*

(It's) nice to have you here. See *(It's) good to have you here.*

(It's) nice to meet you. an expression said just after being introduced to someone. □ TOM: *Sue, this is my sister, Mary.* SUE: *It's nice to meet you, Mary.* MARY: *How are you, Sue?* □ BOB: *I'm Bob. Nice to see you here.* JANE: *Nice to meet you, Bob.*

(It's) nice to see you. an expression said when greeting or saying goodbye to someone. □ MARY: *Hi, Bill. It's nice to see you.* BILL: *Nice to see you, Mary. How are things?* □ JOHN: *Come on in, Jane. Nice to see you.* JANE: *Thanks, and thank you for inviting me.*

(It's) no trouble. Do not worry, this is not a problem. □ MARY: *Do you mind carrying all this up to my apartment?* TOM: *It's no trouble.* □ BOB: *Would it be possible for you to get this* back to me today? BILL: *Sure. No trouble.*

(It's) none of your business! It is nothing that you need to know. It is none of your concern. (Not very polite.) □ ALICE: *How much does a little diamond like that cost?* MARY: *None of your business!* □ JOHN: *Do you want to go out with me Friday night?* MARY: *Sorry, I don't think so.* JOHN: *Well, what are you doing then?* MARY: *None of your business!*

(It's) not half bad. Not as bad as one might have thought. □ MARY: *How do you like this play?* JANE: *Not half bad.* □ JANE: *Well, how do you like college?* FRED: *It's not half bad.*

(It's) not supposed to. AND **(Someone's) not supposed to.** a phrase indicating that someone or something is not meant to do something. (Often with a person's name or a pronoun as a subject.) □ FRED: *This little piece keeps falling off.* CLERK: *It's not supposed to.* □ BILL: *Tom just called from Detroit and says he's coming back tomorrow.* MARY: *That's funny. He's not supposed to.*

It's on me. I will pay this bill. (Usually a bill for a meal or drinks. Similar to *This one's on me.*) □ *As the waiter set down the glasses, Fred said, "It's on me," and grabbed the check.* □ JOHN: *Check, please.* BILL: *No, it's on me this time.*

(It's) out of the question. It cannot be done.; No! (A polite but very firm No!) □ JANE: *I think we should buy a watchdog.* JOHN: *Out of the question.* □ JOHN: *Can we go to the mountains for a vacation this year?* JANE: *It's out of the question.*

(It's) time for a change. an expression announcing a decision to make a change. □ BILL: *Are you really going to take a new job?* MARY: *Yes, it's time for a change.* □ JANE: *Are you going to Florida for your vacation?* FRED: *No. It's time for a change. We're going skiing.*

(It's) time to go. It is now time to leave. (Usually said by guests, but can be said by an adult to children who are guests.) □ JANE: *Look at the clock! Time to go!* JOHN: *Yup! I'm out of here too.* □ MOTHER: *It's four o'clock. The party's over. Time to go.* BILL: *I had a good time. Thank you.*

(It's) time to hit the road. AND **(I'd) better hit the road.; (I've) got to hit the road.** a phrase indicating that it is time that one departed. (See *(I) have to shove off* for other possible variations.) □ HENRY: *Look at the clock. It's past midnight. It's time to hit the road.* ANDREW: *Yeah. We got to go.* SUE: *Okay, good night.* □ BILL: *I've got to hit the road. I have a long day tomorrow.* MARY: *Okay, good night.* BILL: *Bye, Mary.*

(It's) time to move along. See *(It's) time to run.*

(It's) time to push along. See *(It's) time to run.*

(It's) time to push off. See the following entry.

(It's) time to run. AND **(It's) time to move along.; (It's) time to push along.; (It's) time to push off.; (It's) time to split.** an announcement of one's desire or need to depart. (See *(I) have to shove off* for an illustration of other possible variations.) □ ANDREW: *Time to push off. I've got to get home by noon.* HENRY: *See you,* *dude.* □ JOHN: *It's time to split. I've got to go.* SUE: *Okay. See you tomorrow.*

(It's) time to shove off. See *(I) have to shove off.*

(It's) time to split. See *(It's) time to run.*

It's time we should be going. a statement made by one member of a pair (or group) of guests to the other member(s). (Typically, a way for a husband or wife to signal the other spouse that it is time to leave.) □ *Mr. Franklin looked at his wife and said softly, "It's time we should be going."* □ TOM: *Well, I suppose it's time we should be going.* MARY: *Yes, we really should.* ALICE: *So early?*

It's you! It suits you perfectly.; It is just your style. □ JOHN (trying on jacket): *How does this look?* SALLY: *It's you!* □ SUE: *I'm taking a job with the candy company. I'll be managing a store on Maple Street.* MARY: *It's you! It's you!*

It's your funeral. If that is what you are going to do, you will have to endure the consequences. □ TOM: *I'm going to call in sick and go to the ball game instead of to work today.* MARY: *Go ahead. It's your funeral.* □ BILL: *I'm going to take my car to the racetrack and see if I can race against someone.* SUE: *It's your funeral.*

(I've) been getting by. a response to a greeting inquiry into one's well-being indicating that one is having a hard time surviving or that things are just all right, but they could be much better. (See also *(I'm) just getting by.*) □ JOHN: *How are things?* JANE: *Oh, I've been getting by.* □ SUE: *How are you doing?* MARY: *Been getting by. Things could be better.*

(I've) been keeping busy. AND **(I've been) keeping busy.** a response to a specific greeting inquiry asking what one has been doing. □ SUE: *What've you been doing?* JOHN: *Been keeping busy. And you?* SUE: *About the same.* □ MARY: *Been keeping busy?* BOB: *Yeah. Been keeping busy.*

(I've) been keeping cool. AND **(I've been) keeping cool.** an answer to a question about what one has been doing during very hot weather. □ JANE: *How do you like this hot weather?* BILL: *I've been keeping cool.* □ MARY: *Been keeping cool?* BOB: *Yeah. Been keeping cool.*

(I've) been keeping myself busy. AND **(I've been) keeping myself busy.** a typical response to a greeting inquiry asking what one has been doing. □ BILL: *What have you been doing?* BOB: *I've been keeping myself busy. What about you?* BILL: *About the same.* □ JOHN: *Yo! What have you been up to?* BILL: *Been keeping myself busy.*

(I've) been keeping out of trouble. AND **(I've been) keeping out of trouble.** a response to any greeting inquiry that asks what one has been doing. □ JOHN: *What have you been doing, Fred?* FRED: *Been keeping out of trouble.* JOHN: *Yeah. Me too.* □ MARY: *How are things, Tom?* TOM: *Oh, I've been keeping out of trouble.*

(I've) been okay. a response to any greeting inquiry that asks how one has been. □ BILL: *Well, how have you been, good buddy?* JOHN: *I've been okay.* □ SUE: *How you doing?* JANE: *Been okay. And you?* SUE: *The same.*

I've been there. I know exactly what you are talking about.; I know exactly what you are going through.

□ JOHN: *Wow! Those sales meetings really wear me out!* JANE: *I know what you mean. I've been there.* □ SUE: *These employment interviews are very tiring.* BOB: *I know it! I've been there.*

(I've) been under the weather. a greeting response indicating that one has been ill. □ JOHN: *How have you been?* SALLY: *I've been under the weather, but I'm better.* □ DOCTOR: *How are you?* MARY: *I've been under the weather.* DOCTOR: *Maybe we can fix that. What seems to be the trouble?*

(I've) been up to no good. a vague greeting response indicating that one has been doing mischief. □ JOHN: *What have you been doing, Tom?* TOM: *Oh, I've been up to no good, as usual.* JOHN: *Yeah. Me too.* □ MARY: *Been keeping busy as usual?* SUE: *Yeah. Been up to no good, as usual.* MARY: *I should have known.*

(I've) (got) better things to do. There are better ways to spend my time.; I cannot waste any more time on this matter. (Either *I've got* or *I have*.) □ ANDREW: *Good-bye. I've got better things to do than stand around here listening to you brag.* HENRY: *Well, good-bye and good riddance.* □ MARY: *How did things go at your meeting with the zoning board?* SALLY: *I gave up. Can't fight city hall. Better things to do.*

(I've) got to be shoving off. See *(I) have to shove off.*

(I've) got to fly. AND **I('ve) gotta fly.** a phrase announcing one's need to depart. (See *(I) have to shove off* for other possible variations.) □ BILL: *Well, time's up. I've got to fly.* BOB: *Oh, it's early yet. Stay a while.* BILL: *Sorry. I've got to go.* □ *"It's past lunchtime. I've got to fly," said Alice.*

□ *Time's up. I've got to fly.* □ *I've gotta fly. See you later.*

(I've) got to get moving. a phrase announcing one's need to depart. □ BILL: *Time to go. Got to get moving.* SALLY: *Bye, Tom.* □ MARY: *It's late and I've got to get moving.* SUE: *Well, if you must, okay. Come again sometime.* MARY: *Bye.*

(I've) got to go. a phrase announcing one's need to depart. □ ANDREW: *Bye, I've got to go.* RACHEL: *Bye, little brother. See you.* □ SALLY: *Ciao! Got to go.* SUE: *See ya! Take it easy.*

(I've) got to go home and get my beauty sleep. a phrase announcing one's need to depart. (See *(I) have to shove off.* for other possible variations.) □ SUE: *Leaving so early?* JOHN: *I've got to go home and get my beauty sleep.* □ JANE: *I've got to go home and get my beauty sleep.* FRED: *Well, you look to me like you've had enough.* JANE: *Why, thank you.*

(I've) got to hit the road. See *(It's) time to hit the road.*

(I've) got to run. a phrase announcing one's need to depart. □ JOHN: *Got to run. It's late.* JANE: *Me too. See ya, bye-bye.* □ MARY: *Want to watch another movie?* BILL: *No, thanks. I've got to run.*

(I've) got to shove off. See *(I) have to shove off.*

(I've) got to split. a phrase announcing one's need to depart. □ JANE: *Look at the time! Got to split.* MARY: *See you later, Jane.* □ BILL: *It's getting late. I've got to split.* SUE: *Okay, see you tomorrow.* BILL: *Good night.*

(I've) got to take off. a phrase announcing one's need or desire to depart. □ MARY: *Got to take off. Bye.* BOB: *Leaving so soon?* MARY: *Yes. Time to go.* BOB: *Bye.* □ *"Look at the time. I've got to take off!"* shrieked Alice.

I've got work to do. 1. I'm too busy to stay here any longer. □ JANE: *Time to go. I've got work to do.* JOHN: *Me too. See you.* □ BOB: *I have to leave now.* BILL: *So soon?* BOB: *Yes, I've got work to do.* **2.** Do not bother me. I'm busy. □ BILL: *Can I ask you a question?* JANE: *I've got work to do.* □ MARY: *There are some things we have to get straightened out on this Wilson contract.* JOHN: *I've got work to do. It will have to wait.*

I've had a lovely time. AND **We've had a lovely time.** a polite expression said to a host or hostess on departure. □ BOB: *I've had a lovely time. Thanks for asking me.* FRED: *We're just delighted you could come. Good night.* BOB: *Good night.* □ SUE: *We've had a lovely time. Good night.* BILL: *Next time don't stay away so long. Good night.*

I've had enough of this! I will not take any more of this situation! □ SALLY: *I've had enough of this! I'm leaving!* FRED: *Me too!* □ JOHN (glaring at Tom): *I've had enough of this! Tom, you're fired!* TOM: *You can't fire me, I quit!*

I've had it up to here (with someone or something). I will not endure any more of someone or something. □ BILL: *I've had it up to here with your stupidity.* BOB: *Who's calling who stupid?* □ JOHN: *I've had it up to here with Tom.* MARY: *Are you going to fire him?* JOHN: *Yes.*

I've heard so much about you. a polite phrase said upon being introduced to someone you have heard about from a friend or the person's relatives. □ BILL: *This is my cousin Kate.* BOB: *Hello, Kate. I've heard so much about you.* □ SUE: *Hello, Bill. I've heard so much about you.* BILL: *Hello. Glad to meet you.*

(I've) never been better. AND **(I've) never felt better.** a response to a greeting inquiry into one's health or state of being. □ MARY: *How are you, Sally?* SALLY: *Never been better, sweetie.* □ DOCTOR: *How are you, Jane?* JANE: *Never felt better.* DOCTOR: *Then why are you here?*

(I've) never felt better. See the previous entry.

(I've) seen better. a noncommittal and not very positive judgment about something or someone. □ ALICE: *How did you like the movie?* JOHN: *I've seen better.* □ BILL: *What do you think about this weather?* BOB: *Seen better.*

(I've) seen worse. a noncommittal and not totally negative judgment about something or someone. □ ALICE: *How did you like the movie?* JOHN: *I've seen worse.* □ BILL: *What do you think about this weather?* BOB: *Seen worse. Can't remember when, though.*

J

jack around to waste time; to mess around. (Slang.) □ *Stop jacking around and get busy.* □ *The gang was jacking around and broke your window.*

jack someone around to hassle someone; to harass someone. (Slang. Compare to *jerk someone around.*) □ *The I.R.S. is jacking my brother around.* □ *The boss was jacking Gert around, so she just walked out.*

jack someone or something up 1. [with *someone*] to motivate someone; to stimulate someone to do something. (Slang. More at *jacked up.*) □ *I'll jack him up and try to get some action out of him.* □ *What does it take to jack you up?* **2.** [with *something*] to raise the price of something. □ *They kept jacking the price up with various charges, so I walked.* T *How can they jack up the published price?*

jacked (out) angry; annoyed. (Slang.) □ *Boy, was that old guy jacked out at you.* □ *Yup, he was jacked all right.*

jacked up 1. excited. (Slang. More at *jack someone or something up.*) □ *Don was really jacked up about the election.* □ *The gang was jacked up and ready to party.* **2.** arrested. (Underworld.) □ *What time did Reggie get himself jacked up?* □ *He was jacked up at midnight on the dot.* **3.** upset; *stressed.* □ *I was really jacked*

up by the bad news. □ *Don't get jacked up. It'll work out.*

jammed See the following entry.

jammed up 1. AND **jammed** in trouble. (Slang.) □ *He got himself jammed up with the law.* □ *I'm sort of jammed and need some help.* **2.** glutted; full of food or drink. □ *I'm jammed up. I can't eat another bite.* □ *After dinner, I am so jammed up that I need a nap.*

jazz someone or something up to make someone or something more exciting or sexy; to make someone or something appeal more to contemporary and youthful tastes. (Slang.) □ *Let's jazz this up a little bit.* T *They jazzed up the old girl till she looked like a teenager.* T *Don't jazz up the first number too much.*

jazzed (up) 1. alert; having a positive state of mind. (Slang.) □ *I am jazzed up and ready to face life.* □ *Those guys were jazzed and ready for the game.* **2.** alcohol or drug intoxicated. □ *Dave was a bit jazzed up, but not terribly.* □ *Gert was jazzed out of her mind.* **3.** enhanced; with something added; having been made more enticing. □ *The third act was jazzed up with a little skin.* □ *It was jazzed enough to have the police chief around asking questions.*

jerk someone around to hassle someone; to waste someone's time.

(Slang.) □ *Stop jerking me around and give me my money back.* Ⓣ *They sure like to jerk around people in that music shop.*

jerk something away (from someone or something) to snatch something away or pull something back from someone or some creature. □ *I jerked the bone away from the dog.* □ *Kelly jerked the ant poison away from the child.* □ *Mary jerked her hand away from the fire.*

jerk something off ((of) someone or something) to snatch something off someone or something. (The *of* is colloquial.) □ *Alice jerked the top off the box and poured out the contents.* Ⓣ *She jerked off the box top.* □ *She jerked the socks off of Jimmy and put clean ones on him.*

jerk something out (of someone or something) to pull something out of someone or something, quickly. □ *The doctor jerked the arrow out of Bill's leg.* Ⓣ *He jerked out the arrow.* □ *Ted jerked the sword out of Max and wiped it off.*

jerk something up **1.** to pull something up quickly. □ *He jerked his belt up tight.* Ⓣ *He jerked up the zipper to his jacket.* **2.** to lift up something, such as ears, quickly. □ *The dog jerked its ears up.* Ⓣ *The dog jerked up its ears when it heard the floor creak.* □ *The soldier jerked his binoculars up to try to see the sniper.*

jockey someone or something into position to manage to get someone or something into a chosen position. (*Someone* includes *oneself*.) □ *The rider jockeyed his horse into position.* □ *Try to jockey your bicycle into position so you can pass the others.* □ *With*

much effort, she jockeyed herself into position to peek over the transom.

Johnny-come-lately someone who joins in (something) after it is under way. □ *Don't pay any attention to Sally. She's just a Johnny-come-lately and doesn't know what she's talking about.* □ *We've been here for thirty years. Why should some Johnny-come-lately tell us what to do?*

Johnny-on-the-spot someone who is in the right place at the right time. □ *Here I am, Johnny-on-the-spot. I told you I would be here at 12:20.* □ *Bill is late again. You can hardly call him Johnny-on-the-spot.*

join up to become part of some organization. □ *The club has opened its membership roles again. Are you going to join up?* □ *I can't afford to join up.*

join ((up) with someone or something) to bring oneself into association with someone or something. □ *I decided to join up with the other group.* □ *Our group joined with another similar group.*

jolt someone out of something to startle someone out of inertness. (*Someone* includes *oneself*.) □ *The cold water thrown in her face was what it took to jolt Mary out of her deep sleep.* □ *At the sound of the telephone, he jolted himself out of his stupor.*

jot something down to make a note of something. □ *This is important. Please jot this down.* Ⓣ *Jot down this note, please.*

juice something back to drink alcohol. (Slang.) □ *He's been juicing it back since noon.* Ⓣ *Juice back your drink, and let's go.*

jump in ((to) something) to leap into something, such as water, a bed, a problem, etc. □ *She was so cold she just jumped into bed and pulled up the covers.* □ *I jumped in and had a refreshing swim.*

jump off ((of) something) to leap off something. (The *of* is colloquial.) □ *Rachel lost her balance and jumped off the diving board instead of diving.* □ *Better to jump off than to fall off.*

jump off the deep end See *go off the deep end.*

jump off the deep end (over someone or something) to get deeply involved with someone or something. (Often refers to romantic involvement.) □ *Jim is about to jump off the deep end over Jane.* □ *Jane is great, but there is no need to jump off the deep end.*

jump on the bandwagon See *get on the bandwagon.*

jump out of one's skin to react strongly to shock or surprise. (Usually with *nearly, almost*, etc. Never used literally.) □ *Oh! You really scared me. I nearly jumped out of my skin.* □ *Bill was so startled he almost jumped out of his skin.*

jump out of something to leap from something. □ *A mouse jumped out of the cereal box.* □ *I jumped out of bed and ran to answer the telephone.*

jump over something to leap over or across something. □ *The fellow named Jack jumped over a candle placed on the floor.* □ *Puddles are to be jumped over, not waded through.*

jump start 1. the act of starting a car by getting power — through jumper cables — from another car. (Slang.)
□ *I got a jump start from a friend.* □ *Who can give me a jump start?* **2.** to start a car by getting power from another car. □ *I jump started her car for her.* □ *I can't jump start your car. My battery is low.*

jump the gun to start before the starting signal. (Originally used in sports contests that are started by firing a gun.) □ *We all had to start the race again because Jane jumped the gun.* □ *When we took the test, Tom jumped the gun and started early.*

jump the track 1. [for something] to fall or jump off the rails or guides. (Usually said about a train.) □ *The train jumped the track, causing many injuries to the passengers.* □ *The engine jumped the track, but the other cars stayed on.* **2.** to change suddenly from one thing, thought, plan, or activity to another. □ *The entire project jumped the track, and we finally had to give up.* □ *John's mind jumped the track while he was in the play, and he forgot his lines.*

jump to conclusions to move too quickly to a conclusion; to form a conclusion from too little evidence. □ *Please don't jump to any conclusions because of what you have seen.* □ *There is no need to jump to conclusions!*

jump up (on someone or something) to leap upward onto someone or something. □ *A spider jumped up on me and terrified me totally.* □ *The cat jumped up on the sofa.*

Just a minute. AND **Just a moment.; Just a second.; Wait a minute.; Wait a sec(ond).** **1.** Please wait a short time. □ JOHN: *Just a minute.* BOB: *What's the matter?* JOHN: *I dropped* *my wallet.* □ SUE: *Just a sec.* JOHN: *Why?* SUE: *I think we're going in the wrong direction. Let's look at the map.* **2.** Stop there.; *Hold it!* □ JOHN: *Just a minute!* MARY: *What's wrong?* JOHN: *That stick looked sort of like a snake. But it's all right.* MARY: *You scared me to death!* □ MARY: *Wait a minute!* BILL: *Why?* MARY: *We're leaving an hour earlier than we have to.*

Just a moment. See the previous entry.

Just a second. See *Just a minute.*

just let me say See *let me (just) say.*

just like that in just the way it was stated; without any [further] discussion or comment. □ SUE: *You can't walk out on me just like that.* JOHN: *I can too. Just watch!* □ MARY: *And then she slapped him in the face, just like that!* SALLY: *She can be so rude.*

just off the boat to be freshly immigrated and perhaps gullible and naive. (Slang.) □ *I'm not just off the boat. I know what's going on.* □ *He may act like he's just off the boat, but he's all right.*

(just) taking care of business an answer to the question "What are you doing lately?" (Also abbreviated T.C.B.) □ BILL: *Hey, man. What you been doing?* TOM: *Just taking care of business.* □ ANDREW: *Look, officer, I'm just standing here, taking care of business, and this Tom guy comes up and tries to hit me for a loan.* TOM: *That's not true!*

just what the doctor ordered exactly what is required, especially for health or comfort. □ *That meal was delicious, Bob. Just what the doctor ordered.* □ BOB: *Would you like something to drink?* MARY: *Yes, a cold glass of water would be just what the doctor ordered.*

Just (you) wait (and see)! See *You (just) wait (and see)!*

jut out (from something) to stick outward from something. □ *The flagpole juts out from the side of the building.* □ *His nose juts out sharply.*

jut out (into something) to stick outward into an area. □ *The back end of the truck jutted out into the street.* □ *The back end jutted out.*

jut out (over someone or something) to stick out over someone or something. □ *The roof of the house jutted out over the patio.* □ *I'm glad the roof jutted out and kept us dry during the brief storm.*

K

keel over to fall over; to capsize. □ *The boat keeled over.* □ *Tom was so surprised he nearly keeled over.*

keep a civil tongue (in one's head) to speak decently and politely. (Also with *have*.) □ *Please, John. Don't talk like that. Keep a civil tongue in your head.* □ *John seems unable to keep a civil tongue.* □ *He'd be welcome here if he had a civil tongue in his head.*

keep a stiff upper lip to be cool and unmoved by unsettling events. (Also with *have*. See the note at *keep a straight face*.) □ *John always keeps a stiff upper lip.* □ *Now, Billy, don't cry. Keep a stiff upper lip.* □ *Bill can take it. He has a stiff upper lip.*

keep a straight face to make one's face stay free from laughter. (Also with *have*. Note that *keep* implies the exercise of effort, and *have* simply means to possess.) □ *It's hard to keep a straight face when someone tells a funny joke.* □ *I knew it was John who played the trick. He couldn't keep a straight face.* □ *John didn't have a straight face.*

keep after someone (about something) AND **keep at someone (about something)** to nag or harass someone about something. □ *I'll have to keep after him about getting the roof repaired.* □ *He'll get it done if you keep after him.* □ *I will keep at Megan about the meeting until she sets it up.* □ *You will have to keep at her if you want to get anything done.*

keep an eye out (for someone or something) See *have an eye out (for someone or something)*.

keep at someone (about something) See *keep after someone (about something)*.

keep at something to continue to do something; to continue to try to do something. □ *Keep at it until you get it done.* □ *I have to keep at this.*

keep away (from someone or something) to avoid someone or something; to maintain a physical distance from someone or something. □ *Please keep away from me if you have a cold.* □ *Keep away from the construction site, Timmy.*

keep back (from someone or something) to continue to stay in a position away from someone or something. □ *You must keep back from the edge of the crater.* □ *Keep back! It's really dangerous.*

keep body and soul together to feed, clothe, and house oneself. □ *I hardly have enough money to keep body and soul together.* □ *How the old man was able to keep body and soul together is beyond me.*

Keep in there! Keep trying. □ ANDREW: *Don't give up, Sally. Keep in there!* SALLY: *I'm doing my best!* □ JOHN: *I'm not very good, but I keep trying.* FRED: *Just keep in there, John.*

Keep in touch. Good-bye.; Please try to communicate occasionally. (Slang. Sometimes a sarcastic way of saying good-bye to someone one doesn't care about.) □ RACHEL: *Good-bye, Fred. Keep in touch.* FRED: *Bye, Rach.* □ SALLY (throwing kisses): *Good-bye, you two.* MARY (waving good-bye): *Be sure and write.* SUE: *Yes, keep in touch.* □ *Nice talking to you. Keep in touch.* □ *Sorry, we can't use you today. Keep in touch.*

keep (it) in mind that introduces something that the speaker wants remembered. □ BILL: *When we get there I want to take a long hot shower.* FATHER: *Keep it in mind that we are guests, and we have to fit in with the routines of the household.* □ SALLY: *Keep it in mind that you don't work here anymore, and you just can't go in and out of offices like that.* FRED: *I guess you're right.*

Keep it up! **1.** *Keep up the good work!;* Keep on doing it.; *Keep (on) trying.* □ JANE: *I think I'm doing better in calculus.* JOHN: *Keep it up!* □ SALLY: *I can now jog for almost three miles.* FRED: *Great! Keep it up!* **2.** Just keep acting that way and see what happens to you. (Similar to *(Go ahead,) make my day!* See also *keep someone or something up.*) □ JOHN: *You're just not doing what is expected of you.* BILL: *Keep it up! Just keep it up, and I'll quit right when you need me most.* □ *"Your behavior is terrible, young man! You just keep it up and see*

what happens," warned Alice. "Just keep it up!"

keep late hours to stay up or stay out until very late; to work late. □ *I'm always tired because I keep late hours.* □ *If I didn't keep late hours, I wouldn't sleep so late in the morning.*

keep off ((of) something) to remain off something; not to trespass on something. (The *of* is colloquial.) □ *Please keep off the grass.* □ *This is not a public thoroughfare! Keep off!*

keep on someone (about something) to nag someone about something. □ *We will have to keep on him about the report until he turns it in.* □ *Don't worry. I'll keep on him.*

keep on (something) to work to remain mounted on something, such as a horse, bicycle, etc. (Compare to *keep on something.*) □ *It's really hard for me to keep on a horse.* □ *It's hard to keep on when it's moving all over the place.*

keep on something to pay close attention to something. (Compare to *keep on (something).*) □ *Keep on that story until everything is settled.* □ *This is a problem. Keep on it until it's settled.*

Keep (on) trying. AND **Don't quit trying.** a phrase encouraging continued efforts. □ JANE: *I think I'm doing better in calculus.* JOHN: *Keep trying! You can get an A.* □ SUE: *I really want that promotion, but I keep getting turned down.* BILL: *Don't quit trying! You'll get it.*

keep one's cool to remain calm and in control. (Slang. Compare to *blow one's cool.*) □ *Relax, man! Just keep your cool.* □ *It's hard to keep your cool when you've been cheated.*

keep one's ear to the ground See *have one's ear to the ground.*

keep one's eye on the ball **1.** to watch or follow the ball carefully, especially when one is playing a ball game; to follow the details of a ball game very carefully. □ *John, if you can't keep your eye on the ball, I'll have to take you out of the game.* □ *"Keep your eye on the ball," the coach roared at the players.* **2.** to remain alert to the events occurring around one. □ *If you want to get along in this office, you're going to have to keep your eye on the ball.* □ *Bill would do better in his classes if he would just keep his eye on the ball.*

keep one's feet on the ground to remain firmly established. □ *Sally will have no trouble keeping her feet on the ground.*

keep one's head above water to stay ahead of one's responsibilities. □ *Now that I have more space to work in, I can easily keep my head above water.*

keep one's head right to maintain control of oneself. (Slang. Black.) □ *Chill, man, chill. You've got to keep your head right.* □ *I can keep my head right. I'm mellow.*

keep one's nose to the grindstone to keep busy continuously over a period of time. □ *The manager told me to keep my nose to the grindstone or be fired.*

keep one's temper AND **hold one's temper** not to get angry; to hold back an expression of anger. □ *She should have learned to keep her temper when she was a child.* □ *Sally got thrown off the team because she couldn't hold her temper.*

keep one's weather eye open to watch for something (to happen); to be on the alert (for something); to be on guard. □ *Some trouble is brewing. Keep your weather eye open.* □ *Try to be more alert. Learn to keep your weather eye open.*

keep one's word to uphold one's promise. □ *I told her I'd be there to pick her up, and I intend to keep my word.* □ *Keeping one's word is necessary in the legal profession.*

Keep out of my way. AND **Stay out of my way.** **1.** Don't get in my pathway. □ JOHN: *Keep out of my way! I'm carrying a heavy load.* BILL: *Sorry.* □ *"Keep out of my way!" shouted the piano mover.* **2.** Don't cause me any trouble. □ HENRY: *I'm going to get even no matter what. Keep out of my way.* ANDREW: *Keep it up! You'll really get in trouble.* □ JOHN: *I intend to work my way to the top in this business.* MARY: *So do I, so just keep out of my way.*

keep out (of something) **1.** to remain uninvolved with something. □ *Keep out of this! It's my affair.* □ *It's not your affair. Keep out!* **2.** to remain outside something or some place. □ *You should keep out of the darkroom when the door is closed.* □ *The door is closed. Keep out!*

Keep out of this! AND **Stay out of this!** This is not your business, so do not try to get involved. □ JOHN: *Now you listen to me, Fred!* MARY: *That's no way to talk to Fred!* JOHN: *Keep out of this, Mary! Mind your own business!* FRED: *Stay out of this, Mary!* MARY: *It's just as much my business as it is yours.*

Keep quiet. AND **Keep still.** Get quiet and stay that way. □ JOHN: *I'm* *going to go to the store.* BILL: *Keep quiet.* JOHN: *I just said . . .* BILL: *I said, keep quiet!* □ CHILD: *I want some candy!* MOTHER: *Keep still.*

Keep quiet about it. See *Keep still about it.*

Keep smiling. a parting phrase encouraging someone to have good spirits. □ JOHN: *Things are really getting tough.* SUE: *Well, just keep smiling. Things will get better.* □ BILL: *What a day! I'm exhausted and depressed.* BOB: *Not to worry. Keep smiling. Things will calm down.*

keep someone at something to make sure someone continues to work at something. (*Someone* includes *oneself.*) □ *Please keep Walter at his chores.* □ *I was so sick I couldn't keep myself at my work.*

keep someone down to prevent someone from advancing or succeeding. □ *His lack of a degree will keep him down.* □ *I don't think that this problem will keep her down.*

keep someone in stitches to cause someone to laugh loud and hard, over and over. (Also with *have.* See the note at *keep a straight face.*) □ *The comedian kept us in stitches for nearly an hour.* □ *The teacher kept the class in stitches, but the students didn't learn anything.*

keep someone on tenterhooks to keep someone anxious or in suspense. (Also with *have.* See the note at *keep a straight face.*) □ *Please tell me now. Don't keep me on tenterhooks any longer!* □ *Now that we have her on tenterhooks, shall we let her worry, or shall we tell her?*

keep someone or something back 1. to hold someone or something in

reserve. □ *Keep some of the food back for an emergency.* □ *We are keeping Karen back until the other players have exhausted themselves.* **2.** [with someone] to hold a child back in school. □ *We asked them to keep John back a year.* □ *John was kept back a year in school.* **3.** [with someone] to keep someone from advancing in life. □ *I think that your small vocabulary is keeping you back.* □ *Her vocabulary kept her back in life.*

keep someone or something hanging in midair to maintain someone or something waiting to be completed or continued. □ *Please don't keep us hanging in midair.*

keep someone or something in mind AND **bear someone or something in mind** to remember and think about someone or something. □ *When you're driving a car, you must bear this in mind at all times: Keep your eyes on the road.* □ *As you leave home, keep your family in mind.*

keep someone or something off See *hold someone or something off.*

keep someone or something on 1. [with someone] to retain someone in employment longer than is required or was planned. □ *She worked out so well that we decided to keep her on.* □ *Liz was kept on as a consultant.* **2.** [with something] to continue to wear an article of clothing. □ *I'm going to keep my coat on. It's a little chilly in here.* T *I'll keep on my coat, thanks.*

keep someone or something out (of something) 1. to prevent someone or something from getting into something or some place. (*Someone* includes *oneself.*) □ *Keep your kids out of my yard.* □ *Please keep the loose* *papers out of the room.* □ *She just couldn't keep herself out of the cookie jar.* **2.** to keep the subject of someone or something out of a discussion. (*Someone* includes *oneself.*) □ *Keep the kids out of this! I don't want to talk about them.* □ *They kept Dorothy out of the discussion.*

keep someone or something up 1. to hold or prop someone or something upright. □ *Try to keep him up until I can get his bed turned down.* □ *Keep her up for a few minutes longer.* □ *Keep your side of the trunk up. Don't let it sag.* Ⓣ *Keep up your side of the trunk.* **2.** [with *someone*] to prevent someone from going to bed or going to sleep. □ *I'm sorry, was my trumpet keeping you up?* □ *We were kept up by the noise.* **3.** [with *something*] to continue doing something. (More at *Keep it up!*) □ *I love your singing. Don't stop. Keep it up.* Ⓣ *Please keep up your singing.* **4.** [with *something*] to maintain something in good order. □ *I'm glad you keep the exterior of your house up.* Ⓣ *You keep up your house nicely.*

keep someone posted to keep someone informed (of what is happening); to keep someone up to date. □ *If the price of corn goes up, I need to know. Please keep me posted.* □ *Keep her posted about the patient's status.*

keep something to oneself to keep something a secret. (Notice the use of *but* in the examples.) □ *I'm quitting my job, but please keep that to yourself.* □ *Keep it to yourself, but I'm quitting my job.* □ *John is always gossiping. He can't keep anything to himself.*

keep something under one's hat to keep something a secret; to keep something in one's mind (only). (If the secret stays under your hat, it stays in your mind. Note the use of *but* in the examples.) □ *Keep this under your hat, but I'm getting married.* □ *I'm getting married, but keep it under your hat.*

keep something under wraps to keep something concealed (until some future time). □ *We kept the plan under wraps until after the election.* □ *The automobile company kept the new model under wraps until most of the old models had been sold.*

Keep still. See *Keep quiet.*

Keep still about it. AND **Keep quiet about it.** Don't tell it to anyone. □ BILL: *Are you really going to sell your car?* MARY: *Yes, but keep quiet about it.* □ JOHN: *Someone said you're looking for a new job.* SUE: *That's right, but keep still about it.*

keep the home fires burning to keep things going at one's home or other central location. □ *My uncle kept the home fires burning when my sister and I went to school.* □ *The manager stays at the office and keeps the home fires burning while I'm out selling our products.*

keep the wolf from the door to maintain oneself at a minimal level; to keep from starving, freezing, etc. □ *I don't make a lot of money, just enough to keep the wolf from the door.* □ *We have a small amount of money saved, hardly enough to keep the wolf from the door.*

Keep this to yourself. a phrase introducing something that is meant to be a secret. □ ANDREW: *Keep this to yourself, but I'm going to Bora Bora on my vacation.* HENRY: *Sounds great.*

Can I go too? □ JOHN: *Keep this to yourself. Mary and I are breaking up.* SUE: *I won't tell a soul.*

Keep up the good work. Please keep doing the good things that you are doing now. (A general phrase of encouragement.) □ FATHER: *Your grades are fine, Bill. Keep up the good work.* BILL: *Thanks, Dad.* □ *"Nice play," said the coach. "Keep up the good work!"*

keep up (with the Joneses) to stay financially even with one's peers; to work hard to get the same amount of material goods that one's friends and neighbors have. □ *Mr. and Mrs. Brown bought a new car simply to keep up with the Joneses.* □ *Keeping up with the Joneses can take all your money.*

keep up (with the times) to stay in fashion; to keep up with the news; to be contemporary or modern. □ *I try to keep up with the times. I want to know what's going on.* □ *I bought a whole new wardrobe because I want to keep up with the times.* □ *Sally learns all the new dances. She likes to keep up.*

Keep your chin up. an expression of encouragement to someone who has to bear some emotional burdens. □ FRED: *I really can't take much more of this.* JANE: *Keep your chin up. Things will get better.* □ JOHN: *Smile, Fred. Keep your chin up.* FRED: *I guess you're right. I just get so depressed when I think of this mess I'm in.*

Keep your mouth shut (about someone or something). Do not tell anyone about someone or something. □ BOB: *Are you going to see the doctor?* MARY: *Yes, but keep your mouth shut about it.* □ BOB: *Isn't Tom's uncle in tax trouble?* JANE: *Yes, but keep your mouth shut about him.*

Keep your nose out of my business. See *Mind your own business.*

Keep your opinions to yourself! I do not want to hear your opinions! □ JANE: *I think this room looks drab.* SUE: *Keep your opinions to yourself! I like it this way!* □ SALLY: *You really ought to do something about your hair. It looks like it was hit by a truck.* JOHN: *Keep your opinions to yourself. This is the latest style where I come from.* SALLY: *I won't suggest where that might be.*

Keep your shirt on! Be patient!; Just wait a minute! (Colloquial.) □ JOHN: *Hey, hurry up! Finish this!* BILL: *Keep your shirt on! I'll do it when I'm good and ready.* □ JOHN: *Waiter! We've been waiting fifteen minutes! What sort of place is this?* WAITER: *Keep your shirt on!* JOHN (quietly): *Now I know what sort of place this is.*

kick around See *knock around.*

kick back 1. to relax (and enjoy something). (Slang.) □ *Now you just kick back and enjoy this.* □ *I like to kick back and listen to a few tunes.* **2.** money received in return for a favor. (Usually **kickback.**) □ *The kickback the cop got wasn't enough, as it turned out.* □ *You really don't believe that the cops take kickbacks!*

kick back (at someone or something) to kick at someone or something in revenge. □ *She kicked at me, so I kicked back at her.* □ *If you kick me, I'll kick back.*

kick off to die. (Slang.) □ *We've been waiting for years for that cat to kick off.* □ *The old girl finally kicked off.*

kick some ass (around) to take over and start giving orders. (Slang. Use caution with *ass.*) □ *Do I have to* come over there and kick some ass around? □ *Reggie is just the one to kick some ass over there.*

kick something back (to someone or something) to move something back to someone, something, or some place by kicking. □ *I kicked the ball back to Walter.* □ *He kicked it to me, and I kicked it back.*

kick something down to break down something by kicking. □ *I was afraid they were going to kick the door down.* T *Don't kick down the door!*

kick something in to break through something by kicking. □ *Tommy kicked the door in and broke the new lamp.* T *He kicked in the door by accident.*

kick something out (of something) to move something out of something or some place by kicking. □ *The soccer player kicked the ball out of the tangle of legs.* T *She got into the fracas and kicked out the ball.* □ *It looked trapped, but Todd kicked it out.*

kick up a fuss AND **kick up a row; kick up a storm** to become a nuisance; to misbehave and disturb (someone). (*Row* rhymes with *cow*. Note the variations in the examples.) □ *The customer kicked up such a fuss about the food that the manager came to apologize.* □ *I kicked up such a row that they kicked me out.*

kick up a row See the previous entry.

kick up a storm See *kick up a fuss.*

kick up one's heels to act frisky; to be lively and have fun. □ *I like to go to an old-fashioned square dance and really kick up my heels.* □ *For an old man, your uncle is really kicking up his heels.*

kill someone or something off to kill all of a group of people or creatures. □ *Lefty set out to kill Max and his boys off.* T *Something killed off all the dinosaurs.*

kill the fatted calf to prepare an elaborate banquet (in someone's honor). (From the biblical story recounting the return of the prodigal son.) □ *When Bob got back from college, his parents killed the fatted calf and threw a great party.* □ *Sorry this meal isn't much, John. We didn't have time to kill the fatted calf.*

kill the goose that laid the golden egg to destroy the source of one's good fortune. (Proverb. Based on an old fable.) □ *If you fire your best office worker, you'll be killing the goose that laid the golden egg.* □ *He sold his computer, which was like killing the goose that laid the golden egg.*

kill time to waste time. □ *Stop killing time. Get to work!* □ *We went over to the record shop just to kill time.*

kill two birds with one stone to solve two problems with one solution. □ *John learned the words to his part in the play while peeling potatoes. He was killing two birds with one stone.* □ *I have to cash a check and make a payment on my bank loan. I'll kill two birds with one stone by doing them both in one trip to the bank.*

Kind of. See *Sort of.*

kiss and make up to forgive (someone) and be friends again. (Also used literally.) □ *They were very angry, but in the end they kissed and made up.* □ *I'm sorry. Let's kiss and make up.*

kiss of death an act that puts an end to someone or something. □ *The mayor's veto was the kiss of death for* *the new law.* □ *Fainting on stage was the kiss of death for my acting career.*

kiss off the dismissal of someone or something. (Usually **kiss-off**. Slang.) □ *The kiss-off was when I lost the Wilson contract.* □ *Tod got the kiss off and is now looking for a new job.* **2.** death. □ *When the time comes for the kiss-off, I hope I'm asleep.* □ *The kiss-off came wrapped in lead, and it was instant.* **3.** to die. □ *The cat is going to have to kiss off one of these days soon.* □ *The cat kissed off after eighteen years of joy and devotion.*

kiss something good-bye to anticipate or experience the loss of something. (Not literal.) □ *If you leave your camera on a park bench, you can kiss it good-bye.* □ *You kissed your wallet good-bye when you left it in the store.*

kiss the porcelain god to empty one's stomach; to vomit. (Slang.) □ *He fled the room to kiss the porcelain god, I guess.* □ *Who's in there kissing the porcelain god?*

kiss up to someone to flatter someone; to make over someone. (Slang.) □ *I'm not going to kiss up to anybody to get what's rightfully mine.* □ *If I have to kiss up to her, I guess I will.*

kneel down (before someone or something) to show respect by getting down on one's knees in the presence of someone or something. □ *We were told to kneel down in front of a statue of a golden calf.* □ *I'm too old to kneel down comfortably.*

knit one's brow to wrinkle one's brow, especially by frowning. □ *The woman knit her brow and asked us what we wanted from her.* □ *While he read his book, John knit his brow oc-*

casionally. He must not have agreed with what he was reading.

knock around 1. to waste time. (Slang.) □ *Stop knocking around and get to work!* □ *I need a couple of days a week just for knocking around.* **2.** AND **kick around** to wander around; to loiter. □ *I think I'll knock around a few months before looking for another job.* □ *We're just knocking around and keeping out of trouble.*

knock it off 1. to stop talking; to be silent. (Usually a rude command.) □ *Shut up, you guys! Knock it off!* □ *Knock it off and go to sleep!* **2.** Be quiet!; Stop that noise! (Slang. Usually **Knock it off!**) □ JOHN: *Hey, you guys! Knock it off!* BOB: *Sorry.* BILL: *Sorry. I guess we got a little carried away.* □ SUE: *All right. Knock it off!* BILL: *Yeah. Let's get down to business.*

knock on wood a phrase said to cancel out imaginary bad luck. (The same as British "touch wood.") □ *My stereo has never given me any trouble — knock on wood.* □ *We plan to be in Florida by tomorrow evening — knock on wood.*

knock one back See the following entry.

knock one over AND **knock one back** to take a drink of liquor. (Slang.) □ *He knocked one over right away and demanded another.* Ⓣ *He knocked back one and belched grossly.*

knock someone for a loop See *throw someone for a loop.*

knock someone or something down 1. to thrust someone or something to the ground by force. □ *The force of the blast knocked us down.* Ⓣ *It knocked down everyone in the room.*

□ *The wind knocked the fence down.* **2.** [with *something*] to drink a portion of liquor. (Slang.) □ *Here, knock this down and let's go.* ⊤ *He knocked down a bottle of beer and called for another.* **3.** [with *something*] to earn a certain amount of money. □ *I'm lucky to knock twenty thousand down.* ⊤ *She must knock down about forty thousand a year.*

knock someone out 1. to knock someone unconscious. (*Someone* includes oneself.) □ *Max knocked Lefty out and left him there in the gutter.* ⊤ *Max knocked out Lefty.* □ *She fell and knocked herself out.* **2.** to make someone unconscious. (*Someone* includes oneself.) □ *The drug knocked her out quickly.* ⊤ *The powerful medicine knocked out the patient.* **3.** to wear someone out; to exhaust someone. □ *All that exercise really knocked me out.* □ *The day's activities knocked the kids out, and they went right to bed.*

knock someone over to surprise or overwhelm someone. (Figurative.) □ *His statement simply knocked me over.* □ *When she showed me what happened to the car, it nearly knocked me over.*

knock someone some skin to shake hands with someone. (Slang.) □ *Hey, man, knock me some skin!* □ *Tod knocked Sam some skin, and they left the building together.*

knock someone up to make a woman pregnant. (Crude slang.) □ *They say it was Reggie who knocked her up.* ⊤ *He did not knock up Molly. I did.*

knock (up) against someone or something to bump against someone or something. □ *The loose shutter knocked up against the side of the*

house. □ *The large branch knocked against the garage in the storm.* □ *The child's bicycle knocked up against me.*

knocked out 1. exhausted. (Slang.) □ *We were all knocked out at the end of the day.* □ *I'm knocked out after just a little bit of work.* **2.** overwhelmed. □ *We were just knocked out when we heard your news.* □ *Were we surprised? We were knocked out — elated!* **3.** alcohol or drug intoxicated. □ *They were all knocked out by midnight.* □ *Gary was knocked out when we dropped by, so we tried to sober him up.*

knocked up 1. battered; beaten. (Slang.) □ *Sally was a little knocked up by the accident.* □ *This book is a little knocked up, so I'll lower the price.* **2.** alcohol intoxicated. □ *Bill was knocked up and didn't want to drive.* □ *Wow, was that guy knocked up!* **3.** pregnant. □ *Molly got knocked up again.* □ *Isn't she knocked up most of the time?*

know all the tricks of the trade to possess the skills and knowledge necessary to do something. (Also without *all*.) □ *Tom can repair car engines. He knows the tricks of the trade.* □ *If I knew all the tricks of the trade, I could be a better plumber.*

know from something to know about something. (Slang.) □ *Do you know from timers, I mean how timers work?* □ *I don't know from babies! Don't ask me about feeding them!*

know one's ABCs to know the alphabet; to know the most basic things (about something). □ *Bill can't do it. He doesn't even know his ABCs.* □ *You can't expect to write novels when you don't even know your ABCs.*

know someone by sight to know the name and recognize the face of someone. □ *I've never met the man, but I know him by sight.* □ BOB: *Have you ever met Mary?* JANE: *No, but I know her by sight.*

know someone or something like a book See *know someone or something like the palm of one's hand.*

know someone or something like the back of one's hand See the following entry.

know someone or something like the palm of one's hand AND **know someone or something like the back of one's hand; know someone or something like a book** to know someone or something very well. □ *Of course I know John. I know him like the back of my hand.* □ *I know him like a book.*

know something from memory to have memorized something so that one does not have to consult a written version; to know something well from seeing it very often. □ *Mary didn't need the script because she knew the play from memory.* □ *The conductor went through the entire concert without music. He knew it from memory.*

know something in one's bones See *feel something in one's bones.*

know something inside out to know something thoroughly; to know about something thoroughly. □ *I know my geometry inside out.* □ *I studied and studied for my driver's test until I knew the rules inside out.*

know the ropes to know how to do something. □ *I can't do the job because I don't know the ropes.* □ *Ask Sally to do it. She knows the ropes.*

know the score AND **know what's what** to know the facts; to know the facts about life and its difficulties. (Also used literally.) □ *Bob is so naive. He sure doesn't know the score.* □ *I know what you're trying to do. Oh, yes, I know what's what.*

know what's what See the previous entry.

know where one is coming from to understand someone's motivation; to understand and relate to someone's position. (Slang.) □ *I know where you're coming from. I've been there.* □ *We all know where he's coming from. That's why we are so worried.*

know which side one's bread is buttered on to know what is most advantageous for one. □ *He'll do it if his boss tells him to. He knows which side his bread is buttered on.* □ *Since John knows which side his bread is buttered on, he'll be there on time.*

L

lace into someone or something to set to work on someone or something; to attack someone or something. □ *Todd laced into Ralph and scolded him severely.* □ *Elaine laced into the job with the intention of finishing it within an hour.*

Ladies first. an expression indicating that women should go first, as in going through a doorway. □ *Bob stepped back and made a motion with his hand indicating that Mary should go first. "Ladies first," smiled Bob.* □ BOB: *It's time to get in the food line. Who's going to go first?* BILL: *Ladies first, Mary.* MARY: *Why not gentlemen first?* BOB: *Looks like nobody's going first.*

lag behind (someone or something) to linger behind someone or something; to fall behind someone or something. □ *Come on up here. Don't lag behind us or you'll get lost.* □ *Please don't lag behind the donkeys. Come up here with the rest of the hikers.* □ *Don't lag behind too much.*

laid out 1. alcohol or drug intoxicated. (Slang.) □ *Man, you got yourself laid out!* □ *I'm too laid out to go to work today.* 2. well-dressed. (Black.) □ *Look at those silks! Man, are you laid out!* □ *She is all laid out in her Sunday best.*

land (up)on someone or something to light on someone or something.

(*Upon* is formal and less commonly used than *on*.) □ *A bee landed upon her and frightened her.* □ *A butterfly landed on the cake and ruined the icing.*

lap over (something) [for something] to extend or project over the edge or boundary of something. □ *The lid lapped over the edge of the barrel, forming a little table.* □ *The blanket did not lap over enough to keep me warm.*

lap something up 1. [for an animal] to lick something up. □ *The dog lapped the ice cream up off the floor.* ⊤ *The dog lapped up the ice cream.* 2. [for someone] to accept or believe something with enthusiasm. (Figurative.) □ *Of course, they believed it. They just lapped it up.* ⊤ *They lapped up the lies without questioning anything.*

lap (up) against something [for waves] to splash gently against something. □ *The waves lapped up against the shore softly.* □ *The waves lapped against the shore all night long, and I couldn't sleep.*

last but not least last in sequence, but not last in importance. (Often said in introductions.) □ *The speaker said, "And now, last but not least, I'd like to present Bill Smith, who will give us some final words."* □ *And last but not least, here is the loser of the race.*

last something out to endure until the end of something. □ *Ed said that he didn't think he could last the opera out and left.* Ⓣ *He couldn't last out the first act.*

Later, alligator. See *See you later, alligator.*

laugh out of the other side of one's mouth to change sharply from happiness to sadness. □ *Now that you know the truth, you'll laugh out of the other side of your mouth.* □ *He was so proud that he won the election. He's laughing out of the other side of his mouth since they recounted the ballots and found out that he lost.*

laugh someone or something down to cause someone to quit or cause something to end by laughing in ridicule. □ *Her singing career was destroyed when the audience laughed her down as an amateur.* Ⓣ *The cruel audience laughed down the amateur singer.* Ⓣ *They laughed down the magic act also.*

laugh something off to treat a serious problem lightly by laughing at it. □ *Although his feelings were hurt, he just laughed the incident off as if nothing had happened.* Ⓣ *He laughed off the incident.*

laugh up one's sleeve to laugh secretly; to laugh quietly to oneself. □ *Jane looked very serious, but I knew she was laughing up her sleeve.* □ *I told Sally that her dress was darling, but I was laughing up my sleeve because her dress was too small.*

launch into something to start in doing something. □ *Now, don't launch into lecturing me about manners again!* □ *Tim's mother launched into a sermon about how to behave at a concert.*

launch (one's lunch) to empty one's stomach; to vomit. (Slang.) □ *When I saw that mess, I almost launched my lunch.* □ *Watch out! She's going to launch!*

law unto oneself one who makes one's own laws or rules; one who sets one's own standards of behavior. □ *You can't get Bill to follow the rules. He's a law unto himself.* □ *Jane is a law unto herself. She's totally unwilling to cooperate.*

lay a finger on someone or something to touch someone or something, even slightly, even with a finger. (Usually in the negative.) □ *Don't you dare lay a finger on my pencil. Go get your own!* □ *If you lay a finger on me, I'll scream.*

lay a guilt trip on someone See the following entry.

lay a (heavy) trip on someone 1. to criticize someone. (Slang.) □ *There's no need to lay a trip on me. I agree with you.* □ *When he finally does get there, I'm going to lay a heavy trip on him like he'll never forget.* **2.** to confuse or astonish someone. □ *After he laid a heavy trip on me about how the company is almost broke, I cleaned out my desk and left.* □ *After Mary laid a trip on John about her other self, he sat down and stared at his feet.* **3.** AND **lay a guilt trip on someone** to attempt to make someone feel very guilty. □ *Why do you have to lay a guilt trip on me? Why don't you go to a shrink?* □ *Of course, she just had to lay a trip on him about being bossy, self-centered, and aloof.*

lay an egg to give a bad performance. (Also used literally, but only with birds.) □ *The cast of the play really* laid an egg last night. □ I hope I don't lay an egg when it's my turn to sing.

lay down the law **1.** to state firmly what the rules are (for something). □ Before the meeting, the boss laid down the law. We all knew exactly what to do. □ The way she laid down the law means that I'll remember her rules. **2.** to scold someone for misbehaving. □ When the teacher caught us, he really laid down the law. □ Poor Bob. He really got it when his mother laid down the law.

lay it on thick AND **pour it on thick; spread it on thick** to exaggerate praise, excuses, or blame. □ Sally was laying it on thick when she said that Tom was the best singer she had ever heard. □ After Bob finished making his excuses, Sally said that he was pouring it on thick. □ Bob always spreads it on thick.

lay off ((from) something) to cease doing something. (Compare to lay off ((of) someone or something).) □ Lay off from your hammering for a minute, will you? □ That's enough! Please lay off.

lay off ((of) someone or something) to stop doing something to someone or something; to stop bothering someone or something. (The of is colloquial. Compare to lay off ((from) something).) □ Lay off of me! You've said enough. □ Please lay off the chicken. I cooked it as best I could.

lay one's cards on the table See put one's cards on the table.

lay over (some place) to wait somewhere between segments of a journey. □ We were told we would have to lay over in New York. □ I don't mind laying over if it isn't for very long.

lay some sweet lines on someone AND **put some sweet lines on someone** to speak kindly to someone; to flatter someone. (Slang.) □ I just laid some sweet lines on her, and she let me use her car. □ If you put some sweet lines on him, maybe he won't ground you.

lay someone away to bury someone. (Euphemism.) □ Yes, he has passed. We laid him away last week. ⊤ He laid away his uncle in a simple ceremony.

lay someone off (from something) to put an end to someone's employment at something. □ The automobile factory laid five hundred people off from work. ⊤ They laid off a lot of people. □ We knew they were going to lay a lot of people off.

lay something away (for someone or something) to put something in storage for a special occasion or for someone to receive at a later time. (Often said of a purchase that is held until it is paid for.) □ Please lay this away for me. I'll pay for it when I have the money. ⊤ Please lay away this coat until I can get the money together. □ I will lay it away for you. □ She laid the lovely dress away for the next party. ⊤ She laid away the dress. □ Hoping there would be a chance to use it, she laid it away.

lay something in to build up a supply of something. □ We had better lay some firewood in for the winter. ⊤ I will lay in a supply.

lay something on the line See put something on the line.

lay something out to explain something; to go over details of a plan carefully. □ *They laid the sales campaign out after many meetings.* ⊤ *She laid out exactly what she had been thinking so they all could discuss it.*

lay something out for someone or something See the following entry.

lay something out on someone or something AND **lay something out for someone or something** to spend an amount of money on someone or something. □ *We laid out nearly ten thousand dollars on that car.* ⊤ *We laid out a fortune on the children.* ⊤ *I won't lay out another cent for that car!*

lay something to waste AND **lay waste to something** to destroy something. (Both literal and figurative uses.) □ *The invaders laid the village to waste.* □ *The kids came in and laid waste to my clean house.*

lay something up **1.** to acquire and store something. □ *Try to lay as much of it up as you can.* ⊤ *I am trying to lay up some firewood for the winter.* **2.** [for something] to disable something. □ *Engine trouble and a number of other defects laid the ship up.* ⊤ *The accident laid up the ship for repairs.*

lay waste to something See *lay something to waste.*

lead a dog's life AND **live a dog's life** to lead a miserable life. □ *Poor Jane really leads a dog's life.* □ *I've been working so hard. I'm tired of living a dog's life.*

lead back (to some place) [for a pathway] to return to a place. □ *This path leads back to the camp.* □ *I hope it leads back. It seems to be going the wrong way.*

lead down to something [for a pathway or other trail] to run downward

to something. □ *The trail led down to a spring at the bottom of the hill.* □ *These stairs lead down to the furnace room.*

lead off to be the first one to go or leave. (Compare to *lead off (with someone or something).*) □ *You lead off. I'll follow.* □ *Mary led off and the others followed closely behind.*

lead off (with someone or something) to begin with someone or something. (Compare to *lead off.*) □ *The musical revue led off with a bassoon trio.* □ *Sharon, the singer, will lead off tonight.*

lead someone down the garden path to deceive someone. □ *Now, be honest with me. Don't lead me down the garden path.* □ *That cheater really led her down the garden path.*

lead someone on to guide someone onward. □ *We led him on so he could see more of the gardens.* □ *Please lead Mary on. There is lots more to see here.*

lead someone on a merry chase to lead someone in a purposeless pursuit. □ *What a waste of time. You really led me on a merry chase.* □ *Jane led Bill on a merry chase trying to find an antique lamp.*

lead the life of Riley to live in luxury. (No one knows who Riley is.) □ *If I had a million dollars, I could live the life of Riley.* □ *The treasurer took our money to Mexico, where he lived the life of Riley until the police caught him.*

lead up to something **1.** to aim at or route movement to something. □ *A narrow path led up to the door of the cottage.* □ *This road leads up to the house at the top of the hill.* **2.** to prepare to say something; to lay the groundwork for making a point.

(Typically with the present participle.) □ *I was just leading up to telling you what happened when you interrupted.* □ *I knew she was leading up to something, the way she was talking.*

leaf out [for a plant] to open its leaf buds. □ *Most of the bushes leaf out in mid-April.* □ *The trees leafed out early this year.*

leaf through something to look through something, turning the pages. □ *Jan leafed through the catalog, looking for a suitable winter coat.* □ *Leaf through this and see if there is anything you like.*

leak in(to something) [for a fluid] to work its way into something. □ *Some of the soapy water leaked into the soil.* □ *The rainwater is leaking in!*

leak out [for information] to become known. (Compare to *leak out (of something)*.) □ *I hope that news of the new building does not leak out before the contract is signed.* □ *When the story leaked out, my telephone would not stop ringing.*

leak out (of something) [for a fluid] to seep out of something or some place. (Compare to *leak out.*) □ *Some of the brake fluid leaked out of the car and made a spot on the driveway.* □ *Look under the car. Something's leaking out.*

leak something out to permit [otherwise secret] information to become publicly known. □ *Please don't leak this out. It is supposed to be a secret.* T *Someone leaked out the report.*

lean back (against someone or something) to recline backwards, putting weight on someone or something. □ *Just lean back against me. I will prevent you from falling.* □ *Relax and lean back. Nothing bad is going to happen.*

lean over 1. to bend over. □ *Lean over and pick the pencil up yourself! I'm not your servant!* □ *As Kelly leaned over to tie her shoes, her chair slipped out from under her.* **2.** to tilt over. □ *The fence leaned over and almost fell.* □ *As the wind blew, the tree leaned over farther and farther.*

lean toward someone or something 1. to incline toward someone or something. □ *Tom is leaning toward Randy. I think he is going to fall on him.* □ *The tree is leaning toward the edge of the cliff. It will fall eventually.* **2.** to tend to favor [choosing] someone or something. □ *I am leaning toward Sarah as the new committee head.* □ *I'm leaning toward a new committee.*

leap for joy to jump up because one is happy; to be very happy. (Usually figurative.) □ *Tommy leapt for joy because he had won the race.* □ *We all leapt for joy when we heard the news.*

learn something from the bottom up to learn something thoroughly, from the very beginning; to learn all aspects of something, even the most lowly. □ *I learned my business from the bottom up.* □ *I started out sweeping the floors and learned everything from the bottom up.*

leave a bad taste in someone's mouth [for someone or something] to leave a bad feeling or memory with someone. (Also used literally.) □ *The whole business about the missing money left a bad taste in his mouth.* □ *It was a very nice party, but something about it left a bad taste in my mouth.* □ *I'm sorry that Bill was there. He always leaves a bad taste in my mouth.*

leave a sinking ship See *desert a sinking ship.*

Leave it to me. I will attend to it by myself.; I will do it. □ JOHN: *This whole business needs to be straightened out.* SUE: *Leave it to me. I'll get it done.* □ JANE: *Will you do this as soon as possible?* MARY: *Leave it to me.*

Leave me alone! Stop harassing me!; *Don't bother me!* □ JOHN: *You did it. You're the one who always does it.* BILL: *Leave me alone! I never did it.* □ FRED: *Let's give Bill a dunk in the pool.* BILL: *Leave me alone!*

leave no stone unturned to search in all possible places. (As if one might find something under a rock.) □ *Don't worry. We'll find your stolen car. We'll leave no stone unturned.* □ *In searching for a nice place to live, we left no stone unturned.*

leave one to one's fate to abandon someone to whatever may happen — possibly death or some other unpleasant event. □ *We couldn't rescue the miners, and we were forced to leave them to their fate.* □ *Please don't try to help. Just go away and leave me to my fate.*

leave someone for dead to abandon someone as being dead. (The abandoned person may actually be alive.) □ *He looked so bad that they almost left him for dead.* □ *As the soldiers turned — leaving the enemy captain for dead — the captain fired at them.*

leave someone high and dry 1. to leave someone unsupported and unable to maneuver; to leave someone helpless. (Refers to a boat stranded on land or on a reef.) □ *All my workers quit and left me high and dry.*

□ *All the children ran away and left Billy high and dry to take the blame for the broken window.* **2.** to leave someone without any money at all. □ *Mrs. Franklin took all the money out of the bank and left Mr. Franklin high and dry.* □ *Paying the bills always leaves me high and dry.*

leave someone holding the bag to leave someone to take all the blame; to leave someone appearing guilty. □ *They all ran off and left me holding the bag. It wasn't even my fault.* □ *It was the mayor's fault, but he wasn't left holding the bag.*

leave someone in peace to stop bothering someone; to go away and leave someone in peace. (Does not necessarily mean to go away from a person.) □ *Please go — leave me in peace.* □ *Can't you see that you're upsetting her? Leave her in peace.*

leave someone in the lurch to leave someone waiting for or anticipating your actions. □ *Where were you, John? You really left me in the lurch.* □ *I didn't mean to leave you in the lurch. I thought we had canceled our meeting.*

leave someone or something hanging in midair to suspend dealing with someone or something; to leave someone or something waiting to be finished or continued. (Also used literally.) □ *She left her sentence hanging in midair.* □ *She left us hanging in midair when she paused.* □ *Tell me the rest of the story. Don't leave me hanging in midair.* □ *Don't leave the story hanging in midair.*

leave someone or something out (of something) to neglect to include someone or something in something. □ *Please leave me out of it.* □ *Can I* *leave John out this time?* T *Don't leave out Fred's name.*

leave something on 1. to allow something [that can be turned off] to remain on. □ *Who left the radio on?* T *Please leave on the light for me.* **2.** to continue to wear some article of clothing. □ *I think I will leave my coat on. It's chilly in here.* T *I'll leave on my coat.*

leave something up to someone or something to allow someone or something to make a decision about something. □ *We will try to leave that decision up to you.* □ *Can we leave this up to the committee?*

legislate against something to prohibit something; to pass a law against something. □ *You can't just legislate against something. You have to explain to people why they shouldn't do it.* □ *The Congress has just legislated against insolvent banks.*

legislate for something to pass a law that tries to make something happen. □ *The candidate pledged to legislate for tax relief.* □ *We support your efforts to legislate for lower taxes.*

lend an ear (to someone) to listen to someone. □ *Lend an ear to John. Hear what he has to say.* □ *I'd be delighted to lend an ear. I find great wisdom in everything John has to say.*

lend oneself or itself to something [for someone or something] to be adaptable to something; [for someone or something] to be useful for something. □ *This room doesn't lend itself to bright colors.* □ *John doesn't lend himself to casual conversation.*

Let bygones be bygones. One should forget the problems of the past. (Proverb.) □ *Okay, Sally, let bygones*

be bygones. Let's forgive and forget. □ *Jane was unwilling to let bygones be bygones. She still won't speak to me.*

let down to relax one's efforts or vigilance. □ *Now is no time to let down. Keep on your guard.* □ *After the contest was over, Jane let down a bit so she could relax.*

let grass grow under one's feet to do nothing; to stand still. □ *Mary doesn't let the grass grow under her feet. She's always busy.* □ *Bob is too lazy. He's letting the grass grow under his feet.*

Let it be. Leave the situation alone as it is. □ ALICE: *I can't get over the way he just left me there on the street and drove off. What an arrogant pig!* MARY: *Oh, Alice, let it be. You'll figure out some way to get even.* □ JOHN: *You can't!* BILL: *Can too!* JOHN: *Can't!* BILL: *Can too!* JANE: *Stop! Let it be! That's enough!*

Let me get back to you (on that). See *I'll get back to you (on that).*

Let me have it! AND **Let's have it!** Tell me the news. □ BILL: *I'm afraid there's some bad news.* BOB: *Okay. Let me have it! Don't waste time!* BILL: *The plans we made did away with your job.* BOB: *What?* □ JOHN: *I didn't want to be the one to tell you this.* BOB: *What is it? Let's have it!* JOHN: *Your cat was just run over.* BOB: *Never mind that, what's the bad news?*

let me (just) say AND **just let me say** a phrase introducing something that the speaker thinks is important. □ RACHEL: *Let me say how pleased we all are with your efforts.* HENRY: *Why, thank you very much.* □ BOB: *Just let me say that we're extremely pleased* with your activity. BILL: *Thanks loads. I did what I could.*

let off steam AND **blow off steam** to release excess energy or anger. (Also used literally.) □ *Whenever John gets a little angry, he blows off steam.* □ *Don't worry about John. He's just letting off steam.*

let on (about someone or something) to confirm or reveal something about someone or something. □ *You promised you wouldn't let on about Sally and her new job!* □ *I didn't let on. She guessed.*

let one's hair down to become more intimate and begin to speak frankly. □ *Come on, Jane, let your hair down and tell me all about it.* T *I have a problem. Do you mind if I let down my hair?*

let out [for an event that includes many people] to end. (The people are then permitted to come out.) □ *What time does the movie let out? I have to meet someone in the lobby.* □ *The meeting let out at about seven o'clock.* □ *School lets out in June.*

let out (with) something 1. to state or utter something loudly. □ *The man let out with a screaming accusation about the person whom he thought had wounded him.* □ *She let out a torrent of curses.* **2.** to give forth a scream or yell. □ *She let out with a bloodcurdling scream when she saw the snake in her chair.* □ *They let out with shouts of delight when they saw the cake.*

Let sleeping dogs lie. One should not search for trouble.; One should leave well enough alone. (Proverb.) □ *Don't mention that problem with Tom again. It's almost forgotten. Let sleeping dogs lie.* □ *You'll never be able to re-*

form Bill. Leave him alone. *Let sleeping dogs lie.*

let someone off (the hook) to release someone from a responsibility. □ *Please let me off the hook for Saturday. I have other plans.* □ *Okay, I'll let you off.*

let someone off (with something) to give someone a light punishment [for doing something]. □ *The judge let the criminal off with a slap on the wrist.* T *The judge would not let off the criminal with a small fine.* □ *This judge lets too many of these petty crooks off.*

let someone or something down to fail someone or something; to disappoint someone or a group. □ *Please don't let me down. I am depending on you.* T *I let down the entire cast of the play.* □ *I'm sorry I let you down.*

let something out 1. to reveal something; to tell about a secret or a plan. □ *It was supposed to be a secret. Who let it out?* T *Who let out the secret?* **2.** to enlarge the waist of an article of clothing. □ *She had to let her skirts out because she had gained some weight.* T *I see you have had to let out your trousers.*

let something out (to someone) to rent something to someone. □ *I let the back room out to a college boy.* T *I let out the back room to someone.*

let something slide to neglect something. □ *John let his lessons slide.* □ *Jane doesn't let her work slide.*

let something slide by See the following entry.

let something slip by AND **let something slide by 1.** to forget or miss an important time or date. □ *I'm sorry I just let your birthday slip by.* □ *I let it* *slide by accidentally.* **2.** to waste a period of time. □ *You wasted the whole day by letting it slip by.* □ *We were having fun, and we let the time slide by.*

let the cat out of the bag AND **spill the beans** to reveal a secret or a surprise by accident. □ *When Bill glanced at the door, he let the cat out of the bag. We knew then that he was expecting someone to arrive.* □ *We are planning a surprise party for Jane. Don't let the cat out of the bag.* □ *It's a secret. Try not to spill the beans.*

let the chance slip by to lose the opportunity (to do something). □ *When I was younger, I wanted to become a doctor, but I let the chance slip by.* □ *Don't let the chance slip by. Do it now!*

let up 1. to diminish. □ *I hope this rain lets up a little soon.* □ *When the snow lets up so I can see, I will drive to the store.* **2.** to stop [doing something] altogether. □ *The rain let up about noon, and the sun came out.*

let up (on someone or something) to reduce the pressure or demands on someone or something. □ *You had better let up on Tom. He can't handle any more work.* □ *Please let up on the committee. It can only do so much.* □ *Do let up. You are getting too upset.*

Let's call it a day. Let us end what we are doing for the day. □ MARY: *Well, that's the end of the reports. Nothing else to do.* SUE: *Let's call it a day.* □ BOB: *Let's call it a day. I'm tired.* TOM: *Me too. Let's get out of here.*

Let's do lunch (sometime). See *We('ll) have to do lunch sometime.*

Let's do this again (sometime). AND **We must do this again (sometime).** an expression indicating that one member of a group or pair has enjoyed doing something and would like to do it again. □ BILL: *What a nice evening.* MARY: *Yes, let's do this again sometime.* BILL: *Bye.* MARY: *Bye, Bill.* □ SUE (saying good night): *So nice to see both of you.* MARY: *Oh, yes. We must do this again sometime.*

Let's eat. 1. an announcement that a meal is ready to be eaten. □ FATHER: *It's all ready now. Let's eat.* BILL: *Great! I'm starved.* □ JOHN: *Soup's on! Let's eat!* BILL: *Come on, everybody. Let's eat!* **2.** AND **Let's eat something.** a suggestion that it is time to eat. □ MARY: *Look at the clock. We only have a few minutes before the show. Let's eat something.* □ BILL: *What should we do? We have some time to spare.* SUE: *Let's eat something.* BILL: *Good idea.* SUE: *Food is always a good idea with you.*

Let's eat something. See the previous entry.

Let's get down to business. a phrase marking a transition to a business discussion or serious talk. □ JOHN: *Okay, enough small talk. Let's get down to business.* MARY: *Good idea.* □ *"All right, ladies and gentlemen, let's get down to business," said the president of the board.*

Let's get out of here. Let us leave (and go somewhere else). □ ALICE: *It's really hot in this room. Let's get out of here.* JOHN: *I'm with you. Let's go.* □ BILL: *This crowd is getting sort of angry.* BOB: *I noticed that too. Let's get out of here.*

Let's get together (sometime). a vague invitation to meet again, usually said upon departing. (The *sometime* can be a particular time or the word *sometime*.) □ BILL: *Goodbye, Bob.* BOB: *See you, Bill. Let's get together sometime.* □ JANE: *We need to discuss this matter.* JOHN: *Yes, let's get together next week.*

Let's go somewhere where it's (more) quiet. Let us continue our conversation where there is less noise or where we will not be disturbed. □ TOM: *Hi, Mary. It's sure crowded here.* MARY: *Yes, let's go somewhere where it's quiet.* □ BILL: *We need to talk.* SALLY: *Yes, we do. Let's go somewhere where it's more quiet.*

Let's have it! See *Let me have it!*

Let's not go through all that again. We are not going to discuss that matter again. (Compare to *Do we have to go through all that again?*) □ BILL: *Now, I still want to explain again about last night.* SALLY: *Let's not go through all that again!* □ SALLY: *I can't get over the way you spoke to me at our own dinner table.* FRED: *I was only kidding! I said I was sorry. Let's not go through all that again!*

Let's shake on it. Let us mark this agreement by shaking hands on it. □ BOB: *Do you agree?* MARY: *I agree. Let's shake on it.* BOB: *Okay.* □ BILL: *Good idea. Sounds fine.* BOB (extending his hand): *Okay, let's shake on it.* BILL (shaking hands with Bob): *Great!*

Let's talk (about it). Let us talk about the problem and try to settle things. □ TOM: *Bill! Bill! I'm sorry about our argument. Let's talk.* BILL: *Get lost!* □ SALLY: *I've got a real problem.* BOB: *Let's talk about it.*

level off [for variation or fluctuation in the motion of something] to diminish; [for a rate] to stop increasing or decreasing. (More at *level something off*.) □ *The plane leveled off at 10,000 feet.* □ *After a while the work load will level off.* □ *Things will level off after we get through the end of the month.*

level out [for something that was going up and down] to assume a more level course or path. (More at *level something out*.) □ *The road leveled out after a while and driving was easier.* □ *As we got down into the valley, the land leveled out and traveling was easier.*

level something off to make something level or smooth. (More at *level off*.) □ *You are going to have to level the floor off before you put the carpet down.* T *Please level off the floor.*

level something out to cause something to assume a more level course or path. (More at *level out*.) □ *Level this path out before you open it to the public.* T *They have to level out this roadway.*

lie down to recline. □ *Why don't you lie down for a while?* □ *I need to lie down and have a little snooze.*

lie in [for a woman] to lie in bed awaiting the birth of her child. □ *The child is due soon, and the mother is lying in at the present time.* □ *All the women in that particular hospital are lying in.*

lie through one's teeth to lie boldly, obviously, and with no remorse. □ *I knew she was lying through her teeth, but I didn't want to say so just then.* □ *I'm not lying through my teeth! I never do!*

life of the party the type of person who is lively and helps make a party fun and exciting. □ *Bill is always the life of the party. Be sure to invite him.* □ *Bob isn't exactly the life of the party, but he's polite.*

lift off [for a plane or rocket] to move upward, leaving the ground. (Compare to *lift something off (of) someone or something.*) □ *The rocket lifted off exactly on time.* □ *What time will the next one lift off?*

lift something off (of) someone or something to raise something and uncover or release someone or something. (The *of* is colloquial. Compare to *lift off.*) □ *Lift the beam off of him and see if he is still breathing.* Ⓣ *Please lift off the heavy lid.*

light someone or something up to shine lights on someone or something. □ *We lit Fred up with the headlights of the car.* Ⓣ *Light up the stage and let's rehearse.*

light up 1. to become brighter. □ *Suddenly, the sky lit up like day.* □ *The room lit up as the fire suddenly came back to life.* **2.** [for someone] to become interested and responsive in something. □ *We could tell from the way Sally lit up that she recognized the man in the picture.* □ *She lit up when we told her about our team's success.*

light (up)on someone or something 1. to land on someone or something; to settle on someone or something. (*Upon* is formal and less commonly used than *on.*) □ *Three butterflies lit on the baby, causing her to shriek with delight.* □ *The bees lit on the clover blossom and pulled it to the ground.* □ *Her glance lit upon a dress in the store window.* **2.** to arrive at something by chance; to happen upon something. (Figurative. Close to sense 1.) □ *The committee lit upon a solution that pleased almost everyone.* □ *We just happen to light upon this idea as we were talking to each other.*

like a bat out of hell with great speed and force. (Use caution with *hell.*) □ *Did you see her leave? She left like a bat out of hell.* □ *The car sped down the street like a bat out of hell.*

like a bolt out of the blue suddenly and without warning. (Refers to a bolt of lightning coming out of a clear blue sky.) □ *The news came to us like a bolt out of the blue.* □ *Like a bolt out of the blue, the boss came and fired us all.*

like a bump on a log unresponsive; immobile. □ *I spoke to him, but he just sat there like a bump on a log.* □ *Don't stand there like a bump on a log. Give me a hand!*

like a fish out of water awkward; in a foreign or unaccustomed environment. □ *At a formal dance, John is like a fish out of water.* □ *Mary was like a fish out of water at the bowling tournament.*

like a sitting duck AND **like sitting ducks** unguarded; unsuspecting and unaware. (The second phrase is the plural form. Refers to floating rather than flying ducks.) □ *He was waiting there like a sitting duck — a perfect target for a mugger.* □ *The soldiers were standing at the top of the hill like sitting ducks. It's a wonder they weren't all killed.*

like a three-ring circus chaotic; exciting and busy. □ *Our household is* like a three-ring circus on Monday mornings. □ This meeting is like a three-ring circus. Quiet down and listen!

like I was saying See *as I was saying.*

Like it or lump it! There is no other choice. Take that or none. (Slang.) □ JOHN: *I don't like this room. It's too small.* BILL: *Like it or lump it. That's all we've got.* □ JANE: *I don't want to be talked to like that.* SUE: *Well, like it or lump it! That's the way we talk around here.*

like looking for a needle in a haystack engaged in a hopeless search. □ *Trying to find a white dog in the snow is like looking for a needle in a haystack.* □ *I tried to find my lost contact lens on the beach, but it was like looking for a needle in a haystack.*

like sitting ducks See *like a sitting duck.*

like water off a duck's back easily; without any apparent effect. □ *Insults rolled off John like water off a duck's back.* □ *The bullets had no effect on the steel door. They fell away like water off a duck's back.*

like you say See *as you say.*

Likewise(, I'm sure). The same from my point of view. (A hackneyed phrase said in the greeting sequence.) □ ALICE: *I'm delighted to make your acquaintance.* BOB: *Likewise, I'm sure.* □ JOHN: *How nice to see you!* SUE: *Likewise.* JOHN: *Where are you from, Sue?*

line someone or something up 1. to put people or things in line. (*Someone* includes *oneself.* More at *line someone or something up (in something).*) □ *Line everyone up and march them onstage.* ⊤ *Line up the*

kids, please. □ *Please line these books up.* **2.** to schedule someone or something [for something]. □ *Please line somebody up for the entertainment.* ⊤ *We will try to line up a magician and a clown for the party.* ⊤ *They lined up a chorus for the last act.*

line someone or something up (in something) to put people or things into some kind of formation, such as a row, column, ranks, etc. (*Someone* includes *oneself.* More at *line someone or something up.*) □ *The teacher lined the children up in two rows.* ⊤ *Please line up the children in a row.* □ *Yes, line them up.* □ *Let's line ourselves up into two columns.*

line up to form a line; to get into a line. □ *All right, everyone, line up!* □ *Please line up.*

line up for something to form or get into a line and wait for something. □ *Everyone lined up for a helping of birthday cake.* □ *Let's line up for dinner. The doors to the dining room will open at any minute.*

line up in(to) something to form or get into a line, row, rank, column, etc. □ *Please line up in columns of two.* □ *I wish you would all line up into a nice straight line.*

linger on (after someone or something) AND **stay on (after someone or something)** to outlast someone or something; to live longer than someone else or long after an event. □ *Aunt Sarah lingered on only a few months after Uncle Herman died.* □ *She lingered on and was depressed for a while.* □ *She stayed on after her husband for a short time.*

link up to someone or something AND **link (up) with someone or**

something to join up with someone or something. □ *I have a computer modem so I can link up to Bruce.* □ *Now my computer can link up with a computer bulletin board.*

link (up) with someone or something See the previous entry.

listen in (on someone or something)
1. to join someone or a group as a listener. □ *The band is rehearsing. Let's go listen in on them.* □ *It won't hurt to listen in, will it?* **2.** to eavesdrop on someone. □ *Please don't try to listen in on us. This is a private conversation.* □ *I am not listening in. I was here first. You are conversing carelessly.*

little by little slowly, a bit at a time. □ *Little by little, he began to understand what we were talking about.* □ *The snail crossed the stone little by little.*

live a dog's life See *lead a dog's life.*

live and let live not to interfere with other people's business or preferences. □ *I don't care what they do! Live and let live, I always say.* □ *Your parents are strict. Mine just live and let live.*

live beyond one's means to spend more money than one can afford. □ *The Browns are deeply in debt because they are living beyond their means.* □ *I keep a budget so that I don't live beyond my means.*

live by one's wits to survive by being clever. □ *When you're in the kind of business I'm in, you have to live by your wits.* □ *John was orphaned at the age of ten and grew up living by his wits.*

live from hand to mouth to live in poor circumstances. □ *When both my parents were out of work, we lived from hand to mouth.* □ *We lived from hand to mouth during the war. Things were very difficult.*

live in an ivory tower to be aloof from the realities of living. (*Live* can be replaced by several expressions meaning "to dwell" or "spend time," as in the examples. Academics are often said to live in ivory towers.) □ *If you didn't spend so much time in your ivory tower, you'd know what people really think!* □ *Many professors are said to live in ivory towers. They don't know what the real world is like.*

live off (of) someone or something to obtain one's living or means of survival from someone or something. (The *of* is colloquial.) □ *You can't live off your uncle all your life!* □ *I manage to live off of my salary.*

live off the fat of the land to grow one's own food; to live on stored-up resources or abundant resources. □ *If I had a million dollars, I'd invest it and live off the fat of the land.* □ *I'll be happy to retire soon and live off the fat of the land.* □ *Many farmers live off the fat of the land.*

live out of a suitcase to live briefly in a place, never unpacking one's luggage. □ *I hate living out of a suitcase. For my next vacation, I want to go to just one place and stay there the whole time.* □ *We were living out of suitcases in a motel while they repaired the damage the fire caused to our house.*

live something down to overcome some embarrassing or troublesome problem or event. □ *It was so embarrassing! I will never live it down.* ⊤ *I will never live down this incident.*

live through something to endure something; to survive an unpleasant or dangerous time of one's life. □ *I almost did not live through the operation.* □ *I know I can't live through another attack.*

live up to something to be equal to expectations or goals. □ *The dinner did not live up to my expectations.* □ *We will live up to your first impressions of us.*

live with something to put up with something. (Does not mean "to dwell with.") □ *That is not acceptable. I can't live with that. Please change it.* □ *Mary refused to live with the proposed changes.*

live within one's means to spend no more money than one has. □ *We have to struggle to live within our means, but we manage.* □ *John is unable to live within his means.*

live within something 1. to live within certain boundaries. □ *Do you think you can live within your space, or are we going to argue over the use of square footage?* □ *Ted demanded again that Bill live within his assigned area.* 2. to keep one's living costs within a certain amount, especially within one's budget, means, etc. □ *Please try to live within your budget.* □ *You must learn to live within your means.*

live without something to survive, lacking something. □ *I just know I can't live without my car.* □ *I am sure we can live without vegetables for a day or two.*

liven something up to make something more lively or less dull. □ *Some singing might liven things up a bit.* T *The songs livened up the evening.*

load someone or something into something to put someone or some-

thing into something. □ *Load all the boxes into the truck.* □ *Would you load the dishes into the dishwasher?* □ *Let's load the kids into the car and go to the zoo.*

load up (with something) to take or accumulate a lot of something. □ *Don't load up with cheap souvenirs. Save your money.* □ *Whenever I get into a used bookstore, I load up.*

lobby against something to solicit support against something, such as a piece of legislation or a government regulation. □ *We sent a lot of lawyers to the state capital to lobby against the bill, but it passed anyway.* □ *They lobbied against the tax increase.*

lobby for something to solicit support for something among the members of a voting body, such as the Congress. □ *Tom is always lobbying for some bill or other.* □ *The manufacturers lobbied for tax relief.*

lock horns (with someone) to get into an argument with someone. (Like bulls or stags fighting.) □ *Let's settle this peacefully. I don't want to lock horns with the boss.* □ *The boss doesn't want to lock horns either.*

lock someone or something up (somewhere) to lock someone or something within something or some place. (*Someone* includes *oneself*.) □ *The captain ordered the sailor locked up in the brig until the ship got into port.* T *The sheriff locked up the crook in a cell.* □ *Don't lock me up.* □ *She locked herself up in her office where no one could get to her.*

lock something in to take action to fix a rate or price at a certain figure. □ *I can lock the price in for about a* week. T *If you put down a deposit now, I can lock in the price for a week.*

lock, stock, and barrel everything. □ *We had to move everything out of the house — lock, stock, and barrel.* □ *We lost everything — lock, stock, and barrel — in the fire.*

lodge something against someone or something **1.** [with *someone*] to place a charge against someone. □ *The neighbors lodged a complaint against us for parking on their grass.* □ *I want to lodge an assault charge against Max.* **2.** [with *something*] to place or prop something against something. □ *We lodged the chest against the door, making it difficult or impossible to open.* □ *Let's lodge the stone against the side of the barn to help support it.*

log off AND **log out** to record one's exit from a computer system. (This action may be recorded or logged automatically in the computer's memory.) □ *I closed my files and logged off.* □ *What time did you log out?*

log on to attach oneself up to use a computer system. (This action may be recorded or logged automatically in the computer's memory.) □ *What time did you log on to the system this morning?* □ *I always log on before I get my first cup of coffee.*

log out See *log off*.

Long time no see. I have not seen you in a long time.; We have not seen each other in a long time. □ TOM: *Hi, Fred. Where have you been keeping yourself?* FRED: *Good to see you, Tom. Long time no see.* □ JOHN: *It's Bob! Hi, Bob!* BOB: *Hi, John! Long time no see.*

look a sentence opener seeking the attention of the person spoken to. (Words such as this often use intonation to convey the connotation of the sentence that is to follow. The brief intonation pattern accompanying the word may indicate sarcasm, disagreement, caution, consolation, sternness, etc.) □ SUE: *How could you!* FRED: *Look, I didn't mean to.* □ ANDREW: *Look, can't we talk about it?* SUE: *There's no more to be said.* □ JOHN: *I'm so sorry!* ANDREW: *Look, we all make mistakes.* □ *"Look, let me try again," said Fred.* □ ANDREW: *Look, I've just about had it with you!* SALLY: *And I've had it with you.* □ ANDREW: *Look, that can't be right.* RACHEL: *But it is.*

Look alive! Act alert and responsive! □ *"Come on, Fred! Get moving! Look alive!" shouted the coach, who was not happy with Fred's performance.* □ BILL: *Look alive, Bob!* BOB: *I'm doing the best I can.*

look as if butter wouldn't melt in one's mouth to appear to be cold and unfeeling despite any information to the contrary. □ *Sally looks as if butter wouldn't melt in her mouth. She can be so cruel.* □ *What a sour face. He looks as if butter wouldn't melt in his mouth.*

Look (at) what the cat dragged in! *Look who's here!* (A good-humored and familiar way of showing surprise at someone's presence in a place, especially if the person looks a little rumpled. Compare to *(Someone) looks like something the cat dragged in.*) □ *Bob and Mary were standing near the doorway talking when Tom came in. "Look what the cat dragged in!" announced Bob.* □ MARY: *Hello,* *everybody. I'm here!* JANE: *Look at what the cat dragged in!*

look away (from someone or something) to turn one's gaze away from someone. □ *She looked away from him, not wishing her eyes to give away her true feelings.* □ *In embarrassment, she looked away.*

look back (at someone or something) AND **look back (on someone or something)** **1.** to gaze back and try to get a view of someone or something. □ *She looked back at the city and whispered a good-bye to everything she had ever cared for.* □ *I went away and never looked back.* **2.** to think about someone or something in the past. □ *When I look back on Frank, I do remember his strange manner, come to think of it.* □ *When I look back, I am amazed at all I have accomplished.*

look back (on someone or something) See the previous entry.

look daggers at someone to give someone a dirty look. (As if one's line of vision were daggers aimed at someone.) □ *Tom must have been mad at Ann from the way he was looking daggers at her.* □ *Don't you dare look daggers at me. Don't even look cross-eyed at me!*

look down (at someone or something) **1.** to turn one's gaze downward at someone or something. □ *She looked down at me and giggled at the awkward position I was in.* □ *She looked down and burst into laughter.* **2.** AND **look down on someone or something** to view someone or something as lowly or unworthy. □ *She looked down at all the waiters and treated them badly.* □ *They looked down on our humble food.*

look down on someone or something See the previous entry.

look here a phrase emphasizing the point that follows it. (Can indicate some impatience. See also *look.*) □ HENRY: *Look here, I want to try to help you, but you're not making it easy for me.* RACHEL: *I'm just so upset.* □ ANDREW: *Look here, I just asked you a simple question!* BOB: *As I told you in the beginning, there are no simple answers.*

look in (on someone or something) to check on someone or something. □ *I will look in on her from time to time.* □ *I looked in and everything was all right.*

look into something **1.** to gaze into the inside of something. □ *Look into the box and make sure you've gotten everything out of it.* □ *Look into the camera's viewfinder at the little red light.* **2.** to investigate something. □ *I will look into this matter and see what I can do about it.* □ *Please ask the manager to look into it.*

look like a million dollars to look very good. □ *Oh, Sally, you look like a million dollars.* □ *Your new hairdo looks like a million dollars.*

look like the cat that swallowed the canary to appear as if one had just had a great success. (Cats sometimes seem to appear guilty for bad things they have done.) □ *After the meeting John looked like the cat that swallowed the canary. I knew he must have been a success.* □ *What happened? You look like the cat that swallowed the canary.*

Look me up when you're in town. When you next come to my town, try to find me (and we will get together). (A vague and perhaps insincere invitation.) □ BOB: *Nice to see you, Tom. Bye now.* TOM: *Yes, indeed. Look me up when you're in town. Bye.* □ SALLY (on the phone): *Bye. Nice talking to you.* MARY: *Bye, Sally. Sorry we can't talk more. Look me up when you're in town.*

look on to be a spectator. □ *The beating took place while a policeman looked on.* □ *While the kittens played, the mother cat looked on contentedly.*

look on (with someone) to share and read from someone else's notes, paper, book, music, etc. □ *I don't have a copy of the notice, but I will look on with Tom.* □ *Carla has a copy of the music. She doesn't mind if I look on.*

look out 1. to be careful; to think and move fast because something dangerous is about to harm one. □ *When you cross the pond, look out for cracks in the ice.* □ *Look out for falling objects.* **2.** Be careful.; Be aware of the danger near you! (Usually **Look out!**) □ *Bob saw the scenery starting to fall on Tom. "Look out!" cried Bob.* □ *"Look out! That sidewalk is really slick with ice!" warned Sally.*

look out for someone or something 1. to be watchful for the appearance of someone or something. □ *Look out for Sam. He is due any minute.* □ *Look out for the bus. We don't want to miss it.* **2.** to be alert to the danger posed by someone or something. □ *Look out for that last step. It's loose.* □ *Look out for that truck!*

look someone or something over to examine someone or something. (*Someone* includes *oneself.*) □ *I think you had better have the doctor look you over.* ⊤ *Please look over these papers.* □ *They looked themselves over and declared themselves beautiful.*

look someone or something up 1. to seek someone, a group, or something out. □ *I lost track of Sally. I'll try to look her up and get in touch with her.* ⊤ *I am going to look up an old friend when I am in Chicago.* □ *I am going to look that old gang up.* ⊤ *Ted came into town and looked up his favorite pizza place.* **2.** to seek information about someone or something in a book or listing. (*Someone* includes *oneself.*) □ *I don't recognize his name. I'll look him up and see what I can find.* ⊤ *I'll look up this person in a reference book.* ⊤ *Can I use the directory to look up an address?* □ *She looked herself up in the telephone book to make sure her name was spelled correctly.*

look the other way to ignore (something) on purpose. (Also used literally.) □ *John could have prevented the problem, but he looked the other way.* □ *By looking the other way, he actually made the problem worse.*

look through something 1. to gaze through something. □ *Look through the window at what the neighbors are doing.* □ *Look through the binoculars and see if you can get a better view.* **2.** to examine the parts, pages, samples, etc., of something. □ *Look through this report and see what you make of it.* □ *I will look through it when I have time.*

look up to show promise of improving. □ *My prospects for a job are looking up.* □ *Conditions are looking up.*

look up to someone to admire someone. □ *We all look up to Roger. He's authoritative but kind.* □ *I am glad they look up to me.*

look (up)on someone or something as something to view someone or something as something; to consider someone or something to be something. □ *I look upon Todd as a fine and helpful guy.* □ *I look on these requests as an annoyance.*

Look who's here! an expression drawing attention to someone present at a place. □ BILL: *Look who's here! My old friend Fred. How goes it, Fred?* FRED: *Hi, there, Bill! What's new?* BILL: *Nothing much.* □ BILL: *Look who's here!* MARY: *Yeah. Isn't that Fred Morgan?*

Look who's talking! You are guilty of doing what you have criticized someone else for doing or accused someone else of doing. □ ANDREW: *You criticize me for being late! Look who's talking! You just missed your flight!* JANE: *Well, nobody's perfect.* □ MARY: *You just talk and talk, you go on much too long about practically nothing, and you never give a chance for anyone else to talk, and you just don't know when to stop!* SALLY: *Look who's talking!*

loom out of something to appear to come out of or penetrate something. □ *A truck suddenly loomed out of the fog and just missed hitting us.* □ *A tall building loomed out of the mists.*

loom up to appear to rise up [from somewhere]; to take form or definition, usually threatening to some degree. □ *A great city loomed up in the distance. It looked threatening in the dusky light.* □ *A ghost loomed up, but we paid no attention, since it had to be a joke.* □ *The recession loomed up, and the stock market reacted.*

loosen someone or something up 1. to make someone's muscles and joints move more freely by exercising

them. (*Someone* includes *oneself.* More at *loosen up.*) □ *The exercise loosened me up quite nicely.* T *It loosened up my legs.* □ *I have to do some exercises to loosen myself up.* **2.** to make someone or a group more relaxed and friendly. (*Someone* includes *oneself.*) □ *I told a little joke to loosen the audience up.* T *I loosened up the audience with a joke.* □ *Loosen yourself up. Relax and try to enjoy people.* **3.** [with *something*] to make something less tight. □ *Loosen the freshly oiled hinges up by swinging the door back and forth.* T *Try to loosen up those hinges.*

loosen up to become loose or relaxed. (More at *loosen someone or something up.*) □ *Loosen up. Relax.* □ *We tried to get Mary to loosen up, but she did not respond.*

lord it over someone to dominate someone; to direct and control someone. □ *Mr. Smith seems to lord it over his wife.* □ *The boss lords it over everyone in the office.*

Lord knows I've tried. I certainly have tried very hard. □ ALICE: *Why don't you get Bill to fix this fence?* MARY: *Lord knows I've tried. I must have asked him a dozen times — this year alone.* □ SUE: *I can't seem to get to class on time.* RACHEL: *That's just awful.* SUE: *Lord knows I've tried. I just can't do it.*

lose face to lose status; to become less respectable. □ *John is more afraid of losing face than losing money.* □ *Things will go better if you can explain to him where he was wrong without making him lose face.*

lose heart to lose one's courage or confidence. □ *Now, don't lose heart.*

Keep trying. □ *What a disappointment! It's enough to make one lose heart.*

lose one's grip **1.** to lose one's grasp (of something). □ *I'm holding on to the rope as tightly as I can. I hope I don't lose my grip.* □ *This hammer is slippery. Try not to lose your grip.* **2.** to lose control (over something). □ *I can't seem to run things the way I used to. I'm losing my grip.* □ *They replaced the board of directors because it was losing its grip.*

lose one's temper to become angry. □ *Please don't lose your temper. It's not good for you.* □ *I'm sorry that I lost my temper.*

lose one's train of thought to forget what one was talking or thinking about. □ ANDREW: *I had something important on my mind, but that telephone call made me lose my train of thought.* MARY: *Did it have anything to do with money, such as the money you owe me?* ANDREW: *I can't remember.* □ TOM: *Now, let's take a look at, uh. Well, next I want to talk about something that is very important.* MARY: *I think you lost your train of thought.* TOM: *Don't interrupt. You'll make me forget what I'm saying.*

lose out to lose in competition; to lose one's expected reward. □ *Our team lost out because our quarterback broke his leg.* □ *I ran my best race, but I still lost out.* □ *I was hoping for a promotion, but I lost out because of my bad attendance record.*

lose out (on something) to miss enjoying something; to miss participating in something. □ *I would hate to lose out on all the fun.* □ *We'll lose out if we don't get there on time.*

lose out to someone or something to lose in a competition to someone or something. □ *I didn't want to lose out to the other guys.* □ *Our firm lost out to the lowest bidder.*

lost in thought busy thinking. □ *I'm sorry, I didn't hear what you said. I was lost in thought.* □ *Bill — lost in thought as always — went into the wrong room.*

Lots of luck! I wish you luck; you will need it, but it probably will not do any good. □ BILL: *I'm going to try to get my tax bill lowered.* TOM: *Lots of luck!* □ MARY: *I'll go in there and get him to change his mind, you just watch!* SALLY: *Lots of luck!*

lounge around (some place) to lie about some place. □ *I am going to lounge around the house this morning.* □ *Don't lounge around all day.*

love at first sight love established when two people first see one another. □ *Bill was standing at the door when Ann opened it. It was love at first sight.* □ *It was love at first sight when they met, but it didn't last long.*

lovely weather for ducks **1.** rainy weather. □ BOB: *Not very nice out today, is it?* BILL: *It's lovely weather for ducks.* □ *I don't like this weather, but it's lovely weather for ducks.* **2.** a greeting phrase meaning that this unpleasant rainy weather must be good for something. (Usually **Lovely weather for ducks!**) □ BILL: *Hi, Bob. How do you like this weather?* BOB: *Lovely weather for ducks.* □ SALLY: *What a lot of rain!* TOM: *Yeah. Lovely weather for ducks. Don't care for it much myself.*

low man on the totem pole the least important person. (See also *high*

263

man on the totem pole.) □ *I was the last to find out because I'm low man on the totem pole.* □ *I can't be of any help. I'm low man on the totem pole.*

lower one's sights to set one's goals lower. □ *Even though you get frustrated, don't lower your sights.* □ *I shouldn't lower my sights. If I work hard, I can do what I want.*

lower one's voice to speak more softly. □ *Please lower your voice, or you'll disturb the people who are working.* □ *He wouldn't lower his voice, so everyone heard what he said.*

lower the boom on someone to scold or punish someone severely; to crack down on someone. (Originally nautical.) □ *If Bob won't behave better, I'll have to lower the boom on him.* □ *The teacher lowered the boom on the whole class for misbehaving.*

luck out to be fortunate; to strike it lucky. (Slang.) □ *I really lucked out when I ordered the duck. It's excellent.*

□ *I didn't luck out at all. I rarely make the right choice.*

lucky for you a phrase introducing a description of an event that favors the person being spoken to. □ ANDREW: *Lucky for you the train was delayed. Otherwise you'd have to wait till tomorrow morning for the next one.* FRED: *That's luck, all right. I'd hate to have to sleep in the station.* □ JANE: *I hope I'm not too late.* SUE: *Lucky for you, everyone else is late too.*

lunch out to eat lunch away from one's home or away from one's place of work. □ *I think I'll lunch out today. I'm tired of carrying lunches.* □ *I want to lunch out today.*

lure someone or something in(to something) to entice someone or something into something or a place. □ *The thief tried to lure the tourist into an alley to rob him.* □ *The thief led the tourist to an alley and lured him in.* ⊤ *Using an old trick, the thief lured in the tourist.*

M

Ma'am? **1.** Did you call me, ma'am? [said to a woman] □ MOTHER: *Tom!* TOM: *Ma'am?* MOTHER: *Come take out the garbage.* TOM: *Yuck!* □ DOCTOR: *Now, Bill, I need you to do something for me.* BILL: *Ma'am?* DOCTOR: *Stick out your tongue.* **2.** Will you please repeat what you said, ma'am? □ SALLY: *Bring it to me, please.* BILL: *Ma'am?* SALLY: *Bring it to me.* □ *Uncle Fred turned his good ear to the clerk and said, "Ma'am?"*

mac out to overeat, especially the type of food served at McDonald's fast food restaurants. (Slang. From the Big Mac™ sandwich. See also *pig out, pork out, scarf out.*) □ *I've been in Europe for a month, and I just want to get home and mac out.* □ *I mac out every weekend. It's like going to church.*

mace someone's face to do something drastic to someone, such as spraying mace in the face. (Slang. Chemical Mace™ is a brand of tear gas sold in pressurized cans for personal protection.) □ *Do you want me to mace your face? Then shut up!* □ *I look at him, and suddenly I just want to mace his face or something.*

make a beeline for someone or something to head straight toward someone or something. (Also used literally for bees in flight.) □ *Billy came into the kitchen and made a* beeline for the cookies. □ *After the game, we all made a beeline for John, who was serving cold drinks.*

make a check out (to someone or something) to write a check to someone or a group. □ *Please make the check out to Bill Franklin.* Ⓣ *Make out a check to me.* □ *Please make a check out to the bank.*

make a clean breast of something to confess something. □ *You'll feel better if you make a clean breast of it. Now tell us what happened.* □ *I was forced to make a clean breast of the whole affair.*

make a go of it to make something work out all right. □ *It's a tough situation, but Ann is trying to make a go of it.* □ *We don't like living here, but we have to make a go of it.*

make a great show of something to make something obvious; to do something in a showy fashion. □ *Ann made a great show of wiping up the drink that John spilled.* □ *Jane displayed her irritation at our late arrival by making a great show of serving the cold dinner.*

make a hit (with someone or something) to please someone or some group. □ *The singer made a hit with the audience.* □ *She was afraid she wouldn't make a hit.* □ *John made a hit with my parents last evening.*

Make a lap. Sit down. (Slang.) □ ANDREW: *Hey, you're in the way, Tom! Make a lap, why don't you?* TOM: *Sorry.* □ RACHEL: *Come over here and make a lap. You make me tired, standing there like that.* JOHN: *You just want me to sit by you.* RACHEL: *That's right.*

make a long story short to bring a story to an end. (A formula that introduces a summary of a story or a joke.) □ *And — to make a long story short — I never got back the money that I lent him.* □ *If I can make a long story short, let me say that everything worked out fine.*

make a mountain out of a molehill to make a major issue out of a minor one; to exaggerate the importance of something. □ *Come on, don't make a mountain out of a molehill. It's not that important.* □ *Mary is always making mountains out of molehills.*

make a nuisance of oneself to be a constant bother. □ *I'm sorry to make a nuisance of myself, but I do need an answer to my question.* □ *Stop making a nuisance of yourself and wait your turn.*

make a run for it to run fast to get away or get somewhere. □ *When the guard wasn't looking, the prisoner made a run for it.* □ *In the baseball game, the player on first base made a run for it, but he didn't make it to second base.*

make a silk purse out of a sow's ear to create something of value out of something of no value. (Often in the negative.) □ *Don't bother trying to fix up this old bicycle. You can't make a silk purse out of a sow's ear.* □ *My mother made a lovely jacket out of an old coat. She succeeded in making a silk purse out of a sow's ear.*

make cracks (about someone or something) to ridicule or make jokes about someone or something. □ *Please stop making cracks about my haircut. It's the new style.* □ *Some people can't help making cracks. They are just rude.*

make fast work of someone or something See *make short work of someone or something.*

make free with someone or something See *take liberties with someone or something.*

make good money to earn a large amount of money. (*Good* means "plentiful.") □ *Ann makes good money at her job.* □ *I don't know what she does, but she makes good money.*

Make hay while the sun is shining. You should make the most of good times. (Proverb.) □ *There are lots of people here now. You should try to sell them soda pop. Make hay while the sun is shining.* □ *Go to school and get a good education while you're young. Make hay while the sun is shining.*

Make it snappy! *Hurry up!*; Move quickly and smartly. □ ANDREW: *Make it snappy! I haven't got all day.* BOB: *Don't rush me.* □ MARY: *Do you mind if I stop here and get some film?* BOB: *Not if you make it snappy!* MARY: *Don't worry. I'll hurry.*

make it (to something) to manage to attend something; to manage to attend some event. □ *"I'm sorry," said Mary, "I won't be able to make it to your party."* □ RACHEL: *Can you come to the rally on Saturday?* ANDREW: *Sorry. I can't make it.*

Make it two. I wish to order the thing that someone else just now ordered. (Said to food or drink service personnel.) □ BILL (speaking to the waiter): *I'll have the roast chicken.* MARY: *Make it two.* □ WAITER: *Would you like something to drink?* TOM: *Just a beer.* WAITER (turning to Mary): *And you?* MARY: *Make it two.*

make life miserable for someone to make someone unhappy over a long period of time. □ *My shoes are tight, and they are making life miserable for me.* □ *Jane's boss is making life miserable for her.*

make light of something to treat something as if it were unimportant or humorous. □ *I wish you wouldn't make light of his problems. They're quite serious.* □ *I make light of my problems, and that makes me feel better.*

Make mine something. I wish to have something. (The *something* can be a particular food or drink, a flavor of a food, a size of a garment, or a type of almost anything. Most typically used for food or drink.) □ BILL: *I want some pie. Yes, I'd like apple.* TOM: *Make mine cherry.* □ WAITER: *Would you care for some dessert? The ice cream is homemade.* TOM: *Yes, indeed. Make mine chocolate.*

Make my day! "Go ahead, do what you are going to do, and I will be very happy to do what I have to do!" (A catch phrase said typically by a movie police officer who has a gun pointed at a criminal. The police officer wants the criminal to do something that will justify pulling the trigger, which the police officer will do with pleasure. Used in real life in any context, and especially in sarcasm.) □ *Move a muscle! Go for your gun! Go ahead, make my day!* □ *Make my day. Just try it.*

Make no mistake (about it)! Do not be mistaken! □ SALLY: *I'm very angry with you! Make no mistake about it!* FRED: *Whatever it's about, I'm sorry.* □ CLERK: *Make no mistake, this is the finest carpet available.* SALLY: *I'd like something a little less fine, I think.*

make off with someone or something to leave and take away someone or something. □ *The kidnappers made off with the baby in the night.* □ *Max made off with Lady Bracknell's jewels.*

make oneself at home to make oneself comfortable as if one were in one's own home. □ *Please come in and make yourself at home.* □ *I'm glad you're here. During your visit, just make yourself at home.*

make (out) after someone or something to run after someone or something; to start out after someone or something. □ *Paul made out after Fred, who had taken Paul's hat.* □ *The police officer made after the robber.*

make (out) for someone or something to run toward someone, something, or some place. □ *They made out for Sam as soon as they saw him coming.* □ *The boys made for the swimming pool as soon as the coach blew the whistle.*

make out (with someone or something) to manage satisfactorily with someone or something. □ *I know you are negotiating with George on that Franklin deal. How are you making out with him?* □ *How are you making out with school?* □ *He is making out okay.*

make over someone or something to pay a lot of attention to someone or something. □ *Why does she make over your sister so much?* □ *Aunt Em* made over the wedding gifts as if they were for her instead of Susan.

make short work of someone or something AND **make fast work of someone or something** to finish with someone or something quickly. □ I made short work of Tom so I could leave the office to play golf. □ Billy made fast work of his dinner so he could go out and play.

make someone or something over to convert someone or something into a new or different person or thing. (*Someone* includes *oneself*.) □ The hairstylist tried to make Carla over, but she wanted to be the way she has always been. ⊤ She made over Carla. □ I would really like to make this house over.

make someone or something tick to cause someone or something to run or function. (Usually with *what*. Originally the kind of thing that would be said about a clock or a watch.) □ I don't know what makes it tick. □ What makes John tick? I just don't understand him. □ I took apart the radio to find out what made it tick.

make someone the scapegoat for something to make someone take the blame for something. □ They made Tom the scapegoat for the whole affair. It wasn't all his fault. □ Don't try to make me the scapegoat. I'll tell who really did it.

make someone up to put makeup on someone. (*Someone* includes *oneself*.) □ You have to make the clowns up before you start on the other characters in the play. ⊤ Did you make up the clowns? □ He made himself up for the play.

make someone's blood boil to make someone very angry. □ It just makes my blood boil to think of the amount of food that gets wasted around here. □ Whenever I think of that dishonest mess, it makes my blood boil.

make someone's blood run cold to shock or horrify someone. □ The terrible story in the newspaper made my blood run cold. □ I could tell you things about prisons that would make your blood run cold.

make someone's hair stand on end to cause someone to be very frightened. □ The horrible scream made my hair stand on end. □ The ghost story made our hair stand on end.

make someone's head spin See the following entry.

make someone's head swim AND **make someone's head spin** **1.** to make someone dizzy or disoriented. □ Riding in your car makes my head spin. □ Breathing the gas made my head swim. **2.** to confuse or overwhelm someone. □ All these numbers make my head swim. □ The physics lecture made my head spin.

make someone's mouth water to make someone hungry (for something); to cause someone to salivate. (Also used literally.) □ That beautiful salad makes my mouth water. □ Talking about food makes my mouth water.

make something from scratch to make something by starting with the basic ingredients. □ We made the cake from scratch, using no prepared ingredients. □ I didn't have a ladder, so I made one from scratch.

make something off (of) someone or something to make money from someone or something. (The *of* is colloquial.) □ *Are you trying to make your fortune off of me?* □ *We think we can make some money off the sale of the house.*

make something out to see, read, or hear something well enough to understand it. □ *What did you say? I couldn't quite make it out.* T *Can you make out what he is saying?* T *I could just make out the ship in the fog.*

make something up 1. to make a bed. □ *We have to make all the beds up and then vacuum all the rooms.* T *Did you make up the beds?* 2. to fabricate something, such as a story or a lie. □ *That's not true. You are just making that up!* T *You made up that story!* 3. to redo something; to do something that one has failed to do in the past. □ *Can I make the lost time up?* T *Can I make up the test that I missed?*

make something up out of whole cloth to create a story or a lie from no facts at all. □ *I don't believe you. I think you made that up out of whole cloth.* T *Ann made up her explanation out of whole cloth. There was not a bit of truth in it.*

make the feathers fly See the following entry.

make the fur fly AND **make the feathers fly** to cause a fight or an argument. □ *When your mother gets home and sees what you've done, she'll really make the fur fly.* □ *When those two get together, they'll make the feathers fly. They hate each other.*

make the grade to be satisfactory; to be what is expected. □ *I'm sorry, but your work doesn't exactly make the*

grade. □ *This meal doesn't just make the grade. It is excellent.*

make up for lost time to do much of something; to do something fast. □ *Because we took so long eating lunch, we have to drive faster to make up for lost time. Otherwise we won't arrive on time.* □ *At the age of sixty, Bill learned to play golf. Now he plays every day. He's making up for lost time.*

Make up your mind. AND **Make your mind up.** Please make a decision.; Please choose. □ HENRY: *I don't have all day. Make up your mind.* RACHEL: *Don't rush me.* □ BOB: *Make your mind up. We have to catch the plane.* MARY: *I'm not sure I want to go.*

make waves to cause difficulty. (Slang. Often in the negative.) □ *Just relax. Don't make waves.* □ *If you make waves too much around here, you won't last long.*

make with the something to make something visible; to use something. (Slang.) □ *Come on, make with the cash.* □ *I want to know. Come on, make with the answers!*

Make your mind up. See *Make up your mind.*

Make yourself at home. Please make yourself comfortable in my home. (Also a signal that a guest can be less formal.) □ ANDREW: *Please come in and make yourself at home.* SUE: *Thank you. I'd like to.* □ BILL: *I hope I'm not too early.* BOB: *Not at all. Come in and make yourself at home. I've got a few little things to do.* BILL: *Nice place you've got here.*

map something out to plot something out carefully, usually on paper. □ *I have a good plan. I will map it out* *for you.* T *I will map out the plan for you.*

march on [for time] to continue. □ *Time marches on. We are all getting older.* □ *As the day marches on, try to get everything completed.*

march to a different drummer to believe in a different set of principles. □ *John is marching to a different drummer, and he doesn't come to our parties anymore.* □ *Since Sally started marching to a different drummer, she has had a lot of great new ideas.*

mark something down 1. to reduce the price of something. □ *We are going to mark all this merchandise down next Monday.* T *We marked down the merchandise.* 2. to write something down on paper. □ *She marked the number down on the paper.* T *She marked down the number.*

mark something up 1. to make marks all over something. □ *Who marked my book up?* T *I did not mark up the book.* 2. to raise the price of something. □ *I think that they mark everything up once a week at the grocery store.* T *They marked up the prices again last night.* 3. to raise the wholesale price of an item to the retail level. □ *How much do you mark cabbage up?* T *They marked up the cabbage too much.*

mash something up to crush something into a paste or pieces. □ *Mash the potatoes up and put them in a bowl.* T *Mash up the potatoes and put them on the table.*

match up [for things or people] to match, be equal, or complementary. □ *These match up. See how they are the same length?* □ *Sorry, but these two parts don't match up.*

maxed out 1. exhausted; tired. (Slang.) □ *I am just maxed out. I haven't been getting enough sleep.* □ *I had to stop work because I almost maxed out on the keyboard.* 2. alcohol intoxicated. □ *Sam was maxed out and seemed happy enough to sit under the table and whimper.* □ *I hadn't seen Marlowe so maxed out in years. He was nearly paralyzed.*

may as well See *might as well.*

May I help you? See *How may I help you?*

May I speak to someone? See *Could I speak to someone?*

Maybe some other time. AND **We'll try again some other time.** a polite phrase said by a person whose invitation has just been turned down by another person. □ BILL: *Do you think you can come to the party?* BOB: *I'll have to beg off. I have another engagement.* BILL: *Maybe some other time.* □ JOHN: *Can you and Alice come over this Friday?* BILL: *Gee, sorry. We have something else on.* JOHN: *We'll try again some other time.*

measure something off 1. to determine the length of something. □ *He measured the length of the room off and wrote down the figure in his notebook.* T *Fred measured off the width of the house.* 2. to distribute something in measured portions. T *He measured off two feet of the wire.* □ *Fred measured a few feet of string off and cut it with a knife.*

measure up (to someone or something) to compare well to someone or something. □ *He just doesn't measure up to Sarah in intelligence.* □ *He measures up fairly well.*

meet one's end to die. □ *The dog met his end under the wheels of a car.* □ *I don't intend to meet my end until I'm 100 years old.*

meet one's match to meet one's equal. □ *John played tennis with Bill yesterday, and it looks as if John has finally met his match.* □ *Listen to Jane and Mary argue. I always thought that Jane was loud, but she has finally met her match.*

meet someone halfway to offer to compromise with someone. □ *No, I won't give in, but I'll meet you halfway.* □ *They settled the argument by agreeing to meet each other halfway.*

mellow out 1. to calm down; to get less angry. (Slang.) □ *When you mellow out, maybe we can talk.* □ *Come on, man, mellow out!* **2.** to become generally more relaxed; to grow less contentious. □ *Gary was nearly forty before he started to mellow out a little and take life less seriously.* □ *After his illness, he mellowed out and seemed more glad to be alive.*

melt down 1. [for something frozen] to melt. (More at *melt something down.*) □ *The glacier melted down little by little.* □ *When the ice on the streets melted down, it was safe to drive again.* **2.** [for a nuclear reactor] to become hot enough to melt through its container. □ *The whole system was on the verge of melting down.*

melt in one's mouth to taste very good; [for food] to be very rich and satisfying. □ *This cake is so good it'll melt in your mouth.* □ *John said that the food didn't exactly melt in his mouth.*

melt into something to melt and change into a different physical state.

(More at *melt something into something.*) □ *All the ice cream melted into a sticky soup.* □ *The candles melted into a pool of colored wax in all the heat we had last summer.*

melt something down to cause something frozen to become a liquid; to cause something solid to melt. (More at *melt down.*) □ *The rays of the sun melted the candle down to a puddle of wax.* T *The heat melted down the ice.*

melt something into something to cause something to change its physical state when melting. (More at *melt into something.*) □ *The ice melted into a cold liquid that we could drink.* □ *We melted the fat into a liquid that we could deep-fry in.*

mend (one's) fences to restore good relations (with someone). (Also used literally.) □ *I think I had better get home and mend my fences. I had an argument with my daughter this morning.* □ *Sally called up her uncle to apologize and try to mend fences.*

mention something in passing to mention something casually; to mention something while talking about something else. □ *He just happened to mention in passing that the mayor had resigned.* □ *John mentioned in passing that he was nearly eighty years old.*

mesh together to fit together. □ *The various gears mesh together perfectly.* □ *Their ideas don't mesh together too well.*

mesh with something to fit with something. □ *Your idea just doesn't mesh with my plans.* □ *Currently, things don't mesh at all well with our long-range planning.*

mess someone or something up 1. to put someone or something into disarray; to make someone or something dirty or untidy. (*Someone* includes *oneself.*) □ *A car splashed water on me and really messed me up.* T *The muddy water messed up my shirt.* T *Don't mess up the living room.* □ *I messed myself up when I fell.* **2.** to interfere with someone or something; to misuse or abuse someone or something. □ *You really messed me up. I almost got fired for what happened.* T *The new owners messed up the company.* T *Dropping out of school really messed up my life.* □ *Mess him up good so he won't double-cross us again.*

mess someone's face up to beat someone around the face. (Slang.) □ *I had to mess his face up a little, boss, but he's been real cooperative since then.* T *You want me to mess up your face, or do you want to come along quietly?*

might as well AND **may as well** a phrase indicating that it is probably better to do something than not to do it. □ BILL: *Should we try to get there for the first showing of the film?* JANE: *Might as well. Nothing else to do.* □ ANDREW: *May as well leave now. It doesn't matter if we arrive a little bit early.* JANE: *Why do we always have to be the first to arrive?*

millstone about one's neck a continual burden or handicap. □ *This huge and expensive house is a millstone about my neck.* □ *Bill's inability to read is a millstone about his neck.*

mind one's own business to attend only to the things that concern one. □ *Leave me alone, Bill. Mind your own business.* □ *I'd be fine if John would mind his own business.*

mind one's p's and q's to mind one's manners; to pay attention to small details of behavior. (From an old caution to children learning the alphabet or to typesetters to watch carefully for the difference between *p* and *q.*) □ *When we go to the mayor's reception, please mind your p's and q's.* □ *I always mind my p's and q's when I eat at a restaurant with white tablecloths.*

Mind your manners. See *Remember your manners.*

Mind your own business. AND **Get your nose out of my business.; Keep your nose out of my business.** Stop prying into my affairs. (Not at all polite. The expressions with *get* and *keep* can have the literal meanings of removing and keeping removed.) □ ANDREW: *This is none of your affair. Mind your own business.* SUE: *I was only trying to help.* □ BOB: *How much did you pay in federal taxes last year?* JANE: *Good grief, Bob! Keep your nose out of my business!* □ TOM: *How much did it cost?* SUE: *Tom! Get your nose out of my business!* □ *"Hey!" shrieked Sally, jerking the checkbook out of Sue's grasp. "Get your nose out of my business!"*

miss out (on something) not to do something because one is unaware of the opportunity; to fail to or neglect to take part in something. □ *I hope I don't miss out on the January linen sale.* □ *I really don't want to miss out.*

miss (something) by a mile to fail to hit something by a great distance. □ *Ann shot the arrow and missed the target by a mile.* □ *"Good grief, you missed by a mile," shouted Sally.*

miss the point to fail to understand the point, purpose, or intent. □ *I'm* *afraid you missed the point. Let me explain it again.* □ *You keep explaining, and I keep missing the point.*

mix in (with someone or something) to mix or combine with people or substances. (More at *mix someone or something in(to something).*) □ *The band came down from the stage and mixed in with the guests during the break.* □ *The eggs won't mix in with the shortening!*

mix someone or something in(to something) to combine someone or something into something. (More at *mix in (with someone or something).*) □ *We will try to mix the new people into the group.* ⊤ *We will mix in the new people a few at a time.* □ *Ted mixed the flour into the egg mixture slowly.* □ *The cook mixed it in slowly.*

mix someone up to confuse someone. (*Someone* includes *oneself.*) □ *Please don't mix me up!* ⊤ *You mixed up the speaker with your question.* □ *I was so tired I mixed myself up as I spoke.*

mix someone up with someone to confuse one person with another. □ *I'm sorry. I mixed you up with your brother.* ⊤ *I mixed up Ted with his brother.*

mix something up (with something) to mix or stir something with a mixing or stirring device. □ *He mixed the batter up with a spoon.* ⊤ *Please mix up the batter with a spoon.* □ *I will mix it up, if you wish.*

money burns a hole in someone's pocket someone spends as much money as possible. (As if the money were trying as hard as possible to get out.) □ *Sally can't seem to save anything. Money burns a hole in her pocket.* □ *If money burns a hole in your pocket, you never have any for emergencies.*

money is no object it does not matter how much something costs. □ *Please show me your finest automobile. Money is no object.* □ *I want the finest earrings you have. Don't worry about how much they cost because money is no object.*

Money is the root of all evil. Money is the basic cause of all wrongdoing. (Proverb.) □ *Why do you work so hard to make money? It will just cause you trouble. Money is the root of all evil.* □ *Any thief in prison can tell you that money is the root of all evil.*

money talks money gives one power and influence to help get things done or get one's own way. □ *Don't worry. I have a way of getting things done. Money talks.* □ *I can't compete against rich old Mrs. Jones. She'll get her way because money talks.*

mop something down to clean a surface with a mop. □ *Please mop this floor down now.* ⊤ *Please mop down this floor.*

mop something off to wipe the liquid off something. □ *Please mop the counter off.* ⊤ *Mop off the counter.*

mop something up (with something) to clean up something, such as a spill, with a mop or with a mopping motion. □ *Please mop this mess up.* ⊤ *I will mop up this mess.* ⊤ *She will mop up the mess with the rag.*

more or less somewhat. (A vague phrase used to express vagueness or uncertainty.) □ HENRY: *I think this one is what I want, more or less.* CLERK: *A very wise choice, sir.* □ HENRY: *Is this one the biggest, more or* less? JOHN: *Oh, yes. It's the biggest there is.*

More power to you! *Well done!;* You really stood up for yourself!; You really did something for your own benefit! (The stress is on *to,* and the *you* is usually pronounced "ya.") □ BILL: *I finally told her off, but good.* BOB: *More power to you!* □ SUE: *I spent years getting ready for that job, and I finally got it.* MARY: *More power to you!*

more than you('ll ever) know a great deal; more than you suspect. □ BOB: *Why did you do it?* BILL: *I regret doing it. I regret it more than you know.* □ JOHN: *Oh, Mary, I love you.* MARY: *Oh, John, I love you more than you'll ever know.*

motion someone aside to give a hand signal to someone to move aside. □ *He motioned her aside and had a word with her.* ⊤ *I motioned aside the guard and asked him a question.*

motion someone away from someone or something to give a hand signal to someone to move away from someone or something. □ *She motioned me away from Susan.* □ *The police officer motioned the boys away from the wrecked car.*

mount up 1. to get up on a horse. □ *Mount up and let's get out of here!* □ *Please mount up so we can leave.* **2.** [for something] to increase in amount or extent. □ *Expenses really mount up when you travel.* □ *Medical expenses mount up very fast when you're in the hospital.*

move away (from someone or something) 1. to withdraw from someone or something. □ *Please don't move away from me. I like you close.* □ *I*

have to move away from the smoking section. □ *There was too much smoke there, so I moved away.* **2.** to move with one's entire household to another residence. □ *Timmy was upset because his best friend had moved away.* □ *They moved away just as we were getting to know them.*

move back (from someone or something) to move back and away. (Often a command.) □ *Please move back from the edge.* □ *Please move back!*

move heaven and earth to do something to make a major effort to do something. (Not literal.) □ *"I'll move heaven and earth to be with you, Mary," said Bill.* □ *I had to move heaven and earth to get there on time.*

move in (for something) to get closer for some purpose, such as a kill. □ *The big cat moved in for the kill.* □ *As the cat moved in, the mouse scurried away.*

move in (on someone or something) 1. to move closer to someone or something; to make advances or aggressive movements toward someone or something. (Both literal and figurative uses.) □ *The crowd moved in on the frightened guard.* □ *They moved in slowly.* **2.** to attempt to take over or dominate someone or something. □ *The police moved in on the drug dealers.* □ *Max tried to move in on Lefty's territory.* □ *So, you're trying to move in?*

move in(to something) 1. [for someone] to come to reside in something or some place. □ *I moved into a new apartment last week.* □ *When did the new family move in?* **2.** to enter something or some place. □ *The whole* party moved into the house when it started raining. □ All the children just moved in and brought the party with them. **3.** to begin a new line of activity. □ After failing at real estate, he moved into house painting. □ It looked like an area where he could make some money, so he moved in.

move off (from someone or something) to move away from someone or something. □ The doctor moved off from the nurse, satisfied with her work. □ The officer stopped for a minute, looked around, and then moved off.

move on to continue moving; to travel on; to move away and not stop or tarry. □ Move on! Don't stop here! □ Please move on! □ There was no more for him to do in Adamsville, and so he moved on.

move on someone to attempt to pick up someone; to attempt to seduce someone. (Collegiate slang.) □ Don't try to move on my date, old chum. □ Harry is trying to move on Tiffany. They deserve each another.

move on something to do something about something. □ I will move on this matter only when I get some time. □ I have been instructed to move on this and give it the highest priority.

move on (to something) to change to a different subject or activity. □ Now, I will move on to a new question. □ That is enough discussion on that point. Let's move on.

move out (of some place) 1. to leave a place; to begin to depart. (Especially in reference to a large number of persons or things.) □ The crowd started to move out of the area about midnight. □ They had moved out by one o'clock. **2.** to leave a place of

residence permanently. □ We didn't like the neighborhood, so we moved out of it. □ We moved out because we were unhappy.

move someone up to advance or promote someone. □ We are ready to move you up. You have been doing quite well. □ How long will it be before they can move me up?

move up (in the world) to advance (oneself) and become successful. □ The harder I work, the more I move up in the world. □ Keep your eye on John. He's really moving up.

move up (to something) to advance to something; to purchase a better quality of something. □ We are moving up to a larger car. □ There are too many of us now for a small house. We are moving up. □ Isn't it about time that I move up? I've been an office clerk for over a year. □ I had hoped that I would move up faster than this.

mow someone or something down to cut, knock, or shoot someone or something down. □ The speeding car almost mowed us down. ⊤ The car mowed down the pedestrian. ⊤ The lawn mower mowed down the tall grass. □ Machine guns mowed the attackers down.

much ado about nothing a lot of excitement about nothing. (This is the title of a play by Shakespeare. Do not confuse ado with adieu.) □ All the commotion about the new tax law turned out to be much ado about nothing. □ Your promises always turn out to be much ado about nothing.

muddle through (something) to manage to get through something awkwardly. □ We hadn't practiced the song enough, so we just muddled *through it.* □ *We didn't know what we were meant to do, so we muddled through.*

mull something over to think over something; to ponder something. □ *Let me mull this over a little while.* ⊤ *Mull over this matter for a while and see what you think.*

multiply by something to use the arithmetic process of multiplication to expand numerically a certain number of times. □ *To get the amount of your taxes, multiply by .025.* □ *Can you multiply by sixteens?*

multiply something by something to use the arithmetic process of multiplication to expand numerically a particular number a certain number of times. □ *Multiply the number of dependents you are claiming by one thousand dollars.* □ *Multiply twelve by sixteen and tell me what you get.*

Mum's the word. See *The word is mum.*

munch out to eat ravenously. (Slang. See also *pig out.*) □ *I had to munch out after the party. I can't imagine why.* □ *I can munch out for no reason at all.*

mung something up to mess something up. (Slang.) □ *Don't mung it up this time.* ⊤ *The team munged up the play, and the coach blasted them but good.*

muscle in (on someone or something) to interfere with someone or something; to intrude on someone or something. □ *Max tried to muscle in on Lefty, and that made Lefty's gang really mad at Max.* □ *You're not trying to muscle in, are you?*

muscle someone out (of something) to force someone out of something; to push someone out of something. □ *Are you trying to muscle me out of my job?* ⊤ *The younger people are muscling out the older ones.* □ *Lefty "Fingers" Moran had enough competition, and he wanted to muscle Max out.*

mushroom into something to grow suddenly into something large or important. □ *The question of pay suddenly mushroomed into a major matter.* □ *The unpaid bill mushroomed into a nasty argument and, finally, a court battle.*

my a sentence opener expressing a little surprise or amazement. (Words such as this often use intonation to convey the connotation of the sentence that is to follow. The brief intonation pattern accompanying the word may indicate sarcasm, disagreement, caution, consolation, sternness, etc.) □ *"My, what a nice place you have here," gloated Gloria.* □ RACHEL: *My, it's getting late!* JOHN: *Gee, the evening is just beginning.* □ *"My, it's hot!" said Fred, smoldering.*

(My) goodness (gracious)! a general expression of interest or mild amazement. □ BILL: *My goodness! The window is broken!* ANDREW: *I didn't do it!* BILL: *Who did, then?* □ *"Goodness! I'm late!" said Kate, glancing at her watch.* □ *"Goodness gracious! Are you hurt?" asked Sue as she helped the fallen student to his feet.*

(My) heavens! a mild exclamation of surprise or amazement. □ BILL: *Heavens! The clock has stopped.* BOB: *Don't you have a watch?* □ SALLY: *The police are parked in our driveway, and one of them is getting out!* MARY: *My heavens!*

N

nag at someone (about someone or something) to pester someone about someone or something. □ *Don't keep nagging at me about her.* □ *Stop nagging at me!*

nail someone down (on something) See *pin someone down (on something)*.

nail something up 1. to put something up, as on a wall, by nailing. □ *Please nail this up.* ⊤ *I'll nail up this picture for you.* **2.** to nail something closed; to use nails to secure something from intruders. □ *Sam nailed the door up so no one could use it.* ⊤ *Who nailed up the door? I can't get in!*

Name your poison. See *What'll it be?*

narrow something down (to people or things) to reduce a list of possibilities from many to a selected few. □ *We can narrow the choice down to green or red.* ⊤ *We narrowed down the choice to you or Paul.* □ *We can't seem to narrow the choice down.*

nause someone out to nauseate someone. (Slang.) □ *That horrible smell really nauses me out.* □ *Things like that nause me out, too.*

neck and neck exactly even, especially in a race or a contest. □ *John and Tom finished the race neck and neck.* □ *Mary and Ann were neck and neck in the spelling contest. Their scores were tied.*

need I remind you of See the following entry.

need I remind you that AND **need I remind you of** a phrase that introduces a reminder. (A little haughty or parental.) □ BILL: *Need I remind you that today is Friday?* BOB (sarcastically): *Gee, how else would I have known?* □ JOHN: *Need I remind you of our policy against smoking in the office?* JANE: *Sorry, I forgot.*

Need I say more? Is it necessary for me to say any more? □ MARY: *There's grass to be mowed, weeds to be pulled, dishes to be done, carpets to be vacuumed, and there you sit! Need I say more?* TOM: *I'll get right on it.* □ *"This project needs to be finished before anyone sleeps tonight," said Alice, hovering over the office staff, "Need I say more?"*

Neither can I. I cannot do that either. (Any subject pronoun can be used in place of I.) □ BILL: *No matter what they do to them, I just can't stand sweet potatoes!* BOB: *Neither can I.* □ JOHN: *Let's go. I cannot tolerate the smoke in here.* JANE: *Neither can I.*

Neither do I. I do not do that either. (Any subject pronoun can be used in place of I.) □ BILL: *No matter* *what they do to them, I just don't like sweet potatoes!* BOB: *Neither do I.* □ JANE: *I really don't like what the city council is doing.* FRED: *Neither do I.*

neither fish nor fowl not any recognizable thing. □ *The car that they drove up in was neither fish nor fowl. It must have been made out of spare parts.* □ *This proposal is neither fish nor fowl. I can't tell what you're proposing.*

neither hide nor hair no sign or indication (of someone or something). □ *We could find neither hide nor hair of him. I don't know where he is.* □ *There has been no one here—neither hide nor hair—for the last three days.*

nestle down (in something) to settle down in something; to snuggle into something, such as a bed. □ *They nestled down in their warm bed.* □ *Please nestle down and go to sleep.*

nestle (up) against someone or something AND **nestle up (to someone or something)** to lie close to someone or something; to cuddle up to someone or something. □ *The kitten nestled up against its mother.* □ *It nestled up to Kathy.* □ *Kathy nestled against the back seat of the car.*

nestle up (to someone or something) See the previous entry.

Never in a thousand years! See *Not in a thousand years!*

never in my life an emphatic expression showing the depth of the speaker's feelings. □ SALLY: *Never in my life have I seen such a mess!* JOHN: *Well, it's always this way. Where have you been all this time?* SALLY: *I just never noticed before, I suppose.* □ SUE: *Never will I go there again! Never in*

my life! BOB: *That bad, huh?* SUE: *Yes! That bad and worse!*

Never mind! Forget it!; It's not important! □ SALLY: *What did you say?* JANE: *Never mind! It wasn't important.* □ JOHN: *I tried to get the book you wanted, but they didn't have it. Shall I try another store?* MARY: *No, never mind.* JOHN: *I'd be happy to give it a try.*

new lease on life a renewed and revitalized outlook on life; a new start in living. □ *Getting the job offer was a new lease on life.* □ *When I got out of the hospital, I felt as if I had a new lease on life.*

Next question. That is settled, let's move on to something else. (Usually a way of evading further discussion.) □ MARY: *When can I expect this construction noise to stop?* BOB: *In about a month. Next question.* □ BILL: *When will the board of directors raise the dividend again?* MARY: *Oh, quite soon. Next question.*

Nice going! AND **Good job!**; **Nice job!** 1. That was done well. □ JOHN: *Well, I'm glad that's over.* SALLY: *Nice going, John! You did a good job.* □ TOM: *Nice job, Bill!* BILL: *Thanks, Tom!* 2. That was done poorly. (Sarcastic.) □ FRED: *I guess I really messed it up.* BILL: *Nice job, Fred! You've now messed us all up!* FRED: *Well, I'm sorry.* □ *"Nice going," frowned Jane, as Tom upset the bowl of potato chips.*

Nice job! See the previous entry.

Nice place you have here. Your home is nice. (A compliment paid by a guest. The word *place* might be replaced with *home, house, room, apartment,* etc.) □ *Jane came in and* looked around. "Nice place you have here," she said. □ BOB: Come in. Welcome. MARY: Nice place you have here. BOB: Thanks. We like it.

Nice weather we're having. **1.** Isn't the weather nice? (Sometimes used to start a conversation with a stranger.) □ BILL: Nice weather we're having. BOB: Yeah. It's great. □ Mary glanced out the window and said to the lady sitting next to her, "Nice weather we're having." **2.** Isn't this weather bad? (A sarcastic version of sense 1.) □ BILL: Hi, Tom. Nice weather we're having, huh? TOM: Yeah. Gee, it's hot! □ MARY: Nice weather we're having! SALLY: Sure. Lovely weather for ducks.

Nighty-night. Good night. (As said to a child.) □ FATHER: Nighty-night, Bill. BILL: Catch you later, Pop. □ The mother smiled at the tiny sleeping form and whispered, "Nighty-night, little one."

nip and tuck almost even; almost tied. □ The horses ran nip and tuck for the first half of the race. Then my horse pulled ahead. □ In the football game last Saturday, both teams were nip and tuck throughout the game.

nip something in the bud to put an end to something at an early stage. (As if one were pinching the flowering bud from an annoying plant.) □ John is getting into bad habits, and it's best to nip them in the bud. □ There was trouble in the classroom, but the teacher nipped it in the bud.

No can do. I cannot do it. (The opposite of Can do.) □ BOB: Can you do this now? SALLY: Sorry. No can do. □ FRED: Will you be able to fix this, or do I have to buy a new one? ALICE: No can do. You'll have to buy one.

no doubt a transitional or interpretative phrase strengthening the rest of a previous sentence. □ SUE: Mary is giving this party for herself? RACHEL: Yes. She'll expect us to bring gifts, no doubt. □ MARY: All this talk about war has my cousin very worried. SUE: No doubt. At his age, I don't wonder.

No fair! That isn't fair! □ BILL: No fair! You cheated! BOB: I did not! □ "No fair," shouted Tom. "You stepped over the line!"

no (ifs, ands, or) buts about it absolutely no discussion, dissension, or doubt about something. □ I want you there exactly at eight, no ifs, ands, or buts about it. □ This is the best television set available for the money, no buts about it.

No kidding! **1.** You are not kidding me, are you? (An expression of mild surprise.) □ JANE: I got elected vice president. BILL: No kidding! That's great! **2.** Everyone already knows that! Did you just find that out? (Sarcastic.) □ SUE: It looks like taxes will be increasing. TOM: No kidding! What do you expect? □ ALICE: I'm afraid I'm putting on a little weight. JANE: No kidding!

no laughing matter a serious matter. □ Be serious. This is no laughing matter. □ This disease is no laughing matter. It's quite deadly.

No lie? You are not lying, are you? □ BILL: A plane just landed on the interstate highway outside of town! TOM: No lie? Come on! It didn't really, did it? BILL: It did too! TOM: Let's go see it! □ BOB: I'm going to take a trip up the Amazon. SUE: No lie?

No more than I have to. an answer to the greeting question "What are you doing?" or "What have you been doing?" □ BOB: *Hey, Fred. What you been doing?* FRED: *No more than I have to.* □ SUE: *Hi, Bill. How are you?* BILL: *Okay. What have you been doing?* SUE: *No more than I have to.*

No, no, a thousand times no! Very definitely, no! (Jocular.) □ BOB: *Here, have some sweet potatoes.* BILL: *No, thanks.* BOB: *Oh, come on!* BILL: *No, no, a thousand times no!* □ SUE: *The water is a little cold, but it's great. Come on in.* BILL: *How cold?* SUE: *Well, just above freezing, I guess. Come on in!* BILL: *No, no, a thousand times no!*

No siree(, Bob)! Absolutely not! (Not necessarily said to a male, and rarely to any Bob.) □ BILL: *Do you want to sell this old rocking chair?* JANE: *No siree, Bob!* □ BILL: *You don't want sweet potatoes, do you?* FRED: *No siree!*

no skin off someone's nose See the following entry.

no skin off someone's teeth AND **no skin off someone's nose** no difficulty for someone; no concern of someone. □ *It's no skin off my nose if she wants to act that way.* □ *She said it was no skin off her teeth if we wanted to sell the house.*

no spring chicken not young (anymore). □ *I don't get around very well anymore. I'm no spring chicken, you know.* □ *Even though John is no spring chicken, he still plays tennis twice a week.*

no stress no problem; no bother. (Slang.) □ *Don't worry, man, no stress.* □ *Relax. No stress. It doesn't bother me at all.*

no sweat 1. no problem; don't worry; it is no problem. (Slang.) □ *It's no big deal. No sweat.* □ *No sweat, don't fret about it.* **2.** *(That causes) no problem.*; There is no difficulty. (Usually **No sweat.** Slang or colloquial.) □ TOM: *I'm sorry I'm late.* MARY: *No sweat. We're on a very flexible schedule.* □ BILL: *Thanks for carrying this up here.* BOB: *No sweat. Glad to help.*

No, thank you. AND **No, thanks.** a phrase used to decline something. □ BOB: *Would you care for some more coffee?* MARY: *No, thank you.* □ JOHN: *Do you want to go downtown tonight?* JANE: *No, thanks.*

No, thanks. See the previous entry.

no thanks to you I cannot thank you for what happened, because you did not cause it.; I cannot thank you for your help, because you did not give it. □ BOB: *Well, despite our previous disagreement, he seemed to agree to all our demands.* ALICE: *Yes, no thanks to you. I wish you'd learn to keep your big mouth shut!* □ JANE: *It looks like the picnic wasn't ruined despite the fact that I forgot the potato salad.* MARY: *Yes, it was okay. No thanks to you, of course.*

No way! No!; *Absolutely not!* □ BILL: *Will you take my calculus test for me?* BOB: *No way!* □ BOB: *You don't want any more sweet potatoes, do you?* JANE: *No way!*

No way, José! No! (Slang. An elaboration of *No. José* is pronounced with an initial H.) □ BOB: *Can I borrow a hundred bucks?* BILL: *No way, José!* □ SALLY: *Can I get you to take this* *nightgown back to the store for me and get me the same thing in a slightly smaller size?* BOB: *No way, José!*

none the worse for wear no worse because of use or effort. □ *I lent my car to John. When I got it back, it was none the worse for wear.* □ *I had a hard day today, but I'm none the worse for wear.*

Nope. No. (Colloquial. The opposite of *Yup*.) □ BOB: *Tired?* BILL: *Nope.* □ BILL: *Are you sorry you asked about it?* MARY: *Nope.*

nose someone or something out to defeat someone or something by a narrow margin. (Alludes to a horse winning a race "by a nose.") □ *Karen nosed Bobby out in the election for class president.* □ *Our team nosed out the opposing team in last Friday's game.*

Not a chance! There is no chance at all that something will happen. (Similar to *(There is) no chance.*) □ SALLY: *Do you think our team will win today?* MARY: *Not a chance!* □ JANE: *Can I have this delivered by Saturday?* CLERK: *Not a chance!*

not able to see the forest for the trees allowing many details of a problem to obscure the problem as a whole. (*Not able to* is often expressed as *can't*.) □ *The solution is obvious. You missed it because you can't see the forest for the trees.* □ *She suddenly realized that she hadn't been able to see the forest for the trees.*

Not again! I cannot believe that it happened again! □ MARY: *The sink is leaking again.* SALLY: *Not again!* MARY: *Yes, again.* □ FRED: *Here comes Tom with a new girlfriend.* SUE: *Not again!*

Not always. a conditional negative response. □ JOHN: *Do you come here every day?* JANE: *No, not always.* □ JOHN: *Do you find that this condition usually clears up by itself?* DOCTOR: *Not always.*

Not anymore. The facts you mentioned are no longer true.; A previous situation no longer exists. □ MARY: *This cup of coffee you asked me to bring you looks cold. Do you still want it?* SALLY: *Not anymore.* □ TOM: *Do the Wilsons live on Maple Street?* BOB: *Not anymore.*

Not at all. a very polite response to *Thank you*, or some other expression of gratitude. □ JOHN: *Thank you.* JANE: *Not at all.* □ MARY: *I want to thank you very much for all your help.* SUE: *Not at all. Happy to do it.*

Not bad. 1. Someone or something is quite satisfactory. (Similar to *Not half bad*.) □ BILL: *How do you like your new teacher?* JANE: *Not bad.* □ BOB: *Is this one okay?* BILL: *I guess. Yeah. Not bad.* 2. Someone or something is really quite good. (The person or thing can be named, as in the examples.) □ JOHN: *How do you like that new car of yours?* MARY: *Not bad. Not bad at all.* □ TOM: *This one looks great to me. What do you think?* SUE: *It's not bad.*

not born yesterday experienced; knowledgeable in the ways of the world. □ *I know what's going on. I wasn't born yesterday.* □ *Sally knows the score. She wasn't born yesterday.*

Not by a long shot. *under no circumstances; no chance.* (A negative characterization of one's appraisal of someone or something.) □ BILL: *Are you generally pleased with the new* president? MARY: *No, indeed, not by a long shot.* □ JOHN: *Do you find this acceptable?* BILL: *Good grief, no! Not by a long shot.*

Not for love nor money. *Absolutely not!; No way!* □ JOHN: *Would you be willing to drive through the night to get to Florida a day earlier?* MARY: *Not for love nor money!* □ JANE: *Someone needs to tell Sue that her favorite cat was just run over. Would you do it?* BOB: *Not for love nor money!*

Not for my money. Not as far as I'm concerned. (Has nothing to do with money or finance.) □ SUE: *Do you think it's a good idea to build all these office buildings in this part of the city?* MARY: *Not for my money. That's a real gamble.* □ JOHN: *We think that Fred is the best choice for the job. Do you think he is?* MARY: *Not for my money, he's not.*

not have a leg to stand on [for an argument or a case] to have no support. □ *You may think you're in the right, but you don't have a leg to stand on.* □ *My lawyer said I didn't have a leg to stand on, so I shouldn't sue the company.*

not hold water to make no sense; to be illogical. (Said of ideas, arguments, etc., not people. It means that the idea has holes in it.) □ *Your argument doesn't hold water.* □ *This scheme won't work because it won't hold water.*

Not if I see you first. See the following entry.

Not if I see you sooner. AND **Not if I see you first.** a response to *I'll see you later.* This means you will not see me if I see you first, because I will avoid you. □ TOM: *See you later.*

MARY: *Not if I see you sooner.* □ JOHN: *Okay. If you want to argue, I'll just leave. See you later.* MARY: *Not if I see you first.*

Not in a thousand years! AND **Never in a thousand years!** No, never! □ JOHN: *Will you ever approve of her marriage to Tom?* SUE: *No, not in a thousand years.* □ MARY: *Will all this trouble ever subside?* JOHN: *Never in a thousand years.*

Not in my book. Not according to my views. (Compare to *Not for my money*.) □ JOHN: *Is Fred okay for the job, do you think?* MARY: *No, not in my book.* □ SUE: *My meal is great! Is yours a real winner?* BOB: *Not in my book.*

not know enough to come in out of the rain to be very stupid. □ *Bob is so stupid he doesn't know enough to come in out of the rain.* □ *You can't expect very much from somebody who doesn't know enough to come in out of the rain.*

not know someone from Adam not to know someone at all. □ *I wouldn't recognize John if I saw him. I don't know him from Adam.* □ *What does she look like? I don't know her from Adam.*

Not likely. That is probably not so. □ MARY: *Is it possible that you'll be able to fix this watch?* SUE: *Not likely, but we can always try.* □ SALLY: *Will John show up on time, do you think?* BOB: *Not likely.*

not long for this world to be about to die. □ *Our dog is nearly twelve years old and not long for this world.* □ *I'm so tired. I think I'm not long for this world.*

Not on your life! No, *absolutely not!* □ SALLY: *Do you want to go downtown today?* BILL: *Not on your life! There's a parade this afternoon.* □ SUE: *I was cheated out of fifty dollars. Do you think I need to see a lawyer?* JOHN: *Not on your life! You'll pay more than that to walk through a lawyer's door.*

not open one's mouth AND **not utter a word** not to say anything at all; not to tell something (to anyone). □ *Don't worry, I'll keep your secret. I won't even open my mouth.* □ *Have no fear. I won't utter a word.* □ *I don't know how they found out. I didn't even open my mouth.*

Not right now, thanks. No, for the present. (It is hoped that one will be asked again later. Usually used for a [temporary] refusal of a serving of food or drink. There is an implication that more will be wanted later.) □ WAITER: *Do you want some more coffee?* MARY: *Not right now, thanks.* □ JOHN: *Can I take your coat?* SUE: *Not right now, thanks. I'm still a little chilly.*

not set foot somewhere not to go somewhere. □ *I wouldn't set foot in John's room. I'm very angry with him.* □ *He never set foot here.*

not show one's face not to appear (somewhere). □ *After what she said, she had better not show her face around here again.* □ *If I don't say I'm sorry, I'll never be able to show my face again.*

not sleep a wink not to sleep at all; not to close one's eyes in sleep even as long as it takes to blink. □ *I couldn't sleep a wink last night.* □ *Ann hasn't been able to sleep a wink for a week.*

not someone's cup of tea not something one prefers. □ *Playing cards isn't her cup of tea.* □ *Sorry, that's not my cup of tea.*

not to put too fine a point on it a phrase introducing a fine or important point, apologetically. □ RACHEL: *Not to put too fine a point on it, Mary, but you're still acting a little rude to Tom.* MARY: *I'm sorry, but that's the way I feel.* □ JOHN: *I think, not to put to fine a point on it, you ought to do exactly as you are told.* ANDREW: *And I think you ought to mind your own business.*

Not to worry. Please do not worry. □ BILL: *The rain is going to soak all our clothes.* TOM: *Not to worry, I put them all in plastic bags.* □ SUE: *I think we're about to run out of money.* BILL: *Not to worry. I have some more traveler's checks.*

Not (too) much. a response to greeting inquiries into what one has been doing. □ JOHN: *What have you been doing?* MARY: *Not much.* □ SUE: *Been keeping busy? What are you up to?* BOB: *Not too much.* SUE: *Yeah. Me too.*

not under any circumstances See *under no circumstances.*

not up to scratch AND **not up to snuff** not adequate. □ *Sorry, your paper isn't up to scratch. Please do it over again.* □ *The performance was not up to snuff.*

not up to snuff See the previous entry.

not utter a word See *not open one's mouth.*

Nothing. 1. I did not say anything. □ MARY: *What did you say?* SUE:

Nothing. □ TOM: *Did you have something to say? What do you want?* MARY: *Nothing.* **2.** a response to greeting inquiries into what one has been doing. □ BOB: *What you been doing?* MARY: *Nothing.* □ BILL: *What have you been up to?* MARY: *Nothing, really.*

nothing but skin and bones AND **all skin and bones** very thin or emaciated. □ *Bill has lost so much weight. He's nothing but skin and bones.* □ *That old horse is all skin and bones. I won't ride it.*

Nothing doing! I will not permit it!; I will not participate in it! □ JOHN: *Can I put this box in your suitcase?* BILL: *Nothing doing! It's too heavy now.* □ SUE: *We decided that you should drive us to the airport. Do you mind?* JANE: *Nothing doing! I've got work to do.*

Nothing for me, thanks. I do not want any of what was offered. (Typically to decline a serving of food or drink.) □ WAITER: *Would you care for dessert?* BOB: *Nothing for me, thanks.* □ BOB: *We have beer and wine. Which would you like?* MARY: *Nothing for me, thanks.*

Nothing much. Not much.; Hardly anything.; Nothing of importance. □ JOHN: *Hey, man! How's by you?* BOB: *Hiya! Nothing much.* □ BILL: *What have you been doing?* TOM: *Nothing much.*

Nothing ventured, nothing gained. you cannot achieve anything if you do not try. (Proverb.) □ *Come on, John. Give it a try. Nothing ventured, nothing gained.* □ *I felt as if I had to take the chance. Nothing ventured, nothing gained.*

now a sentence opener having no specific meaning. (Words such as this often use intonation to convey the connotation of the sentence that is to follow. The brief intonation pattern accompanying the word may indicate sarcasm, disagreement, caution, consolation, sternness, etc. See also *now, now*.) □ JOHN: *I'm totally disgusted with you.* BOB: *Now, don't get angry!* □ ANDREW: *I'm fighting mad. Why did you do that?* BILL: *Now, let's talk this over.* □ ANDREW: *Now, try it again, slowly this time.* SALLY: *How many times do I have to rehearse this piece?* □ FRED: *Now, who do you think you are?* TOM: *Well, who do you think you are, asking me that question?*

now, now a calming and consoling phrase that introduces good advice. □ *"Now, now, don't cry,"* said the mother to the tiny baby. □ JANE: *I'm so upset!* ANDREW: *Now, now, everything will work out all right.*

now then a sentence opener indicating that a new topic is being opened or that the speaker is getting down to business. (Expressions such as this often use intonation to convey the connotation of the sentence that is to follow. The brief intonation pattern accompanying the expression may indicate sarcasm, disagreement, caution, consolation, sternness, etc.) □ *"Now then, where's the pain?"* asked the doctor. □ MARY: *Now then, let's talk about you and your interests.* BOB: *Oh, good. My favorite subject.* □ SUE: *Now then, what are your plans for the future?* ALICE: *I want to become a pilot.* □ *"Now then, what did you have in mind when you took this money?"* asked the police investigator.

Now what? AND **What now?** What is going to happen now?; What kind of new problem has arisen? □ *The doorbell rang urgently, and Tom said, rising from the chair, "Now what?"* □ BOB: *There's a serious problem — sort of an emergency — in the mail room.* SUE: *What now?* BOB: *They're out of stamps or something silly like that.*

Now you're cooking (with gas)! Now you are doing what you should be doing! □ *As Bob came to the end of the piece, the piano teacher said, "Now you're cooking with gas!"* □ TOM (painting a fence): *How am I doing with this painting? Any better?* JANE: *Now you're cooking.* TOM: *Want to try it?*

Now you're talking! Now you are saying the right things. □ TOM: *I won't put up with her behavior any longer. I'll tell her exactly what I think of it.* BILL: *Now you're talking!* □ JOHN: *When I get back to school, I'm going to study harder than ever.* MOTHER: *Now you're talking!*

number off (by something) to say a number in a specified sequence when it is one's turn. (More at *number someone off*.) □ *Please number off by tens.* □ *Come on, number off!*

number someone off to provide people with numbers. (More at *number off (by something)*.) □ *I had to number the children off.* T *I numbered off the contestants.*

nurse someone through (something) to care for a sick person during the worst part of a sickness or recovery. □ *There was no one there to nurse him through the worst part of his illness.* □ *It was a horrible ordeal, but John nursed her through.*

nut up to go crazy; to go nuts. (Slang.) □ *I've got to have a vacation soon, or I'm going to nut up.* □ *Poor Sue nutted up and had to take it easy for a few months.*

O

odd man out an unusual or atypical person or thing. □ *I'm odd man out because I'm not wearing a tie.* □ *You had better learn to work a computer unless you want to be odd man out.*

Of all the nerve! See *What (a) nerve!*

of course yes; *Certainly!; For sure.* □ SALLY: *Are you ready to go?* BOB: *Of course.* SALLY: *Then let's go.* □ JANE: *Are you coming with us?* JOHN: *Of course. I wouldn't miss this for the world.* □ *"And you'll be there, of course?" asked Alice.* □ *"I would be happy to help, of course," confided Tom, a little insincerely.*

of the first water of the finest quality. (Originally a measurement of the quality of a pearl.) □ *This is a very fine pearl—a pearl of the first water.* □ *Tom is of the first water—a true gentleman.*

off base unrealistic; inexact; wrong. (Also used literally in baseball.) □ *I'm afraid you're off base when you state that this problem will take care of itself.* □ *You're way off base!*

off-color 1. not the exact color (that one wants). □ *The book cover used to be red, but now it's a little off-color.* □ *The wall was painted off-color. I think it was meant to be orange.* **2.** rude, vulgar, or impolite. □ *That joke you told was off-color and embarrassed me.* □ *The nightclub act was a bit off-color.*

off duty not working at one's job. □ *I'm sorry, I can't talk to you until I'm off duty.* □ *The police officer couldn't help me because he was off duty.*

off the air not broadcasting (a radio or television program). □ *The radio audience won't hear what you say when you're off the air.* □ *When the performers were off the air, the director told them how well they had done.*

off the record unofficial; informal. □ *This is off the record, but I disagree with the mayor on this matter.* □ *Although her comments were off the record, the newspaper published them anyway.*

off the top of one's head [to state something] rapidly and without having to think or remember. □ *I can't think of the answer off the top of my head.* □ *Jane can tell you the correct amount off the top of her head.*

off to a running start with a good, fast beginning, possibly a head start. □ *I got off to a running start in math this year.* □ *The horses got off to a running start.*

Oh, boy. 1. Wow! (Usually **Oh, boy!** It has nothing to do with boys.) □ BILL: *Oh, boy! An old-fashioned* circus! BOB: *So what?* □ *"Oh, boy!"* shouted John. *"When do we eat?"* **2.** I dread this!; This is going to be awful! □ *"Oh, boy!"* moaned Fred. *"Here we go again."* □ DOCTOR: *It looks like something fairly serious.* JANE: *Oh, boy.* DOCTOR: *But nothing modern medicine can't handle.*

Oh, sure (someone or something will)! a sarcastic expression claiming that someone or something will do something or that something will happen. □ ANDREW: *Don't worry. I'll do it.* RACHEL: *Oh, sure you will. That's what you always say.* □ BOB: *I'll fix this fence the first chance I get.* MARY: *Oh, sure. When will that be? Next year?*

Oh, yeah? Is that what you think? (Rude and hostile.) □ TOM: *You're getting to be sort of a pest.* BILL: *Oh, yeah?* TOM: *Yeah.* □ BOB: *This sauce tastes bad. I think you ruined it.* BILL: *Oh, yeah? What makes you think so?* BOB: *My tongue tells me!*

O.K. See *Okay.*

OK See the following entry.

Okay. AND **OK; O.K. 1.** Yes.; *All right.* □ JOHN: *Can we go now?* SUE: *Okay. Let's go.* □ MARY: *Can I have one of these?* FRED: *Okay.* MARY: *Thanks.* **2.** an expression indicating that the speaker accepts the current situation. (Not an answer to a question.) □ *"Okay, we're all here. Let's go now,"* said Tom. □ BILL: *Okay, I can see the house now.* RACHEL: *This must be where we turn then.* **3.** a question word asking if the person spoken to accepts the current situation. (Usually **Okay?** Very close to sense 1.) □ BILL: *I'm going to turn here, okay?* RACHEL: *Sure. It looks like the*

right place. □ ANDREW: *I'll take this one, okay?* MARY: *Yes, that's okay.*

on a waiting list [for someone's name to be] on a list of people waiting for an opportunity to do something. (A can be replaced with *the*.) □ *I couldn't get a seat on the plane, but I got on a waiting list.* □ *There is no room for you, but we can put your name on the waiting list.*

on active duty in battle or ready to go into battle. (Military.) □ *The soldier was on active duty for ten months.* □ *That was a long time to be on active duty.*

on all fours on one's hands and knees. □ *I dropped a contact lens and spent an hour on all fours looking for it.* □ *The baby can walk, but is on all fours most of the time anyway.*

on balance See *all in all.*

on cloud nine very happy. □ *When I got my promotion, I was on cloud nine.* □ *When the check came, I was on cloud nine for days.*

on duty at work; currently doing one's work. □ *I can't help you now, but I'll be on duty in about an hour.* □ *Who is on duty here? I need some help.*

on one's feet 1. standing up, standing on one's feet. □ *Get on your feet. They are playing the national anthem.* □ *I've been on my feet all day, and they hurt.* **2.** well and healthy, especially after an illness. □ *I hope to be back on my feet next week.* □ *I can help out as soon as I'm back on my feet.*

on one's honor on one's solemn oath; promised sincerely. □ *On my honor, I'll be there on time.* □ *He promised on his honor that he'd pay me back next week.*

on one's mind occupying one's thoughts; currently being thought about. □ *You've been on my mind all day.* □ *Do you have something on your mind? You look so serious.*

on one's toes alert. □ *You have to be on your toes if you want to be in this business.* □ *My boss keeps me on my toes.*

on pins and needles anxious; in suspense. □ *I've been on pins and needles all day, waiting for you to call with the news.* □ *We were on pins and needles until we heard that your plane landed safely.*

on second thought having given something more thought; having reconsidered something. □ *On second thought, maybe you should sell your house and move into an apartment.* □ *On second thought, let's not go to a movie.*

on someone's doorstep See *at someone's doorstep.*

on someone's head on someone's own self. (Usually with *blame. On* can be replaced with *upon.*) □ *All the blame fell on their heads.* □ *I don't think that all the criticism should be on my head.*

on someone's or something's last legs for someone or something to be almost finished. □ *This building is on its last legs. It should be torn down.* □ *I feel as if I'm on my last legs. I'm really tired.*

on someone's say-so on someone's authority; with someone's permission. □ *I can't do it on your say-so. I'll have to get a written request.* □ BILL: *I canceled the contract with the A.B.C. Company.* BOB: *On whose say-so?*

on someone's shoulders on someone's own self. (Usually with responsibility. On can be replaced with *upon.*) □ *Why should all the responsibility fall on my shoulders?* □ *She carries a tremendous amount of responsibility on her shoulders.*

on target on schedule; exactly as predicted. □ *Your estimate of the cost was right on target.* □ *My prediction was not on target.*

on the air broadcasting (a radio or television program). □ *The radio station came back on the air shortly after the storm.* □ *We were on the air for two hours.*

on the average generally; usually. □ *On the average, you can expect about a 10 percent failure.* □ *This report looks okay, on the average.*

on the bench 1. directing a session of court. (Said of a judge.) □ *I have to go to court tomorrow. Who's on the bench?* □ *It doesn't matter who's on the bench. You'll get a fair hearing.* 2. sitting, waiting for a chance to play in a game. (In sports, such as basketball, football, soccer, etc.) □ *Bill is on the bench now. I hope he gets to play.* □ *John played during the first quarter, but now he's on the bench.*

on the block 1. on a city block. □ *John is the biggest kid on the block.* □ *We had a party on the block last weekend.* 2. on sale at auction; on the auction block. □ *We couldn't afford to keep up the house, so it was put on the block to pay the taxes.* □ *That's the finest painting I've ever seen on the block.*

on the button exactly right; in exactly the right place; at exactly the right time. □ *That's it! You're right on the button.* □ *He got here at one o'clock on the button.*

on the contrary a phrase disagreeing with a previous statement. □ TOM: *It's rather warm today.* BOB: *On the contrary, I find it too cool.* □ MARY: *I hear that you aren't too happy about my decision.* SUE: *On the contrary, I find it fair and reasonable.*

on the dot at exactly the right time. □ *I'll be there at noon on the dot.* □ *I expect to see you here at eight o'clock on the dot.*

on the go busy; moving about busily. □ *I'm usually on the go all day long.* □ *I hate being on the go all the time.*

on the heels of something soon after something. □ *There was a rainstorm on the heels of the windstorm.* □ *The team held a victory celebration on the heels of their winning season.*

on the horizon soon to happen. (Also used literally.) □ *Do you know what's on the horizon?* □ *Who can tell what's on the horizon?*

on the horns of a dilemma having to decide between two things, people, etc.; balanced between one choice and another. □ *Mary found herself on the horns of a dilemma. She didn't know which to choose.* □ *I make up my mind easily. I'm not on the horns of a dilemma very often.*

on the hour at each hour on the hour mark. □ *I have to take this medicine every hour on the hour.* □ *I expect to see you there on the hour, not one minute before and not one minute after.*

on the house [something that is] given away free by a merchant. (Also used literally.) □ *"Here," said the waiter, "have a cup of coffee on the house."* □ *I went to a restaurant last night. I was the ten thousandth customer, so my dinner was on the house.*

on the level honest; dependably open and fair. (Also with *strictly.*) □ *How can I be sure you're on the level?* □ *You can trust Sally. She's on the level.*

on the market available for sale; offered for sale. □ *I had to put my car on the market.* □ *This is the finest home computer on the market.*

on the mend getting well; healing. □ *My cold was terrible, but I'm on the mend now.* □ *What you need is some hot chicken soup. Then you'll really be on the mend.*

on the move moving; happening busily. □ *What a busy day. Things are really on the move at the store.* □ *When all the buffalo were on the move across the plains, it must have been very exciting.*

on the other hand a phrase introducing an alternate view. □ JOHN: *I'm ready to go; on the other hand, I'm perfectly comfortable here.* SALLY: *I'll let you know when I'm ready, then.* □ MARY: *I like this one. On the other hand, this is nice too.* SUE: *Why not get both?*

on the QT quietly; secretly. □ *The company president was making payments to his wife on the QT.* □ *The mayor accepted a bribe on the QT.*

on the spot 1. at exactly the right place; at exactly the right time. □ *It's noon, and I'm glad you're all here on the spot. Now we can begin.* □ *I expect you to be on the spot when and where trouble arises.* **2.** in trouble; in a difficult situation. □ *There is a problem in the department I manage, and*

I'm really on the spot. □ *I hate to be on the spot when it's not my fault.*

on the spur of the moment suddenly; spontaneously. □ *We decided to go on the spur of the moment.* □ *I had to leave town on the spur of the moment.*

on the tip of one's tongue about to be said; almost remembered. (As if a word were about to leap from one's tongue and be spoken.) □ *I have his name right on the tip of my tongue. I'll think of it in a second.* □ *John had the answer on the tip of his tongue, but Ann said it first.*

on the wagon not drinking alcohol; no longer drinking alcohol. (Also used literally. Refers to a "water wagon.") □ *None for me, thanks. I'm on the wagon.* □ *Look at John. I don't think he's on the wagon anymore.*

on the wrong track going the wrong way; following the wrong set of assumptions. (Also used literally for trains, hounds, etc.) □ *You'll never get the right answer. You're on the wrong track.* □ *They won't get it figured out because they are on the wrong track.*

on thin ice in a risky situation. □ *If you try that you'll really be on thin ice. That's too risky.* □ *If you don't want to find yourself on thin ice, you must be sure of your facts.*

on tiptoe standing or walking on the front part of the feet (the balls of the feet) with no weight put on the heels. (This is done to gain height or to walk quietly.) □ *I had to stand on tiptoe in order to see over the fence.* □ *I came in late and walked on tiptoe so I wouldn't wake anybody up.*

on top victorious over something; famous or notorious for something.

□ *I have to study day and night to keep on top.* □ *Bill is on top in his field.*

on top of the world feeling wonderful; glorious; ecstatic. □ *Wow, I feel on top of the world.* □ *Since he got a new job, he's on top of the world.*

on trial being tried in court. □ *My sister is on trial today, so I have to go to court.* □ *They placed the suspected thief on trial.*

on vacation away, taking a vacation; on holiday. □ *Where are you going on vacation this year?* □ *I'll be away on vacation for three weeks.*

once and for all finally; permanently. □ SUE: *I'm going to get this place organized once and for all!* ALICE: *That'll be the day!* □ *"We need to get this straightened out once and for all,"* said Bob, for the fourth time today.

once in a blue moon very rarely. □ *I seldom go to a movie — maybe once in a blue moon.* □ *I don't go into the city except once in a blue moon.*

once more AND **one more time** Please do it one more time. □ MARY: *You sang that line beautifully, Fred. Now, once more.* FRED: *I'm really tired of all this rehearsing.* □ JOHN (finishing practicing his speech): *How was that?* SUE: *Good! One more time, though.* JOHN: *I'm getting bored with it.*

one final thing See the following entry.

one final word AND **one final thing** a phrase introducing a parting comment or the last item in a list. □ JOHN: *One final word, keep your chin up.* MARY: *Good advice!* □ SUE: *And one final thing, don't haul around a lot of expensive camera stuff. It just tells* the thieves who to rob. JOHN: *There are thieves here?* SUE: *Yeah. Everywhere.*

One good turn deserves another. A good deed should be repaid with another good deed. (Proverb.) □ *If he does you a favor, you should do him a favor. One good turn deserves another.* □ *Glad to help you out. One good turn deserves another.*

one in a hundred See *one in a thousand.*

one in a million See the following entry.

one in a thousand AND **one in a hundred; one in a million** unique; one of a very few. □ *He's a great guy. He's one in million.* □ *Mary's one in a hundred — such a hard worker.*

One man's meat is another man's poison. One person's preference may be disliked by another person. (Proverb.) □ *John just loves his new fur hat, but I think it is horrible. Oh, well, one man's meat is another man's poison.* □ *The neighbors are very fond of their dog even though it's ugly, loud, and smelly. I guess one man's meat is another man's poison.*

One moment, please. Please wait a minute.; *Just a minute.* □ JOHN: *Can you help me?* CLERK: *One moment, please. I will be with you shortly.* □ BILL (answering the phone): *Hello?* BOB: *Hello. Can I speak to Tom?* BILL: *One moment, please.* (handing phone to Tom) *It's for you.* TOM: *Hello, this is Tom.*

one more time See *once more.*

one way or another somehow. □ TOM: *Can we fix this radio, or do I have to buy a new one?* MARY: *Don't fret! We'll get it repaired one way or another.* □ JOHN: *I think we're lost.* ALICE: *Don't worry. We'll get there one way or another.*

One's bark is worse than one's bite. One may threaten, but not do much damage. (Proverb.) □ *Don't worry about Bob. He won't hurt you. His bark is worse than his bite.* □ *She may scream and yell, but have no fear. Her bark is worse than her bite.*

one's better half one's spouse. (Usually refers to a wife.) □ *I think we'd like to come for dinner, but I'll have to ask my better half.* □ *I have to go home now to my better half. We are going out tonight.*

one's days are numbered [for someone] to face death or dismissal. □ *If I don't get this contract, my days are numbered at this company.* □ *Uncle Tom has a terminal disease. His days are numbered.*

one's eyes are bigger than one's stomach [for one] to take more food than one can eat. □ *I can't eat all this. I'm afraid that my eyes were bigger than my stomach.* □ *Try to take less food. Your eyes are bigger than your stomach at every meal.*

one's heart is in one's mouth [for one] to feel strongly emotional. □ *It was a touching scene. My heart was in my mouth the whole time.*

one's heart is set on something to desire and expect something. □ *Jane's heart is set on going to London.*

one's number is up one's time to die — or to suffer some other unpleasantness — has come. □ *John is worried. He thinks his number is up.* □ *When my number is up, I hope it all goes fast.*

one's tail is between one's legs one is acting frightened or cowed. □ *He should have stood up and argued, but — as usual — his tail was between his legs.*

one's words stick in one's throat to find it difficult to speak because of emotion. □ *My words stick in my throat whenever I try to say something kind or tender.*

open a can of worms to uncover a set of problems; to create unnecessary complications. (*Can of worms* means "mess." Also with *open up* and with various modifiers such as *new, whole, another,* as in the examples.) □ *Now you are opening a whole new can of worms.* □ *How about cleaning up this mess before you open up a new can of worms?*

open one's heart (to someone) to reveal one's inmost thoughts to someone. □ *I always open my heart to my spouse when I have a problem.* □ *It's a good idea to open your heart every now and then.*

open (out) on(to) something [for a building's doors] to exit toward something. □ *The French doors opened out onto the terrace.* □ *The doors opened on a lovely patio.*

open Pandora's box to uncover a lot of unsuspected problems. □ *When I asked Jane about her problems, I didn't know I had opened Pandora's box.* □ *You should be cautious with people who are upset. You don't want to open Pandora's box.*

open something up 1. to open something that was closed. □ *They opened Peru's border up recently.* T *They opened up the border.* 2. to begin working on something for which there are paper records, such as a case, investigation, file, etc. □ *I'm afraid we are going to have to open the case up again.* T *They opened up the case again.*

open something up (to someone) to make something available to someone; to permit someone to join something or participate in something. □ *We intend to open the club up to everyone.* T *We will open up our books to the auditors.* □ *We had to open the books up.*

open up (to someone) 1. to tell [everything] to someone; to confess to someone. □ *If she would only open up to me, perhaps I could help her.* □ *She just won't open up. Everything is "private."* □ *After an hour of questioning, Thomas opened up.* 2. [for opportunities] to become available to someone. (Figurative.) □ *After Ann's inquiries, doors began to open up to me.* □ *An agent helps. After I got one, all sorts of doors opened up.*

open up (to someone or something) 1. [for doors] to become open so someone, something, or some creature can enter; to open for someone or something. □ *The doors to the supermarket opened up to me, so I went in.* □ *The automatic doors opened up to the dog, and it came into the store.* 2. [for someone] to become more accepting of someone or something. □ *Finally, he opened up to the suggestion that he should leave.* □ *Finally the boss opened up to Tom as a manager.*

operate on someone to perform a surgical operation on someone. □ *They decided not to operate on her.* □ *She wasn't operated on after all.*

or what? a way of adding emphasis to a yes-or-no question the speaker has asked. (In effect, if it wasn't what I said, what is it?) □ BOB: *Now, is this a fine day or what?* JOHN: *Looks okay to me.* □ TOM: *Look at Bill and Mary. Do they make a fine couple or what?* BOB: *Sure, they look great.*

or words to that effect or similar words meaning about the same thing. □ JOHN: *It says right here in the contract, "You are expected to attend without fail," or words to that effect.* MARY: *That means I have to be there, huh?* JOHN: *You got it!* □ SALLY: *She said that I wasn't doing my job well, or words to that effect.* JANE: *Well, you ought to find out exactly what she means.* SALLY: *I'm afraid I know.*

order someone in(to something) to command someone to get into something. □ *The officer ordered Ann into the wagon.* □ *She didn't want to go, but the cop ordered her in.*

order something in to have something, usually food, brought into one's house or place of business. □ *Do you want to order pizza in?* Ⓣ *Shall I order in pizza?*

other side of the tracks the poorer part of a town, often near the railroad tracks. (Especially with *from the* or *live on the.*) □ *Who cares if she's from the other side of the tracks?* □ *I came from a poor family — we lived on the other side of the tracks.*

Our house is your house. See *My house is your house.*

out and about able to go out and travel around; well enough to go out. □ *Beth has been ill, but now she's out and about.* □ *As soon as I feel better, I'll be able to get out and about.*

out cold AND **out like a light** unconscious. □ *I fell and hit my head. I was out cold for about a minute.* □ *Tom fainted! He's out like a light!*

out in left field offbeat; unusual and eccentric. □ *Sally is a lot of fun, but she's sort of out in left field.* □ *What a strange idea. It's really out in left field.*

out like a light See *out cold.*

out of a clear blue sky AND **out of the blue** suddenly; without warning. □ *Then, out of a clear blue sky, he told me he was leaving.* □ *Mary appeared on my doorstep out of the blue.*

out of (all) proportion of an exaggerated proportion; of an unrealistic proportion compared to something else; lopsided. □ *This problem has grown out of all proportion.* □ *Yes, this thing is way out of proportion.*

out of circulation 1. no longer available for use or lending. (Usually said of library materials.) □ *I'm sorry, but the book you want is temporarily out of circulation.* □ *How long will it be out of circulation?* **2.** not interacting socially with other people. □ *I don't know what's happening because I've been out of circulation for a while.* □ *My cold has kept me out of circulation for a few weeks.*

out of commission 1. [for a ship] to be not currently in use or under command. □ *This vessel will remain out of commission for another month.* □ *The ship has been out of commission since repairs began.* **2.** broken, unserviceable, or inoperable. □ *My watch is out of commission and is running slowly.* □ *I can't run in the marathon because my knees are out of commission.*

out of gas 1. having no more gasoline (in a car, truck, etc.). □ *We can't go any farther. We're out of gas.* □ *This*

293

car will be completely *out of gas in a few more miles.* **2.** tired; exhausted; worn out. □ *What a day! I've been working since morning, and I'm really out of gas.* □ *This electric clock is out of gas. I'll have to get a new one.*

out of hand immediately and without consulting anyone; without delay. □ *I can't answer that out of hand. I'll check with the manager and call you back.* □ *The offer was so good that I accepted it out of hand.*

out of luck without good luck; having bad fortune. □ *If you wanted some ice cream, you're out of luck.* □ *I was out of luck. I got there too late to get a seat.*

out of one's element not in a natural or comfortable situation. □ *When it comes to computers, I'm out of my element.* □ *Sally's out of her element in math.*

out of one's head See the following entry.

out of one's mind AND **out of one's head; out of one's senses** silly and senseless; crazy; irrational. □ *Why did you do that? You must be out of your mind!* □ *Good grief, Tom! You have to be out of your head!* □ *She's acting as if she were out of her senses.*

out of one's senses See the previous entry.

out of order 1. not in the correct order. □ *This book is out of order. Please put it in the right place on the shelf.* □ *You're out of order, John. Please get in line after Jane.* **2.** not following correct parliamentary procedure. □ *I was declared out of order by the president.* □ *Ann inquired, "Isn't a motion to table the question out of order at this time?"*

out of practice performing poorly due to a lack of practice. □ *I used to be able to play the piano extremely well, but now I'm out of practice.* □ *The baseball players lost the game because they were out of practice.*

out of print [for a book] to be no longer available for sale. (Compare to *in print.*) □ *The book you want is out of print, but perhaps I can find a used copy for you.* □ *It was published nearly ten years ago, so it's probably out of print.*

out of season 1. not now available for sale. □ *Sorry, oysters are out of season. We don't have any.* □ *Watermelon is out of season in the winter.* **2.** not now legally able to be hunted or caught. □ *Are salmon out of season?* □ *I caught a trout out of season and had to pay a fine.*

out of service inoperable; not now operating. □ *Both elevators are out of service, so I had to use the stairs.* □ *The washroom is temporarily out of service.*

Out of sight, out of mind. If you do not see something, you will not think about it. (Proverb.) □ *When I go home, I put my schoolbooks away so I won't worry about doing my homework. After all, out of sight, out of mind.* □ *Jane dented the fender on her car. It's on the right side, so she doesn't have to look at it. Like they say, out of sight, out of mind.*

out of sorts not feeling well; grumpy and irritable. □ *I've been out of sorts for a day or two. I think I'm coming down with something.* □ *The baby is out of sorts. Maybe she's getting a tooth.*

out of the blue See *out of a clear blue sky.*

out of the corner of one's eye [seeing something] at a glance; glimpsing (something). □ *I saw someone do it out of the corner of my eye. It might have been Jane who did it.* □ *I only saw the accident out of the corner of my eye. I don't know who is at fault.*

out of the frying pan into the fire from a bad situation to a worse situation. (If it was hot in the pan, it is hotter in the fire.) □ *When I tried to argue about my fine for a traffic violation, the judge charged me with contempt of court. I really went out of the frying pan into the fire.* □ *I got deeply in debt. Then I really got out of the frying pan into the fire when I lost my job.*

out of the hole out of debt. (Also used literally.) □ *I get paid next week, and then I can get out of the hole.* □ *I can't seem to get out of the hole. I keep spending more money than I earn.*

out of the question not possible; not permitted. □ *I'm sorry, but it's out of the question.* □ *You can't go to Florida this spring. We can't afford it. It's out of the question.*

out of the red out of debt. □ *This year our firm is likely to get out of the red before fall.* □ *If we can cut down on expenses, we can get out of the red fairly soon.*

out of the running no longer being considered; eliminated from a contest. □ *After the first part of the diving meet, three members of our team were out of the running.* □ *After the scandal was made public, I was no longer in the running. I pulled out of the election.*

out of the woods past a critical phase; out of the unknown. □ *When the patient got out of the woods, every-one relaxed.* □ *I can give you a better prediction for your future health when you are out of the woods.*

out of thin air out of nowhere; out of nothing. □ *Suddenly—out of thin air—the messenger appeared.* □ *You just made that up out of thin air.*

out of this world wonderful; extraordinary. (Also used literally.) □ *This pie is just out of this world.* □ *Look at you! How lovely you look—simply out of this world.*

out of tune (with someone or something) 1. not in musical harmony with someone or something. □ *The oboe is out of tune with the flute.* □ *The flute is out of tune with John.* □ *They are all out of tune.* 2. not in harmony or agreement. (Figurative.) □ *Your proposal is out of tune with my ideas of what we should be doing.* □ *Let's get all our efforts in tune.*

out of turn not at the proper time; not in the proper order. □ *We were permitted to be served out of turn, because we had to leave early.* □ *Bill tried to register out of turn and was sent away.*

out on a limb in a dangerous position; taking a chance. □ *I don't want to go out on a limb, but I think I'd agree to your request.* □ *She really went out on a limb when she agreed.*

out on the town celebrating at one or more places in a town. □ *I'm really tired. I was out on the town until dawn.* □ *We went out on the town to celebrate our wedding anniversary.*

Out, please. Please let me get out. (Said by someone trying to get out of an elevator. Similar to *Coming through(, please).*) □ *The elevator stopped again, as it had at every floor,* *and someone said, "Out, please," as someone had said at every floor.* □ JANE: *Out, please. This is my floor.* JOHN: *I'll get out of your way.* JANE: *Thanks.*

out to lunch eating lunch away from one's place of work. □ *I'm sorry, but Sally Jones is out to lunch. May I take a message?* □ *She's been out to lunch for nearly two hours. When will she be back?*

Over my dead body! a defiant phrase indicating the strength of one's opposition to something. (A joking response is "That can be arranged.") □ SALLY: *Alice says she'll join the circus no matter what anybody says.* FATHER: *Over my dead body!* SALLY: *Now, now. You know how she is.* □ BILL: *I think I'll rent out our spare bedroom.* SUE: *Over my dead body!* BILL (smiling): *That can be arranged.*

over the hill aged; too old to do something. □ *Now that Mary's forty, she thinks she's over the hill.* □ *My grandfather was over eighty before he felt as if he was over the hill.*

over the hump over the difficult part. □ *This is a difficult project, but we're over the hump now.* □ *I'm halfway through — over the hump — and it looks as if I may get finished after all.*

over the long haul for a relatively long period of time. □ *Over the long haul, it might be better to invest in stocks.* □ *Over the long haul, everything will turn out all right.*

over the short haul for the immediate future. □ *Over the short haul, you'd be better off to put your money in the bank.* □ *Over the short haul, you may wish you had done something different. But things will work out all right.*

over the top having gained more than one's goal. □ *Our fund-raising campaign went over the top by $3,000.* □ *We didn't go over the top. We didn't even get half of what we set out to collect.*

own up to someone or something 1. [with *someone*] to confess or admit something to someone. □ *Finally, he owned up to his boss.* □ *We had hoped he would own up to us sooner.* **2.** [with *something*] to admit something; to confess to something. □ *He refused to own up to doing it.* □ *I will own up to my mistakes.*

P

pace something out 1. to deal with a problem by pacing around. □ *When she was upset, she walked and walked while she thought through her problem.* *When Ed came into the room, she was pacing a new crisis out.* ⊤ *She usually paced out her anxiety.* **2.** to measure a distance by counting the number of even strides taken while walking. □ *He paced the distance out and wrote it down.* ⊤ *He paced out the distance from the door to the mailbox.*

pack something up (in something) to prepare something to be transported by placing it into a container. (More at *pack up*.) □ *Gerry will pack the dishes up in a strong box, using lots of crumpled paper.* ⊤ *Please pack up the dishes carefully.*

pack up to prepare one's belongings to be transported by placing them into a container; to gather one's things together for one's departure. (More at *pack something up (in something)*.) □ *If we are going to leave in the morning, we should pack up now.* □ *I think you should pack up and be ready to leave at a moment's notice.* □ *He didn't say good-bye. He just packed up and left.*

packed (in) like sardines packed very tightly. (Many variations are possible, as in the examples.) □ *It was terribly crowded there. We were* *packed in like sardines.* □ *The bus was full. The passengers were packed like sardines.* □ *They packed us in like sardines.*

pad out to go to bed or to sleep. (Slang.) □ *Man, if I don't pad out by midnight, I'm a zombie.* □ *Why don't you people go home so I can pad out?*

pad the bill to put unnecessary items on a bill to make the total cost higher. □ *The plumber had padded the bill with things we didn't need.* □ *I was falsely accused of padding the bill.*

paddle one's own canoe to do (something) by oneself; to be alone. (Could also be used literally.) □ *I've been left to paddle my own canoe too many times.* □ *Sally isn't with us. She's off paddling her own canoe.*

pain in the ass AND **pain in the butt; pain in the rear** a very annoying thing or person. (Crude slang. An elaboration of *pain*. Use caution with *ass*. *Butt* is less offensive. *Rear* is euphemistic.) □ *That guy is a real pain in the ass.* □ *Things like that give me a pain in the butt.* □ *You are nothing but a pain in the rear.*

pain in the butt See the previous entry.

pain in the neck a difficult or annoying thing or person. (Slang. Compare to *pain in the ass*.) □ *This tax form is* *a pain in the neck.* □ *My boss is a pain in the neck.*

pain in the rear See *pain in the ass.*

paint over something to cover something up with a layer of paint. □ *Sam painted over the rusty part of the fence.* □ *The work crew was told to paint over the graffiti.*

paint something out to cover something up or obliterate something by applying a layer of paint. □ *The worker painted the graffiti out.* ⊤ *They had to paint out the graffiti.*

paint the town red to have a wild celebration during a night on the town. (Not literal.) □ *Let's all go out and paint the town red!* □ *Oh, do I feel awful. I was out all last night, painting the town red.*

pair up (with someone) to join with someone to make a pair. □ *Sally decided to pair up with Jason for the dance contest.* □ *Sally and Jason paired up with each other.* □ *Sally and Jason paired up.* □ *All the kids paired up and gave gifts to one another.*

pal around (with someone) to associate with someone as a good friend. □ *I like to pal around with my friends on the weekends.* □ *They like to pal around.* □ *They often palled around with each other.*

pan in (on someone or something) See *zoom in (on someone or something).*

parade someone or something out to bring or march someone or some creature out in public. □ *He parades his children out every Sunday as they go to church.* ⊤ *He paraded out all his children.* □ *The owners paraded their dogs out, and the judge got ready to choose the best one.*

Pardon (me). See *Excuse me.*

Pardon (me)? See *Excuse me?*

Pardon me for living! a very indignant response to a criticism or rebuke. □ FRED: *Oh, I thought you had already taken yourself out of here!* SUE: *Well, pardon me for living!* □ TOM: *Butt out, Mary! Bill and I are talking.* MARY: *Pardon me for living!*

park it (somewhere) to sit down somewhere; to sit down and get out of the way. (Slang.) □ *Hey, park it! You're in the way.* □ *Carl, park it over there in the corner. Stop pacing around. You make me nervous.*

part and parcel See *bag and baggage.*

part someone's hair to come very close to someone. (Usually an exaggeration. Also used literally.) □ *That plane flew so low that it nearly parted my hair.* □ *He punched at me and missed. He only parted my hair.*

pass away to die. (Euphemistic.) □ *Uncle Herman passed away many years ago.* □ *He passed away in his sleep.*

pass go to complete a difficult or dangerous task successfully. (Slang. From "pass go and collect $200" in the game Monopoly™.) □ *Man, I tried to get there on time, but I just couldn't pass go.* □ *You had better pass go with this job, or you've had it.*

pass on to die. □ *When did your uncle pass on?* □ *Uncle Herman passed on nearly thirty years ago.*

pass on (to someone or something) to leave the person or thing being dealt with and move on to another person or thing. □ *I am finished with Henry. I will pass on to Jerry.* □ *I will pass on when I am finished.*

pass over (someone or something)
1. to skip over someone or something; to fail to select someone or something. □ *I was next in line for a promotion, but they passed over me.* □ *I passed over the bruised apples and picked out the nicest ones.* **2.** to pass above someone or something. □ *A cloud passed over our little group, cooling us a little.* □ *The huge blimp passed over the little community.*

pass someone or something up 1. to fail to select someone or something. □ *The committee passed Jill up and chose Kelly.* T *They passed up Jill.* □ *We had to pass your application up this year.* **2.** to travel past someone or something. □ *We had to pass her up, thinking we could visit her the next time we were in town.* T *We passed up a hitchhiker.* T *You passed up a nice restaurant near the edge of town when you left.*

pass something along (to someone)
1. to give or hand something to someone. □ *Would you kindly pass this along to Hillary?* T *Please pass along my advice to Wally over there.* □ *I would be happy to pass it along.* **2.** to relay some information to someone. □ *I hope you don't pass this along to anyone, but I am taking a new job next month.* T *Could you pass along my message to Fred?* □ *I will pass it along as you ask.*

pass something back (to someone) to return something by hand to someone. □ *Kelly passed the pictures back to Betty.* □ *They weren't Betty's and she passed them back to Beth.*

pass something down (to someone) AND **pass something on (to someone) 1.** to send something down a line of people to someone. (Each per-son hands it to the next.) □ *Please pass this down to Mary at the end of the row.* T *Pass down this box to Mary.* □ *Mary wants this. Please pass it down.* □ *Mary is expecting this. Please pass it on.* **2.** to will something to someone. □ *My grandfather passed this watch down to me.* T *He passed on the watch to me.* □ *I have always wanted it and I'm so glad he passed it down.*

pass something on (to someone) See the previous entry.

pass something out (to someone) to distribute something to someone. □ *Please pass these out to everyone.* T *Pass out these papers to everyone.* □ *Please pass them out.*

pass something over (to someone) to send something to someone farther down in a line of people. (Each person hands it to the next.) □ *Please pass this paper over to Jane.* T *Would you pass over this paper to Jane?* □ *I would be happy to pass it over.*

pass the buck to pass the blame (to someone else); to give the responsibility (to someone else). □ *Don't try to pass the buck! It's your fault, and everybody knows it.* □ *Some people try to pass the buck whenever they can.*

pass the hat to attempt to collect money for some (charitable) project. □ *Bob is passing the hat to collect money to buy flowers for Ann.* □ *He's always passing the hat for something.*

paste something up 1. to repair something with paste. □ *See if you can paste this book up so it will hold together.* T *Paste up the book and hope it holds together for a while.* **2.** to assemble a complicated page of material by pasting the parts together.

□ *There is no way a typesetter can get this page just the way you want it. You'll have to paste it up yourself.* T *Paste up this page again and let me see it.*

patch something together (with something) to use something to repair something hastily or temporarily. □ *I think I can patch the exhaust pipe together with some wire.* □ *See if you can patch this engine together well enough to run for a few more hours.*

patch something up to repair something in a hurry; to make something temporarily serviceable again. □ *Can you patch this up so I can use it again?* T *I'll patch up the hose for you.*

pay an arm and a leg (for something) AND **pay through the nose (for something)** to pay too much money for something. □ *I hate to have to pay an arm and a leg for a tank of gas.* □ *If you shop around, you won't have to pay an arm and a leg.* □ *Why should you pay through the nose?*

pay off to yield profits; to result in benefits. □ *My investment in those stocks has really paid off.* □ *The time I spent in school paid off in later years.*

pay one's debt (to society) to serve a sentence for a crime, usually in prison. □ *The judge said that Mr. Simpson had to pay his debt to society.* □ *Mr. Brown paid his debt in state prison.*

pay one's dues 1. to pay the fees required to belong to an organization. □ *If you haven't paid your dues, you can't come to the club picnic.* □ *How many people have paid their dues?* 2. to have earned one's right to something through hard work or suf-fering. □ *He worked hard to get to where he is today. He paid his dues and did what he was told.* □ *I have every right to be here. I paid my dues!*

pay someone back 1. to return money that was borrowed from a person. □ *You owe me money. When are you going to pay me back?* □ *You must pay John back. You have owed him money for a long time.* 2. to get even with someone [for doing something]. (Figurative.) □ *I will pay her back for what she said about me.* □ *Max will pay Lefty back. He bears a grudge for a long time.*

pay something back (to someone) to repay someone. □ *I paid the money back to Jerry.* T *Can I pay back the money to George now?* □ *Please pay the money back now.*

pay something down 1. to make a deposit of money on a purchase. □ *You will have to pay a lot of money down on a car that expensive.* T *I only paid down a few thousand dollars.* 2. to reduce a bill by paying part of it, usually periodically. □ *I think I can pay the balance down by half in a few months.* T *I will pay down the balance a little next month.*

pay something in(to something) to pay an amount of money into an account. □ *Mary paid forty dollars into my account by mistake.* T *She paid in a lot of money.* □ *I have an account here and I want to pay something in.*

pay something off to pay the total amount of a bill; to settle an account by paying the total sum. □ *You should pay the total off as soon as possible to avoid having to pay more interest.* T *I will pay off the entire amount.*

pay something out to unravel or unwind wire or rope as it is needed. □ *One worker paid the cable out, and another worker guided it into the conduit.* T *The worker paid out the cable.*

pay something out (for someone or something) to disburse money for something or someone. □ *We have already paid too much money out for your education.* T *We paid out too much money.* □ *How much did you pay out?*

pay something out (to someone) to pay money to someone. □ *The grocery store paid one hundred dollars out to everyone who had become ill.* T *They paid out money to people who claimed illness.* □ *Alice, the cashier, paid the money out as it was requested.*

pay something up to pay all of whatever is due; to complete all the payments on something. □ *Please pay all your bills up.* T *Would you pay up your bills, please?* □ *Your dues are all paid up.*

pay the piper to face the results of one's actions; to receive punishment for something. □ *You can put off paying your debts only so long. Eventually you'll have to pay the piper.* □ *You can't get away with that forever. You'll have to pay the piper someday.*

pay through the nose (for something) See *pay an arm and a leg (for something).*

peal out [for bells or voices] to sound forth musically. □ *The bells pealed out to announce that the wedding had taken place.* □ *All six of the bells seemed to peal out at once.*

peek in (on someone or something) to glance quickly into a place to see someone or something. □ *Would you please peek in on the baby?* □ *Yes, I'll peek in in a minute.*

peel something off from something See the following entry.

peel something off ((of) something) AND **peel something off from something** to remove the outside surface layer from something. (The *of* is colloquial.) □ *She carefully peeled the skin off the apple.* T *She peeled off the apple's skin.* □ *Please peel the skin off.*

peer in(to something) to stare into something; to look deep into something. □ *I peered into the room, hoping to get a glimpse of the lovely furnishings.* □ *I tried to peer into the room when my host wasn't looking, but only had time to get a glimpse around.*

peer out at someone or something to stare out at someone or something. □ *A little puppy peered out at them from the cage.* □ *When I looked under the box, Timmy peered out at me with a big smile.*

pelt down (on someone or something) [for something] to fall down on someone or something. (Typically rain, hail, sleet, stones, etc.) □ *The rain pelted down on the children as they ran to their school bus.* □ *The ashes from the volcanic eruption pelted down on the town, covering the houses in a gray shroud.*

pen someone or something in (some place) to confine someone or some creature in a pen. □ *We penned all the kids in the backyard while we got the party things ready in the house.* T *We had to pen in the kids to keep them away from the traffic.* □ *Alice penned her dog in.*

pen someone or something up to confine someone or something to a pen. ☐ *He said he didn't want them to pen him up in an office all day.* ⊤ *They penned up the dog during the day.*

pencil someone or something in to write in something with a pencil. (Implies that the writing is not final.) ☐ *I will pencil you in for a Monday appointment.* ☐ *This isn't the final answer, so I will just pencil it in.* ⊤ *I penciled in a tentative answer.*

penny-wise and pound-foolish It is foolish to lose a lot of money to save a little money. (Proverb.) ☐ *Sally shops very carefully to save a few cents on food, then charges the food to a charge card that costs a lot in annual interest. That's being penny-wise and pound-foolish.* ☐ *John drives thirty miles to buy gas for three cents a gallon less than it costs here. He's really penny-wise and pound-foolish.*

Perhaps a little later. Not now, but possibly later. ☐ WAITER: *Would you like your coffee now?* BOB: *Perhaps a little later.* WAITER: *All right.* ☐ SALLY: *Hey, Bill, how about a swim?* BOB: *Sounds good, but not now. Perhaps a little later.* SALLY: *Okay. See you later.*

Perish the thought. Do not even consider thinking of something. (Literary.) ☐ *If you should become ill—perish the thought—I'd take care of you.* ☐ *I'm afraid that we need a new car. Perish the thought.*

perk up to be invigorated; to become more active. ☐ *After a bit of water, the plants perked up nicely.* ☐ *About noon, Andy perked up and looked wide-awake.*

Permit me. See *Allow me.*

permit someone out (of something) to allow someone to go out of something or some place. ☐ *His mother won't permit him out of his room all weekend.* ☐ *I didn't do anything, but she won't permit me out!*

pick someone or something out (for someone or something) to choose someone or something to serve as someone or something. ☐ *I picked one of the new people out for Santa Claus this year.* ⊤ *I picked out several large potatoes for the stew.* ⊤ *Sally picked out a ripe one.* ☐ *I picked her out myself.*

pick someone or something out (of something) 1. to lift or pull someone or something out of something. ☐ *The mother picked her child out of the fray and took him home.* ⊤ *I picked out the mushrooms before eating the soup.* ☐ *Larry fell off the boat into the water, and I picked him out.* 2. to select someone or something out of an offering of selections. ☐ *I picked Jerry out of all the boys in the class.* ⊤ *I picked out Jerry.* ☐ *I picked Jerry out.*

pick someone or something up (from something) 1. to lift up or raise someone or something from a lower place. (*Someone* includes *oneself*. See also *pick up.*) ☐ *Please help me pick this guy up from the pavement. He passed out and fell down.* ⊤ *Help me pick up this guy from the ground, will you?* ☐ *Slowly, she picked herself up from the ground.* 2. to fetch someone or something from something or some place. ☐ *I picked her up from the train station.* ⊤ *Please pick up my cousin from the airport.* ☐ *I have to pick my dog up from the vet.* 3. to acquire someone or something. ☐ *They picked some valuable antiques up at an auction.* ⊤ *She picked up a cold last* *week.* T *I picked up a little German while I was in Austria.*

pick up to increase, as with business, wind, activity, etc. (See also *pick someone or something up (from something)*.) □ *Business is beginning to pick up as we near the holiday season.* □ *The wind picked up about midnight.*

pick up (after someone or something) to tidy up after someone or a group. (*Someone* includes *oneself*.) □ *I refuse to pick up after you all the time.* □ *I refuse to pick up after your rowdy friends.* □ *Why do I always have to pick up?* □ *You have to learn to pick up after yourself.*

pick up the tab to pay the bill. □ *Whenever we go out, my father picks up the tab.* □ *Order whatever you want. The company is picking up the tab.*

piddle (around) to waste time; to work aimlessly or inefficiently. (Slang.) □ *Stop piddling around! Get to work!* □ *Can't you get serious and stop piddling?*

pie in the sky a future reward, especially after death. (From a longer phrase, "pie in the sky by and by when you die.") □ *Are you nice to people just because of pie in the sky, or do you really like them?* □ *Don't hold out for a big reward, you know — pie in the sky.*

piece of cake 1. something easy to do. (Slang.) □ *No problem. When you know what you're doing, it's a piece of cake.* □ *Glad to help. It was a piece of cake.* **2.** It's easy! (Usually **Piece of cake!**) □ *No problem, piece of cake!* □ *Rescuing drowning cats is my specialty. Piece of cake!*

piece something together to fit something together; to assemble the pieces of something, such as a puzzle or something puzzling, and make sense of it. □ *The police were unable to piece the story together.* T *The detective tried to piece together the events leading up to the crime.*

pig out to overeat; to overindulge in food or drink. (Slang. Similar to *mac out, pork out, scarf out*.) □ *I always pig out on Fridays.* □ *I can't help myself when I see ice cream. I have to pig out.*

pile in(to something) to climb into something in a disorderly fashion. □ *Everyone piled into the car, and we left.* □ *Come on. Pile in!*

pile off (something) to get down off something; to clamber down off something. □ *All the kids piled off the wagon and ran into the barn.* □ *She stopped the wagon, and they piled off.*

pile on((to) someone or something) to make a heap of people on someone or something. □ *The football players piled onto the poor guy holding the ball.* □ *They ran up to the ball-carrier and piled on.*

pile out (of something) to climb out of something, such as a car. □ *All the kids piled out of the van and ran into the school.* □ *The van pulled up, and the kids piled out.*

pile someone in(to something) to bunch people into something in a disorderly fashion. (*Someone* includes *oneself*.) □ *She piled the kids into the van and headed off for school.* T *She piled in the kids and closed the doors.* □ *Pile them in and let's go.* □ *They piled themselves into the car and sped off towards town.*

pile something up to make something into a heap. (More at *pile up*.) □ *Carl piled all the leaves up and set them afire.* T *Please pile up the leaves.*

pile up 1. to gather or accumulate. (More at *pile something up*.) □ *The newspapers began to pile up after a few days.* □ *Work is really piling up around here.* 2. [for a number of vehicles] to crash together. □ *Nearly twenty cars piled up on the tollway this morning.*

pilot someone or something through (something) to guide or steer someone or something through something, especially through a waterway. (Literal or figurative with people or things.) □ *We hired someone to pilot us through the harbor entrance.* □ *The channel was treacherous, and we hired someone to pilot the ship through.* □ *John offered to pilot us through the bureaucracy when we went to the courthouse.*

pilot something in(to something) to steer or guide something into something. (Usually refers to steering a ship.) □ *We need to signal for a pilot to pilot our ship into the harbor.* T *Fred piloted in the freighter.* □ *Mary piloted the ship in.*

pilot something out (of something) to steer or guide something out of something. (Usually refers to steering a ship.) □ *The chubby little man with a pipe piloted the huge ship out of the harbor.* □ *The storm made it very difficult to pilot the ship out.*

pin someone down (on something) AND **nail someone down (on something)** to demand and receive a firm answer from someone to some question. □ *I tried to pin him down on a time and place, but he was very evasive.* T *Don't try to pin down the mayor on anything!* □ *I want to nail her down on a meeting time.* □ *It's hard to pin her down. She is so busy.*

pin something up to raise something and hold it up with pins. □ *I will pin this hem up and then sew it later.* T *Please pin up the hem so I can see where to sew it.*

pinch something back to pinch off a bit of the top of a plant so it will branch out and grow more strongly. □ *You should pinch this back so it will branch.* T *Pinch back the new leaves at the top.*

pipe up (with something) to interject a comment; to interrupt with a comment. □ *Nick piped up with an interesting thought.* □ *You can always count on Alice to pipe up.*

piss someone off to make someone angry. (Crude slang. Use caution with *piss*.) □ *She really pissed me off!* T *That's enough to piss off anybody.*

pissed (off) angry. (Crude slang. Use caution with *piss*. More at *piss someone off*.) □ *I was so pissed off I could have screamed.* □ *He's come back, and he's sure pissed.*

pitch a bitch to make a complaint. (Crude slang.) □ *You really love to pitch a bitch, don't you? What makes you happy?* □ *Complain, complain! You could pitch a bitch all day long.*

pitch in (and help) (with something) to join in and help someone with something. □ *Would you please pitch in and help with the party?* □ *Come on! Pitch in!* □ *Please pitch in with the dishes!* □ *Can't you pitch in and help?*

pitch someone a curve (ball) to surprise someone with an unexpected act or event. (Also used literally referring to a curve ball in baseball.) □ *You really pitched me a curve ball when you said I had done a poor job. I did my best.* □ *You asked Tom a hard question. You certainly pitched him a curve.*

pitch someone or something out ((of) something) to throw someone or something out of something or some place. □ *The usher pitched the drunk out of the theater.* T *The usher pitched out the annoying person.* □ *The officer arrested the driver because he pitched a can out the car window.*

plan something out to make thorough plans for something. □ *Let us sit down and plan our strategy out.* T *We sat down and planned out our strategy.*

plane something down to smooth something down with a plane. □ *I will have to plane the door down before I hang it again.* T *I planed down the edge of the door for you.*

play along (with someone or something) 1. to play a musical instrument with someone or a group. □ *The trombonist sat down and began to play along with the others.* □ *Do you mind if I play along?* **2.** to pretend to cooperate with someone or something in a joke, scam, etc. □ *I decided that I would play along with Larry for a while and see what would happen.* □ *I don't think I want to play along.*

play ball (with someone) 1. to play a ball game with someone. (Note the special baseball use in the second example.) □ *When will our team play ball with yours?* □ *Suddenly, the umpire shouted "Play ball!" and the game began.* **2.** to cooperate with someone. □ *Look, friend, if you play ball with me, everything will work out all right.* □ *Things would go better for you if you'd learn to play ball.*

play both ends (against the middle) [for one] to scheme in a way that pits two sides against each other (for one's own gain). □ *I told my brother that Mary doesn't like him. Then I told Mary that my brother doesn't like her. They broke up, so now I can have the car this weekend. I succeeded in playing both ends against the middle.* □ *If you try to play both ends, you're likely to get in trouble with both sides.*

play by ear to play a musical instrument well, without formal training. □ *John can play the piano by ear.* □ *If I could play by ear, I wouldn't have to take lessons — or practice!*

play cat and mouse (with someone) to capture and release someone over and over. (Both literal and figurative uses.) □ *The police played cat and mouse with the suspect until they had sufficient evidence to make an arrest.* □ *Tom had been playing cat and mouse with Ann. Finally she got tired of it and broke up with him.*

play fast and loose (with someone or something) to act carelessly, thoughtlessly, and irresponsibly. □ *I'm tired of your playing fast and loose with me. Leave me alone.* □ *Bob got fired for playing fast and loose with the company's money.* □ *If you play fast and loose like that, you can get into a lot of trouble.*

play it cool 1. to do something without revealing insecurities or incompetence. (Slang.) □ *Play it cool, man. Look like you belong there.* □ *If the boss walks in, just play it cool.* **2.** to hold one's temper. □ *Come on now.*

Let it pass. Play it cool. □ *Don't let them get you mad. Play it cool.*

play it safe to be or act safe; to do something safely. □ *You should play it safe and take your umbrella.* □ *If you have a cold or the flu, play it safe and go to bed.*

play one's cards close to one's vest See the following entry.

play one's cards close to the chest AND **play one's cards close to one's vest** [for someone] to work or negotiate in a careful and private manner. (Refers to holding one's playing cards close so that no one can possibly see what one is holding.) □ *It's hard to figure out what John is up to because he plays his cards close to his chest.* □ *Don't let them know what you're up to. Play your cards close to your vest.*

play out to run out; to finish. □ *The whole incident is about to play out. Then it all will be forgotten.* □ *When the event plays out, everything will return to normal.*

play second fiddle (to someone) to be in a subordinate position to someone. □ *I'm tired of playing second fiddle to John.* □ *I'm better trained than he, and I have more experience. I shouldn't play second fiddle.*

play someone or something up to emphasize someone or something; to support or boost someone or something. □ *Her mother kept playing Jill up, hoping she would get chosen.* Ⓣ *She played up her daughter to anyone who would listen.* □ *Don't play our weak points up so much.*

play something back (to someone) to play a recording to someone. □ *Can you play the speech back to me?* Ⓣ

Please play back the speech to me, so I can hear how I sound. □ *Let me play it back.*

play something by ear to be able to play a piece of music without looking at the notes after just listening to it a few times. □ *I can play "Stardust" by ear.* □ *Some people can play Chopin's music by ear.*

play something through to play something, such as a piece of music or a record, from beginning to end. □ *I played the album through, hoping to find even one song I liked.* Ⓣ *As I played through the album, I didn't hear anything I liked.*

play the field to date many different people rather than going steady with one person. □ *When Tom told Ann good-bye, he said he wanted to play the field.* □ *He said he wanted to play the field while he was still young.*

play to the gallery to perform in a manner that will get the strong approval of the audience; to perform in a manner that will get the approval of the lower elements in the audience. □ *John is a competent actor, but he has a tendency to play to the gallery.* □ *When he made the rude remark, he was just playing to the gallery.*

play up to someone to flatter someone; to try to gain influence with someone. □ *It won't do any good to play up to me. I refuse to agree to your proposal.* □ *I played up to him and he still wouldn't let me go.*

play (up)on something 1. to make music on a musical instrument. (*Upon* is formal and less commonly used than *on.*) □ *Can you play upon this instrument, or only the one you are holding?* □ *I can't play on this! It's* broken. **2.** to exploit something — including a word — for some purpose; to develop something for some purpose. (*Upon* is formal and less commonly used than *on*.) □ *You are just playing on words!* □ *You are playing on a misunderstanding.* **3.** [for light] to sparkle on something. □ *The reflections of the candles played on the surface of the soup.* □ *The lights played on the crystal goblets.*

play with fire to take a big risk. (Also used literally.) □ *If you accuse her of stealing, you'll be playing with fire.* □ *I wouldn't try that if I were you — unless you like playing with fire.*

played (out) **1.** having to do with a portion of marijuana (in a cigarette or a pipe) that has had all of the effective substance smoked out of it. (Slang.) □ *This stuff is played. Get rid of it.* □ *You gave me pot that was played out!* **2.** worn-out; exhausted; no longer effective. □ *This scenario is played out. It no longer makes sense.* □ *I'm played. I have no new ideas.*

Please. **1.** a response to a denial or refusal. □ BILL: *Can I go to the picnic on the Fourth of July?* MOTHER: *No, you can't go to the picnic.* BILL: *Please!* □ TOM: *No, Bill. You can't have a raise.* BILL: *Please. I can hardly afford to live.* TOM: *You'll manage.* **2.** You go first.; Give yourself priority.; Attend to your interests first. □ *Bob stepped back and made a motion with his hand indicating that Mary should go first. "Please," smiled Bob.* □ MARY: *Do you mind if I take the last piece of cake?* BOB: *Please.* MARY: *Thanks.* **3.** Please stop what you are doing.; Please do not do that.; Please do not say that. (Compare to *I beg your pardon.*) □ MARY: *You always make a mess where*

ever you go. ALICE: *Please! I do not!* □ *Andrew kept bumping up against Mary in line. Finally Mary turned to him and said, "Please!"*

Please hold. See *Hold the wire(, please).*

plot something out to map something out; to outline a plan for something. □ *I have an idea about how to remodel this room. Let me plot it out for you.* ⊤ *I plotted out my ideas for the room.*

plow something back into something to put something, such as a profit, back into an investment. □ *We plowed all the profits back into the expansion of the business.* ⊤ *Bill and Ted plowed back everything they earned into the company.*

plow something in to work something into the soil by plowing. □ *Lay the fertilizer down and plow it in.* ⊤ *Plow in the fertilizer as soon as you can.*

plow something under (something) to push something under the surface of soil or water. □ *The farmer plowed the wheat stubble under the surface of the soil.* □ *The farmer plowed the stubble under.*

plow through something to work through something laboriously. □ *I have to plow through all the paperwork this weekend.* □ *Will you help me plow through all these contracts?*

pluck something off ((of) someone or something) to pick something off someone or something. (The *of* is colloquial.) □ *She plucked the mosquito off his back before it could bite him.* ⊤ *She plucked off the bud.* □ *There is an unnecessary branch on the plant. Please pluck it off.*

pluck something out (of something) to snatch something out of something. □ She plucked the coin out of his hand and put it in her shoe. ⊤ Reaching into the fountain, Jane plucked out the coin. □ Mary plucked it out.

pluck up someone's courage to bolster someone's courage. (*Someone* includes *oneself*.) □ I hope you are able to pluck up your courage so that you can do what has to be done. □ Some good advice from a friend helped pluck up my courage.

plug away (at someone or something) to keep working at someone or something. □ I will just keep plugging away at Fred. I will convince him yet. □ I won't leave him alone. I'll keep plugging away.

plug something in(to something) to connect something to something else, usually by connecting wires together with a plug and socket. □ Plug this end of the wire into the wall. ⊤ Plug in the lamp and turn it on. □ Please plug this in. □ Is the vacuum cleaner plugged in?

plug something up to fill up a hole; to block a hole or opening. □ Please plug this hole up so the cold air doesn't get in. ⊤ Can you plug up the hole?

plump something up to pat or shake something like a pillow into a fuller shape. □ Todd plumped his pillow up and finished making the bed. ⊤ He plumped up his pillow.

plunge in(to something) to dive or rush into something; to immerse oneself in something. (Compare to *plunge something in(to someone or something)*.) □ Ned took off his shoes and plunged into the river, hoping to rescue Frank. □ He plunged into his work and lost track of time. □ Barry strode to the side of the pool and plunged in.

plunge something in(to someone or something) to drive or stab something into someone or something. (Compare to *plunge in(to something)*.) □ The murderer plunged the knife into his victim. ⊤ She plunged in the dagger. □ Ken plunged the cooked pasta into cold water.

point someone or something out to identify someone or something in a group; to select someone or something from a group. □ I don't know what June looks like, so you will have to point her out. ⊤ Will you point out June, please? □ I pointed the door out to her.

poke fun (at someone) to make fun of someone; to ridicule someone. □ Stop poking fun at me! It's not nice. □ Bob is always poking fun.

poke one's nose in(to something) AND **stick one's nose in(to something)** to interfere with something; to be nosy about something. (Not literal.) □ I wish you'd stop poking your nose into my business. □ She was too upset for me to stick my nose in and ask what was wrong.

poke out (of something) to stick out of something; to extend out of something. □ The bean sprouts were beginning to poke out of the soil of the garden. □ I knew there were little birds in the birdhouse, because a little head poked out now and then.

poke something in(to something) to stick or cram something into something. □ He poked his finger into the jam, pulled it out again, and licked it.

T *Jeff poked in his finger.* ☐ *Don't poke your finger in!*

polish something off to eat, consume, exhaust, or complete all of something. ☐ *Who polished the cake off?* T *Who polished off the juice?* T *She polished off her chores in record time.*

polish something up to rub something until it shines. ☐ *Polish the silver up and make it look nice and shiny.* T *If you will polish up the silver, I will put it away.*

ponder (up)on something to think on something; to consider something. (*Upon* is formal and less commonly used than *on.*) ☐ *Ponder upon this awhile. See what you come up with.* ☐ *I need to ponder on this.*

poop out to quit; to wear out and stop. (Slang. More at *pooped (out).*) ☐ *He pooped out after about an hour.* ☐ *I think I'm going to poop out pretty soon.*

pooped (out) 1. exhausted; worn-out. (Slang. Said of a person or an animal. More at *poop out.*) ☐ *I'm really pooped out.* ☐ *The horse looked sort of pooped in the final stretch.* **2.** alcohol intoxicated. ☐ *How much of that stuff does it take to get pooped?* ☐ *He's been drinking all night and is totally pooped out.*

pop for something to pay for a treat (for someone). (Slang. See also *spring for something.*) ☐ *Let's have some ice cream. I'll pop for it.* ☐ *It's about time you popped for coffee.*

pop off 1. to make an unnecessary remark; to interrupt with a remark; to sound off. (Slang.) ☐ *Please don't pop off all the time.* ☐ *Bob keeps popping off when he should be listening.* **2.** to

lose one's temper. (Compare to *pop one's cork.*) ☐ *Now, don't pop off. Keep cool.* ☐ *I don't know why she popped off at me. All I did was say hello.* **3.** to die. ☐ *My uncle popped off last week.* ☐ *I hope I'm asleep when I pop off.*

pop one's cork to release one's anger; to have an angry outburst. (Slang.) ☐ *I'm just about to pop my cork.* ☐ *She tried to hold it back, but suddenly she popped her cork.*

pop out (of something) to jump out of something; to burst out of something. ☐ *Suddenly, a little mouse popped out of the drawer.* ☐ *I opened the drawer and a mouse popped out.*

pop something in(to something) to fit, snap, or press something into place in something. ☐ *Lee popped the lever into place, and the machine began to function.* T *Lee popped in the plastic part, and the toy ran beautifully.* ☐ *He popped the part in.*

pop something on((to) something) to snap something onto something. ☐ *Denise took one more sip of the medicine and popped the lid onto the bottle.* T *She popped on the lid when she was finished.* ☐ *Mary popped the top on and put the box away.*

pop something out (of something) to release something from something so that it jumps or bursts out, possibly with a popping sound. ☐ *Sue popped the cork out of the champagne bottle.* ☐ *It took a little effort to pop the cork out.*

pop the question to ask someone to marry you. ☐ *I was surprised when he popped the question.* ☐ *I've been waiting for years for someone to pop the question.*

pop up (some place) to appear suddenly and unexpectedly some place. □ *I never know where Henry is going to pop up next.* □ *A new problem has popped up.* □ *Guess who popped up at the office today?*

pork out to overindulge in food and drink. (Slang. A play on *pig out*.) □ *Whenever I see French fries, I know I'm going to pork out.* □ *We porked out on pizza.*

pounce (up)on someone or something to spring or swoop upon someone or something; to seize someone or something. (*Upon* is formal and less commonly used than *on*.) □ *As Gerald came into the room, his friend Daniel pounced on him and frightened him to death.* □ *The cat pounced upon a mouse.* □ *The preacher pounced on me after church and talked my ear off.* □ *The teacher pounced on all my spelling errors immediately.*

pound a beat to walk a route. (Usually said of a police patrol officer.) □ *The patrolman pounded the same beat for years and years.* □ *Pounding a beat will wreck your feet.*

pound a beer AND **pound some beers** to drink beer. (Slang.) □ *On a hot day like this, I want to go home and pound a beer.* □ *Let's go down to the tavern and pound some beers.*

pound away (at someone or something) to hammer or batter constantly on someone or something. □ *The cops pounded away at the poor guy, and then they put him in handcuffs.* □ *The jackhammer kept pounding away at the pavement.* □ *Two jackhammers pounded away all morning.*

pound one's ear to sleep. (Slang.) □ *I've got to spend more time pounding my ear.* □ *She went home to pound her ear an hour or two before work.*

pound some beers See *pound a beer.*

pound something down to hammer, flatten, or batter something. □ *Please pound that nail down so that no one gets hurt on it.* ⊤ *Yes, please pound down that nail!* □ *The butcher pounded the chicken breasts down.*

pound something in(to someone) See *hammer something in(to someone)*.

pound something in(to something) See *hammer something in(to something)*.

pound the books See *hit the books.*

pound the pavement to walk through the streets looking for a job. □ *I spent two months pounding the pavement after the factory I worked for closed.* □ *Hey, Bob. You'd better get busy pounding those nails unless you want to be out pounding the pavement.*

pour cold water on something AND **dash cold water on something; throw cold water on something** to discourage doing something; to reduce enthusiasm for something. (Not literal in this sense.) □ *When my father said I couldn't have the car, he poured cold water on my plans.* □ *John threw cold water on the whole project by refusing to participate.*

pour it on thick See *lay it on thick.*

pour money down the drain to waste money; to throw money away. □ *What a waste! You're just pouring money down the drain.* □ *Don't buy any more of that low-quality merchandise. That's just throwing money down the drain.*

pour oil on troubled water to calm things down. (If oil is poured onto rough seas during a storm, the water will become more calm.) ☐ *That was a good thing to say to John. It helped to pour oil on troubled water. Now he looks happy.* ☐ *Bob is the kind of person who pours oil on troubled water.*

pour out (of something) [for someone or something] to stream or gush out of something or some place. ☐ *The water poured out of the broken pipe and flooded the basement.* ☐ *The pipe split and the water just poured out.*

pour something off ((of) something) to spill liquid off the top of something. (The *of* is colloquial.) ☐ *Valerie poured the cream off the milk.* ⊤ *Valerie poured off the cream.* ☐ *She poured the water off.*

power something up to start something, such as an engine. (More at *power up*.) ☐ *You should power the engine up and let it run awhile before you drive away.* ⊤ *Power up the engine and mow the grass.*

power up to start an engine. (More at *power something up*.) ☐ *Well, let's power up so we will be ready to leave with the others.* ☐ *It's time to power up and get going.*

practice what you preach to do what you advise other people to do. ☐ *If you'd practice what you preach, you'd be better off.* ☐ *You give good advice. Why not practice what you preach?*

pray to the porcelain god to empty one's stomach; to vomit. (Slang. Refers to being on one's knees (praying) in front of a porcelain toilet bowl.) ☐ *Boy, was I sick. I was praying to the porcelain god for two* hours. ☐ *I think I'd better go home and pray to the porcelain god.*

press against someone or something to push or bear upon someone or something. ☐ *I pressed against Henry, trying gently to get him to move out of the way.* ☐ *Don't press against the glass door!*

press down on someone or something to push down on someone or something. ☐ *The weight of all the covers was pressing down on me, and I couldn't sleep.* ☐ *Press down on this lever and the recorder will start.*

press on something to push or depress something, such as a button, catch, snap, etc. ☐ *Press on this button if you require room service.* ☐ *Don't press on this because it rings a loud bell.*

press one's luck See *push one's luck.*

press someone to the wall See *push someone to the wall.*

press something against someone or something to push or force something against someone or something. ☐ *The person in line behind Betty kept pressing his elbow against her.* ☐ *I pressed my hand against the door and it opened.*

press something in(to something) 1. to force something into something, such as a mold. ☐ *Now, you need to press the clay into the mold carefully.* ⊤ *Now, hold the mold with one hand and press in the clay.* ☐ *Press it in.* 2. to force or drive something into the surface of something. ☐ *You are standing on my chewing gum, and you have pressed it into the carpet!* ⊤ *Don't press in the gum by standing on it.* ☐ *You pressed the gum in!*

press something on (to something) to put pressure on something and cause it to stick to the surface of something. □ *I pressed the label onto the envelope and took it to the post office.* ⊤ *I pressed on the label.* □ *With much effort, I pressed the label on so it would stick.*

press something out (of something) to squeeze something out of something by applying pressure. □ *The Indians press the acid out of the manioc before they use it as food.* □ *Gene used an iron to press the wrinkles out of his suit coat.* ⊤ *They pressed out the acid.* □ *Gerald pressed the wrinkles out.*

press (up)on someone or something to put pressure on someone or something. (*Upon* is formal and less commonly used than *on*.) □ *The crowd pressed upon the child, squeezing out all his breath.* □ *The load presses on your car's springs very heavily.*

presume (up)on someone or something to take unwelcome advantage of someone or something. □ *I didn't mean to seem to presume upon you. I apologize.* □ *I did not feel that you presumed on me.*

Pretty is as pretty does. You should do pleasant things if you wish to be considered pleasant. □ *Now, Sally. Let's be nice. Pretty is as pretty does.* □ *My great-aunt always used to say, "Pretty is as pretty does," to my sister.*

prevail (up)on someone or something (to do something) to appeal to someone or a group to do something. (*Upon* is formal and less commonly used than *on*.) □ *I will prevail upon her to attend the meeting.* □ *I prevailed on the committee to no avail.*

prey (up)on someone or something to take advantage of someone or something. (*Upon* is formal and less commonly used than *on*.) □ *The people of that island prey on tourists and do not give them good treatment.* □ *I really don't want to seem to prey on your kindness.*

prick up one's ears to listen more closely. □ *At the sound of my voice, my dog pricked up her ears.* □ *I pricked up my ears when I heard my name mentioned.*

print something out **1.** to write something out by drawing letters. □ *Please print it out. I can't read your handwriting.* ⊤ *Print out your name, please.* **2.** to use a computer printer to print something. □ *I will print a copy out and send it to you.* ⊤ *Please print out another copy.*

print something up to set something in type and print it; to print something by any process. □ *This looks okay to me. Let's print it up now.* ⊤ *Print up the final version.*

promise someone the moon See the following entry.

promise the moon (to someone) AND **promise someone the moon** to make extravagant promises to someone. □ *Bill will promise you the moon, but he won't live up to his promises.* □ *My boss promised the moon, but only paid the minimum wage.*

prune something off ((of) something) to cut something off something. (The *of* is colloquial.) □ *Claire pruned the dead branch off the apple tree.* ⊤ *She pruned off the dead branch.*

pry into something to snoop into something; to get into someone else's business. □ *Why are you prying into my affairs all the time?* □ *I wish you wouldn't pry into things.*

pry something off ((of) something) to use a lever to get something off something. (The *of* is colloquial.) □ *Tom pried the top off the jelly jar.* ⊤ *He pried off the jar top.* □ *Tom pried it off.*

pry something up to raise something, as with a lever. □ *See if you can pry that trapdoor up.* ⊤ *Pry up that lid.*

psych out to have a nervous or emotional trauma; to go mad for a brief time. (Slang. Similar to *freak (out)*. More at *psych someone out*.) □ *Another day like this one and I'll psych out for sure.* □ *He looked at the bill and psyched out.*

psych someone out to try to figure out what someone is likely to do. (Slang. More at *psych out*.) □ *Don't try to psych me out.* ⊤ *The batter tried to psych out the pitcher, but it didn't work.*

psych someone up to get someone excited or mentally prepared for something. (Slang.) □ *I psyched myself up to sing in front of all those people.* ⊤ *The coach psyched up the team for the game.*

psyched (out) excited; overwhelmed; thrilled. (Slang.) □ *She's really psyched out.* □ *That's great. I'm really psyched!* □ *What a psyched-out way to talk!*

psyched (up) completely mentally ready (for something). (Slang.) □ *I'm really psyched for this test.* □ *The team isn't psyched up enough to do a good job.*

puff out to swell out. □ *The frog's throat puffed out, and we expected to* hear a croak. □ *The sail puffed out, and the boat began to move.*

puff someone or something up to boost or promote someone or something. (*Someone* includes *oneself*.) □ *Judy puffed Nell up so much that Nell could not begin to live up to her own reputation.* ⊤ *Don't puff up your own interests so much.* □ *Wally puffed himself up so much that he couldn't live up to his own image.*

puff something out to cause something to swell out or expand outward. □ *The frog puffed its throat out and croaked.* ⊤ *The frog puffed out its throat and croaked a mighty croak.*

puff up (into something) to assume a larger shape by filling up with air or water; to swell up into something. □ *The strange-looking fish puffed up into a round ball.* □ *The fish puffed up and stuck out its spines.*

pull in(to some place) to drive into some place. □ *A strange car just pulled into our driveway.* □ *Some stranger just pulled in.*

pull off (something) to steer or turn a vehicle off the road. □ *I pulled off the road and rested for a while.* □ *I had to pull off and rest.*

pull oneself up (by one's own bootstraps) to achieve (something) through one's own efforts. □ *They simply don't have the resources to pull themselves up by their own bootstraps.* □ *If I could have pulled myself up, I'd have done it by now.*

pull out (of something) 1. to withdraw from something. □ *For some reason, he pulled out of the coalition and went his own way.* □ *The other side got impatient with the negotiations and pulled out.* **2.** to drive out of

313

something, such as a driveway, parking space, garage, etc. □ *The car pulled out of the driveway and nearly hit a truck.* □ *Look out! A car is about to pull out!*

pull someone in(to something) to get someone involved in something. □ *Please don't pull me into this argument.* T *Don't pull in anyone else.* □ *It's not my affair. Don't pull me in!*

pull someone or something up to drag or haul someone or something upward or to an upright position. (*Someone* includes *oneself*.) □ *Bob had slipped down into the creek, so I reached down and pulled him up.* T *I pulled up Bob and nearly fell in myself.* □ *Nick pulled the cushion up and propped it against the back of the sofa.* □ *The injured soldier pulled himself up with the greatest of difficulty.*

pull someone's leg to kid, fool, or trick someone. □ *You don't mean that. You're just pulling my leg.* □ *Don't believe him. He's just pulling your leg.*

pull someone's or something's teeth to reduce the power of someone or something. (Also used literally.) □ *The mayor tried to pull the teeth of the new law.* □ *The city council pulled the teeth of the new mayor.*

pull something down to tear something down; to raze something, such as a building. □ *The developers decided not to pull the historic house down.* T *They tried to pull down the old house.*

pull something down over someone or something to draw something down over someone or something. □ *Lucy's mother pulled the dress down over Lucy and buttoned it up in back.*

□ *Sarah pulled the cover down over the bird cage and turned out the lights.*

pull something off ((of) something) to tug or drag something off something else. (The *of* is colloquial.) □ *Sam pulled the covers off the bed and fell into it, dead tired.* T *He pulled off the covers.* □ *Sam pulled them off.*

pull something out to withdraw something. □ *Arthur pulled his sword out and saluted the knight.* T *He pulled out his sword.*

pull something out of a hat AND **pull something out of thin air** to produce something as if by magic. □ *This is a serious problem, and we just can't pull a solution out of a hat.* □ *I'm sorry, but I don't have a pen. What do you want me to do, pull one out of thin air?*

pull something out of thin air See the previous entry.

pull something up (out of something) to draw something upward out of something. □ *The worker pulled a cold wet dog up out of the well.* T *He pulled up the dog out of the well.* □ *Sam reached down and pulled the dog up.*

pull the rug out (from under someone) to make someone ineffective. □ *The treasurer pulled the rug out from under the mayor.* □ *Things were going along fine until the treasurer pulled the rug out.*

pull the wool over someone's eyes to deceive someone. □ *You can't pull the wool over my eyes. I know what's going on.* □ *Don't try to pull the wool over her eyes. She's too smart.*

pull through (something) to survive something. □ *I am sure that your* uncle will pull through the illness. □ I'm glad he pulled through.

Pull up a chair. Please get a chair and sit down and join us. (Assumes that there is seating available. The speaker does not necessarily mean that the person spoken actually has to move a chair.) □ TOM: *Well, hello, Bob!* BOB: *Hi, Tom. Pull up a chair.* □ *The three men were sitting at a table for four. Bob came up and said hello. Bill said, "Pull up a chair." Bob sat in the fourth chair at the table.*

pull up (some place) to arrive at a place in a vehicle; [for a vehicle] to arrive some place. □ *She pulled up at the front door exactly on time.* □ *Alice pulled up exactly on time.*

pull up stakes to move to another place. (As if one were pulling up tent stakes.) □ *I've been here long enough. It's time to pull up stakes.* □ *I hate the thought of having to pull up stakes.*

pump something in(to someone or something) to try to force something, such as a gas, liquid, information, or money into someone or something. □ *First you have to pump some air into the ball to make it hard.* T *I pumped in the air.* □ *The hospital oxygen system pumped life-giving oxygen into Karen's lungs.* □ *The small pump near the aquarium pumped air in.* □ *I helped pump anatomical terms into Fred for the big test he was having the next day.* T *I pumped in the knowledge.* □ *Congress tried to pump money into the economy, but only created inflation.* □ *The young teacher worked hard to pump new life into the classroom.*

pump something out to empty something by pumping. □ *I need to buy a large pump to pump my basement out.* T *I have to pump out my basement.*

pump something out (of someone or something) to remove something from someone or something by force or suction. □ *The doctors pumped the poison out of her.* T *They pumped out the poison.* □ *They used electric pumps to pump the water out.*

pump something up to flex and tense a muscle until it is expanded to its fullest size, as with thighs and forearms. (Bodybuilding slang.) □ *She pumped her thighs up and struck a pose.* T *He really can pump up his pecs.*

pumped (up) excited; physically and mentally ready. (Sports slang.) □ *The team is really pumped up for Friday's game.* □ *She really plays well when she's pumped!*

punch in to record one's arrival at one's workplace at a certain time. □ *What time did you punch in?* □ *I punched in at the regular time.*

punch out to record that one has left one's workplace at a certain time. □ *Why didn't you punch out when you left last night?* □ *I punched out at the regular time.*

punch something out (of something) to press on something and make it pop out of something. □ *She punched the stickers out of the page and stuck them onto her schoolbooks.* T *Jane punched out the stickers.* □ *Punch another one out for me.*

punch something up to register a figure on a cash register. □ *Jake punched the total up, and the register drawer opened.* T *He punched up the total too carelessly.*

punk out 1. to chicken out. (Slang.) □ *He was supposed to ask her out, but he punked out at the last minute, of*

315

course. □ *Come on! Stick with it! Don't punk out!* **2.** to become a punker. □ *If I punked out, my parents would probably clobber me.* □ *If my kids ever punked out and looked like that, I think I'd clobber them.*

push off AND **shove off** to leave. (Slang. As if one were pushing away from a dock.) □ *Well, it looks like it's time to push off.* □ *It's time to go. Let's shove off.*

push one's luck AND **press one's luck** to expect continued good fortune; to expect to continue to escape bad luck. □ *You're okay so far, but don't push your luck.* □ *Bob pressed his luck too much and got into a lot of trouble.*

push (oneself) away (from something) to move oneself back and away from something. □ *The skater pushed herself away from the wall.* □ *Tom pushed himself away from the table when he had eaten enough.*

push out to spread out; to expand outward. □ *The sides of the box pushed out, and I was afraid it would break.* □ *His little tummy pushed out when he was full.*

push someone or something out (of something) to force someone or something out of something. (*Someone* includes *oneself*.) □ *Nick pushed the intruder out of the house.* T *Nick pushed out the intruder.* □ *Elaine opened the door and pushed the dog out.* □ *He pushed himself out of the door of the plane and parachuted to the ground.*

push someone or something up to raise or lift someone or something. □ *Jake is sliding down again. Push him up.* T *Push up the window, please.*

push someone to the wall AND **press someone to the wall** to force some-

one into a position where there is only one choice to make; to put someone in a defensive position. (Also used literally.) □ *There was little else I could do. They pushed me to the wall.* □ *When we pressed him to the wall, he told us where the cookies were hidden.*

push something off on(to) someone to place one's task onto another person; to make someone else do an unwanted job. □ *Don't push the dirty work off onto me.* □ *Kelly pushed her job off on me.* □ *I will try to push the cleaning off onto Sally and Todd.*

put a bee in someone's bonnet to give someone an idea (about something). □ *Somebody put a bee in my bonnet that we should go to a movie.* □ *Who put a bee in your bonnet?*

put a con on someone to attempt to deceive someone; to attempt to swindle someone. (Underworld. Slang.) □ *Don't try to put a con on me, Buster! I've been around too long.* □ *I wouldn't try to put a con on you. I'm not that dumb.*

put all one's eggs in one basket to risk everything at once. (Often negative. If the basket is dropped, all the eggs are lost.) □ *Don't put all your eggs in one basket. Then everything won't be lost if there is a catastrophe.* □ *John only applied to the one college he wanted to go to. He put all his eggs in one basket.*

put another way See *to put it another way.*

Put 'er there. See *Put it there.*

put in a good word (for someone) to say something (to someone) in support of someone. □ *I hope you get the job. I'll certainly put in a good word for* you. □ *Yes, I want the job. If you see the boss, please put in a good word.*

put in one's oar See *put one's oar in.*

put in one's two cents (worth) to add one's comments (to something). (Implies that one's comments may not be of great value, but need to be stated anyway.) □ *Can I put in my two cents worth?* T *Sure, go ahead — put your two cents in.*

Put it there. AND **Put 'er there.** Shake hands with me. (Literally, put your hand there, in mine. Colloquial. The apostrophe on *'er* is not always used.) □ BOB (extending his hand): *Sounds great to me, old buddy. Put it there.* FRED: *Thanks, Bob. I'm glad we could close the deal.* □ BOB: *Good to see you, Fred.* FRED: *Put 'er there, Bob.*

put on to pretend; to deceive. (More at *put someone on.*) □ *She is not really that way. She is just putting on.* □ *Stop putting on. Act yourself.*

put on airs to act superior. □ *Stop putting on airs. You're just human like the rest of us.* □ *Ann is always putting on airs. You'd think she was a queen.*

put on one's thinking cap to start thinking in a serious manner. (Not literal. Usually used with children.) □ *All right now, let's put on our thinking caps and do some arithmetic.* □ *It's time to put on our thinking caps, children.*

put one through one's paces to make one demonstrate what one can do; to make one do one's job thoroughly. □ *The boss really put me through my paces today. I'm tired.* □ *I tried out for a part in the play, and the director really put me through my paces.*

put one's best foot forward to act or appear at one's best; to try to make a good impression. □ *When you apply for a job, you should always put your best foot forward.* □ *I try to put my best foot forward whenever I meet someone for the first time.*

put one's cards on the table AND **lay one's cards on the table** to reveal everything; to be open and honest with someone. (As one might do at certain points in a number of different card games to make an accounting of the cards one has been holding.) □ *Come on, John, lay your cards on the table. Tell me what you really think.* □ *Why don't we both put our cards on the table?*

put one's dibs on something See *have dibs on something.*

put one's foot in it See the following entry.

put one's foot in one's mouth AND **put one's foot in it; stick one's foot in one's mouth** to say something that you regret; to say something stupid, insulting, or hurtful. □ *When I told Ann that her hair was more beautiful than I had ever seen it, I really put my foot in my mouth. It was a wig.* □ *I put my foot in it by telling John's secret.*

put one's hand to the plow to begin to do a big and important task; to undertake a major effort. (Rarely literal.) □ *If John would only put his hand to the plow, he could do an excellent job.* □ *You'll never accomplish anything if you don't put your hand to the plow.*

put one's nose to the grindstone to keep busy doing one's work. (Never literal. Also with *have* and *get*, as in the examples.) □ *The boss told me to* put my nose to the grindstone. □ I've had my nose to the grindstone ever since I started working here. □ If the other people in this office would get their noses to the grindstone, more work would get done.

put one's oar in AND **put in one's oar** to give help; to interfere by giving advice; to add one's assistance to the general effort. □ You don't need to put your oar in. I don't need your advice. □ I'm sorry. I shouldn't have put in my oar.

put one's shoulder to the wheel to get busy. (Not literal.) □ You won't accomplish anything unless you put your shoulder to the wheel. □ I put my shoulder to the wheel and finished the job quickly.

put oneself out to inconvenience oneself. □ I just don't know why I put myself out for you! □ No, I did not put myself out at all. It was no trouble, in fact. □ She refused to put herself out even one little bit.

put out to generate lots of something. (Colloquial. Compare to put someone out.) □ What a great machine. It really puts out! □ The outlet of the dam really puts out!

put some sweet lines on someone See lay some sweet lines on someone.

put someone off 1. to delay action with someone. □ I hate to keep putting you off, but we are not ready to deal with you yet. Ⓣ I had to put off the plumber again. He really wants his money. 2. to repel someone. □ You really put people off with your scowling face. Ⓣ You put off people with your frown.

put someone on to tease or deceive someone. (More at put on.) □ You can't be serious! You're just putting me on! □ Stop putting me on!

put someone or something out to pasture to retire someone or something. (Originally said of a horse that was too old to work.) □ Please don't put me out to pasture. I have lots of good years left. □ This car has reached the end of the line. It's time to put it out to pasture.

put someone or something over to succeed in making someone or something be accepted. (Someone includes oneself.) □ The public relations expert helped put John over to the public. □ Do you think we can put this over? □ Do you think I put myself over all right?

put someone or something to bed 1. [with someone] to help someone — usually a child — get into a bed. □ Come on, Billy, it's time for me to put you to bed. □ I want grandpa to put me to bed. 2. [with something] to complete work on something and send it on to the next step in production, especially in publishing. □ This edition is finished. Let's put it to bed. □ Finish the editing of this book and put it to bed.

put someone or something to sleep 1. to kill someone or something. (Euphemistic.) □ We had to put our dog to sleep. □ The robber said he'd put us to sleep forever if we didn't cooperate. 2. to cause someone or something to sleep, perhaps through drugs or anesthesia. □ The doctor put the patient to sleep before the operation. □ I put the cat to sleep by stroking its tummy. 3. [with someone] to bore someone. (Literal.) □ That dull lecture put me to sleep. □ Her long story almost put me to sleep.

put someone out to annoy or irritate someone. (More at *put out*.) □ *He really put me out when he used a saucer for an ashtray.* □ *I didn't mean to put you out. I had no idea you were so touchy.*

put someone through the wringer to give someone a difficult time. (As one squeezes water from clothing in an old-fashioned wringer washing machine.) □ *They are really putting me through the wringer at school.* □ *The boss put Bob through the wringer over this contract.*

put someone to shame to show someone up; to embarrass someone; to make someone ashamed. □ *Your excellent efforts put us all to shame.* □ *I put him to shame by telling everyone about his bad behavior.*

put someone to the test to test someone; to see what someone can achieve. □ *I think I can jump that far, but no one has ever put me to the test.* □ *I'm going to put you to the test right now!*

put someone up (for something) to nominate or offer someone for some office or task. □ *I put Henry up for dogcatcher.* ⊤ *We put up Shannon for treasurer.*

put someone's nose out of joint to offend someone; to cause someone to feel slighted or insulted. (Not literal.) □ *I'm afraid I put his nose out of joint by not inviting him to the picnic.* □ *There is no reason to put your nose out of joint. I meant no harm.*

put something across (to someone) to make something clear to someone. □ *I don't know how to put this point across to my class. Can you help?* □ *Can you help me put this across?*

put something down to take the life of a creature mercifully. □ *It's kind to put fatally ill animals down.* ⊤ *We put down our old dog last year.*

put something off (until something) to postpone or delay something until something happens or until some future time. □ *I can't put this off until tomorrow.* ⊤ *I will put off the review until next week.* □ *I can put it off forever if you want.*

put something on to dress in an article of clothing. □ *Put your coat on, and let's go.* ⊤ *Put on your coat, and let's go.*

put something on ice AND **put something on the back burner** to delay or postpone something; to put something on hold. (Neither phrase is literal in these senses.) □ *I'm afraid that we'll have to put your project on ice for a while.* □ *Just put your idea on ice and keep it there till we get some money.*

put something on paper to write something down; to write or type an agreement on paper. □ *You have a great idea for a novel. Now put it on paper.* □ *I'm sorry, I can't discuss your offer until I see something in writing. Put it on paper, and then we'll talk.*

put something on the back burner See *put something on ice.*

put something on the cuff to buy something on credit; to add to one's credit balance. (As if one were making a note of the purchase on one's shirt cuff.) □ *I'll take two of those, and please put them on the cuff.* □ *I'm sorry, Tom. We can't put anything more on the cuff.*

put something on the line AND **lay something on the line** to speak very firmly and directly about something.

(Perhaps this refers to a battle line.) □ *She was very mad. She put it on the line, and we have no doubt about what she meant.* □ *All right, you kids! I'm going to lay it on the line. Don't ever do that again if you know what's good for you.*

put something on the street to make something known publicly; to tell everyone one's troubles. (Slang.) □ *Man, can't you keep a secret? Don't put everything on the street.* □ *She gets a little problem, and she puts it on the street right away!*

put something through its paces to demonstrate how well something operates; to demonstrate all the things something can do. □ *I was down by the barn, watching Sally put her horse through its paces.* □ *This is an excellent can opener. Watch me put it through its paces.*

put something up (for sale) to offer something for sale. □ *We had to put the farm up for sale because the crops failed once too often.* T *They put up their house for sale.* □ *They are going to sell the house themselves. They put it up last Saturday.*

put the cart before the horse to have things in the wrong order; to have things confused and mixed up. (Refers to an imaginary hitching up of a horse cart in a way that it would move in front of the horse rather than being pulled behind. Also with have.) □ *You're eating your dessert! You've put the cart before the horse.* □ *Slow down and get organized. Don't put the cart before the horse!* □ *John has the cart before the horse in most of his projects.*

put the chill on someone AND **put the freeze on someone** to ignore someone. (Slang.) □ *She was pretty snooty till we all put the chill on her.* □ *Let's put the freeze on Ted until he starts acting better.*

put the freeze on someone See the previous entry.

put the moves on someone to attempt to seduce someone. (Slang. With *any* in the negative.) □ *At least he didn't try to put any moves on me.* □ *If somebody doesn't try to put the moves on her, she thinks she's a failure.*

put the pedal to the metal to press a car's accelerator to the floor. (Slang.) □ *Let's go, man. Put the pedal to the metal.* □ *Put the pedal to the metal, and we're out of here.*

put to it in trouble or difficulty; hard up (for something such as money). (Slang. As if one's back were put to the wall.) □ *Sorry, I can't lend you anything. I'm a bit put to it this month.* □ *What a day. I'm really put to it.*

put two and two together to figure something out from the information available. □ *Well, I put two and two together and came up with an idea of who did it.* □ *Don't worry. John won't figure it out. He can't put two and two together.*

put up a (brave) front to appear to be brave (even if one is not). □ *Mary is frightened, but she's putting up a brave front.* □ *If she weren't putting up a front, I'd be more frightened than I am.*

put words into someone's mouth to speak for another person without permission. □ *Stop putting words into my mouth. I can speak for myself.* □ *The lawyer was scolded for putting words into the witness's mouth.*

Put your money where your mouth is! a command to stop talking big and make a bet. (Not literal.) □ *I'm tired of your bragging about your skillat betting. Put your money where your mouth is!* □ *You always talk about betting, but you don't ever place a bet. Put your money where your mouth is!*

putz around to fiddle around; to mess around. (Slang.) □ *Stop putzing around and get to work.* □ *Those guys spend most of their time just putzing around.*

puzzle something out to figure something out. □ *It took me a while to puzzle it out.* T *I puzzled out the answer to the question.*

Q

quaff a brew to drink a beer. (Slang.)
□ *I went down to the bar to quaff a brew.* □ *Let's go somewhere and quaff a brew.*

quake in one's boots See *shake in one's boots.*

quarrel (with someone) (about someone or something) to have an argument with someone about the subject of someone or something. □ *Please don't quarrel with me about money.* □ *You are always quarreling with Claire.* □ *They are quarreling about Donna.*

quarrel (with someone) (over someone or something) to have an argument with someone about who is going to have someone or something. □ *Todd quarreled with Carl over who was going to get the new secretary.* □ *They are quarreling over Sally.* □ *Don't quarrel over money.*

queue up (for something) to line up for something. (Typically British.) □ *We had to queue up for tickets to the play.* □ *You must queue up.*

quick-and-dirty rapidly and carelessly done. (Slang.) □ *I'm selling this car, so all I want is a quick-and-dirty repair job.* □ *They only do quick-and-dirty work at that shop.*

quick on the draw See the following entry.

quick on the trigger AND **quick on the draw** 1. quick to draw or shoot a gun. □ *Some of the old cowboys were known to be quick on the trigger.* □ *Wyatt Earp was particularly quick on the draw.* 2. quick to respond to anything. □ *John gets the right answer before anyone else. He's really quick on the trigger.* □ *Sally will probably win the quiz game. She's really quick on the draw.*

quick on the uptake quick to understand something. □ *Just because I'm not quick on the uptake, it doesn't mean I'm stupid.* □ *Mary understands jokes before anyone else because she's so quick on the uptake.*

quiet down to become quiet; to become less noisy. □ *Please quiet down.* □ *Ask them to quiet down.*

quiet someone or something down to make someone or some creature more quiet. (*Someone* includes oneself.) □ *Please go and quiet the children down.* Ⓣ *Try to quiet down the children.* □ *He was able to quiet himself down by taking a tranquilizer.*

quit on someone 1. [for something] to quit while someone is using it. □ *This stupid car quit on me.* □ *I hope this thing doesn't quit on me.* 2. to leave one's job, usually unannounced or suddenly. □ *Wally, the mayor, quit* on us at the last minute. □ My boss quit on me. □ I don't know what to do. Both of my waitresses quit on me over the weekend.

R

race with someone or something to enter a contest of speed with someone or something. □ *I refuse to race with Carla. She is much too fast for me.* □ *I can't race with a horse!*

rack one's brain(s) to try very hard to remember or think of something. □ *I racked my brains all afternoon, but couldn't remember where I put the book.* □ *Don't waste any more time racking your brain. Go borrow the book from the library and look it up.*

rack (out) to go to sleep or to bed. (Slang.) □ *What time do you rack out?* □ *I've got to rack out or drop from exhaustion.* □ *If I don't rack by midnight, I'm dead the next day.*

rack something up 1. to accumulate something; to collect or acquire something, particularly a score, a win, etc. □ *The Bears racked their fourth victory up.* T *They hope to rack up a few more points before the end of the game.* □ *We racked a lot of money up in the stock market.* 2. to wreck something. □ *Fred racked his car up.* T *He racked up his arm in the football game.* 3. to place something onto or into its rack. □ *You had better rack the billiard balls up when you finish this time.* T *Please rack up the balls.*

racked (up) alcohol or drug intoxicated. (Slang.) □ *They drank till they were good and racked.* □ *Man, are you*

racked. *What did you drink? A gallon?* □ *They all got racked up last weekend.*

raffle something off to dispose of something through a drawing or raffle. □ *They will raffle a television set off.* T *They are going to raffle off a television set this weekend at the school.*

rag out to dress up. (Slang.) □ *I like to rag out and go to parties.* □ *I hate to rag out. I like comfortable clothes.*

rage through something 1. [for a fire] to burn rapidly through an area or a building. □ *The fire raged through the unoccupied building.* □ *When the fire began to rage through the forest, we knew we had better head for the river.* 2. [for someone] to move rapidly through some sequence or process, as if in a rage. □ *Harry raged through the contract, looking for more errors.* □ *She raged through the book, angry with everything she read.*

railroad someone into something to force someone into doing something in great haste. □ *The committee tried to railroad me into signing the contract.* □ *You can't railroad me into doing anything!*

railroad something through (something) to force something through some organization or legislative body without due consideration. □ *The committee railroaded the new* *constitution through the ratification process.* □ *Mary felt she could railroad the legislation through.*

rain cats and dogs to rain very hard. (Not literal.) □ *It's raining cats and dogs. Look at it pour!* □ *I'm not going out in that storm. It's raining cats and dogs.*

rain down on someone or something to fall or drop down on someone or something like rain. □ *The ashes from the incinerator rained down on us, getting our clothes dirty.* □ *The hail rained down on us— some of it quite large.*

rain in on someone or something [for rain] to enter a window or other opening and get someone or something wet. □ *Carol left the window open, and it rained in on her in the night.* □ *The storm rained in on my carpet!*

rain on someone or something See the following entry.

rain on someone's parade AND **rain on someone or something** to spoil something for someone or something. (Slang.) □ *I hate to rain on your parade, but your plans are all wrong.* □ *She really rained on our parade.* □ *Did anyone rain on the meeting?*

rain or shine no matter whether it rains or the sun shines. □ *Don't worry. I'll be there rain or shine.* □ *We'll hold the picnic — rain or shine.*

rain something down (on someone or something) to pour something, such as criticism or praise, onto someone or something. □ *The employees rained criticism down on the*

manager for the new policy on sick leave. ⊤ *The audience rained down compliments on the performers.*

rain something out [for rain] to force the cancellation of an outdoor event. □ *It looked as if the storm would rain the picnic out, but it blew over before causing any trouble.* ⊤ *The storm rained out the game.*

raise one's sights to set higher goals for oneself. □ *When you're young, you tend to raise your sights too high.* □ *On the other hand, some people need to raise their sights.*

raise some eyebrows to shock or surprise people mildly (by doing or saying something). (*Some* can be replaced with *a few, someone's, a lot of*, etc.) □ *What you just said may raise some eyebrows, but it shouldn't make anyone really angry.* □ *John's sudden marriage to Ann raised a few eyebrows.*

raise someone or something up to lift someone or something up; to lift oneself up. (*Someone* includes *oneself.*) □ *The aides raised the dying man up while the nurse spread clean linen beneath him.* ⊤ *Jane raised up the lid.* □ *He raised himself up with the greatest of difficulty.*

raise up to get up or begin to get up. □ *She raised up and then fell back onto her bed.* □ *I could not raise up enough to see out the window.*

rake someone over the coals AND **haul someone over the coals** to give someone a severe scolding. □ *My mother hauled me over the coals for coming in late last night.* □ *The manager raked me over the coals for being late again.*

rake something in to take in a lot of something, usually money. (Slang.) □ *Our candidate will rake votes in by the thousand.* ⊤ *They were raking in money by the bushel.*

rake something off ((of) something) to remove something from something by raking. (The *of* is colloquial.) □ *Please rake the leaves off the lawn.* ⊤ *Rake off the leaves.* □ *Please rake them off.*

rake something out to clean something by raking. □ *Please rake the gutter out.* ⊤ *You ought to rake out the flower beds. They are a mess.*

rake something out (of something) to clean something out of something by raking. □ *You ought to rake the leaves out of the gutter so the water will flow.* ⊤ *Please rake out the leaves.*

rake something up 1. to gather and clean up something with a rake. □ *Would you please rake these leaves up before it rains?* ⊤ *Please rake up the leaves.* **2.** to clean something up by raking. □ *Would you rake the yard up?* ⊤ *I will rake up the yard.* **3.** to find some unpleasant information. □ *His opposition raked an old scandal up and made it public.* ⊤ *That is ancient history. Why did you have to rake up that old story?*

rally around someone or something to unite or assemble in support of someone or something. □ *All the other workers rallied around Fred in his fight with management.* □ *They rallied around the principle that Fred stood for.*

ralph something up to vomit (something). (Teen and collegiate slang.) □ *The doctor gave him some stuff that made him ralph it up.* ⊤ *He ralphed up his dinner.*

ram something through (something) 1. to force something through something. □ *He rammed his fist through the window, cutting himself in the process.* □ *Harry put the brick up to the window glass and rammed it through. Next time he would remember his key.* ⊤ *The brick rammed through the glass.* **2.** to force something through a deliberative body, usually not allowing due consideration. □ *They rammed the bill through the city council.* □ *The President was unable to ram the measure through Congress.* ⊤ *They rammed through the bill.*

ram through something to crash or pound through something. □ *The car rammed through the back of the garage.* □ *I was afraid that the truck would ram through the fence.*

ramble on to go on and on aimlessly; to wander about aimlessly. (Usually figurative. As with a road, a speaker, a speech, etc. More at *ramble on (about someone or something)*.) □ *The road rambled on through mile after mile of wilderness.* □ *The speaker rambled on for almost an hour without really saying anything.*

ramble on (about someone or something) [for someone] to talk endlessly and aimlessly about someone or something. (More at *ramble on*.) □ *I wish you wouldn't ramble on about your first husband all the time.* □ *Must you ramble on so?*

range from something to something to vary from one thing to another. □ *The weather ranges from bad to terrible in this part of the north.* □ *The appraisals of the property ranged from high to low.*

rank someone (out) to annoy or chastise someone. (Slang.) □ *He* *really ranks me out. What a pest!* ⊤ *I ranked out the whole gang, but good!*

rap something out (on something) to tap out the rhythm of something on something. □ *Try to rap the rhythm out on the table.* ⊤ *He rapped out the rhythm on the table.* □ *Rap it out and hum the song as you do.*

rat around to waste time loafing around; to loiter. (Collegiate slang.) □ *I didn't do anything but rat around all summer.* □ *If kids don't have jobs, they just rat around.*

rat (on someone) to inform (on someone). (Slang.) □ *Bill said he was going to rat on that punk.* □ *If you rat on me, I'll get you!* □ *Who ratted?*

rat out to quit (on someone or something). (Slang.) □ *It's too late to rat out.* □ *He tried to rat out at the last minute.*

rattle around in something 1. to make a rattling noise inside something. □ *What is rattling around in this package?* □ *There is something rattling around in my glove compartment.* 2. to ride about in a rattly vehicle. □ *I am perfectly happy to rattle around in my ten-year-old car.* □ *Todd rattles around in his grandfather's old car.* 3. to live in a place that is much too big. (Figurative.) □ *We have been rattling around in this big old house for long enough. Let's move to a smaller place.* □ *I can't afford to rattle around in a three-story house any longer.*

rattle something off to recite something with ease; to recite a list quickly and easily. □ *He rattled the long list of names off without even taking a breath.* ⊤ *He rattled off the long list of names without even taking a breath.*

reach back (in)to something to extend back into a particular period in time. □ *This policy reaches back into the last century.* □ *Our way of making fine candies reaches back to the recipes used by the founder of the company.*

reach down to extend downward. (See also *reach something down*.) □ *The stems of the plant reached down almost to the floor.* □ *The drapes don't quite reach down to the floor.*

reach first base (with someone or something) See *get to first base (with someone or something)*.

reach in(to something) to stick one's hand into something in order to grasp something. □ *Bob reached into the cookie jar and found it empty.* □ *Bob went to the cookie jar and reached in.*

reach out 1. to extend one's grasp outward. □ *He reached out, but there was no one to take hold of.* □ *I reached out and grabbed onto the first thing I could get hold of.* 2. to enlarge one's circle of friends and experiences. □ *If you are that lonely, you ought to reach out. Get to know some new friends.* □ *I need to reach out more and meet people.*

reach out (after someone or something) to extend one's grasp to someone or something. □ *Don reached out after Doris, but she slipped away before he could get a good hold on her.* □ *Doris reached out after the door, but it slammed closed.* □ *As she reached out, the door closed.*

reach out into something to extend one's grasp out into something, such as the darkness. □ *Laura reached out into the darkness, looking for the light switch.* □ *Jane reached out into the* night, hoping to find a lamp or even a candle.

reach out to someone 1. to offer someone a helping hand. □ *You reached out to me just when I needed help the most.* □ *I reach out to other people in trouble because I would want someone to do that for me.* **2.** to seek someone's help and support. □ *When I reached out to Don for help, he turned me down.* □ *Jane reached out to her friends for the help and support that she needed.*

reach something down to hand something down. (Colloquial. See also *reach down.*) □ *Please reach the hammer down to me.* ⊤ *Would you reach down the hammer to Jane?*

read between the lines to infer something (from something); to try to understand what is meant by something that is not written clearly or openly. (Usually figurative. Does not necessarily refer to written or printed information.) □ *After listening to what she said, if you read between the lines, you can begin to see what she really means.* □ *Don't believe everything you hear. Learn to read between the lines.*

read someone like a book to understand someone very well. □ *I've got John figured out. I can read him like a book.* □ *Of course I understand you. I read you like a book.*

read someone out (for something) to chastise someone verbally for doing something wrong. □ *The coach read the player out for making a silly error.* □ *She really read the players out.* ⊤ *The coach read out the whole team.*

read someone out of something to make a case for the removal of some-one from something. □ *The chairman read the absent members out of the organization.* □ *Dave was read out of the club.*

read someone the riot act to give someone a severe scolding. □ *The manager read me the riot act for coming in late.* □ *The teacher read the students the riot act for their failure to do their assignments.*

read something back (to someone) to read back some information to the person who has just given it. □ *Yes, I have written the telephone number down. Let me read it back to you to make sure I have it right.* ⊤ *Please read back the letter to me.* □ *Did you copy the number correctly? Please read it back.*

read something in((to) something) to presume inferences as one reads something; to imagine that additional messages, ideas, or biases are present in something that one is reading. □ *Just accept the words for what they mean. Don't read something else into it.* □ *Don't read anything in.*

read something off to read aloud a list. □ *Nick read the list of the names off, and I wasn't on the list.* ⊤ *Jane read off the names.*

read something over to read something, concentrating on form as well as content. □ *Please read this over and report back to me when you are finished.* ⊤ *I will read over the report and talk to you later.*

read through something to look through some reading material. □ *I read through your proposal and find that it has merits.* □ *Please read through this at your convenience.*

read up (on someone or something) to study about someone or something by reading. □ *I have to read up on Milton Berle for a report I have to write.* □ *I can't write a word about him until I read up.*

Really. 1. I agree with what you just said. □ RACHEL: *This cake is just too dry.* MARY: *Really. I guess it's getting stale.* □ HENRY: *Taxes are just too high.* MARY: *Really. It's out of hand.* **2.** Do you really mean what you just said? (Usually **Really?**) □ HENRY: *I'm going to join the army.* MARY: *Really?* HENRY: *Yes, I'm really going to do it.* □ SALLY: *This will cost over two hundred dollars.* RACHEL: *Really? I paid half that the last time.* **3.** I can't believe what has just been said or done.; I'm shocked. (Usually **Really!**) □ FRED: *Then I punched him in the nose.* HENRY: *Really!* FRED: *Well, I had too.* HENRY: *Really!* □ *"Really!" cried Sally, seeing the jogger knock down the elderly lady.*

ream someone out to scold someone severely. (Slang.) □ *The teacher really reamed him out.* T *The coach reamed out the whole team.*

rear back 1. [for a horse] to pull back onto its hind legs in an effort to move backwards rapidly. □ *The animal reared back in terror.* □ *The horse reared back and almost threw its rider.* **2.** [for a person] to pull back and stand up or sit up straighter. □ *He reared back in his chair and looked perturbed.* □ *Tom reared back in his chair, waiting for something else to happen.*

rear up 1. [for a horse] to lean back on its hind legs and raise its front part up, assuming a threatening pos-

ture or avoiding something on the ground, such as a snake. □ *The horse reared up suddenly, throwing the rider onto the ground.* □ *When the horse reared up, I almost fell off.* **2.** [for something, especially a problem] to arise suddenly. (Figurative.) □ *A new problem reared up and cost us a lot of time.* □ *A lot of new costs reared up toward the end of the month.*

reason something out to figure something out; to plan a reasonable course of action. □ *Now let's be calm and try to reason this out.* T *Let us reason out our difficulties.*

record something on something to make a record of something on the surface of something. □ *Nancy recorded the appointment on the calendar that served as a blotter on the top of her desk.* □ *Please record this on your calendar.*

recount something to someone to tell something to someone; to narrate a series of events, in order. □ *Carl recounted the events of the day to his wife.* □ *The strange events were recounted by a number of people.*

recruit someone into something to seek out and induct someone into something. □ *The colonel tried to recruit ten people a week into the army.* □ *The army recruited almost no one during the month of December.*

recuperate from something to recover from something; to be cured or to heal after something. □ *I hope that you recuperate from your illness soon.* □ *Has she recuperated from her surgery yet?*

reel something in to bring in something, such as a fish, by winding up the line on a reel. □ *With great effort,* *she reeled the huge fish in.* T *Hurry and reel in the fish!*

reel something off to recite a list or sequence of words, rapidly, from memory. □ *Jane reeled her speech off flawlessly.* T *Tony reeled off his speech as fast as he could.*

reel under something 1. to stagger under the weight of something. □ *Tony reeled under the weight of the books.* □ *She knew she would reel under the heavy load.* **2.** to stagger because of a blow. □ *The boxer reeled under the blow to his chin.* □ *Max reeled under the beating that Lefty gave him.* **3.** to suffer because of a burden. (Figurative.) □ *Gary reeled under the responsibilities he had been given.* □ *I was just reeling under the burdens of my new job.*

refer someone back to someone or something to suggest that someone go back to someone or something, such as the source. □ *I referred the client back to the lawyer she had originally consulted.* □ *Tom referred the customer back to the manufacturer who had made the shoddy product.*

refer someone to someone or something to direct someone to someone or something; to send someone to someone or something. □ *The front office referred me to you, and you are now referring me to someone else!* □ *They should have referred you to the personnel department.*

refer something back (to someone or something) to send something back to someone or a group for action. □ *The senate referred the bill back to committee.* □ *John had not seen it, so I referred it back to him.* T *They referred back all the bills.*

refrain from something to hold back from doing something; to choose not to do something as planned. □ *I wish you would refrain from shouting.* □ *Please refrain from hollering.*

regain something from someone or something to take back possession of one's property or right from someone or something. □ *I intend to regain my money from Herb.* □ *The used car agency regained the car from the delinquent buyer.*

rely (up)on someone or something to depend on someone or something; to trust in someone or something. (*Upon* is formal and less commonly used than *on.*) □ *I know I can rely upon you to do a good job.* □ *Can we rely on this old car to get us there?*

remain up to stay awake and out of bed. □ *I remained up throughout most of the night.* □ *I cannot remain up much longer.*

remain within (something) to stay inside something or some place. □ *Please try to remain within the boundaries of the campus.* □ *Everyone else went out, but I decided to remain within.*

remark (up)on someone or something to comment on someone or something. (*Upon* is formal and less commonly used than *on.*) □ *She remarked upon his tardiness and then continued the lesson.* □ *There is no need to remark on me or anything I do or don't do.*

Remember me to someone. Please carry my good wishes to someone. (The *someone* can be a person's name or a pronoun.) □ TOM: *My brother says hello.* BILL: *Oh, how nice. Please remember me to him.* TOM: *I will.* □

FRED: *Bye.* JOHN: *Good-bye, Fred. Remember me to your Uncle Tom.*

Remember to write. AND **Don't forget to write.** **1.** a final parting comment made to remind someone going on a journey to write to those remaining at home. □ ALICE: *Bye.* MARY: *Good-bye, Alice. Remember to write.* ALICE: *I will. Bye.* □ SALLY: *Remember to write!* FRED: *I will!* SALLY: *I miss you already!* **2.** a parting comment made to someone in place of a regular good-bye. (Jocular.) □ JOHN: *See you tomorrow. Bye.* JANE: *See you. Remember to write.* □ JOHN: *Okay. See you after lunch.* JANE: *Yeah. Bye. Remember to write.*

Remember your manners. **1.** a parting instruction, usually to a child, encouraging proper behavior. □ *As Jimmy was going out the door, his mother said, "Have a good time and remember your manners."* □ JOHN: *It's time for me to go to the party, Mom.* MOTHER: *Yes, it is. Remember your manners. Good-bye.* **2.** AND **Mind your manners.** a comment intended to remind someone of proper behavior, such as saying *thank you* or *excuse me.* □ *After Mary gave a cookie to little Bobby, Bobby's mother said to him, "Remember your manners."* □ BOB: *Here, Jane. Have one of these.* JANE (*taking one*): *Wow!* BOB: *Okay. Have another.* MOTHER: *What do you say? Remember your manners.* JANE: *Thanks a lot!*

rend something from someone or something to tear something from someone or something. □ *Harry rent the burning clothing from the man who had just fled from the burning building.* □ *God rent the veil from the temple.*

report back (on someone or something) to return with information or an explanation about someone or something. □ *I need you to report back on Walter by noon.* □ *I'll report back as soon as I can.*

report back (to someone or something) **1.** to go back to someone or something and present oneself. □ *Report back to me at once!* □ *I'll report back immediately.* **2.** to present information or an explanation to someone or some group. □ *Please report back to me when you have the proper information.* □ *I'll report back as soon as I have all the information.*

report for something to present oneself for something. □ *Please report for duty on Monday morning at eight o'clock sharp.* □ *I can't report for my examination at the time we agreed upon.*

rest up (for something) to take it easy in advance of something tiring. □ *Excuse me, but I have to go rest up for the concert tonight.* □ *I really need to rest up awhile.*

rest up (from something) to recover or recuperate from something tiring. □ *I need about a week to rest up from my vacation.* □ *I'll need a few days to rest up.*

rest (up)on something to lie on something; to take it easy on something. (*Upon* is formal and less commonly used than *on.*) □ *Here, rest upon this mat.* □ *I'll just rest on this chair, thanks.* □ *She rested upon the couch for a while and then went out to weed the garden.*

retaliate against someone or something to take revenge against someone or something. □ *The* *administration will retaliate against the students by closing down the cafeteria.* □ *The students retaliated against the administration.*

retire from something to withdraw from something. (Usually to terminate a working career permanently.) □ *I retired from the company early.* □ *When do you intend to retire from your job?*

retire someone or something from something to take someone or something out of service permanently. □ *The company retired the vice president from the job and gave it to someone else.* □ *It is time to retire my automobile from service.*

rev something up to race an engine in one or more short bursts. (More at *rev up.*) □ *George revved the engine up and took off.* ⊤ *He revved up the engine.*

rev up to increase in amount or activity. (More at *rev something up.*) □ *Production revved up after the strike.* □ *We're hoping business will rev up soon.*

revenge oneself (up)on someone or something to retaliate against someone or something. (*Upon* is formal and less commonly used than *on.*) □ *There is no need for you to revenge yourself upon Walter. It was an accident.* □ *I will revenge myself on the whole world!* □ *She did not know how she would revenge herself on Joe, but she knew she would.*

reverberate through something [for sound] to roll or pass through a space. □ *The thunder reverberated through the valley.* □ *The sound of the organ reverberated through the church.*

reverberate with something to echo or resound with something. □ *The hall reverberated with the rich basso voice of Walter Rogers.* □ *The church reverberated with the roar of the pipe organ.*

ricochet off something [for some rapidly moving object, such as a bullet] to bounce off something at an oblique angle. □ *The bullet ricocheted off the wall and struck the gunman.* □ *Bullets were ricocheting off the walls from all angles.*

ride away to depart, riding a bike or a horse or similar animal. □ *She got on her horse and rode away.* □ *They rode away without even saying good-bye.*

ride off to depart, riding something such as a horse or a bicycle. □ *Betty said good-bye and rode off.* □ *We rode off, each one in a different direction.*

ride on to continue to ride, traveling onward. □ *We rode on for at least an hour before finding a rest stop.* □ *They rode on for a while.*

ride roughshod over someone or something to treat someone or something with disdain or scorn. □ *Tom seems to ride roughshod over his friends.* □ *You shouldn't have come into our town to ride roughshod over our laws and our traditions.*

ride shotgun to accompany and guard someone or something. (Slang. A term from the days of stagecoaches and their armed guards.) □ *I have to take the beer over to the party. Why don't you come along and ride shotgun?* □ *Who's going to ride shotgun with Bill?*

ride someone or something down 1. to chase down someone or some creature while riding on horseback.

□ *The mounted policeman rode the mugger down and captured him.* T *The rider rode down the thief.* T *We had to ride down the runaway horse.* **2.** [with *something*] to ride on something that is going down, such as an elevator. □ *You take the stairs, and I will ride the elevator down.* □ *I don't want to ride the cable car down. I will walk.*

ride something out to endure something; to remain with something until its termination. □ *Things are rough in my department at the office, but I think I can ride it out.* T *I can ride out the storm if I can remember to be patient.*

ride the gravy train to live in luxury. □ *If I had a million dollars, I sure could ride the gravy train.* □ *I wouldn't like loafing. I don't want to ride the gravy train.*

ride up (on someone) 1. [for someone on a horse] to approach someone, riding. □ *I rode up on him and frightened him.* □ *I guess I was in the house when you rode up.* **2.** [for clothing, especially underpants] to keep moving higher on one's body. □ *I don't like it when my pants ride up on me.* □ *I hate it when my underpants ride up.*

ride (up)on someone or something to use someone or something as a beast of burden. (*Upon* is formal and less commonly used than *on*.) □ *As a game, the children used to ride on their father.* □ *We rode upon burros along the narrow mountain trails.*

riding for a fall risking failure or an accident, usually due to overconfidence. □ *Tom drives too fast, and he seems too sure of himself. He's riding*

for a fall. □ *Bill needs to eat better and get more sleep. He's riding for a fall.*

rifle through something to ransack something; to search through something looking for something to steal. □ *The teenager quickly rifled through the cabinets, looking for something worth eating.* □ *The soldiers rifled through every house they could break into.*

rig someone or something out (in something) to outfit someone or something in something; to decorate or dress someone or something in something. (*Someone* includes oneself.) □ *Joan rigged her daughter out in a witch's costume for the Halloween party.* T *He rigged out his car with lights for the parade.* □ *Alice rigged her bicycle out in festive colors.* □ *She rigged herself out in a clown suit and joined the circus for a day.*

rig something up to prepare something, perhaps on short notice or without the proper materials. □ *We don't have what's needed to make the kind of circuit you have described, but I think we can rig something up anyway.* T *We will rig up whatever you need.*

Right. Correct.; What you said is right. □ JANE: *It's really hot today.* JOHN: *Right.* JANE: *Keeping cool?* JOHN: *No way.* □ SALLY: *Let's go over to Fred's room and cheer him up.* SUE: *Right.*

Right away. AND **Right now.** Immediately. □ JOHN: *Take this over to Sue.* BILL: *Right away.* □ JOHN: *How soon can you do this?* SUE: *Right away.*

Right now. See the previous entry.

right off the bat immediately; first thing. (Seems to refer to a ball leaving the baseball bat, but probably referred to a cricket bat originally.) □ *When he was learning to ride a bicycle, he fell on his head right off the bat.* □ *The new manager demanded new office furniture right off the bat.*

(right) off the top of one's head without giving it too much thought or without the necessary knowledge. □ MARY: *How much do you think this car would be worth on a trade?* FRED: *Well, right off the top of my head, I'd say about a thousand.* □ TOM: *What time does the morning train come in?* BILL: *Off the top of my head, I don't know.*

Righto. Yes.; I will comply. □ FRED: *Can you handle this project for me today?* SUE: *Righto.* □ JOHN: *Is that you, Tom?* TOM: *Righto. What do you want?*

ring in the New Year to celebrate the beginning of the New Year at midnight on December 31st. (As if ringing church bells to celebrate the New Year.) □ *We are planning a big party to ring in the New Year.* □ *How did you ring in the New Year?*

ring someone back to call someone back on the telephone. □ *I will have to ring you back later.* □ *Please ring me back when you have a moment.* T *I will ring back the caller when I have time.*

ring someone up to call someone on the telephone. (Chiefly British.) □ *I will ring her up when I get a chance.* T *I have to ring up a whole list of people.*

ring something up (on something) to record the amount of a sale on a cash register. □ *Jane rang the purchases up one by one on the cash register.* T *She rang up the purchases on the*

register *as quick as lightning.* □ *She rang them up and collected the money.*

rinse someone or something down to wash or clean someone or something with water or other fluid. □ *I rinsed him down for an hour and still didn't get the smell of skunk off him.* T *I had to rinse down the driveway.*

rinse someone or something off to wash or clean someone or something by flushing with water or other fluid. (*Someone* includes *oneself.*) □ *Mother rinsed the baby off and dried him with a soft towel.* T *She rinsed off the baby.* □ *Coming out of the sea, she rinsed herself off with fresh water.*

rinse something out 1. to clean cloth or clothing partially by immersing it in water and squeezing it out. □ *Can you please rinse this rag out? It's all dirty.* T *Please rinse out your clothes to make sure there is no soap left in them.* 2. to launder something delicate, such as feminine underwear, using a mild soap. □ *I have to go rinse a few things out.* T *After I rinse out some things, I will be right with you.* 3. to clean the inside of a container partially by flushing it out with water. □ *Rinse the bottle out and throw it away.* T *Rinse out the bottle and throw it away.*

rinse something out (of something) to remove something from something by flushing it with water. □ *See if you can rinse the dirt out of this jacket.* T *I can't rinse out the dirt.* □ *Then I'll rinse it out.*

rip into someone or something 1. to attack someone or something. □ *The raccoons ripped into the trash bags, scattering papers and stuff all over the street.* □ *The horrid murderer ripped* *into the helpless victim.* **2.** to criticize or censure someone or something severely. □ *The drama critic ripped into Larry.* □ *The critics really ripped into Larry's poor performance.*

rip off [for something] to tear or peel off. □ *My pocket ripped off and my money is gone now!* □ *A piece of the bumper ripped off my car.*

rip on someone to give someone a hard time; to annoy someone. (Slang.) □ *Fred was ripping on me, and I heard about it.* □ *Stop ripping on my friend!*

rip someone or something off **1.** [with *someone*] to assault, kill, beat, rob, rape, or cheat someone. (Slang. Note the *for* in the example.) □ *They ripped me off, but they didn't hurt me.* □ *Man, they ripped me off for three hundred dollars.* **2.** [with *something*] to steal something. □ *They ripped them all off.* T *The crooks ripped off the hubcaps of my car.*

rip someone or something up **1.** to tear someone or something into bits; to mutilate someone or something. (*Someone* includes *oneself*.) □ *Careful! That machine will rip you up if you fall in.* T *I ripped up the contract and threw the pieces in the air.* □ *The dog fell into the lawn mower and ripped itself up badly.* **2.** [with *something*] to take something up by force and remove it. (Usually refers to something on the floor or ground, such as carpeting or pavement.) □ *They are going to rip all the broken sidewalk up.* T *The workers ripped up the pavement and loaded the pieces into a truck.*

rip something down to tear something down. (Refers to something that has been posted or mounted.)

□ *The custodian ripped all the posters down at the end of the day.* T *He ripped down the posters.*

rip something off ((of) someone or something) to tear something away from someone or something. (The *of* is colloquial.) □ *I ripped the cover off of the book accidentally.* T *I ripped off the book cover.* □ *He ripped the shirt off the injured man and began to treat the wound.* □ *Alice ripped the cover off.*

rip something out (of someone or something) to tear something out of someone or something. □ *The high priest ripped the beating heart out of the sacrificial victim.* T *He ripped out the heart and kicked the victim down the steep side of the pyramid.*

rise up **1.** to come up; to ascend. □ *The water is rising up fast. You had better get to higher ground.* □ *As the water rose up, it covered the houses and streets.* **2.** to get up from lying down. □ *The deer rose up and darted off into the woods.* □ *I rose up and brushed my clothing.*

rise (up) against someone or something to challenge someone or something; to rebel against someone or something. □ *The citizens rose up against their elected officials.* □ *They rose against the abusive power of the government.*

risk one's neck (to do something) to risk physical harm in order to accomplish something. □ *Look at that traffic! I refuse to risk my neck just to cross the street to buy a paper.* □ *I refuse to risk my neck at all.*

rivet something on(to) something to attach something to something with rivets. □ *The pockets of these jeans* *are riveted onto the body of the pants.* ⊤ *You should rivet on this part of the frame to the wall.* □ *Okay. I'll rivet it on the wall.*

roar something out to bellow something out loudly. □ *Walter roared his protest out so everyone knew how he felt.* ⊤ *Jane roared out her criticism.*

rob Peter to pay Paul to take from one in order to give to another. □ *Why borrow money to pay your bills? That's just robbing Peter to pay Paul.* □ *There's no point in robbing Peter to pay Paul. You will still be in debt.*

rob the cradle to marry or date someone who is much younger than you are. (As if one were consorting with an infant.) □ *I hear that Bill is dating Ann. Isn't that sort of robbing the cradle? She's much younger than he is.* □ *Uncle Bill — who is nearly eighty — married a thirty-year-old woman. That is really robbing the cradle.*

rock the boat to cause trouble where none is welcome; to disturb a situation that is otherwise stable and satisfactory. (Often negative.) □ *Look, Tom, everything is going fine here. Don't rock the boat!* □ *You can depend on Tom to mess things up by rocking the boat.*

Roger (wilco). Yes. (From aircraft radio communication. *Wilco* means "will comply.") □ JOHN: *Can you do this right now?* BOB: *Roger.* □ MARY: *I want you to take this over to the mayor's office.* BILL: *Roger wilco.*

roll about to move about, turning or rotating, as a wheel or a ball. □ *The ball rolled about awhile and then came to rest.* □ *His eyes rolled about in amazement before he spoke.*

roll away to move away, rotating, turning over, turning, or moving on wheels. □ *The ball rolled away and fell down a storm sewer.* □ *The cart rolled away, and we had to chase it down the hill.*

roll back [for something] to return, rotating, turning, or moving on wheels. □ *I rolled the ball away, thinking it would roll back. It didn't.* □ *I struck the golf ball away from the sand trap, but it rolled back.*

roll by 1. to pass by, rotating, as a wheel or a ball; to move past, rolling on wheels. □ *The wheel of a car rolled by, all by itself. It must have come off a car somewhere down the road.* □ *The traffic rolled by relentlessly.* 2. to move past, as if rolling. □ *The years rolled by, and soon the two people were old and gray.* □ *The clouds were rolling by, spreading patterns of light and dark across the land.*

roll down to move downward, rotating, as a wheel or a ball; to move downward on wheels. □ *I pushed the wagon up the driveway, and it rolled down again.* □ *Don't place the cart at the top of the hill. It will roll down.*

roll down (something) to move downward, rotating, as a wheel or a ball; to move downward on wheels. □ *The ball rolled down the hall to the end.* □ *The cart went rolling down the hill all by itself.*

roll off (someone or something) to flow or fall off someone or something. (Both literal and figurative.) □ *The ball rolled off the shelf and bounced across the room.* □ *The ball rolled off and made a hole in the* *lampshade.* □ *The insults rolled off Walter like water off a duck's back.*

roll on 1. [for something] to continue rolling. □ *The ball rolled on and on.* □ *The cart came rolling down the hill and rolled on for a few yards at the bottom.* **2.** [for something] to be applied by rolling. □ *This kind of deodorant just rolls on.* □ *She rolled on too much paint and it dripped from the ceiling.* **3.** to move on slowly and evenly. (Figurative.) □ *The years rolled on, one by one.* □ *As the hours rolled on, I learned just how bored I could get without going to sleep.*

roll out the red carpet for someone to provide special treatment for someone. □ *There's no need to roll out the red carpet for me.* □ *We rolled out the red carpet for the king and queen.*

roll over to turn over; to rotate once. □ *The old man rolled over and started snoring again.* □ *Please roll over and give me some more space in the bed.*

roll something away to cause something to move away, rotating, turning over, turning, or moving on wheels. □ *Jane rolled the ball away and it was lost.* T *Jane rolled away the ball.* □ *Please roll the cart away.*

roll something back 1. to return something to someone by rotating it, as with a wheel or a ball, or moving it back on wheels. □ *I intercepted the ball and rolled it back.* T *Jane rolled back the ball.* **2.** to reduce prices. □ *The store rolled all its prices back for the sale.* T *The protesters demanded that they roll back their prices.*

roll something down 1. to move something down, making it rotate like a wheel or a ball, or moving it on

wheels. □ *Don't carry the ball down; roll it down!* T *I rolled down the ball as you asked.* **2.** to crank down something, such as a car window. □ *Please roll the window down and get some air in this car.* T *Please roll down the car window.*

roll something off ((of) someone or something) to cause something to roll away, off someone or something. (The *of* is colloquial.) □ *The other workers quickly rolled the wheel off of the injured man.* T *Please roll off the wheel quickly!* □ *We had to roll the heavy stone off the neighbor's lawn.*

roll something on(to something) to apply something or a coat of a substance by rolling something saturated with the substance on the thing to be coated. □ *You should roll another coat of paint onto this wall over here.* T *Roll on another coat.* □ *Okay, I'll roll it on.*

roll something out 1. to bring or take something out by rolling it; to push something out on wheels. □ *Jane rolled her bike out to show it off.* T *Alice rolled out her bicycle for us to see.* **2.** to flatten something by rolling it. □ *You should roll the pastry out first.* T *They rolled out the steel in a huge mill.*

roll something up to coil or rotate something into a coil or roll of something. □ *I rolled the poster up and put it back in its mailing tube.* T *I have to roll up this paper.*

Rome wasn't built in a day. Important things don't happen overnight. (Proverb.) □ *Don't expect a lot to happen right away. Rome wasn't built in a day, you know.* □ *Don't be anxious about how fast you are growing. Rome wasn't built in a day.*

romp through something to run through something fast and playfully. □ *The conductor romped through the slow movement of the symphony as if it were a march.* □ *The cast romped through the last act, knowing that the play would be closed that very night.*

room together [for two or more people] to share a room, as in a college dormitory. □ *Sarah and I roomed together in college.* □ *We don't want to room together anymore.*

root around (for something) to dig or shuffle in or through something, looking for something. □ *Alice rooted around in her desk drawer for a pen.* □ *I'll root around here and see if I can find it.* □ *The pigs rooted around, looking for something to eat.* □ *I opened the drawer and began to root around to see if I could find a screwdriver.*

root someone or something out (of something) to seek and remove someone or something from something or some place; to seek to discover and bring someone or something to light. □ *The committee wanted to root all the lazy people out of the club.* Ⓣ *The manager rooted out all the deadwood.* Ⓣ *We rooted out all the problem files and gave them to Walter to fix.*

root something up [for a pig] to find something in the ground by digging with its nose. □ *The pigs will root your plants up if they get out of their pen.* Ⓣ *The pigs will root up your plants if they get out of their pen.*

rope someone in(to something) to persuade or trick someone into doing something. □ *You can't rope me into doing it. I'm wise to your tricks.* Ⓣ *The*

con artists roped in the unsuspecting tourist. □ *They tried to rope me in.*

rope someone or something up to tie someone or some creature up with a rope. □ *Rope this guy up tight so he won't get away.* Ⓣ *The sheriff roped up the bandit.* Ⓣ *The cowboy roped up the calf in a few seconds.*

rope something off to isolate something with a rope barrier. □ *The police roped the scene of the accident off.* Ⓣ *The police roped off the scene of the accident.*

rot off to decompose and fall off. □ *If you don't clean your smelly feet, they'll rot off!* □ *A few old branches finally rotted off, but the ancient tree looked as if it would survive the wet spell.*

rot out to decompose. □ *If you don't brush your teeth, they'll rot out!* □ *Some of the rafters in the shed rotted out, but we replaced them easily.*

rough someone up to treat someone roughly. □ *Max wanted to rough Lefty up a bit, but the boss said no.* Ⓣ *Lefty roughed up Max.*

rough something in to construct or draw something initially, temporarily, or crudely. □ *The carpenter roughed the doorways in without consulting the plans.* Ⓣ *The carpenter roughed in the doorways without consulting the plans.*

rough something out to make a rough sketch of something. □ *I will rough it out and have one of the staff artists attend to the details.* Ⓣ *Jane roughed out a picture of the proposed building.*

rough something up to scrape or rub something in a way that makes it rough. □ *All you have to do is rough the ground up, sow the seeds, and then* water them. T *Rough up the surface a little before you paint it.*

round down to something to discard a fractional part of a number. (More at *round something down.*) □ *You should round down to whole numbers.* □ *Round down to the next number if the fraction is less than half.*

round someone or something up to locate and gather someone or something. □ *Please round the suspects up for questioning.* T *The police rounded up the usual suspects.* □ *They failed to round Max and Lefty up, however.* T *The cowboys rounded up all the cattle for market.* □ *It takes many reporters to round the news up for television.*

round something down to reduce a fractional part of a number to the next lowest whole number. (More at *round down to something.*) □ *You can round this figure down if you want. It won't affect the total all that much.* T *Please round down all figures having fractions less than one-half.*

round something off to change a fractional part of a number to the closest whole number. □ *Please round all your figures off* T *Round off everything.*

round something off (with something) to finish something with something; to complement something with something. □ *We rounded the meal off with a sinful dessert.* T *We rounded off the meal with coffee.*

round something out to complete or enhance something. □ *We will round the evening out with dessert at a nice restaurant.* T *They rounded out the meal with dessert.* T *That's a fine way to round out a meal.*

rub (away) at something to chafe or scrape something, repeatedly. □ *The side of his shoe rubbed away at the side of his desk until the paint wore off.* □ *Don't rub at your sore. It will get worse.*

rub elbows with someone AND **rub shoulders with someone** to associate with someone; to work closely with someone. □ *I don't care to rub elbows with someone who acts like that!* □ *I rub shoulders with John at work. We are good friends.*

rub off ((of) something) [for something] to become detached from something because of incidental rubbing or scraping. (The *of* is colloquial.) □ *The label rubbed off this can. What do you think it is?* □ *I can't tell what it is. The label rubbed off.*

rub off on(to) someone or something 1. [for something, such as a coating] to become transferred to someone or something through the contact of rubbing. □ *Look what rubbed off on me!* □ *The wet paint rubbed off onto my pants leg.* **2.** [for a trait] to transfer from one person to another. □ *I hope that your good humor rubs off on our children.* □ *I wish it would rub off on Mary.*

rub shoulders with someone See *rub elbows with someone.*

rub someone or something down to stroke or smooth someone or some creature, for muscular well-being. □ *Sam rubbed his horse down after his ride.* T *He rubbed down his horse.* □ *The trainer rubbed Sam down.*

rub someone the wrong way See the following entry.

rub someone's fur the wrong way AND **rub someone the wrong way**

339

to irritate someone. (As if one were stroking an animal's fur, such as that of a pet cat, in the wrong direction, thus irritating the animal. The second entry form is derived from the first.) □ *I'm sorry I rubbed your fur the wrong way. I didn't mean to upset you.* □ *Don't rub her the wrong way!*

rub something away to remove something by chafing or rubbing. □ *See if you can rub some of the dirt away.* T *Rub away the dirt if you can.*

rub something in(to something) to cause something to penetrate a surface by rubbing it against the surface. □ *Rub this lotion into your muscles. It will stop the aching.* T *Try rubbing in this lotion.* □ *Please rub it in.*

rub something off ((of) something) to remove something from something by rubbing. (The *of* is colloquial.) □ *The butler rubbed the tarnish off the pitcher.* T *The butler rubbed off the dark tarnish.* □ *Yes, please rub that stuff off.*

rub something out to obliterate something by rubbing. □ *See if you can rub those stains out.* T *Rub out the graffiti on the side of the car if you can.*

rub (up) against someone or something to bump or scrape against someone or something. □ *The cat rubbed up against me and seemed friendly.* □ *The side of the car rubbed against the fence.*

rule against someone or something [for a judge or deliberating body] to give a judgment against someone or something. □ *The judge ruled against the prosecutor.* □ *The judge ruled against my motion.* □ *I hope the board doesn't rule against my proposal.*

rule for someone or something See the following entry.

rule in favor of someone or something AND **rule for someone or something** [for a judge or deliberating body] to award a decision to someone or something or to render a decision favoring someone or something. □ *The judge ruled for the defendant.* □ *The examining board ruled in favor of dismissing George.*

rule on something to give a decision or judgment about something. □ *How long will it be before the court rules on your petition?* □ *The boss will rule on your request tomorrow.*

rule someone or something out to eliminate someone or something from consideration. (*Someone* includes *oneself.*) □ *I can rule Tom out as a suspect. He was in Denver.* T *Don't rule out Tom.* □ *You can rule this one out.* □ *I'll have to rule myself out. I can't run for office.*

rule the roost to be the boss or manager, especially at home. □ *Who rules the roost at your house?* □ *Our new office manager really rules the roost.*

rummage through something to toss things about while searching through something. □ *I rummaged through my top drawer, looking for any two socks that matched.* □ *Mary spent some time rummaging through the toolbox before she found what she was looking for.*

rumple someone or something up to bring disorder to someone['s clothing] or something. (*Someone* includes *oneself.*) □ *One of the little boys knocked another boy down and rumpled him up.* T *He rumpled up Dan's shirt.*

□ *I have to keep from rumpling myself up before the party.*

run a fever AND **run a temperature** to have a body temperature higher than normal; to have a fever. □ *I ran a fever when I had the flu.* □ *The baby is running a temperature and is grouchy.*

run a taut ship See *run a tight ship.*

run a temperature See *run a fever.*

run a tight ship AND **run a taut ship** to run a ship or an organization in an orderly and disciplined manner. (*Taut* and *tight* mean the same thing. *Taut* is correct nautical use.) □ *The new office manager really runs a tight ship.* □ *Captain Jones is known for running a taut ship.*

run (around) in circles See the following entry.

run around like a chicken with its head cut off AND **run (around) in circles** to run around frantically and aimlessly; to be in a state of chaos. □ *I spent all afternoon running around like a chicken with its head cut off.* □ *If you run around in circles, you'll never get anything done.* □ *Get organized and stop running in circles.*

run around with someone to go places with someone; to socialize with someone. □ *I used to run around with Alice and Jill before we all graduated.* □ *Carl and Jane used to run around with each other.*

run away (from someone or something) to flee someone or something. □ *Please don't run away from me. I mean you no harm.* □ *Our dog ran away from the lawn mower.*

run down 1. to come down, running; to go down, running. □ *I need to talk to you down here. Can you run down?* □ *I will run down and talk to you.* **2.** [for something] to lose power and stop working. □ *The clock ran down because no one was there to wind it.* □ *The toy ran down and wouldn't go again until it had been wound.* **3.** to become worn or dilapidated. □ *The property was allowed to run down, and it took a lot of money to fix it up.* □ *The old neighborhood has certainly run down since we moved away.*

run down some lines 1. to converse (with someone). (Slang. See also *run one's rhymes.*) □ *I was running down some lines with Fred when the bell rang.* □ *Hey, man, let's run down some lines.* **2.** to try to seduce someone; to go through a talk leading to seduction. □ *Go run down some lines with someone else.* □ *I was just standing there running down some lines with Mary when those guys broke in.*

run down to someone or something to come or go down to someone or something rapidly. □ *Sally ran down the slope to Bob, who stood waiting for her with outstretched arms.* □ *I ran down to the well to get some water for Ed, who had the hiccups.*

run for one's life to run away in order to save one's life. □ *The dam has burst! Run for your life!* □ *The captain told us all to run for our lives.*

run in the family [for a characteristic] to appear in all (or most) members of a family. □ *My grandparents lived well into their nineties, and it runs in the family.* □ *My brothers and I have red hair. It runs in the family.*

run into a stone wall to come to a barrier against further progress. (Also used literally.) □ *We've run into a stone wall in our investigation.* □ *Algebra was hard for Tom, but he really ran into a stone wall with geometry.*

run in (to something) 1. [for a liquid] to flow into something or a place. □ *The water is running into the basement!* □ *It's running in very fast.* **2.** to enter something or a place on foot, running. □ *The boys ran into the room and out again.* □ *They ran in and knocked over a lamp.* **3.** to stop by a place for a quick visit or to make a purchase quickly. □ *I have to run in the drugstore for a minute.* □ *I ran into the store for some bread.* □ *I want to visit Mrs. Potter. I can't stay long. I can only run in for a minute.* □ *All right. If you just run in.*

Run it by (me) again. See *Run that by (me) again.*

run it down to tell the whole story; to tell the truth. (Slang.) □ *Come on! What happened? Run it down for me!* □ *I don't care what happened. Run it down. I can take it.*

run off 1. to flee. □ *The children rang our doorbell and then ran off.* □ *They ran off as fast as they could.* **2.** [for a fluid] to drain away from a flat area. □ *By noon, all the rainwater had run off the playground.* **3.** to have diarrhea. (Slang.) □ *Jimmy has been running off since midnight.* □ *At least he's not running off now.*

run off at the mouth to talk too much; to have "diarrhea of the mouth." (Slang.) □ *I wish you would stop running off at the mouth.* □ *Tom runs off at the mouth too much. I wish he would temper his remarks.*

run off with someone or something 1. to take someone or something

away, possibly running. □ *Fred ran off with Ken. They'll be back in a minute.* □ *Who ran off with my dictionary?* **2.** to capture and take away someone or something; to steal someone or something. □ *The kidnappers ran off with little Valerie.* □ *The kids ran off with a whole box of candy, and the storekeeper is going to press charges.*

run on 1. to continue running. □ *I wanted to stop her and ask her something, but she just ran on.* □ *The joggers had a chance to stop and rest, but they just ran on.* **2.** to continue on for a long time. □ *The lecture ran on and bored everyone to tears.* □ *How long is this symphony likely to run on?*

run one's rhymes to say what you have to say; to give one's speech or make one's plea. (Collegiate slang. See also *run down some lines.*) □ *Go run your rhymes with somebody else!* □ *I told him to run his rhymes elsewhere.*

run out of gas 1. to use up all the gasoline available. □ *I hope we don't run out of gas.* **2.** to lose momentum or interest. (Slang. Figurative.) □ *His program is running out of gas.* □ *I hope I don't run out of gas before I finish what I set out to do.*

run out (of something) 1. to leave something or a place, running. □ *Everyone ran out of the theater when they smelled smoke.* □ *They ran out screaming.* **2.** to use all of something and have none left. □ *I am afraid that we have run out of eggs.* □ *Check again. I don't think we have run out.*

run out of time to have used up most of the allotted time; to have no time left. □ *You have just about run out of* time. □ *I ran out of time before I could finish the test.*

run out on someone to depart and leave someone behind. □ *My date ran out on me at the restaurant, and I had to pay the bill.* □ *Her boyfriend ran out on her when she needed him the most.*

run over 1. to come by for a quick visit. □ *Can you run over for a minute after work?* □ *I will run over for a minute as soon as I can.* **2.** to overflow. □ *The bathtub ran over and there was water all over the floor.* □ *She poured the coffee until the cup ran over.*

run over someone or something 1. to drive, steer, or travel so as to pass over someone or something. □ *The bus ran over the fallen man.* □ *That car almost ran over my toe.* **2.** [with *something*] to exceed a limit. □ *The lecture ran over the allotted time.* □ *The students ran over the time allotted for the exam.* □ *I thought I had our order for food exactly right, but when the people showed up, we ran over.*

run over something with someone to review something with someone. □ *I would like to run over this with you one more time.* □ *I want to run over the proposal with Carl again.*

run someone or something down 1. to criticize or deride someone or something. (*Someone* includes oneself.) □ *Please stop running me down all the time. I can't be that bad!* T *You run down everybody!* □ *All the critics ran the play down.* □ *Poor Sally is always running herself down.* **2.** to collide with and knock down someone or something. □ *The driver ran three pedestrians down.* T *Mary ran down a*

stop sign. **3.** to hunt for and locate someone or something. □ *Could you run some information down for me?* T *I was finally able to run down my old friend.* **4.** [with *something*] to use something having batteries, a motor, or an engine until it has no more power and stops. □ *Who ran my electric toothbrush down?* T *Someone ran down my batteries.*

run someone or something in(to something) to take or drive someone or something into something or some place. (*Someone* includes oneself.) □ *Let me run you into the city this morning. I need the car today.* T *Do you want to go to town? I have to run in George, and you can come along.* □ *As soon as I run George in, I'll talk to you.* □ *Bill ran himself into town to get the medicine.*

run someone or something off 1. to drive someone or something away from something. □ *The defenders ran the attackers off time after time.* T *We had to run off the attackers.* T *The police came and ran off the raccoons.* **2.** [with *something*] to duplicate something, using a mechanical duplicating machine. □ *If the master copy is ready, I will run some other copies off.* T *I'll run off some more copies.* **3.** [with *something*] to get rid of something, such as fat or energy, by running. □ *The little boys are very excited. Send them outside to run it off.* T *They need to run off their energy.*

run someone or something out (of something) to chase someone or something out of something or some place. □ *The old man ran the kids out of his orchard.* T *He ran out the kids.*

run someone ragged to run someone hard and fast; to keep someone or something very busy. □ *This busy season is running us all ragged at the store.* □ *What a busy day. I ran myself ragged.*

run something in (to something) to guide or route something, such as a wire or a pipe, into something or a place. □ *The worker ran the circuit into each room.* □ *He ran the circuit in as instructed.* Ⓣ *He ran in the circuit as specified.*

run something out (of something) to drive or steer something out of something or some place. □ *The cowboys ran the cattle out of the corral.* Ⓣ *They ran out the cattle.* □ *They ran the horses out, too.*

run something up 1. to raise or hoist something, such as a flag. □ *Harry ran the flag up the flagpole each morning.* Ⓣ *Will you please run up the flag today?* **2.** to cause something to go higher, such as the price of stocks or commodities. □ *A rumor about higher earnings ran the price of the computer stocks up early in the afternoon.* Ⓣ *They ran up the price too high.* **3.** to stitch something together quickly. Ⓣ *She's very clever. I'm sure she can run up a costume for you.* □ *The seamstress ran a party dress up in one afternoon.* **4.** to accumulate indebtedness. □ *I ran a huge phone bill up last month.* Ⓣ *Walter ran up a hotel bar bill that made his boss angry.*

Run that by (me) again. AND **Run it by (me) again.** Please repeat what you just said.; Please go over that one more time. (Slang.) □ ALICE: *Do you understand?* SUE: *No. I really didn't understand what you said. Run that by me again, if you don't mind.* □ JOHN: *Put this piece into the longer slot and the remaining piece into the slot on*

the bottom. SUE: *Run that by again. I got lost just after* put. □ MARY: *Keep to the right, past the fork in the road, then turn right at the crossroads. Do you follow?* JANE: *No. Run it by me again.*

run to seed AND **go to seed** to become worn out and uncared for. (Said especially of a lawn that needs care.) □ *Look at that lawn. The whole thing has run to seed.* □ *Pick things up around here. This place is going to seed. What a mess!*

rush in (to something) 1. to run or hurry into a thing or a place. □ *Everyone rushed into the shelter when the rain started.* □ *They all rushed in at once.* **2.** to begin doing something without the proper preparation. □ *Don't rush into this job without thinking it through.* □ *Mary rushed in without thinking.*

rush off (from some place) to hurry away from some place. □ *I'm sorry, but I will have to rush off from this meeting before it's over.* □ *Mary had to rush off before the party was over.*

rush out (of something) to exit in a hurry. □ *Everyone rushed out of the room at the same time.* □ *They rushed out because they smelled smoke.*

rush someone or something in (to something) to lead or carry someone or something into something or some place hurriedly. □ *I rushed her into the hospital emergency room, and everything was soon all right.* Ⓣ *The nurse rushed in the emergency medical equipment.*

rush someone or something out (of something) to lead or guide someone or something out of something or some place hurriedly. □ *The ushers rushed everyone out of the church so they could clean the place before the next wedding.* T *They rushed out another edition of the newspaper that afternoon.* □ *We will have to rush another edition out.*

rush something off (to someone or something) to send something quickly to someone or something. □ *I will rush your order off to you immediately.* T *I need to rush off this package to Walter.*

rush something through (something) to move something through some process or office in a hurry. □ *He was in a hurry so we rushed his order through the order department.* □ *He asked us to rush it through.*

rush through something to hurry to get something finished; to race through something. □ *Please don't rush through this business. Get it right.* □ *Timmy rushed through dinner so he could go out and play.*

rustle something up to manage to prepare a meal, perhaps on short notice. (Folksy.) □ *I think I can rustle something up for dinner.* T *I'll rustle up some ham and eggs.*

S

sack out to go to bed or go to sleep. (Slang.) □ *It's time for me to sack out.* □ *Let's sack out early tonight.*

safe and sound secure, whole, and healthy. □ *It was a rough trip, but we got there safe and sound.* □ *I'm glad to see you here safe and sound.*

sail into someone or something 1. to crash into someone or something with a boat or ship. □ *The boat sailed into the dock, causing considerable damage.* □ *I was in my skiff when a larger boat sailed into me.* **2.** to crash into someone or something. □ *The missile sailed into the soldiers, injuring a few.* □ *The car sailed into the lamppost.*

sail (right) through something 1. to travel through something in a boat or ship. □ *The line of boats sailed right through the Grenadines in the daylight hours.* □ *We sailed through the narrows without a pilot.* **2.** to go through something very quickly and easily. (Figurative.) □ *The kids just sailed right through the ice cream and cake. There was not a bit left.* □ *You have sailed through your allowance already.*

salt something away 1. to store and preserve a foodstuff by salting it. □ *The farmer salted a lot of fish and hams away for the winter.* T *She salted away a lot of food.* **2.** to store something; to

place something in reserve. (Figurative.) □ *I need to salt some money away for my retirement.* T *I will salt away some money for emergencies.*

save something for a rainy day to reserve something — usually money — for some future need. (Also used literally. *Save something* can be replaced with *put something aside, hold something back, keep something,* etc.) □ *I've saved a little money for a rainy day.* □ *Keep some extra candy for a rainy day.*

save something up (for something) to accumulate something, usually an amount of money, for the purchase of something. (More at *save up for something.*) □ *I'm saving my money up for a car.* T *Save up your money for a car.* □ *You should save it up.*

save the day to produce a good result when a bad result was expected. □ *The team was expected to lose, but Sally made many points and saved the day.* □ *Your excellent speech saved the day.*

save up for something to accumulate something for some purpose. (More at *save something up (for something).*) □ *I can't buy a car because I am saving up for college.* □ *I don't have the money now, but I am starting to save up.*

346

say a word used to catch someone's attention and announce that a sentence — probably a question — follows. (Words such as this often use intonation to convey the connotation of the sentence that is to follow. The brief intonation pattern accompanying the word may indicate sarcasm, disagreement, caution, consolation, sternness, etc.) □ BOB: *Say, don't I know you from somewhere?* RACHEL: *I hope not.* □ *"Say, why don't you stay on your side?" screamed Tom at the other boys.* □ ANDREW: *Say, where did I see that can opener?* RACHEL: *You saw it where you left it after you last used it.*

Say cheese! an expression used by photographers to get people to smile, which they must do while saying the word *cheese*. □ *"All of you please stand still and say cheese!" said the photographer.* □ *"Is everybody ready? Say cheese!" asked Mary, holding the camera to her face.*

Say hello to someone (for me). Please convey my good wishes to someone. (The *someone* can be a person's name or a pronoun. See also *Give my best to someone.; Remember me to someone.*) □ ANDREW: *Good-bye, Tom. Say hello to your brother.* TOM: *Sure. Bye, Andy.* □ SALLY: *Well, good-bye.* MARY: *Bye.* SALLY: *And say hello to Jane.* MARY: *Sure. Bye-bye.*

Say no more. I agree.; I will do it.; I concede, no need to continue talking. □ JOHN: *Someone ought to take this stuff outside.* BILL: *Say no more. Consider it done.* □ MARY: *Shouldn't we turn here if we plan to visit Jane?* ALICE: *Say no more. Here we go.*

Say what? What did you say?; Please repeat what you said. □ SALLY: *Would you like some more salad?* FRED: *Say what?* SALLY: *Salad? Would you like some more salad?* □ JOHN: *Put this one over there.* SUE: *Say what?* JOHN: *Never mind, I'll do it.*

Say when. Tell me when I have given you enough of something, usually a liquid. (Sometimes answered with **When.**) □ TOM (pouring milk into Fred's glass): *Say when, Fred.* FRED: *When.* □ JOHN: *Do you want some more juice?* MARY: *Yes.* JOHN: *Okay. Say when.*

Says me! the contentious response to *Says who?* □ BILL: *I think you're making a mess of this project.* BOB: *Says who?* BILL: *Says me!* □ JOHN: *What do you mean I shouldn't have done it? Says who?* MARY: *Says me!*

Says who? Who do you think you are to say that? □ TOM: *Fred, you sure can be dumb sometimes.* FRED: *Says who?* TOM: *Says me!* □ BILL: *You take this dog out of here right now!* BOB: *Says who?* BILL: *Says me!*

Says you! It is just you who are saying that, so it does not matter. □ BILL: *I think you're headed for some real trouble.* BOB: *Says you!* FRED: *Says who?* TOM: *Says me!* FRED: *Aw, says you!*

scale something down to reduce the size or cost of something. □ *The bad economy forced us to scale the project down.* ⊤ *Liz scaled down the project.*

scarcer than hens' teeth See *(as) scarce as hens' teeth.*

scare someone or something off to frighten someone or some creature away. □ *The dog's barking scared the burglar off.* ⊤ *The barking scared off*

347

the prowler. □ My dog scared the skunk off.

scarf out to overeat. (Slang. See also *pig out, pork out, mac out*.) □ *I scarf out every weekend.* □ *My brother scarfs out every day—around the clock!*

scarf something down to eat something, perhaps in a hurry; to swallow something, perhaps in a hurry. (Slang.) □ *Are you going to scarf this whole thing down?* T *Here, scarf down this sandwich.*

scheme against someone or something to plot or conspire against someone or something. □ *A group of generals was plotting against the government.* □ *They schemed against Roger until he caught them and put an end to it.*

schiz(z) out to freak out; to lose mental control. (Slang.) □ *What a day! I nearly schizzed out.* □ *I schizzed out during the test. Failed it.*

scour something off ((of) something) to clean something off something else by scouring. (The *of* is colloquial.) □ *See if you can scour the rust off the cookie sheet.* T *I will scour off the rust.* □ *Please help me scour it off.*

scour something out to clean something out by scouring. □ *Would you scour the pans out?* T *Please scour out the pans — don't just wash them.*

scout around (for someone or something) to look around for someone or something. □ *I don't know who would do a good job for you, but I'll scout around for a likely candidate.* □ *You stay here. I'll scout around.*

scout someone or something up to search for and find someone or something. □ *I'll scout a costume up for the Halloween party.* T *Can you scout up a date for Friday night?*

scrape by (on something) AND scrape by (with something) to manage just to get by with something. □ *There is not really enough money to live on, and we just have to scrape by on what we get.* □ *We can't scrape by with only that amount of money.* □ *I think we can just scrape by again this month.*

scrape by (something) to manage just to get by something. □ *I scraped by the man standing at the gate and got into the theater without a ticket.* □ *Mary scraped by the cart that was blocking the crowded hallway.*

scrape by (with something) See *scrape by (on something)*.

scrape something away (from something) to scratch or rasp something off something. □ *Ted scraped the rough places away from the fender he was repairing.* T *Ted scraped away the rough places.* □ *Mary couldn't polish her shoes until she scraped the mud away.*

scrape something off ((of) someone or something) to rub or stroke something off someone or something. (The *of* is colloquial.) □ *I sat down and scraped the caked mud off of me. It was everywhere!* T *Jake scraped off the caked mud.* □ *Mary scraped the mud off.*

scrape something out to empty something by scraping. □ *Scrape the pan out. Don't leave any of that good sauce inside.* T *Please scrape out the pan and wash it.*

scrape something out (of something) to remove something by scraping. □ *Scrape all the peanut butter out of the jar before you discard it.* T *Scrape out the peanut butter.* □ *Please scrape it out.*

scrape the bottom of the barrel to select from among the worst; to choose from what is left over. (As if one were down to the very last and worst choices.) □ *You've bought a bad-looking car. You really scraped the bottom of the barrel to get that one.* □ *The worker you sent over was the worst I've ever seen. Send me another — and don't scrape the bottom of the barrel.*

scrape through (something) 1. to move through something, scraping or rubbing the sides. □ *The car, going at a very high speed, scraped through the tunnel.* □ *It just managed to scrape through.* **2.** to get by something just barely; to pass a test just barely. □ *Alice passed the test, but she just scraped through it.* □ *I just scraped through my calculus test.*

scratch someone or something out to mark out the name of someone or something. □ *I scratched John out and wrote in George instead.* T *I scratched out John and forgot about him.* □ *Donna scratched the name of the defunct company out.*

scratch someone or something up to damage or mar someone or something by scratching. □ *Being thrown clear of the car in the accident didn't break any bones, but it scratched her up a lot.* T *Who scratched up my coffee table?* □ *I didn't scratch it up.*

scratch the surface to begin to find out about something; to examine only the superficial aspects of something. □ *The investigation of the* governor's staff revealed some suspicious dealing. It is thought that the investigators have just scratched the surface. □ We don't know how bad the problem is. We've only scratched the surface.*

scream bloody murder See *cry bloody murder.*

screen someone or something out (of something) to filter someone or something out of something. □ *The test screened all the unqualified candidates out of the group.* T *We screened out the suppliers who were not financially sound.* □ *We screened some of the applicants out.* T *Walter screened out the rocks from the soil.*

screw around to waste time. (Slang.) □ *Stop screwing around and get busy.* □ *John's always screwing around and never does anything on time.*

screw someone over to give someone a very bad time; to scold someone severely. (Slang.) □ *Those guys really screwed you over. What started it?* T *Let's get those kids in here and screw over every one of them. This stuff can't continue.*

screw something down to secure something to the floor or a base by the use of screws. □ *You had better screw these seats down or someone will knock them over.* T *Please screw down the threshold.*

screw up 1. to mess up. (Slang.) □ *I hope I don't screw up this time.* □ *The waiter screwed up again.* **2.** a mess; a blunder; utter confusion. (Usually **screw-up.**) □ *This is the chef's screw-up, not mine.* □ *One more screw up like that and you're fired.*

screw up one's courage to build up one's courage. □ *I guess I have to* screw up my courage and go to the dentist. □ I spent all morning screwing up my courage to take my driver's test.

scrub someone or something down to clean someone or something thoroughly by rubbing. (*Someone* includes *oneself*.) □ *The mother scrubbed the baby down gently and put lotion on her.* T *Please scrub down this floor.* □ *He scrubbed himself down and put on clean clothes.*

scrub someone or something off to clean someone or something by rubbing. (*Someone* includes *oneself*.) □ *Mother scrubbed Timmy off.* T *Liz scrubbed off the countertop.* □ *He scrubbed himself off and went to work.*

scrub something off ((of) something) to clean something off something by scrubbing. (The *of* is colloquial.) □ *I have to scrub the mud off the porch steps.* □ *Did you scrub all the grease off?* T *Tina scrubbed off the grease.*

scrub something out to clean out the inside of something by rubbing or brushing. □ *Please scrub these pots out and put them away.* T *Jim will scrub out the pots.*

scrub something out (of something) to clean something out of something by scrubbing. □ *Please scrub the gravy out of the pot.* T *Are you going to scrub out the burned material?*

scrub up 1. to clean oneself up. □ *You have to scrub up before dinner.* □ *Please go scrub up before you come to the table.* **2.** to clean oneself, especially one's hands and arms, as a preparation for performing a surgical procedure. (A special use of sense 1.) □ *The surgeon scrubbed up thoroughly before the operation.* □ *When you fin-*

ish scrubbing up, someone will help you on with sterile clothing.

'Scuse (me). See *Excuse me.*

'Scuse me? See *Excuse me?*

'Scuse, please. See *Excuse me.*

scuzz someone out to nauseate someone. (Slang.) □ *He had this unreal face that almost scuzzed me out!* T *It's not nice to scuzz out people like that, especially when you hardly know them.*

seal something off (from someone or something) to make something inaccessible to someone or something. □ *The police sealed the building off from everyone.* T *They sealed off the building from all the reporters.* □ *We sealed the room off from the outside air.*

Search me. I do not know.; You can search my clothing and my person, but you won't find the answer to your question anywhere near me. (Colloquial and not too polite. The two words have equal stress.) □ JANE: *What time does Mary's flight get in?* SALLY: *Search me.* □ JOHN: *What kind of paint should I use on this fence?* BILL: *Search me.*

search something with a fine-tooth comb See *go over something with a fine-tooth comb.*

second nature to someone easy and natural for someone. □ *Swimming is second nature to Jane.* □ *Driving is no problem for Bob. It's second nature to him.*

see eye to eye (about something) AND **see eye to eye on something** to view something in the same way (as someone else). □ *John and Ann see eye to eye about the new law. Neither of* them likes it. □ *That's interesting because they rarely see eye to eye.*

see eye to eye on something See the previous entry.

See if I care! I do not care if you do it. □ MARY: *That does it! I'm going home to Mother!* JOHN: *See if I care!* □ SUE: *I'm putting the sofa here, whether you like it or not.* BILL: *Go ahead! See if I care!*

see someone off to accompany one to the point of departure for a trip and say good-bye upon departure. □ *We went to the train station to see Andy off.* ⊤ *We saw off all the scouts going to camp.*

see something through to stay with a project all the way to its completion. □ *They will see the job through.* □ *I will see this whole thing through, don't worry.*

see the (hand)writing on the wall to know that something is certain to happen. □ *If you don't improve your performance, they'll fire you. Can't you see the writing on the wall?* □ *I know I'll get fired. I can see the handwriting on the wall.*

see the light (at the end of the tunnel) to foresee an end to one's problems after a long period of time. □ *I had been horribly ill for two months before I began to see the light at the end of the tunnel.* □ *I began to see the light one day in early spring. At that moment, I knew I'd get well.*

see the light (of day) to come to the end of a very busy time. □ *Finally, when the holiday season was over, we could see the light of day. We had been so busy!* □ *When business lets up for a while, we'll be able to see the light.*

see through someone or something to recognize the deception involved with someone or something. □ *I know what you're up to! I see through you!* □ *I see through this proposal.*

see to someone or something to tend to or care for someone or something. □ *Please go see to the baby. She's crying again.* □ *Ted went to see to whoever was at the door.*

See ya! Good-bye! (Colloquial.) □ ANDREW: *Good-bye, Tom. See ya!* TOM: *Bye. Take it easy.* □ MARY: *Bye, Jane! See you later.* JANE: *See ya!*

See ya, bye-bye. Bye. (Colloquial and slang.) □ BILL: *I have to be off.* BOB: *See ya, bye-bye.* □ MARY: *See ya, bye-bye.* SUE: *Toodle-oo.*

See you around. I will see you again somewhere. □ BOB: *Bye for now.* JANE: *See you around.* □ TOM: *See you around, Fred.* FRED: *Sure, Tom. See you.*

(See you) later. See *I'll see you later.*

See you later, alligator. AND **Later, alligator.** Good-bye. (A natural mate to *After while(, crocodile).*) □ BOB: *See you later, alligator.* JANE: *After while, crocodile.* □ BOB: *Bye, Tom.* TOM: *See you later, alligator.* BOB: *Later.*

seep in(to something) [for a fluid] to trickle or leak out of something. □ *Water is seeping into the basement.* □ *Water is seeping in very slowly.*

seep out (of something) [for a fluid] to trickle or leak out of something. □ *A lot of oil has seeped out of the car onto the driveway.* □ *There is oil seeping out. There must be a leak.*

seep through something [for a fluid] to permeate something and escape.

☐ *The oil seeped through the gasket onto the ground.* ☐ *Some water seeped through the ceiling, ruining our carpet as well as the ceiling.*

seize onto someone or something to grab onto someone or something. ☐ *The beggar seized onto the well-dressed gentleman and demanded money.* ☐ *Tony seized onto the doorknob and gave it a hard jerk.*

seize up to freeze or halt; to grind suddenly to a stop. ☐ *The engine seized up, and we were almost thrown out of the car.* ☐ *My knee seized up in the middle of a football game.*

seize (up)on something **1.** to grasp something tightly. (*Upon* is formal and less commonly used than *on*.) ☐ *Dave seized upon the knob of the door and yanked hard.* ☐ *I seized on the railing and held on tight.* **2.** to take hold of something, such as a plan, idea, etc. (Figurative.) ☐ *I heard her ideas and seized upon them immediately.* ☐ *The committee seized on the proposal at once.* ☐ *The plan was seized upon at once.*

sell like hot cakes [for something] to be sold very fast. ☐ *The delicious candy sold like hot cakes.* ☐ *The fancy new cars were selling like hot cakes.*

sell out (to someone) **1.** to sell everything to someone. ☐ *The farmer finally gave up and sold out to a large corporation.* ☐ *I refuse to sell out no matter what they offer me.* **2.** to betray someone or something to someone. ☐ *I think that you have sold out to the enemy!*

sell someone a bill of goods to get someone to believe something that isn't true; to deceive someone. ☐ *Don't pay any attention to what John* says. *He's just trying to sell you a bill of goods.* ☐ *I'm not selling you a bill of goods. What I say is true.*

sell someone or something out to betray someone or something. (*Someone* includes *oneself*.) ☐ *The small country didn't know how to conduct espionage. They sold their own agent out.* ⊤ *They sold out their own agent.* ☐ *The agent sold her country out.* ☐ *You're asking me to sell myself out!*

sell someone or something short to underestimate someone or something; to fail to see the good qualities of someone or something. ☐ *This is a very good restaurant. Don't sell it short.* ☐ *When you say that John isn't interested in music, you're selling him short. Did you know he plays the violin quite well?*

sell something off to sell all of something. ☐ *We ended up with a large stock of out-of-style coats, and we had to sell them all off at a loss.* ⊤ *We sold off all the excess stock.*

send away (for something) to order something to be brought or sent from some distance. ☐ *I sent away for a new part to replace the one that was broken.* ☐ *I couldn't find the part locally. I had to send away for it.*

send for someone or something to make a request that someone or something be brought. ☐ *Mr. Franklin sent for his secretary.* ☐ *I think we should send for an ambulance.*

send off for something to dispatch an order for something to a distant place. ☐ *I sent off for the proper contest entry forms.* ☐ *Did you send off for a new license?*

send one about one's business to send someone away, usually in an unfriendly way. □ *Is that annoying man on the telephone again? Please send him about his business.* □ *Ann, I can't clean up the house with you running around. I'm going to have to send you about your business.*

send out (for someone or something) to send an order by messenger, telephone, cable, or fax that someone or something is to come or be delivered. (More at *send someone out (for someone or something)*.) □ *We sent out for a public stenographer to record the will as Uncle Herman dictated it.* □ *There was no one there who could take dictation, so we had to send out.* □ *We sent out for sandwiches.*

send someone in for someone to send someone into a game as a replacement for someone else. □ *The coach sent Jill in for Alice, who was beginning to tire.* □ *Ted sent Bill in for Wally.*

send someone in(to something) to make someone go into something or some place. □ *George sent me into the house for a hammer.* ⊤ *The boys know where it is. He should have sent in the boys.* □ *George sent me in.*

send someone off (to something) to send someone away to something or some place, especially away on a journey; to be present when someone sets out on a journey to something or some place. □ *We sent both kids off to camp this summer and had peace in the house for the first time in years.* ⊤ *Liz sent off Karen to the store.* □ *I had to send them off. They were getting to be annoying.*

send someone out (for someone or something) to send someone out to search for someone or something.

(More at *send out (for someone or something)*.) □ *We sent Gerald out for Walter, who was supposed to have been there already.* ⊤ *Karen sent out Liz for some medicine.*

send someone over ((to) some place) to order someone to go to some place. □ *I sent Dave over to the main office.* □ *I will send someone else over.* ⊤ *Please send over someone else.*

send someone packing to send someone away; to dismiss someone, possibly rudely. □ *I couldn't stand him anymore, so I sent him packing.* □ *The maid proved to be so incompetent that I had to send her packing.*

send someone to the showers to send a player out of the game and off the field, court, etc. (From sports.) □ *John played so badly that the coach sent him to the showers after the third quarter.* □ *After the fistfight, the coaches sent both players to the showers.*

send something by something 1. to dispatch something by a particular carrier. □ *I will send it to you by special messenger.* □ *We sent the package by air freight.* **2.** to deliver something to something or some place. (Informal.) □ *I will send the parcel by your office this afternoon.* □ *We sent your order by your house, but no one was there to receive it.*

send something off (to someone or something) to dispatch something to someone, something, or some place. □ *I will send the package off to you in tomorrow's mail.* ⊤ *Karen sent off a letter to her aunt.* □ *She sent it off only yesterday.*

separate something out (of something) to remove something out

353

from something. □ *She used a filter to separate the dirt particles out of the water.* ⊤ *A filter separated out the impurities.* □ *It separated the sand out.*

separate the men from the boys to separate the competent from those who are less competent. □ *This is the kind of task that separates the men from the boys.* □ *This project requires a lot of thinking. It'll separate the men from the boys.*

separate the sheep from the goats to divide people into two groups. □ *Working in a place like this really separates the sheep from the goats.* □ *We can't go on with the game until we separate the sheep from the goats. Let's see who can jump the farthest.*

serve as a guinea pig [for someone] to be experimented on; to allow some sort of test to be performed on someone. □ *Try it on someone else! I don't want to serve as a guinea pig!* □ *Jane agreed to serve as a guinea pig. She'll be the one to try out the new flavor of ice cream.*

serve someone right [for an act or event] to punish someone fairly (for doing something). □ *John copied off my test paper. It would serve him right if he fails the test.* □ *It'd serve John right if he got arrested.*

serve something up to distribute or deliver food for people to eat. □ *The cook served the stew up and then passed around the bread.* ⊤ *Can you serve up the food now?*

serve under someone or something to carry out one's responsibility under the direction or in the employment of someone or something. □ *I served under the president of the com-*

pany as special assistant. □ *Jane served under the court as an investigator.*

set foot somewhere to go or enter somewhere. (Often in the negative.) □ *If I were you, I wouldn't set foot in that town.* □ *I wouldn't set foot in her house! Not after the way she spoke to me.*

set great store by someone or something to have positive expectations for someone or something; to have high hopes for someone or something. □ *I set great store by my computer and its ability to help me in my work.* □ *We set great store by John because of his quick mind.*

set in to begin; to become fixed for a period of time. □ *A severe cold spell set in early in November.* □ *When high temperatures set in, the use of electricity went up considerably.*

set off (for something) to leave for something or some place. □ *We set off for Springfield three hours late.* □ *It was after noon before we could set off.*

set off on something to begin on a journey or expedition. □ *When do you plan to set off on your journey?* □ *We will set off on our adventure tomorrow morning.*

set one (back) on one's feet AND **set one on one's feet again** to reestablish someone; to help someone become active and productive again. □ *Gary's uncle helped set him back on his feet.* □ *We will all help set you on your feet again.*

set one back on one's heels to surprise, shock, or overwhelm someone. □ *Her sudden announcement set us all back on our heels.* □ *The manager scolded me, and that really set me back on my heels.*

set one on one's feet again See *set one (back) on one's feet.*

set one's heart on something to become determined about something. □ *Jane set her heart on going to London.*

set one's sights on something to select something as one's goal. □ *I set my sights on a master's degree from the state university.* □ *Don't set your sights on something you cannot possibly do.*

set out (on something) to begin a journey; to begin a project. □ *We set out on our trip exactly as planned.* □ *We set out as planned.*

set out to do something to begin to do something; to intend to do something. □ *Jill set out to weed the garden, but pulled up a few valuable plants in the process.* □ *I set out to repair the door, not rebuild the whole house.*

set someone down (on (to) something) to place a person one is carrying or lifting onto something. □ *I set the small boy down onto the desk and gave him a piece of candy.* T *I set down the child on the chair.* □ *Jane set her down.*

set someone off 1. to cause someone to become very angry; to ignite someone's anger. □ *That kind of thing really sets me off!* T *Your behavior set off Mrs. Franklin.* □ *When I mentioned high taxes it really set Walter off. He went into a rage.* **2.** to cause someone to start talking or lecturing about a particular subject. □ *When I mentioned high taxes it really set Walter off. He talked and talked.* □ *The subject set Karen off, and she talked on endlessly.*

set someone or something up to place someone or something in an upright position. □ *He was asleep, but we tried to set him up anyway.* T *I set up the lamp, which had fallen over again.*

set someone or something up (for something) 1. [with *someone*] to prepare someone for a deception. (*Someone* includes *oneself*.) □ *The crooks set the old lady up for their standard scam.* T *They set up their victim for the scam.* □ *It didn't take much to set Max up.* □ *They set themselves up to be cheated.* **2.** [with *someone*] to make someone become part of a joke. (*Someone* includes *oneself*.) □ *The comedian was highly skilled at setting members of the audience up for a gag.* T *The joker set up a friend for the butt of the joke.* □ *So, you thought you could set me up!* □ *You really set yourself up for that one!* **3.** [with *something*] to arrange something for a particular time or event. □ *I will set a meeting up for tomorrow.* T *Can you set up a meeting for tomorrow?* □ *Yes, I'll set it up.*

set someone's teeth on edge 1. [for a sour or bitter taste] to irritate one's mouth and make it feel funny. □ *Have you ever eaten a lemon? It'll set your teeth on edge.* □ *I can't stand food that sets my teeth on edge.* **2.** [for a person or a noise] to be irritating or get on one's nerves. □ *Please don't scrape your fingernails on the blackboard! It sets my teeth on edge!* □ *Here comes Bob. He's so annoying. He really sets my teeth on edge.*

set something down (on something) 1. to place something on the surface of something. □ *Andy set the hot skillet down on the countertop and burned* a hole in it. ⊤ *He set down the skillet on the counter.* □ *Please set it down carefully.* **2.** to write something on paper. □ *Let me set this down on paper so we will have a record of what was said.* ⊤ *I will set down this note on paper.* □ *She set it down in a very neat hand.* **3.** to land an airplane on something. □ *The pilot set the plane down on the runway.* □ *I can't set the plane down on this field!*

set something down to something to blame something on something; to regard something as the cause of something. □ *She set his rude behavior down to indigestion.* □ *I just set her crankiness down to lack of sleep.*

set something in(to something) to install something into its place. □ *The movers set the stove into its proper place, and the plumber hooked it up two weeks later.* ⊤ *They set in the stove.* □ *It was difficult, but they set it in properly.*

set something off **1.** to ignite something, such as fireworks. □ *The boys were setting firecrackers off all afternoon.* ⊤ *They set off bomb after bomb.* **2.** to cause something to begin. □ *The coach set the race off with a shot from the starting pistol.* ⊤ *She set off the race with a gunshot.* **3.** to make something distinct or outstanding. □ *The lovely stonework sets the fireplace off quite nicely.* ⊤ *The white hat really sets off Betsy's eyes.*

set something (up)on something to place something on the surface of something. □ *Mrs. Franklin set a bowl of fruit upon the table.* □ *I set my empty glass on the counter.*

set the world on fire to do exciting things that bring fame and glory.

(Not literal. Frequently negative.) □ *I'm not very ambitious. I don't want to set the world on fire.* □ *You don't have to set the world on fire. Just do a good job.*

settle down **1.** to become calm. □ *Please settle down. Relax.* □ *I will try to settle down so I can think straight.* **2.** to get quiet. (More at *settle someone down.*) □ *Will you all please settle down so we can begin?* □ *Settle down! Let's get this meeting over with!* **3.** to abandon a carefree life-style and take up a more stable and disciplined one. (Often with thoughts of marriage, home-ownership, and child-bearing.) □ *I wish Charles would settle down.* □ *Haven't you ever thought of settling down and raising a family?*

settle down somewhere to establish a residence somewhere. □ *After retiring, they settled down in a little cabin near a lake.* □ *We really wanted to settle down in a small town in the South.*

settle in(to something) **1.** to become accustomed to something, such as a new home, job, status, etc. □ *By the end of the first week he had settled into his new job.* □ *He settled in with no problems.* **2.** to get comfortable in something. □ *I love to settle back into my new reclining chair.* □ *Jan sat down in the chair and settled in.*

settle someone down to make someone become quiet. (*Someone* includes oneself. More at *settle down.*) □ *The principal had to go into the classroom and settle the students down.* □ *At last the little boys settled themselves down and went to sleep.*

shag (off) to depart. (Slang.) □ *I gotta shag. It's late.* □ *Go on! Shag* off! □ *I gotta shag. Somebody's calling my name.*

shake in one's boots AND **quake in one's boots** to be afraid; to shake from fear. □ *I was shaking in my boots because I had to go see the manager.* □ *Stop quaking in your boots, Bob. I'm not going to fire you.*

Shake it (up)! *Hurry up!;* Move faster!; Run faster! □ *FRED: Move it, Tom! Shake it up! TOM: I can't go any faster!* □ *JANE: Move, you guys. Shake it! BILL: Hey, I'm doing the best I can!*

shake something down See the following entry.

shake something out **1.** to clean something of dirt or crumbs by shaking. □ *Please shake the tablecloth out.* T *Can you shake out your coat? It's really dusty.* **2.** AND **shake something down** to test something to find out what the problems are. (Figurative.) □ *I need to spend some time driving my new car to shake it out.* T *We need to shake out this car before I make the final payment.* □ *The ship ran well when I shook it down.*

shake something up **1.** to mix something by shaking. □ *I am going to shake the salad dressing up before I serve it.* T *Please shake up the salad dressing.* **2.** to upset an organization or group of people by some administrative action. □ *The board of directors shook middle management up by firing a few of the old-timers.* T *They shook up the firm by taking the company public.*

Shake the lead out! See *Get the lead out!*

Shame on you! a phrase scolding someone for being naughty. (Typically said to a child or to an adult for a childish infraction.) □ *JOHN: I think I broke one of your figurines. MARY: Shame on you! JOHN: I'll replace it, of course. MARY: Thanks, I sort of liked it.* □ *"Shame on you!" said Mary. "You should have known better!"*

shank it to use one's legs to get somewhere; to walk. (Slang.) □ *My car needs fixing so I had to shank it to work today.* □ *I like to shank it every now and then.*

shape someone up **1.** to cause someone to get into good physical condition. (More at *shape up.*) □ *The jogging shaped him up, but it harmed his joints.* T *The jogging shaped up Karen in about three weeks.* **2.** to cause someone to become productive, efficient, competent, etc. (More at *shape up.*) □ *The manager decided she had to shape everyone in the office up.* T *The new director shaped up the salespeople virtually overnight.*

shape up **1.** to get into good physical condition. (More at *shape someone up.*) □ *I really need to shape up. I get out of breath too easily.* □ *If you don't shape up, you might develop heart trouble.* **2.** to become productive, efficient, competent, etc. (More at *shape someone up.*) □ *You are going to have to shape up if you want to keep your job.* □ *The boss told her to shape up or find another job.*

Shape up or ship out. to either improve one's performance (or behavior) or leave or quit. □ *Okay, Tom. That's the end. Shape up or ship out!* □ *John was late again, so I told him to shape up or ship out.*

shed crocodile tears to shed false tears; to pretend that one is weeping. □ *The child wasn't hurt, but she shed* crocodile tears anyway. □ He thought he could get his way if he shed crocodile tears.

shift out of something to change out of a particular mode, time, gear, attitude, etc. □ She quickly shifted out of second gear into third. □ I hope you can shift out of that bad attitude into a more pleasant state before the guests arrive.

shine out 1. to shine or radiate light; to shine forth. □ She snapped on the flashlight and a reassuring light shone out. □ The hallway was cheery and a bright light shone out, inviting us in. **2.** [for a characteristic] to make itself very evident. □ His good humor shone out, especially when he was surrounded by grouches. □ Sarah's basically good character shone out almost all the time.

shine something up to polish something. □ Tom shined his shoes up. ⊤ Fred shined up the furniture.

shine something (up)on someone or something to cast a beam of light onto someone or something. (Upon is formal and less commonly used than on.) □ Please shine your flashlight on Sam so we can see him. □ The sun shone its rays on the fields.

shine through (something) 1. [for rays of light] to penetrate something. □ The bright light of day shone through the windows. □ The light shone through and lit up the room. **2.** [for something that was obscured or hidden] to become visible or evident. □ Her basic intelligence shone through in spite of her country ways. □ Her intelligence shone through in most instances.

shine up to someone to flatter someone; to try to get into someone's

favor. □ The cat shined up to the man every day, but it still got thrown out of the house every night. □ Are you trying to shine up to me? What will that accomplish?

Shoot! Say what you have to say!; Ask your question! □ BOB: Can I ask you a question? BILL: Sure. Shoot! □ MARY: There are a few things I want to say before we go on. TOM: Shoot!

shoot from the hip 1. to fire a gun that is held at one's side, against one's hip. (This increases one's speed in firing a gun.) □ When I lived at home on the farm, my father taught me to shoot from the hip. □ I quickly shot the snake before it bit my horse. I'm glad I learned to shoot from the hip. **2.** to speak directly and frankly. □ John has a tendency to shoot from the hip, but he generally speaks the truth. □ Don't pay any attention to John. He means no harm. It's just his nature to shoot from the hip.

shoot in(to something) to run or dart into something or some place. □ A mouse shot into the crack in the wall of the barn. □ A little mouse shot in.

shoot one's breakfast See the following entry.

shoot one's cookies AND **shoot one's breakfast; shoot one's supper** to empty one's stomach; to vomit. (Slang.) □ I think I'm gonna shoot my cookies. □ I shot my supper, and I was glad to get rid of it.

shoot one's supper See the previous entry.

shoot out to pop or dart out. □ A car shot out right in front of me. □ The frog's tongue shot out.

shoot the bull AND **shoot the crap; shoot the shit** to chat and gossip. (Slang. Use caution with *crap, shit.*) □ *Let's get together sometime and shoot the bull.* □ *You spend too much time shooting the crap.*

shoot the crap See the previous entry.

shoot the shit See *shoot the bull.*

shoot up to grow rapidly. □ *The seeds germinated and sprouts shot up almost overnight.* □ *Tim shot up just after he turned twelve.*

short out [for an electrical circuit] to go out because of a short circuit. □ *All the lights in the house shorted out when lightning struck.* □ *This radio has shorted out, I think.*

shot down 1. demolished; destroyed. (Slang.) □ *Her idea was shot down after all her work.* □ *I felt shot down, even though I was sure of what I was getting into.* **2.** rejected by a person of the opposite sex. □ *Tiffany is a cruel chick. I was shot down from day one.* □ *Fred's shot down, thanks to his best girl. He'll get over it.*

shot in the arm a boost; something that gives someone energy. □ *Thank you for cheering me up. It was a real shot in the arm.* □ *Your friendly greeting card was just what I needed—a real shot in the arm.*

should have stood in bed should have stayed in bed. (Has nothing to do with standing up.) □ *What a horrible day! I should have stood in bed.* □ *The minute I got up and heard the news this morning, I knew I should have stood in bed.*

shout someone down to stop someone from speaking by shouting, yelling, or jeering. □ *The audience shouted the politician down.* T *They shouted down the speaker.*

shove off See *push off.*

shove off (for something) 1. to begin a journey to something or some place by pushing a boat or ship out onto the water. □ *We will shove off at about noon, headed for Barbados.* □ *Go up to the bow of the boat and shove off when I tell you.* **2.** to depart for something or some place, using any form of transportation. □ *The car is all warmed up and ready to go. Let's shove off.* □ *Let's shove off pretty soon.*

show off (to someone) to make an exhibition of oneself to someone. □ *Ed was making a nuisance of himself, showing off to the girls.* □ *Stop showing off, Ed.*

show one's (true) colors to show what one is really like or what one is really thinking. □ *Whose side are you on, John? Come on. Show your colors.* □ *It's hard to tell what Mary is thinking. She never shows her true colors.*

show someone around (something) to give someone a tour of something or some place; to lead someone in an examination of something or some place. (*Someone* includes *oneself.*) □ *I would be happy to show you around the factory.* □ *Can I show you around?* □ *I'll show myself around. Don't worry. I can find the way.*

show someone or something off (to someone) to show someone or something to someone proudly. □ *She was very pleased to show her daughter off to everyone.* T *Liz showed off her daughter to Karen.* T *Richard showed off his new shoes to everyone in the office.*

show someone out (of something) to usher or escort someone out of something or some place. □ *The butler showed Roger out of the main hall into the orangery.* □ *May I show you out, sir?*

show someone the ropes to tell or show someone how something is to be done. □ *Since this was my first day on the job, the manager spent a lot of time showing me the ropes.*

show someone through (something) to give someone a tour of something or some place. □ *I would be happy to show you through the office complex.* □ *This is our office area. Let me show you through.*

shrink up to shrivel; to recede. □ *My shirt shrank up when you washed it!* □ *The bruise on Tom's arm shrank up when he put ice on it.*

shrivel up to contract; to shrink. □ *The goldfish must have jumped out of its bowl during the night. Anyway, it's on the floor all shriveled up this morning.* □ *The new plants shriveled up in the burning sun.*

shrug something off to ignore something; to dismiss something. □ *No, you didn't hurt my feelings. I just shrugged your comment off.* ⊤ *Liz couldn't shrug off the remark.*

shut off to stop operating; to turn off. □ *The machine shuts off automatically.* □ *What time do the lights shut off?*

shut someone or something down 1. to close a business; to force someone who runs a business to close. □ *Sam's business was failing, and finally the bank shut him down.* ⊤ *The bank shut down Tom's shop.* **2.** [with *something*] to turn something off. □ *They*

shut the machine down so they could repair it. ⊤ *They had to shut down the machine.*

shut someone up to cause someone to stop talking or making other noise. □ *I don't know how to shut him up. He just talks on and on.* ⊤ *Shut up that loudmouth!*

shut up 1. to be quiet. (Rude slang.) □ *Shut up! You talk too much!* □ *Please shut up when I am on the phone.* **2.** Be quiet! (Usually **Shut up!** Impolite.) □ BOB: *And another thing.* BILL: *Oh, shut up, Bob!* □ ANDREW: *Shut up! I've heard enough!* BOB: *But I have more to say!* □ *"Shut up! I can't hear anything because of all your noise!" shouted the director.*

Shut up about it. Do not tell anyone about it. □ BILL: *I heard that you had a little trouble with the police.* TOM: *Just shut up about it! Do you hear?* □ ANDREW: *Didn't you once appear in a movie?* ALICE: *Shut up about it. No one has to know.*

Shut your face! Be quiet!; *Shut up!* (Rude.) □ HENRY: *Shut your face! I'm tired of your constant chatter.* BOB: *I didn't say a single word!* □ MARY: *You make me sick!* SALLY: *Shut your face!*

shy away (from someone or something) to draw away from someone or something that is frightening or startling; to avoid dealing with someone or something. □ *The child shied away from the doctor.* □ *I won't hurt you. Don't shy away.*

sift something out (of something) to get rid of something in something else by sifting. □ *Dan sifted the impurities out of the flour.* ⊤ *Walter sifted out the foreign matter.*

sign in to indicate that one has arrived somewhere and at what time by signing a piece of paper or a list. □ *Please sign in so we will know you are here.* □ *Did you remember to sign in this time?*

sign off 1. [for a broadcaster] to announce the end of programming for the day; [for an amateur radio operator] to announce the end of a transmission. □ *Wally signed off and turned the transmitter off.* □ *Wally failed to sign off at the scheduled time last night.* **2.** to quit doing what one has been doing and leave to go to bed. (Figurative.) □ *I have to sign off and get to bed. See you all.* □ *When you finally sign off tonight, please turn out all the lights.*

sign off on something to sign a paper, indicating that one has finished with something or agrees with the state of something. □ *Michael signed off on the book and sent it to be printed.* □ *I refuse to sign off on this project until it is done correctly.*

sign on to announce the beginning of a broadcast transmission. □ *The announcer signed on and then played "The Star-Spangled Banner."* □ *We usually sign on at six in the morning.*

sign on the dotted line to place one's signature on a contract or other important paper. □ *This agreement isn't properly concluded until we both sign on the dotted line.* □ *Here are the papers for the purchase of your car. As soon as you sign on the dotted line, that beautiful, shiny automobile will be all yours!*

sign one's own death warrant to sign a paper that calls for one's death. (Figurative.) □ *I wouldn't ever gamble a large sum of money. That would be signing my own death warrant.* □

The killer signed his own death warrant when he walked into the police station and gave himself up.

sign out to indicate in writing that one is leaving or going out temporarily. (More at *sign someone out (of some place)*.) □ *I forgot to sign out when I left.* □ *Please sign out every time you leave.*

sign someone or something in 1. [with *someone*] to record that someone has arrived somewhere and at what time by recording the information on a paper or a list. (*Someone* includes *oneself*.) □ *I will sign you in. What is your name?* T *Do I have to sign in everyone?* □ *I'll sign myself in. You don't need to.* **2.** [with *something*] to record that something has been received at a particular time by recording the information on a paper or a list. □ *I have to sign this tape recorder in, then I will be right with you.* T *Should I sign in this tape recorder now?*

sign someone or something out (of some place) 1. [with *someone*] to make a record of someone's departure from some place. (*Someone* includes *oneself*.) □ *Did someone sign you out of the factory, or did you just open the door and leave?* T *I signed out those two who just left.* □ *Please sign me out. I have to leave in a hurry.* □ *Do I have to sign myself out?* **2.** [with *something*] to make a record of the borrowing of something from some place. □ *Dave signed the tape recorder out of the library.* T *Dave signed out the tape recorder.* □ *Mary signed a projector out.*

sign someone up (for something) to record the agreement of someone to participate in something. (*Someone* includes *oneself*. More at *sign up (for something).*) □ *Has anyone signed you up for the party?* T *Can you sign up Liz for the party?* □ *I would be happy to sign her up.* □ *I signed myself up for the class.*

sign someone up (with someone or something) to record the agreement of someone to join someone, a group of people, or an organization. (*Someone* includes *oneself.*) □ *I found Tom in the hall, and we went to sign him up with Alice.* T *Tom signed up his friends with the agency.* □ *Tom signed all his friends up with his newly started bicycle club.* □ *I signed myself up with the crew of the Felicity Ann.*

sign something away to sign a paper in which one gives away one's rights to something. □ *Valerie signed her rights away.* T *She signed away her claim to the money.*

sign something over (to someone) to sign a paper granting the rights to or ownership of something to a specific person. □ *Larry signed all the rights to his book over to the publisher.* T *He signed over all the rights to the publisher.* □ *Steve signed all rights over.*

sign up (for something) to record one's agreement to participate in something. (More at *sign someone up (for something).*) □ *I want to sign up for guitar lessons.* □ *We will sign up as soon as possible.*

signed, sealed, and delivered formally and officially signed; [for a formal document to be] executed. □ *Here is the deed to the property — signed, sealed, and delivered.* □ *I can't begin work on this project until I have the contract in my hand signed, sealed, and delivered.*

Since when? When was that decided?; *That's news to me.*; When was that done? □ TOM: *You've been assigned to the night shift.* JOHN: *Since when?* □ JANE: *Fred is now the assistant manager.* JOHN: *Since when?* JANE: *Since I appointed him, that's when.*

sing out to sing louder. (More at *sing something out.*) □ *Sing out, please. This is a very large hall.* □ *The sopranos will have to sing out more.*

sing something out to sing or announce something loudly. (More at *sing out.*) □ *He sang the names out loud and clear.* T *She sang out "The Star-Spangled Banner" in a loud voice.*

single someone or something out (for something) to choose or pick someone or something for something; to select an eligible person or thing for something. □ *The committee singled her out for a special award.* T *We singled out Liz for special honors.* T *They singled out my entry for special mention.*

sink back (into something) to lean back and relax in something, such as a soft chair. □ *I can't wait to get home and sink back into my easy chair.* □ *He sank back and went to sleep almost immediately.*

sink down to sink or submerge. □ *The sun sank down and darkness spread across the land.* □ *She sat in the chair and sank down, enjoying her moment of relaxation.*

sink in (to someone or something) to penetrate someone or something. (Used figuratively in reference to someone's brain or thinking.) □ *It finally began to sink into me that we were really, totally lost.* □ *When what* *she said finally sank in, I was shocked and amazed.*

sink one's teeth into something 1. to take a bite of some kind of food, usually a special kind of food. □ *I can't wait to sink my teeth into a nice juicy steak.* □ *Look at that chocolate cake! Don't you want to sink your teeth into that?* **2.** to get a chance to do, learn, or control something. □ *That appears to be a very challenging assignment. I can't wait to sink my teeth into it.* □ *Being the manager of this department is a big task. I'm very eager to sink my teeth into it.*

sink or swim fail or succeed. □ *After I've studied and learned all I can, I have to take the test and sink or swim.* □ *It's too late to help John now. It's sink or swim for him.*

sink something in((to) someone or something) 1. to drive or push something into someone or something. □ *The brave hero sank the wooden stake into the vampire.* Ⓣ *The hero sank in the stake.* □ *Jamie sank it in, and the movie ended.* **2.** to invest time or money in someone or something. (Sometimes implying that it was wasted.) □ *You would not believe how much money I've sunk into that guy!* □ *She sank a lot of money in the stock market.*

siphon something off (from something) to suck or draw a liquid off from something. □ *Harry siphoned the cream off the milk.* Ⓣ *He siphoned off the cream.* □ *He siphoned it off.* □ *Frank siphoned all the water off from the fish tank.*

Sir? 1. Did you call me, sir? (Compare to *Ma'am*.) □ JOHN: *Tom!* TOM: *Sir?* JOHN: *Get over here!* □ FRED: *Bill!* BILL: *Sir? Did you call me?* FRED: *Yes.*

Have a seat. I want to talk to you. **2.** I did not hear what you said, sir. □ JOHN: *I want you to take this to Mr. Franklin.* CHILD: *Sir?* JOHN: *Please take this to Mr. Franklin.* □ BOB: *Can you wait on me?* CLERK: *Sir?* BOB: *Can you wait on me?* CLERK: *Oh, yes, sir.*

sit around to sit and relax; to waste time sitting. □ *Don't just sit around! Get moving!* □ *I need to sit around every now and then and reorganize my thoughts.*

sit back to push oneself back in one's seat; to lean against the back of one's seat. □ *Please sit back. I can't see around you.* □ *I sat back and made myself comfortable, assuming that the movie would bore me to sleep.*

sit down to be seated; to sit on something, such as a chair. □ *Please sit down and make yourself comfortable.* □ *Can I sit down here?*

sit in (for someone) to act as a substitute for someone. □ *I am not a regular member of this committee. I am sitting in for Larry Smith.* □ *Do you mind if I sit in? My representative can't be here.*

sit in (on something) to attend something as a visitor; to act as a temporary participant in something. □ *Do you mind if I sit in on your discussion?* □ *Please do sit in.*

sit on its hands [for an audience] to refuse to applaud. (Not literal.) □ *We saw a very poor performance of the play. The audience sat on its hands for the entire play.*

sit on one's hands to do nothing; to fail to help. (Not literal.) □ *When we needed help from Mary, she just sat on her hands.* □ *We need the* *cooperation of everyone. You can't sit on your hands!*

sit out to refrain from participation. □ *I'm not playing, thanks. I'll just sit out.* □ *John played, but his brother sat out.*

sit (something) out to elect not to participate in something. □ *I think I will not join in this game. I'll sit it out.*

sit through something to remain seated and in attendance for all of something. □ *I can't stand to sit through that class one more time!* □ *Do I have to sit through the whole lecture?*

sit tight to wait; to wait patiently. (Does not necessarily refer to sitting.) □ *Just relax and sit tight. I'll be right with you.* □ *We were waiting in line for the gates to open when someone came out and told us to sit tight because it wouldn't be much longer before we could go in.*

sit up 1. to rise from a lying to a sitting position. □ *When the alarm went off, he sat up and put his feet on the floor.* □ *She couldn't sleep, so she sat up and read a book.* **2.** to sit straighter in one's seat; to hold one's posture more upright while seated. □ *Please sit up. Don't slouch!* □ *You wouldn't get backaches if you would sit up.*

sit up and take notice to become alert and pay attention. □ *A loud noise from the front of the room caused everyone to sit up and take notice.* □ *The company wouldn't pay any attention to my complaints. When I had my lawyer write them a letter, they sat up and took notice.*

sit up with someone to remain awake and attend someone throughout the

night. □ *I sat up with a sick friend all night.* □ *I had to sit up with Timmy because he had a tummyache.*

sitting on a powder keg in a risky or explosive situation; in a situation where something serious or dangerous may happen at any time. (Not literal. A *powder keg* is a keg of gunpowder.) □ *Things are very tense at work. The whole office is sitting on a powder keg.* □ *The fire at the oil field seems to be under control for now, but all the workers there are sitting on a powder keg.*

six of one and half a dozen of the other about the same one way or another. □ *It doesn't matter to me which way you do it. It's six of one and half a dozen of the other.* □ *What difference does it make? They're both the same — six of one and half a dozen of the other.*

size someone or something up to scrutinize someone or something and form a judgment. Ⓣ *The boxer had sized up his opponent by watching videotapes of previous fights.* Ⓣ *He came into the house and sized up the kitchen and dining room.*

skate on thin ice to be in a risky situation. (Also used literally.) □ *I try to stay well informed so I don't end up skating on thin ice when the teacher asks me a question.*

skeleton in the closet a hidden and shocking secret; a secret fact about oneself. (Often in the plural. As if one had hidden the grisly results of murder in the closet.) □ *You can ask anyone about how reliable I am. I don't mind. I don't have any skeletons in the closet.* □ *My uncle was in jail for a day once. That's our family's skeleton in the closet.*

skim through something to go through something hastily; to read through something hastily. □ *She skimmed through the catalogs, looking for a nice gift for Gary.* □ *I will skim through your manuscript and see if it looks promising.*

Skin me! See *Give me five!*

Skin me! Give me some skin!; Shake my hand! (Originally black slang.) □ *Hey, man, skin me!* □ *Hey, old buddy. Don't walk on! Skin me!*

Skip it! *Never mind!; Forget it!* (Shows impatience or disappointment.) □ JOHN: *I need some help on this project.* MARY: *What?* JOHN: *Oh, skip it!* □ JANE: *Will you be able to do this, or should I get someone with more experience?* BOB: *What did you say?* JANE: *Oh, skip it!*

skip over someone or something not to choose someone or something next in line. □ *She skipped over me and chose the next one in line.* □ *I skipped over the red ones and took a blue one.*

Skoal! See *Bottoms up.*

slack off to wane or decline; to decrease in intensity. □ *Finally the rains slacked off, and we could go outside and walk around.* □ *When business slacks off a bit, we have a sale.*

slam some beers to drink beer; to drink a number of beers. (Slang.) □ *Fred and Larry went out to slam some beers.* □ *Let's slam some beers sometime.*

slap something on to dress in something hastily. □ *Henry slapped a shirt on and went out to say something to the garbage hauler.* ⊤ *He slapped on a shirt and ran to the bus stop.*

slap something on(to someone or something) to place something onto someone or something by slapping. □ *Tim slapped a sign onto Gary that said "kick me."* ⊤ *Tim came up to Gary's back and slapped on a sign.* □ *Tim slapped a sign on.*

slap something together to make up something very quickly. □ *This is very carelessly done. Someone has just slapped it together.* □ *This house was just slapped together. It is really poorly constructed.*

sleep in to remain in bed, sleeping past one's normal time of arising. □ *I really want to sleep in this morning.* □ *I slept in both Saturday and Sunday.*

sleep like a log to sleep very soundly. (Not literal, of course.) □ *Nothing can wake me up. I usually sleep like a log.* □ *Everyone in our family sleeps like a log, so no one heard the fire engines in the middle of the night.*

sleep on something to think about something overnight; to weigh a decision overnight. □ *I don't know whether I agree to do it. Let me sleep on it.* □ *I slept on it, and I've decided to accept your offer.*

sleep something off to sleep away the effect of alcohol or drugs. □ *Jeff is in his room, sleeping it off.* ⊤ *Jeff is sleeping off the effects of the night before.*

sleep through something to remain sleeping through some event. □ *I didn't hear the storm. I guess I slept through it.* □ *Wally slept through the entire opera — even the loud part.*

slice in(to something) to cut into something, usually with a knife or something similar. □ *Betty sliced into the cake and discovered it was chocolate all the way through.* □ *It wasn't until* she sliced in that she found out what kind of cake it was.

slice something off to cut something off with slicing motions. □ *Sue sliced the dead branches off with a rusty machine.* ⊤ *Karen sliced off a nice piece of turkey.*

slice through something to cut through something with slicing motions. □ *The chef sliced through the ham as if it were butter.* □ *The knife was too dull to slice through the tomato.*

slide out of something to slip or glide out of something without much effort. □ *Mary slid out of the car and ran to the front door.* □ *The floppy disk slid out of the computer.*

slide something in (to something) to insert something into something effortlessly. □ *Henry slid the end of the seat-belt buckle into its holder and started the car.* ⊤ *Slide in the buckle and make sure it's tight.* □ *Slide it in quickly so we can start up.*

slide something out (of something) to cause something to slip or glide out of something without much effort. □ *The hunter slid his knife out of its sheath and got ready to skin the deer.* ⊤ *He slid out the heavy box.* □ *Tony slid the box out.*

slim down to become thinner; to become narrower. (More at *slim someone down.*) □ *You have really slimmed down a lot since I last saw you.* □ *I need to eat less so I can slim down.* □ *He slimmed down quite a bit after he had his health problem.*

slim someone down to cause someone to lose weight. (*Someone* includes *oneself*. More at *slim down.*) □ *They started to slim her down in the hospital, but she gained the weight back*

as soon as she got out. ⊤ *The dietician slimmed down all the patients under his care.*

slip in (to something) to slide or glide into something, such as clothing, a sleeping bag, a tight place, etc. □ *I don't want to slip into a cold sleeping bag. How can I warm it up?* □ *I opened the bag and slipped in.*

Slip me five! See *Give me five!*

Slip me some skin! See *Give me five!*

slip of the tongue an error in speaking where a word is pronounced incorrectly, or where something that the speaker did not mean to say is said. (As if one's tongue had made a misstep.) □ *I didn't mean to tell her that. It was a slip of the tongue.* □ *I failed to understand the instructions because the speaker made a slip of the tongue at an important point.*

slip off ((of) someone or something) to fall away from or off someone or something. (The *of* is colloquial.) □ *The jacket slipped off of Sally, but she grabbed it before it hit the floor.* □ *She hung the jacket on the back of the chair, but it slipped off.*

slip off (to some place) to sneak away to some place. □ *Judy and Jeff slipped off to the movies unnoticed.* □ *They slipped off and no one cared.*

slip one's mind [for something that was to be remembered] to be forgotten. (As if a thought had slipped out of one's brain.) □ *I meant to go to the grocery store on the way home, but it slipped my mind.* □ *My birthday slipped my mind. I guess I wanted to forget it.*

slip out (of something) 1. to sneak out of a place unnoticed. □ *Gloria* *slipped out of the theater at intermission.* □ *She slipped out and went home.* **2.** to slide out of an article of clothing. □ *She slipped out of her dress and hung it neatly in the closet.* □ *Ted slipped out of his T-shirt and left it on the floor where it fell.*

slip someone five to shake someone's hand. (Slang.) □ *Billy slipped me five, and we sat down to discuss old times.* □ *Come on, man, slip me five!*

slip something off to let an item of clothing slide off one's body; to remove an item of clothing. □ *He slipped his coat off and put it on a chair.* ⊤ *She slipped off her shoes and relaxed.*

slip something on to put on an article of clothing, possibly casually or in haste. □ *I will go in and slip my bathing suit on and join you in a minute.* ⊤ *She slipped on her shoes and we left.*

slip through someone's fingers to get away from someone; for someone to lose track (of something or someone). □ *I had a copy of the book you want, but somehow it slipped through my fingers.* □ *There was a detective following me, but I managed to slip through his fingers.*

slip up to make an error. □ *I hope you don't slip up again. Try to be more careful.* □ *I will try not to slip up.*

slip up (on something) to make an error (in something). □ *I guess I slipped up on that last job.* □ *Fred slipped up on that list — there are a lot of names missing.*

slouch down to slump or droop down. □ *Don't always slouch down, Timmy! Stand up straight.* □ *I slouch down because I am tired.*

slouch over to lean or crumple and fall to one side; [for someone] to collapse while in a sitting position. □ *He slouched over and went to sleep in his chair.* □ *When he slouched over, I thought something was wrong.*

Slow and steady wins the race. Deliberateness and determination will lead to success. (Proverb.) □ *I worked my way through college in six years. Now I know what they mean when they say, "Slow and steady wins the race."* □ *Ann won the race because she started off slowly and established a good pace. The other runners tried to sprint the whole distance, and they tired out before the final lap. Ann's trainer said, "You see! I told you! Slow and steady wins the race."*

slow down to decrease speed; to go slower. □ *Please slow down. You are going too fast.* □ *Slow down or you will skid.*

slow someone or something down to cause someone or something to decrease speed or go slower. □ *Slow him down if you can. He is going too fast.* ⊤ *Slow down that car!* □ *Please slow your car down!* □ *Slow yourself down a little. You are working too hard and too fast.*

slow up to go slower; to reduce speed in order for someone or something to catch up. □ *Slow up a little! I can't keep up with you!* □ *Please slow up. I can't follow your lecture when you talk so fast.*

slump over **1.** [for someone] to collapse and fall over in a sitting position. □ *Just after the gunshot, Bruno slumped over and slid from his chair to the floor.* **2.** to fall over heavily; to collapse and droop from an upright

367

position. □ *How can you work when you slump over your desk that way?* □ *He slumped over suddenly, and we were afraid that he was ill.*

smack-dab in the middle right in the middle. □ *I want a big helping of mashed potatoes with a glob of butter smack-dab in the middle.* □ *Tom and Sally were having a terrible argument, and I was trapped — smack-dab in the middle.*

smash into something to crash into something; to bump or crash into something. □ *Judy smashed into the coffee table and hurt her leg.* □ *The car smashed into the side of a bus and caused a lot of damage.*

smash out of something to break [one's way] out of something. □ *The prisoner smashed out of his cell.* □ *The horse smashed out of its stable.*

smash something in to crush something inward; to make something collapse inward by striking it. □ *Andy gave one good kick and smashed the drum in.* T *Liz smashed in the window.*

smash something up to break something up; to destroy something. □ *I hope the children don't smash the good china up if we use it tonight.* T *The angry worker smashed up the bucket.*

smash through something to break [one's way] through some sort of barrier. □ *The fleeing car smashed through the police barrier.* □ *Max got angry and smashed through the office door.*

Smile when you say that. I will be happy to interpret that remark as a joke or as kidding. □ JOHN: *You're a real pain in the neck.* BOB: *Smile when you say that.* □ SUE: *I'm going to bop*

you on the head! JOHN: *Smile when you say that!*

smooth something down to make something flat or smooth by pressing. □ *She smoothed her skirt down, fluffed her hair, and went into the boardroom.* T *Karen smoothed down the bedclothes.*

smooth something out 1. to flatten or even something out by smoothing or pressing. □ *Wally smoothed the bedspread out.* T *Wally finished making the bed by smoothing out the spread.* **2.** to polish and refine something. (Figurative.) □ *The editor smoothed John's style out.* T *You need to smooth out your delivery when you are speaking.*

snap back (after something) to return to normal after an accident or similar event. □ *He is upset now, but he will snap back after things settle down.* □ *Things will snap back in no time at all.*

snap back (at someone) to give a sharp or angry response to someone. □ *The telephone operator, unlike in the good old days, snapped back at the caller.* □ *Please don't snap back. I've had a bad day.*

Snap it up! *Hurry up!* (Colloquial.) □ JOHN: *Come on, Fred. Snap it up!* FRED: *I'm hurrying! I'm hurrying!* □ SALLY: *Snap it up! You're going to make us late.* JOHN: *That's exactly what I had in mind.*

snap one's cookies to vomit; to regurgitate. (Slang.) □ *I think I'm gonna snap my cookies.* □ *Some jerk snapped his cookies on the sidewalk.*

Snap to it! Move faster!; Look alert! □ BILL: *Snap to it! MARY: Don't rush me!* □ JOHN: *Get in line there. Snap* *to it!* SALLY: *What is this, the army? You just wait till I'm ready!*

sneak in(to some place) to enter a place quietly and in secret, perhaps without a ticket or permission. □ *The kids tried to sneak into the rock concert, but they were stopped by the guards.* □ *Never try to sneak in. Sometimes they arrest you for trespassing.*

sneak out (of some place) to go out of a place quietly and in secret. □ *I sneaked out of the meeting, hoping no one would notice.* □ *Jamie saw me and sneaked out with me.*

sneak up on someone or something to approach someone or something quietly and in secret. □ *Please don't sneak up on me like that.* □ *I sneaked up on the cake, hoping no one would see me. Someone did.*

snoop around (something) to look around in a place, trying to find out something secret or learn about someone else's affairs. □ *Why are you snooping around my house?* □ *I am not snooping around.*

snow someone or something in [for a heavy snowfall] to block someone or something in a place. □ *The sudden storm snowed us in.* T *The storm snowed in most of the people in town.* T *We hoped it hadn't snowed in the fire engines.*

snuff it to die. (Slang.) □ *The cat leapt straight up in the air and snuffed it.* □ *I was so sick they thought I was going to snuff it.*

so 1. a sentence opener used to break a silence in a conversation or aggressively start a new topic. (Words such as this often use intonation to convey the connotation of the sentence that is to follow. The brief in-tonation pattern accompanying the word may indicate sarcasm, disagreement, caution, consolation, sternness, etc.) □ ANDREW: *So, I'm new around here. Where's the fun?* BOB: *You must be new. There's never been any fun around here.* □ *"So, how are you?" asked Kate.* □ ANDREW: *So, when do we eat?* RACHEL: *Don't you have any manners?* □ BOB: *So, what you been doing?* BILL: *Not much.* □ ANDREW: *So, been keeping busy?* BOB: *No. I been taking it easy.* **2.** a defensive sentence opener that takes an offensive tone. □ FRED: *So I made a mistake. So what?* JOHN: *It caused us all a lot of trouble. That's what.* □ ALICE: *So I'm not perfect! What does that prove?* ANDREW: *Nothing, I guess.*

So do I. I do too. □ MARY: *I want some more cake.* SALLY: *So do I.* □ BOB: *I have to go home now.* TOM: *So do I.* BOB: *Bye.*

So much for that. That is the end of that.; We will not be dealing with that anymore. □ *John tossed the stub of a pencil into the trash. "So much for that," he muttered, fishing through his drawer for another.* □ MOTHER: *Here, try some carrots.* CHILD (brushing the spoon aside): *No! No!* MOTHER: *Well, so much for that.*

so quiet you could hear a pin drop See the following entry.

so still you could hear a pin drop AND **so quiet you could hear a pin drop** very quiet. (Also with *can.*) □ *When I came into the room, it was so still you could hear a pin drop. Then everyone shouted, "Happy birthday!"* □ *Please be quiet. Be so quiet you can hear a pin drop.*

So (what)? Why does that matter? (Colloquial or familiar. Can be considered rude.) □ BOB: *Your attitude always seems to lack sincerity.* MARY: *So what?* □ JOHN: *Your car sure is dusty.* SUE: *So?*

(So) what else is new? This isn't new. It has happened before.; Not this again. □ MARY: *Taxes are going up again.* BOB: *So what else is new?* □ JOHN: *Gee, my pants are getting tight. Maybe I'm putting on a little weight.* SALLY: *What else is new?*

soak in (to something) [for moisture] to penetrate something. □ *The rain soaked into the parched ground as fast as it fell.* □ *I'm glad it soaked in. I was afraid it would run off.*

soak something off ((of) something) to remove something, such as a label or surface soil, from something by soaking it in a liquid. (The *of* is colloquial.) □ *She soaked the labels off the bottles and jars.* ⊤ *Please soak off the label.* □ *Soak the labels off, don't scrape them off.*

soak something out (of something) to remove something, such as a stain, from something by soaking in a liquid. □ *Dan soaked the stain out of his shirt and then washed it.* ⊤ *Dan soaked out the stain.* □ *I couldn't soak the stain out.*

soak through something [for liquid] to work its way through something, such as cloth or paper. □ *Please wipe up that mess before it soaks through the tablecloth.* □ *It's too late. The grape juice has soaked through the carpet into the mat.*

soap someone or something down to cover someone or something thoroughly with soap or suds. (*Someone* includes *oneself*.) □ *Mother soaped*

Timmy *down and rinsed him off in warm water.* ⊤ *She soaped down the floor.* □ *He soaped himself down and then rinsed off.*

sober someone up 1. to take actions that will cause a drunken person to become sober. (*Someone* includes *oneself*. More at *sober up*.) □ *Some coffee ought to sober him up.* ⊤ *They tried to sober up the guys who had been out all night.* **2.** to cause someone to face reality. □ *The harsh reality of what had happened sobered him up immediately.* ⊤ *The lecture sobered up all the revelers.*

sober up to return to sobriety from a drunken state. (More at *sober someone up*.) □ *Jeff sobered up in an hour and could function again.* □ *I don't think that Tex has sobered up since the 1960's.*

soil one's hands See *get one's hands dirty.*

Some people (just) don't know when to give up. See the following entry.

Some people (just) don't know when to quit. AND **Some people (just) don't know when to give up. 1.** You, or someone being talked about, should stop doing something, such as talking, arguing, scolding, etc. (Often directed toward the person being addressed.) □ BILL: *I hate to say it again, but that lipstick is all wrong for you. It brings out the wrong color in your eyes, and it makes your mouth larger than it really is.* JANE: *Oh, stop, stop! That's enough! Some people just don't know when to quit.* □ JOHN: *Those bushes out in the backyard need trimming.* SALLY: *You keep criticizing! Is there no end to it? Some people don't know when to quit!* **2.** Some people do not know when to slow down and stop working so hard. □ BOB: *We were afraid that John had suffered a heart attack.* BILL: *I'm not surprised. He works so hard. Some people just don't know when to give up.* □ JANE: *He just kept on gambling. Finally, he had no money left.* SALLY: *Some people don't know when to quit.*

(Someone had) better keep quiet about it. See the following entry.

(Someone had) better keep still about it. AND **(Someone had) better keep quiet about it.** an admonition that a particular person ought not to tell about or discuss something. (The *someone* can stand for any person's name, any pronoun, or even the word *someone* meaning "you-know-who." If there is no *Someone had*, the phrase is a mild admonition to keep quiet about something.) □ MARY: *I saw you with Bill last night.* JANE: *You'd better keep quiet about it.* □ JANE: *Tom found out what you're giving Sally for her birthday.* BILL: *He had better keep quiet about it!*

(Someone) looks like something the cat dragged in. Someone looks rumpled or worn out. (Jocular. Compare to *Look (at) what the cat dragged in!*) □ ALICE: *Tom just came in. He looks like something the cat dragged in. What do you suppose happened to him?* □ RACHEL: *Wow! Did you see Sue?* JANE: *Yes. Looks like something the cat dragged in.*

(Someone or something is) supposed to. an expression meaning that someone or something was meant to do something. (Frequently, in speech, *supposed* is reduced to *'sposed*. The words *someone* or *something* can be replaced with nouns or

pronouns, or used themselves.) □ MARY: *They didn't deliver the flowers we ordered.* SUE: *Supposed to. Give them a call.* □ SALLY: *This screw doesn't fit into hole number seven in the way the instructions say it should.* BILL: *It's supposed to. Something is wrong.*

(Someone will) be with you in a minute. AND **With you in a minute.** Please be patient, someone will attend to you very soon. (The *someone* can be any person's name or a pronoun, typically *I*. If there is no one mentioned, *I* is implied. The *minute* can be replaced by *moment* or *second*.) □ SUE: *Oh, Miss?* CLERK: *Someone will be with you in a minute.* □ BILL: *Please wait here. I'll be with you in a minute.* BOB: *Please hurry.*

(Someone's) not supposed to. See *(It's) not supposed to.*

Something has got to give. Emotions or tempers are strained, and there is going to be an outburst. □ ALICE: *There are serious problems with Mary and Tom. They fight and fight.* SUE: *Yes, something has got to give. It can't go on like this.* □ BILL: *Things are getting difficult at the office. Something has got to give.* MARY: *Just stay clear of all the bickering.*

Sooner than you think. an expression stating something will happen quicker than one expects. □ SALLY: *I'm going to have to stop pretty soon for a rest.* MARY: *Sooner than you think, I'd say. I think one of our tires is low.* □ TOM: *The stock market is bound to run out of steam pretty soon.* BOB: *Sooner than you think from the look of today's news.*

Sorry (that) I asked. Now that I have heard the answer, I regret asking the question. □ ALICE: *Can we get a new car soon? The old one is a wreck.* JOHN: *Are you kidding? There's no way that we could ever afford a new car!* ALICE: *Sorry I asked.* □ *After he heard the long list of all the reasons he wouldn't be allowed to go to the concert, Fred just shrugged and said, "Sorry that I asked."*

Sort of. AND **Kind of.** Yes, but only to a small degree. □ BOB: *Do you like what you're doing in school?* ALICE: *Kind of.* □ HENRY: *What do you think about all these new laws? Do they worry you?* JOHN: *Sort of.*

sort something out 1. to sort something; to arrange something according to class or category. □ *Let's sort these cards out.* T *Would you please sort out your socks?* **2.** to study a problem and figure it out. □ *I can't sort this out without some more time.* T *Let's sort out this mess and settle it once and for all.*

sound off to speak something loudly; to call out one's name or one's place in a numerical sequence. □ *All right, sound off, you guys!* □ *Each one sounded off.*

sound off (about something) to complain loudly about something; to make a fuss over something. □ *She is always sounding off about something.* □ *Betty sounds off all the time.*

Soup's on! The meal is ready to eat. (Said for any food, not just soup.) □ TOM: *Soup's on!* BILL: *The camp chef has dished up another disaster. Come on, we might as well face the music.* □ JOHN: *Soup's on! Come and get it!* MARY: *Well, I guess it's time to eat again.* SUE: *Yeah, no way to avoid it, I guess.*

sow one's wild oats to do wild and foolish things in one's youth. (Often assumed to have some sort of sexual meaning, with *wild oats* referring to a young man's semen.) □ *Dale was out sowing his wild oats last night, and he's in jail this morning.* □ *Mrs. Smith told Mr. Smith that he was too old to be sowing his wild oats.*

space someone out to cause someone to become giddy. (Slang.) □ *The whole business just spaced me out.* T *The spectacle spaced out the entire audience.*

spaced (out) AND **spacy** silly; giddy. (Slang. Hyphenated before a nominal.) □ *I have such spaced-out parents!* □ *He's so spaced!* □ *I love my spacy old dad.*

spacy See the previous entry.

spaz around to waste time; to mess around. (Slang.) □ *You kids are always spazzing around. Why don't you get a job?* □ *We're just spazzing around. Leave us alone.*

spaz out 1. to overreact to something; to become overly excited about something. (Slang.) □ *I knew you would spaz out! It's not that bad!* □ *Come on, don't spaz out!* **2.** an emotional display. (Usually **spaz-out.**) □ *There's no need for a spaz-out!* □ *She threw a hell of a spaz-out.*

Speak of the devil. a phrase said when someone whose name has just been mentioned suddenly appears on the scene. (Similar to *We were just talking about you.*) □ TOM: *Speak of the devil, here comes Bill.* MARY: *We were just talking about you, Bill.* □ JOHN: *I wonder how Fred is doing in his new job.* FRED: *Hi, you two. What's* *up?* JOHN: *Speak of the devil. Look who's here!*

speak out to speak loudly; to speak to be heard. □ *Please speak out. We need to hear you.* □ *They won't hear you in the back row if you don't speak out.*

speak out (about someone or something) to express oneself about someone or something; to tell what one knows about someone or something. □ *I could keep silent no longer. I had to speak out about the alleged accident.* □ *I had to speak out!*

speak out (against someone or something) to speak negatively and publicly about someone or something; to reveal something negative, in speech, about someone or something. □ *I don't want to speak out against my friends, but I am afraid I have to.* □ *The citizens spoke out against corruption in government.* □ *They felt that they had to speak out.*

speak up **1.** to speak loudly. □ *Please speak up. I can't hear you.* □ *No one will be able to hear you if you do not speak up.* **2.** Please speak louder.; Do not be shy, speak louder. (Usually **Speak up.**) □ *"Speak up. I can hardly hear you," said Uncle Henry, cupping his hand to his ear.* □ MARY: *I'm sorry.* TEACHER: *Speak up.* MARY: *I'm sorry, ma'am. I won't do it again.*

speak up for someone or something to speak in favor of someone or something; to come forward and express favorable things about someone or something. □ *I hope you will speak up for me when the time comes.* □ *I will speak up for the proposed legislation.*

Speaking. AND **This is someone.** I am the person you have just asked for (on the telephone). (The *someone* can be a person's name or *he* or *she*.) □ TOM: *Hello?* MARY: *Is Tom there?* TOM: *Speaking.* □ TOM: *Hello?* MARY: *Is Tom there?* TOM: *This is he.*

speaking (quite) candidly an expression introducing a frank or forthright statement. □ *"Speaking quite candidly, I find your behavior a bit offensive," stated Frank, obviously offended.* □ MARY: *Tell me what you really think about this skirt.* SALLY: *Speaking candidly, I think you should get your money back.*

(speaking) (quite) frankly AND **frankly speaking** a transitional phrase announcing that the speaker is going to talk in a more familiar and totally forthright manner. □ TOM: *Speaking quite frankly, I'm not certain she's the one for the job.* MARY: *I agree.* □ BOB: *We ought to be looking at housing in a lower price bracket.* BILL: *Quite frankly, I agree.* □ *"Frankly speaking," said John, "I think you're out of your mind!"*

speed someone or something up to cause someone or something to move faster. (More at *speed up.*) □ *We tried to speed him up, but he is just a very slow person.* T *We sped up the process, but it still took too long.*

speed up to go faster. (More at *speed someone or something up.*) □ *Please speed up. We are late.* □ *All the cars sped up.*

spice something up **1.** to make some food more spicy. □ *Judy spiced the cider up by adding cinnamon and nutmeg.* T *She spiced up the chili too much.* **2.** to make something more interesting, lively, or sexy. (Figurative.) □ *I'm afraid that they spiced the musical up too much. Some people walked out.* □ *Judy liked to spice her lectures up by telling jokes.* ⊤ *She spiced up each lecture with a joke.* ⊤ *They spiced up the play too much.*

spiffed out nicely dressed; decked out. (Slang.) □ *I like to get all spiffed out every now and then.* □ *Wow, you look spiffed out! Where are you going?*

spiffed up dressed up, brushed up, and polished up nicely. (Slang.) □ *See if you can get yourself a little spiffed up before we get to the front door. We wouldn't want the Wilmington-Thorpes to think you only have one suit.* □ *The house doesn't have to be too spiffed up for the Franklins. They are used to clutter.*

spill the beans See *let the cat out of the bag.*

spin off [for something] to part and fly away from something that is spinning; [for something] to detach or break loose from something. □ *The blade of the lawn mower spun off, but fortunately no one was injured.* □ *The lid to the pickle jar spun off easily after I got it loosened.*

splash down [for a space capsule] to land in the water. □ *The capsule splashed down very close to the pickup ship.* □ *It splashed down at noon.*

split off (from something) to separate away from something; to sever connection with and separate from something. □ *A large iceberg split off from the glacier and made an enormous splash.* □ *A giant ice cube split off and floated away.*

split people up to separate two or more people. □ *I am going to have to*

split you two up if you don't stop talking to each other. ⊤ *I will have to split up those two.*

split someone or something up (into something) to divide people or things up into something, such as groups. (*Someone* includes *oneself.*) □ *I had to split the group up into two sections — there were so many who showed up.* ⊤ *I split up the class into two discussion sections.* □ *I split them up.* □ *They split themselves up into smaller groups.*

split something off ((of) something) to sever connection with something and separate. (The *of* is colloquial.) □ *Dave split a piece of wood off the log to use for kindling.* ⊤ *He split off a stick of wood.* □ *Jamie took a log and split a stave of wood off.*

split the difference to divide the difference between two things (with someone else). □ *You want to sell for $120, and I want to buy for $100. Let's split the difference and close the deal at $110.* □ *I don't want to split the difference. I want $120.*

sponge someone or something down to remove the [excess] moisture from someone or something. □ *The fight manager sponged his boxer down.* ⊤ *I will sponge down the countertop.*

sponge something away to absorb, wipe up, or wipe away something. □ *Try sponging the stain away with some soda water.* ⊤ *I will sponge away the mess.*

spot someone (something) 1. to give an advantage to someone. (Slang.) □ *I'll spot you twenty points.* □ *No need to spot me. I'm the greatest!* **2.** to lend someone something. □ *Can you* spot me a few bucks? □ I can spot you a whole hundred!

spread it on thick See *lay it on thick.*

spread like wildfire [for something] to spread rapidly and without control. □ *The epidemic is spreading like wildfire. Everyone is getting sick.* □ *John told a joke that was so funny it spread like wildfire.*

spread oneself too thin to do so many things that you can do none of them well; to spread one's efforts or attention too widely. □ *It's a good idea to get involved in a lot of activities, but don't spread yourself too thin.* □ *I'm too busy these days. I'm afraid I've spread myself too thin.*

spread out to separate and distribute over a wide area. (More at *spread something out.*) □ *The sheriff told the members of the posse to spread out and continue their search.* □ *The grease spread out and stained a large area of the carpet.*

spread something on(to something) to distribute a coating of something onto something. □ *Spread the butter onto the bread evenly.* ⊤ *Spread on the butter evenly.* □ *Donna spread the paint on with a roller.*

spread something out to open, unfold, or lay something over a wider area. (More at *spread out.*) □ *Spread the wet papers out so they will dry.* ⊤ *She spread out the papers to dry them.*

spring for something AND **bounce for something** to treat (someone) by buying something. (Slang.) □ *I'm bouncing for pizza. Any takers?* □ *Ralph sprang for drinks, and we all had a great time.*

spring up to appear or develop suddenly; to sprout, as with a seedling. □ *We knew it was really spring when all the flowers sprang up.* □ *It seems as if the tulips sprang up overnight.* □ *The dog's ears sprang up when the refrigerator opened.* □ *A little breeze sprang up and cooled things off.*

spruce someone or something up 1. to tidy up and groom someone or something. (*Someone* includes oneself.) □ *Laura's mother took a few minutes to spruce her daughter up for the party.* ⊤ *She spruced up her daughter.* □ *Let's spruce the house up this spring.* □ *He spruced himself up a bit and then rang the doorbell.* **2.** to refurbish or renew someone or something. (*Someone* includes oneself.) □ *Do you think we should spruce this room up a little?* ⊤ *Yes, let's spruce up this room.* ⊤ *We spruced up the house for the holidays.* □ *She bought all new clothes so she could spruce herself up for her new job.*

square peg in a round hole a misfit. □ *John can't seem to get along with the people he works with. He's just a square peg in a round hole.* □ *I'm not a square peg in a round hole. It's just that no one understands me.*

squash something down to crush something down; to pack something down. □ *Squash the ice cream down so the air will be pushed out.* ⊤ *Who squashed down my hat?*

squeak by (someone or something) 1. to manage just to squeeze past someone or something. □ *I squeaked by the fat man in the hallway only to find myself blocked by another.* □ *I just barely squeaked by.* **2.** to manage just to get past a barrier represented by a person or thing, such as a teacher or an examination. □ *Judy just squeaked by Professor Smith, who has a reputation for flunking just about everyone.* □ *I took the test and just squeaked by.*

squeak something through to manage just to get something accepted or approved. □ *I just managed to squeak the proposal through.* □ *Tom squeaked the application through at the last minute.*

squeak through (something) **1.** to manage just to squeeze through an opening. □ *The child squeaked through the opening and escaped.* □ *Sally squeaked through and got away.* **2.** to manage just to get past a barrier, such as an examination or interview. □ *Sally just barely squeaked through the interview, but she got the job.* □ *I wasn't too alert, and I just squeaked through.*

squeeze someone or something up to press people or things close together. □ *The usher tried to squeeze us up so she could seat more people.* ⊤ *Don't squeeze up the cars too tight in the parking area.*

squeeze (themselves) up [for people] to press themselves closely together. (Also in other persons, as in the examples.) □ *Everyone squeezed themselves up in the tiny car so there would be room for one more.* □ *Let's squeeze up so Jamie can sit down.* □ *They squeezed themselves up so they would take less space.* □ *Let's squeeze ourselves up to make more room.*

squiff out to collapse from alcoholic drink. (Slang.) □ *Hank squiffed out at midnight, right on the dot.* □ *She kept from squiffing out because she didn't trust her date.*

squirm out (of something) **1.** to crawl or wiggle out of something. □ *The worm squirmed out of its hole and was gobbled up by a bird.* □ *The worm squirmed out.* **2.** to escape doing something; to escape the responsibility for having done something. □ *You can't squirm out of it. You have to do it.* □ *He agreed to go but squirmed out at the last minute.* □ *You did it and you can't squirm out of it by denying it!*

stab someone in the back to betray someone. (Also used literally.) □ *I thought we were friends! Why did you stab me in the back?* □ *You don't expect a person whom you trust to stab you in the back.*

stack something up to make a stack of some things. (More at *stack up.*) □ *Please stack these books up.* ⊤ *Liz stacked up the papers and took them to the garage.*

stack up [for something] to accumulate, as in stacks. (Often used figuratively in reference to vehicular traffic. More at *stack something up.*) □ *Your work is stacking up. You will have to work late to finish it.* □ *I hate to let my work stack up. I have to do it sooner or later.* □ *Traffic is stacking up on the expressway.*

stake someone out (on someone) to assign someone to watch someone or to spy on someone. □ *The police staked a detective out on Fred.* ⊤ *They staked out a detective on Fred.* □ *Fred needed watching, so the police staked someone out.*

stake something off to mark out the boundaries of an area of land with stakes. □ *The prospectors staked an area off for themselves.* ⊤ *The prospectors staked off an area in which they would look for gold.*

stalk in(to some place) to stride into a place indignantly. □ *Carl stalked into the manager's office and began his tirade.* □ *He stalked in and began to complain.*

stalk out of some place to stride out of a place indignantly. □ *Jeff stalked out of the store and went straight to the police.* □ *Mary got angry and stalked out of the meeting.*

stall someone or something off to hold someone or something off; to postpone the action of someone or something. □ *Please stall them off while I try to get out the back door.* ⊤ *I will stall off the bill collector for a while.*

stammer something out to manage to say something, but only haltingly. □ *Fred stammered the words out haltingly.* ⊤ *He stammered out the name of the winner.*

stampede out of some place [for a crowd of people or other creatures] to move rapidly out of a place, as if in panic. □ *The patrons stampeded out of the smoky theater.* □ *The cattle stampeded out of the corral.*

stand around to wait around, standing; to loiter. □ *Please don't stand around. Get busy!* □ *Why are all these people standing around doing nothing?*

stand aside 1. to step aside; to get out of the way. □ *Please stand aside while the bridal party passes by.* □ *The guests stood aside while the bride and groom left.* **2.** to withdraw and ignore something; to remain passive while something happens. □ *He just stood aside and let his kids get away with murder.* □ *She stood aside and did not try to come between them.*

stand back (from someone or something) to stand or move well away and to the rear of someone or something. □ *Stand back from Sam. He is really angry.* □ *Would you please stand back from the edge?* □ *Stand back!*

stand by to wait in a state of readiness. □ *I may need your help in a minute. Please stand by.* □ *Stand by while I find your records in this computer.*

stand down to step down, particularly from the witness stand in a courtroom. □ *The bailiff told the witness to stand down.* □ *Please stand down and take your seat.*

stand in (for someone) to represent someone; to substitute for someone. □ *I will stand in for Roger in tonight's performance of the play. He is sick.* □ *He is sick, so I will stand in.*

stand on one's own two feet to be independent and self-sufficient rather than being supported by someone else. □ *I'll be glad when I have a good job and can stand on my own two feet.* □ *When Jane gets out of debt, she'll be able to stand on her own two feet again.*

stand one's ground AND **hold one's ground** to stand up for one's rights; to resist an attack. □ *The lawyer tried to confuse me when I was giving testimony, but I managed to stand my ground.* □ *Some people were trying to crowd us off the beach, but we held our ground.*

stand out (from someone or something) 1. to be prominent when compared to someone or something. □ *As a programmer, she stands out from all the others.* □ *This one stands out from all the rest.* □ *It really stands out.* **2.** [with *something*] to protrude from something. □ *One very straight branch in particular stood out from the* *tree and looked suitable for a post.* □ *The branch stood out and made a perfect place to hang my shirt while I worked.*

stand up **1.** to arise from a sitting or reclining position. □ *He stood up and looked across the valley.* □ *She had been sitting for so long that it was a pleasure to stand up.* **2.** to be in a standing position. □ *I've been standing up all day, and I'm exhausted.* □ *I stood up throughout the whole trip because there were no more seats on the train.* **3.** to wear well; to remain sound and intact. □ *This material just doesn't stand up well when it's washed.* □ *Her work doesn't stand up under close scrutiny.* **4.** [for an assertion] to remain believable. (Figurative.) □ *His testimony will not stand up in court.* □ *When the police checked the story, it did not stand up.*

stand up against someone or something to challenge or hold one's own against someone or something. □ *He's good, but he can't stand up against Jill.* □ *Can this tent stand up against the wind?*

stand up and be counted to state one's support (for someone or something); to come out for someone or something. □ *If you believe in more government help for farmers, write your representative — stand up and be counted.* □ *I'm generally in favor of what you propose, but not enough to stand up and be counted.*

stare someone down to pressure someone to capitulate, back down, or yield by staring. □ *Don't try to stare me down. I have nerves of steel.* T *I tried to stare down my opponent, but it didn't work.*

start from scratch to start from the beginning; to start from nothing. □ *Whenever I bake a cake, I start from scratch. I never use a cake mix in a box.* □ *I built every bit of my own house. I started from scratch and did everything with my own hands.*

start off to begin; to set out on a journey. □ *When do you want to start off?* □ *We will start off as soon as we can get ready.*

start off (by doing something) to begin a process by doing a particular thing first. □ *Can I start off by singing the school song?* □ *That's a good way to start off.*

start off (on something) **1.** to begin a series or sequence. □ *Today I start off on the first volume of my trilogy.* □ *I am ready to start off now.* **2.** to begin a journey. □ *When do we start off on our trip?* □ *I'm ready to start off. What about you?*

start (off) with a clean slate to start out again afresh; to ignore the past and start over again. □ *I plowed under all last year's flowers so I could start with a clean slate next spring.* □ *If I start off with a clean slate, then I'll know exactly what each plant is.*

start out to begin. □ *Whenever you are ready, we will start out.* □ *We can't start out until Tom is here.*

start out as something to begin one's career as something. □ *I started out as a clerk and I'm still a clerk!* □ *I wanted to start out as an assistant manager.*

start over to begin again. □ *I have messed this up so much that there is nothing to do now but start over.* □ *When you start over, try to do it right this time.*

start someone off (on something) to cause someone to begin on a task or job. □ *I have to start Jeff off on this task, then I will talk to you.* T *I will start off my workers on the job tomorrow.* □ *Let me know what time to start them off.*

start something up to start something, such as an engine or a motor. (More at *start up.*) □ *Start your lawn mower up and get that grass cut!* T *Start up your car and let's go.*

start up to begin; to begin running, as with an engine. (More at *start something up.*) □ *The car started up without a problem.* □ *The engines of the plane started up one by one.*

stay away (from someone or something) to avoid someone or something. □ *Stay away from me!* □ *Please stay away!*

stay back (from something) to keep one's distance from someone or something. □ *Stay back from the lawn mower!* □ *This is dangerous. Stay back!*

stay on (after someone or something) See *linger on (after someone or something).*

Stay out of my way. See *Keep out of my way.*

stay out (of something) 1. to keep out of something or some place. □ *Stay out of here!* □ *Please stay out until we are ready.* **2.** to remain uninvolved in some piece of business. □ *I decided to stay out of it and let someone else handle it.* □ *My help wasn't needed there, so I just stayed out.*

Stay out of this! See *Keep out of this!*

stay up (for something) to remain awake and out of bed for some nighttime event. □ *I will stay up for her arrival.* □ *I can't stay up that late.*

steal a base to sneak from one base to another in baseball. □ *The runner stole second base, but he nearly got put out on the way.* □ *Tom runs so slowly that he never tries to steal a base.*

steal a march (on someone) to get some sort of an advantage over someone without being noticed. □ *I got the contract because I was able to steal a march on my competitor.* □ *You have to be clever and fast — not dishonest — to steal a march.*

steal away to sneak away quietly. □ *She stole away in the still of the night.* □ *I plan to steal away during the second act because I have to get to bed early.*

steal someone's thunder to lessen someone's force or authority. (Not literal.) □ *What do you mean by coming in here and stealing my thunder? I'm in charge here!* □ *Someone stole my thunder by leaking my announcement to the press.*

steal the show See the following entry.

steal the spotlight AND **steal the show** to give the best performance in a show, play, or some other event; to get attention for oneself. □ *The lead in the play was very good, but the butler stole the show.* □ *Ann always tries to steal the spotlight when she and I make a presentation.*

steam someone's beam to make someone angry. (Slang.) □ *Being stood up really steams my beam!* □ *Come on, don't steam your beam. Remember how hard times are now.*

steam something off ((of) something) to loosen and remove something by an application of steam. (The *of* is colloquial.) □ *Toby steamed the old paper off the wall.* T *Toby steamed off the old paper.* □ *It is hard to steam the paper off.*

steam something out (of something) to remove something embedded, through an application of steam. □ *The cleaner was not able to steam the wrinkles out of my jacket.* T *I tried to steam out the gum.* □ *I will try to steam them out.*

steam something up to cause something to be covered with water vapor due to the presence of steam. (More at *steam up.*) □ *Our breaths steamed the windows up.* T *Our breaths steamed up the windows.*

steam up to become covered with a film of steam or water vapor. (More at *steam something up.*) □ *The windows steamed up, and we had to wipe them so we could see out.* □ *The window has steamed up, and I can't see.*

steamed (up) 1. angry. (Slang.) □ *Now, now, don't get so steamed up!* □ *She is really massively steamed.* 2. alcohol intoxicated and angry. □ *He was really steamed—and could hardly stand up.* □ *By midnight, Larry was too steamed to drive home, and he had to spend the night.*

step aside 1. to step out of the way. □ *Please step aside. You are in the way.* □ *I stepped aside just in time.* 2. Please move out of the way so there is a pathway. (Usually **Step aside.**) □ *"Step aside. Let the mayor through, please," called out the mayor's bodyguard.* □ TOM (blocking the boss's door): *Just a moment, sir.* BOSS (trying to exit): *Step aside, please.* TOM: *But, sir!* BOSS: *Step aside, please.* TOM: *But, sir, the tax people are here with an arrest warrant.*

step back (from someone or something) to move back from someone or something; to move back so as to provide space around someone or something. □ *Please step back from the injured woman. Give her some air.* □ *Step back and give her some air.*

step off the curb to die. (Slang.) □ *Ralph almost stepped off the curb during his operation.* □ *I'm too young to step off the curb.*

step on it See *step on the gas.*

step on someone's toes AND **tread on someone's toes** to interfere with or offend someone. (Also used literally. Note examples with *anyone.*) □ *When you're in public office, you have to avoid stepping on anyone's toes.* □ *Ann trod on someone's toes during the last campaign and lost the election.*

step on the gas AND **step on it** hurry up. □ *I'm in a hurry, driver. Step on it!* □ *I can't step on the gas, mister. There's too much traffic.*

step out into something to go out from a place into a different set of conditions. □ *Julie stepped out of her previous job into a whole new world.* □ *Wally stepped out into the bright sunlight.*

step out of line 1. to move briefly out of a line where one was standing. (Literal.) □ *I stepped out of line for a minute and lost my place.* □ *It's better not to step out of line if you aren't sure you can get back in again.* 2. to misbehave; to do something offensive. (Figurative.) □ *I'm terribly sorry. I hope I didn't step out of line.* □ *John is* a lot of fun to go out with, but he has a tendency to step out of line.

step out (of something) 1. to go out of a place. □ *She stepped out of the house without a coat and nearly froze to death.* □ *Jamie stepped out and nearly froze her nose.* 2. to take one step to get out of clothing that has dropped from one's body to the floor. □ *He stepped out of his pants and pulled off his shirt.* □ *Joan took off her skirt and stepped out.*

step out (on someone) to be unfaithful to a spouse or lover. □ *Jeff has been stepping out on Judy.* □ *I was not stepping out!*

step outside 1. to go outside, as if to get some fresh air. □ *I need to step outside for a minute to get a breath of air.* □ *Tom and Harry stepped outside for a moment.* 2. to go outside to fight or settle an argument. □ *I find that insulting. Would you care to step outside?* □ *Max invited Lefty to step outside.*

step over (to) some place to move to a place a few steps away. □ *Please step over here and I'll show you some other merchandise.* □ *If you will step over to the display case, I will show you some earrings.*

step right up to come right to where the speaker is; to come forward to the person speaking. (Used by people selling things.) □ *Please step right up and buy a ticket to see the show.* □ *Don't be shy! Step right up and buy one of these.*

step something up 1. to make something more active; to increase something. (More at *step up*.) □ *I hope we can step the pace of business up in the next few days.* T *We can step up busi-*ness considerably by putting out a larger sign. 2. to make something go or run faster. □ *The engineer stepped the motors up and the production line moved even faster.* T *Please step up the speed of your activity.* □ *The new manager stepped production up considerably.*

step up to increase. (More at *step something up*.) □ *Industrial production stepped up a large amount this last quarter.* □ *Traffic has stepped up since the road was paved.*

step up to something to walk to something, especially a counter or a bar. □ *Jake stepped up to the ticket counter and bought a single ticket for the balcony.* □ *When Wally stepped up to the ticket window, he learned that the show was sold out.*

stew in one's own juice to be left alone to suffer one's anger or disappointment. □ *John has such a terrible temper. When he got mad at us, we just let him go away and stew in his own juice.* □ *After John stewed in his own juice for a while, he decided to come back and apologize to us.*

stick around to remain in the general vicinity. (Colloquial.) □ *Please stick around. I need to talk to you after the meeting.* □ *I will stick around for a while, but I have another appointment.*

stick one's foot in one's mouth See *put one's foot in one's mouth*.

stick one's neck out to take a risk. □ *Why should I stick my neck out to do something for her? What's she ever done for me?* □ *He made a risky investment. He stuck his neck out because he thought he could make some money.*

stick one's nose in(to something)
See *poke one's nose in(to something)*.

stick out to project outward. (More at *stick something out*.) ☐ *You can't lock your suitcase because there is a bit of cloth sticking out.* ☐ *Some cloth stuck out of the top of the drawer.*

stick out (from someone or something) to project outward from someone or something. ☐ *His right arm, which was in a cast, stuck out from him like a crane.* ☐ *His arm stuck out.*

stick out (of someone or something) to protrude from someone or something. ☐ *The arrow stuck out of him, wobbling as he staggered.* ☐ *A dollar bill stuck out of the book. What a strange bookmark.*

stick someone or something up to rob someone or a business establishment. (Presumably with the aid of a gun.) ☐ *Max tried to stick the drugstore up.* ⊤ *Max stuck up the store.* ☐ *He stuck the store up.*

stick something down to fasten something down, as with glue or paste. ☐ *Get some glue and stick this wallpaper down, please.* ⊤ *Stick down this wallpaper, would you?*

stick something in(to someone or something) to insert something into someone or something. ☐ *The lab technician stuck a needle into my arm and took some blood out.* ⊤ *She stuck in the needle.* ☐ *Harry stuck the needle in with great care.*

stick something out **1.** to cause something to project outward. (More at *stick out*.) ☐ *Don't stick your tongue out at me!* ⊤ *She stuck out her tongue at me!* **2.** to endure something;

to stay with something. (The *something* is usually *it*.) ☐ *I will stick it out as long as I can.* ☐ *She stuck it out as long as she could; then she started looking for another job.*

stick to one's guns to remain firm in one's convictions; to stand up for one's rights. ☐ *I'll stick to my guns on this matter. I'm sure I'm right.* ☐ *Bob can be persuaded to do it our way. He probably won't stick to his guns on this point.*

stick together **1.** to adhere to one another. ☐ *The noodles are sticking together. What shall I do?* ☐ *You need to keep the pieces separate while you fry them or else they will stick together.* **2.** to remain in one another's company. (Figurative.) ☐ *Let us stick together so we don't get lost.* ☐ *They stuck together through thick and thin.*

Stick with it. Do not give up. Stay with your task. ☐ BILL: *I'm really tired of calculus.* FATHER: *Stick with it. You'll be a better person for it.* ☐ BILL: *This job is getting to be such a pain.* SUE: *True, but it pays well, doesn't it? Stick with it.*

Still waters run deep. A quiet person is probably thinking deep or important thoughts. (Proverb.) ☐ *Jane is so quiet. She's probably thinking. Still waters run deep, you know.* ☐ *It's true that still waters run deep, but I think that Jane is really half asleep.*

stink on ice to be really rotten. (Slang. So rotten as to reek even when frozen.) ☐ *This show stinks on ice.* ☐ *The whole idea stank on ice.*

stir someone or something up **1.** [with *someone*] to get someone excited; to get someone angry. ☐ *The march music really stirred the audience* up. ⊤ *The march stirred up the audience.* **2.** [with *something*] to mix something by stirring. □ *Please stir the pancake batter up before you use it.* ⊤ *Please stir up the batter.* **3.** [with *something*] to bring about trouble. □ *Why are you always trying to stir trouble up?* ⊤ *Are you stirring up trouble again?*

stir up a hornet's nest to create trouble or difficulties. □ *What a mess you have made of things. You've really stirred up a hornet's nest.* □ *Bill stirred up a hornet's nest when he discovered the theft.*

stitch something up to sew something together; to mend a tear or a ripped seam. □ *I tore my shirt. Would you stitch it up, please?* ⊤ *Please stitch up my shirt.*

stock up (on something) to build up a supply of something in particular. □ *I need to stock up on food for the party.* □ *We need fresh vegetables. We will have to stock up before the weekend.*

stoked (on someone or something) excited by someone or something. (Slang.) □ *We were stoked on Mary. She is the greatest.* □ *Everyone is stoked on spring.* □ *Now, don't get too stoked, you are the one who has to run.*

stoked out exhausted. (Slang.) □ *I ran all the way and got stoked out.* □ *Alex is totally stoked out.*

stoned (out) alcohol or drug intoxicated. (Slang.) □ *Fred is really stoned out.* □ *I have never seen anybody so stoned who could still talk.*

stoop down to dip, duck, or squat down. □ *I had to stoop down to enter the tiny door.* □ *Stoop down so you don't bump your head.*

stoop over to bend over. □ *Carl stooped over to pick up his napkin and lost his balance.* □ *As he stooped over, he lost his balance and fell.*

stop by (some place) to go to a place and stop and then continue on. (The *some place* may be any expression of a location.) □ *Stop by my place for dinner sometime.* □ *Please stop by before the end of the day.*

stop in (some place) to pay a brief visit to a place. □ *Do you want to stop in Adamsville or just drive on through?* □ *Let's stop in for a few minutes.*

stop over (some place) to stay one or more nights at a place. □ *We stopped over in Miami for one night.* □ *We had to stop over, but we stayed in a very nice hotel.*

stop something up (with something) to plug something with something. (More at *stop up*.) □ *Gary stopped the sink up with bacon grease.* ⊤ *He stopped up the sink with bacon grease.* □ *Try not to stop the sink up.*

Stop the music! AND **Stop the presses!** Stop everything!; Hold it! (*Presses* refers to the printing presses used to print newspapers. This means that there is recent news of such magnitude that the presses must be stopped so a new edition can be printed immediately.) □ JOHN (entering the room): *Stop the music! There's a fire in the kitchen!* MARY: *Good grief! Let's get out of here!* □ *"Stop the presses!" shouted Jane. "I have an announcement."*

Stop the presses! See the previous entry.

stop up [for something] to become clogged. (More at *stop something up* *(with something).)* □ *The sink stopped up again!*

storm in (to some place) to burst into something or some place angrily. □ *The army stormed into the town and took many of the citizens as prisoners.* □ *Leonard stormed in, shouting at everyone.*

storm out (of some place) to burst out of some place angrily. □ *Carol stormed out of the office in a rage.* □ *She got mad and stormed out.*

straight from the horse's mouth from an authoritative or dependable source. (Not literal.) □ *I know it's true! I heard it straight from the horse's mouth!* □ *This comes straight from the horse's mouth, so it has to be believed.*

straight from the shoulder sincerely; frankly; holding nothing back. □ *Sally always speaks straight from the shoulder. You never have to guess what she really means.* □ *Bill gave a good presentation — straight from the shoulder and brief.*

straighten out 1. to become straight. (More at *straighten someone or something out.*) □ *The road finally straightened out.* □ *The train tracks straightened out on the plain.* **2.** to improve one's behavior or attitude. (More at *straighten someone or something out.*) □ *I hope he straightens out before he gets himself into real trouble.* □ *Fred had better straighten out soon if he wants to get a job.*

straighten someone or something out 1. to make someone's body or something straight or orderly. (*Someone* includes *oneself.* More at *straighten out.*) □ *The undertaker straightened Sam out in his coffin.* Ⓣ *The under-*

taker straightened out the corpse in the coffin. □ *Can you straighten this spoon out?* □ *Straighten yourself out and see if your bed is going to be long enough.* **2.** [with *something*] to make something straighter. (More at *straighten out.*) □ *I can't straighten this row of books out.* Ⓣ *Please straighten out this line of people.* **3.** [with *something*] to bring order to something that is disorderly. (More at *straighten out.*) □ *See if you can straighten this mess out.* Ⓣ *Will you straighten out this mess?*

straighten something up to make something less messy. (Compare to *straighten up.*) □ *This room is a mess. Please straighten it up.* Ⓣ *Can you straighten up this room?*

straighten up 1. to sit or stand more vertically. □ *Please straighten up. Don't slouch.* □ *I have to remind Timmy constantly to straighten up.* **2.** to behave better. (Compare to *straighten something up.*) □ *Come on! Straighten up or I will send you home!* □ *I wish you would straighten up. Your behavior is very bad.*

stream down (on someone or something) [for a liquid or light] to flow downward onto someone or something. □ *The water streamed down on all of them.* □ *The light broke through the clouds and streamed down on all of them.* □ *It streamed down and soaked them all.*

stream in (to something) to flow or rush into something. □ *The people streamed into the hall, each seeking the best possible seat.* □ *Water streamed into the room from the broken pipe.* □ *Complaints about the performance streamed in.*

stretch out [for one] to extend and stretch one's body to its full length.

(More at *stretch someone or something out*.) □ *She lay down, stretched out, and relaxed for the first time in days.* □ *I need a bigger bed. I can't stretch out in this one.*

stretch someone or something out to extend or draw out someone or something. (*Someone* includes *oneself*. More at *stretch out*.) □ *Molly stretched the baby out to change his clothes.* T *She stretched out the baby, who had rolled into a ball.* □ *Stretch the chicken out and skin it.*

stretch something out (to someone or something) to reach something out to someone or something. □ *Jeff stretched his hand out to Tiffany.* T *He stretched out his hand to the visitor.* □ *The visitor approached and stretched her hand out.*

strike a happy medium AND **hit a happy medium** to find a compromise position; to arrive at a position halfway between two unacceptable extremes. □ *Ann likes very spicy food, but Bob doesn't care for spicy food at all. We are trying to find a restaurant that strikes a happy medium.* □ *Tom is either very happy or very sad. He can't seem to hit a happy medium.*

strike a match to light a match. □ *Mary struck a match and lit a candle.* □ *When Sally struck a match to light a cigarette, Jane said quickly, "No smoking, please."*

strike a sour note AND **hit a sour note** to signify something unpleasant. □ *Jane's sad announcement struck a sour note at the annual banquet.* □ *News of the crime hit a sour note in our holiday celebration.*

strike back (at someone or something) to return the blows of some-one or something; to return the attack of someone or something. □ *The victim struck back at the mugger and scared him away.* □ *The victim struck back in the courts.*

strike for something to conduct a work stoppage in order to gain something. □ *The workers were striking for longer vacations.* □ *We are striking for fundamental human rights.*

strike it rich to acquire wealth suddenly. □ *If I could strike it rich, I wouldn't have to work anymore.* □ *Sally ordered a dozen oysters and found a huge pearl in one of them. She struck it rich!*

strike out 1. [for a baseball player] to accumulate three strikes. □ *Jeff struck out for the fourth time this season.* □ *I knew I would strike out this inning.* **2.** to have a series of failures. (Figurative.) □ *It was a hard job. Finally I struck out and had to go into another line of work.* □ *I keep striking out when it comes to the opposite sex.*

strike out (at someone or something) to hit at someone or something with the intention of threatening or harming them. □ *Dave would strike out at anyone who came near him, but it was all bluff.* □ *He was mad, and when anyone came close, he struck out.*

strike someone funny to seem funny to someone. □ *Sally has a great sense of humor. Everything she says strikes me funny.* □ *Why are you laughing? Did something I said strike you funny?*

strike someone's fancy to appeal to someone. □ *I'll have some ice cream, please. Chocolate strikes my fancy right now.* □ *Why don't you go to the store* and buy a record album that strikes your fancy?

strike something down [for a court] to invalidate a law. □ *The higher court struck the ruling of the lower court down.* T *The court struck down the ruling.*

strike up a friendship to become friends (with someone). □ *I struck up a friendship with John while we were on a business trip together.* □ *If you're lonely, you should go out and try to strike up a friendship with someone you like.*

strike while the iron is hot to do something at the best possible time; to do something when the time is ripe. □ *He was in a good mood, so I asked for a loan of $200. I thought I'd better strike while the iron was hot.* □ *Please go to the bank and settle this matter now! They are willing to be reasonable. You've got to strike while the iron is hot.*

string someone along to maintain someone's attention or interest, probably insincerely. □ *You are just stringing me along because you like to borrow my car. You are not a real friend.* □ *Rachel strung her along for the sake of old times.*

strip down to remove one's clothing. □ *The doctor told Joe to strip down for his examination.* □ *Joe stripped down for the examination.*

struggle through (something) to get through something in the best way possible. □ *I am going to struggle through this dull book to the very end.* □ *The book was dull, but I struggled through.*

Stuff a sock in it! *Shut up!*; Stop talking! (Literally, stuff a sock in your mouth to stop the noise.) □ TOM: *Hey, Henry! Can you hear me?* HENRY: *Be quiet, Tom. Stuff a sock in it!* □ FRED: *Hey, you still here? I want to tell you a few things!* JOHN: *Oh, stuff a sock in it! You're a pain.*

stuff and nonsense nonsense. □ *Come on! Don't give me all that stuff and nonsense!* □ *I don't understand this book. It's all stuff and nonsense as far as I am concerned.*

stuff the ballot box to put fraudulent ballots into a ballot box; to cheat in counting the votes in an election. □ *The election judge was caught stuffing the ballot box during the election yesterday.* □ *Election officials are supposed to guard against stuffing the ballot box.*

stumble through something to get through a sequence of something awkwardly and falteringly. □ *The cast stumbled through the first act and barely finished the second.* □ *Mary stumbled through her speech and fled from the stage.*

subsist on something to exist on something; to stay alive on something. □ *We can only subsist on this amount of money. We need more!* □ *They are able to do no more than subsist on what Mrs. Harris is paid.*

succumb to something to yield to something, especially a temptation, fatal disease, a human weakness, etc. □ *He finally succumbed to his pneumonia.* □ *She did not succumb to the disease until the last.*

suck something up to pick something up by suction, as with a vacuum cleaner, or through a straw. □ *Will this vacuum suck all this dirt up?* T *The vacuum cleaner sucked up all the dog hair.*

suit someone to a T AND **fit someone to a T** to be very appropriate for someone. □ *This kind of job suits me to a T.* □ *This is Sally's kind of house. It fits her to a T.*

Suit yourself. You decide the way you want it.; *Have it your way.* □ MARY: *I think I want the red one.* TOM: *Suit yourself.* □ JOHN (reading the menu): *The steak sounds good, but I'm helpless in the face of fried chicken.* SALLY: *Suit yourself. I'll have the steak.*

sum something up to give a summary of something. □ *I would like to sum this lecture up by listing the main points I have covered.* T *She summed up the president's speech in three sentences.*

sum up to summarize. □ *It is time for me to sum up.* □ *The events of the day took some time to sum up.*

suppose See *supposing.*

Suppose I do? AND **Supposing I do?** And what does it matter if I do, and what are you going to do about it? (Not usually with question intonation.) □ ALICE: *Do you really think it's right to do something like that?* SUE: *Suppose I do?* □ FRED: *Are you going to drive up into the mountains as you said you would?* SALLY: *Supposing I do?* FRED: *I'm just asking.*

Suppose I don't? AND **Supposing I don't?** And what will happen if I don't? (Not usually with question intonation.) □ BILL: *You'd better get yourself over to the main office.* TOM: *Suppose I don't?* □ FATHER: *You simply must do better in school.* TOM: *Supposing I don't?* FATHER: *Your clothing and personal belongings will be placed on the curb for the garbage pickup, and we will have the locks changed. Next question.*

supposing AND **suppose** a word introducing a hypothesis. □ FRED: *Supposing I was to walk right out of here, just like that.* MARY: *I'd say good-bye and good riddance.* □ SUE: *Suppose all the electricity suddenly stopped. What would we do?* BOB: *It doesn't matter, the television can run on batteries too.*

Supposing I do? See *Suppose I do?*

Supposing I don't? See *Suppose I don't?*

Sure. Yes, certainly. (See also *Oh, sure (someone or something will)!*) □ MARY: *This okay?* JANE: *Sure.* □ BILL: *Want to go to a movie with me Saturday?* SUE: *Sure, why not?*

Sure as shooting! *Absolutely yes!* (An elaboration of *Sure.*) □ BILL: *Are you going to be there Monday night?* BOB: *Sure as shooting!* □ BOB: *Will you take this over to the main office.* BILL: *Sure as shooting!*

Sure thing. I certainly will. □ SUE: *Will you be at the reception?* BOB: *Sure thing.* □ BILL: *You remember my cousin, Tom, don't you?* BOB: *Sure thing. Hi, Tom.*

surge in(to something) to burst or gush into something or some place. □ *The water surged into the valley after the dam broke.* □ *The doors opened, and the people surged in.*

surge out (of something) to burst forth or gush out of something or some place. □ *The water surged out of the huge crack in the dam.* □ *We saw the crack where the water surged out.*

surge up to rush or gush upwards. □ *A spring of fresh water surged up under the stone and flowed out on the ground.* □ *The oil surged up and blew out into* the open air in a tall column of living blackness.

swallow someone or something up
1. to eat or gobble up someone or something. □ *The fairy-tale wolf threatened to swallow Gwen up in one bite.* T *The wolf swallowed up the meat in one bite.* **2.** to engulf or contain something. (Figurative.) □ *The garage seemed to swallow the cars up.* T *The huge sweater swallowed up the tiny child.*

swallow something down to swallow something. □ *Here, take this pill and swallow it down.* T *Liz swallowed down the pill.*

swear at someone or something to curse someone or something. □ *Please don't swear at the children.* □ *Scott swore at the police station as he drove by.*

swear by someone or something 1. to utter an oath on someone or something. □ *I swear by Jupiter that I will be there on time.* □ *She swore by her sainted mother that she would never do it again.* □ *The sheriff swore by his badge that he would lock her up if she ever did it again.* **2.** to announce one's full faith and trust in someone or something. □ *I would swear by Roger any time. He is a great guy, and anything he does is super.* □ *I swear by this computer. It has always served me well.*

swear someone in (as something) to administer an oath to someone who then becomes something. □ *The judge swore Alice in as street commissioner.* T *The judge swore in Alice as the new director.* □ *She swore Alice in.*

sweep something off ((of) something) to clean something by sweep-

ing. (The *of* is colloquial.) □ *The waiter swept the crumbs off the tablecloth.* □ *Jake swept the counter off and wiped it clean.* T *He swept off the back porch.* T *He swept off the crumbs from the tablecloth.*

sweep something out to clean something out by sweeping. □ *Someone has to sweep the garage out.* T *Don't sweep out this room. I'll do it.*

sweep something up 1. to clean up and remove something, such as dirt, by sweeping. (More at *sweep up*.) □ *Please sweep these crumbs up.* T *Can you sweep up these crumbs?* **2.** to clean up some place by sweeping. (More at *sweep up*.) □ *Please sweep this room up.* T *Can you sweep up this room, please?* **3.** to arrange something, such as hair, into a curve or wave. □ *The hairstylist swept her hair up over the top. No one liked it.* T *Sweep up my hair the way it looks in this picture.*

sweep up to clean up by sweeping. (More at *sweep something up*.) □ *Would you sweep up this time?* □ *Please give me a few minutes to sweep up before you come to visit.*

swell up to enlarge; to inflate; to bulge out. □ *I struck my thumb with a hammer, and it swelled up something awful.* □ *During the rainy season, we anxiously watched the water in the dam swell up.*

swim against the current See the following entry.

swim against the tide AND **swim against the current** to do the opposite of everyone else; to go against the trend. □ *Bob tends to do what everybody else does. He isn't likely to swim against the tide.* □ *Mary always* *swims against the current. She's a very contrary person.*

swish something off ((of) someone or something) to brush something off someone or something. (The *of* is colloquial.) □ *The barber swished the loose hairs off of Paul's collar.* T *The barber swished off the loose hairs.* □ *Jamie swished the hairs off.*

switch back (to something) **1.** to return to using or doing something. □ *I decided to switch back to my old shampoo.* □ *I switched back and was glad I did.* **2.** [for a road] to reverse upon itself. □ *The road switched back twenty times in three miles.* □ *It switched back every now and then.*

switch off **1.** [for something] to turn itself off. (More at *switch someone or something off.*) □ *At midnight, all the lights switched off automatically.* □ *The television switched off after I went to sleep.* **2.** [for someone] to stop paying attention. (Figurative.) □ *I got tired of listening and switched off.* □ *You could see that the audience was switching off.*

switch someone or something off to cause someone or something to be quiet or stop doing something. (More at *switch off.*) □ *I got tired of listening to her, so I punched the button and switched her off.* T *I switched off the television set.*

switch something back (to something) to return something to the way it was. □ *I switched the television back to the previous channel.* T *I switched back the channel to what I was watching before.* □ *I switched it back and then went to sleep.*

switch something on to close an electrical circuit that causes something to start functioning or operating. □ *Please switch the fan on.* T *I switched on the fan.*

swoop down (up)on someone or something to dive or plunge downward on someone or something. (Both literal and figurative uses.) □ *The eagle swooped down upon the lamb.* □ *The children swooped down on the ice cream and cake.*

T

Ta-ta. See *Toodle-oo*.

Tah-dah! a phrase introducing or pointing to something that is supposed to be exciting. □ *"Tah-dah,"* *said Alice, pretending to be a trumpet.* *"This is my new car!"* □ BILL: *Tah-dah! Everyone, meet Mrs. Wilson!* MARY: *Hello, Mrs. Wilson.*

tail wagging the dog a situation where a small part is controlling the whole thing. □ *John was just hired yesterday, and today he's bossing everyone around. It's a case of the tail wagging the dog.* □ *Why is this small matter so important? Now the tail is wagging the dog!*

take a backseat (to someone) to defer to someone; to give control to someone. □ *I decided to take a backseat to Mary and let her manage the project.* □ *I had done the best I could, but it was time to take a backseat and let someone else run things.*

take a dirt nap to die and be buried. (Slang.) □ *I don't want to end up taking a dirt nap during this operation.* □ *Isn't Tom a little young to take a dirt nap?*

take a hike AND **take a walk** to leave; to beat it. (Slang.) □ *Okay, I've had it with you. Take a hike! Beat it!* □ *I had enough of the boss and the whole place, so I cleaned out my desk and took a walk.*

take a leaf out of someone's book to behave or to do something in the way that someone else would. (A *leaf* is a page.) □ *When you act like that, you're taking a leaf out of your sister's book, and I don't like it!* □ *You had better do it your way. Don't take a leaf out of my book. I don't do it well.*

take a load off one's feet See *get a load off one's feet*.

take a nosedive See *go into a nosedive*.

take a walk See *take a hike*.

Take care (of yourself). 1. Good-bye and keep yourself healthy. □ JOHN: *I'll see you next month. Good-bye.* BOB: *Good-bye, John. Take care of yourself.* □ MARY: *Take care.* SUE: *Okay. See you later.* **2.** Take care of your health and get well. □ MARY: *Don't worry. I'll get better soon.* SUE: *Well, take care of yourself. Bye.* □ JANE: *I'm sorry you're ill.* BOB: *Oh, it's nothing.* JANE: *Well, take care of yourself.*

take cold See *catch cold*.

take five to take a five-minute break. (Slang.) □ *Okay, gang, take five. Be back here in five minutes, or else.* □ *She told them to take five, but they turned the five into fifty.*

take forty winks to take a nap; to go to sleep. □ *I think I'll go to bed and* take forty winks. See you in the morning. □ Why don't you go take forty winks and call me in about an hour?

Take it easy. **1.** Good-bye and be careful. □ MARY: *Bye-bye.* BILL: *See you, Mary. Take it easy.* □ SUE: *Take it easy, Tom. Don't do anything I wouldn't do.* TOM: *Could you give me a short list of things you wouldn't do?* **2.** Be gentle.; Treat someone carefully. □ SUE: *Then I want you to move the piano and turn all the mattresses.* ANDREW: *Come on. Take it easy! I'm not made of steel, you know.* □ HENRY: *Oh, I'm pooped.* ALICE: *You just need a little rest and you'll feel as good as new. Just take it easy.* **3.** Calm down.; Relax.; Do not get excited. □ ANDREW: *I am so mad I could blow my top!* RACHEL: *Now, now. Take it easy. What's wrong?* □ *Mary could see that Sally was very upset at the news. "Now, just take it easy," said Mary. "It can't be all that bad."*

take it or leave it **1.** to accept something the way it is or forget about it. □ *This is my last offer. Take it or leave it.* □ *It's not much, but it's the only food we have. You can take it or leave it.* **2.** That is all there is. There is no choice. Take this one or none. (Usually **Take it or leave it.**) □ BILL: *That's my final offer. Take it or leave it.* BOB: *Aw, come on! Take off a few bucks.* □ BILL: *Aw, I want eggs for breakfast, Mom.* MOTHER: *There's only Sweet Wheets left. Take it or leave it.*

take liberties with someone or something AND **make free with someone or something** to use or abuse someone or something. □ *You are overly familiar with me, Mr. Jones. One might think you were taking liberties with me.*

□ *I don't like it when you make free with my lawn mower. You should at least ask when you want to borrow it.*

Take my word for it. Believe me.; *Trust me,* I am telling you the truth. □ BILL: *Take my word for it. These are the best encyclopedias you can buy.* BOB: *But I don't need any encyclopedias.* □ RACHEL: *No one can cook better than Fred. Take my word for it.* BILL: *Really?* FRED: *Oh, yes. It's true.*

take names to make a list of wrongdoers. (Often figuratively, as with a schoolteacher whose major weapon is to take names and send them to the principal.) □ *The boss is madder than hell, and he's taking names.* □ *Gary is coming by to talk about the little riot last night, and I think he's taking names.*

take off **1.** to take flight. □ *When does this plane take off?* □ *We took off on time.* **2.** [for someone] to leave. (Colloquial.) □ *It's late. I've got to take off now.* □ *We will have to take off about midnight, since we have to get up early in the morning.* **3.** to become active and exciting. (Colloquial.) □ *Did the party ever take off, or was it dull all night?* □ *Things began to take off about midnight.*

take off from something to take flight from something or some place. □ *The plane took off from the busy airport right on schedule.* □ *We will take off from the airport on one side of town, fly across the city, and land at our destination within three hours.*

take one's death of cold See *catch one's death (of cold).*

take one's medicine to accept the punishment or the bad fortune that one deserves. (Also used literally.) □ *I know I did wrong, and I know I have to take my medicine.* □ *Billy knew he was going to get spanked, and he didn't want to take his medicine.*

take out after someone or something to set out chasing or running after someone or something. □ *Mary took out after Claire but couldn't catch her.* □ *The dog took out after the rabbit.*

take over (from someone) to assume the role or job of someone. □ *I take over for the manager next month.* □ *Liz takes over and will be in charge.*

take someone in 1. to give someone shelter. □ *Do you think you could take me in for the night?* T *I don't take in strangers.* **2.** to deceive someone. □ *Those crooks really took me in. I was a fool.* T *The con artists took in a lot of innocent people.*

take someone or something away to remove someone or something. □ *The police came and took her away.* T *He took away the extra food.*

take someone or something by storm to overwhelm someone or something; to attract a great deal of attention from someone or something. □ *Jane is madly in love with Tom. He took her by storm at the office party, and they've been together ever since.* □ *The singer took the world of opera by storm with her performance in* La Boheme.

take someone or something for granted to accept someone or something — without gratitude — as a matter of course. □ *We tend to take a lot of things for granted.* □ *Mrs. Franklin complained that Mr. Franklin takes her for granted.*

take someone or something off (something) to remove someone or something from the surface of something. □ *Bob helped take his children off the merry-go-round.* □ *Please take your books off the table.* □ *I'll take them off.*

take someone or something on to agree to deal with someone or something; to begin to handle someone or something. □ *I did not agree to take him on.* T *I wouldn't have taken on this project if I had thought there would be no help.*

take someone or something out 1. [with *someone*] to block someone, as in a football game. □ *I was supposed to take the left end out, but I was trapped under the center.* T *Okay, Andy, you take out the center this time.* **2.** [with *something*] to bomb or destroy something. □ *The enemy took one of the tanks out, but not the one carrying the medicine.* T *The last flight took out two enemy bunkers and a radar installation.* **3.** [with *someone*] to date someone. □ *I hope he'll take me out soon.* T *She wanted to take out the new guy for an evening.*

take someone or something out (of something) to carry, lead, or guide someone or something out of something or some place. □ *He was becoming quite ill from the smoke, and I had to take him out of the room.* T *They took out the people.* □ *Let's take them out as soon as we can.*

take someone under one's wing(s) to take over and care for a person. □ *John wasn't doing well in geometry until the teacher took him under her wing.* □ *I took the new workers under my wings, and they learned the job in no time.*

take someone's breath away **1.** to cause someone to be out of breath due to a shock or hard exercise. □ *Walking this fast takes my breath away.* □ *Mary frightened me and took my breath away.* **2.** to overwhelm someone with beauty or grandeur. □ *The magnificent painting took my breath away.* □ *Ann looked so beautiful that she took my breath away.*

take something apart to break something to pieces; to disassemble something. □ *Tim took his watch apart, and that was the end of it.* ⊤ *Don't take apart every mechanical device you own!*

take something at face value to accept something just as it is presented. □ *John said he wanted to come to the party, and I took that at face value. I'm sure he'll arrive soon.* □ *He made us a promise, and we took his word at face value.*

take something down (in something) to write something down in something, such as writing, a notebook, etc. □ *Please take these figures down in your notebook.* ⊤ *Take down these figures in your record of this meeting.* □ *I will ask my secretary to take some notes down about what happens at this meeting.* ⊤ *Please take down some notes on this.* □ *I will take them down and type them later.*

take something in **1.** to reduce the size of a garment. □ *This is too big. I'll have to take it in around the waist.* ⊤ *I'll have to take in these pants.* **2.** to bring something or a creature into shelter. □ *I didn't want Joan to take the stray cat in, but she did it anyway.* ⊤ *Joan always takes in stray animals.* **3.** to view and study something; to attend something involving viewing.

□ *The mountains are so beautiful! I need an hour or so to take it all in.* ⊤ *I want to sit here a minute and take in the view.* ⊤ *Would you like to take in a movie?* **4.** to receive money as payment or proceeds. □ *How much did we take in today?* ⊤ *The box office took in nearly a thousand dollars in just the last hour.* **5.** to receive something into the mind, usually visually. □ *The woodcut was so detailed, I couldn't take it all in.* ⊤ *I could hardly take in everything she said.*

take something in stride to accept something as natural or expected. □ *The argument surprised him, but he took it in stride.* □ *It was a very rude remark, but Mary took it in stride.*

take something lying down to endure something unpleasant without fighting back. □ *He insulted me publicly. You don't expect me to take that lying down, do you?* □ *I'm not the kind of person who'll take something like that lying down.*

take something off to remove something, such as an article of clothing. □ *Please take your coat off and stay awhile.* ⊤ *Please take off your coat.*

take something on faith to accept or believe something on the basis of little or no evidence. □ *Please try to believe what I'm telling you. Just take it on faith.* □ *Surely you can't expect me to take a story like that on faith.*

take something on the chin to experience and endure a direct blow or assault. (Both literal and figurative uses.) □ *The bad news was a real shock, and John took it on the chin.* □ *The worst luck comes my way, and I always end up taking it on the chin.*

393

take something over 1. to assume responsibility for a task. □ *It looks as if I'm going to have to take the project over.* ⊤ *I will take over the project.* **2.** to acquire all of an asset. □ *Carl set out to take the failing airline over.* ⊤ *He took over the failing company.*

take something up 1. [for someone or a group] to deliberate something. □ *When will the board of directors take this issue up?* ⊤ *Let's take up that matter now.* **2.** to raise something, such as the height of a hem. □ *The skirt is too long. I'll have to take it up.* ⊤ *Can you take up this skirt for me?* **3.** to continue with something after an interruption. □ *They took it up where they left off.* ⊤ *Let's take up this matter at the point we were at when we were interrupted.* ⊤ *We must take up our work again.* **4.** to begin something; to start to acquire a skill in something. □ *When did you take this hobby up?* ⊤ *I took up skiing last fall.*

take something with a grain of salt See the following entry.

take something with a pinch of salt AND **take something with a grain of salt** to listen to a story or an explanation with considerable doubt. □ *You must take anything she says with a grain of salt. She doesn't always tell the truth.* □ *They took my explanation with a pinch of salt. I was sure they didn't believe me.*

take the bitter with the sweet to accept the bad things along with the good things. □ *We all have disappointments. You have to learn to take the bitter with the sweet.* □ *There are good days and bad days, but every day you take the bitter with the sweet. That's life.*

take the bull by the horns to meet a challenge directly. □ *If we are going to solve this problem, someone is going to have to take the bull by the horns.* □ *This threat isn't going to go away by itself. We are going to take the bull by the horns and settle this matter once and for all.*

take the law into one's own hands to attempt to administer the law; to act as a judge and jury for someone who has done something wrong. □ *Citizens don't have the right to take the law into their own hands.* □ *The shopkeeper took the law into his own hands when he tried to arrest the thief.*

take the spear (in one's chest) to accept full blame for something; to accept the full brunt of the punishment for something. (Slang.) □ *The admiral got the short straw and had to take the spear in his chest.* □ *I sure didn't want to take the spear.*

take the stand to go to and sit in the witness chair on the witness stand in a courtroom. □ *I was in court all day, waiting to take the stand.* □ *The lawyer asked the witness to take the stand.*

take the words out of one's mouth [for someone else] to say what you were going to say. (Also with *right*.) □ *John said exactly what I was going to say. He took the words out of my mouth.* □ *I agree with you, and I wanted to say the same thing. You took the words right out of my mouth.*

take to one's heels to run away. □ *The little boy said hello and then took to his heels.* □ *The man took to his heels to try to get to the bus stop before the bus left.*

take too much on to accept too many tasks; to accept a task that is too big a burden for one. □ *Nancy has a tendency to take too much on and then get exhausted.* ⊤ *I always take on too much, and then I have no time of my own.*

take up one's abode somewhere to settle down and live somewhere. (Literary.) □ *I took up my abode downtown near my office.* □ *We decided to take up our abode in a warmer climate.*

taking care of business doing what one is meant to do; coping with life as it is. (Black.) □ *If the dude is taking care of business, what else do you want out of him?* □ *Walter is taking care of business. Back in a minute.*

talk a blue streak to say very much and talk very rapidly. □ *Billy didn't talk until he was six, and then he started talking a blue streak.* □ *I can't understand anything Bob says. He talks a blue streak, and I can't follow his thinking.*

talk around something to talk, but avoid talking directly about the subject. □ *You are just talking around the matter! I want a straight answer!* □ *He never really said anything. He just talked around the issue.*

talk back (to someone) to challenge verbally a parent, an older person, or one's superior. □ *Please don't talk back to me!* □ *I've told you before not to talk back!*

talk down to someone to speak to someone condescendingly. □ *You would be more convincing if you didn't talk down to your audience.* □ *Please don't talk down to me. I can understand anything that you are likely to say.*

talk in circles to talk in a confusing or roundabout manner. □ *I couldn't understand a thing he said. All he did was talk in circles.* □ *We argued for a long time and finally decided that we were talking in circles.*

talk on the big white phone to vomit into a toilet. (Slang.) □ *One more beer and I'm gonna have to go talk on the big white phone.* □ *She was talking on the big white phone all night.*

talk oneself out to talk until one can talk no more. □ *She talked herself out and was silent for the rest of the day.* □ *I talked until I talked myself out.*

talk shop to talk about business matters at a social event (where business talk is out of place). □ *All right, everyone, we're not here to talk shop. Let's have a good time.* □ *Mary and Jane stood by the punch bowl, talking shop.*

talk someone into something to convince someone to do something through discussion. (*Someone* includes *oneself.*) □ *I think I can talk June into it.* □ *She finally talked herself into making the dive.*

talk something out to settle something by discussion. □ *Let's not get mad. Let's just talk it out.* ⊤ *Please, let's talk out this matter.*

talk something up to promote or advertise something by saying good things about it to as many people as possible. □ *Let's talk the play up around campus so we can get a good audience.* ⊤ *I will talk up the play all I can.*

talk through one's hat to talk nonsense; to brag or boast; to tell small lies casually. □ MARY: *I've got the fastest feet in the dorm and they're going* *to carry me all the way to the Olympics.* SALLY: *Oh, Mary, you're just talking through your hat.* □ "*Bill is always talking through his hat,*" *said Fred.* "*Don't pay any attention to his bragging.*"

talk until one is blue in the face to talk until one is exhausted. □ *I talked until I was blue in the face, but I couldn't change her mind.* □ *She had to talk until she was blue in the face in order to convince him.*

tall in the saddle proud. (Often with *sit.*) □ *I'll still be tall in the saddle when you are experiencing the results of your folly.* □ *Despite her difficulties, she still sat tall in the saddle.*

tally something up to add something up. □ *Please tally everything up and tell me the total.* T *Let's tally up everything and ask for donations.*

tap dance like mad to be busy continuously; to have to move fast to distract someone. (Slang.) □ *When things get tough, Congress tap dances like mad.* □ *Any public official knows how to tap dance like mad and still seem honest.*

tap out to lose one's money in gambling or in the financial markets. (Slang.) □ *I'm gonna tap out in about three more rolls—just watch.* □ *I really tapped out on that gold-mining stock.*

taper off to slack off gradually; to cease something gradually; to reduce gradually. □ *Activity finally tapered off in the middle of the afternoon.* □ *I hope that business doesn't taper off in the summer this year.*

team up against someone or something to join with someone else against someone or something. □

Let's team up against Paul and Tony in the footrace. □ *We teamed up against the group from the other school.*

team up (with someone) to join with one or more persons; to collaborate with two or more persons. □ *I intend to team up with a friend and go into the painting business.* □ *I do better by myself. I don't want to team up.*

tear away (from someone or something) to leave someone or something, running. □ *Dave tore away from Jill, leaving her to find her own way home.* □ *Roger tore away from the meeting, trying to make his train.*

tear down something to race down something very fast. (Compare to *tear someone or something down.*) □ *The girls tore down the hallway as fast as they could run.* □ *They tore down the stairs and ran out the door.*

tear off (from someone or something) to leave someone or something in a great hurry. □ *I hate to tear off from you guys, but I'm late for dinner.* □ *It's time for me to go. I have to tear off.*

tear one's hair to be anxious, frustrated, or angry. (Not literal.) □ *I was so nervous, I was about to tear my hair.* □ *I had better get home. My parents will be tearing their hair.*

tear (oneself) away (from someone or something) to force oneself to leave someone or something. □ *Do you think you can tear yourself away from your friends for dinner?* □ *I could hardly tear myself away from the concert.*

tear out (of some place) to leave a place in a great hurry. □ *The kids tore out of the house after they broke the* *window.* □ *They saw what they had done and tore out.*

tear someone or something down 1. to criticize someone or something mercilessly. (*Someone* includes *oneself.* Compare to *tear down something.*) □ *What is the point in tearing Frank down? He is doing his best and it's as good as anyone else can do, too.* T *Don't tear down Frank or the others!* □ *Ann tore our efforts down mercilessly.* □ *You are always tearing yourself down!* **2.** to raze something. □ *The workers tore the building down and carried the debris away.* T *They tore down the building.*

tear someone or something up 1. to rip someone or something into many pieces. □ *Don't get close to that machine. It can tear you up.* T *The lawn mower tore up the paper left in the yard.* **2.** [with *someone*] to cause someone to grieve seriously. □ *The news of the accident really tore her up.* T *The news tore up the whole family.*

tear something away (from someone or something) 1. to peel something from someone or something. □ *The paramedic tore the clothing away from the burn victim and began to treat the wounds immediately.* T *She tore away the clothing from the victim.* □ *She tore the clothing away.* **2.** to snatch something away from someone or something. □ *I tore the grenade away from the child and threw it in the lake.* T *Liz tore away the cover from the book.* □ *She tore it away.*

tear something off ((of) someone or something) to peel or rip something off someone or something. (The *of* is colloquial.) □ *Max tore the tie off his victim and ran away with it.* T *He tore*

off the tie. □ *Max tore the label off the can.*

tear something out (of something) to remove something from something by ripping or tearing. □ *Tear the coupons out of the magazine and save them.* T *Please tear out the coupons.* □ *I tore them all out.*

tee someone off to make someone angry. (Slang.) □ *That really teed me off!* T *Well, you sure managed to tee off everybody!*

Tell me another (one)! What you just told me was a lie, so tell me another lie! □ BILL: *Did you know that the football coach was once a dancer in a movie?* TOM: *Go on! Tell me another one!* □ *"Tell me another one!" laughed Bill at Tom's latest exaggeration*

tell one to one's face to tell (something) to someone directly. □ *I'm sorry that Sally feels that way about me. I wish she had told me to my face.* □ *I won't tell Tom that you're mad at him. You should tell him to his face.*

tell someone where to get off to rebuke someone; to put one in one's place. (Idiomatic. Also literal uses, as with a train conductor indicating a debarkation point to a passenger.) □ *You really told him where to get off!* □ *If she keeps acting like that to me, I will tell her where to get off.*

tell tales out of school to tell secrets or spread rumors. □ *I wish that John would keep quiet. He's telling tales out of school again.* □ *If you tell tales out of school a lot, people won't know when to believe you.*

tempest in a teapot an uproar about practically nothing. □ *This isn't a* *serious problem — just a tempest in a teapot.* □ *Even a tempest in a teapot can take a lot of time to get settled.*

tense up (for something) to become rigid or firm; to become anxious and ready for something. (Both literal and figurative uses.) □ *Liz tensed up for the game and was very nervous.* □ *He tensed up and that made it hard to give him the injection he needed.*

test out (of something) to score high enough on a placement test that one does not need to take a particular course in school. □ *I tested out of calculus.* □ *I don't know enough to test out.*

test something out to try something out; to test something to see if it works. □ *I can't wait to test my new stereo out.* ⊤ *I will test out the stereo.*

Thank goodness! AND **Thank heavens!** Oh, I am so thankful! □ JOHN: *Well, we finally got here. Sorry we're so late.* MOTHER: *Thank goodness! We were all so worried.* □ JANE: *There was a fire on Maple Street, but no one was hurt.* BILL: *Thank heavens!*

Thank heavens! See the previous entry.

thank one's lucky stars to be thankful for one's luck. □ *You can thank your lucky stars that I was there to help you.* □ *I thank my lucky stars that I studied the right things for the test.*

Thank you. I am grateful to you and offer you my thanks. □ BILL: *Here, have some more cake.* BOB: *Thank you.* □ JOHN: *Your hair looks nice.* MARY: *Thank you.*

Thank you a lot. See *Thanks (a lot).*

Thank you for a lovely evening. an expression said by a departing guest to the host or hostess at the end of an evening. (Other adjectives, such as *nice*, can be used in place of *lovely*.) □ MARY: *Thank you for a lovely evening.* JOHN: *Will I see you again?* □ BILL: *Thank you for a nice evening.* MARY: *Thank you so much for coming. Good night.*

Thank you for a lovely time. an expression said by a departing guest to the host or hostess. (Other adjectives, such as *nice*, can be used in place of *lovely*.) □ BILL: *Thank you for a nice time.* MARY: *Thank you so much for coming. Bye now.* □ JOHN: *Thank you so much for coming.* JANE: *Well, thank you for a lovely evening.* JOHN: *Don't stay away so long next time.*

Thank you for calling. Thank you for calling on the telephone. (Said when the call is helpful or a bother to the caller.) □ MARY: *Good-bye.* SUE: *Good-bye, thanks for calling.* □ JOHN: *Okay. Well, I have to get off the phone. I just wanted you to know what was happening with your order.* JANE: *Okay. Bye. Thanks for calling.*

Thank you for having me. See *Thank you for inviting me.*

Thank you for having us. See the following entry.

Thank you for inviting me. AND **Thank you for inviting us.; Thank you for having me.; Thank you for having us.** a polite expression said to a host or hostess on departure. □ MARY: *Good-bye, glad you could come.* BILL: *I had a great time. Thank you for inviting me.* □ JOHN: *I had a good time. Thank you for having me.* SALLY: *Come back again, John. It was good talking to you.*

Thank you for inviting us. See the previous entry.

Thank you so much. See the following entry.

Thank you very much. AND **Thank you so much.** a more polite and emphatic way of saying *Thank you.* □ TOM: *Welcome. Come in.* BOB: *Thank you very much.* □ BILL: *Here's the book I promised you.* SUE: *Thank you so much.*

Thanks (a lot). AND **Thank you a lot. 1.** Thank you, I am grateful. □ BILL: *Here, take mine.* BOB: *Thanks a lot.* □ MARY: *Well, here's your pizza.* BILL: *Thanks.* **2.** That is not worth much.; That is nothing to be grateful for. (Sarcasm is indicated by the tone of voice used with this expression.) □ JOHN: *I'm afraid that you're going to have to work the night shift.* BOB: *Thanks a lot.* □ FRED: *Here's your share of the money. We had to take out nearly half to make up for the damage you did to the car.* BILL: *Thanks a lot.*

Thanks a million. *Thank you a lot.* □ BILL: *Oh, thanks a million. You were very helpful.* BOB: *Just glad I could help.* □ JOHN: *Here's your book.* JANE: *Thanks a million. Sorry I needed it back in such a rush.*

Thanks awfully. *Thank you very much.* □ JOHN: *Here's one for you.* JANE: *Thanks awfully.* □ MARY: *Here, let me help you with all that stuff.* SUE: *Thanks awfully.*

Thanks, but no thanks. *Thank you, but I am not interested.* (A way of turning down something that is not very desirable.) □ ALICE: *How would you like to buy my old car?* JANE: *Thanks, but no thanks.* □ JOHN: *What do you think about a trip over to see the*

Wilsons? SALLY: *Thanks, but no thanks. We don't get along.*

Thanks for the lift. See the following entry.

Thanks for the ride. AND **Thanks for the lift.** Thank you for giving me a ride in your car. □ JOHN (stopping the car): *Here we are.* BOB: *Thanks for the ride. Bye.* JOHN: *Later.* □ As Fred got out of the car, he said, "*Thanks for the lift.*"

Thanks loads. *Thanks a lot.* (Colloquial.) □ MARY: *Here, you can have these. And take these too.* SALLY: *Thanks loads.* □ JOHN: *Wow! You look great!* SALLY: *Thanks loads. I try.*

That ain't the way I heard it. That is not the way I heard the story told. (A catch phrase. The grammar error, *ain't*, is built into the expression.) □ JOHN: *It seemed like a real riot, then Sally called the police and things calmed down.* SUE: *That ain't the way I heard it.* JOHN: *What?* SUE: *Somebody said the neighbors called the police.* □ FRED: *Four of us went fishing and were staying in this cabin. These women stopped and said they were having car trouble. What could we do?* SALLY: *That ain't the way I heard it.*

That (all) depends. My answer depends on factors that have yet to be discussed. □ TOM: *Will you be able to come to the meeting on Thursday night?* MARY: *That all depends.* □ BOB: *Can I see you again?* SALLY: *That depends.*

That beats everything! See *If that don't beat all!*

that brings me to the (main) point a transitional expression that introduces the main point of a conversation. (See also *which brings me to* *the (main) point.*) □ FATHER: *It's true. All of us had to go through something like this when we were young, and that brings me to the point. Aren't you old enough to be living on your own and making your own decisions and supporting yourself?* TOM: *Well, yes, I guess so.* □ FRED: *Yes, things are very expensive these days, and that brings me to the main point. You simply have to cut back on spending.* BILL: *You're right. I'll do it!*

(That causes) no problem. That will not cause a problem for me or anyone else. □ MARY: *Do you mind waiting for just a little while?* BOB: *No problem.* □ SUE: *Does this block your light? Can you still read?* JANE: *That causes no problem.*

That does it! 1. That completes it!; It is now done just right! □ *When Jane got the last piece put into the puzzle, she said, "That does it!"* □ JOHN (signing a paper): *Well, that's the last one! That does it!* BILL: *I thought we'd never finish.* **2.** That's the last straw.; Enough is enough! □ BILL: *We're still not totally pleased with your work.* BOB: *That does it! I quit!* □ SALLY: *That does it! I never want to see you again!* FRED: *I only put my arm around you!*

That (really) burns me (up)! That makes me very angry! □ BOB: *Did you hear that interest rates are going back up?* MARY: *That really burns me up!* □ SUE: *Fred is telling everyone that you are the one who lost the party money.* MARY: *That burns me! It was John who had the money in the first place.*

That takes care of that. That is settled. □ *That takes care of that, and I'm glad it's over.* □ *I spent all morning dealing with this matter, and that takes care of that.*

That takes the cake! 1. That is good, and it wins the prize! (Assuming that the prize is a cake.) □ *"What a performance!" cheered John. "That takes the cake!"* □ SUE: *Wow! That takes the cake! What a dive!* RACHEL: *She sure can dive!* **2.** That is the end!; That does it! □ BOB: *What a dumb thing to do, Fred!* BILL: *Yeah, Fred. That takes the cake!* □ BOB: *Wow! That takes the cake!* BILL: *What is it? Why are you slowing down?* BOB: *That stupid driver in front of me just hit the car on the left and then swung over and hit the car on the right.*

That tears it! That's the absolute end!; That does it! (*Tears* rhymes with *stairs*.) □ RACHEL: *Okay, that tears it! I'm going to complain to the landlord. Those people make noise day and night!* SUE: *Yes, this is too much.* □ TOM: *The boss thinks maybe you should work on the night shift.* MARY: *That tears it! I quit!*

That'll be the day! It will be an unusually amazing day when that happens! □ BILL: *I think I'll fix that lamp now.* ANDREW: *When you finally get around to fixing that lamp, that'll be the day!* □ SUE: *I'm going to get this place organized once and for all!* ALICE: *That'll be the day!*

That'll teach someone! What happened to someone is a suitable punishment! (The *someone* is usually a pronoun.) □ BILL: *Tom, who has cheated on his taxes for years, finally got caught.* SUE: *That'll teach him.* □ BILL: *Gee, I got a ticket for speeding.* FRED: *That'll teach you!*

That's a new one on me! I had not heard that before. □ BOB: *Did you* hear? They're building a new highway that will bypass the town. FRED: *That's a new one on me! That's terrible!* □ SUE: *All of us will have to pay our taxes monthly from now on.* MARY: *That's a new one on me!*

That's about the size of it. That is the way it is. □ BOB: *We only have grocery money left in the bank.* SALLY: *That means that there isn't enough money for us to go to Jamaica?* BOB: *That's about the size of it.* □ BOB: *I'm supposed to take this bill to the county clerk's office and pay them four hundred dollars?* SALLY: *That's about the size of it.*

That's all someone needs. AND **It's all someone needs.; (It's) just what you need.; That's just what you need.** Someone does not need that at all.; *That's the last straw!* (Always sarcastic. The *someone* can be a person's name or a pronoun.) □ JANE: *The dog died and the basement is just starting to flood.* FRED: *That's all we need.* □ SALLY: *Bill, the check you wrote to the Internal Revenue Service was returned. There's no more money in the bank.* BILL: *That's all we need.* □ BOB: *On top of all that, now I have car trouble!* MARY: *That's just what you need!*

That's easy for you to say. You can say that easily because it really does not affect you the way it affects others. □ WAITER: *Here's your check.* MARY: *Thanks.* (turning to others) *I'm willing to just split the check evenly.* BOB: *That's easy for you to say. You had lobster!* □ SALLY: *Let's each chip in ten bucks and buy him a sweater.* SUE: *That's easy for you to say. You've got ten bucks to spare.*

That's enough! No more!; Stop that! □ SUE: *Here, I'll stack another one on*

top. MARY: *That's enough! It will fall.* □ JOHN: *I could go on with complaint after complaint. I could talk all week, in fact.* BOB: *That's enough!*

That's enough for now. No more of that for now.; Please stop for a while. □ MARY: *Here, have some more cake. Do you want a larger piece?* BILL: *Oh, no. That's enough for now.* □ BILL: *Shall I cut a little more off this tree, lady, or save the rest till spring?* JANE: *No, that's enough for now.*

(That's) enough (of this) foolishness! 1. Stop this foolishness. □ BILL: *Enough of this foolishness. Stop it!* SALLY: *Sorry.* □ FATHER: *That's enough of this foolishness. You two stop fighting over nothing.* BOB: *Okay.* BILL: *Sorry.* 2. I have had enough of this. (Does not refer to something that is actual foolishness.) □ ANDREW: *Enough of this foolishness. I hate ballet. I'm leaving.* SUE: *Well, sneak out quietly.* ANDREW: *No, I'll lead an exodus.* □ SALLY: *That's enough foolishness. I'm leaving and I never want to see you again!* BOB: *Come on! I was only teasing.*

(That's) fine by me. See the following entry.

(That's) fine with me. AND **(That's) fine by me.; (That's) okay by me.; (That's) okay with me.** That is agreeable as far as I am concerned. (The expressions with *by* are colloquial.) □ SUE: *I'm giving away your old coat.* BOB: *That's fine with me.* □ SALLY: *Can I take twenty dollars out of your wallet?* FRED: *That's okay by me —if you can find it, of course.*

That's funny. That is strange or peculiar. □ BILL: *Tom just called from Detroit and says he's coming back tomorrow.* MARY: *That's funny. He's* not supposed to. □ SUE: *The sky is turning very gray.* MARY: *That's funny. There's no bad weather forecast.*

That's (just) too much! 1. That is unpleasant and unacceptable!; That is more than I can bear! □ *"That's just too much!" exclaimed Sue, and she walked out.* □ BILL: *I'm afraid this movie isn't what we thought it was going to be.* SUE: *Did you see that? That's too much! Let's go!* **2.** That is just too funny. (Compare to *You're too much!*) □ *After Fred finished the joke, and Bill had stopped howling with laughter, Bill said, "That's too much! Tell a sad one for a change."* □ *When Tom stopped laughing, his sides ached and he had tears in his eyes. "Oh, that's too much!" he moaned.*

That's just what you need. See *That's all someone needs.*

That's more like it. That is better.; That is a better response this time. □ WAITER: *Here is your order, sir. Roast chicken as you requested. Sorry about the mix-up.* JOHN: *That's more like it.* □ CLERK: *Now, here's one that you might like.* SALLY: *Now, that's more like it!*

That's news to me. I did not know that.; I had not been informed of that. □ BILL: *They've blocked off Maple Street for some repairs.* TOM: *That's news to me.* □ SALLY: *The telephones are out. None of them work.* BILL: *That's news to me.*

(That's) no skin off my nose. AND **(That's) no skin off my teeth.** That does not embarrass me.; That causes me no difficulty or harm. (Colloquial. The second form is borrowed from the metaphor *by the skin of someone's teeth* meaning "just barely." The first form has additional

variations—most of them vulgar.) □ BILL: *Everybody around here seems to think you're the one to blame.* BOB: *So what? I'm not to blame. That's no skin off my teeth, whatever they think.* □ BILL: *Sally is going to quit her job and go to Tampa.* BOB: *No skin off my nose! I don't care what she does.*

(That's) no skin off my teeth. See the previous entry.

(That's) okay by me. See *(That's) fine with me.*

(That's) okay with me. See *(That's) fine with me.*

That's that! That is the end of that! Nothing more can be done. □ TOM: *Well, that's that! I can do no more.* SALLY: *That's the way it goes.* □ DOCTOR (finishing an operation): *That's that! Would you close for me, Sue?* SUE: *Nice job, doctor. Yes, I'll close.*

That's the last straw. AND **That's the straw that broke the camel's back.** That is the final thing. □ *Now it's raining! That's the last straw. The picnic is canceled!* □ *When Sally came down sick, that was the straw that broke the camel's back.* □ BOB: *Now they say I have to have a tutor to pass calculus.* MARY: *That's the last straw! I'm going straight up to that school and find out what they aren't doing right.* □ *"That's the last straw!" cried Fred when he got another special tax bill from the city.*

That's the straw that broke the camel's back. See the previous entry.

That's the stuff! That is the right attitude or action. □ BOB: *I'm positive I can do it!* FRED: *That's the stuff!* □

"That's the stuff!" cried the coach as Mary crossed the finish line.

That's the ticket! That is what is required! □ MARY: *I'll just get ready and drive the letter directly to the airport!* SUE: *That's the ticket. Take it right to the airport post office.* □ BOB: *I've got it! I'll buy a new computer!* BILL: *That's the ticket!*

That's the way it goes. That is fate. □ MARY: *All my roses died in the cold weather.* SUE: *That's the way it goes.* □ SALLY: *Someone stole all the candy we left out in the front office.* JANE: *That's the way it goes.*

That's the way the ball bounces. See the following entry.

That's the way the cookie crumbles. AND **That's the way the ball bounces.; That's the way the mop flops.** That is life.; *That's the way it goes.* □ SUE: *I lost out on the chance for a promotion.* ALICE: *That's the way the cookie crumbles.* □ JOHN: *This entire week was spent on this project. Then they canceled it.* SALLY: *That's the way the ball bounces.*

That's the way the mop flops. See the previous entry.

(That's the) way to go! a phrase encouraging someone to continue the good work. □ *As John ran over the finish line, everyone cried, "That's the way to go!"* □ *"Way to go!" said Mary when Bob finally got the car started.*

(That's) too bad. It is unfortunate.; *I'm sorry to hear that.* □ TOM: *I hurt my foot on our little hike.* FRED: *That's too bad. Can I get you something for it?* TOM: *No, I'll live.* □ BOB: *My uncle just passed away.* TOM: *That's too bad. I'm sorry to hear that.* BOB: *Thanks.*

That's what I say. I agree with what was just said. □ TOM: *We've got to get in there and stand up for our rights!* MARY: *That's what I say.* □ BOB: *They shouldn't do that!* MARY: *That's what I say!* BOB: *They should be put in jail!* MARY: *That's what I say!*

that's why! a tag on the end of a statement that is an answer to a question beginning with *why.* (Shows a little impatience.) □ SUE: *Why do you always put your right shoe on first?* BOB: *Because, when I get ready to put on my shoes, I always pick up the right one first, that's why!* □ MARY: *Why do you eat that awful peppermint candy?* TOM: *Because I like it, that's why!*

thaw out to warm up from being frozen. (More at *thaw someone or something out.*) □ *How long will it take for the chicken to thaw out?* □ *I can't wait for the cake to thaw out. I want some now!*

thaw someone or something out to raise the temperature of someone or something above freezing. (More at *thaw out.*) □ *We need to get inside so I can thaw my brother out. His toes are almost frozen.* ⊤ *Did you thaw out the chicken?*

(The) best of luck (to someone). I wish good luck to someone. □ ALICE: *Good-bye, Bill.* BILL: *Good-bye, Alice. Best of luck.* ALICE: *Thanks. Bye.* □ *"Good-bye, and the best of luck to you," shouted Mary, waving and crying at the same time.*

The coast is clear. There is no visible danger. □ *I'm going to stay hidden here until the coast is clear.* □ *You can come out of your hiding place now. The coast is clear.*

The early bird gets the worm. The early person will get the reward. (Proverb.) □ *Don't be late again! Don't you know that the early bird gets the worm?* □ *I'll be there before the sun is up. After all, the early bird gets the worm.*

The fat is in the fire. Serious trouble has broken out. (Proverb.) □ *Now that Mary is leaving, the fat is in the fire. How can we get along without her?* □ *The fat's in the fire! There's $3,000 missing from the office safe.*

The honeymoon is over. The early pleasant beginning has ended. □ *Okay, the honeymoon is over. It's time to settle down and do some hard work.* □ *I knew the honeymoon was over when they started yelling at me to work faster.*

the pot calling the kettle black an instance of someone with a fault accusing someone else of having the same fault. □ *Ann is always late, but she was rude enough to tell everyone when I was late. Now that's the pot calling the kettle black!* □ *You're calling me thoughtless? That's really a case of the pot calling the kettle black.*

The rest is history. Everyone knows the rest of the story that I am telling. □ BILL: *Then they arrested all the officers of the corporation, and the rest is history.* SUE: *Can't trust anybody these days.* □ BOB: *Hey, what happened between you and Sue?* BILL: *We finally realized that we could never get along, and the rest is history.*

The same for me. See *I'll have the same.*

(The) same to you. 1. AND **You too.** a polite way of returning good wishes to someone. □ CLERK: *Have a nice day.* SALLY: *The same to you.* □ BOB: *I hope things work out for you. Happy New Year!* BILL: *Same to you. Bye.* **2.** an impolite way of returning a curse or epithet to someone. (Slang. The stress is on *to.* Often **Same to ya.**) □ TOM: *You're such a pest!* BILL: *Same to ya!* □ TOM: *I hope you go out and fall in a hole.* BILL: *The same to you.*

The shame of it (all)! That is so shameful!; I am so embarrassed. (Considerable use as a parody. Compare to *For shame!*) □ JOHN: *Good grief! I have a pimple! Always, just before a date.* ANDREW: *The shame of it all!* □ TOM: *John claims that he cheated on his taxes.* BILL: *Golly! The shame of it!*

The shoe is on the other foot. One is experiencing the same things that one caused another person to experience. (Proverb. Note the variations in the examples.) □ *The teacher is taking a course in summer school and is finding out what it's like when the shoe is on the other foot.* □ *When the policeman was arrested, he learned what it was like to have the shoe on the other foot.*

The sooner the better. The sooner something gets done, the better things will be. □ BOB: *When do you need this?* MARY: *The sooner the better.* □ BOB: *Please get the oil changed in the station wagon. The sooner the better.* ALICE: *I'll do it today.*

the way I see it See *from my perspective.*

the way it plays the way it is; the way things are. (Slang.) □ *The world is a rough place, and that's the way it plays.* □ *It's tough, but it's the way it plays.*

The word is mum. AND **Mum's the word.** a pledge not to reveal a secret or to tell about something or someone. □ BOB: *I hope you won't tell all this to anyone.* BILL: *Don't worry, the word is mum.* □ *"Mum's the word," said Jane to let Mary know she would keep the secret.*

then as a consequence; therefore; because of that. (Often this word seems to be filler with no clear or needed meaning.) □ BILL: *I've taken a job in New York.* ALICE: *You'll be leaving Toledo then?* BILL: *Yes, I have to move.* □ *"All right then, what sort of car were you thinking about?" asked the sales manager.*

There are plenty of other fish in the sea There are other choices. (Used to refer to persons.) □ *When John broke up with Ann, I told her not to worry. There are plenty of other fish in the sea.* □ *It's too bad that your secretary quit, but there are plenty of other fish in the sea.*

(There is) no chance. There is no chance that something will happen. □ TOM: *Do you think that some little country like that will actually attack England?* JOHN: *There's no chance.* □ BILL: *No chance you can lend me a few bucks, is there?* BILL: *Nope. No chance.*

(There is) no doubt about it. It cannot be doubted.; It is obvious. □ JANE: *It's really cold today.* FRED: *No doubt about it!* □ SUE: *Things seem to be getting more and more expensive.* TOM: *There's no doubt about it. Look at the price of oranges!*

(There is) no need (to). You do not have to.; It is not necessary. □ MARY: *Shall I try to save all this wrapping paper?* SUE: *No need. It's all torn.*

□ BOB: *Would you like me to have it repaired? I'm so sorry I broke it.* BILL: *There is no need to. I can just glue it, thanks.*

There will be hell to pay. There will be a lot of trouble if something is done or if something is not done. □ FRED: *If you break another window, there will be hell to pay.* ANDREW: *I didn't do it! I didn't.* □ BILL: *I'm afraid there's no time to do this one. I'm going to skip it.* BOB: *There will be hell to pay if you do.*

There will be the devil to pay. There will be lots of trouble. □ *If you damage my car, there will be the devil to pay.* □ *Bill broke a window, and now there will be the devil to pay.*

There you are. That's the way things are.; This is the way things have worked out. (A fatalistic dismissal.) □ *"There's nothing more that can be done. We've done what we could. So there you are," said Fred, dejected.* □ ANDREW: *Then what happened?* BOB: *Then they put me in a cell until they found I was innocent. Somebody stole my watch in there, and I cut myself on a broken wine bottle left on a bench. And now I've got lice. All because of mistaken identity. So there you are.*

There you go! Now you are doing it right!; Now you have the right attitude! □ ALICE: *I know I can do it. I just need to try harder.* JANE: *There you go!* □ BOB: *I'll devote my full time to studying and stop messing around.* FATHER: *There you go! That's great!*

There's more than one way to skin a cat. There is more than one way to do something. (Proverb.) □ *If that way won't work, try another way. There's more than one way to skin a* cat. □ *Don't worry, I'll figure out a way to get it done. There's more than one way to skin a cat.*

There's no accounting for taste. There is no explanation for people's preferences. (Proverb.) □ *Look at that purple and orange car! There's no accounting for taste.* □ *Some people seemed to like the music, although I thought it was worse than noise. There's no accounting for taste.*

(There's) no way to tell. No one can find out the answer. □ TOM: *How long are we likely to have to wait before the plane takes off?* CLERK: *Sorry, sir. There's no way to tell.* □ BILL: *Will the banks be open when we arrive?* BOB: *No way to tell. They don't keep regular hours.*

(There's) nothing to it! It is easy! □ JOHN: *Is it hard to learn to fly a small plane?* SUE: *There's nothing to it!* □ BILL: *Me? I can't dive off a board that high! I can hardly dive off the side of the pool!* BOB: *Aw, come on! Nothing to it!*

They must have seen you coming. You were really cheated.; They saw you coming and decided they could cheat you easily. □ ANDREW: *It cost two hundred dollars.* RACHEL: *You paid two hundred dollars for that thing? Boy, they must have seen you coming.* □ BOB: *Do you think I paid too much for this car? It's not as good as I thought it was.* TOM: *It's almost a wreck. They must have seen you coming.*

thin down to become thinner or slimmer. □ *He stopped eating altogether so he could thin down.* □ *I have to thin down so I can get into my new suit.*

thin out to spread out; to become less dense. (More at *thin something out*.)

□ *The trees began to thin out as we got higher up the mountain.* □ *The crowd began to thin out as we got a little farther from the theater.*

thin something out to make something less dense; to scatter something. (More at *thin out*.) □ *You will have to thin the young plants out, because there is not room for all of them.* ⊤ *Can you thin out these young plants?*

(Things) could be better. AND **(I) could be better.; (Things) might be better.** a greeting inquiry response meaning "My state is not as good as it might be." (Not necessarily a direct answer.) □ JOHN: *How are things going, Fred?* FRED: *Things could be better. And you?* JOHN: *About the same.* □ BOB: *Hi, Bill! How are you?* BILL: *I could be better. What's new with you?* BOB: *Nothing much.*

(Things) could be worse. AND **(I) could be worse.** a greeting inquiry response meaning "My state is not as bad as it might be." (Not necessarily a direct answer.) □ JOHN: *How are you, Fred?* FRED: *Things could be worse. And you?* JOHN: *Okay, I guess.* □ BILL: *Hi, Bob! What's happening?* BOB: *I could be worse. What's new with you?*

(Things) couldn't be better. See *(It) couldn't be better.*

Things haven't been easy. See *(It) hasn't been easy.*

(Things) might be better. See *(Things) could be better.*

Things will work out (all right). AND **Everything will work out (all right).; Everything will work out for the best.; Things will work out for the best.** The situation will reach a satisfactory conclusion.; The problem(s) will be resolved. □ *"Cheer up!" Mary said to a gloomy Fred. "Things will work out all right."* □ MARY: *Oh, I'm so miserable!* BILL: *Don't worry. Everything will work out for the best.* □ *"Now, now, don't cry. Things will work out," consoled Sally, hoping that what she was saying was really true.*

Things will work out for the best. See the previous entry.

think back (on someone or something) to contemplate someone or something in the past. □ *I like to think back on my family and the way we used to do things together.* □ *It makes me feel good to think back on those things.* □ *I like to think back and relive those days.*

think back (to something) to remember back to something in the past. □ *Now, try and think back to the night of January 16th.* □ *I can't think back. My mind is preoccupied with other things.*

Think nothing of it. AND **Don't give it another thought.; Don't give it a (second) thought. 1.** *You're welcome.*; It was nothing.; I was glad to do it. □ MARY: *Thank you so much for driving me home.* JOHN: *Think nothing of it.* □ SUE: *It was very kind of you to bring these all the way out here.* ALICE: *Think nothing of it. I was delighted to do it.* **2.** You did no harm at all. (A very polite way of reassuring someone that an action has not caused any great harm to the speaker.) □ SUE: *Oh, sorry. I didn't mean to bump you!* BOB: *Think nothing of it.* □ JANE: *I hope I didn't hurt your feelings when I said you were*

too loud. BILL: *Don't give it a second thought. I was too loud.*

think on one's feet to think while one is talking. □ *If you want to be a successful teacher, you must be able to think on your feet.* □ *I have to write out everything I'm going to say, because I can't think on my feet too well.*

think something out to go through something in one's mind; to think through something. □ *I have to take some time and think this out before I can respond to you.* [T] *I thought out this proposal very carefully before I presented it to you.*

think something over to think about something and whether one will choose to do it. □ *I need a few minutes to think it over.* [T] *Let me think over your request for a day or so.*

think something through to consider carefully and try to settle something in one's mind. □ *Let me think this through and call you in the morning.* [T] *I will think through this matter and get back to you.*

think something up to invent something. □ *I don't have a good excuse, but I'll think something up.* [T] *I'll think up a good answer.*

This doesn't quite suit me. AND **It doesn't quite suit me.** This is not quite what I want.; This does not please me. (Compare to *(It) suits me (fine).*) □ CLERK: *How do you like this one?* MARY: *It doesn't quite suit me.* □ BOB: *This doesn't quite suit me. Let me see something a little darker.* CLERK: *How's this?* BOB: *Better.*

This is it! I have discovered the right thing!; This is the one! □ *"This is it!" shouted the scientist, holding a test* tube in the air. □ SUE: This is it! This is the book that has all the shrimp recipes. MARY: Well, happy birthday! I never saw anybody get so happy about shrimp.

This is my floor. a phrase said by someone at the back of an elevator suggesting that people make way for an exit at a particular floor. □ Mary said, "This is my floor," and everyone made room for her to get out of the elevator. □ "Out, please," said Tom loudly. "This is my floor!"

This is someone. See Speaking.

This is where I came in. I have heard all this before. (When someone begins watching a film after it has begun, this phrase is said when the reshowing of the film reaches familiar scenes.) □ John sat through a few minutes of the argument, and when Tom and Alice kept saying the same thing over and over John said, "This is where I came in," and left the room. □ The speaker stood up and asked again for a new vote on the proposal. "This is where I came in," muttered Jane as she headed for the door.

This one's on me. I will pay for the treat this time. (Usually said in reference to buying drinks. Similar to It's on me.) □ As the waiter set down the glasses, Fred said, "This one's on me." □ JOHN: Check, please. BILL: No, this one's on me.

thrash something out to argue something through to a settlement. □ We will have to get together and thrash this out. ⊤ We will thrash out this disagreement together.

throng in(to something) [for a crowd] to swarm into some place. □ The eager crowd thronged into the de-

partment store to partake in the advertised sale. □ The doors opened, and they thronged in.

throng out (of something) [for a crowd] to swarm out of something or some place. □ The people thronged out of the concert hall at the end of the program. □ At half past ten, the crowd thronged out.

through thick and thin through good times and bad times. □ We've been together through thick and thin, and we won't desert each other now. □ Over the years, we went through thick and thin and enjoyed every minute of it.

throw a map to empty one's stomach; to vomit. (Slang.) □ Somebody threw a map on the sidewalk. □ I felt like I was going to throw a map.

throw a monkey wrench in the works to cause problems for someone's plans. □ I don't want to throw a monkey wrench in the works, but have you checked your plans with a lawyer? □ When John refused to help us, he really threw a monkey wrench in the works.

throw caution to the wind to become very careless. □ Jane, who is usually cautious, threw caution to the wind and went windsurfing. □ I don't mind taking a little chance now and then, but I'm not the type of person who throws caution to the wind.

throw cold water on something See pour cold water on something.

throw down the gauntlet to challenge someone to an argument or combat. (Both literal and figurative uses.) □ When Bob challenged my conclusions, he threw down the gauntlet. I was ready for an argument. □ Frowning at Bob is the same as *throwing down the gauntlet. He loves to get into a fight about something.*

throw good money after bad to waste additional money after wasting money once. □ *I bought a used car and then had to spend $300 on repairs. That was throwing good money after bad.* □ *The Browns are always throwing good money after bad. They bought an acre of land that turned out to be swamp and then had to pay to have it filled in.*

throw in the sponge See the following entry.

throw in the towel AND **throw in the sponge** to quit (doing something). □ *When John could stand no more of Mary's bad temper, he threw in the towel and left.* □ *Don't give up now! It's too soon to throw in the sponge.*

throw one's cookies See *toss one's cookies.*

throw one's toenails up to wretch; to vomit a lot. (Slang.) □ *Who's in the john throwing her toenails up?* ⊤ *It sounded like he was throwing up his toenails.*

throw one's voice to empty one's stomach; to vomit. (Slang.) □ *Wally's in the john throwing his voice.* □ *Another drink of that stuff and Don'll be throwing his voice all night.*

throw oneself at someone's feet to bow down humbly at someone's feet. (Both literal and figurative uses.) □ *Do I have to throw myself at your feet in order to convince you that I'm sorry?* □ *I love you sincerely, Jane. I'll throw myself at your feet and await your command. I'm your slave!*

throw oneself at the mercy of the court See the following entry.

throw oneself on the mercy of the court AND **throw oneself at the mercy of the court** to plead for mercy from a judge in a courtroom. □ *Your honor, please believe me, I didn't do it on purpose. I throw myself on the mercy of the court and beg for a light sentence.* □ *Jane threw herself at the mercy of the court and hoped for the best.*

throw someone a curve 1. to pitch a curve ball to someone in baseball. □ *The pitcher threw John a curve, and John swung wildly against thin air.* □ *During that game, the pitcher threw everyone a curve at least once.* **2.** to confuse someone by doing something unexpected. (Figurative.) □ *When you said "house" you threw me a curve. The password was supposed to be "home."* □ *John threw me a curve when we were making our presentation, and I forgot my speech.*

throw someone for a loop AND **knock someone for a loop** to confuse or shock someone. □ *When Bill heard the news, it threw him for a loop.* □ *The manager knocked Bob for a loop by firing him on the spot.*

throw someone over (for someone else) to break up with a lover in favor of someone else. □ *Sarah threw Jason over for Larry.* ⊤ *She threw over Jason for Walter.* □ *I knew she would throw him over.*

throw someone to the wolves to sacrifice someone. (Figurative.) □ *The press was demanding an explanation, so the mayor blamed the mess on John and threw him to the wolves.* □ *I wouldn't let them throw me to the wolves! I did nothing wrong, and I won't take the blame for their errors.*

throw something back to eat or drink something. (Slang.) □ *Did you throw that whole pizza back?* Ⓣ *Jed threw back a quick snort and went on with his complaining.*

throw something into the bargain to include something in a deal. □ *To encourage me to buy a new car, the car dealer threw a free radio into the bargain.* □ *If you purchase three pounds of chocolates, I'll throw one pound of salted nuts into the bargain.*

throw something off to cast something, such as a coat, off one's body. Ⓣ *He threw off his jacket and dived into the icy water.* □ *He threw his jacket off.*

throw something together to assemble or create something in a hurry. □ *I think I can throw something acceptable together for dinner.* Ⓣ *I can throw together something that is quite edible.*

throw something up **1.** to build or erect something in a hurry. □ *They sure threw that building up in a hurry.* Ⓣ *They threw up the building in only a few weeks.* **2.** to vomit something. (More at *throw up*.) □ *Poor Wally threw his dinner up.* Ⓣ *He threw up his dinner.*

throw up to vomit. (More at *throw something up*.) □ *I was afraid I would throw up, the food was so horrible.* □ *This food is bad enough to make you throw up.*

thrust out to stick out; to stab outward; to protrude outward. □ *A deck thrust out from the back of the house, offering a lovely view of the stream far below.* □ *As he grew angrier, his chin thrust out farther and farther.*

thrust someone or something back to push someone or something backward and away. □ *Tom moved forward, but the guard thrust him back.* Ⓣ *He thrust back the door, which had closed on his foot.*

thumb a ride AND **hitch a ride** to get a ride from a passing motorist; to make a sign with one's thumb that indicates to passing drivers that one is begging for a ride. □ *My car broke down on the highway, and I had to thumb a ride to get back to town.* □ *Sometimes it's dangerous to hitch a ride with a stranger.*

thumb one's nose at someone or something to make a rude gesture of disgust with one's thumb and nose at someone or something. (Both literal and figurative uses.) □ *The tramp thumbed his nose at the lady and walked away.* □ *You can't just thumb your nose at people who give you trouble. You've got to learn to get along.*

ticked (off) angry. (Slang.) □ *Wow, was she ticked off!* □ *Kelly was totally ticked.*

tickle someone's fancy to interest someone; to make someone curious. □ *I have an interesting problem here that I think will tickle your fancy.* □ *This doesn't tickle my fancy at all. This is dull and boring.*

tide someone over (until something) to supply someone until a certain time or until something happens. □ *Will this amount tide us over until next week?* Ⓣ *There is enough food here to tide over the entire camp until next month.* □ *Yes, this will tide us over.*

tidy something up to clean something up; to make something more orderly. (More at *tidy up*.) □ *Please* tidy this room up. □ This room needs to be tidied up immediately.

tidy up to clean up oneself or a place. (More at *tidy something up.*) □ *Please tidy up. This place is a mess.* □ *Please tidy up. You are a mess.*

tie in (with someone or something) to join with someone or something; to connect with someone or something. □ *I would like to tie in with you and see if we can solve this together.* □ *We would like for you to tie in and share your expertise.* □ *I tied in with a manufacturer who will produce the toy I invented.*

tie in (to something) to fasten or connect to something. □ *Can you fix it so my computer can tie into Rachel's?* □ *This one will not tie into her computer.* □ *It just won't tie in.*

tie someone down (to someone or something) to encumber someone with someone or something; to make someone responsible to or for someone or something. (*Someone* includes *oneself.*) □ *Please don't tie me down to your uncle. Let your sister help out.* □ *Yes, don't tie me down all week.* □ *I'll be tied down until I'm fifty!* □ *I don't want to tie myself down to a dog.*

tie someone in knots to become anxious or upset. □ *John tied himself in knots worrying about his wife during the operation.* □ *This waiting and worrying really ties me in knots.*

tie someone or something down to fasten someone or something down by tying or binding. (*Someone* includes *oneself.*) □ *The robbers tied Gary down so he couldn't get up and get away.* T *They tied down Gary.* □ *Please tie the chairs down so they don't fall off the boat in the storm.* □ *It was*

so windy, I almost had to tie myself down to stay on deck.

tie someone or something in (to something) to seek to establish a connection between someone or something and something. □ *The police tried to tie Sarah into the crime.* T *They tried to tie in Liz, too.* □ *Can we tie your computer into the system?* □ *Yes, you can tie it in.*

tie someone or something up to keep someone or something busy or occupied. T *Sally tied up the photocopy machine all afternoon.* □ *The well-wishers tied my telephone up all day long.* □ *The meeting tied me up all afternoon.*

tie someone's hands to prevent someone from doing something. (Also used literally.) □ *I'd like to help you, but my boss has tied my hands.* □ *Please don't tie my hands with unnecessary restrictions. I'd like the freedom to do whatever is necessary.*

tie something back to bind or fasten something back out of the way. □ *George tied the curtains back to let a little more light in.* □ *Let me tie the vines back out of the way.*

tie something off to tie the ends of blood vessels closed to prevent bleeding. □ *The surgeons tied all the blood vessels off — one by one — as they were exposed.* T *They tied off all the vessels very quickly.*

tie something up to block or impede something, such as traffic or progress. □ *The stalled bus tied traffic up for over an hour.* T *The stalled bus tied up traffic.*

tie the knot to get married. □ *Well, I hear that you and John are going to tie* *the knot.* □ *My parents tied the knot almost forty years ago.*

tied to one's mother's apron strings dominated by one's mother; dependent on one's mother. □ *Tom is still tied to his mother's apron strings.* □ *Isn't he a little old to be tied to his mother's apron strings?*

tighten one's belt to manage to spend less money. □ *Things are beginning to cost more and more. It looks like we'll all have to tighten our belts.* □ *Times are hard, and prices are high. I can tighten my belt for only so long.*

tighten something up to make something tighter. (More at *tighten up.*) □ *Tighten your seat belt up. It looks loose.* Ⓣ *Can you tighten up all the bolts?*

tighten up **1.** [for something] to get tighter. (More at *tighten something up.*) □ *The door hinges began to tighten up, making the door hard to open and close.* □ *His grip around the handle tightened up and he refused to let go.* **2.** [for someone or a group] to become miserly. □ *The government tightened up, and our budget was slashed.* □ *We almost went out of business when we couldn't get credit because the bank tightened up.* **3.** [for someone or something] to become more restrictive or better enforced. □ *The boss is tightening up on matters of this type.* □ *There are more rules, and the people who enforce them are tightening up.*

Till next time. See *Good-bye for now.*

Till we meet again. See *Good-bye for now.*

tilt at windmills to fight battles with imaginary enemies; to fight against

unimportant enemies or issues. (As with the fictional character, Don Quixote, who attacked windmills.) □ *Aren't you too smart to go around tilting at windmills?* □ *I'm not going to fight this issue. I've wasted too much of my life tilting at windmills.*

Time hangs heavy on someone's hands. Time seems to go slowly when one has nothing to do. (Not literal. Note the variations in the examples.) □ *I don't like it when time hangs so heavily on my hands.* □ *John looks so bored. Time hangs heavy on his hands.*

time in to record one's arrival time. (More at *time someone in.*) □ *Did you remember to time in this morning?* □ *When did she time in?*

Time is money. [My] time is valuable, so don't waste it. (Proverb.) □ *I can't afford to spend a lot of time standing here talking. Time is money, you know!* □ *People who keep saying time is money may be working too hard.*

time out **1.** to record one's departure time. □ *Did you remember to time out when you left work?* □ *I timed out at the regular time.* **2.** Stop everything for just a minute!; Stop talking for a minute! (Usually **Time (out)!** A way of interrupting someone.) □ *"Hey, stop a minute! Time out!" yelled Mary as the argument grew in intensity.* □ *Right in the middle of the discussion, Alice said, "Time!" Then she announced that dinner was ready.*

time someone in to record someone's arrival time. (More at *time in.*) □ *I timed you in at noon. Where were you?* Ⓣ *My job is to time in people.*

time someone out to record someone's departure time. □ *Harry had to* time everyone out because the time clock was broken. T I had to time out everyone.

Time to call it a day. It's time to quit for the day. □ JANE: Well, I'm done. Time to call it a day. SUE: Yes, let's get out of here. □ JANE: Well, I've done too much work. SUE: Yes, it's late. Time to call it a day.

Time to call it a night. It's time to quit one's activities for the night. (Can refer to work or partying.) □ BOB: Wow, it's late! Time to call it a night. MARY: Yes, it's really dark! Good night. □ FRED: Gee, I'm tired. Look at the time! JANE: Yes, it's time to call it a night.

time to cruise an expression indicating that it is time to leave. (Slang.) □ See ya. It's time to cruise. □ Time to cruise. We're gone.

Times are changing. a response to a surprising piece of news from someone. □ SUE: They paid nearly five hundred thousand for their first house! RACHEL: Well, I shouldn't be so surprised. Times are changing, I guess. □ "Times are changing," warned Mary. "You can't expect the world to stand still."

tinker (around) (with something) to meddle with something; to play with something, trying to get it to work or work better. □ Let me tinker around with it for a while and see if I can get it to work. □ Please don't tinker with the controls. □ I have the stereo set just the way I want it. Don't tinker around.

tip someone off (about someone or something) AND **tip someone off (on someone or something)** to give someone a valuable piece of news about someone or something. □ I

tipped the cops off about Max and where he was going to be that night. T I tipped off the mayor about the financial crisis. □ Yes, I am the one who did it. What tipped you off?

tip someone off (on someone or something) See the previous entry.

tip something over to cause something to fall over. □ Did you tip this chair over? T Who tipped over the chair?

tip the scales at something to weigh some amount. □ Tom tips the scales at nearly 200 pounds. □ I'll be glad when I tip the scales at a few pounds less.

tire out to become exhausted. (More at tire someone out.) □ I tire out easily. □ When I had the flu I found that I tired out easily.

tire someone out to exhaust someone. (More at tire out.) □ The extra work tired him out a lot. T Too much work will tire out the horses.

(To) hell with that! I reject that! □ MARY: I think we ought to go to the dance Friday night. TOM: To hell with that! □ FRED: Don't you want to drive me down to school? JOHN: To hell with that!

to one's heart's content as much as one wants. □ John wanted a week's vacation so he could go to the lake and fish to his heart's content. □ I just sat there, eating chocolate to my heart's content.

to put it another way AND **put another way** a phrase introducing a restatement of what someone, usually the speaker, has just said. □ FATHER: You're still very young, Tom. To put it another way, you don't have any idea about what you're getting into. TOM: *But I still want to get married, so can I borrow fifty dollars?* □ JOHN: *Could you go back to your own room now, Tom? I have to study.* TOM: *(no answer)* JOHN: *Put another way, get out of here!* TOM: *Okay, okay. Don't get your bowels in an uproar!*

to the best of my knowledge See *(as) far as I know.*

to the ends of the earth to the remotest and most inaccessible points on the earth. □ *I'll pursue him to the ends of the earth.* □ *We've almost explored the whole world. We've traveled to the ends of the earth trying to learn about our world.*

to the max maximally. (Slang.) □ *She is happy to the max.* □ *They worked to the max their whole shift.*

To the victors belong the spoils. The winners achieve power over people and property. (Proverb.) □ *The mayor took office and immediately fired many workers and hired new ones. Everyone said, "To the victors belong the spoils."* □ *The office of President includes the right to live in the White House and at Camp David. To the victors belong the spoils.*

toe the line See the following entry.

toe the mark AND **toe the line** to do what one is expected to do; to follow the rules. □ *You'll get ahead, Sally. Don't worry. Just toe the mark, and everything will be okay.* □ *John finally got fired. He just couldn't learn to toe the line.*

tone something down to cause something to have less of an impact on the senses of sight or sound; to lessen the impact of something prepared for public performance or consumption.

□ *This is rather shocking. You had better tone it down a bit.* T *Tone down this paragraph.* T *Tone down the color of the walls. They're very red.*

tongue-in-cheek insincere; joking. □ *Ann made a tongue-in-cheek remark to John, and he got mad because he thought she was serious.* □ *The play seemed very serious at first, but then everyone saw that it was tongue-in-cheek, and they began laughing.*

too good to be true almost unbelievable; so good as to be unbelievable. □ *The news was too good to be true.* □ *When I finally got a big raise, it was too good to be true.*

Too many cooks spoil the broth. See the following entry.

Too many cooks spoil the stew. AND **Too many cooks spoil the broth.** Too many people trying to manage something simply spoil it. (Proverb.) □ *Let's decide who is in charge around here. Too many cooks spoil the stew.* □ *Everyone is giving orders, but no one is following them! Too many cooks spoil the broth.*

Toodle-oo. AND **Ta-ta.; Toodles.** Good-bye. □ FRED: *Bye, you guys. See you.* SALLY: *It's been. Really it has. Toodle-oo.* □ MARY: *See ya, bye-bye.* SUE: *Ta-ta.*

Toodles. See the previous entry.

tool around to drive or cruise around. (Slang.) □ *We tooled around for a while and then rented a horror flick.* □ *Let's tool around on the way home.*

tool something up to equip a factory or production line with tools and machines. □ *The manager closed down the factory so she could tool it up for the new models.* T *She tooled up the factory in record time.*

tool up to become equipped with tools. □ *I need some money so I can tool up to do the job.* □ *The factory tooled up to make the new cars in only two weeks.*

toot one's own horn AND **blow one's own horn** to boast or praise oneself. □ *Tom is always tooting his own horn. Is he really as good as he says he is?* □ *I find it hard to blow my own horn, but I manage.*

top something off (with something) to celebrate an end to something with something; to complete the top of something, such as a building. □ *They topped the evening off with dessert.* T *They topped off the evening with a bottle of champagne.* □ *The workers topped the building off with a flag.*

topple over [for something very tall] to fall over. □ *I was afraid that Jimmy's stack of blocks would topple over.* □ *The stack of books toppled over and ended up as a jumbled mess on the floor.*

toss one's cookies AND **throw one's cookies; toss one's lunch; toss one's tacos** to empty one's stomach; to vomit. (Slang.) □ *Right then and there, with no warning, he tossed his cookies.* □ *If you feel like throwing your cookies, please leave quietly.*

toss one's hat into the ring to state that one is running for an elective office. □ *Jane wanted to run for treasurer, so she tossed her hat into the ring.* □ *The mayor never tossed his hat into the ring. Instead he announced his retirement.*

toss one's lunch See *toss one's cookies.*

toss one's tacos See *toss one's cookies.*

toss something off 1. to do something quickly without much time or effort. (Slang.) □ *It was no big deal. I tossed it off in thirty minutes.* T *We can toss off the entire order in — let's say — three hours.* **2.** to drink something quickly. □ *He tossed it off and ordered another.* T *She tossed off a scotch in one big swig.* **3.** to ignore criticism; to ignore defeat or a setback. □ *She just tossed it off like nothing had happened.* T *How could she just toss off that rude remark?*

toss something together to assemble something hastily. □ *This report is useless. You just tossed it together!* □ *This meal was just tossed together, but it was delicious.*

total something up to add up the total of something. □ *Please total the bill up and let me see the cost.* T *Total up the bill and give it to me.*

touch down [for an airplane] to come in contact with the ground. □ *Flight twelve is due to touch down at midnight.* □ *When will this plane touch down?*

touch someone or something off to ignite or excite someone or something. □ *She is very excitable. The slightest thing will touch her off.* T *The appearance of the fox touched off a furor in the henhouse.*

touch something up to fix up the minor flaws in something. □ *It's only a little scratch in the finish. We can touch it up easily.* T *I can touch up the paint on your car easily.*

touch (up)on something to mention something; to discuss something briefly. (*Upon* is formal and less commonly used than *on.*) □ *The lecturer* *only touched upon the question of new technology.* □ *She only touched on the main issue.*

tough act to follow a difficult presentation or performance to follow with one's own performance. □ *Bill's speech was excellent. It was a tough act to follow, but my speech was good also.* □ *In spite of the fact that I had a tough act to follow, I did my best.*

tough row to hoe a difficult task to undertake. □ *It was a tough row to hoe, but I finally got a college degree.* □ *Getting the contract signed is going to be a tough row to hoe, but I'm sure I can do it.*

tough something out to carry on with or endure something despite difficulties or setbacks. (Slang.) □ *Sorry, you'll just have to tough it out.* □ *I think I can tough this job out for another month.* □ *I will tough this out to the very end.* T *I can tough out anything for a few days.*

toughen someone or something up to cause someone or something to be stronger, less compromising, or more severe. (*Someone* includes *oneself.* More at *toughen up.*) □ *A few days behind the counter at the discount store will toughen her up quickly.* T *Having to deal with people toughened up the clerk quickly.* □ *She tried to toughen the skin on her palms up.* □ *I need to toughen myself up if I am going to deal with the public.*

toughen up to become tougher, stronger, or more severe. (More at *toughen someone or something up.*) □ *She will toughen up after a while. You have to be tough around here to survive.* □ *You are going to have to toughen up if you want to play on the team.*

Tout suite! right away; with all haste. (From French *Toute de Suite.* Pronounced "toot sweet.") □ JOHN: *Come on, get this finished!* BOB: *I'm trying.* JOHN: *Tout suite! Get moving!* □ *"I want this mess cleaned up, tout suite!" shouted Sally, hands on her hips and steaming with rage.*

tow someone or something away to pull something, such as a car or a boat, away with another car, boat, etc. (The *someone* refers to the property of someone, not the person.) □ *If I don't get back to my car, they will tow me away.* T *The truck towed away my car.* □ *A big truck came and towed the illegally parked car away.*

tow someone or something in(to something) to pull something, such as a car or a truck, into something, such as a garage. (The *someone* refers to the property of someone, not the person.) □ *They had to tow my car into the garage to be repaired.* T *They towed in my car.* □ *They towed me in!*

tow someone or something out (of some place) to pull something, such as a car, out of something, such as a ditch. (The *someone* refers to the property of someone, not the person.) □ *The farmer used his tractor to tow Andrew out of the ditch.* □ *He towed the car out of the ditch.* T *He towed out the car.*

track someone or something down to search out where someone or something is. □ *I don't know where Anne is. I'll try to track her down.* T *I'll track down Anne for you.* □ *I will try to track the book down for you.*

track something in(to some place) to bring something, such as mud, into a place on the bottom of one's feet. □ *Please don't track mud into the office.* T *Don't track in any mud!* □ *You tracked it in!*

track something up to mess something up by spreading around something dirty or messy with one's feet. □ *Please don't track the floor up!* T *Claire tracked up the floor.*

trade something in (for something) AND **trade something in (on something)** to return something, such as a car, to a place where cars are sold as partial payment on a new car. □ *I traded my old car in on a new one.* T *I traded in my old jalopy for a newer car.* □ *This car is old. It's time to trade it in.*

trade something in (on something) See the previous entry.

trade something off 1. to get rid of something in an exchange. □ *I traded my car off.* T *I traded off my old car for a new one.* **2.** to sacrifice something in an exchange. □ *You end up trading security off for more money.* T *Don't trade off your job security.*

tread on someone's toes See *step on someone's toes.*

trick someone into something to deceive someone into doing something. □ *She tried to trick him into doing it her way.* □ *I didn't want to do it, but I was tricked into it.*

trick someone out of something AND **trick something out of someone** to get something from someone by trickery. □ *You can't trick me out of my money. I'm not that dumb!* □ *Stay alert so that no one tricks you out of your money.* □ *They tricked the information out of Bob.*

trick something out of someone See the previous entry.

trigger someone or something off 1. to cause someone or something to go into action. □ *Your rude comments triggered her off.* T *Your comments triggered off quite an uproar.* **2.** [with something] to set something off, such as an explosion. □ *We were afraid that the sparks from the engine would trigger an explosion off.* T *The sparks triggered off an explosion.*

trim something away (from something) to cut something away (from something). □ *The butcher trimmed the fat away from the steak.* T *Please trim away the fat from the meat.* □ *Oh, yes. Trim it away.*

trim something off ((of) someone or something) to cut something off someone or something. □ *I asked the barber to trim the beard off of Ralph.* T *The barber trimmed off Ralph's beard.* □ *Please trim it off.*

trip someone up 1. to cause someone to trip; to entangle someone's feet. (*Someone* includes *oneself.*) □ *The rope strewn about the deck tripped him up.* T *The lines tripped up the crew.* □ *He tripped himself up in the lines.* **2.** to cause someone to falter. (Figurative. *Someone* includes *oneself.*) □ *Mary came in while the speaker was talking, and the distraction tripped him up.* T *The noise in the audience tripped up the speaker.* □ *Take care and do not trip yourself up.*

trot someone or something out to bring out and display someone or something. (Figurative.) □ *The boss trotted the new vice president out for us to meet.* T *The boss trotted out his daughter and introduced her as a new* *vice president.* T *Fred trotted out his favorite project for everyone to see.*

true to one's word keeping one's promise. □ *True to his word, Tom showed up at exactly eight o'clock.* □ *We'll soon know if Jane is true to her word. We'll see if she does what she promised.*

Trust me! Honestly!; I am telling you the truth.; Please believe me. (Slang.) □ *Tom said with great conviction, "Trust me! I know exactly what to do!"* □ MARY: *Do you really think we can keep this party a secret until Thursday?* SALLY: *Trust me! I know how to plan a surprise party.*

try as I may a phrase that introduces an expression of regret or failure. □ BILL: *Try as I may, I cannot get this thing put together right.* ANDREW: *Did you read the instructions?* □ RACHEL: *Wow! This place is a mess!* MOTHER: *Try as I may, I can't get Andrew to clean up after himself.*

try one's wings (out) to try to do something one has recently become qualified to do. (Like a young bird uses its wings to try to fly.) □ *You've read about it enough. It's time to try your wings.* T *John just got his driver's license and wants to borrow the car to try out his wings.* T *I learned to skin dive, and I want to go to the seaside to try out my wings.*

try out (for something) to audition for a part in some performance or other activity requiring skill. □ *I intend to try out for the play.* □ *I'm going to try out too.*

try someone's patience to do something annoying that may cause someone to lose patience; to cause someone to be annoyed. □ *Stop*

whistling. *You're trying my patience. Very soon I'm going to lose my temper.* □ *Some students think it's fun to try the teacher's patience.*

try something out on someone to see how someone responds to something or some idea. □ *Let me try this idea out on you and see what you think.* T *Let me try out this new medicine on her.*

Tsup? What's up? (Slang.) □ BILL: *Tsup?* TOM: *Nothing. What's new with you?* BILL: *Nothing.* □ BOB: *Tsup?* FRED: *I'm getting a new car.* BOB: *Excellent!*

tuck something in((to) something) to fold or stuff something into something. □ *Please tuck your shirttail into your pants.* T *Tuck in your shirttail.* □ *When you make the bed, you have to tuck the sheets in.* □ *I tucked a handkerchief into the breast pocket of my jacket.* □ *She tucked a note into the box with my present.*

tumble out of something to fall, topple, or drop out of something. □ *Don't let the baby tumble out of the chair!* □ *The children tumbled out of the car and ran for the school building.*

tumble over (something) to fall over the edge of something. □ *Stay away from the edge. I don't want any of you tumbling over it.* □ *Don't go too close. You'll tumble over.*

tune up [for one or more musicians] to bring their instruments into tune. □ *You could hear them behind the curtain, tuning up.* □ *We have to tune up before the concert.*

turn a blind eye to someone or something to ignore someone or something and pretend you do not see them or it. □ *The usher turned a blind eye to the little boy who sneaked* *into the theater.* □ *How can you turn a blind eye to all those starving children?*

turn a deaf ear (to something) to ignore what someone says; to ignore a cry for help. □ *How can you just turn a deaf ear to their cries for food and shelter?* □ *The government has turned a deaf ear.*

turn about See *turn around.*

turn against someone or something to attack, defy, or revolt against someone or something. □ *You wouldn't think that your own family would turn against you!* □ *In the last days, everyone turned against the government.*

turn around AND **turn about** to reverse; to face the opposite direction; to change the direction of motion. □ *The bus turned around and went the other way.* □ *Please turn around so I can see who you are.* □ *The bus turned about and returned to the station.*

turn back (from some place) to stop one's journey and return. □ *We turned back from the amusement park so we could go home and get the tickets we had forgotten.* □ *We turned back at the last minute.*

turn belly-up AND **go belly-up** 1. to fail. (Slang.) □ *I sort of felt that the whole thing would go belly-up, and I was right.* □ *The computer — on its last legs anyway — turned belly-up right in the middle of an important job.* 2. to die. (As a fish does when it dies. See also *belly-up.*) □ *The cat was friendly for a moment before she turned belly-up.* □ *Every fish in Greg's tank went belly-up last night.*

turn in((to) some place) to walk or steer one's vehicle into a place. □ *Turn into the next service station for*

some gas. □ *I'll turn in for gas now.* □ *She walked down the street and turned into the drugstore.*

turn off [for something] to go off; to switch off. □ *All the lights turn off automatically.* □ *What time do the streetlights turn off?*

turn on [for something] to switch on and start running. □ *The lights turned on right at dusk.* □ *At what time do the streetlights turn on?*

turn on a dime to turn in a very tight turn. □ *This car handles very well. It can turn on a dime.* □ *The speeding car turned on a dime and headed in the other direction.*

turn one's nose up at someone or something to sneer at someone or something; to reject someone or something. □ *John turned his nose up at Ann, and that hurt her feelings.* Ⓣ *I never turn up my nose at dessert, no matter what it is.*

turn out (for something) [for people, especially an audience] to [leave home to] attend some event. □ *A lot of people turned out for our meeting.* □ *Almost all the residents turned out for the meeting.*

turn over a new leaf to start again with the intention of doing better; to begin again, ignoring past errors. □ *Tom promised to turn over a new leaf and do better in school from now on.* □ *After a minor accident, Sally decided to turn over a new leaf and drive more carefully.*

turn over in one's grave [for a dead person] to be shocked or horrified. (Not used literally.) □ *If Beethoven heard Mary play one of his sonatas, he'd turn over in his grave.* □ *If Aunt Jane knew what you were doing with*

419

her favorite chair, she would turn over in her grave.

turn someone or something back to cause someone or something to stop and go back; to cause someone or something to retreat. □ *The border guards turned us back because we had no passports.* ⊤ *They turned back the train because the bridge was down.*

turn someone or something down 1. [with *someone*] to issue a refusal to someone. □ *We had to turn Joan down, even though her proposal was okay.* ⊤ *We turned down Joan, even though her credentials were good.* **2.** [with *something*] to bend or fold something down. □ *He turned his coat collar down when he got inside the house.* ⊤ *Timmy had turned down his cuffs and caught one of them in his bicycle chain.* **3.** [with *something*] to decrease the volume of something. □ *Please turn the radio down.* ⊤ *Can't you turn down that stereo?* **4.** [with *something*] to reject something. □ *The board turned our proposal down.* ⊤ *They turned down our offer.*

turn someone or something over to someone or something to release or assign someone or something to someone or something; to transfer or deliver someone or something to someone or something. □ *The deputy turned the bank robber over to the sheriff.* ⊤ *I turned over the money I found to the police.* □ *The police officer turned Max over to the court.*

turn someone or something up 1. to increase the volume of a device emitting the sound of someone or something. □ *I can't hear the lecturer. Turn her up.* ⊤ *Turn up the radio, please.* **2.** to discover or locate someone or something. ⊤ *See if you can*

turn up any evidence of his presence in the apartment on the night of January 16th. ⊤ *Have you been able to turn up a date for Friday night?* **3.** [with *something*] to bend or fold something up. (More at *turn up.*) □ *Please turn your cuffs up. They are getting muddy.* ⊤ *He turned up his coat collar to keep the rain off his neck.* **4.** [with *something*] to turn playing cards face up. □ *Please turn all the cards up.* ⊤ *Sally turned up the cards one at a time.*

turn someone or something out 1. [with *someone*] to train or produce someone with certain skills or talents. □ *The state law school turns lawyers out by the dozen.* ⊤ *A committee accused the state university of turning out too many veterinarians.* **2.** [with *something*] to manufacture or produce something in numbers. □ *The factory turns too few cars out.* ⊤ *The factory turns out about seventy-five cars a day.* **3.** [with *something*] to turn off a light. □ *Please turn the hall light out.* ⊤ *Turn out the lights on the Christmas tree.*

turn someone's stomach to make someone ill. (Both figurative and literal uses.) □ *This milk is spoiled. The smell of it turns my stomach.* □ *The play was so bad that it turned my stomach.*

turn something on to switch on something to make it run. □ *I turned the microwave oven on and cooked dinner.* ⊤ *I turned on the lights when the sun went down.*

turn something to one's advantage to make an advantage for oneself out of something (that might otherwise be a disadvantage). □ *Sally found a way to turn the problem to her advantage.* □ *The ice-cream store manager* was able to turn the hot weather to her advantage.

turn the other cheek to ignore abuse or an insult. (Biblical.) ☐ When Bob got mad at Mary and yelled at her, she just turned the other cheek. ☐ Usually I turn the other cheek when someone is rude to me.

turn the tide to cause a reversal in the direction of events; to cause a reversal in public opinion. ☐ It looked as if the team was going to lose, but near the end of the game, our star player turned the tide. ☐ At first, people were opposed to our plan. After a lot of discussion, we were able to turn the tide.

turn to to start working; to start doing one's job. ☐ Get going, you guys! Come on! Turn to! ☐ It's time you all turned to and gave us a hand.

turn turtle to turn over, as with a ship. (When a ship is upside down in the water, its hull looks like the shell of a huge turtle.) ☐ The old dog finally turned turtle, and that was the end. ☐ The car struck a pole and turned turtle.

turn up 1. [for part of something] to point upward. (More at turn someone or something up.) ☐ The ends of the elf's funny little shoes turned up. **2.** to happen. ☐ Something always turns up to prevent their meeting. ☐ I am sorry I was late. Something turned up at the last minute.

turn up one's toes to die. (Slang.) ☐ I'm too young to turn my toes up. T The cat turned up its toes right after church. Ah, the power of prayer.

turn up (somewhere) [for someone or something] to appear in a place. ☐ Her name is always turning up in the gossip columns. ☐ He turned up an hour late. ☐ Guess who turned up today? ☐ Tom turned up in my office today. ☐ Someone I did not expect to see turned up. ☐ My glasses turned up in the dishwasher.

twiddle one's thumbs to pass time by playing with one's fingers. ☐ What am I supposed to do while waiting for you? Sit here and twiddle my thumbs? ☐ Don't sit around twiddling your thumbs. Get busy!

twist someone around one's little finger to manipulate and control someone. ☐ Bob really fell for Jane. She can twist him around her little finger. ☐ Billy's mother has twisted him around her little finger. He's very dependent on her.

twist someone's arm to force or persuade someone to do or say something. ☐ At first she refused, but after I twisted her arm a little, she agreed to help. ☐ I didn't want to run for mayor, but everyone twisted my arm.

type something up to type a handwritten document. ☐ I will give this to you as soon as I type it up. T Please type up this paper.

U

under a cloud (of suspicion) to be suspected of (doing) something. □ *Someone stole some money at work, and now everyone is under a cloud of suspicion.* □ *Even the manager is under a cloud.*

under construction in the process of being built or repaired. □ *We cannot travel on this road because it's under construction.* □ *Our new home has been under construction all summer. We hope to move in next month.*

under fire during an attack. □ *There was a scandal in city hall, and the mayor was forced to resign under fire.* □ *John is a good lawyer because he can think under fire.*

under no circumstances AND **not under any circumstances** never. □ ANDREW: *Under no circumstances will I ever go back there again!* RACHEL: *Why? What happened?* □ SUE: *Can I talk you into serving as a referee again?* MARY: *Heavens, no! Not under any circumstances!*

under normal circumstances normally; usually; typically. □ *"We'd be able to keep the dog at home under normal circumstances," said Mary to the vet.* □ *"Under normal circumstances you'd be able to return to work in a week," explained the doctor.*

under one's own steam by one's own power or effort. □ *I missed my ride to class, so I had to get there under my own steam.* □ *John will need some help with this project. He can't do it under his own steam.*

under the counter [for something to be bought or sold] in secret or illegally. (Also used literally.) □ *The drugstore owner was arrested for selling liquor under the counter.* □ *This owner was also selling dirty books under the counter.*

under the table in secret, as with the giving of a bribe. (Also used literally.) □ *The mayor had been paying money to the construction company under the table.* □ *Tom transferred the deed to the property to his wife under the table.*

under the weather ill. □ *I'm a bit under the weather today, so I can't go to the office.* □ *My head is aching, and I feel a little under the weather.*

under the wire just barely in time or on time. □ *I turned in my report just under the wire.* □ *Bill was the last person to get in the door. He got in under the wire.*

unite against someone or something to join against someone or something. □ *We will unite against the opposing forces.* □ *We must unite against the incumbent legislators.*

unite someone against someone or something to cause people to join together against someone or something. (*Someone* includes *oneself.*) □ *The mayor united his people against the federal investigators.* □ *Ted united us against John.* □ *They united themselves against the enemy.*

Until we meet again. See *Good-bye for now.*

up a blind alley at a dead end; on a route that leads nowhere. □ *I have been trying to find out something about my ancestors, but I'm up a blind alley. I can't find anything.* □ *The police are up a blind alley in their investigation of the crime.*

up for grabs 1. available for anyone; not yet claimed. (Slang.) □ *It's up for grabs. Everything is still very chancy.* □ *I don't know who will get it. It's up for grabs.* 2. in total chaos. □ *This is a madhouse. The whole place is up for grabs.* □ *When the market crashed, the whole office was up for grabs.*

up for something agreeable to something. (Slang.) □ *I'm up for a pizza. Anybody want to chip in?* □ *Who's up for a swim?*

up front 1. at the beginning; in advance. (Slang.) □ *She wanted $200 up front.* □ *The more you pay up front, the less you'll have to finance.* 2. open; honest; forthcoming. (Usually **up-front.**) □ *She is a very up-front gal — trust her.* □ *I wish the salesman had been more up-front about it.* 3. in the forefront; under fire (at the front). □ *You guys who are up front are gonna get the most fire.* □ *You two go up front and see if you can help.*

up in arms rising up in anger; armed with weapons. (Both literal and figurative uses.) □ *My father was really up in arms when he got his tax bill this year.* □ *The citizens were up in arms, pounding on the gates of the palace, demanding justice.*

up in the air undecided; uncertain. (Also used literally.) □ *I don't know what Sally plans to do. Things were sort of up in the air the last time we talked.* □ *Let's leave this question up in the air until next week.*

up to one's ears (in something) See the following entry.

up to one's neck (in something) AND **up to one's ears (in something)** very much involved in something. □ *I can't come to the meeting. I'm up to my neck in these reports.* □ *Mary is up to her ears in her work.*

up to par as good as the standard or average; up to a certain standard. □ *I'm just not feeling up to par today. I must be coming down with something.* □ *The manager said that the report was not up to par and gave it back to Mary to do over again.*

upgrade someone or something to something to raise someone or something to a higher grade or rank. (*Someone* includes *oneself.*) □ *Please upgrade me to first-class seating on the plane.* □ *They upgraded the crisis to code red.* □ *She upgraded herself to a higher rank.*

upset the apple cart to mess up or ruin something. □ *Tom really upset the apple cart by telling Mary the truth about Jane.* □ *I always knew he'd upset the apple cart.*

use every trick in the book to use every method possible. □ *I used every* trick in the book, but I still couldn't manage to get a ticket to the game Saturday. □ Bob tried to use every trick in the book, but he still failed.

use something up to consume or use all of something. □ *Use it up. I have more in the cupboard.* Ⓣ *Use up every bit of it. Go ahead.*

Use your head! AND **Use your noggin!; Use your noodle!** Start thinking.; Use your brain. □ TOM: *I just don't know what to do.* MARY: *Use your head! You'll figure out something.* □ ANDREW: *Come on, John, you can figure it out. A kindergartner could do it. Use your noggin!* JOHN: *I'm doing my best.*

Use your noggin! See the previous entry.

Use your noodle! See *Use your head!*

usher someone or something in (to some place) to escort or lead a person, a group, or something into a place. □ *The guard ushered the group into the palace.* Ⓣ *They ushered in the visitors.* □ *They ushered the children into the theater.*

usher someone or something out (of some place) to escort or lead someone or a group out of a place. □ *The woman ushered the guest out.* □ *We ushered the children out of the room.* □ *They ushered the birthday party out.*

V

vacuum something up (from something) to clean something up from something using a vacuum cleaner. □ *Fred vacuumed the dirt up from the carpet.* ⊤ *He vacuumed up the birdseed from the kitchen floor.* ⊤ *He vacuumed up the dirt.*

Vamoose! Get out!; Go away! (From Spanish *vamos*, "let's go.") □ BOB: *Go on. Get out of here! Vamoose!* BILL: *I'm going! I'm going!* □ TOM: *Go away!* BILL: *What?* BOB: *Vamoose! Scram! Beat it!* BILL: *Why?* BOB: *Because you're a pain.*

vanish into thin air to disappear without leaving a trace. □ *My money gets spent so fast. It seems to vanish into thin air.* □ *When I came back, my car was gone. I locked it, and it couldn't have vanished into thin air!*

Variety is the spice of life. Differences and changes make life interesting. (Proverb.) □ *Mary reads all kinds of books. She says variety is the spice of life.* □ *The Franklins travel all over the world so they can learn how different people live. After all, variety is the spice of life.*

veg (out) to cease working and take it easy; to vegetate. (Slang.) □ *Someday, I just want to veg out and enjoy life.* □ *I think I'll just veg this weekend.*

Very good. 1. It is good. □ JOHN: *How do you like your lobster?* ALICE: *Mmm. Very good.* □ JANE: *What did you think of the movie?* FRED: *Very good.* JANE: *Is that all?* FRED: *Yeah.* **2.** As you say.; Thank you for your instructions. (Typically said by someone in a serving role, such as a clerk, waiter, waitress, butler, maid, etc.) □ WAITER: *What are you drinking, madam?* SUE: *It's just soda. No more, thanks.* WAITER: *Very good.* □ MARY: *Would you charge this to my account?* CLERK: *Very good.*

volunteer for something to submit oneself for some task. □ *I volunteered for the job.* □ *I didn't volunteer for this.*

vote a straight ticket to cast a ballot with all the votes for members of the same political party. □ *I'm not a member of any political party, so I never vote a straight ticket.* □ *I usually vote a straight ticket because I believe in the principles of one party and not in the other's.*

vote someone or something down to defeat someone or something in an election. □ *The community voted the proposal down.* ⊤ *They voted down the proposal.* □ *The citizens voted Roger down.*

W

wade in(to something) 1. to walk into an area covered by water. □ *The horse waded right into the stream.* □ *It waded right in.* 2. to get quickly and directly involved in something. □ *Don't just wade into things. Stop and think about what you are doing.* □ *Just wade in and get started.*

Wait a minute. See *Just a minute.*

Wait a sec(ond). See *Just a minute.*

wait-and-see attitude a skeptical attitude; an uncertain attitude where someone will just wait and see what happens. □ *John thought that Mary couldn't do it, but he took a wait-and-see attitude.* □ *His wait-and-see attitude didn't influence me at all.*

wait on someone hand and foot to serve someone very well, attending to all personal needs. □ *I don't mind bringing you your coffee, but I don't intend to wait on you hand and foot.* □ *I don't want anyone to wait on me hand and foot. I can take care of myself.*

Wait up (a minute)! Wait for me while I catch up with you! □ *Tom, who was following Mary down the street, said, "Wait up a minute! I need to talk to you."* □ JOHN: *Hey, Sally! Wait up!* SALLY: *What's happening?*

wait up (for someone or something) 1. to slow down and pause for some- one or something to catch up. □ *Wait up for me. You are too fast.* □ *Please wait up for the bus.* □ *Wait up, you guys!* 2. to delay going to bed for someone or something or until someone or something does something. □ *I won't wait up for you.* □ *There is no need to wait up.* □ *We chose to wait up for the coming of the New Year.*

wait (up)on someone to pay homage to someone. (Stilted.) □ *Do you expect me to wait upon you like a member of some medieval court?* □ *She waited on her grown children as if they were gods and goddesses.*

wake someone or something up to cause someone or some creature to awaken. (More at *wake up.*) □ *Please don't wake me up until noon.* T *Wake up your brother at noon.* □ *Don't wake the dog up unless you want to take her for a walk.*

wake up to awaken; to become alert. (More at *wake someone or something up.*) □ *Wake up! We have to get on the road.* □ *It's time to wake up!*

walk a tightrope to be in a situation where one must be very cautious. (Also used literally.) □ *I've been walking a tightrope all day. I need to relax.* □ *Our business is about to fail. We've been walking a tightrope for three months.*

walk heavy to conduct oneself with an air of importance. (Black slang.) □ Harry's been walking heavy since he graduated. □ Why have you been walking heavy, man?

walk in on someone or something to interrupt someone or something by entering a place. □ I didn't mean to walk in on you. I didn't know anyone was in here. □ Alice walked in on the meeting by accident.

walk off to walk away; to leave on foot abruptly. □ She didn't even say good-bye. She just walked off. □ He walked off and never looked back.

walk on air to be very happy; to be euphoric. (Never used literally.) □ Ann was walking on air when she got the job. □ On the last day of school, all the children are walking on air.

walk on eggs to be very cautious. (Never used literally.) □ The manager is very hard to deal with. You really have to walk on eggs. □ I've been walking on eggs ever since I started working here.

walk out (of something) 1. to exit something or some place. □ We walked out of the shop when we had made our purchases. □ She went to the door and walked out. **2.** to exit the workplace on strike. □ The workers walked out because of a jurisdictional dispute. □ The workers walked out in sympathy with another union.

walk out (on someone or something) to leave or abandon someone or something in anger, disgust, or aversion. □ Sally walked out on Tom because she was fed up with him. □ Sally finally walked out.

walk tall to be brave and self-assured. (Slang.) □ I know I can walk tall because I'm innocent. □ You go out on that stage and walk tall. There is no reason to be afraid.

walk the floor to pace nervously while waiting. □ While Bill waited for news of the operation, he walked the floor for hours on end. □ Walking the floor won't help. You might as well sit down and relax.

walls have ears we may be overheard. □ Let's not discuss this matter here. Walls have ears, you know. □ Shhh. Walls have ears. Someone may be listening.

want in((to) something) to want to come into something or some place. □ It's cold out here! I want into the house. □ The dog wants in.

want out (of something) 1. to desire to get out of something or some place. (More at want someone or something out of something.) □ I want out of this stuffy room. □ Where's the door? I want out. **2.** to desire to be relieved of a responsibility. □ I want out of this responsibility. I don't have the time to do it right. □ This job is no good for me. I want out.

want someone or something out of something to desire that someone or something leave or be removed from something or some place. (More at want out (of something).) □ I want you out of here immediately. □ I want this box out of here now!

warm someone or something up 1. to make someone or something warmer; to take the chill off someone or something. (Someone includes oneself. More at warm up.) □ I put him by the fire to warm him up a little. T We warmed up our feet before the fire. T Could you warm up my coffee, *please?* □ *Is dinner warmed up yet?* □ *I need to get in there and warm myself up.* **2.** [with *someone*] to help someone get physically prepared to perform in an athletic event. (More at *warm up (for something).*) □ *The referee told the coach to warm his team up so the game could begin.* Ⓣ *You have to warm up the team before a game.* □ *Be sure to warm yourself up before playing.*

warm the bench [for a player] to remain out of play during a game — seated on a bench. □ *John spent the whole game warming the bench.* □ *Mary never warms the bench. She plays from the beginning to the end.*

warm the cockles of someone's heart to make someone warm and happy. □ *It warms the cockles of my heart to hear you say that.* □ *Hearing that old song again warmed the cockles of her heart.*

warm up 1. [for the weather or a person] to become warmer or hotter. (More at *warm someone or something up.*) □ *I think it is going to warm up next week.* □ *Will it ever warm up?* **2.** [for someone] to become more friendly. □ *Todd began to warm up halfway through the conference.* □ *After he had worked there for a while, he began to warm up.*

warm up (for something) to prepare for some kind of performance or competition. (More at *warm someone or something up, warm up.*) □ *The team had to warm up before the game.* □ *They have to warm up.*

warm up to someone or something to become more fervent and earnest toward someone, something, or a group; to become more responsive and receptive to someone, a group, or something. □ *After we talked, he began to warm up to us a little.* □ *I warmed up to the committee as the interview went on.* □ *Jane warmed up to the idea, so she may approve it.*

warn someone against someone or something to advise someone against someone, something, or doing something. □ *We warned them all against going to Turkey at this time.* □ *I warned her against Gerald.*

warn someone away from someone or something to advise someone to avoid someone or something. □ *We warned her away from the danger, but she did not heed our warning.* □ *Why didn't you warn me away from Roger?*

warn someone off to advise a person to stay away. □ *We placed a guard outside the door to warn people off until the gas leak could be fixed.* Ⓣ *The guards warned off everyone in the vicinity.*

wash away to be carried away by water or some other liquid. (More at *wash someone or something away.*) □ *The bridge washed away in the flood.* □ *All the soil washed away and left the rocks exposed.*

wash off ((of) someone or something) to be carried off of or away from someone or something by the action of water or another liquid. (The *of* is colloquial. More at *wash someone or something off.*) □ *The dirt washed off of the floor easily.* □ *The label washed off this can, and now I don't know what's in it.*

wash one's hands of someone or something to end one's association with someone or something. □ *I washed my hands of Tom. I wanted no* *more to do with him.* □ *That car was a real headache. I washed my hands of it long ago.*

wash someone or something away 1. [for a flood of water] to carry someone or something away. (More at *wash away.*) □ *The flood washed the boats away.* Ⓣ *The high water washed away the shoreline.* □ *The storm washed some people on the shore away.* **2.** [with *something*] to clean something by scrubbing and flushing away the dirt. (More at *wash away.*) □ *Fresh water will wash the seawater away.* Ⓣ *Let's wash away these muddy footprints.*

wash someone or something off to clean someone or something by washing. (*Someone* includes *oneself.* More at *wash off ((of) someone or something), wash something off ((of) someone or something).*) □ *She washed the muddy children off with a hose and put their clothes right into the washing machine.* Ⓣ *Jane washed off the children.* □ *She washed them off.* □ *She washed herself off and then went down to dinner.*

waste one's breath to waste one's time talking; to talk in vain. □ *Don't waste your breath talking to her. She won't listen.* □ *You can't persuade me. You're just wasting your breath.*

Watch it! 1. Be careful. □ RACHEL: *Watch it! There's a broken stair there.* JANE: *Gee, thanks.* □ MARY: *Watch it! There's a pothole in the street.* BOB: *Thanks.* **2.** Do not act or talk that way. □ SALLY: *I really hate John!* SUE: *Watch it! He's my brother!* □ BILL: *You girls always seem to take so long to do a simple thing like getting dressed.* MARY: *Watch it!*

watch out (for someone or something) to keep looking for someone or something. □ *Watch out for Millie. She's mad at you.* □ *You had better watch out!* □ *I'll wait here out of the rain. You watch out for the bus.*

Watch your mouth! See the following entry.

Watch your tongue! AND **Watch your mouth!** Do not talk like that!; Do not say those things!; Do not say those bad words! □ ANDREW: *Don't talk to me like that! Watch your tongue!* BILL: *I'll talk to you any way I want.* □ *"Watch your mouth!" warned Sue. "I will not listen to any more of this slime!"*

water under the bridge past and forgotten □ *Please don't worry about it anymore. It's all water under the bridge.* □ *I can't change the past. It's water under the bridge.*

We aim to please. We are happy to try to please you. (Usually a commercial slogan, but can be said in jest by one person, often in response to *Thank you.*) □ MARY: *This meal is absolutely delicious!* WAITER: *We aim to please.* □ TOM: *Well, Sue, here's the laundry detergent you wanted from the store.* SUE: *Oh, thanks loads. You saved me a trip.* TOM: *We aim to please.*

(We) don't see you around here much anymore. See the following entry.

(We) don't see you much around here anymore. AND **(We) don't see you around here much anymore.** We haven't seen you for a long time. (The *we* can be replaced with *I*.) □ BILL: *Hello, Tom. Long time no see.* TOM: *Yes, Bill. We don't see you much* around here anymore. □ "We don't see you around here much anymore," said the old pharmacist to John, who had just come home from college.

We had a lovely time. See *I had a lovely time.*

We must do this again (sometime). See *Let's do this again (sometime).*

We need to talk about something. an expression inviting someone to discuss something. □ BILL: *Can I come over tonight? We need to talk about something.* MARY: *I guess so.* □ *"Mr. Franklin," said Bill's boss sort of sternly, "I want to see you in my office for a minute. We need to talk about something."*

We were just talking about you. a phrase said when a person being discussed appears on the scene. (Similar to *Speak of the devil.*) □ TOM: *Speak of the devil, here comes Bill.* MARY: *We were just talking about you, Bill.* □ SALLY (approaching Tom and Bill): *Hi, Tom. Hi, Bill. What's new?* BILL: *Oh, Sally! We were just talking about you.*

wear more than one hat to have more than one set of responsibilities; to hold more than one office. □ *The mayor is also the police chief. She wears more than one hat.* □ *I have too much to do to wear more than one hat.*

wear off [for the effects of something] to dissipate or go away. □ *The effects of the morphine began to wear off, and Dave began to feel the pain.* □ *As the drug wore off, she was more alert.*

wear out to become worn from use; to become diminished or useless from use. □ *My car engine is about to wear out.* □ *It takes a lot of driving to wear out an engine.*

wear out one's welcome to stay too long (at an event to which one has been invited); to visit somewhere too often. □ *Tom visited the Smiths so often that he wore out his welcome.* □ *At about midnight, I decided that I had worn out my welcome, so I went home.*

wear someone or something down **1.** [with *someone*] to exhaust someone. □ *This hot weather wears me down.* T *The weather wore down the tourists.* **2.** [with *someone*] to reduce someone to submission or agreement by constant badgering. □ *Finally they wore me down, and I told them what they wanted to know.* T *The agents wore down the suspect.* **3.** [with *something*] to grind something away; to erode something. □ *The constant rubbing of the door wore the carpet down.* T *The rubbing of the door wore down the carpet.*

wear someone or something out **1.** [with *someone*] to exhaust or annoy someone. (*Someone* includes *oneself.*) □ *All this shopping is wearing me out.* T *The shopping trip wore out the tourists.* □ *They will wear themselves out before the game. They should take it easy.* **2.** [with *something*] to make something worthless or nonfunctional from use. □ *I wore my shoes out in no time at all.* T *I wore out my shoes in less than a month.*

wear (up)on someone to diminish someone's energy and resistance; to bore or annoy someone. (*Upon* is formal and less commonly used than *on.*) □ *You could see that the lecture was beginning to wear upon the audience.* □ *This kind of thing really wears on me.*

weird out to become emotionally disturbed or unnerved; to flip out.

(Slang.) □ *The day was just gross. I thought I would weird out at noon.* □ *I weirded out at the news of Frankie's death.*

Welcome. Come into this place. You are welcome here. □ MARY: *Welcome. Please come in.* TOM: *Thank you so much.* □ BILL: *I'm glad you could make it. Come in. Welcome.* MARY: *Thanks. My, what a nice place you have here.*

Welcome to our house. an expression said by a host or hostess when greeting guests and bringing them into the house. □ ANDREW: *Hello, Sally. Welcome to our house. Come on in.* SALLY: *Thanks. It's good to be here.* □ TOM: *Welcome to our house. Make yourself at home.* HENRY: *Thanks, I'm really tired.*

well a sentence opener, having no specific meaning, sometimes expressing reservation or indecision. (Words such as this often use intonation to convey the connotation of the sentence that is to follow. The brief intonation pattern accompanying the word may indicate sarcasm, disagreement, caution, consolation, sternness, etc.) □ SALLY: *Can you take this downtown for me?* ANDREW: *Well, I don't know.* □ *"Well, I guess," answered Tom, sort of unsure of himself.* □ *"Well, if you think you can treat me that way, you've got another think coming," raged Betty.* □ BILL: *What do you think about my haircut?* JANE: *Well, it looks okay to me.* □ SUE: *I've decided to sell my car.* MARY: *Well, if that's what you want.* □ *"Well, hello," smiled Kate.*

Well done! You did that nicely! □ SALLY: *Well done, Tom. Excellent speech.* TOM: *Thanks.* □ *In the lobby* after the play, Tom was met with a chorus of well-wishers saying, "Well done, Tom!"

well-fixed See *well-heeled.*

We('ll) have to do lunch sometime. AND **Let's do lunch (sometime).** We must have lunch together sometime. (A vague statement that may lead to lunch plans.) □ RACHEL: *Nice to talk to you, Tom. We have to do lunch sometime.* TOM: *Yes, good to see you. I'll give you a ring.* □ TOM: *Can't talk to you now. Catch you later.* MARY: *We'll have to do lunch sometime.* □ JOHN: *Good to see you, Tom.* TOM: *Right. Let's do lunch sometime.* JOHN: *Good idea. I'll call you. Bye.* TOM: *Right. Bye.* □ MARY: *Catch you later.* SUE: *Sure. Let's do lunch.* MARY: *Okay. Call me. Bye.*

well-heeled AND **well-fixed; well-off** wealthy; with a sufficient amount of money. □ *My uncle can afford a new car. He's well-heeled.* □ *Everyone in his family is well-off.*

(Well,) I never! 1. I have never been so insulted! □ BILL: *Just pack up your things and get out!* JANE: *Well, I never!* □ TOM: *Look, your manners with the customers are atrocious!* JANE: *Well, I never!* 2. *I never heard of such a thing.* □ TOM: *Now they have machines that will do all those things at the press of a button.* SALLY: *Well, I never! I had no idea!* □ JOHN: *Would you believe I have a whole computer in this pocket?* ALICE: *I never!*

well-off See *well-heeled.*

Well said. You said that very well, and I agree. □ *As Sally sat down, Mary complimented her, "Well said, Sally. You made your point very well."* □ JOHN: *And I for one will never* stand for this kind of encroachment on my rights again! MARY: *Well said!* BOB: *Well said, John!* FRED: *Yes, well said.*

well-to-do wealthy and of good social position. (Often with *quite*, as in the examples.) □ *The Jones family is quite well-to-do.* □ *There is a gentleman waiting for you at the door. He appears quite well-to-do.*

We'll try again some other time. See *Maybe some other time.*

(Well,) what do you know! a way of expressing surprise at finding something that is unexpected; an expression of mild surprise at something someone has said. (No answer is expected or desired.) □ ANDREW: *Well, what do you know! Here's a brand new shirt in this old trunk.* BOB: *I wonder how it got there.* □ TOM: *These two things fit together like this.* JOHN: *Well, what do you know!*

(We're) delighted to have you (here). See *(I'm) delighted to have you (here).*

(We're) glad you could come. See *(I'm) glad you could come.*

(We're) glad you could drop by. See *(I'm) glad you could drop by.*

(We're) glad you could stop by. See *(I'm) glad you could drop by.*

Were you born in a barn? an expression chiding someone who has left a door open or who is disorderly. □ ANDREW: *Close the door! Were you born in a barn?* BOB: *Sorry.* □ FRED: *Can't you clean this place up a little? Were you born in a barn?* BOB: *I call it the messy look.*

wet behind the ears young and inexperienced. (Compare to *dry be-*

hind *the ears.*) □ *John's too young to take on a job like this! He's still wet behind the ears!* □ *He may be wet behind the ears, but he's well trained and totally competent.*

We've had a lovely time. See *I've had a lovely time.*

What (a) nerve! AND **Of all the nerve!** How rude!; How dare someone! □ BOB: *Lady, get the devil out of my way!* MARY: *What a nerve!* □ JANE: *You can't have that one! I saw it first!* SUE: *Of all the nerve! I can too have it!*

What a pity! AND **What a shame!** an expression of consolation meaning *That's too bad.* (Can also be used sarcastically.) □ BILL: *I'm sorry to tell you that the cat died today.* MARY: *What a pity!* □ MARY: *The cake is ruined!* SALLY: *What a shame!*

What a shame! See the previous entry.

What about it? So what?; Do you want to argue about it? (Contentious.) □ BILL: *I heard you were the one accused of breaking the window.* TOM: *Yeah? So, what about it?* □ MARY: *Your piece of cake is bigger than mine.* SUE: *What about it?*

What about you? **1.** What is your choice? (Compare to *How about you?*) □ TOM: *I'm having the pot roast and a cup of coffee. What about you?* MARY: *I want something fattening and unhealthy.* □ SALLY: *I prefer reds and purple for this room. What about you?* MARY: *Well, purple's okay, but reds are a little warm for this room.* **2.** What will happen to you? □ MARY: *My parents are taking my brothers to the circus.* SUE: *What about you?* MARY: *I have a piano rehearsal.*

□ MARY: *All my friends have been accepted to colleges.* SUE: *What about you?* MARY: *Oh, I'm accepted too.*

What are you drinking? **1.** a phrase inquiring what someone is already drinking so that the person who asks the question can offer another drink of the same thing. □ BILL: *Hi, Tom. Nice to see you. Can I get you something to drink?* TOM: *Sure. What are you drinking?* BILL: *Scotch and water.* TOM: *That works for me.* □ WAITER: *What are you drinking, madam?* SUE: *It's just soda. No more, thanks.* WAITER: *Very good.* **2.** a phrase inquiring what is being drunk at a particular gathering, so that the person asking can request the same drink. (A way of finding out what drinks are available.) □ MARY: *Do you want a drink?* SUE: *Yes, thanks. Say, that looks good. What are you drinking?* MARY: *It's just ginger ale.* □ BILL: *Can I get you something to drink?* JANE: *What are you drinking?* BILL: *I'm having gin and tonic.* JANE: *I'll have that too, thanks.*

What are you having? What food or drink are you planning to order? (Either part of a conversation or a request from food service personnel. In a restaurant, sometimes the host or hostess will signal to a guest to order first by saying this. Sometimes a guest will ask this of a host or hostess to determine the price range that is appropriate.) □ WAITER: *Would you care to order now?* TOM: *What are you having?* MARY: *You order. I haven't made up my mind.* □ WAITER: *May I help you?* TOM: *What are you having, Pop?* FATHER: *I'll have the roast chicken, I think, with fries.* TOM: *I'll have the same.*

What brings you here? What is your reason for being here? (A polite request for this information. More polite than "Why are you here?") □ TOM: *Hello, Mary. What brings you here?* MARY: *I was invited, just like you.* □ DOCTOR: *Well, John, what brings you here?* JOHN: *I've had this cough for nearly a month, and I think it needs looking into.*

What can I do for you? See *How may I help you?*

What can I say? I have no explanation or excuse. What do you expect me to say? (See also *What do you want me to say?*) □ BILL: *Why on earth did you lose that big order?* SALLY: *What can I say? I'm sorry!* □ BOB: *You're going to have to act more aggressive if you want to make sales. You're just too timid.* TOM: *What can I say? I am what I am.*

What can I tell you? **1.** What kind of information do you want? □ BILL: *I have a question.* BOB: *What can I tell you?* BILL: *When do we arrive at Chicago?* □ MARY: *I would like to ask a question about the quiz tomorrow.* BILL: *What can I tell you?* MARY: *The answers, if you know them.* **2.** I haven't any idea of what to say. (Compare to *What can I say?*) □ JOHN: *Why on earth did you do a dumb thing like that?* BILL: *What can I tell you? I just did it, that's all.* □ MARY: *I'm so disappointed with you, Fred.* FRED: *What can I tell you? I am too.*

What do you know? a typical greeting inquiry. (Informal. A specific answer is not expected. Often pronounced "Wha-da-ya know?") □ BOB: *Hey, Tom! What do you know?* TOM: *Hey! Look who's here! Hello, Bob!*

□ JOHN: *What do you know?* MARY: *Nothing. How are you?* JOHN: *Okay.*

What do you know for sure? *How are you?; What do you know?* (Familiar. An elaboration of *What do you know?* Does not require a direct answer.) □ TOM: *Hey, man! What do you know for sure?* BILL: *Howdy, Tom. What's new?* □ JOHN: *How are you doing, old buddy?* BILL: *Great, you ugly beast!* JOHN: *What do you know for sure?* BILL: *Nothing.*

What do you say? **1.** Hello, how are you? (Informal.) □ BOB: *What do you say, Tom?* TOM: *Hey, man. How are you doing?* □ BILL: *What do you say, man?* FRED: *What's the good word, you old so-and-so?* **2.** What is your answer or decision? □ BILL: *I need an answer from you now. What do you say?* BOB: *Don't rush me!* □ SUE: *I can offer you seven hundred dollars for your old car. What do you say?* BOB: *I'll take it!* **3.** an expression urging a child to say "please" or "thank you." □ *When Aunt Sally gave Billy some candy, his mother said to Billy, "What do you say?" "Thank you," said Billy.* □ MOTHER: *Here's a nice glass of milk.* CHILD: *Good.* MOTHER: *What do you say?* CHILD: *Very good.* MOTHER: *No. What do you say?* CHILD: *Thank you.*

What do you think? What is your opinion? □ MARY: *This is our new company stationery. What do you think?* BILL: *Stunning. Simply stunning.* □ MARY: *We're considering moving out into the country. What do you think?* SUE: *Sounds good to me.*

What do you think about that? See the following entry.

What do you think of that? AND **What do you think about that?**

Isn't that remarkable?; What is your opinion of that? □ BOB: *I'm leaving tomorrow and taking all these books with me. What do you think of that?* MARY: *Not much.* □ SUE: *I'm going to start taking cooking lessons. What do you think about that?* BILL: *I'm overjoyed!* JOHN: *Thank heavens!* MARY: *Fortune has smiled on us, indeed!*

What do you think of this weather? a phrase used to open a conversation with someone, often someone one has just met. □ SUE: *Glad to meet you, Mary.* MARY: *What do you think about this weather?* SUE: *I've seen better.* □ BILL: *What do you think about this weather?* JANE: *Lovely weather for ducks.*

What do you think you are doing here? Why are you in this place? (Stern and threatening.) □ JOHN: *Mary!* MARY: *John!* JOHN: *What do you think you're doing here?* □ *"What do you think you're doing here?" said Fred to a frightened rabbit trapped in the garage.*

What do you want me to say? I have no response.; I have no answer, do you have one for me to say? (Almost the same as *What can I say?; What can I tell you?*) □ TOM: *You've really made a mess of all of this!* BILL: *Sorry. What do you want me to say?* □ BOB: *All of these problems should have been settled some time ago. Why are they still plaguing us?* TOM: *What do you want me to say?*

What does that prove? *So what?; That does not mean anything.* (A defensive expression. The heaviest stress is on *that.* Often with *so,* as in the examples.) □ TOM: *It seems that you were in the apartment the same night that it was robbed.* BOB: *So, what* *does that prove?* TOM: *Nothing, really. It's just something we need to keep in mind.* □ RACHEL: *You're late again on your car payment.* JANE: *What does that prove?* RACHEL: *Simply that you can't afford the car, and we are going to repossess it.*

What else can I do? See *What more can I do?*

What else can I do for you? In what other way can I serve you? (Said by shopkeepers, clerks, and service personnel.) □ BILL: *What else can I do for you?* BOB: *Please check the oil.* □ *"Here's your prescription. What else can I do for you?" said the pharmacist.*

What gives? *What happened?;* What went wrong?; What's the problem? □ BILL: *Hi, you guys. What gives?* BOB: *Nothing, just a little misunderstanding. Tom's a little angry.* □ BOB: *Where's my wallet? What gives?* TOM: *I think one of those roughnecks who just walked by us has borrowed it for a little while.*

What happened? What went wrong here? □ BOB (approaching a crowd): *What happened?* TOM (with Bob): *What's wrong?* BYSTANDER: *Just a little mix-up. A car wanted to drive on the sidewalk, that's all.* □ *There was a terrible noise, an explosion that shook the house. Bob looked at Jane and said, "What happened?"*

What (have) you been up to? a greeting inquiry. (A detailed answer may be expected.) □ MARY: *Hello, Jane. What have you been up to?* JANE: *Been up to no good. What about you?* MARY: *Yeah. Me too.* □ JOHN: *Bill, baby! What you been up to?* BILL: *Nothing really. What about you?* JOHN: *The same, I guess.*

What if I do? Does it matter to you if I do it?; What difference does it make if I do it? (Saucy and colloquial.) □ TOM: *Are you really going to sell your leather coat?* BOB: *What if I do?* □ JANE: *You're not going to go out dressed like that, are you?* SUE: *So what if I do?*

What if I don't? Does it matter to you if I do not do it?; What difference does it make if I do not do it? (Saucy and colloquial.) □ BOB: *You're certainly going to tidy up a bit before going out, aren't you?* TOM: *What if I don't?* □ FATHER: *You are going to get in by midnight tonight or you're grounded.* FRED: *So what if I don't?* FATHER: *That's enough! You're grounded as of this minute!*

What is it? What do you want from me?; Why do you want to get my attention? (There is also a literal meaning.) □ TOM: *John, can I talk to you for a minute?* JOHN: *What is it?* □ SUE: *Jane?* JANE: *What is it?* SUE: *Close the door, please.*

What is sauce for the goose is sauce for the gander. What is appropriate for one is appropriate for the other. (Proverb.) □ *If John gets a new coat, I should get one, too. After all, what is sauce for the goose is sauce for the gander.* □ *If I get punished for breaking the window, so should Mary. What is sauce for the goose is sauce for the gander.*

what makes someone tick what motivates someone; what makes someone behave in a certain way. □ *William is sort of strange. I don't know what makes him tick.* □ *When you get to know people, you find out what makes them tick.*

What makes you think so? 1. Why do you think that?; What is your evidence for that conclusion? □ TOM: *This bread may be a little old.* ALICE: *What makes you think so?* TOM: *The green spots on the edges.* □ BOB: *Congress is in session again.* TOM: *What makes you think so?* BOB: *My wallet is empty.* **2.** Is that not totally obvious? (Sarcastic.) □ JOHN: *I think I'm putting on a little weight.* MARY: *Oh, yeah? What makes you think so?* □ MARY (shivering): *Gee, I think it's going to be winter soon.* SUE (also shivering): *Yeah? What makes you think so?*

What more can I do? AND **What else can I do?** I am at a loss to know what else to do.; Is there any thing else I can do? (An expression of desperation, not an inquiry.) □ BOB: *Did you hear about the death in the Wilson family?* BILL: *Yes, I feel so helpless. I sent flowers. What more can I do?* □ BILL: *Is your child still sick?* MARY: *Yes. I'm giving her the right medicine. What more can I do?*

What now? See *Now what?*

What number are you calling? an expression used when one suspects that a telephone caller may have gotten the wrong number. □ BOB (on the telephone): *Hello?* MARY: *Hello, is Sally there?* BOB: *Uh, what number are you calling?* MARY: *I guess I have the wrong number. Sorry.* BOB: *No problem. Good-bye.* □ When the receptionist asked, "What number are you calling?" I realized I had made a mistake.

What of it? What does it matter?; Why treat it as if it were important?; Why do you think that this is any of your business? (Colloquial and a bit contentious.) □ JOHN: *I hear you've been having a little trouble at the office.*

BOB: *What of it?* □ SUE: *You missed a spot shaving.* FRED: *What of it?*

What say? What did you say? (Widely used.) □ TOM: *My coat is there on the chair. Could you hand it to me?* BOB: *What say?* TOM (pointing): *Could you hand me my coat?* □ SUE: *Here's your paper.* FRED: *What say?* SUE (louder): *Here is your newspaper!*

What was the name again? Please tell me your name again. (More typical of a clerk than of someone just introduced.) □ CLERK: *What was the name again?* BILL: *Bill.* □ "*What was the name again? I didn't write it down,*" confessed Fred.

What would you like to drink? an offer to prepare a drink. □ BILL: *Come in and sit down. What would you like to drink?* ANDREW: *Nothing, thanks. I just need to relax a moment.* □ WAITER: *What would you like to drink?* ALICE: *Do you have any grape soda?* WAITER: *I'll bring you some ginger ale, if that's all right.* ALICE: *Well, okay. I guess.*

What would you say if? an expression introducing a request for an opinion or a judgment. □ BILL: *What would you say if I ate the last piece of cake?* BOB: *Go ahead. I don't care.* □ MARY: *What would you say if we left a little early?* SALLY: *It's okay with me.*

Whatever. Anything, it doesn't matter.; Either one. □ BOB: *Which do you want, red or green?* TOM: *Whatever.* □ MARY: *Do you want to go with me to the seashore or stay here?* JANE: *Whatever.*

Whatever turns you on. 1. Whatever pleases or excites you is okay. □ MARY: *Do you mind if I buy some of these flowers?* BILL: *Whatever turns* *you on.* □ MARY: *I just love to hear a raucous saxophone play some smooth jazz.* BOB: *Whatever turns you on, baby.* **2.** a comment implying that it is strange to get so excited about something. (Essentially sarcastic.) □ BOB: *I just go wild whenever I see pink gloves on a woman. I don't understand it.* BILL: *Whatever turns you on.* □ JANE: *You see, I never told anybody this, but whenever I see dirty snow at the side of the road, I just go sort of wild inside.* SUE: *Weird, Jane, weird. But, whatever turns you on.*

What'll it be? AND **Name your poison.; What'll you have?; What's yours?** What do you want to drink?; What do you want?; How can I serve you? (Typically said by a bartender or bar waiter or waitress.) □ TOM: *What'll it be, friend?* BILL: *I'll just have a Coke, if you don't mind.* □ WAITRESS: *What'll you have?* BOB: *Nothing, thanks.*

What'll you have? See the previous entry.

What's coming off? AND **What's going down?** What is happening here?; What is going to happen? (Slang. Also a greeting inquiry.) □ BILL: *Hey, man! What's coming off?* TOM: *Oh, nothing, just a little car fire.* □ BOB: *Hey, we just got here! What's going down?* BILL: *What does it look like? This is a party, dude!*

What's cooking? What is happening?; How are you? (Colloquial or slang.) □ BOB: *Hi, Bill! What's cooking?* BILL: *How are you doing, Bob?* □ BOB: *Hi, Fred! What's cooking?* FRED: *Nothing. Anything happening with you?*

What's eating someone? What is bothering someone? (Slang.) □ TOM: *Go away!* BOB: *Gee, Tom,* *what's eating you?* □ BILL: *Tom's so grouchy lately. What's eating him?* BOB: *Beats me!*

What's going down? See *What's coming off?*

What's going on (around here)? What is happening in this place?; What is the explanation for the strange things that are happening here? □ BILL: *There was an accident in the factory this morning.* BOB: *That's the second one this week. What's going on around here?* □ MARY: *What's all the noise? What's going on?* SUE: *We're just having a little party.*

What's happ(ening)? Hello, what's new?; a general and vague greeting inquiry. (Slang.) □ *Hey, dude! What's happening?* □ *What's happ? How's it goin'?* □ BOB: *Hey, man! What's happening?* BILL: *Nothing. How you be?* □ BILL: *Hi, Tom.* TOM: *Hi, Bill, what's happening?* BILL: *Nothing much.*

What's in it for me? What is the benefit for me in this scheme? □ BOB: *Now that plan is just what is needed.* BILL: *What's in it for me? What do I get out of it?* □ SUE: *We signed the Wilson contract yesterday.* MARY: *That's great! What's in it for me?*

What's it to you? Why does it matter to you?; It's none of your business. (Colloquial and a bit contentious.) □ TOM: *Where are you going?* JANE: *What's it to you?* □ MARY: *Bill's pants don't match his shirt.* JANE: *Does it matter? What's it to you?*

What's keeping someone? What is delaying someone? (The *someone* is replaced by a person's name or a pronoun.) □ BOB: *Wasn't Mary supposed to be here?* BILL: *I thought so.*

BOB: *Well, what's keeping her?* BILL: *How should I know?* □ BILL: *I've been waiting here for an hour for Sally.* SUE: *What's keeping her?*

What's new? What things have happened since we last talked or met? □ MARY: *Greetings, Jane. What's new?* JANE: *Nothing much.* □ BOB: *What's new?* TOM: *Not a whole lot.*

What's new with you? a typical response to *What's new?* □ MARY: *What's new?* SALLY: *Oh, nothing. What's new with you?* MARY: *The same.* □ FRED: *Hi, John! How you doing?* JOHN: *Great! What's new with you?*

What's on tap for today? What is on the schedule for today?; What is going to happen today? (As a beer that is on tap and ready to be served.) □ TOM: *Good morning, Fred.* FRED: *Morning. What's on tap for today?* TOM: *Trouble in the morning and difficulty in the afternoon.* FRED: *So nothing is new.* □ SALLY: *Can we have lunch today?* SUE: *I'll have to look at my schedule and see what's on tap for today.*

What's shakin' (bacon)? How are you?; What is new? (Slang.) □ *What's shakin' bacon? What's going down?* □ *Hi, Jim. What's shakin'?*

What's the catch? What is the drawback?; What are the negative factors? (Colloquial.) □ BILL: *How would you like to have these seven books for your very own?* SALLY: *What's the catch?* BILL: *There's no catch. You have to pay for them, but there's no catch.* □ BOB: *Here, take this dollar bill.* SUE: *So, what's the catch?* BOB: *No catch. It's counterfeit.*

What's the damage? What are the charges?; How much is the bill? (Slang.) □ BILL: *That was delicious. Waiter, what's the damage?* WAITER: *I'll get the check, sir.* □ WAITER: *Your check sir.* TOM: *Thanks.* BILL: *What's the damage, Tom? Let my pay my share.* TOM: *Nonsense, I'll get it.* BILL: *Okay this time, but I owe you one.*

What's the deal? See *What's the scam?*

What's the drill? **1.** What is going on here? □ BILL: *I just came in. What's the drill?* TOM: *We have to carry all this stuff out to the truck.* □ *"What's the drill?" asked Mary. "Why are all these people sitting around like this?"* **2.** What are the rules and procedures for doing this? □ BILL: *I need to apply for new license plates. What's the drill? Is there a lot of paperwork?* CLERK: *Yes, there is.* □ BILL: *I have to get my computer repaired. Who do I talk to? What's the drill?* BOB: *You have to get a purchase order from Fred.*

What's the good word? a vague greeting inquiry. (Colloquial and familiar. A direct answer is not expected.) □ BOB: *Hey, Tom! What's the good word?* TOM: *Hi, Bob! How are you doing?* □ SUE: *What's happening?* JANE: *Hi, Sue. What's the good word?*

What's the matter (with you)? **1.** Is there something wrong with you?; Are you ill? □ BILL: *What's the matter with you?* FRED: *I have this funny feeling in my chest.* BILL: *Sounds serious.* □ BOB: *I have to stay home again today.* BILL: *What's the matter with you? Have you seen a doctor?* □ MARY: *Oh, I'm so miserable!* SUE: *What's the matter?* MARY: *I lost my* *contact lenses and my glasses.* □ JOHN: *Ouch!* ALICE: *What's the matter?* JOHN: *I bit my tongue.* **2.** How very stupid of you! How can you be so stupid? (Usually said in anger.) □ *As Fred stumbled over the step and dumped the birthday cake on the floor, Jane screamed, "What's the matter with you? The party is in fifteen minutes, and we have no cake!"* □ MARY: *I think I just lost the Wilson account.* SUE: *What! What's the matter with you? That account pays your salary!*

What's the problem? **1.** What problem are you presenting to me? □ BILL (coming in): *I need to talk to you about something.* TOM: *What's the problem, Bill?* □ *"What's the problem?" said Mary, peering at her secretary over her glasses.* **2.** a question asking what the problem is and implying that there should not be a problem. □ CHILD (crying): *He hit me!* FATHER: *What's the problem?* CHILD: *He hit me!* FATHER: *Are you hurt?* CHILD: *No.* FATHER: *Then stop crying.* □ BOB: *Hi, Fred.* FRED: *What's the problem?* BOB: *There's no problem. Why do you ask?* FRED: *I've had nothing but problems today.*

What's the scam? AND **What's the deal?** What is going on around here?; Why are you doing this? (Slang.) □ *There's a big rumpus down the hall. What's the scam?* □ *I gave you a twenty, and you give me five back? What's the deal? Where's my other five?*

What's the scoop? What is the news?; *What's new with you?* (Slang.) □ BOB: *Did you hear about Tom?* MARY: *No, what's the scoop?* □ *"Hi, you guys!" beamed John's little brother. "What's the scoop?"*

What's (there) to know? This doesn't require any special knowledge, so what are you talking about? □ BILL: *Do you know how to wind a watch?* BOB: *Wind a watch? What's there to know?* □ SUE: *We must find someone who knows how to repair a broken lawn mower.* TOM: *What's to know? Just a little tightening here and there. That's all it needs.*

What's up? What is happening?; What have you been doing lately? □ BOB: *Hi, Bill. What's up?* BILL: *Yo, Bob! Nothing going on around here.* □ TOM (answering the telephone): *Hello.* BILL: *Hi, this is Bill.* TOM: *What's up?* BILL: *You want to go camping?* TOM: *Sure.*

What's with someone or something? Why is someone or something in that condition?; What's going on with someone or something? □ MARY: *What's with Tom? He looks depressed.* BILL: *He broke up with Sally.* □ *"What's with this stupid coffeepot? It won't get hot!" groused Alice.*

What's wrong? There is something wrong here. What has happened? □ MARY: *Oh, good grief!* BILL: *What's wrong?* MARY: *I forgot to feed the cat.* □ SUE (crying): *Hello, Sally?* SALLY: *Sue, what's wrong?* SUE: *Oh, nothing. Tom left me.*

What's yours? See *What'll it be?*

When do we eat? What time is the next meal served? (Familiar. The speaker is hungry.) □ BILL: *This is a lovely view, and your apartment is great. When do we eat?* MARY: *We've already eaten. Weren't you just leaving?* BILL: *I guess I was.* □ ANDREW: *Wow! Something really smells good! When do we eat?* RACHEL: *Oh, mind your manners.*

when I'm good and ready not until I want to and no sooner. (A bit contentious.) □ MARY: *When are you going to rake the leaves?* FATHER: *When I'm good and ready.* □ BOB: *When are you going to help me move this piano?* FRED: *When I'm good and ready and not a minute before.*

When in Rome, do as the Romans do. One should behave in the same way that the local people behave. (Proverb.) □ *I don't usually eat lamb, but I did when I went to Australia. When in Rome, do as the Romans do.* □ *I always carry an umbrella when I visit London. When in Rome, do as the Romans do.*

When the cat's away the mice will play. Some people will get into mischief when they are not being watched. □ *The students behaved very badly for the substitute teacher. When the cat's away the mice will play.* □ *John had a wild party at his house when his parents were out of town. When the cat's away the mice will play.*

when the time is ripe at exactly the right time. □ *I'll tell her the good news when the time is ripe.* □ *When the time is ripe, I'll bring up the subject again.*

when you get a chance See the following entry.

when you get a minute AND **when you get a chance** a phrase introducing a request. □ BILL: *Tom?* TOM: *Yes.* BILL: *When you get a minute, I'd like to have a word with you.* □ *"Please drop over for a chat when you get a chance," said Fred to Bill.*

Whenever. At whatever time, it really doesn't matter. □ BILL: *When should I pick you up?* SUE: *Oh, whenever. I don't care. Just come on up, and*

we'll take it from there. □ MARY: *Well, Uncle Harry, how nice to have you for a visit. We need to book your return flight. When will you be leaving?* UNCLE: *Oh, whenever.*

Where can I wash up? AND **Is there some place I can wash up?** a way of asking where the toilet or bathroom is without referring to one's need to use it. (Of course, this is also appropriate to ask where one can wash one's hands.) □ *The minute he got to the house he asked Fred, "Where can I wash up?"* □ FRED: *Welcome. Come in.* BILL: *Oh, is there some place I can wash up?*

Where have you been all my life? an expression of admiration usually said to a lover. □ MARY: *I feel very happy when I'm with you.* JOHN: *Oh, Mary, where have you been all my life?* □ *John, who always seemed to sound like a paperback novel, grasped her hand, stared directly at her left ear, and stuttered, "Where have you been all my life?"*

Where (have) you been keeping yourself? I haven't seen you for a long time. Where have you been? □ BILL: *Hi, Alice! Where you been keeping yourself?* ALICE: *Oh, I've been around. How are you doing?* BILL: *Okay.* □ JOHN: *Tsup?* BILL: *Hi, man. Where you been keeping yourself?* JOHN: *Oh, I've been busy.*

Where is the rest room? the appropriate way of asking for the toilet in a public building. □ BOB: *'Scuse me.* WAITER: *Yes, sir.* BOB: *Where is the rest room?* WAITER: *To your left, sir.* □ MARY: *Where is the rest room, please?* CLERK: *Behind the elevators, ma'am.*

Where is your powder room? See *Could I use your powder room?*

Where there's a will there's a way. One can do something if one really wants to. (Proverb.) □ *Don't give up, Ann. You can do it. Where there's a will there's a way.* □ *They told John he'd never walk again after his accident. He worked at it, and he was able to walk again! Where there's a will there's a way.*

Where there's smoke there's fire. Evidence of a problem probably indicates that there really is a problem. (Proverb.) □ *There is a lot of noise coming from the classroom. There is probably something wrong. Where there's smoke there's fire.* □ *I think there is something wrong at the house on the corner. The police are there again. Where there's smoke there's fire.*

Where will I find you? Please give me directions for finding you. (Said when people are arranging a meeting somewhere.) □ SUE: *Where will I find you?* BOB: *I'll be sitting in the third row somewhere.* □ TOM: *We'll get to the farm about noon. Where will we find you?* SALLY: *Probably in the barn. If you can't find me, just go up to the house and make yourself comfortable on the porch.*

Where's the fire? Where are you going in such a hurry? (Typically said by a police officer to a speeding driver.) □ OFFICER: *Okay, where's the fire?* MARY: *Was I going a little fast?* □ *"Where's the fire?" Bob called ahead to Sue, who had gotten well ahead of him in her excitement.*

which brings me to the (main) point a transitional phrase that introduces the main point of a discussion. □

BILL: *Keeping safe at times like this is very important — which brings me to the main point. Does your house have an adequate burglar alarm?* SALLY: *I knew you were trying to sell me something! Out!* □ LECTURER: *... which brings me to the point.* JOHN (whispering): *Thank heavens! I knew there was a point to all this.*

Who cares? Does anyone really care?; It is of no consequence. □ JOHN: *I have some advice for you. It will make things easier for you.* BOB: *Who cares?* JOHN: *You might.* □ SUE: *You missed a spot shaving.* FRED: *Who cares?*

Who could have thought? See *Who would have thought?*

Who do you think you are? Why do you think you can lord it over people that way?; Why are you so arrogant? (Usually in anger.) □ TOM: *Just a minute! Who do you think you are? You can't talk to me that way!* BOB: *Says who?* □ *"Who do you think you are, bursting in here like that?" sputtered the doorman as Fred bolted into the club lobby.*

Who do you think you're kidding? You aren't fooling anyone.; Surely, you do not think you can fool me, do you? □ BILL: *I must pull down about eighty thou a year.* BOB: *You? Who do you think you're kidding?* □ MARY: *This carpet was made in Persia by children.* TOM: *Who do you think you're kidding?*

Who do you think you're talking to? Why do you think you can address me in that manner?; You can't talk to me that way! □ TOM: *Get out of the way!* SUE: *Who do you think you're talking to?* TOM: *Then move please.* □ CLERK: *Look, take it or leave it. Isn't it* *good enough for you?* SUE: *Who do you think you're talking to? I want to see the manager!*

Who do you want to speak to? See the following entry.

Who do you want (to talk to)? AND **Who do you want to speak to?;** **Who do you wish to speak to?;** **Who do you wish to talk to?** Who do you want to speak to over the telephone? (All these questions can also begin with *whom.* Compare to *With whom do you wish to speak?*) □ SUE: *Wilson residence. Who do you want to speak to?* BILL: *Hi, Sue. I want to talk to you.* □ TOM (answering the phone): *Hello?* SUE: *Hello, who is this?* TOM: *Who do you wish to speak to?* SUE: *Is Sally there?* TOM: *Just a minute.*

Who do you wish to speak to? See the previous entry.

Who do you wish to talk to? See *Who do you want (to talk to)?*

Who is it? See *Who's there?*

Who is this? Who is making this telephone call?; Who is on the other end of this telephone line? □ TOM (answering the phone): *Hello?* FRED: *Hello. Do you have any fresh turkeys?* TOM: *Who is this?* FRED: *Isn't this the Harrison Poultry Shop?* TOM: *No.* FRED: *I guess I have the wrong number.* □ MARY (answering the phone): *Hello?* SUE: *Hello, who is this?* MARY: *Well, who did you want?* SUE: *I want Grandma.* MARY: *I'm sorry, I think you have the wrong number.*

Who knows? Who knows the answer to that question? □ TOM: *When will this train get in?* RACHEL: *Who know?* □ ANDREW: *Why can't someone put*

this stuff away? RACHEL: *Who knows? Why don't you put it away?*

Who was it? Who called on the telephone or who was at the door? (Assumes that the caller is not waiting on the telephone or at the door.) □ SUE (as Mary hangs up the telephone): *Who was it?* MARY: *None of your business.* □ BILL (as he leaves the door): *What a pest!* SUE: *Who was it?* BILL: *Some silly survey.*

who would have thought? AND **who could have thought?** a question phrase indicating surprise or amazement. (No answer is expected.) □ TOM: *Fred just quit his job and went to Africa.* BILL: *Who would have thought he could do such a thing?* □ ANDREW: *They say Bill jogs and runs in his spare time.* RACHEL: *Who would have thought?*

Whoa! Stop! (An instruction — usually said to a horse — to stop, said to a person.) □ BOB: *First, slip the disk into this slot and then do a directory command to see what's on it.* JOHN: *Whoa! You lost me back at "slip the disk . . . "* □ *"Whoa!" shouted Tom at Bill. "Don't move any more in that direction. The floor is rotten there."*

whole ball of wax everything; the whole thing. (Slang. Always with the.) □ *Well, that just about ruins the whole ball of wax.* □ *Your comments threatened the whole ball of wax, that's what.*

Whoops! a phrase indicating that an error has been made by the previous speaker or by someone else. □ *"Whoops! I think you meant flout, not flaunt," corrected Sally.* □ *"Whoops! I meant to say mature, not old," said Kate.*

Who's calling(, please)? Who is making this telephone call? □ RACHEL: *Yes, Tom is here. Who's calling, please?* TOM: *Who is it?* RACHEL: *It's Fred.* □ FRED (answering the phone): *Hello?* TOM: *Hello, is Bill there?* FRED: *Who's calling, please?* TOM: *This is Tom Wilson returning his call.*

Who's on the line? See the following entry.

Who's on the phone? AND **Who's on the line?** Who is on the telephone line now?; Who just called on the telephone? (The caller may still be waiting.) □ *Bill was on the telephone, and Mary walked by. "Who's on the phone?" asked Mary, hoping the call was for her.* □ *Tom asked, "Who's on the line?" Mary covered the receiver and said, "None of your business!"*

Who's there? AND **Who is it?** a question asking who is on the other side of a door or concealed in some other place. □ *Hearing a noise, Tom called out in the darkness, "Who's there?"* □ *Hearing a knock on the door, Mary went to the door and said, "Who is it?"*

Who's your friend? Who is that following along behind you? □ JOHN: *Hi, Tom. Who's your friend?* TOM: *Oh, this is my little brother, Willie.* JOHN: *Hi, Willie.* □ *Looking at the little dog almost glued to Bob's pants cuff, Sally asked, "Who's your friend?"*

why a sentence opener expressing surprise. (The *why* is pronounced like the name of the letter Y.) □ *"Why, it's just a little boy!" said the old sea captain.* □ BOB: *Why, what are you doing here?* MARY: *I was going to ask you the same thing.* □ MARY: *Why, your hair has turned white!*

ANDREW: *No, I'm in the school play. This is just temporary.* □ RACHEL: *Why, this page is torn!* ANDREW: *I didn't do it!*

why don't you? a question tag that is put onto the end of a command. □ ANDREW: *Make a lap, why don't you?* BOB: *Okay. Sorry. I didn't know I was in the way.* □ *"Just keep bugging me, why don't you?" threatened Wally.* □ ANDREW: *Try it again, why don't you?* SUE: *I hope I get it right this time.*

Why not? **1.** Please explain your negative answer. □ MARY: *No, you can't.* SALLY: *Why not?* □ SUE: *Could I have another piece of cake?* MARY: *No.* SUE: *Why not?* MARY: *I want it.* **2.** I cannot think of a reason not to, so yes. □ BOB: *You want to go to see a movie next Friday?* JANE: *Why not?* □ FRED: *Do you feel like wandering over to the bowling alley?* TOM: *Why not?*

wide of the mark **1.** far from the target. □ *Tom's shot was wide of the mark.* □ *The pitch was quite fast, but wide of the mark.* **2.** inadequate; far from what is required or expected. □ *Jane's efforts were sincere, but wide of the mark.* □ *He failed the course because everything he did was wide of the mark.*

wild-goose chase a worthless hunt or chase; a futile pursuit. □ *I wasted all afternoon on a wild-goose chase.* □ *John was angry because he was sent out on a wild-goose chase.*

Will I see you again? a question asked toward the end of a date implying that further dating would please the speaker if it would please the other party. (This question seeks to find out if there is interest in another date, leaving it open to the other party to confirm that the interest is mutual by requesting a further date. Compare to *Can I see you again?*) □ TOM: *I had a wonderful time tonight, Mary. Good night.* MARY: *Will I see you again?* TOM: *That would be nice. Can I call you tomorrow?* MARY: *That would be nice.* □ *"Will I see you again?" asked Sally, cautiously and hopefully.*

Will that be all? See the following entry.

(Will there be) anything else? AND **Is that everything?; Is there anything else?; Will that be all?** Is there anything else you want?; Is there any other matter you wish to discuss?; Is there any other request? (These phrases are used by shopkeepers, clerks, and food service personnel to find out if the customer wants anything more.) □ CLERK: *Here's the roast you ordered. Will there be anything else?* RACHEL: *No, that's all.* □ WAITER: *Anything else?* BILL: *Just coffee.* □ *The clerk rang up the last item and asked, "Anything else?"* □ WAITER: *Anything else?* JANE: *No, that's everything.*

Will you excuse us, please? See *Could you excuse us, please?*

Will you hold? See *Could you hold?*

wimp out (of something) to chicken out (of something); to get out of something, leaving others to carry the burden. (Slang.) □ *Come on! Don't wimp out now that there's all this work to be done.* □ *Ted wimped out on us.*

Win a few, lose a few. Sometimes one succeeds, and sometimes one fails. □ TOM: *Well, I lost out on that Wilson contract, but I got the Jones job.* SALLY: *That's life. Win a few, lose a few.* □ *"Win a few, lose a few," said Fred, staring at yesterday's stock prices.*

win by a nose to win by the slightest amount of difference. (As in a horse race where one horse wins with only its nose ahead of the horse that comes in second.) □ *I ran the fastest race I could, but I only won by a nose.* □ *Sally won the race, but she only won by a nose.*

win someone over (to something) to succeed in making someone favorable to something. □ *I hope I can win them all over to our side.* T *I won over the mayor to our side.* □ *We can win the voters over!*

wind down to start running or operating slower. □ *Things will begin to wind down at the end of the summer.* □ *As things wind down, life will be a lot easier.* □ *The clock wound down and finally stopped.*

wind something on (to something) to coil or wrap something onto something. □ *Wind this string onto the ball and save it.* T *If you find the string ball, please wind on this string.* □ *Here, wind some more on.*

wind something up to tighten the spring in something, such as a watch or a clock. □ *Please wind your watch up now — before it runs down.* T *Wind up your watch before you forget.*

wind up (by) doing something to end by doing something [anyway]. □ *I wound up by going home early.* □ *I wound up eating out.*

wing it to improvise; to do something extemporaneously. (Slang.) □ *I lost my lecture notes, so I had to wing it* *today.* □ *Don't worry. Just go out there and wing it.*

wipe someone or something off to clean someone or something off of something by wiping. (*Someone* includes *oneself.*) □ *She wiped the baby off and put clean clothes on him.* ⊤ *Please wipe off your shoes.* □ *John fell in the mud, and Sam wiped him off.* □ *She wiped herself off, getting all the mud off her shoes, at least.*

wipe something off ((of) someone or something) to remove something from someone or something by wiping. (The *of* is colloquial.) □ *The mother wiped the ice cream off of her child.* ⊤ *She wiped off the ice cream.* □ *Tony wiped the mud off.*

wipe something up 1. to clean something up by wiping. □ *Please wipe that spilled milk up.* ⊤ *Jim wiped up the spill.* **2.** to clean something by wiping. □ *The floor was sticky so I wiped it up.* ⊤ *Please wipe up the countertop.*

wired into someone or something concerned with someone or something; really involved with someone or something. (Slang.) □ *Mary is really wired into classical music.* □ *Sam and Martha are totally wired into one another.*

with all one's heart and soul very sincerely. □ *Oh, Bill, I love you with all my heart and soul, and I always will!* □ *She thanked us with all her heart and soul for the gift.*

with both hands tied behind one's back See *with one hand tied behind one's back.*

with every (other) breath [saying something] repeatedly or continually. □ *Bob was out in the yard, raking leaves and cursing with every other breath.* □ *The child was so grateful that she was thanking me with every breath.*

with flying colors easily and excellently. □ *John passed his geometry test with flying colors.* □ *Sally qualified for the race with flying colors.*

with my blessing a phrase expressing consent or agreement; yes. □ BOB: *Can I take this old coat down to the rummage sale?* SUE: *With my blessing.* □ MARY: *Shall I drive Uncle Tom to the airport a few hours early?* SUE: *Oh, yes! With my blessing!*

with no strings attached AND **without any strings attached** unconditionally; with no obligations attached. □ *My parents gave me a computer without any strings attached.* □ *I want this only if there are no strings attached.*

with one hand tied behind one's back AND **with both hands tied behind one's back** under a handicap; easily. □ *I could put an end to this argument with one hand tied behind my back.* □ *John could do this job with both hands tied behind his back.*

With pleasure. a phrase indicating eager consent to do something. □ FRED: *Would you please take this note over to the woman in the red dress?* WAITER: *With pleasure, sir.* □ SUE: *Would you kindly bring in the champagne now?* JANE: *With pleasure.*

With whom do you wish to speak? a polite phrase used by telephone answerers to find out whom the caller wants to speak to. (Compare to *Who do you want to talk to?*) □ *John answered the telephone and then* said, "With whom do you wish to speak?" □ TOM (answering the phone): *Good morning, Acme Air Products. With whom do you wish to speak?* SUE: *Sorry, I have the wrong number.* TOM: *That's perfectly all right. Have a nice day.*

With you in a minute. See *(Someone will) be with you in a minute.*

wither on the vine AND **die on the vine** [for something] to decline or fade away at an early stage of development. (Also used literally in reference to grapes or other fruit.) □ *You have a great plan, Tom. Let's keep it alive. Don't let it wither on the vine.* □ *The whole project died on the vine when the contract was canceled.*

within an inch of one's life very close to taking one's life; almost to death. □ *The accident frightened me within an inch of my life.* □ *When Mary was seriously ill in the hospital, she came within an inch of her life.*

without a doubt a phrase expressing certainty or agreement; yes. □ JOHN: *This cheese is as hard as a rock. It must have been in the fridge for weeks.* FRED: *Without a doubt.* □ MARY: *Taxes will surely go up before I retire.* JANE: *Without a doubt!*

without any strings attached See *with no strings attached.*

without batting an eye without showing alarm or response; without blinking an eye. □ *I knew I had insulted her, but she turned to me and asked me to leave without batting an eye.* □ *Right in the middle of the speech — without batting an eye — the speaker walked off the stage.*

without further ado without further talk. (An overworked phrase usually heard in public announcements.) □ *And without further ado, I would like to introduce Mr. Bill Franklin!* □ *The time has come to leave, so without further ado, good evening and good-bye.*

wolf in sheep's clothing something threatening disguised as something kind. □ *Beware of the police chief. He seems polite, but he's a wolf in sheep's clothing.* □ *This proposal seems harmless enough, but I think it's a wolf in sheep's clothing.*

Won't you come in? the standard phrase used to invite someone into one's home or office. □ BILL: *Won't you come in?* MARY: *I hope I'm not early.* □ *Tom stood in the doorway of Mr. Franklin's office for a moment. "Won't you come in?" said Mr. Franklin without looking up.*

work away (at something) to continue to work industriously at something. □ *All the weavers were working away at their looms.* □ *They just kept working away.*

work like a horse to work very hard. □ *I've been working like a horse all day, and I'm tired.* □ *I'm too old to work like a horse. I'd prefer to relax more.*

work on someone **1.** [for a physician] to treat someone; [for a surgeon] to operate on someone. □ *The doctor is still working on your uncle. There is no news yet.* □ *They are still working on the accident victims.* **2.** to try to convince someone of something. □ *I'll work on her, and I am sure she will agree.* □ *They worked on Max for quite a while, but he still didn't speak.* **3.** [for something, such as medication] to have the desired effect on someone. □ *This medicine just doesn't* work on me. □ *Your good advice doesn't seem to work on Sam.*

work one's fingers to the bone to work very hard. □ *I worked my fingers to the bone so you children could have everything you needed. Now look at the way you treat me!* □ *I spent the day working my fingers to the bone, and now I want to relax.*

work out 1. [for something] to turn out all right in the end. □ *Don't worry. Everything will work out.* □ *This will work out. Don't worry.* **2.** [for someone] to do a program of exercise. □ *I work out at least twice a week.* □ *I need to work out more often.*

work out for the best to end up in the best possible way. □ *Don't worry. Things will work out for the best.* □ *It seems bad now, but it'll work out for the best.*

work something in(to something) to press, mix, or force a substance into something. □ *You should work the butter into the dough carefully.* T *Work in the butter carefully.* □ *Work it in bit by bit.* □ *Work the lard into the flour with a fork.*

work something off 1. to get rid of body fat by doing strenuous work. □ *I was able to work a lot of weight off by jogging.* T *I need to work off some fat.* **2.** to get rid of anger, anxiety, or energy by doing physical activity. □ *I was so mad! I went out and played basketball to work my anger off.* T *I need to work off some fat.* **3.** to pay off a debt through work rather than by money. □ *I had no money so I had to work the bill off by washing dishes.* T *I have to work off my debt.*

work something up to prepare something, perhaps on short notice. □

There are some special clients coming in this weekend. We need to make a presentation. Do you think you can work something up by then? T *I will work up something for this weekend.*

work up to something 1. [for something] to build or progress to something. (Usually concerning the weather.) □ *The sky is working up to some kind of storm.* □ *The weather is working up to something severe.* **2.** [for someone] to lead up to something. □ *You are working up to telling me something unpleasant, aren't you?* □ *I think I am working up to a good cry.*

work (up)on something 1. to repair or tinker with something. (*Upon* is formal and less commonly used than *on.*) □ *He's out in the kitchen, working upon his tax forms.* □ *He's working on his car.* **2.** [for something] to have the desired effect on something. (*Upon* is formal and less commonly used than *on.*) □ *This medicine should work well upon your cold.* □ *I hope it will work on your cold.*

worship the porcelain god to empty one's stomach; to vomit. (Collegiate slang.) □ *Somebody was in the john worshiping the porcelain god till all hours.* □ *I think I have to go worship the porcelain god. See ya.*

worth its weight in gold very valuable. □ *This book is worth its weight in gold.* □ *Oh, Bill. You're wonderful. You're worth your weight in gold.*

worth one's salt worth one's salary. □ *Tom doesn't work very hard, and he's just barely worth his salt, but he's very easy to get along with.* □ *I think he's more than worth his salt. He's a good worker.*

Would you believe! Isn't that unbelievable?; How shocking! □ TOM: *Jane has run off and married Fred!* SALLY: *Would you believe!* □ JANE: *Then the manager came out and asked us to leave. Would you believe?* MARY: *It sounds just awful. I'd sue.*

(Would you) care for another (one)? Do you want another drink or serving? □ *Tom stood there with an almost empty glass. Bill said, "Would you care for another one?"* □ WAITER: *Care for another one, madam?* SUE: *No, thank you.*

(would you) care to? a polite phrase introducing an inquiry as to whether someone wishes to do something. □ JOHN: *Would you care to step out for some air?* JANE: *Oh, I'd love it.* □ SUE: *Care to go for a swim?* MARY: *Not now, thanks.*

(Would you) care to dance? Do you want to dance with me?; Would you please dance with me? □ JOHN: *Would you care to dance?* MARY: *I don't dance, but thank you for asking.* □ *"Care to dance?" asked Bill, politely, hoping desperately that the answer would be no, preferably an emphatic and devastating no that would send him to the sidelines, crushed.*

(Would you) care to join us? Do you want to join us? □ *Tom and Mary saw Fred and Sally sitting at another table in the restaurant. Tom went over to them and said, "Would you care to join us?"* □ MARY: *Isn't that Bill and Sue over there?* JOHN: *Yes, it is. Shall I ask them to join us?* MARY: *Why not?* JOHN (after reaching the other table): *Hi, you guys! Care to join us?* BILL: *Love to, but Sue's mom is going to be along any minute. Thanks anyway.*

Would you excuse me? **1.** a polite question that essentially announces one's departure. (Compare to *Could I be excused?; Excuse me.*) □ JANE: *Would you excuse me? I have to get home now.* ANDREW: *Oh, sure. I'll see you to the door.* □ *Rising to leave, Jane said, "Would you excuse me?" and left by the rear door.* **2.** a polite way to request passage through or by a group of people; a way to request space to exit an elevator. □ *There were two people talking in the corridor, blocking it. Tom said, "Would you excuse me?" They stepped aside.* □ FRED: *Would you excuse me? This is my floor.* SALLY: *Sure. It's mine too.*

Would you excuse us, please? See *Could you excuse us, please?*

Would you please? a phrase that agrees that what was offered to be done should be done. □ BILL: *Do you want me to take this over to the bank?* MARY: *Would you please?* □ TOM: *Can I take your coat?* SALLY: *Would you please?*

Wow! an exclamation of surprise and amazement. □ *"Wow! A real shark!" said Billy.* □ SALLY: *Wow! I won the contest! What do I get?* RACHEL: *A stuffed doll.* SALLY: *Oh, goodie.* □ JANE: *Wow! I just made it. I thought I would miss this flight for sure.* SUE: *Well, you almost did.*

wrap something up to complete work on something; to bring something to an end. □ *I will wrap the job up this morning. I'll call you when I finish.* ⊤ *I can wrap up this little project in a week.*

write away to write a lot; to continue writing. □ *There he was, writing away, not paying attention to anything else.* □ *I spent the entire afternoon* *writing away, having a fine, productive time.*

write away for something to send for something in writing, from a distant place. □ *I wrote away for a book on the rivers of the world.* □ *You will have to write away for another copy of the instruction manual.*

write off (to someone) (for something) to send away a written request for something. □ *I wrote off to my parents for some money, but I think they are ignoring me.* □ *I wrote off for money.* □ *I need money so I wrote off to my parents.*

write someone in (on something) to write the name of someone in a special place on a ballot, indicating a vote for the person. □ *Please write my name in on the ballot.* T *I wrote in your name on the ballot.* □ *I wrote you in.*

write someone or something off (as a something) 1. to give up on turning someone or something into something. (*Someone* includes *oneself.*) □ *I had to write Jill off as a future dancer.* T *The inventor almost wrote off the automobile as a dependable means of transportation.* □ *He would never work out. We wrote him off.* □ *Don't write yourself off just yet.* 2. to give up on someone or something as a dead loss, waste of time, hopeless case, etc. (*Someone* includes *oneself.*) □ *Don't write me off as a has-been.* T *We almost wrote off the investment as a dead loss.* □ *We wrote the cash loss off.* □ *They wrote themselves off as a loss.* 3. to take a charge against one's taxes. □ *Can I write this off as a deduction, or is it a dead loss?* T *Can I write off this expense as a tax deduction?* □ *Write it off and see what happens.*

write someone or something up to write a narrative or description of someone or something. □ *The reporter wanted to write me up, but I think I am just too dull.* T *The reporter wrote up the charity ball.* □ *The reporter wrote Sam and June up.*

write something back to someone to write a letter answering someone. □ *I wrote an answer back to her the same day that I received the letter.* □ *Will you please write something back to Julie? She complains that you are ignoring her.* □ *I wrote a letter back to Harry, explaining what had happened.*

write something down to make a note of something; to record something on paper in writing. □ *Please write this down.* T *Please write down what I tell you.*

write something in (to something) 1. to write information into something. □ *I wrote her telephone number into my notebook.* T *I wrote in her number.* □ *I took out my notebook and wrote it in.* 2. to include a specific statement or provision in a document, such as a contract or agreement. □ *I want you to write a stronger security clause into my contract.* T *I will write in a stronger clause.* □ *There is no security clause, so I will write one in.*

write something off (on something) to deduct something from one's federal income taxes. □ *Can I write this off on my income taxes?* T *I'll write off this trip on my taxes.* □ *Oh, yes! Write it off!*

write something out to put thoughts into writing, rather than keeping them in memory. □ *Let me write it out. Then I won't forget it.* T *Karen wrote out her objections.*

X

X marks the spot this is the exact spot. (Can be used literally when someone draws an X to mark an exact spot.) □ *This is where the rock struck my car—X marks the spot.* □ *Now, please move that table over here. Yes, right here—X marks the spot.*

x someone or something out to mark out someone or something printed or in writing, with x's. (*Someone* includes *oneself.*) □ *Sally x'd the incorrect information out.* Ⓣ *Sally x'd out the incorrect information.* □ *You should x Tom out. He's not coming.* Ⓣ *Please x out this line of print.* □ *He x'd himself out with a pen.*

Y

yank someone around to harass someone; to give someone a hard time. (Slang. Similar to *jerk someone around*.) □ *Listen, I don't mean to yank you around all the time, but we have to have the drawings by Monday.* □ *Please stop yanking me around.*

yank someone's chain to harass someone; to give someone a hard time. (Slang. As if one were a dog wearing a choker collar, on a leash.) □ *Stop yanking my chain!* □ *Do you really think you can just yank my chain whenever you want?*

year in, year out all year long, year after year. □ *I seem to have hay fever year in, year out. I never get over it.* □ *John wears the same old suit, year in, year out.*

yell out to cry out; to shout loudly. □ *The pain caused the child to yell out.* □ *I yelled out, but no one heard me.*

Yes siree(, Bob)! *Absolutely!; Without a doubt!* (Not necessarily said to a male and not necessarily to Bob.) □ MARY: *Do you want some more cake?* TOM: *Yes siree, Bob!* □ *"That was a fine turkey dinner. Yes siree!" said Uncle Henry.*

Yesterday wouldn't be too soon. an answer to the question "When do you want this?" □ MARY: *Mr. Franklin, when do you want this?* FRED: *Well, yesterday wouldn't be too soon.* □ ALICE: *When am I supposed to have this finished?* SUE: *Yesterday wouldn't be too soon.*

yield something to someone 1. to give the right-of-way to someone. □ *You must yield the right-of-way to pedestrians.* □ *You failed to yield the right-of-way to the oncoming car.* **2.** to give up something to someone. □ *The army yielded the territory to the invading army.* □ *We yielded the territory to the government.*

yo a word used to get someone's attention or signal that the speaker is in a particular location. □ ANDREW: *Yo, Tom. I'm over here!* TOM: *I can't see you. Oh, there you are!* □ BOB: *Let's see who's here. I'll call the role. Bill Franklin.* BILL: *Yo!*

You ain't seen nothing yet! The best, most exciting, or cleverest part is yet to come! (The use of *ain't* is a fixed part of this idiomatic expression.) □ ALICE: *Well, the first act was simply divine.* SUE: *Stick around. You ain't seen nothing yet!* □ MARY: *This part of the city is really beautiful.* BILL: *You ain't seen nothing yet!*

You (always) give up too eas(il)y. You don't stand up for your rights.; You give up without a fight. □ BILL: *Well, I guess she was right.* BOB: *No, she was wrong. You always give up too*

451

easily. □ BOB: *I asked her to go out with me Friday, but she said she thought she was busy.* TOM: *Ask her again. You give up too easy.*

You and what army? See the following entry.

You and who else? AND **You and what army?** a phrase that responds to a threat by implying that the threat is a weak one. □ BILL: *I'm going to punch you in the nose!* BOB: *Yeah? You and who else?* □ TOM: *Our team is going to slaughter your team.* BILL: *You and what army?* □ BILL: *If you don't stop doing that, I'm going to hit you.* TOM: *You and who else?*

You are something else (again)! You are amazing or entertaining! □ *After Sally finished telling her joke, everyone laughed and someone said, "Oh, Sally, you are something else!"* □ *"You are something else again," said Fred, admiring Sue's presentation.*

You asked for it! **1.** You are getting what you requested! □ *The waiter set a huge bowl of ice cream, strawberries, and whipped cream in front of Mary, saying apologetically, "You asked for it!"* □ BILL: *Gee, this escargot stuff is gross!* MARY: *You asked for it!* **2.** You are getting the punishment you deserve! □ BILL: *The tax people just ordered me to pay a big fine.* BOB: *The careless way you do your tax forms caused it. You asked for it!* □ MOTHER: *I'm sorry to have to punish you in this fashion, but you asked for it!* BILL: *I did not!*

You been keeping busy? See *(Have you) been keeping busy?*

You been keeping cool? See *(Have you) been keeping cool?*

You been keeping out of trouble? See *(Have you) been keeping out of trouble?*

You been okay? See *(Have you) been okay?*

You bet. AND **You betcha.** You can be quite certain. □ BILL: *Can I take one of these apples?* BOB: *You bet.* □ BILL: *Do you like this movie?* TOM: *You betcha.*

You bet your boots! See *You bet your (sweet) life!*

You bet your life! See *You bet your (sweet) life!*

You bet your (sweet) bippy. See the following entry.

You bet your (sweet) life! AND **You bet your boots!; You bet your life!; You bet your (sweet) bippy.** You can be absolutely certain of something! (Informal and colloquial.) □ MARY: *Will I need a coat today?* BILL: *You bet your sweet life! It's colder than an iceberg out there.* □ BILL: *Will you be at the game Saturday?* TOM: *You bet your boots!*

You betcha. See *You bet.*

You called? **1.** a phrase used when returning a telephone call, meaning "What did you want to talk about when you called before?" □ BILL (answering the phone): *Hello?* BOB: *This is Bob. You called?* □ TOM: *You called? It's Tom.* MARY: *Hi, Tom. Yes, I wanted to ask you about these estimates.* **2.** a phrase said by someone who has been summoned into a person's presence. (Often used in jest, in the way a servant might answer an employer.) □ MARY: *Oh, Tom. Come over here a minute.* TOM (coming to where Mary is standing): *You* called? □ TOM: *Bill! Bill! Over here, Bill, across the street.* BILL (panting from running and with mock deference): *You called?*

You can say that again! AND **You said it!** That is true.; You are correct.; That is so true or so insightful that it bears repeating. (The word *that* is emphasized.) □ MARY: *It sure is hot today.* JANE: *You can say that again!* □ BILL: *This cake is yummy!* BOB: *You said it!*

(You) cannot! See the following entry.

(You) can't! AND **(You) cannot!** You are wrong, you cannot!; Don't say you can, because you cannot. (The second form is the typical response to *(I) can too.*) □ BILL: *Don't tell me I can't, because I can!* BOB: *Cannot!* BILL: *Can too!* BOB: *Cannot!* BILL: *Can too!* □ TOM: *I want to go to the rock concert. Bill can go and so can I, can't I?* MOTHER: *No, you can't!*

(You) can't beat that. AND **(You) can't top that.** No one can do better than that. (This *you* represents both personal and impersonal antecedents. That is, it means second person singular or plural, and *anyone*.) □ MARY: *Wow! Look at the size of that lobster! It looks yummy!* BILL: *Yeah. You can't beat that. I wonder what it's going to cost.* □ *"What a view! Nothing like it anywhere! You can't top this!" said Jeff, admiring the view he was paying two hundred dollars a night to enjoy.*

You can't expect me to believe that. AND **You don't expect me to believe that.** That is so outrageous that no one could believe it. □ BILL: *My father is running for president.* BOB: *You can't expect me to believe that.* □ JANE: *Everyone in our family has one extra toe.* MARY: *You don't expect me to believe that!*

(You) can't fight city hall. There is no way to win in a battle against a bureaucracy. □ BILL: *I guess I'll go ahead and pay the tax bill.* BOB: *Might as well. You can't fight city hall.* □ MARY: *How did things go at your meeting with the zoning board?* SALLY: *I gave up. Can't fight city hall. Better things to do.*

(You) can't get there from here. a catch phrase said jokingly when someone asks directions to get to a place that can be reached only by a circuitous route. □ BILL: *How far is it to Adamsville?* TOM: *Adamsville? Oh, that's too bad. You can't get there from here.* □ *"Galesburg? Galesburg, you say?" said the farmer. "By golly, you can't get there from here!"*

You can't mean that! Surely you do not mean what you said! □ BILL: *I hate you! I hate you! I hate you!* MARY: *You can't mean that.* □ SALLY: *The cake burned and there's no time to start another before the party.* MARY: *You can't mean that!*

(You) can't take it with you. Since you cannot take your wealth with you when you die, you ought to enjoy it while you're alive. (Proverb.) □ JANE: *Go ahead, enjoy it while you've got it. You can't take it with you.* ANDREW: *I love logic like that.* □ HENRY: *Sure, I spent a fortune on this car. Can't take it with you, you know.* RACHEL: *And this way, you can share it with your friends.* □ *My uncle is a wealthy miser. I keep telling him, "You can't take it with you."* □ *If you have* *money, you should make out a will. You can't take it with you, you know!*

You can't teach an old dog new tricks. Old people cannot learn anything new. (Proverb. Also used literally for dogs.) □ *"Of course I can learn," bellowed Uncle John. "Who says you can't teach an old dog new tricks?"* □ *I'm sorry. I can't seem to learn to do it right. Oh, well. You can't teach an old dog new tricks.*

(You) can't top that. See *(You) can't beat that.*

(You) can't win 'em all. See the following entry.

(You) can't win them all. AND **(You) can't win 'em all.** a catch phrase said when someone, including the speaker, has lost in a contest or failed at something. (The *you* is impersonal, meaning *one, anyone.* The apostrophe on *'em* is not always used.) □ MARY: *Gee, I came in last again!* JANE: *Oh, well. You can't win them all.* □ *"Can't win 'em all,"* muttered Alice as she left the boss's office with nothing accomplished.

You changed your mind? See *(Have you) changed your mind?*

(You) could have fooled me. I would have thought otherwise.; I would have thought the opposite. □ HENRY: *Did you know that this land is among the most productive in the entire state?* JANE: *You could have fooled me. It looks quite barren.* □ JOHN: *I really do like Mary.* ANDREW: *Could have fooled me. You treat her rather badly sometimes.*

You could have knocked me over with a feather. I was extremely surprised.; I was so surprised that I was disoriented and could have been knocked over easily. □ ANDREW: *When she told me she was going to get married, you could have knocked me over with a feather.* SALLY: *I can see why.* □ JOHN: *Did you hear that they are going to tear down city hall and build a new one—price tag twelve million dollars?* SALLY: *Yes, and when I did, you could have knocked me over with a feather.*

You couldn't (do that)! AND **You wouldn't (do that)!** an indication of disbelief that someone might do something. □ BILL: *I'm going to run away from home!* JANE: *You couldn't!* □ BILL: *I get so mad at my brother, I could just strangle him.* TOM: *You couldn't do that!*

You doing okay? See *(Are you) doing okay?*

You don't expect me to believe that. See *You can't expect me to believe that.*

You don't know the half of it. You really don't know how bad it is.; You might think that what you have heard is bad, but you do not know the whole story. □ MARY: *They say you've been having a bad time at home.* SALLY: *You don't know the half of it.* □ SALLY: *The company has no cash, they are losing orders right and left, and the comptroller is cooking the books.* MARY: *Sounds bad.* SALLY: *You don't know the half of it.*

You don't know where it's been. It may be dirty, so do not touch it or put it in your mouth, because you do not know where it has been and what kind of dirt it has picked up. (Most often said to children.) □ MOTHER: *Don't put that money in your mouth. You don't know where it's* been. BILL: *Okay.* □ FATHER: *Take that stick out of your mouth. You don't know where it's been.* BOB: *It's been on the ground.*

You don't say. **1.** a general response to something that someone has said. (Expresses a little polite surprise or interest, but not disbelief.) □ BILL: *I'm starting work on a new job next Monday.* BOB: *You don't say.* □ SALLY: *The Jones boys are keeping a pet snake.* ALICE: *You don't say.* **2.** You have just said something that everybody already knows. □ BILL: *I think I'm beginning to put on a little weight.* JANE: *You don't say.* □ JOHN: *My goodness, prices are getting high.* SUE: *You don't say.*

You first. an invitation for someone to precede the speaker. □ BILL: *Let's try some of this goose liver stuff.* JANE: *You first.* □ BILL: *The water sure looks cold. Let's jump in.* BOB: *You first.*

You got it! Good, you understand it!; Finally, you understand it! □ BILL: *Does that mean I can't have the car tonight?* FATHER: *You got it!* □ BOB: *You're fired! You don't work here any longer! There are no more paychecks coming to you.* BILL: *In other words, I'm out of a job.* BOB: *You got it!*

You got me beat. See *(It) beats me.*

You heard someone. Don't argue. You heard your instructions from someone. (The *someone* can be a person's name, a title, or a pronoun.) □ ANDREW: *You heard the man. Get moving.* HENRY: *Don't rush me!* □ BILL: *What makes her think she can tell me what to do?* BOB: *She's the boss. Do it! You heard her!*

You (just) wait (and see)! AND **Just (you) wait (and see)!** Wait and see what will happen.; If you wait, you will see that what I predict will be true. □ JOHN: *You'll get what you deserve! Just you wait!* JANE: *Mind your own business.* □ BILL: *Things will get better. Just wait!* SUE: *Sure, but when?*

(You) (just) watch! Just pay attention to what I do, and you will see that what I said is true! □ RACHEL: *I'll get her to change! You just watch!* ANDREW: *Good luck!* □ ANDREW: *You watch! You'll see I'm right.* SALLY: *Sure, you are.* □ BOB: *Watch! This is the way it's done.* BILL: *You don't know what you're doing.* BOB: *Just watch!*

you know an expression placed on the end of a statement for emphasis. (This expression is often overused, in which case it is totally meaningless and irritating.) □ ANDREW: *Sure, I spent a fortune on this car. Can't take it with you, you know.* RACHEL: *But there are better things to do with it here and now.* □ BILL: *Do you always lock your door?* TOM: *Usually. There's a lot of theft around here, you know.*

You know what? See *(Do you) know what?*

(You) know what I mean? See *You know (what I'm saying)?*

You know what I mean? See *(Do you) know what I'm saying?*

You know (what I'm saying)? AND **(You) know what I mean?; (You) know what I'm saying?** You can figure out what I'm trying to say, besides I forgot the right words, so I won't explain further. (The *You know* is frowned on by many people, especially when it is overused.) □ JOHN: *I'm going to Florida, on the gulf side. You know what I'm saying?* MARY: *Yeah, that's great!* □ FRED:

I've got to get some of those things that hold up the back of the car. You know what I mean? BOB: *Yeah, springs. I need some too.*

(You) know what I'm saying? See the previous entry.

You leaving so soon? See *(Are you) leaving so soon?*

You make me laugh! What you said is totally ridiculous.; You are totally ridiculous. (Compare to *Don't make me laugh!*) □ BILL: *I have this plan to make electricity from garbage.* SALLY: *What a dumb idea! You make me laugh!* □ BILL: *I'm really sorry. Give me another chance. I'll never do it again!* JANE: *You make me laugh!*

You (really) said a mouthful. You said exactly what needed to be said.; What you said was very meaningful and had great impact. (Colloquial and folksy.) □ BILL: *Did you hear what I said to her?* JANE: *Yes. You said a mouthful. Was she mad?* □ BILL: *This is the worst food I have ever eaten. It is either stale, wilted, dry, or soggy!* TOM: *You said a mouthful!*

You said it! See *You can say that again!*

You too. See *(The) same to you.*

(You) took the words right out of my mouth. You said exactly what I meant to say before I had a chance to say it, and, therefore, I agree with you very much. □ BILL: *I think she's old enough to know better.* TOM: *You took the words right out of my mouth.* □ MARY: *This movie is going to put me to sleep.* JANE (yawning): *You took the words right out of my mouth.*

(You want to) know something? See *(Do you) want to know something?*

You want to make something of it? See *(Do you) want to make something of it?*

You wouldn't be trying to kid me, would you? You are not lying, are you? □ BILL: *There's a mouse sitting on the toe of your shoe.* TOM: *You wouldn't be trying to kid me, would you?* □ BILL: *The history final examination was changed to yesterday. Did they tell you?* BOB: *You wouldn't be trying to kid me, would you?*

You wouldn't dare (to do something)! an exclamation that shows disbelief about something that the speaker has stated an intention of doing. □ BILL: *I'm going to leave school.* TOM: *You wouldn't dare leave!* □ BILL: *Be quiet or I'll slap you.* JANE: *You wouldn't dare!*

You wouldn't (do that)! See *You couldn't (do that)!*

You('d) better believe it! a way of emphasizing a previous statement. □ BILL: *Man, you're the best goalie this team has ever had!* TOM: *You better believe it!* □ BILL: *This food is so bad. It will probably stunt my growth.* TOM: *You'd better believe it!*

(You'd) better get moving. an expression encouraging someone to leave. □ JANE: *It's nearly dark. Better get moving.* MARY: *Okay. I'm leaving right now.* □ BOB: *I'm off. Good night.* BILL: *Yes, it's late. You'd better get moving.*

You'll be sorry you asked. The answer to the question you just asked is so bad that you will be sorry you asked it. (Compare to *(Are you) sorry you asked?*) □ FATHER: *What are your grades going to be like this semester?* SALLY: *You'll be sorry you* asked. □ MARY: *How much did you pay for that lamp?* JANE: *You'll be sorry you asked.*

You'll be the death of me (yet). You and your problems may, in fact, kill me. (An exaggeration, of course.) □ HENRY: *You'll be the death of me yet. Why can't you ever do anything right?* ANDREW: *I got a talent for it, I guess.* □ BILL: *Mom, the teacher says you have to go to school again for a conference.* MOTHER: *Oh, Billy, you'll be the death of me.*

You'll get onto it. Don't worry. You will become more comfortable with this situation soon.; You will catch the spirit of the situation soon. □ BILL: *I just can't seem to do this right.* BOB: *You'll get onto it.* □ MARY: *How long does it take to learn to work this computer?* JANE: *Don't fret. You'll get onto it.*

You'll get the hang of it. Don't worry. You will learn soon how it is done. □ MARY: *It's harder than I thought to glue these things together.* TOM: *You'll get the hang of it.* □ BILL: *I can't seem to swing this club the way you showed me.* SALLY: *You'll get the hang of it. Don't worry. Golf is easy.*

You'll never get away with it. You will never succeed with that illegal or outrageous plan. □ BILL: *I have a plan to cheat on the exam.* MARY: *You'll never get away with it.* □ JANE: *I think I can trick everybody into walking out on the performance.* MARY: *That's awful. You'll never get away with it.*

Your guess is as good as mine. Your answer is likely to be as correct as mine.; I really do not know. □ *I don't know where the scissors are. Your*

guess is as good as mine. □ *Your guess is as good as mine as to when the train will arrive.* □ MARY: *What time do we eat around here?* BOB: *Your guess is as good as mine.* □ BILL: *Why would anyone build a house like that way out here in the woods?* BOB: *Your guess is as good as mine.*

Your place or mine? an expression of inquiry regarding whose dwelling should be the site of a rendezvous. (Often associated with a sudden or spontaneous sexual encounter.) □ BILL: *So, do you want to go somewhere?* MARY: *Your place or mine?* □ BILL: *I was thinking of a movie. What's this "You're place or mine?"* MARY: *Okay, I'll rent the movie and we'll watch it at your place.*

You're dern tootin'! You are absolutely right! (Colloquial and folksy. Never the full form *tooting*.) □ TOM: *Are you really going to take up boxing?* BOB: *You're dern tootin'!* □ FATHER: *Do you really want to buy that droopy-looking puppy?* BILL: *You're dern tootin'!*

You're excused. **1.** You may leave the room, the table, etc. (Said in response to *May I be excused?*) □ MOTHER: *Are you finished, Tom?* TOM: *Yes, ma'am.* MOTHER: *You're excused.* □ BILL (raising his hand): *Can I leave the room? I have to go get my books off my bike.* TEACHER: *You're excused.* BILL: *Thanks.* **2.** You must leave the room or the premises. (Typically said at the end of a scolding.) □ FATHER: *I've heard quite enough of this nonsense, Tom. You're excused.* TOM: *Sorry.* □ ANDREW: *That is the end of this conversation. You're excused.* BOB: *But, there's more.* **3.** You are forgiven for belching or for some other breach of strict etiquette. (Said in response to *Excuse me*.) □ TOM (after belching): *Excuse me.* FATHER: *You're excused.* □ SALLY: *Excuse me for being so noisy.* MOTHER: *You're excused.*

You're (just) wasting my time. What you have to say is of no interest to me. □ RACHEL: *I've heard enough. You're just wasting my time. Good-bye.* MARY: *If that's the way you feel about it, good-bye.* □ BOB: *Come on, Bill. I'll show you what I mean.* BILL: *No, you're wasting my time.*

You're out of your mind! AND **You've got to be out of your mind!** You must be crazy for saying or doing that! (Said to someone who has said or done something silly or stupid.) □ ANDREW: *Go to the Amazon? You're out of your mind!* JANE: *Maybe so, but doesn't it sound like fun?* □ MARY: *Come on, Jane. Let's go swimming in the river.* JANE: *Look at that filthy water. Swim in it? You've got to be out of your mind!*

You're telling me! I know all too well the truth of what you are saying. □ TOM: *Man, it's hot today!* BOB: *You're telling me!* □ JANE: *This food is really terrible.* SALLY: *Wow! You're telling me!*

You're the doctor. You are in a position to tell me what to do.; I yield to you and your knowledge of this matter. (The person being addressed is most likely not a physician.) □ BILL: *Eat your dinner, then you'll feel more like playing ball. Get some energy!* TOM: *Okay, you're the doctor.* □ TEACHER: *You'd better study the first two chapters more thoroughly.* BOB: *You're the doctor.*

You're too much! **1.** You are too much of a problem for me. □ ANDREW: *You're too much! I'm going to report you to the head office!* BOB: *Go ahead. See if I care.* □ BOB: *Get out! Just go home! You're too much!* ANDREW: *What did I do?* BOB: *You're a pest!* **2.** You are just too funny, clever, entertaining, etc. □ ALICE: *Oh, Fred, that was really funny. You're too much!* FRED: *I do my best.* □ SALLY: *What a clever thing to say! You're too much!* ANDREW: *Actually, I didn't make it up myself.*

You're welcome. a phrase that follows *Thanks* or *Thank you*. (Made emphatic and more gracious with an adjective, such as *quite* or *very*.) □ FATHER: *Thank you.* MOTHER: *You're welcome.* □ BOB: *We all thank you very much.* SALLY: *You're quite welcome.*

Yourself? See *And you?*

You've got another think coming. You will have to rethink your position. (The second part of an expression something like, "If you think so-and-so, then *you've got another think coming.*" Also with *thing* rather than *think*.) □ RACHEL: *If you think I'm going to stand here and listen to your complaining all day, you've got another think coming!* BILL: *Frankly, I don't care what you do.* □ ANDREW: *If you think you can get away with it, you've got another think coming!* BOB: *Get away with what? I didn't do anything!*

(You've) got me stumped. I can't possible figure out the answer to your question. □ BILL: *How long is the Amazon River?* JANE: *You've got me stumped.* □ BOB: *Do you know of a book that would interest a retired* *sea captain?* SALLY: *You've got me stumped.*

You've got to be kidding! This cannot be the truth. Surely you are kidding me! □ BOB: *Sally is getting married. Did you hear?* MARY: *You've got to be kidding!* □ BILL: *I think I swallowed my gold tooth!* MOTHER: *You've got to be kidding!*

You've got to be out of your mind! See *You're out of your mind!*

Yup. Yes. (Colloquial and folksy. Considered rude or disrespectful in some situations, such as a child speaking to an adult.) □ BILL: *Want some more?* TOM: *Yup.* □ MARY: *Tired?* JANE: *Yup.*

Z

zero in (on someone or something)
1. to aim directly at someone or
something. □ *The television camera
zeroed in on the little boy scratching his
head.* □ *It zeroed in on the glass of
cola.* □ *Zero in when I tell you.* □
*Let's zero in on the important points in
this discussion.* **2.** [with *something*] to
aim or focus directly on something.
□ *"Now," said Mr. Smith, "I would
like to zero in on another important
point."* □ *Mary is very good about
zeroing in on the most important and
helpful ideas.*

Zip it up! See *Zip (up) your lip!*

zip something up **1.** to close a zipper.
□ *You should zip that zipper up.* ⊤
You should zip up that zipper. **2.** to
close a garment by zipping a zipper
closed. □ *You had better zip your
jacket up.* ⊤ *You had better zip up your
jacket.* **3.** to close one's mouth.
(Usually **Zip it up!**) □ *Zip your
mouth up, Fred!* ⊤ *Zip up your mouth,
Fred.*

Zip (up) your lip! AND **Zip it up!** Be
quiet!; Close your mouth and be
quiet! (Slang and slightly rude.) □
*"I've heard enough. Zip your lip!"
hollered the coach.* □ ANDREW: *All
right, you guys. Shut up! Zip it up!*
BOB: *Sorry.* BILL: *Be quiet.* ANDREW:
That's better.

zonk out to collapse from exhaustion;
to go into a stupor from drugs or
exhaustion. (Slang.) □ *I'm gonna go
home and zonk out.* □ *I went home
after the trip and just zonked out.*

zonked (out) AND **zounked (out)** **1.**
alcohol or drug intoxicated. (Slang.)
□ *She's too zonked to drive.* □ *Jed
was almost zounked out to unconscious-
ness.* **2.** exhausted; asleep. □ *She was
totally zonked out by the time I got
home.* □ *I'm zounked. Good night.*

zoom in (on someone or something)
AND **pan in (on someone or something)** **1.** to move in to get a
close-up picture of someone or something, using a zoom lens or a similar
lens. □ *The camera zoomed in on the
love scene.* □ *The camera operator
panned in slowly.* **2.** to focus sharply
on a matter related to someone or a
problem. □ *Let's zoom in on this matter of debt.* □ *She zoomed in and dealt
quickly with the problem at hand.* □
*Sally zoomed in on Tom and demanded
an explanation.*

zoom off to leave in a hurry. □ *Sorry,
I have to zoom off.* □ *We will zoom off
soon.*

zoom through (something) **1.** to pass
through a town or some other location very fast. □ *Don't just zoom
through these little towns. Stop and ex-
plore one or two.* □ *We didn't stop. We*

just *zoomed through.* **2.** to work one's way through something very rapidly. □ *She zoomed through the reading assignment and went on to something else.* □ *Jeff can open a book and zoom through in record time.*

zoom up to pull up some place in a vehicle rapidly. □ *The car zoomed up and came to a stop.* □ *The bus zoomed up and let a few people off.*

zounked (out) See *zonked (out).*

PHRASE-FINDER INDEX

Use this index to find the form of the phrase or compound that you want to look up in this dictionary. First, pick out any main word in the phrase you are seeking. Second, look that word up in this index to find the form of the phrase used in this dictionary. Third, look up the phrase in the main body of this dictionary. See *Uses* and *Hints* below.

Some of the words occurring in this dictionary do not occur as entries in this index. Single word entries are not indexed here and should be looked up in the dictionary directly. Some words are omitted because they occur so frequently that their lists would cover many pages. Most grammar words — prepositions, personal pronouns, conjunctions, etc. — and the following words do not occur as entries in the index: *get, let, make, one's, place, someone, something.* In these instances, you should look up the phrase under some other word.

Uses

This index provides a convenient way of finding the words that follow the first word in a phrasal entry. For instance, there are a number of entries beginning with *act*, but the index lists three additional entries that include *act* in some other form or position: **clean one's act up, read someone the riot act,** and **tough act to follow.**

If you were trying to find an expression that includes something about spoiled stew, you could look up either word in the index. At both *spoil* and *stew* you would find listed **Too many cooks spoil the stew.** You would turn to the **T** section of this dictionary to find the entry for this expression. In fact, the index lists this expression at *cook, many, spoil,* and *stew.*

Hints

1. This is an index of forms, not meanings. The expressions in an index entry do not necessarily have any meaning in common. Consult the dictionary definitions for information about meaning.

2. When you are trying to find an expression in this index, try first to look up any nouns that may be part of the expression.

3. When you are looking for a noun, try first to find its singular or simplest form.

4. When you are looking for a verb, try first to find its present tense or simplest form.

5. In most expressions where a noun or pronoun is a variable part of the expression, it will be represented by the words *someone* or *something*. If you do not find the noun you want in the index, it may, in fact, be a variable word and you should look up another word.

6. When you locate the phrase you want, look it up in the main body of the dictionary.

ABLE
not able to see the forest for the trees

ABODE
take up one's abode somewhere

ABSENCE
conspicuous by one's absence

ACCEPT
I can accept that. □ I can't accept that.

ACCORDING
according to Hoyle

ACCOUNT
cook the accounts □ give a good account of oneself □ There's no accounting for taste.

ACE
ace in(to something) □ ace out □ ace someone out

ACQUAINTANCE
(I'm) delighted to make your acquaintance.

ACT
act (up)on something □ act high-and-mighty □ act of God □ act one's age □ act something out □ act up □ Act your age! □ clean one's act up □ read someone the riot act □ tough act to follow

ACTION
Actions speak louder than words.

ACTIVE
on active duty

ADAM
not know someone from Adam

ADD
add fuel to the fire □ add insult to injury

ADMIT
admit something into something

ADO
much ado about nothing □ without further ado

ADVANCE
advance (up)on someone or something

ADVANTAGE
turn something to one's advantage

ADVISE
advise someone against someone or something

AFRAID
(I'm) afraid not. □ (I'm) afraid so. □ afraid of one's own shadow

AFTERNOON
(Good) afternoon.

AGAIN
(I) hope to see you again (sometime). □ (It's) good to see you (again). □ Again(, please). □ Call again. □ Come again. □ Could I see you again? □ Do we have to go through all that again? □ Don't make me say it again! □ go and never darken my door again □ Here we go again. □ How's that again? □ Let's do this again (sometime). □ Let's not go through all that again. □ Not again! □ Run that by (me) again. □ What was the name again? □ Will I see you again? □ You are something else (again)! □ You can say that again!

AGE
act one's age □ Act your age! □ Age before beauty. □ come of age □ in this day and age

AGREE
agree (up)on someone or something □ agree to something □ agree with someone (about someone or something) □ agree with someone or something

AHEAD

(Go ahead,) make my day! □ come out ahead □ Go ahead.

AIM

aim something at someone or something □ We aim to please.

AIR

air someone's dirty linen in public □ air something out □ build castles in the air □ give oneself airs □ in the air □ leave someone or something hanging in midair □ off the air □ on the air □ out of thin air □ put on airs □ up in the air □ vanish into thin air □ walk on air

ALARM

I don't want to alarm you, but

ALIVE

Look alive!

ALL

(I) haven't got all day. □ (You) can't win them all. □ all in a day's work □ all in all □ all over but the shouting □ All right(y) already! □ All right. □ All roads lead to Rome. □ All systems are go. □ All that glitters is not gold. □ All the more reason for doing something. □ all thumbs □ all walks of life □ all wet □ All work and no play makes Jack a dull boy. □ All's well that ends well. □ as bad as all that □ blow something out of all proportion □ Do we have to go through all that again? □ Don't spend it all in one place. □ Everything's going to be all right. □ first of all □ for all intents and purposes □ free-for-all □ get (all) dolled up □ have it all together □ hope against all hope □ I was up all night with a sick friend. □ If that don't beat all! □ Let's not go through all that again. □ Money is

the root of all evil. □ Not at all. □ of all the nerve □ on all fours □ once and for all □ out of all proportion □ put all one's eggs in one basket □ That (all) depends. □ That's all someone needs. □ The shame of it (all)! □ Things will work out (all right). □ Where have you been all my life? □ with all one's heart and soul

ALLEY

up a blind alley

ALLIGATOR

See you later, alligator.

ALLOW

allow for someone or something □ Allow me. □ allow someone or something in (something)

ALONE

Leave me alone!

ALREADY

All right(y) already!

ALWAYS

Not always. □ You (always) give up too eas(il)y.

AMOUNT

amount to something □ amount to the same thing (as something)

ANOTHER

(Would you) care for another (one)? □ dance to another tune □ horse of another color □ One good turn deserves another. □ One man's meat is another man's poison. □ one way or another □ Tell me another (one)! □ to put it another way □ You've got another think coming.

ANY

(It) doesn't bother me any. □ (It) won't bother me any. □ Any friend of someone('s) (is a friend of mine). □ in any case

ANYMORE

(We) don't see you much around here anymore. □ Not anymore.

ANYONE

Anyone I know? □ Don't breathe a word of this to anyone.

ANYTHING

(Is) anything going on? □ (Will there be) anything else? □ Anything new down your way? □ Anything you say. □ Don't do anything I wouldn't do. □ If there's anything you need, don't hesitate to ask.

ANYTIME

Anytime you are ready. □ Come back anytime.

APART

be poles apart □ come apart at the seams □ fall apart □ take something apart

APPEAR

appear before someone

APPLE

(as) easy as (apple) pie □ apple of someone's eye □ upset the apple cart

APPLY

apply something to something

APPOINT

appoint someone to something

APRON

tied to one's mother's apron strings

ARCH

arch over someone or something

ARGUE

(I) can't argue with that. □ argue against someone or something □ argue one's way out (of something) □ argue someone or something down

ARM

arm in arm □ armed to the teeth □ cost an arm and a leg □ give one's right arm (for someone or something) □ pay an arm and a leg (for something) □ shot in the arm □ twist someone's arm □ up in arms

AROUSE

arouse someone from something

ARRANGE

arrange something with someone or something

ARRIVE

arrive (up)on the scene (of something) □ arrive at something

ASIDE

as an aside □ elbow someone aside □ motion someone aside □ stand aside □ step aside

ASK

(Are you) sorry you asked? □ (I'm) sorry you asked (that). □ (I) couldn't ask for more. □ (It) doesn't hurt to ask. □ ask after someone □ ask for the moon □ ask for trouble □ ask someone in((to) some place) □ ask someone out (to something) □ ask someone over □ ask someone up □ Don't ask. □ I couldn't ask you to do that. □ If there's anything you need, don't hesitate to ask. □ If you don't see what you want, please ask (for it). □ Sorry (that) I asked. □ You asked for it! □ You'll be sorry you asked.

ASLEEP

asleep at the switch

ASS

pain in the ass

ASSIGN

assign someone or something to someone or something □ assign something to someone

ATTACH
attach oneself to someone or something □ with no strings attached

ATTITUDE
wait-and-see attitude

AUCTION
auction something off

AUDITION
audition for something □ audition someone for something

AVERAGE
average out □ on the average

AWFULLY
Thanks awfully.

AX
have an ax to grind

BABY
(as) soft as a baby's bottom □ babe in the woods

BACON
What's shakin' (bacon)?

BAD
(It's) not half bad. □ (That's) too bad. □ as bad as all that □ come to a bad end □ in bad faith □ in bad shape □ in bad sorts □ in bad taste □ leave a bad taste in someone's mouth □ Not bad. □ throw good money after bad

BAG
bag and baggage □ Bag it! □ bag of tricks □ in the bag □ leave someone holding the bag □ let the cat out of the bag

BAGGAGE
bag and baggage

BAIL
bail out (of something) □ bail someone or something out (of something)

BAIT
Fish or cut bait.

BALANCE
catch someone off-balance □ hang in the balance

BALL
carry the ball □ drop the ball □ Have a ball! □ pitch someone a curve (ball) □ play ball (with someone) □ whole ball of wax

BALLOT
stuff the ballot box

BAND
(as) tight as Dick's hatband □ band together (against someone or something)

BANDWAGON
climb on the bandwagon □ get on the bandwagon

BANG
bang into someone or something □ go over with a bang

BARGAIN
bargain for something □ drive a hard bargain □ hold one's end (of the bargain) up □ in the bargain □ throw something into the bargain

BARGE
barge in on someone or something □ barge into someone or something

BARK
bark up the wrong tree □ One's bark is worse than one's bite.

BARN
Were you born in a barn?

BARREL
get someone over a barrel □ lock, stock, and barrel □ scrape the bottom of the barrel

BASE
get to first base (with someone or something) □ off base □ steal a base

BASKET
put all one's eggs in one basket

BASTARD
Don't let the bastards wear you down.

BAT
(as) blind as a bat □ go to bat for someone □ have bats in one's belfry □ like a bat out of hell □ right off the bat □ without batting an eye

BAWL
bawl someone out

BEAM
steam someone's beam

BEAR
(as) hungry as a bear □ bear (up)on something □ bear down (on someone or something) □ bear one's cross □ bear someone or something up □ bear the brunt (of something) □ bear up (under something) □ bear watching □ bear with someone or something □ grin and bear it

BEARD
beard the lion in his den

BEAT
(I) can't beat that. □ (It) beats me. □ (You) can't beat that. □ beat a dead horse □ beat a path to someone's door □ beat around the bush □ beat down on someone or something □ Beat it! □ beat one's head against the wall □ beat someone or something down □ beat something into something □ beat something up □ beat the gun □ If that don't beat all! □ pound a beat

BEAUTY
(I've) got to go home and get my beauty sleep. □ Age before beauty. □ Beauty is only skin deep.

BEAVER
(as) busy as a beaver

BED
bed down (for something) □ Early to bed, early to rise(, makes a man healthy, wealthy, and wise). □ get up on the wrong side of the bed □ put someone or something to bed □ should have stood in bed

BEE
birds and the bees □ have a bee in one's bonnet □ make a beeline for someone or something □ put a bee in someone's bonnet

BEEF
beef something up

BEELINE
make a beeline for someone or something

BEER
pound a beer □ slam some beers

BEG
(I) beg your pardon, but □ (I) beg your pardon. □ beg off ((on) something) □ beg something off □ I'll have to beg off.

BEGGAR
Beggars can't be choosers.

BEGIN
begin to see daylight □ begin to see the light □ Charity begins at home.

BELFRY
have bats in one's belfry

BELIEVE
(I) don't believe I've had the pleasure. □ believe it or not □ Believe you me! □ Do you expect me to believe that? □ I believe we've met. □ I can't believe (that)! □ I don't believe it! □ I don't believe this! □ Would you believe! □ You

can't expect me to believe that. □ You('d) better believe it!

BELL
Hell's bells (and buckets of blood)!

BELLY
turn belly-up

BELONG
To the victors belong the spoils.

BELT
belt up □ get something under one's belt □ tighten one's belt

BENCH
on the bench □ warm the bench

BEND
bend down □ bend over □ bend someone's ear □ go (a)round the bend

BENEFIT
get the benefit of the doubt □ give someone the benefit of the doubt

BERTH
give someone or something a wide berth

BEST
(The) best of luck (to someone). □ come off second-best □ Give my best to someone. □ put one's best foot forward □ work out for the best

BET
(I) wouldn't bet on it. □ I('ll) bet □ You bet your (sweet) life! □ You bet.

BETTER
(I'd) better be going. □ (I'd) better get moving. □ (I'd) better get on my horse. □ (I've) (got) better things to do. □ (I've) never been better. □ (I've) seen better. □ (I) couldn't be better. □ (It's) better than nothing. □ (It) couldn't be better. □ (Someone had) better keep still about it. □ (Things) could be better. □ (You'd)

better get moving. □ Better late than never. □ better left unsaid □ Better luck next time. □ Half a loaf is better than none. □ one's better half □ The sooner the better. □ You('d) better believe it!

BIG
big frog in a small pond □ have a big mouth □ have eyes bigger than one's stomach □ one's eyes are bigger than one's stomach □ talk on the big white phone

BILL
fill the bill □ foot the bill □ get a clean bill of health □ give someone a clean bill of health □ pad the bill □ sell someone a bill of goods

BIND
bind someone or something up (with something) □ bind someone over (to someone or something)

BIRD
(as) free as a bird □ A bird in the hand is worth two in the bush. □ a little bird told me □ birds and the bees □ Birds of a feather flock together. □ eat like a bird □ The early bird gets the worm.

BIRTHDAY
in one's birthday suit

BIT
champ at the bit □ hair of the dog that bit one

BITCH
pitch a bitch

BITE
bite off more than one can chew □ bite on something □ bite one's nails □ bite one's tongue □ bite the dust □ bite the hand that feeds one □ Bite your tongue! □ I'll bite. □ One's bark is worse than one's bite.

BITTER
take the bitter with the sweet

BLACK
black out □ black sheep of the family □ black something out □ get a black eye □ give someone a black eye □ in black and white □ in the black □ the pot calling the kettle black

BLAME
blame someone for something □ blame something on someone

BLANK
blank something out □ draw a blank □ Fill in the blanks.

BLAST
blast off (for some place)

BLAZE
blaze down (on someone or something) □ blaze up

BLEND
blend in (with someone or something) □ blend in(to something) □ blend something in(to something)

BLESSING
with my blessing

BLIND
(as) blind as a bat □ blind leading the blind □ turn a blind eye to someone or something □ up a blind alley

BLINK
blink back one's tears

BLOCK
a chip off the old block □ block something off □ block something out □ block something up □ on the block

BLOOD
cry bloody murder □ draw blood □ flesh and blood □ Hell's bells (and buckets of blood)! □ in the blood □

make someone's blood boil □ make someone's blood run cold

BLOT
blot someone or something out

BLOW
blow away □ blow in □ blow itself out □ blow off □ blow over □ blow someone or something away □ blow someone or something down □ blow someone or something over □ blow someone or something up □ blow someone's cover □ blow something out □ blow something out of all proportion □ blow the whistle (on someone) □ blow up □ It blows my mind!

BLUE
burn with a low blue flame □ get the blues □ like a bolt out of the blue □ once in a blue moon □ out of a clear blue sky □ talk a blue streak □ talk until one is blue in the face

BOARD
back to the drawing board

BOAT
in the same boat □ just off the boat □ rock the boat

BOB
No siree(, Bob)! □ Yes siree(, Bob)!

BODY
I don't want to sound like a busybody, but □ Over my dead body!

BOGGLE
boggle someone's mind

BOIL
A watched pot never boils. □ boil down to something □ boil over □ boil something out (of something) □ have a low boiling point □ make someone's blood boil

BOLT
like a bolt out of the blue

BONE

bone of contention □ cut someone or something to the bone □ feel something in one's bones □ have a bone to pick (with someone) □ nothing but skin and bones □ work one's fingers to the bone

BONNET

have a bee in one's bonnet □ put a bee in someone's bonnet

BOOK

book someone through (to some place) □ have one's nose in a book □ hit the books □ Not in my book. □ read someone like a book □ take a leaf out of someone's book □ use every trick in the book

BOOM

boom out □ lower the boom on someone

BOOT

boot someone out (of something) □ boot something up □ boot up □ shake in one's boots

BOOTSTRAPS

pull oneself up (by one's own bootstraps)

BORDER

border (up)on something

BOREDOM

die of boredom

BORN

born with a silver spoon in one's mouth □ not born yesterday □ Were you born in a barn?

BOSS

boss someone around

BOTCH

botch something up

BOTH

burn the candle at both ends □ play both ends (against the middle)

BOTHER

(It) doesn't bother me any. □ (It) don't bother me none. □ (It) won't bother me any. □ Don't bother me! □ Don't bother.

BOTTLE

bottle something up (inside (someone))

BOTTOM

(as) soft as a baby's bottom □ at the bottom of the ladder □ bottom out □ Bottoms up. □ from the bottom of one's heart □ from top to bottom □ get to the bottom of something □ hit bottom □ learn something from the bottom up □ scrape the bottom of the barrel

BOUNCE

bounce off ((of) something) □ bounce out (of something) □ bounce something off (of) someone or something

BOUND

bound hand and foot □ by leaps and bounds

BOW

bow and scrape □ bow out (of something)

BOWELS

Don't get your bowels in an uproar!

BOWL

bowl someone over

BOX

box someone or something in □ open Pandora's box □ stuff the ballot box

BOY

All work and no play makes Jack a dull boy. □ boy (oh boy) □ Boy howdy! □ How's my boy? □ Oh, boy. □ separate the men from the boys

BRACE
brace someone or something up

BRAIN
rack one's brain(s)

BRANCH
branch off (from something) □ branch out (from something) □ branch out (into something) □ hold out the olive branch

BRASS
get down to brass tacks

BRAVE
put up a (brave) front

BREAD
bread and butter

BREADTH
by a hair's breadth

BREAK
break (out) into tears □ Break a leg! □ break away (from someone) □ break camp □ break down □ break down (and do something) □ break in (on someone or something) □ break in(to something or some place) □ Break it up! □ break new ground □ break off (from something) □ break one's neck (to do something) □ break out □ break out (with something) □ break out in a cold sweat □ break out of something □ break someone down □ break someone in □ break someone up □ break someone's fall □ break someone's heart □ break something down □ break something in □ break something off ((of) something) □ break something up □ break something up (into something) □ break the ice □ break the news (to someone) □ break through (something) □ break up □ break up (into something) □ break up (with someone) □ Give me a break!

BREAST
make a clean breast of something

BREATH
Don't hold your breath. □ Don't waste your breath. □ get time to catch one's breath □ I don't have time to catch my breath. □ in the same breath □ take someone's breath away □ waste one's breath □ with every (other) breath

BREATHE
(I) won't breathe a word (of it). □ breathe down someone's neck □ breathe one's last □ breathe something in □ breathe something out □ Don't breathe a word of this to anyone. □ hardly have time to breathe

BREED
Familiarity breeds contempt.

BREEZE
breeze along □ breeze in(to some place) □ breeze through (something)

BREW
brew something up □ brew up □ quaff a brew

BRICK
hit (someone) like a ton of bricks □ hit the bricks

BRIDE
give the bride away

BRIDGE
burn one's bridges (behind one) □ cross a bridge before one comes to it □ cross a bridge when one comes to it □ water under the bridge

BRING
bring a verdict in □ bring someone down □ bring someone in (on something) □ bring someone or something up □ bring someone to □ bring someone up for something

☐ bring someone up on something ☐ bring something about ☐ bring something back ☐ bring something back (to someone) ☐ bring something down ☐ bring something in ☐ bring something on ☐ bring something on someone ☐ bring something out ☐ bring something out (in someone) ☐ bring something to light ☐ bring the house down ☐ bring up the rear ☐ That brings me to the (main) point. ☐ What brings you here? ☐ which brings me to the (main) point

BROAD
in broad daylight

BROKE
die of a broken heart ☐ flat broke

BROW
by the sweat of one's brow

BROWN
brown out

BRUNT
bear the brunt (of something)

BRUSH
brush (up) against someone or something ☐ brush by someone or something ☐ brush someone off ☐ brush something away (from something) ☐ brush something down ☐ brush something off ((of) someone or something) ☐ brush up (on something) ☐ have a brush with something

BUBBLE
bubble over

BUCK
pass the buck

BUCKET
Hell's bells (and buckets of blood)!

BUCKLE
buckle someone in ☐ buckle someone or something up ☐ buckle up

BUD
nip something in the bud

BUDDY
buddy up (to someone) ☐ buddy up (with someone)

BUG
(as) snug as a bug in a rug

BUILD
build castles in the air ☐ build on ((to) something) ☐ build someone in(to something) ☐ build someone or something up ☐ build someone up (for something) ☐ build something in(to something) ☐ build something out of something ☐ build up ☐ Rome wasn't built in a day.

BULL
bull in a china shop ☐ cock-and-bull story ☐ hit the bull's-eye ☐ shoot the bull ☐ take the bull by the horns

BULLPEN
in the bullpen

BULLY
Bully for you!

BUMP
bump (up) against someone or something ☐ get goose bumps ☐ like a bump on a log

BUNCH
bunch someone or something up ☐ bunch up

BUNDLE
bundle (oneself) up (against something) ☐ bundle off ☐ bundle someone in(to something) ☐ bundle someone up (in something) ☐ bundle something off (to someone or some place)

BUOY

buoy someone or something up

BURN

burn (itself) out □ burn away □ burn down □ burn off □ burn one's bridges (behind one) □ burn someone at the stake □ burn someone or something out □ burn someone or something to a crisp □ burn someone or something up □ burn something away □ burn something down □ burn something off ((of) something) □ burn the candle at both ends □ burn the midnight oil □ burn up □ burn with a low blue flame □ get one's fingers burned □ have money to burn □ money burns a hole in someone's pocket □ That (really) burns me (up)!

BURST

burst (out) into something □ burst (up)on someone □ burst (up)on the scene □ burst at the seams □ burst in ((up)on someone or something) □ burst in (with something) □ burst in(to some place) □ burst out □ burst out (of some place) □ burst out doing something □ burst out of something □ burst out with something □ burst through something □ burst with joy

BURY

bury one's head in the sand □ bury someone or something away (some place) □ bury the hatchet □ dead and buried

BUSH

A bird in the hand is worth two in the bush. □ beat around the bush □ bush out

BUSHEL

hide one's light under a bushel

BUSINESS

(I'm just) minding my own business. □ (It's) none of your business! □ (just) taking care of business □ do a land-office business □ drum some business up □ go about one's business □ How's business? □ I'll thank you to mind your own business. □ Let's get down to business. □ mind one's own business □ Mind your own business. □ send one about one's business □ taking care of business

BUSY

(as) busy as a beaver □ (as) busy as Grand Central Station □ (Have you) been keeping busy? □ (I've) been keeping busy. □ (I've) been keeping myself busy. □ I'm busy.

BUSYBODY

I don't want to sound like a busybody, but

BUTT

butt (up) against someone or something □ butt in (on someone or something) □ butt into something □ Butt out!

BUTTER

bread and butter □ butter someone up □ look as if butter wouldn't melt in one's mouth

BUTTON

button one's lip □ button something up □ button up □ on the button

BUTTRESS

buttress something up

BUY

(Could I) buy you a drink? □ buy a pig in a poke □ buy in(to something) □ buy one's way out (of something) □ buy someone off □ buy someone or something out □ buy something □ buy something back (from someone) □ buy something for a song □ buy something sight unseen □ buy something up

BUZZ
buzz in(to some place) □ have a buzz on

BYE
(Good-bye) until then. □ Bye-bye. □ good-bye and good riddance □ Good-bye for now. □ Good-bye. □ See ya, bye-bye.

BYGONES
Let bygones be bygones.

CAKE
have one's cake and eat it too □ piece of cake □ sell like hot cakes □ That takes the cake!

CALL
call (up)on someone □ call (up)on someone (for something) □ call a spade a spade □ Call again. □ call in (to some place) □ call it a day □ call it quits □ call out (to someone) □ call someone down □ call someone in (for something) □ call someone on the carpet □ call someone or something back □ call someone or something out □ call someone or something up □ call someone over (to some place) □ call something (back) in □ call something off □ call the dogs off □ Could I call you? □ Could I have someone call you? □ Could I tell someone who's calling? □ Don't call us, we'll call you. □ Give me a call. □ I'll call back later. □ Let's call it a day. □ Thank you for calling. □ the pot calling the kettle black □ Time to call it a day. □ Time to call it a night. □ What number are you calling? □ Who's calling(, please)? □ You called?

CALM
calm down □ calm someone or something down

CAMP
break camp □ camp out

CANARY
look like the cat that swallowed the canary

CANCEL
cancel out (of something)

CANDIDLY
speaking (quite) candidly

CANDLE
burn the candle at both ends □ can't hold a candle to someone

CANOE
paddle one's own canoe

CAP
feather in one's cap □ put on one's thinking cap

CARD
Cash or credit (card)? □ in the cards □ play one's cards close to the chest □ put one's cards on the table

CARE
(I) could(n't) care less. □ (just) taking care of business □ (Would you) care for another (one)? □ (Would you) care to dance? □ (Would you) care to join us? □ (would you) care to? □ I don't care. □ See if I care! □ Take care (of yourself). □ taking care of business □ That takes care of that. □ Who cares?

CAREFUL
Be careful.

CARPET
call someone on the carpet □ get the red-carpet treatment □ give someone the red-carpet treatment □ roll out the red carpet for someone

CARRY

can't carry a tune □ carry a torch (for someone) □ carry coals to Newcastle □ carry on (about someone or something) □ carry on (with someone or something) □ carry over (to something) □ carry someone or something about □ carry someone or something away □ carry someone or something off □ carry something on □ carry something on (to something) □ carry the ball □ carry the torch □ carry the weight of the world on one's shoulders □ carry through (on something) □ carry weight (with someone) □ cash-and-carry

CART

cart someone or something off □ put the cart before the horse □ upset the apple cart

CARVE

carve something in (to something) □ carve something into something □ carve something out □ carve something out (of something) □ carve something up

CASE

case in point □ in any case □ live out of a suitcase

CASH

cash (one's chips) in □ cash in (on something) □ Cash or credit (card)? □ cash-and-carry

CAST

cast (one's) pearls before swine □ cast off (from something) □ cast someone or something off □ cast someone or something out □ cast someone or something up □ cast the first stone

CASTLES

build castles in the air

CAT

(Someone) looks like something the cat dragged in. □ Curiosity killed the cat. □ let the cat out of the bag □ Look (at) what the cat dragged in! □ look like the cat that swallowed the canary □ play cat and mouse (with someone) □ rain cats and dogs □ There's more than one way to skin a cat. □ When the cat's away the mice will play.

CATCH

(I'll) catch you later. □ (I'll) try to catch you some other time. □ catch cold □ Catch me later. □ catch on (to someone or something) □ catch on (with someone) □ catch one's death (of cold) □ catch someone off-balance □ catch someone up (on someone or something) □ catch someone up in something □ catch someone's eye □ catch up (on someone or something) □ catch up (to someone or something) □ catch up (with someone or something) □ caught in the cross fire □ caught short □ get time to catch one's breath □ I didn't (quite) catch that (last) remark. □ I didn't catch the name. □ I don't have time to catch my breath. □ What's the catch?

CAUSE

(That causes) no problem. □ cause (some) eyebrows to raise □ cause (some) tongues to wag

CAUTION

throw caution to the wind

CAVE

cave in (on someone or something) □ cave in (to someone or something)

CENTER

center something on someone or something

CENTRAL
(as) busy as Grand Central Station

CENTS
put in one's two cents (worth)

CEREMONY
Don't stand on ceremony.

CHAIN
yank someone's chain

CHAIR
Pull up a chair.

CHALK
chalk something out □ chalk something up □ chalk something up to something

CHAMP
champ at the bit

CHANCE
(There is) no chance. □ chance (up)on someone or something □ Give me a chance! □ let the chance slip by □ Not a chance!

CHANGE
(Have you) changed your mind? □ (I) changed my mind. □ (It's) time for a change. □ change horses in midstream □ change out of something □ Times are changing.

CHANNEL
go through channels

CHARGE
charge in(to some place) □ charge off □ charge out of some place □ charge someone or something up □ charge something (up) to someone or something

CHARITY
Charity begins at home.

CHARM
Charmed(, I'm sure).

CHART
chart something out (for someone or something)

CHASE
chase someone or something down □ Go chase yourself! □ lead someone on a merry chase □ wild-goose chase

CHEAT
cheat someone out of something

CHECK
check back (on someone or something) □ check back (with someone) □ check in (at something) □ check in on someone or something □ check into something □ check on someone or something □ check out □ check out (from something) □ check out (of something) □ check someone or something in □ check someone or something off □ check someone or something out □ check someone or something over □ check up (on someone or something) □ Check, please. □ honor someone's check □ make a check out (to someone or something)

CHEEK
tongue-in-cheek □ turn the other cheek

CHEER
cheer someone up □ cheer up

CHEESE
Say cheese!

CHEST
get something off one's chest □ play one's cards close to the chest □ take the spear (in one's chest)

CHEW
bite off more than one can chew □ chew something off ((of) something) □ chew something up

table □ Clear the way! □ clear up □ Do I make myself (perfectly) clear? □ out of a clear blue sky □ The coast is clear.

CLIMB
climb on the bandwagon

CLIP
clip someone's wings □ clip something on((to) someone or something) □ clip something out (of something)

CLOCK
against the clock □ clock in □ clock out □ clock someone in □ clock someone out

CLOCKWORK
(as) regular as clockwork □ go like clockwork

CLOG
clog something up □ clog up

CLOSE
close at hand □ close down □ close in (on someone or something) □ close ranks □ close someone or something down □ close someone or something up □ close someone out of something □ close something out □ close up □ have a close shave □ play one's cards close to the chest

CLOSET
come out of the closet □ skeleton in the closet

CLOTH
make something up out of whole cloth

CLOTHING
wolf in sheep's clothing

CLOUD
cloud up □ Every cloud has a silver lining. □ have one's head in the clouds □ on cloud nine □ under a cloud (of suspicion)

CLOWN
clown around (with someone)

CLUE
clue someone in (on something)

CLUTTER
clutter something up

COAL
carry coals to Newcastle □ rake someone over the coals

COAST
coast-to-coast □ The coast is clear.

COCK
cock-and-bull story

COCKLES
warm the cockles of someone's heart

COIL
coil something up

COLD
(Is it) cold enough for you? □ break out in a cold sweat □ catch cold □ catch one's death (of cold) □ get cold feet □ make someone's blood run cold □ out cold □ pour cold water on something

COLLAPSE
collapse into something □ collapse under someone or something

COLLAR
hot under the collar

COLOR
horse of another color □ off-color □ show one's (true) colors □ with flying colors

COMB
comb something out □ comb something out (of something) □ go over something with a fine-tooth comb

COME
(I'm) glad you could come. □ Come (on) in. □ come a cropper □ come about □ Come again. □ Come and

get it! □ come apart at the seams □ come around □ come away (from someone or something) □ come away empty-handed □ come back □ come back (to someone or something) □ Come back and see us. □ Come back anytime. □ Come back when you can stay longer. □ come by something □ come down in the world □ come down with something □ come home (to roost) □ come in □ Come in and make yourself at home. □ Come in and sit a spell. □ come in out of the rain □ come into one's or its own □ come of age □ come off □ come off ((of) something) □ Come off it! □ come off second-best □ come on □ come on ((to) someone or something) □ come out □ come out ahead □ come out in the wash □ come out of the closet □ come out with something □ come over □ come over (to our side) □ come over someone or something □ come over to something □ Come right in. □ come through □ come through (for someone or something) □ come through (something) □ come through (with something) □ come to □ come to a bad end □ come to a dead end □ come to a head □ come to a standstill □ come to an end □ come to an untimely end □ come to grief □ come to grips with something □ come to light □ come to one's senses □ come to pass □ come to the point □ come to think of it □ come true □ come up □ come up against someone or something □ come up in the world □ come up something □ come what may □ Coming through(, please). □ Could I come in? □ cross a bridge before one comes to it □ cross a bridge when one comes to it □ dream come

true □ easy come, easy go □ First come, first served. □ How come? □ if worst comes to worst □ Johnny-come-lately □ not know enough to come in out of the rain □ They must have seen you coming. □ This is where I came in. □ What's coming off? □ Won't you come in? □ You've got another think coming.

COMEDY
Cut the comedy!

COMFORTABLE
(as) comfortable as an old shoe

COMMISSION
out of commission

COMPLAIN
(I) can't complain.

COMPLIMENT
fish for a compliment

CON
put a con on someone

CONCERNED
(as) far as I'm concerned

CONCLUSION
jump to conclusions

CONDITION
in mint condition □ in the pink (of condition)

CONNECT
connect (up) to something

CONSPICUOUS
conspicuous by one's absence

CONSTRUCTION
under construction

CONTEMPT
Familiarity breeds contempt.

CONTENT
to one's heart's content

CONTENTION
bone of contention

CONTINUE
Could we continue this later?

CONTRACT
contract something out

CONTRARY
on the contrary

CONTROL
control the purse strings

COOK
cook out □ cook someone's goose □ cook something out □ cook something up (with someone) □ cook the accounts □ Now you're cooking (with gas)! □ Too many cooks spoil the stew. □ What's cooking?

COOKIE
shoot one's cookies □ snap one's cookies □ That's the way the cookie crumbles. □ toss one's cookies

COOL
(as) cool as a cucumber □ (Have you) been keeping cool? □ (I've) been keeping cool. □ cool down □ cool one's heels □ cool someone or something down □ I'm cool. □ play it cool

COPYCAT
be a copycat

CORK
pop one's cork

CORNER
out of the corner of one's eye

COST
cost a pretty penny □ cost an arm and a leg

COUNT
count (up)on someone or something □ count down □ count noses □ count off □ count one's chickens before they hatch □ count someone or something off □ count someone out (for something) □ count some-

thing in □ count something out □ every minute counts □ stand up and be counted

COUNTER
under the counter

COUPLE
couple up (with someone)

COURAGE
pluck up someone's courage □ screw up one's courage

COURSE
of course

COURT
throw oneself on the mercy of the court

COVER
blow someone's cover □ cover (up) for someone □ cover a lot of ground □ cover for someone □ cover someone or something up

CRACK
crack a joke □ crack a smile □ crack down (on someone or something) □ crack someone or something up □ crack up □ make cracks (about someone or something)

CRADLE
rob the cradle

CRAMP
cramp someone's style

CRASH
crash into someone or something □ crash through something

CRAZY
(as) crazy as a loon

CREAM
cream of the crop

CREDIT
Cash or credit (card)? □ give credit where credit is due

481

CREEP
creep by

CRIME
Crime doesn't pay.

CRISP
burn someone or something to a crisp

CROCODILE
After while(, crocodile). □ shed crocodile tears

CROP
cream of the crop □ crop out □ crop up

CROPPER
come a cropper

CROSS
bear one's cross □ caught in the cross fire □ cross a bridge before one comes to it □ cross a bridge when one comes to it □ cross one's heart (and hope to die) □ cross someone or something off ((of) something) □ cross someone or something out □ cross swords (with someone) □ cross-examine someone

CROUCH
crouch down

CROW
as the crow flies

CROWD
crowd in (on someone or something) □ crowd in(to some place) □ crowd together

CRUISE
time to cruise

CRUMBLE
crumble something (up) (into something) □ That's the way the cookie crumbles.

CRUMPLE
crumple someone or something up

CRUNCH
crunch someone or something up

CRUSH
crush (up) against someone or something □ crush something out □ crush something up (into something)

CRUTCH
(as) funny as a crutch

CRUX
crux of the matter

CRY
cry before one is hurt □ cry bloody murder □ cry one's eyes out □ cry over spilled milk □ cry wolf □ For crying out loud!

CUCUMBER
(as) cool as a cucumber

CUDDLE
cuddle up (to someone or something)

CUE
cue someone in

CUFF
put something on the cuff

CUP
not someone's cup of tea

CURB
step off the curb

CURE
An ounce of prevention is worth a pound of cure.

CURIOSITY
Curiosity killed the cat.

CURL
curl someone's hair □ curl something up □ curl up (in(to) something) □ curl up and die

CURVE
pitch someone a curve (ball) □ throw someone a curve

CUT

cut back (on something) □ cut class □ cut down (on something) □ cut in (on someone or something) □ cut in (with something) □ Cut it out! □ cut off □ cut off one's nose to spite one's face □ cut one's (own) throat □ cut someone or something (off) short □ cut someone or something off from something □ cut someone or something to the bone □ cut someone to the quick □ cut someone's losses □ cut something away (from something) □ cut something back □ cut something down □ cut something in(to something) □ cut something off □ cut something out □ cut something out (of something) □ Cut the comedy! □ cut the ground out from under someone □ Fish or cut bait. □ run around like a chicken with its head cut off

DAB

dab something on((to) something) □ smack-dab in the middle

DAGGER

look daggers at someone

DAM

dam something up

DAMAGE

What's the damage?

DANCE

(Would you) care to dance? □ dance to another tune □ go into one's song and dance about something □ tap dance like mad

DANDER

get someone's dander up

DANGEROUS

A little knowledge is a dangerous thing.

DARE

You wouldn't dare (to do something)!

DARKEN

go and never darken my door again

DASH

dash off □ dash out (for something) □ dash something off

DATE

date back (to someone or something) □ date back (to sometime)

DAVY

go to Davy Jones's locker

DAWN

dawn (up)on someone

DAY

(as) plain as day □ (Go ahead,) make my day! □ (I) haven't got all day. □ all in a day's work □ as different as night and day □ call it a day □ Every dog has its day. □ Have a nice day. □ in this day and age □ Let's call it a day. □ Make my day! □ one's days are numbered □ Rome wasn't built in a day. □ save something for a rainy day □ save the day □ see the light (of day) □ That'll be the day! □ Time to call it a day.

DAYLIGHT

begin to see daylight □ in broad daylight

DEAD

(as) dead as a dodo □ (as) dead as a doornail □ beat a dead horse □ come to a dead end □ dead and buried □ dead to the world □ have someone dead to rights □ in a dead heat □ leave someone for dead □ Over my dead body!

DEAF

turn a deaf ear (to something)

DEAL
deal something out □ What's the deal?

DEAR
Dear me!

DEATH
at death's door □ be death on something □ catch one's death (of cold) □ death on someone or something □ sign one's own death warrant □ You'll be the death of me (yet).

DEBT
pay one's debt (to society)

DECIDE
decide (up)on someone or something

DECK
deck someone or something out (in something)

DECLARE
I (do) declare!

DEEP
Beauty is only skin deep. □ go off the deep end □ in deep □ in deep water □ jump off the deep end (over someone or something) □ Still waters run deep.

DELIGHT
(I'm) delighted to have you (here). □ (I'm) delighted to make your acquaintance.

DELIVER
signed, sealed, and delivered

DEN
beard the lion in his den

DENT
dent something up

DEPEND
That (all) depends.

DEPOSIT
deposit something in(to) something

DEPTH
beyond one's depth

DERN
You're dern tootin'!

DESERT
desert a sinking ship

DESERTS
get one's just deserts

DESERVE
One good turn deserves another.

DESK
away from one's desk

DEVIL
for the devil of it □ give the devil his due □ Speak of the devil. □ There will be the devil to pay.

DIAMOND
diamond in the rough

DIBS
have dibs on something

DIE
cross one's heart (and hope to die) □ curl up and die □ die away □ die back □ die down □ die of a broken heart □ die of boredom □ die off □ die on someone □ die out

DIFFERENCE
(It) makes no difference to me. □ split the difference

DIFFERENT
as different as night and day □ march to a different drummer

DIG
dig down □ Dig in! □ dig in(to something) □ dig out (of something) □ dig some dirt up on someone □ dig someone or something out (of something) □ dig something in(to something) □ Dig up!

DIGGETY
Hot diggety (dog)!

DILEMMA
on the horns of a dilemma

DIM
dim out □ dim something down □ dim something up

DIME
turn on a dime

DIN
din something in(to someone)

DINE
dine in □ dine off something □ dine out

DINNER
Dinner is served.

DIP
dip in((to) something) □ dip something in((to) something)

DIRT
dig some dirt up on someone □ take a dirt nap

DIRTY
air someone's dirty linen in public □ dirty something up □ get one's hands dirty □ quick-and-dirty

DISEASE
have foot-in-mouth disease

DISH
dish something out (to someone) □ do the dishes

DISTANCE
go the distance

DIVE
dive in(to something) □ go into a nosedive

DIVIDE
divide something into something

DOCTOR
just what the doctor ordered □ You're the doctor.

DODO
(as) dead as a dodo

DOG
(as) sick as a dog □ call the dogs off □ Every dog has its day. □ hair of the dog that bit one □ Hot diggety (dog)! □ lead a dog's life □ Let sleeping dogs lie. □ rain cats and dogs □ tail wagging the dog □ You can't teach an old dog new tricks.

DOGHOUSE
in the doghouse

DOLDRUMS
in the doldrums

DOLE
dole something out (to someone)

DOLL
doll someone up □ get (all) dolled up

DOLLAR
dollar for dollar □ feel like a million (dollars) □ look like a million dollars

DOOR
at death's door □ beat a path to someone's door □ get one's foot in the door □ go and never darken my door again

DOORNAIL
(as) dead as a doornail

DOORSTEP
at someone's doorstep

DOSE
dose of one's own medicine

DOT
on the dot □ sign on the dotted line

DOUBLE
double back (on something) □ double over □ double someone or something over □ double up (on someone or something) □ double up (with someone or something)

DOUBT

(There is) no doubt about it. □ get the benefit of the doubt □ give someone the benefit of the doubt □ I doubt it. □ I doubt that. □ no doubt □ without a doubt

DOZE

doze off (to sleep)

DOZEN

six of one and half a dozen of the other

DRAG

(Someone) looks like something the cat dragged in. □ drag behind □ drag on □ drag out □ drag someone or something in(to something) □ drag someone or something off (to someone or something) □ drag someone up □ drag something behind one □ drag something out □ drag something out of someone □ Look (at) what the cat dragged in!

DRAIN

down the drain □ drain away □ drain out □ drain something away (from something) □ drain something off (from something) □ drain something out of something □ pour money down the drain

DRAW

back to the drawing board □ draw (up) alongside ((of) someone or something) □ draw a blank □ draw a line between something and something else □ draw away (from someone or something) □ draw back (from someone or something) □ draw blood □ draw near □ draw near (to someone or something) □ draw on someone or something □ draw oneself up (to something) □ draw people together □ draw someone or something in(to something)

□ draw someone or something out (of something) □ draw someone or something to(ward) someone or something □ draw someone out (on someone or something) □ draw something off (from something) □ draw something out □ draw something out (of someone) □ draw something up □ draw up

DREAM

dream about someone or something □ dream come true □ dream something up

DREDGE

dredge someone or something up

DRESS

dress (up) as someone or something □ dress someone down □ dress someone or something (up) (in something)

DRIFT

(Do you) get my drift? □ drift back (to someone or something) □ drift in(to something) □ drift off □ drift out □ drift to(ward) someone or something

DRILL

drill into something □ drill something in(to someone or something) □ What's the drill?

DRINK

(Could I) buy you a drink? □ (Could I) get you something (to drink)? □ drink something down □ drink something in □ drink something up □ drink to excess □ drink up □ Drop by for a drink (sometime). □ I'll drink to that! □ What are you drinking? □ What would you like to drink?

DRIP

drip something in(to something)

DRIVE

(as) white as the driven snow □ drive a hard bargain □ drive away □ drive down (to some place) □ drive off □ drive on □ drive out (to some place) □ drive over (to some place) □ Drive safely. □ drive someone down (to some place) □ drive someone on (to something) □ drive someone or something (away) (from some place) □ drive someone or something back □ drive someone or something off □ drive someone or something out (of something) □ drive someone up (to some place) □ drive something down □ drive something down (to some place) □ drive something up □ drive through (something) □ drive up to something

DRIZZLE

drizzle down (on someone or something)

DRONE

drone on (about someone or something)

DROP

(I'm) glad you could drop by. □ at the drop of a hat □ drop away □ drop back □ drop behind (in something) □ drop behind (someone or something) □ drop below someone or something □ drop by (some place) □ Drop by for a drink (sometime). □ drop by the wayside □ drop down □ drop in (on someone) □ drop in (to say hello) □ drop in one's tracks □ Drop in sometime. □ Drop me a line. □ Drop me a note. □ drop off □ drop out (of something) □ drop over □ drop someone a line □ drop someone or something down □ drop someone or something in(to something) □ drop someone or

something off ((at) some place) □ drop someone or something off (of something) □ drop the ball □ drop the other shoe □ Drop the subject! □ drop up (some place) □ so still you could hear a pin drop

DROWN

drown one's troubles □ drown someone or something out

DRUG

drug on the market

DRUM

drum some business up □ drum someone out of something □ drum something in(to someone) □ drum something out

DRUMMER

march to a different drummer

DRY

dry behind the ears □ dry out □ dry someone or something off □ dry something out □ dry something up □ dry up □ leave someone high and dry

DUB

dub something in

DUCK

(as) easy as duck soup □ as a duck takes to water □ duck down □ duck out (of some place) □ duck out of something □ get one's ducks in a row □ like a sitting duck □ like water off a duck's back □ lovely weather for ducks

DUE

give credit where credit is due □ give the devil his due □ in due time □ pay one's dues

DULL

All work and no play makes Jack a dull boy.

DUMB

How dumb do you think I am?

DUMP

down in the dumps

DUST

bite the dust □ dust someone or something off □ dust something out

DUTCH

go Dutch

DUTY

in the line of duty □ off duty □ on active duty □ on duty

EAR

bend someone's ear □ dry behind the ears □ get someone's ear □ go in one ear and out the other □ have one's ear to the ground □ in one ear and out the other □ lend an ear (to someone) □ make a silk purse out of a sow's ear □ play by ear □ play something by ear □ pound one's ear □ prick up one's ears □ turn a deaf ear (to something) □ walls have ears □ wet behind the ears

EARLY

Early to bed, early to rise(, makes a man healthy, wealthy, and wise). □ The early bird gets the worm.

EARN

A penny saved is a penny earned. □ earn one's keep

EARTH

move heaven and earth to do something □ on earth □ to the ends of the earth

EASE

ease away (from someone or something) □ ease back on something □ ease off □ ease off (from someone or something) □ ease off (on someone or something) □ ease someone or something out (of something) □ ease up (on someone or something)

EASILY

Don't give up too eas(il)y! □ You (always) give up too eas(il)y.

EASY

(as) easy as (apple) pie □ (as) easy as duck soup □ (It) hasn't been easy. □ Don't give up too eas(il)y! □ easy come, easy go □ Easy does it. □ free and easy □ get off easy □ I'm easy (to please). □ Take it easy. □ That's easy for you to say. □ You (always) give up too eas(il)y.

EAT

(I) hate to eat and run. □ eat (away) at someone or something □ eat (something) out of something □ eat humble pie □ eat in □ eat in(to something) □ eat like a bird □ eat like a horse □ eat one's hat □ eat one's heart out □ eat one's words □ eat out □ eat out of someone's hands □ eat someone out of house and home □ eat someone or something up □ eat something away □ eat something off ((of) something) □ eat something out □ eat up □ have one's cake and eat it too □ Let's eat. □ What's eating someone? □ When do we eat?

ECHO

echo back to something

EDGE

edge away (from someone or something) □ set someone's teeth on edge

EDGEWISE

get a word in edgewise

EEL

(as) slippery as an eel

EFFECT

or words to that effect

EFFIGY

hang someone in effigy

EGG
egg someone on □ have egg on one's face □ lay an egg □ put all one's eggs in one basket □ walk on eggs

EKE
eke something out

ELBOW
elbow (one's way) through something □ elbow someone aside □ rub elbows with someone

ELEMENT
out of one's element

ELEVEN
at the eleventh hour

ELSE
(So) what else is new? □ (Will there be) anything else? □ draw a line between something and something else □ throw someone over (for someone else) □ What else can I do for you? □ You and who else? □ You are something else (again)!

EMBLAZON
emblazon something on(to) something

EMPTY
come away empty-handed □ empty something out □ go away empty-handed

END
All's well that ends well. □ at loose ends □ at one's wit's end □ at the end of one's rope □ burn the candle at both ends □ can't see beyond the end of one's nose □ come to a bad end □ come to a dead end □ come to an end □ come to an untimely end □ end in itself □ end of the road □ end something up □ end up □ end up at something □ end up doing something □ end up somehow □ end up something □ get the

short end of the stick □ go off the deep end □ hold one's end (of the bargain) up □ jump off the deep end (over someone or something) □ make someone's hair stand on end □ meet one's end □ play both ends (against the middle) □ see the light (at the end of the tunnel) □ to the ends of the earth

ENGRAVE
engrave something (up)on something

ENJOY
Enjoy your meal.

ENLARGE
enlarge (up)on something

ENLIST
enlist someone in something

ENOUGH
(I) can't thank you enough. □ (Is it) cold enough for you? □ (Is it) hot enough for you? □ (That's) enough (of this) foolishness! □ Enough is enough! □ get up enough nerve (to do something) □ Good enough. □ I've had enough of this! □ not know enough to come in out of the rain □ That's enough for now. □ That's enough!

ENTER
enter (up)on something □ enter in something □ enter into something □ enter one's mind □ enter someone or something in((to) something)

ENTOMB
entomb someone or something in something

ENVY
green with envy

ERASE
erase something from something

ERUPT
erupt from something □ erupt into something

ESCALATE
escalate into something

EVEN
Don't even look like something! □ Don't even think about (doing) it. □ Don't even think about it (happening). □ even something off □ even something out □ even something up

EVENING
(Good) evening. □ Thank you for a lovely evening.

EVER
more than you('ll ever) know

EVERY
Every cloud has a silver lining. □ Every dog has its day. □ every living soul □ every minute counts □ hang on someone's every word □ How's every little thing? □ use every trick in the book □ with every (other) breath

EVERYTHING
(Is) everything okay? □ everything but the kitchen sink □ everything from soup to nuts □ Everything's going to be all right. □ Hold everything!

EVIL
Money is the root of all evil.

EXACT
exact something from someone

EXAMINE
cross-examine someone

EXCESS
drink to excess

EXCLUDE
exclude someone or something from something

EXCUSE
Could I be excused? □ Could you excuse us, please? □ Excuse me. □ Would you excuse me? □ You're excused.

EXEMPT
exempt someone from something

EXPAND
expand (up)on something □ expand into something □ expand something into something

EXPECT
Do you expect me to believe that? □ expecting (a child) □ You can't expect me to believe that.

EXPEDITION
go on a fishing expedition

EXPERIMENT
experiment (up)on someone or something

EXPLAIN
explain something away

EXTEND
extend across something

EYE
An eye for an eye, a tooth for a tooth. □ apple of someone's eye □ catch someone's eye □ cry one's eyes out □ feast one's eyes (on someone or something) □ get a black eye □ get stars in one's eyes □ give someone a black eye □ give someone the eye □ have an eye out (for someone or something) □ have eyes bigger than one's stomach □ have eyes in the back of one's head □ hit someone between the eyes □ hit the bull's-eye □ in one's mind's eye □ in the public eye □ in the twinkling of an eye □ one's eyes are bigger than one's stomach □ out of the corner of one's eye □ pull the wool over someone's eyes □ see eye to eye

(about something) □ turn a blind eye to someone or something □ without batting an eye

EYEBROW

cause (some) eyebrows to raise □ raise some eyebrows

FACE

(as) plain as the nose on one's face □ can't see one's hand in front of one's face □ cut off one's nose to spite one's face □ face off □ face someone down □ face the music □ face up (to someone or something) □ fall flat (on one's face) □ fly in the face of someone or something □ Get out of my face! □ have egg on one's face □ lose face □ mace someone's face □ mess someone's face up □ not show one's face □ Shut your face! □ take something at face value □ talk until one is blue in the face □ tell one to one's face

FADE

fade away into something □ fade down

FAIR

Fair to middling. □ fair-weather friend □ No fair!

FAITH

in bad faith □ take something on faith

FALL

break someone's fall □ fall (down) to something □ fall (up)on someone (to do something) □ fall apart □ fall back □ fall back on(to) someone or something □ fall behind (in something) □ fall down □ fall down on the job □ fall flat (on one's face) □ fall in □ fall in love □ fall in love (with someone or something) □ fall in(to step) □ fall in(to) line (with someone or something) □ fall in(to)

place □ fall off □ fall off ((of) something) □ fall outside something □ fall over □ fall over backwards (to do something) □ fall over someone or something □ fall short (of something) □ fall through □ fall to □ fall to pieces □ fall to someone or something □ riding for a fall

FAMILIAR

have a familiar ring

FAMILIARITY

Familiarity breeds contempt.

FAMILY

black sheep of the family □ How's the family? □ run in the family

FAN

be a fan of someone □ fan out (from some place) □ fan something out □ hit the fan

FANCY

Fancy meeting you here! □ Fancy that! □ strike someone's fancy □ tickle someone's fancy

FAR

(as) far as I know □ (as) far as I'm concerned □ as far as it goes

FARM

farm someone or something out

FAST

hard-and-fast rule □ play fast and loose (with someone or something)

FASTEN

fasten (up)on someone or something □ fasten something up

FAT

live off the fat of the land □ The fat is in the fire.

FATE

leave one to one's fate

FATTEN
fatten someone or something up (with something)

FAVOR
rule in favor of someone or something

FEAR
for fear of something

FEAST
feast one's eyes (on someone or something)

FEATHER
(as) light as a feather □ Birds of a feather flock together. □ feather in one's cap □ feather one's (own) nest □ in fine feather □ You could have knocked me over with a feather.

FEED
bite the hand that feeds one □ feed off (of) something □ feed the kitty □ I'm (really) fed up (with someone or something).

FEEL
(Are you) feeling okay? □ (I'm) feeling okay. □ feel for someone □ feel like a million (dollars) □ feel like a new person □ feel out of place □ feel out of something □ feel someone out (about someone or something) □ feel something in one's bones □ feel up to something □ have mixed feelings (about someone or something) □ How (are) you feeling?

FEET
get a load off one's feet □ get back on one's feet □ get cold feet □ get one's feet on the ground □ get one's feet wet □ get to one's feet □ have feet of clay □ let grass grow under one's feet □ on one's feet □ set one (back) on one's feet □ stand on one's own two feet □ think on one's

feet □ throw oneself at someone's feet

FELICITATIONS
Greetings and felicitations!

FELL
at one fell swoop

FELLOW
hail-fellow-well-met

FENCE
fence someone or something off (from something) □ fence something in □ mend (one's) fences

FEND
fend someone or something off

FEVER
run a fever

FEW
I have to wash a few things out. □ Win a few, lose a few.

FIDDLE
(as) fit as a fiddle □ fiddle around (with someone or something) □ play second fiddle (to someone)

FIELD
out in left field □ play the field

FIGHT
(You) can't fight city hall. □ fight (one's way) back to something □ fight (one's way) through something □ fight against someone or something □ fight back (at someone or something) □ fight one's way out of something □ fight someone or something down □ fight someone or something hammer and tongs □ fight something through (something) □ I won't give up without a fight.

FIGURE
figure on something □ figure someone or something in((to) something)

☐ figure someone or something out
☐ figure something up

FILE

file in((to) something) ☐ file out (of something) ☐ file something away

FILL

fill in (for someone or something) ☐ Fill in the blanks. ☐ fill out ☐ fill someone in (on someone or something) ☐ fill someone's shoes ☐ fill something in ☐ fill something out ☐ fill the bill ☐ fill up ☐ get one's fill of someone or something

FINAL

one final word

FIND

find for someone or something ☐ find it in one's heart (to do something) ☐ find one's or something's way somewhere ☐ Finders keepers (,losers weepers). ☐ Where will I find you?

FINE

(It) suits me (fine). ☐ (That's) fine with me. ☐ fine kettle of fish ☐ go over something with a fine-tooth comb ☐ in fine feather ☐ not to put too fine a point on it

FINGER

get one's fingers burned ☐ have one's finger in the pie ☐ lay a finger on someone or something ☐ slip through someone's fingers ☐ twist someone around one's little finger ☐ work one's fingers to the bone

FINGERTIPS

have something at one's fingertips

FINISH

finish someone or something up ☐ finish something off ☐ finish up ☐ from start to finish ☐ I'm not finished with you.

FIRE

add fuel to the fire ☐ caught in the cross fire ☐ fire (something) back at someone or something ☐ have too many irons in the fire ☐ out of the frying pan into the fire ☐ play with fire ☐ set the world on fire ☐ spread like wildfire ☐ The fat is in the fire. ☐ under fire ☐ Where there's smoke there's fire. ☐ Where's the fire?

FIRM

firm something up ☐ firm up

FIRST

cast the first stone ☐ first and foremost ☐ First come, first served. ☐ first of all ☐ first thing (in the morning) ☐ first things first ☐ get to first base (with someone or something) ☐ in the first place ☐ Ladies first. ☐ love at first sight ☐ of the first water ☐ You first.

FISH

Fish or cut bait. ☐ fine kettle of fish ☐ fish for a compliment ☐ fish someone or something out (of something) ☐ fish something up (out of something) ☐ go on a fishing expedition ☐ have other fish to fry ☐ like a fish out of water ☐ neither fish nor fowl ☐ There are plenty of other fish in the sea

FIST

hand over fist

FIT

(as) fit as a fiddle ☐ fit for a king ☐ fit in((to) something) ☐ fit like a glove ☐ fit someone or something in ((to) something) ☐ fit someone or something out (for something) ☐ fit something on((to) something) ☐ If the shoe fits, wear it.

FIVE

Give me five! □ slip someone five □ take five

FIX

fix someone or something up □ fix someone's wagon □ fix something over

FLAG

flag someone or something down

FLAME

burn with a low blue flame □ flame up □ go up in flames

FLARE

flare up □ flare up (at someone or something)

FLASH

flash back (on someone or something) □ flash in the pan □ in a flash

FLAT

(as) flat as a pancake □ fall flat (on one's face) □ flat broke □ flatten someone or something out □ in nothing flat

FLESH

flesh and blood □ flesh out □ flesh something out (with something) □ in the flesh

FLICK

flick something off □ flick something off ((of) someone or something) □ flick something on □ flicker out

FLIGHT

Have a nice flight.

FLING

fling something off (of oneself)

FLIP

flip through something

FLOAT

float a loan

FLOCK

Birds of a feather flock together. □ flock in((to) some place) □ flock together

FLOOD

flood in(to something) □ flood out (of something) □ flood someone or something out (of something)

FLOOR

This is my floor. □ walk the floor

FLOW

flow in(to something) □ flow out (of something)

FLUSH

flush something away

FLY

(I've) got to fly. □ (My,) how time flies. □ as the crow flies □ fly by □ fly in the face of someone or something □ fly in the ointment □ fly in (to something) □ fly off □ fly off the handle □ Have a nice flight. □ make the fur fly □ with flying colors

FOAM

foam at the mouth

FOB

fob someone or something off (on (to) someone)

FOG

fog over □ fog something up □ fog up

FOLD

fold something back □ fold something in(to something) □ fold something over □ fold something up □ fold up

FOLLOW

Do you follow? □ follow one's heart □ follow someone up □ follow something up □ follow through (on something) □ follow through (with something) □ tough act to follow

FOOD
food for thought

FOOL
(You) could have fooled me. □ A fool and his money are soon parted. □ fool around

FOOLISH
(That's) enough (of this) foolishness! □ penny-wise and pound-foolish

FOOT
bound hand and foot □ foot the bill □ get a load off one's feet □ get back on one's feet □ get cold feet □ get one's feet on the ground □ get one's feet wet □ get one's foot in the door □ get to one's feet □ have feet of clay □ have foot-in-mouth disease □ have the shoe on the other foot □ let grass grow under one's feet □ not set foot somewhere □ on one's feet □ put one's best foot forward □ put one's foot in one's mouth □ set foot somewhere □ set one (back) on one's feet □ stand on one's own two feet □ The shoe is on the other foot. □ think on one's feet □ throw oneself at someone's feet □ wait on someone hand and foot

FORBID
God forbid!

FORCE
force someone or something out (of something) □ force someone to the wall □ force someone's hand □ force something down □ force something through something

FOREMOST
first and foremost

FOREST
not able to see the forest for the trees

FORGET
Forget (about) it! □ forgive and forget

FORGIVE
forgive and forget

FORK
fork money out (for something) □ fork something over (to someone)

FORM
form an opinion

FORT
hold the fort

FORTH
hold forth (on someone or something)

FORTY
take forty winks

FORWARD
put one's best foot forward

FOUL
foul play

FOUR
on all fours

FOWL
neither fish nor fowl

FOX
(as) sly as a fox

FRANKLY
(speaking) (quite) frankly

FREE
(as) free as a bird □ free and easy □ free-for-all □ go scot-free

FREEDOM
give one one's freedom

FREEZE
freeze over □ freeze up

FRESH
freshen someone or something up □ get fresh (with someone)

FRET
Fret not!

too eas(il)y! □ Don't give up! □ give a good account of oneself □ give as good as one gets □ give credit where credit is due □ give in □ give in (to someone or something) □ Give it a rest! □ Give it up! □ Give me a break! □ Give me a call. □ Give me a chance! □ Give me a rest! □ Give me five! □ Give my best to someone. □ Give one an inch, and one will take a mile. □ give one one's freedom □ give one's right arm (for someone or something) □ give oneself airs □ give out □ give someone a black eye □ give someone a clean bill of health □ give someone a piece of one's mind □ give someone a ring □ give someone or something a wide berth □ give someone or something back (to someone or something) □ give someone or something up (to someone) □ give someone the benefit of the doubt □ give someone the eye □ give someone the red-carpet treatment □ give someone the runaround □ give someone the shirt off one's back □ give someone tit for tat □ give something a lick and a promise □ give something away (to someone) □ give something out □ give something over (to someone or something) □ give the bride away □ give the devil his due □ give up □ give up (on someone or something) □ give up the ghost □ I won't give up without a fight. □ Something has got to give. □ What gives? □ You (always) give up too eas(il)y.

GLAD

(I'm) (very) glad to meet you. □ (I'm) glad to hear it. □ (I'm) glad you could come. □ (I'm) glad you could drop by. □ Am I glad to see you!

GLANCE

glance back (at someone) □ glance down (at something) □ glance off ((of) someone or something) □ glance over someone or something □ glance through something

GLITTER

All that glitters is not gold.

GLORY

Glory be!

GLOVE

fit like a glove □ hand in glove (with someone) □ handle someone with kid gloves

GNAW

gnaw (away) at someone or something □ gnaw on something

GOATS

separate the sheep from the goats

GOD

act of God □ God forbid! □ God only knows! □ God willing. □ pray to the porcelain god □ worship the porcelain god

GOLD

(as) good as gold □ All that glitters is not gold. □ have a heart of gold □ worth its weight in gold

GONE

I'm gone.

GOOD

(as) good as done □ (as) good as gold □ (Good) afternoon. □ (Good) evening. □ (Good) heavens! □ (Good) morning. □ (Good) night. □ (Goodbye) until then. □ (I've) been up to no good. □ (It's been) good talking to you. □ (It's) good to be here. □ (It's) good to have you here. □ (It's) good to hear your voice. □ (It's) good to see you (again). □ Be good.

□ do someone's heart good □ give a good account of oneself □ give as good as one gets □ good-bye and good riddance □ Good-bye for now. □ Good-bye. □ Good enough. □ Good for you! □ Good grief! □ Good luck! □ have a good head on one's shoulders □ Have a good time. □ Have a good trip. □ have good vibes □ I must say good night. □ if you know what's good for you □ in good shape □ make good money □ One good turn deserves another. □ put in a good word (for someone) □ sell someone a bill of goods □ throw good money after bad □ too good to be true □ Very good. □ What's the good word? □ when I'm good and ready □ Your guess is as good as mine.

GOODNESS
(My) goodness (gracious)! □ Thank goodness!

GOOSE
cook someone's goose □ get goose bumps □ What is sauce for the goose is sauce for the gander. □ wild-goose chase

GRAB
grab on(to someone or something) □ up for grabs

GRACIOUS
(My) goodness (gracious)!

GRADE
grade someone or something down □ make the grade

GRADUATE
graduate from something

GRAIN
go against the grain

GRAND
(as) busy as Grand Central Station

GRANTED
take someone or something for granted

GRASS
let grass grow under one's feet

GRAVE
turn over in one's grave

GRAVY
ride the gravy train

GRAZE
graze on something

GREAT
Great Scott! □ make a great show of something □ set great store by someone or something

GREEN
green with envy □ have a green thumb

GREETINGS
Greetings and felicitations!

GRIEF
come to grief □ Good grief!

GRIN
grin and bear it

GRIND
grind someone down □ grind something away □ grind something down □ grind something out □ grind something up □ grind to a halt □ have an ax to grind

GRINDSTONE
put one's nose to the grindstone

GRIP
come to grips with something □ lose one's grip

GRIT
grit one's teeth

GROUND
break new ground □ cover a lot of ground □ cut the ground out from

under someone □ from the ground up □ get one's feet on the ground □ get something off (the ground) □ have one's ear to the ground □ stand one's ground

GROW
let grass grow under one's feet

GUESS
Guess what! □ I guess □ I guess (so). □ I guess not. □ Your guess is as good as mine.

GUEST
Be my guest.

GUINEA
serve as a guinea pig

GUN
beat the gun □ gun for someone □ jump the gun □ ride shotgun □ stick to one's guns

GUT
hate someone's guts

GUTTER
in the gutter

HACK
hack something down □ hack something up

HAIL
hail-fellow-well-met

HAIR
by a hair's breadth □ curl someone's hair □ get in someone's hair □ hair of the dog that bit one □ hang by a hair □ let one's hair down □ make someone's hair stand on end □ neither hide nor hair □ part someone's hair □ tear one's hair

HALE
hale and hearty

HALF
(It's) not half bad. □ at half-mast □ Half a loaf is better than none. □

one's better half □ six of one and half a dozen of the other □ You don't know the half of it.

HALFHEARTED
be halfhearted (about someone or something)

HALFWAY
meet someone halfway

HALL
(You) can't fight city hall.

HALT
grind to a halt

HAM
ham something up

HAMMER
fight someone or something hammer and tongs □ hammer (away) at someone □ hammer something down □ hammer something in(to someone) □ hammer something in (to something)

HAND
A bird in the hand is worth two in the bush. □ bite the hand that feeds one □ bound hand and foot □ can't see one's hand in front of one's face □ close at hand □ come away empty-handed □ do something by hand □ do something hands down □ eat out of someone's hands □ force someone's hand □ from hand to hand □ get one's hands dirty □ get the upper hand (on someone) □ go away empty-handed □ hand in glove (with someone) □ hand over fist □ hand over hand □ hand something down □ hand something down (to someone) □ hand something off (to someone) □ hand something out (to someone) □ have clean hands □ have one's hand in the till □ have one's hands full (with someone or something) □ have

499

one's hands tied □ have someone or something in one's hands □ live from hand to mouth □ on the other hand □ out of hand □ put one's hand to the plow □ sit on its hands □ sit on one's hands □ take the law into one's own hands □ tie someone's hands □ Time hangs heavy on someone's hands. □ wait on someone hand and foot □ wash one's hands of someone or something □ with one hand tied behind one's back

HANDLE
Can you handle it? □ fly off the handle □ handle someone with kid gloves

HANDWRITING
see the (hand)writing on the wall

HANG
get the hang of something □ hang around (some place) □ hang around with someone □ hang back (from someone or something) □ hang by a hair □ hang in the balance □ Hang in there. □ hang on □ Hang on (a minute). □ hang on (to someone or something) □ hang on someone's every word □ Hang on to your hat! □ hang out (with someone or something) □ hang someone in effigy □ hang together □ hang up □ have something hanging over one's head □ leave someone or something hanging in midair □ Time hangs heavy on someone's hands. □ You'll get the hang of it.

HAPPEN
Don't even think about it (happening). □ happen (up)on someone or something □ What happened? □ What's happening?

HAPPY
(as) happy as a clam □ (as) happy as

a lark □ (I'd be) happy to (do something). □ strike a happy medium

HARD
(as) hard as nails □ between a rock and a hard place □ Don't work too hard. □ drive a hard bargain □ hard on someone's heels □ hard-and-fast rule □ hardly have time to breathe

HARE
(as) mad as a March hare

HARP
harp on someone or something

HASH
hash something over (with someone)

HASTE
Haste makes waste.

HAT
(as) mad as a hatter □ (as) tight as Dick's hatband □ at the drop of a hat □ be old hat □ eat one's hat □ Hang on to your hat! □ pass the hat □ pull something out of a hat □ talk through one's hat □ toss one's hat into the ring □ wear more than one hat

HATBAND
(as) tight as Dick's hatband

HATCH
count one's chickens before they hatch

HATCHET
bury the hatchet

HATE
(I) hate to eat and run. □ hate someone's guts

HATTER
(as) mad as a hatter

HAUL
haul someone in □ over the long haul □ over the short haul

HAY

Make hay while the sun is shining.

HAYSTACK

like looking for a needle in a haystack

HEAD

(right) off the top of one's head □ beat one's head against the wall □ bury one's head in the sand □ can't make heads or tails (out) of someone or something □ come to a head □ get one's head above water □ go over someone's head □ go to someone's head □ have a good head on one's shoulders □ have a price on one's head □ have eyes in the back of one's head □ have one's head in the clouds □ have something hanging over one's head □ head and shoulders above someone or something □ head back (some place) □ head someone or something off □ head something up □ Heads up! □ hit the nail (right) on the head □ hold one's head up □ in over one's head □ make someone's head swim □ off the top of one's head □ on someone's head □ run around like a chicken with its head cut off □ Use your head!

HEAL

heal over □ heal up

HEALTH

Early to bed, early to rise(, makes a man healthy, wealthy, and wise). □ get a clean bill of health □ give someone a clean bill of health

HEAP

heap something (up)on someone or something □ heap something up

HEAR

(Do) you hear? □ (I'm) glad to hear it. □ (I'm) sorry to hear that. □ (I)

never heard of such a thing. □ (It's) good to hear your voice. □ have you heard? □ hear someone out □ I hear what you're saying. □ I've heard so much about you. □ so still you could hear a pin drop □ That ain't the way I heard it. □ You heard someone.

HEART

be halfhearted (about someone or something) □ break someone's heart □ cross one's heart (and hope to die) □ die of a broken heart □ do someone's heart good □ eat one's heart out □ find it in one's heart (to do something) □ follow one's heart □ from the bottom of one's heart □ get to the heart of the matter □ hale and hearty □ have a heart □ have a heart of gold □ have a heart of stone □ have a soft spot in one's heart for someone or something □ have one's heart in one's mouth □ have one's heart set on something □ lose heart □ one's heart is in one's mouth □ one's heart is set on something □ open one's heart (to someone) □ set one's heart on something □ to one's heart's content □ warm the cockles of someone's heart □ with all one's heart and soul

HEAT

heat up □ in a dead heat □ in heat

HEAVEN

(Good) heavens! □ (My) heavens! □ in seventh heaven □ move heaven and earth to do something

HEAVY

heavy into someone or something □ lay a (heavy) trip on someone □ Time hangs heavy on someone's hands. □ walk heavy

HEEL

cool one's heels □ hard on someone's heels □ on the heels of something □ set one back on one's heels □ take to one's heels □ well-heeled

HELL
(To) hell with that! □ Hell's bells (and buckets of blood)! □ like a bat out of hell □ There will be hell to pay.

HELLO
drop in (to say hello) □ Say hello to someone (for me).

HELP
(I) can't help it. □ (I) couldn't help it. □ (It) can't be helped. □ Could I help you? □ help (someone) out □ help out (with something) □ help out some place □ help someone back (to something) □ help someone off with something □ Help yourself. □ How may I help you? □ pitch in (and help) (with something)

HEN
(as) mad as a wet hen □ (as) scarce as hens' teeth

HESITATE
If there's anything you need, don't hesitate to ask.

HIDE
hide one's light under a bushel □ hide out (from someone or something) □ hide someone or something away (some place) □ neither hide nor hair

HIGH
(as) high as a kite □ act high-and-mighty □ high man on the totem pole □ leave someone high and dry

HIKE
hike something up □ take a hike

HILL
make a mountain out of a molehill □ over the hill

HINGE
hinge (up)on someone or something

HIP
shoot from the hip

HIRE
hire someone away (from someone or something)

HISTORY
go down in history □ The rest is history.

HIT
(It's) time to hit the road. □ hit (someone) like a ton of bricks □ hit (up)on someone or something □ hit a snag □ hit back (at someone or something) □ hit bottom □ hit it off (with someone) □ hit someone (up) for something □ hit someone between the eyes □ hit something off □ hit the books □ hit the bricks □ hit the bull's-eye □ hit the fan □ hit the nail (right) on the head □ hit the spot □ make a hit (with someone or something)

HOE
tough row to hoe

HOLD
can't hold a candle to someone □ Could you hold? □ Don't hold your breath. □ hold back (on something) □ Hold everything! □ hold forth (on someone or something) □ Hold it! □ hold off ((from) doing something) □ hold on □ hold one's end (of the bargain) up □ hold one's head up □ hold one's own □ hold one's peace □ hold one's tongue □ hold out □ hold out (against someone or something) □ hold out (for someone or something) □ hold out the olive branch □ hold someone or something down □ hold someone or something off □ hold someone or

something out (of something) □
hold someone or something over □
hold someone or something up □
hold something out (to someone) □
hold the fort □ Hold the wire(,
please). □ hold true □ hold up (for
someone or something) □ hold up
(on someone or something) □ Hold
your horses! □ Hold your tongue!
□ leave someone holding the bag □
not hold water

HOLE
hole in one □ hole up □ in the hole
□ money burns a hole in someone's
pocket □ out of the hole □ square
peg in a round hole

HOLLOW
hollow something out

HOME
(I've) got to go home and get my
beauty sleep. □ Charity begins at
home. □ come home (to roost) □
Come in and make yourself at home.
□ eat someone out of house and
home □ home in (on someone or
something) □ make oneself at home
□ Make yourself at home.

HONEYMOON
The honeymoon is over.

HONOR
do the honors □ honor someone's
check □ on one's honor

HOOK
get (someone) off the hook □ hook
in(to something) □ hook someone
or something up (to someone or
something) □ hook something into
something □ hook something up □
let someone off (the hook)

HOP
hop in(to something) □ Hop to it!

HOPE
(I) hope not. □ (I) hope so. □ (I)
hope to see you again (sometime). □
cross one's heart (and hope to die)
□ hope against all hope

HORIZON
on the horizon

HORN
horn in (on someone) □ lock horns
(with someone) □ on the horns of a
dilemma □ take the bull by the
horns □ toot one's own horn

HORNET
(as) mad as a hornet □ stir up a hornet's nest

HORSE
(I'd) better get on my horse. □ beat
a dead horse □ change horses in
midstream □ Don't look a gift horse
in the mouth. □ eat like a horse □
Hold your horses! □ horse of
another color □ put the cart before
the horse □ straight from the horse's
mouth □ work like a horse

HOT
(Is it) hot enough for you? □ Hot
diggety (dog)! □ hot under the collar □ sell like hot cakes □ strike
while the iron is hot

HOUR
at the eleventh hour □ on the hour

HOUSE
bring the house down □ eat someone out of house and home □ in the
doghouse □ My house is your house.
□ on the house □ Welcome to our
house.

HOWDY
Boy howdy!

HOYLE
according to Hoyle

HUDDLE
huddle (up) (together)

HUFF
in a huff

HUMBLE
eat humble pie □ in my humble opinion

HUMP
over the hump

HUNCH
hunch up

HUNGRY
(as) hungry as a bear

HUNT
hunt someone or something down □
hunt someone or something out □
hunt someone or something up □
hunt through something

HURL
hurl someone or something down

HURRY
hurry away □ hurry back (to someone or something) □ Hurry on! □
hurry someone or something in(to
something) □ hurry someone or something up □ hurry up

HURT
(It) doesn't hurt to ask. □ cry before
one is hurt

HUSH
hush someone or something up □
hush up

HYPE
hyped (up)

ICE
break the ice □ ice over □ ice something down □ ice up □ on thin ice
□ put something on ice □ skate on
thin ice □ stink on ice

IDENTIFY
identify someone or something with
someone or something

IDLE
idle something away

IMAGE
be the spit and image of someone

IMMUNIZE
immunize someone against something

IMPLANT
implant something in(to) someone or
something

IMPLICATE
implicate someone in something

IMPOSE
impose (up)on someone □ impose
something (up)on someone

IMPRESS
impress someone with someone or
something □ impress something
(up)on someone

IMPRINT
imprint something into something □
imprint something on(to) something

IMPRISON
imprison someone in something

IMPROVE
improve (up)on something

IMPROVISE
improvise on something

INCARCERATE
incarcerate someone in something

INCH
Give one an inch, and one will take a
mile. □ inch by inch □ within an
inch of one's life

INCLINE
incline toward someone or something

INCLUDE
include someone in (something)

INCORPORATE
incorporate someone or something in
(to) something

INDEED
A friend in need is a friend indeed.

INFORMATION
for your information

INJURY
add insult to injury

INNOCENT
(as) innocent as a lamb

INOCULATE
inoculate someone against something

INSCRIBE
inscribe something on(to) something

INSIDE
bottle something up (inside (someone)) □ get the inside track

INSIST
insist (up)on something

INSTILL
instill something in(to) something

INSULT
add insult to injury

INTENT
for all intents and purposes

INTEREST
in the interest of saving time

INTERVENE
intervene in something

INTRODUCE
introduce someone to someone

INTRUDE
intrude (up)on someone or something

INVEST
invest in someone or something

INVITE
invite someone in(to some place) □
invite someone out □ invite someone over (for something) □ Thank
you for inviting me.

IRON
have too many irons in the fire □
iron something out □ strike while
the iron is hot

ITCHY
have an itchy palm

IVORY
live in an ivory tower

JACK
All work and no play makes Jack a
dull boy. □ before you can say Jack
Robinson □ jack around □ jack
someone around □ jack someone or
something up □ jacked (out) □
jacked up

JAMM
jammed up

JAZZ
jazz someone or something up □
jazzed (up)

JERK
jerk someone around □ jerk something away (from someone or something) □ jerk something off ((of)
someone or something) □ jerk something out (of someone or something)
□ jerk something up

JOB
fall down on the job

JOCKEY
jockey someone or something into
position

JOHNNY
Johnny-come-lately □ Johnny-on-
the-spot

JOIN

(Would you) care to join us? □ Could I join you? □ join ((up) with someone or something) □ join up

JOINT

put someone's nose out of joint

JOKE

crack a joke

JOLT

jolt someone out of something

JONES

go to Davy Jones's locker

JOT

jot something down

JOY

burst with joy □ leap for joy

JUDGE

(as) sober as a judge

JUICE

juice something back □ stew in one's own juice

JUMP

get the jump on someone □ jump in ((to) something) □ jump off ((of) something) □ jump off the deep end (over someone or something) □ jump out of one's skin □ jump out of something □ jump over something □ jump start □ jump the gun □ jump the track □ jump to conclusions □ jump up (on someone or something)

JUST

(I was) just wondering. □ (I'm just) minding my own business. □ (I'm) (just) plugging along. □ (I'm) (just) thinking out loud. □ (I'm) just getting by. □ (I) just want(ed) to □ (It) just goes to show (you) (something). □ (just) taking care of business □ (You) (just) watch! □ get one's just deserts □ I know (just)

what you mean. □ Just a minute. □ just like that □ just off the boat □ just what the doctor ordered □ let me (just) say □ Some people (just) don't know when to quit. □ That's (just) too much! □ We were just talking about you. □ You (just) wait (and see)! □ You're (just) wasting my time.

JUT

jut out (from something) □ jut out (into something) □ jut out (over someone or something)

KEEP

(Have you) been keeping busy? □ (Have you) been keeping cool? □ (Have you) been keeping out of trouble? □ (I've) been keeping busy. □ (I've) been keeping cool. □ (I've) been keeping myself busy. □ (I've) been keeping out of trouble. □ (Someone had) better keep still about it. □ Could you keep a secret? □ earn one's keep □ Finders keepers(, losers weepers). □ I'll thank you to keep your opinions to yourself. □ What's keeping someone? □ Where (have) you been keeping yourself?

KEG

sitting on a powder keg

KETTLE

fine kettle of fish □ the pot calling the kettle black

KID

handle someone with kid gloves □ I kid you not. □ I'm not kidding. □ No kidding! □ Who do you think you're kidding? □ You wouldn't be trying to kid me, would you? □ You've got to be kidding!

KILL

Curiosity killed the cat.

KING
fit for a king

KITCHEN
everything but the kitchen sink

KITE
(as) high as a kite

KITTEN
(as) weak as a kitten

KITTY
feed the kitty

KNOCKED
You could have knocked me over with a feather.

KNOT
tie someone in knots □ tie the knot

KNOW
(as) far as I know □ (Do you) know what I'm saying? □ (Do you) know what? □ (Do you) want to know something? □ (I) wouldn't know. □ (Well,) what do you know! □ Anyone I know? □ Don't I know it! □ Don't I know you from somewhere? □ Don't you know it! □ Don't you know? □ God only knows! □ How do you know? □ How should I know? □ I don't know. □ I know (just) what you mean. □ if you know what's good for you □ in the know □ Lord knows I've tried. □ more than you('ll ever) know □ not know enough to come in out of the rain □ not know someone from Adam □ Some people (just) don't know when to quit. □ What do you know for sure? □ What do you know? □ What's (there) to know? □ Who knows? □ You don't know the half of it. □ You don't know where it's been. □ you know □ You know (what I'm saying)?

KNOWLEDGE
A little knowledge is a dangerous thing.

LACE
lace into someone or something

LADDER
at the bottom of the ladder

LADY
Ladies first.

LAG
lag behind (someone or something)

LAMB
(as) innocent as a lamb □ in two shakes of a lamb's tail

LAND
do a land-office business □ land (up)on someone or something □ live off the fat of the land

LAP
in the lap of luxury □ lap (up) against something □ lap over (something) □ lap something up □ Make a lap.

LARK
(as) happy as a lark

LAST
at the last minute □ breathe one's last □ get the last laugh □ get the last word □ He who laughs last, laughs longest. □ I didn't (quite) catch that (last) remark. □ last but not least □ last something out □ on someone's or something's last legs □ That's the last straw.

LATE
Better late than never.

LATELY
Johnny-come-lately

LATER
(I'll) catch you later. □ Catch me later. □ Could we continue this

507

later? □ I'll call back later. □ I'll see you later. □ Perhaps a little later. □ See you later, alligator.

LAUGH

Don't make me laugh! □ get the last laugh □ He who laughs last, laughs longest. □ laugh out of the other side of one's mouth □ laugh someone or something down □ laugh something off □ laugh up one's sleeve □ no laughing matter □ You make me laugh!

LAUNCH

launch (one's lunch) □ launch into something

LAW

law unto oneself □ lay down the law □ take the law into one's own hands

LAY

laid out □ lay a (heavy) trip on someone □ lay a finger on someone or something □ lay an egg □ lay down the law □ lay it on thick □ lay off ((from) something) □ lay off ((of) someone or something) □ lay over (some place) □ lay some sweet lines on someone □ lay someone away □ lay someone off (from something) □ lay something away (for someone or something) □ lay something in □ lay something out □ lay something out on someone or something □ lay something to waste □ lay something up

LEAD

All roads lead to Rome. □ blind leading the blind □ Get the lead out! □ lead a dog's life □ lead back (to some place) □ lead down to something □ lead off □ lead off (with someone or something) □ lead someone down the garden path □ lead someone on □ lead someone on

a merry chase □ lead the life of Riley □ lead up to something

LEAF

leaf out □ leaf through something □ take a leaf out of someone's book □ turn over a new leaf

LEAK

leak in(to something) □ leak out □ leak out (of something) □ leak something out

LEAN

lean back (against someone or something) □ lean over □ lean toward someone or something

LEAP

by leaps and bounds □ leap for joy

LEARN

learn something from the bottom up

LEASE

new lease on life

LEAST

last but not least

LEAVE

better left unsaid □ Could I leave a message? □ leave a bad taste in someone's mouth □ Leave it to me. □ Leave me alone! □ leave no stone unturned □ leave one to one's fate □ leave someone for dead □ leave someone high and dry □ leave someone holding the bag □ leave someone in peace □ leave someone in the lurch □ leave someone or something hanging in midair □ leave someone or something out (of something) □ leave something on □ leave something up to someone or something □ take it or leave it

LEAVING

(Are you) leaving so soon?

LEFT

better left unsaid □ out in left field

LEG

Break a leg! □ cost an arm and a leg □ have one's tail between one's legs □ not have a leg to stand on □ on someone's or something's last legs □ one's tail is between one's legs □ pay an arm and a leg (for something) □ pull someone's leg

LEGISLATE

legislate against something □ legislate for something

LEND

lend an ear (to someone) □ lend oneself or itself to something

LESS

(I) could(n't) care less. □ in less than no time □ more or less

LEVEL

level off □ level out □ level something off □ level something out □ on the level

LIBERTY

take liberties with someone or something

LICK

give something a lick and a promise

LIE

Let sleeping dogs lie. □ lie down □ lie in □ lie through one's teeth □ No lie? □ take something lying down

LIFE

(I'm) having the time of my life. □ all walks of life □ get the shock of one's life □ have the time of one's life □ in the prime of life □ lead a dog's life □ lead the life of Riley □ life of the party □ make life miserable for someone □ never in my life □ new lease on life □ Not on your

life! □ run for one's life □ Variety is the spice of life. □ Where have you been all my life? □ within an inch of one's life □ You bet your (sweet) life!

LIFT

(Could I) give you a lift? □ Could I have a lift? □ lift off □ lift something off (of) someone or something

LIGHT

(as) light as a feather □ begin to see the light □ bring something to light □ come to light □ hide one's light under a bushel □ light (up)on someone or something □ light someone or something up □ light up □ make light of something □ see the light (at the end of the tunnel) □ see the light (of day)

LIKE

(Someone) looks like something the cat dragged in. □ Don't even look like something! □ eat like a bird □ eat like a horse □ feel like a million (dollars) □ feel like a new person □ fit like a glove □ go like clockwork □ hit (someone) like a ton of bricks □ How do you like school? □ How do you like that? □ How do you like this weather? □ I don't want to sound like a busybody, but □ I would like you to meet someone. □ I'd like (for) you to meet someone. □ I'd like (to have) a word with you. □ I'd like to speak to someone (, please). □ I'm like you □ just like that □ like a bat out of hell □ like a bolt out of the blue □ like a bump on a log □ like a fish out of water □ like a sitting duck □ like a three-ring circus □ Like it or lump it! □ like looking for a needle in a haystack □ like water off a duck's back □ look like a million dollars □ look like the cat that swallowed the canary □ packed (in) like sardines □ read someone like a book □ run around like a chicken with its head cut off □ sell like hot cakes □ sleep like a log □ spread like wildfire □ tap dance like mad □ That's more like it. □ What would you like to drink? □ work like a horse

LIKELY
as likely as not □ Not likely.

LIKEWISE
Likewise(, I'm sure).

LILY
gild the lily

LIMB
out on a limb

LIMELIGHT
in the limelight

LIMIT
go the limit

LINE
draw a line between something and something else □ Drop me a line. □ drop someone a line □ Every cloud has a silver lining. □ fall in(to) line (with someone or something) □ in the line of duty □ lay some sweet lines on someone □ line someone or something up □ line someone or something up (in something) □ line up □ line up for something □ line up in(to) something □ put something on the line □ read between the lines □ run down some lines □ sign on the dotted line □ step out of line

LINEN
air someone's dirty linen in public

LINGER
linger on (after someone or something)

LINING
Every cloud has a silver lining.

LINK
link up to someone or something

LION
beard the lion in his den

LIP
button one's lip □ My lips are sealed. □ Zip (up) your lip!

LIST
on a waiting list

LISTEN
I'm listening. □ listen in (on someone or something)

LITTLE
(I'll) see you in a little while. □ a little bird told me □ A little knowledge is a dangerous thing. □ How's every little thing? □ little by little □ Perhaps a little later. □ twist someone around one's little finger

LIVE
every living soul □ I can live with that. □ live and let live □ live beyond one's means □ live by one's wits □ live from hand to mouth □ live in an ivory tower □ live off (of) someone or something □ live off the fat of the land □ live out of a suitcase □ live something down □ live through something □ live up to something □ live with something □ live within one's means □ live within something □ live without something □ Pardon me for living!

LIVEN
liven something up

LOAD
get a load off one's feet □ get a load off one's mind □ load someone or something into something □ load up (with something) □ Thanks loads.

LOAF

Half a loaf is better than none.

LOAN

float a loan

LOBBY

lobby against something □ lobby for something

LOCK

lock horns (with someone) □ lock someone or something up (somewhere) □ lock something in □ lock, stock, and barrel

LOCKER

go to Davy Jones's locker

LODGE

lodge something against someone or something

LOG

like a bump on a log □ log off □ log on □ sleep like a log

LOGGERHEADS

at loggerheads

LOINS

gird (up) one's loins

LONG

(I) haven't seen you in a long time. □ Come back when you can stay longer. □ Don't be gone (too) long. □ Don't stay away so long. □ He who laughs last, laughs longest. □ in the long run □ Long time no see. □ make a long story short □ Not by a long shot. □ not long for this world □ over the long haul

LOOK

(Someone) looks like something the cat dragged in. □ Don't even look like something! □ Don't look a gift horse in the mouth. □ I'll look you up when I'm in town. □ I'm only looking. □ like looking for a needle in a haystack □ Look (at) what the cat dragged in! □ look (up)on someone or something as something □ Look alive! □ look as if butter wouldn't melt in one's mouth □ look away (from someone or something) □ look back (at someone or something) □ look daggers at someone □ look down (at someone or something) □ look here □ look in (on someone or something) □ look into something □ look like a million dollars □ look like the cat that swallowed the canary □ Look me up when you're in town. □ look on □ look on (with someone) □ look out □ look out for someone or something □ look someone or something over □ look someone or something up □ look the other way □ look through something □ look up □ look up to someone □ Look who's here! □ Look who's talking!

LOOM

loom out of something □ loom up

LOON

(as) crazy as a loon

LOOP

throw someone for a loop

LOOSE

at loose ends □ loosen someone or something up □ loosen up □ play fast and loose (with someone or something)

LORD

lord it over someone □ Lord knows I've tried.

LOSE

Finders keepers(, losers weepers). □ Get lost! □ lose face □ lose heart □ lose one's grip □ lose one's temper □ lose one's train of thought □ lose out □ lose out (on something) □ lose out to someone or something

□ lost in thought □ make up for lost time □ Win a few, lose a few.

LOSS
cut someone's losses

LOST
Get lost! □ lost in thought □ make up for lost time

LOT
cover a lot of ground □ have a lot going (for one) □ Lots of luck! □ Thanks (a lot).

LOUD
(I'm) (just) thinking out loud. □ (I) read you loud and clear. □ Actions speak louder than words. □ For crying out loud!

LOUNGE
lounge around (some place)

LOVE
(I) love it! □ fall in love □ fall in love (with someone or something) □ love at first sight □ Not for love nor money.

LOVELY
I had a lovely time. □ I've had a lovely time. □ lovely weather for ducks □ Thank you for a lovely evening. □ Thank you for a lovely time.

LOW
burn with a low blue flame □ have a low boiling point □ low man on the totem pole □ lower one's sights □ lower one's voice □ lower the boom on someone

LUCK
(The) best of luck (to someone). □ as luck would have it □ Better luck next time. □ Good luck! □ Lots of luck! □ luck out □ out of luck □ push one's luck

LUCKY
lucky for you □ thank one's lucky stars

LUMP
get a lump in one's throat □ Like it or lump it!

LUNCH
launch (one's lunch) □ lunch out □ out to lunch □ We('ll) have to do lunch sometime.

LURCH
leave someone in the lurch

LURE
lure someone or something in(to something)

LUXURY
in the lap of luxury

LYING
take something lying down

MAC
mac out

MACE
mace someone's face

MAD
(as) mad as a hatter □ (as) mad as a hornet □ (as) mad as a March hare □ (as) mad as a wet hen □ in a mad rush □ tap dance like mad

MAIL
by return mail

MAIN
in the main □ That brings me to the (main) point. □ which brings me to the (main) point

MAN
Early to bed, early to rise(, makes a man healthy, wealthy, and wise). □ high man on the totem pole □ low man on the totem pole □ odd man out □ One man's meat is another

man's poison. □ separate the men from the boys

MANNERS
Remember your manners.

MANY
have too many irons in the fire □ How many times do I have to tell you? □ Too many cooks spoil the stew.

MAP
map something out □ throw a map

MARCH
(as) mad as a March hare □ march on □ march to a different drummer □ steal a march (on someone)

MARK
mark something down □ mark something up □ toe the mark □ wide of the mark □ X marks the spot

MARKET
drug on the market □ on the market

MASH
mash something up

MAST
at half-mast

MATCH
match up □ meet one's match □ strike a match

MATTER
(It) (really) doesn't matter to me. □ crux of the matter □ get to the heart of the matter □ no laughing matter □ What's the matter (with you)?

MAX
maxed out □ to the max

MAY
be that as it may □ come what may □ How may I help you? □ try as I may

MAYBE
I don't mean maybe! □ Maybe some other time.

MEAL
Enjoy your meal.

MEAN
(Do) you mean to say something? □ beyond one's means □ I don't mean maybe! □ I know (just) what you mean. □ live beyond one's means □ live within one's means □ You can't mean that!

MEASURE
measure something off □ measure up (to someone or something)

MEAT
One man's meat is another man's poison.

MEDICINE
dose of one's own medicine □ take one's medicine

MEDIUM
strike a happy medium

MEET
(I'm) (very) glad to meet you. □ (I'm) pleased to meet you. □ (It's) nice to meet you. □ Fancy meeting you here! □ hail-fellow-well-met □ Have you met someone? □ I believe we've met. □ I would like you to meet someone. □ I'd like (for) you to meet someone. □ meet one's end □ meet one's match □ meet someone halfway

MELLOW
mellow out

MELT
look as if butter wouldn't melt in one's mouth □ melt down □ melt in one's mouth □ melt into something □ melt something down □ melt something into something

MEN

separate the men from the boys

MEND

mend (one's) fences □ on the mend

MENTION

mention something in passing

MERCY

throw oneself on the mercy of the court

MERRY

lead someone on a merry chase

MESH

mesh together □ mesh with something

MESS

mess someone or something up □ mess someone's face up

MESSAGE

Could I leave a message? □ Could I take a message?

METAL

put the pedal to the metal

MICE

When the cat's away the mice will play.

MIDAIR

leave someone or something hanging in midair

MIDDLE

Fair to middling. □ play both ends (against the middle) □ smack-dab in the middle

MIDDLING

Fair to middling.

MIDNIGHT

burn the midnight oil

MIDSTREAM

change horses in midstream

MIGHT

act high-and-mighty □ might as well

MILE

Give one an inch, and one will take a mile. □ miss (something) by a mile

MILK

cry over spilled milk

MILL

been through the mill □ tilt at windmills

MILLION

feel like a million (dollars) □ look like a million dollars □ Thanks a million.

MILLSTONE

millstone about one's neck

MIND

(do you) mind if? □ (Have you) changed your mind? □ (I'm just) minding my own business. □ (I) changed my mind. □ (I) don't mind if I do. □ boggle someone's mind □ Do you mind? □ Don't mind me. □ enter one's mind □ get a load off one's mind □ give someone a piece of one's mind □ I'll thank you to mind your own business. □ if you don't mind □ in one's mind's eye □ in one's right mind □ It blows my mind! □ Make up your mind. □ mind one's own business □ mind one's p's and q's □ Mind your own business. □ Never mind! □ on one's mind □ out of one's mind □ Out of sight, out of mind. □ slip one's mind □ You're out of your mind!

MINE

Any friend of someone('s) (is a friend of mine). □ back to the salt mines □ Make mine something. □ Your guess is as good as mine. □ Your place or mine?

MINT

in mint condition

MINUTE
(Someone will) be with you in a minute. □ at the last minute □ every minute counts □ Hang on (a minute). □ Just a minute. □ Wait up (a minute)! □ when you get a minute

MISERABLE
make life miserable for someone

MISS
miss (something) by a mile □ miss out (on something) □ miss the point

MISSOURI
be from Missouri

MISTAKE
Make no mistake (about it)!

MIX
have mixed feelings (about someone or something) □ mix in (with someone or something) □ mix someone or something in(to something) □ mix someone up □ mix someone up with someone □ mix something up (with something)

MOLEHILL
make a mountain out of a molehill

MOMENT
on the spur of the moment □ One moment, please.

MONEY
A fool and his money are soon parted. □ fork money out (for something) □ have money to burn □ in the money □ make good money □ money burns a hole in someone's pocket □ money is no object □ Money is the root of all evil. □ money talks □ Not for love nor money. □ Not for my money. □ pour money down the drain □ Put your money where your mouth is! □ throw good money after bad □ Time is money.

MONKEY
throw a monkey wrench in the works

MONTH
(I) haven't seen you in a month of Sundays.

MOOD
in no mood to do something

MOON
ask for the moon □ once in a blue moon □ promise the moon (to someone)

MOP
mop something down □ mop something off □ mop something up (with something)

MORE
(Do) have some more. □ (I) couldn't ask for more. □ All the more reason for doing something. □ bite off more than one can chew □ Let's go somewhere where it's (more) quiet. □ more or less □ More power to you! □ more than you('ll ever) know □ Need I say more? □ No more than I have to. □ once more □ Say no more. □ That's more like it. □ There's more than one way to skin a cat. □ wear more than one hat □ What more can I do?

MORNING
(Good) morning. □ first thing (in the morning)

MOSS
A rolling stone gathers no moss.

MOTHER
tied to one's mother's apron strings

MOTION
go through the motions □ motion someone aside □ motion someone away from someone or something

MOUNT
mount up

MOUNTAIN
make a mountain out of a molehill

MOUSE
(as) poor as a church mouse □ (as) quiet as a mouse □ play cat and mouse (with someone) □ When the cat's away the mice will play.

MOUTH
(You) took the words right out of my mouth. □ born with a silver spoon in one's mouth □ by word of mouth □ Don't look a gift horse in the mouth. □ down in the mouth □ foam at the mouth □ have a big mouth □ have foot-in-mouth disease □ have one's heart in one's mouth □ laugh out of the other side of one's mouth □ leave a bad taste in someone's mouth □ live from hand to mouth □ look as if butter wouldn't melt in one's mouth □ make someone's mouth water □ melt in one's mouth □ not open one's mouth □ one's heart is in one's mouth □ put one's foot in one's mouth □ put words into someone's mouth □ Put your money where your mouth is! □ run off at the mouth □ straight from the horse's mouth □ take the words out of one's mouth

MOUTHFUL
You (really) said a mouthful.

MOVE
(I'd) better get moving. □ (I've) got to get moving. □ (I) have to be moving along. □ (You'd) better get moving. □ move away (from someone or something) □ move back (from someone or something) □ move heaven and earth to do something □ move in (for something) □ move in (on someone or something) □ move in(to something) □ move off (from someone or something) □ move on □ move on (to something) □ move on someone □ move on something □ move out (of some place) □ move someone up □ move up (in the world) □ move up (to something) □ on the move □ put the moves on someone

MOW
mow someone or something down

MUCH
(We) don't see you much around here anymore. □ I've heard so much about you. □ much ado about nothing □ Not (too) much. □ Nothing much. □ So much for that. □ take too much on □ Thank you very much. □ That's (just) too much! □ You're too much!

MUD
(as) clear as mud

MUDDLE
muddle through (something)

MULE
(as) stubborn as a mule

MULL
mull something over

MULTIPLY
multiply by something □ multiply something by something

MUM
The word is mum.

MUNCH
munch out

MUNG
mung something up

MURDER
cry bloody murder

MUSCLE
muscle in (on someone or something) □ muscle someone out (of something)

MUSHROOM
mushroom into something

MUSIC
face the music □ Stop the music!

MUST
(I) really must go. □ I must be off. □ I must say good night. □ if you must □ They must have seen you coming.

NAG
nag at someone (about someone or something)

NAIL
(as) dead as a doornail □ (as) hard as nails □ bite one's nails □ hit the nail (right) on the head □ nail something up

NAME
I didn't catch the name. □ in name only □ take names □ What was the name again?

NAP
take a dirt nap

NAPE
by the nape of the neck

NARROW
narrow something down (to people or things)

NATURE
second nature to someone

NAUSE
nause someone out

NEAR
draw near □ draw near (to someone or something)

NECK
break one's neck (to do something) □ breathe down someone's neck □ by the nape of the neck □ millstone about one's neck □ neck and neck □ pain in the neck □ risk one's neck (to do something) □ stick one's neck out □ up to one's neck (in something)

NEED
(There is) no need (to). □ A friend in need is a friend indeed. □ I need it yesterday. □ If there's anything you need, don't hesitate to ask. □ need I remind you that □ Need I say more? □ That's all someone needs. □ We need to talk about something.

NEEDLE
like looking for a needle in a haystack □ on pins and needles

NEITHER
Neither can I. □ Neither do I. □ neither fish nor fowl □ neither hide nor hair

NERVE
get on someone's nerves □ get up enough nerve (to do something) □ of all the nerve □ What (a) nerve!

NEST
feather one's (own) nest □ stir up a hornet's nest

NESTLE
nestle (up) against someone or something □ nestle down (in something)

NEVER
(I've) never been better. □ (I) never heard of such a thing. □ (I) never thought I'd see you here! □ (Well,) I never! □ A watched pot never boils. □ Better late than never. □ go and never darken my door again □ It never rains but it pours. □ never in my life □ Never mind! □ You'll never get away with it.

NEW
(So) what else is new? □ Anything new down your way? □ break new ground □ feel like a new person □

new lease on life □ ring in the New Year □ That's a new one on me! □ turn over a new leaf □ What's new with you? □ What's new? □ You can't teach an old dog new tricks.

NEWCASTLE

carry coals to Newcastle

NEWS

break the news (to someone) □ That's news to me.

NEXT

(I'll) see you next year. □ Better luck next time. □ Next question.

NICE

(I) had a nice time. □ (It's) nice to meet you. □ (It's) nice to see you. □ Have a nice day. □ Have a nice flight. □ Nice going! □ Nice place you have here. □ Nice weather we're having.

NICK

in the nick of time

NIGHT

(Good) night. □ as different as night and day □ burn the midnight oil □ I must say good night. □ I was up all night with a sick friend. □ Nighty-night. □ Time to call it a night.

NINE

on cloud nine

NIP

nip and tuck □ nip something in the bud

NOD

get the nod

NONE

(It's) none of your business! □ (It) don't bother me none. □ Half a loaf is better than none. □ none the worse for wear

NONSENSE

stuff and nonsense

NOR

neither fish nor fowl □ neither hide nor hair □ Not for love nor money.

NORMAL

under normal circumstances

NOSE

(as) plain as the nose on one's face □ (That's) no skin off my nose. □ can't see beyond the end of one's nose □ count noses □ cut off one's nose to spite one's face □ have one's nose in a book □ nose someone or something out □ poke one's nose in (to something) □ put one's nose to the grindstone □ put someone's nose out of joint □ stick one's nose in (to something) □ thumb one's nose at someone or something □ turn one's nose up at someone or something □ win by a nose

NOSEDIVE

go into a nosedive

NOTE

Drop me a note. □ strike a sour note

NOTHING

(It's) better than nothing. □ (There's) nothing to it! □ in nothing flat □ much ado about nothing □ nothing but skin and bones □ Nothing doing! □ Nothing for me, thanks. □ Nothing much. □ Nothing ventured, nothing gained. □ Think nothing of it. □ You ain't seen nothing yet!

NOTICE

sit up and take notice

NOW

(I) have to go now. □ Could I take your order (now)? □ Good-bye for now. □ Not right now, thanks. □

now then □ Now what? □ Now you're cooking (with gas)! □ Now you're talking! □ now, now □ That's enough for now.

NUISANCE
make a nuisance of oneself

NUMBER
in round numbers □ number off (by something) □ number someone off □ one's days are numbered □ one's number is up □ What number are you calling?

NURSE
nurse someone through (something)

NUT
everything from soup to nuts □ nut up

OAR
put one's oar in

OATS
sow one's wild oats

OBJECT
money is no object

ODD
for the odds to be against one □ odd man out

OFFICE
Could I see you in my office? □ do a land-office business

OIL
burn the midnight oil □ pour oil on troubled water

OINTMENT
fly in the ointment

OKAY
(Are you) doing okay? □ (Are you) feeling okay? □ (Have you) been okay? □ (I'm) doing okay. □ (I'm) feeling okay. □ (I've) been okay. □ (Is) everything okay?

OLD
(as) comfortable as an old shoe □ a chip off the old block □ be old hat □ You can't teach an old dog new tricks.

OLIVE
hold out the olive branch

ONCE
if I've told you once, I've told you a thousand times □ once and for all □ once in a blue moon □ once more

ONLY
Beauty is only skin deep. □ God only knows! □ I'm only looking. □ in name only

OPEN
be (out) in the open □ not open one's mouth □ open (out) on(to) something □ open a can of worms □ open one's heart (to someone) □ open Pandora's box □ open something up □ open something up (to someone) □ open up (to someone or something) □ open up (to someone)

OPERATE
operate on someone

OPINION
form an opinion □ I'll thank you to keep your opinions to yourself. □ in my humble opinion

ORDER
(Are you) ready to order? □ Could I take your order (now)? □ in short order □ just what the doctor ordered □ order someone in(to something) □ order something in □ out of order

OTHER
(I'll) try to catch you some other time. □ drop the other shoe □ go in one ear and out the other □ have other fish to fry □ have the shoe on

the other foot □ in one ear and out the other □ in other words □ laugh out of the other side of one's mouth □ look the other way □ Maybe some other time. □ on the other hand □ other side of the tracks □ six of one and half a dozen of the other □ The shoe is on the other foot. □ There are plenty of other fish in the sea □ turn the other cheek □ with every (other) breath

OUNCE
An ounce of prevention is worth a pound of cure.

OUT
Out of sight, out of mind. □ Out, please.

OUTSIDE
(Do) you want to step outside? □ at the outside □ fall outside something □ step outside

OVERBOARD
go overboard

OWE
I owe you one.

OWL
(as) wise as an owl

OWN
(I'm just) minding my own business. □ afraid of one's own shadow □ come into one's or its own □ cut one's (own) throat □ dose of one's own medicine □ feather one's (own) nest □ hold one's own □ I'll thank you to mind your own business. □ in a world of one's own □ mind one's own business □ Mind your own business. □ own up to someone or something □ paddle one's own canoe □ pull oneself up (by one's own bootstraps) □ sign one's own death warrant □ stand on one's own two feet □ stew in one's own juice

□ take the law into one's own hands □ toot one's own horn □ under one's own steam

OX
(as) strong as an ox

PACE
at a snail's pace □ pace something out □ put one through one's paces □ put something through its paces

PACK
pack something up (in something) □ pack up □ packed (in) like sardines □ send someone packing

PAD
pad out □ pad the bill

PADDLE
paddle one's own canoe

PAIN
pain in the ass □ pain in the neck

PAINT
paint over something □ paint something out □ paint the town red

PAIR
pair up (with someone)

PAL
pal around (with someone)

PALE
beyond the pale

PALM
have an itchy palm

PAN
flash in the pan □ out of the frying pan into the fire

PANCAKE
(as) flat as a pancake

PANDORA'S
open Pandora's box

PANTS
by the seat of one's pants

PAPER

get something down (on paper) □ put something on paper

PAR

up to par

PARADE

parade someone or something out □ rain on someone's parade

PARDON

(I) beg your pardon, but □ (I) beg your pardon. □ Pardon me for living!

PARK

park it (somewhere)

PART

A fool and his money are soon parted. □ part someone's hair

PARTY

life of the party

PASS

come to pass □ mention something in passing □ pass away □ pass go □ pass on □ pass on (to someone or something) □ pass over (someone or something) □ pass someone or something up □ pass something along (to someone) □ pass something back (to someone) □ pass something down (to someone) □ pass something out (to someone) □ pass something over (to someone) □ pass the buck □ pass the hat

PASTE

paste something up

PASTURE

put someone or something out to pasture

PATCH

patch something together (with something) □ patch something up

PATH

beat a path to someone's door □ lead someone down the garden path

PATIENCE

try someone's patience

PAUL

rob Peter to pay Paul

PAVEMENT

pound the pavement

PAY

Crime doesn't pay. □ pay an arm and a leg (for something) □ pay off □ pay one's debt (to society) □ pay one's dues □ pay someone back □ pay something back (to someone) □ pay something down □ pay something in(to something) □ pay something off □ pay something out □ pay something out (for someone or something) □ pay something out (to someone) □ pay something up □ pay the piper □ rob Peter to pay Paul □ There will be hell to pay. □ There will be the devil to pay.

PEA

(as) thick as pea soup

PEACE

hold one's peace □ leave someone in peace

PEACOCK

(as) proud as a peacock

PEAL

peal out

PEARLS

cast (one's) pearls before swine

PEDAL

put the pedal to the metal

PEEK

peek in (on someone or something)

PEEL

peel something off ((of) something)

PEER
peer in(to something) □ peer out at someone or something

PEG
square peg in a round hole

PELT
pelt down (on someone or something)

PEN
in the bullpen □ pen someone or something in (some place) □ pen someone or something up

PENCIL
pencil someone or something in

PENNY
A penny saved is a penny earned. □ cost a pretty penny □ penny-wise and pound-foolish

PEOPLE
draw people together □ narrow something down (to people or things) □ Some people (just) don't know when to quit. □ split people up

PERFECTLY
Do I make myself (perfectly) clear?

PERHAPS
Perhaps a little later.

PERISH
Perish the thought.

PERK
perk up

PERMIT
permit someone out (of something)

PERSON
feel like a new person

PERSPECTIVE
from my perspective

PET
be the teacher's pet

PETER
rob Peter to pay Paul

PHONE
talk on the big white phone □ Who's on the phone?

PICK
have a bone to pick (with someone) □ pick someone or something out (for someone or something) □ pick someone or something out (of something) □ pick someone or something up (from something) □ pick up □ pick up (after someone or something) □ pick up the tab

PICTURE
(as) pretty as a picture □ (Do you) get the picture?

PIDDLE
piddle (around)

PIE
(as) easy as (apple) pie □ eat humble pie □ have one's finger in the pie □ pie in the sky

PIECE
fall to pieces □ give someone a piece of one's mind □ piece of cake □ piece something together

PIG
buy a pig in a poke □ pig out □ serve as a guinea pig

PILE
pile in(to something) □ pile off (something) □ pile on((to) someone or something) □ pile out (of something) □ pile someone in(to something) □ pile something up □ pile up

PILLAR
from pillar to post

PILOT
pilot someone or something through (something) □ pilot something in(to

something) □ pilot something out (of something)

PIN

on pins and needles □ pin someone down (on something) □ pin something up □ so still you could hear a pin drop

PINCH

pinch something back □ take something with a pinch of salt

PINK

in the pink (of condition)

PIPE

pipe up (with something)

PIPER

pay the piper

PISS

piss someone off □ pissed (off)

PITCH

pitch a bitch □ pitch in (and help) (with something) □ pitch someone a curve (ball) □ pitch someone or something out ((of) something)

PITY

For pity('s) sake(s)! □ What a pity!

PLAIN

(as) plain as day □ (as) plain as the nose on one's face

PLAN

plan something out

PLANE

plane something down

PLAY

All work and no play makes Jack a dull boy. □ foul play □ in play □ play (up)on something □ play along (with someone or something) □ play ball (with someone) □ play both ends (against the middle) □ play by ear □ play cat and mouse (with someone) □ play fast and loose (with someone or something) □ play it cool □ play it safe □ play one's cards close to the chest □ play out □ play second fiddle (to someone) □ play someone or something up □ play something back (to someone) □ play something by ear □ play something through □ play the field □ play to the gallery □ play up to someone □ play with fire □ played (out) □ the way it plays □ When the cat's away the mice will play.

PLEASE

(I'm) pleased to meet you. □ Again(, please). □ Check, please. □ Coming through(, please). □ Could I get by, please? □ Could you excuse us, please? □ Hold the wire(, please). □ I'd like to speak to someone (, please). □ I'm easy (to please). □ If you don't see what you want, please ask (for it). □ if you please □ One moment, please. □ Out, please. □ We aim to please. □ Who's calling(, please)? □ Would you please?

PLEASURE

(I) don't believe I've had the pleasure. □ My pleasure. □ With pleasure.

PLENTY

There are plenty of other fish in the sea

PLOT

plot something out

PLOW

plow something back into something □ plow something in □ plow something under (something) □ plow through something □ put one's hand to the plow

PLUCK

pluck something off ((of) someone or

something) □ pluck something out (of something) □ pluck up someone's courage

PLUG
(I'm) (just) plugging along. □ plug away (at someone or something) □ plug something in(to something) □ plug something up

PLUMP
plump something up

PLUNGE
plunge in(to something) □ plunge something in(to someone or something)

POCKET
have someone in one's pocket □ money burns a hole in someone's pocket

POINT
case in point □ come to the point □ have a low boiling point □ miss the point □ not to put too fine a point on it □ point someone or something out □ That brings me to the (main) point. □ which brings me to the (main) point

POISON
One man's meat is another man's poison.

POKE
buy a pig in a poke □ poke fun (at someone) □ poke one's nose in(to something) □ poke out (of something) □ poke something in(to something)

POLE
be poles apart □ high man on the totem pole □ low man on the totem pole

POLISH
polish something off □ polish something up

POND
big frog in a small pond

PONDER
ponder (up)on something

POOP
poop out □ pooped (out)

POOR
(as) poor as a church mouse

POP
pop for something □ pop off □ pop one's cork □ pop out (of something) □ pop something in(to something) □ pop something on((to) something) □ pop something out (of something) □ pop the question □ pop up (some place)

PORCELAIN
pray to the porcelain god □ worship the porcelain god

PORK
pork out

POSITION
jockey someone or something into position

POSSIBLE
(as) soon as possible

POST
from pillar to post

POT
A watched pot never boils. □ go to pot □ the pot calling the kettle black

POUNCE
pounce (up)on someone or something

POUND
An ounce of prevention is worth a pound of cure. □ penny-wise and pound-foolish □ pound a beat □ pound a beer □ pound away (at

someone or something) □ pound one's ear □ pound something down □ pound the pavement

POUR

It never rains but it pours. □ pour cold water on something □ pour money down the drain □ pour oil on troubled water □ pour out (of something) □ pour something off ((of) something)

POWDER

Could I use your powder room? □ sitting on a powder keg

POWER

More power to you! □ power something up □ power up

PRACTICE

out of practice □ practice what you preach

PRAY

pray to the porcelain god

PREACH

practice what you preach

PREMIUM

at a premium

PRESENT

at the present time

PRESS

press (up)on someone or something □ press against someone or something □ press down on someone or something □ press on something □ press something against someone or something □ press something in(to something) □ press something on(to something) □ press something out (of something)

PRESUME

presume (up)on someone or something

PRETTY

(as) pretty as a picture □ cost a pretty penny □ Pretty is as pretty does.

PREVAIL

prevail (up)on someone or something (to do something)

PREVENTION

An ounce of prevention is worth a pound of cure.

PREY

prey (up)on someone or something

PRICE

have a price on one's head

PRICK

prick up one's ears

PRIME

in one's or its prime □ in the prime of life

PRINT

in print □ out of print □ print something out □ print something up

PROBLEM

(I have) no problem with that. □ (That causes) no problem. □ What's the problem?

PROMISE

give something a lick and a promise □ I promise you! □ promise the moon (to someone)

PROPORTION

blow something out of all proportion □ out of all proportion

PROUD

(as) proud as a peacock

PROVE

What does that prove?

PRUNE

prune something off ((of) something)

PRY
pry into something □ pry something off ((of) something) □ pry something up

PSYCH
psych out □ psych someone out □ psych someone up □ psyched (out) □ psyched (up)

PUBLIC
air someone's dirty linen in public □ in the public eye

PUFF
puff out □ puff someone or something up □ puff something out □ puff up (into something)

PULL
pull in(to some place) □ pull off (something) □ pull oneself up (by one's own bootstraps) □ pull out (of something) □ pull someone in(to something) □ pull someone or something up □ pull someone's leg □ pull someone's or something's teeth □ pull something down □ pull something down over someone or something □ pull something off ((of) something) □ pull something out □ pull something out of a hat □ pull something up (out of something) □ pull the rug out (from under someone) □ pull the wool over someone's eyes □ pull through (something) □ pull up (some place) □ Pull up a chair. □ pull up stakes

PUMP
pump something in(to someone or something) □ pump something out □ pump something out (of someone or something) □ pump something up □ pumped (up)

PUNCH
punch in □ punch out □ punch something out (of something) □ punch something up

PUNK
punk out

PURPOSE
for all intents and purposes

PURSE
control the purse strings □ make a silk purse out of a sow's ear

PUSH
Don't push (me)! □ push (oneself) away (from something) □ push off □ push one's luck □ push out □ push someone or something out (of something) □ push someone or something up □ push someone to the wall □ push something off on (to) someone

PUT
I'll put a stop to that. □ not to put too fine a point on it □ put a bee in someone's bonnet □ put a con on someone □ put all one's eggs in one basket □ put in a good word (for someone) □ put in one's two cents (worth) □ Put it there. □ put on □ put on airs □ put on one's thinking cap □ put one through one's paces □ put one's best foot forward □ put one's cards on the table □ put one's foot in one's mouth □ put one's hand to the plow □ put one's nose to the grindstone □ put one's oar in □ put one's shoulder to the wheel □ put oneself out □ put out □ put someone off □ put someone on □ put someone or something out to pasture □ put someone or something over □ put someone or something to bed □ put someone or something to sleep □ put someone out □ put someone through the wringer □ put someone to shame □ put someone to the test □ put someone up (for something) □ put someone's nose out of joint □ put

something across (to someone) □ put something down □ put something off (until something) □ put something on □ put something on ice □ put something on paper □ put something on the cuff □ put something on the line □ put something on the street □ put something through its paces □ put something up (for sale) □ put the cart before the horse □ put the chill on someone □ put the moves on someone □ put the pedal to the metal □ put to it □ put two and two together □ put up a (brave) front □ put words into someone's mouth □ Put your money where your mouth is! □ to put it another way

PUTZ
putz around

PUZZLE
puzzle something out

QT
on the QT

QUAFF
quaff a brew

QUARREL
quarrel (with someone) (about someone or something) □ quarrel (with someone) (over someone or something)

QUESTION
(It's) out of the question. □ Next question. □ out of the question □ pop the question

QUEUE
queue up (for something)

QUICK
(as) quick as a wink □ cut someone to the quick □ quick on the trigger □ quick on the uptake □ quick-and-dirty

QUIET
(as) quiet as a mouse □ Be quiet! □ Let's go somewhere where it's (more) quiet. □ quiet down □ quiet someone or something down

QUIT
call it quits □ quit on someone □ Some people (just) don't know when to quit.

QUITE
(speaking) (quite) frankly □ I didn't (quite) catch that (last) remark. □ I'm having quite a time □ speaking (quite) candidly □ This doesn't quite suit me.

RACE
race with someone or something □ Slow and steady wins the race.

RACK
go to rack and ruin □ rack (out) □ rack one's brain(s) □ rack something up □ racked (up)

RAFFLE
raffle something off

RAG
from rags to riches □ in rags □ rag out

RAGE
rage through something

RAGGED
run someone ragged

RAILROAD
railroad someone into something □ railroad something through (something)

RAIN
come in out of the rain □ It never rains but it pours. □ not know enough to come in out of the rain □ rain cats and dogs □ rain down on someone or something □ rain in on someone or something □ rain on

someone's parade □ rain or shine □ rain something down (on someone or something) □ rain something out □ save something for a rainy day

RAISE

cause (some) eyebrows to raise □ raise one's sights □ raise some eyebrows □ raise someone or something up □ raise up

RAKE

rake someone over the coals □ rake something in □ rake something off ((of) something) □ rake something out □ rake something out (of something) □ rake something up

RALLY

rally around someone or something

RALPH

ralph something up

RAM

ram something through (something) □ ram through something

RAMBLE

ramble on □ ramble on (about someone or something)

RANGE

range from something to something

RANK

close ranks □ rank someone (out)

RAP

rap something out (on something)

RAT

rat (on someone) □ rat around □ rat out

RATTLE

rattle around in something □ rattle something off

REACH

reach back (in)to something □ reach down □ reach in(to something) □ reach out □ reach out

(after someone or something) □ reach out into something □ reach out to someone □ reach something down

READ

(I) read you loud and clear. □ Do you read me? □ read between the lines □ read someone like a book □ read someone out (for something) □ read someone out of something □ read someone the riot act □ read something back (to someone) □ read something in((to) something) □ read something off □ read something over □ read through something □ read up (on someone or something)

READY

(Are you) ready for this? □ (Are you) ready to order? □ Anytime you are ready. □ when I'm good and ready

REAL

(I'll) see you (real) soon.

REALLY

(I) really must go. □ (It) (really) doesn't matter to me. □ I'm (really) fed up (with someone or something). □ That (really) burns me (up)! □ You (really) said a mouthful.

REAM

ream someone out

REAR

bring up the rear □ rear back □ rear up

REASON

All the more reason for doing something. □ reason something out

RECOGNIZE

How will I recognize you?

RECORD
for the record □ off the record □ record something on something

RECOUNT
recount something to someone

RECRUIT
recruit someone into something

RECUPERATE
recuperate from something

RED
get the red-carpet treatment □ give someone the red-carpet treatment □ in the red □ out of the red □ paint the town red □ roll out the red carpet for someone

REEL
reel something in □ reel something off □ reel under something

REFER
refer someone back to someone or something □ refer someone to someone or something □ refer something back (to someone or something)

REFRAIN
refrain from something

REGAIN
regain something from someone or something

REGULAR
(as) regular as clockwork

RELY
rely (up)on someone or something

REMAIN
remain up □ remain within (something)

REMARK
I didn't (quite) catch that (last) remark. □ remark (up)on someone or something

REMEMBER
Remember me to someone. □ Remember to write. □ Remember your manners.

REMIND
need I remind you that

REND
rend something from someone or something

REPORT
report back (on someone or something) □ report back (to someone or something) □ report for something

REST
Give it a rest! □ Give me a rest! □ rest (up)on something □ rest up (for something) □ rest up (from something) □ The rest is history. □ Where is the rest room?

RETALIATE
retaliate against someone or something

RETIRE
retire from something □ retire someone or something from something

RETURN
by return mail

REV
rev something up □ rev up

REVENGE
revenge oneself (up)on someone or something

REVERBERATE
reverberate through something □ reverberate with something

RHYME
run one's rhymes

RICH
from rags to riches □ strike it rich

RICOCHET
ricochet off something

RIDDANCE
good-bye and good riddance

RIDE
go along for the ride □ ride (up)on someone or something □ ride away □ ride off □ ride on □ ride roughshod over someone or something □ ride shotgun □ ride someone or something down □ ride something out □ ride the gravy train □ ride up (on someone) □ riding for a fall □ Thanks for the ride. □ thumb a ride

RIFLE
rifle through something

RIG
rig someone or something out (in something) □ rig something up

RIGHT
(I'll) be right there. □ (I'll) be right with you. □ (I) can't rightly say. □ (right) off the top of one's head □ (You) took the words right out of my mouth. □ All right(y) already! □ All right. □ Am I right? □ Come right in. □ Everything's going to be all right. □ give one's right arm (for someone or something) □ have someone dead to rights □ have the right-of-way □ hit the nail (right) on the head □ I'll get right on it. □ in one's right mind □ in the right □ Not right now, thanks. □ Right away. □ right off the bat □ sail (right) through something □ serve someone right □ step right up □ Things will work out (all right).

RILEY
lead the life of Riley

RING
give someone a ring □ have a familiar ring □ like a three-ring circus □ ring in the New Year □ ring someone back □ ring someone up

□ ring something up (on something) □ toss one's hat into the ring

RINSE
rinse someone or something down □ rinse someone or something off □ rinse something out □ rinse something out (of something)

RIOT
read someone the riot act

RIP
rip into someone or something □ rip off □ rip on someone □ rip someone or something off □ rip someone or something up □ rip something down □ rip something off ((of) someone or something) □ rip something out (of someone or something)

RIPE
when the time is ripe

RISE
Early to bed, early to rise(, makes a man healthy, wealthy, and wise). □ rise (up) against someone or something □ rise up

RISK
risk one's neck (to do something)

RIVET
rivet something on(to) something

ROAD
(It's) time to hit the road. □ All roads lead to Rome. □ end of the road

ROAR
roar something out

ROB
rob Peter to pay Paul □ rob the cradle

ROBINSON
before you can say Jack Robinson

ROCK
between a rock and a hard place □ rock the boat

ROGER

Roger (wilco).

ROLL

A rolling stone gathers no moss. □ roll about □ roll away □ roll back □ roll by □ roll down □ roll down (something) □ roll off (someone or something) □ roll on □ roll out the red carpet for someone □ roll over □ roll something away □ roll something back □ roll something down □ roll something off ((of) someone or something) □ roll something on (to something) □ roll something out □ roll something up

ROMAN

When in Rome, do as the Romans do.

ROME

All roads lead to Rome. □ Rome wasn't built in a day. □ When in Rome, do as the Romans do.

ROMP

romp through something

ROOF

go through the roof

ROOM

Could I use your powder room? □ room together □ Where is the rest room?

ROOST

come home (to roost) □ rule the roost

ROOT

Money is the root of all evil. □ root around (for something) □ root someone or something out (of something) □ root something up

ROPE

at the end of one's rope □ rope someone in(to something) □ rope someone or something up □ rope

something off □ show someone the ropes □ walk a tightrope

ROT

rot off □ rot out

ROUGH

diamond in the rough □ rough someone up □ rough something in □ rough something out □ rough something up

ROUGHSHOD

ride roughshod over someone or something

ROUND

in round numbers □ round down to something □ round someone or something up □ round something down □ round something off □ round something off (with something) □ round something out □ square peg in a round hole

ROW

get one's ducks in a row □ tough row to hoe

RUB

rub (away) at something □ rub (up) against someone or something □ rub elbows with someone □ rub off ((of) something) □ rub off on(to) someone or something □ rub someone or something down □ rub someone's fur the wrong way □ rub something away □ rub something in(to something) □ rub something off ((of) something) □ rub something out

RUG

(as) snug as a bug in a rug □ pull the rug out (from under someone)

RUIN

go to rack and ruin

RULE

hard-and-fast rule □ rule against someone or something □ rule in favor of someone or something □ rule on something □ rule someone or something out □ rule the roost

RUMMAGE

rummage through something

RUMPLE

rumple someone or something up

RUN

(I've) got to run. □ (I) hate to eat and run. □ (I) have to run along. □ (It's) time to run. □ in the long run □ make a run for it □ make someone's blood run cold □ off to a running start □ out of the running □ run a fever □ run a tight ship □ run around like a chicken with its head cut off □ run around with someone □ run away (from someone or something) □ run down □ run down some lines □ run down to someone or something □ run for one's life □ run in the family □ run in(to something) □ run into a stone wall □ run it down □ run off □ run off at the mouth □ run off with someone or something □ run on □ run one's rhymes □ run out (of something) □ run out of gas □ run out of time □ run out on someone □ run over □ run over someone or something □ run over something with someone □ run someone or something down □ run someone or something in(to something) □ run someone or something off □ run someone or something out (of something) □ run someone ragged □ run something in (to something) □ run something out (of something) □ run something up □ Run that by (me) again. □ run to seed □ Still waters run deep.

RUNAROUND

get the runaround □ give someone the runaround

RUSH

Don't rush me! □ in a mad rush □ rush in(to something) □ rush off (from some place) □ rush out (of something) □ rush someone or something in(to something) □ rush someone or something out (of something) □ rush something off (to someone or something) □ rush something through (something) □ rush through something

RUSTLE

rustle something up

SACK

sack out

SADDLE

tall in the saddle

SAFE

Drive safely. □ Have a safe trip. □ play it safe □ safe and sound

SAIL

sail (right) through something □ sail into someone or something

SAKE

For pity('s) sake(s)!

SALE

put something up (for sale)

SALT

back to the salt mines □ salt something away □ take something with a pinch of salt □ worth one's salt

SAME

(The) same to you. □ amount to the same thing (as something) □ by the same token □ I'll have the same. □ in the same boat □ in the same breath

SAND

bury one's head in the sand

SARDINES

packed (in) like sardines

SAUCE

What is sauce for the goose is sauce for the gander.

SAVE

A penny saved is a penny earned. □ in the interest of saving time □ save something for a rainy day □ save something up (for something) □ save the day □ save up for something

SAY

(Do you) know what I'm saying? □ (Do) you mean to say something? □ (I) can't rightly say. □ (I) can't say for sure. □ (I) can't say that I do. □ (I) can't say that I have. □ Anything you say. □ as I was saying □ as you say □ before you can say Jack Robinson □ better left unsaid □ Don't make me say it again! □ Don't say it! □ drop in (to say hello) □ I hear what you're saying. □ I must say good night. □ I wish I'd said that. □ let me (just) say □ Need I say more? □ on someone's say-so □ Say cheese! □ Say hello to someone (for me). □ Say no more. □ Say what? □ Say when. □ Says me! □ Says who? □ Says you! □ Smile when you say that. □ That's easy for you to say. □ That's what I say. □ Well said. □ What can I say? □ What do you say? □ What do you want me to say? □ What say? □ what would you say if? □ You (really) said a mouthful. □ You can say that again! □ You don't say. □ You know (what I'm saying)? □ You said it!

SCALE

scale something down □ tip the scales at something

SCAM

What's the scam?

SCAPEGOAT

make someone the scapegoat for something

SCARCE

(as) scarce as hens' teeth

SCARE

scare someone or something off

SCARF

scarf out □ scarf something down

SCENE

arrive (up)on the scene (of something) □ burst (up)on the scene

SCHEME

scheme against someone or something

SCHOOL

How do you like school? □ tell tales out of school

SCOOP

What's the scoop?

SCOT

go scot-free

SCOTT

Great Scott!

SCOUR

scour something off ((of) something) □ scour something out

SCOUT

scout around (for someone or something) □ scout someone or something up

SCRAPE

bow and scrape □ have a scrape (with someone or something) □ scrape by (on something) □ scrape by (something) □ scrape something away (from something) □ scrape something off ((of) someone or something) □ scrape something out □ scrape something out (of something) □ scrape the bottom of the barrel □ scrape through (something)

SCRATCH

make something from scratch ☐ not up to scratch ☐ scratch someone or something out ☐ scratch someone or something up ☐ scratch the surface ☐ start from scratch

SCREEN

screen someone or something out (of something)

SCREW

screw around ☐ screw someone over ☐ screw something down ☐ screw up ☐ screw up one's courage

SCRUB

scrub someone or something down ☐ scrub someone or something off ☐ scrub something off ((of) something) ☐ scrub something out ☐ scrub something out (of something) ☐ scrub up

SEA

at sea (about something) ☐ There are plenty of other fish in the sea

SEAL

My lips are sealed. ☐ seal something off (from someone or something) ☐ signed, sealed, and delivered

SEAM

burst at the seams ☐ come apart at the seams

SEASON

in season ☐ out of season

SEAT

(Is) this (seat) taken? ☐ by the seat of one's pants

SECOND

come off second-best ☐ get one's second wind ☐ get second thoughts about someone or something ☐ in one's second childhood ☐ on second thought ☐ play second fiddle (to someone) ☐ second nature to someone

SECRET

Could you keep a secret?

SEE

(I'll) be seeing you. ☐ (I'll) see you (real) soon. ☐ (I'll) see you in a little while. ☐ (I'll) see you next year. ☐ (I'll) see you then. ☐ (I'll) see you tomorrow. ☐ (I've) seen better. ☐ (I've) seen worse. ☐ (I) haven't seen you in a long time. ☐ (I) haven't seen you in a month of Sundays. ☐ (I) hope to see you again (sometime). ☐ (I) never thought I'd see you here! ☐ (It's) good to see you (again). ☐ (It's) nice to see you. ☐ (We) don't see you much around here anymore. ☐ Am I glad to see you! ☐ as I see it ☐ begin to see daylight ☐ begin to see the light ☐ buy something sight unseen ☐ can't see beyond the end of one's nose ☐ can't see one's hand in front of one's face ☐ Come back and see us. ☐ Could I see you again? ☐ Could I see you in my office? ☐ Haven't I seen you somewhere before? ☐ I'll see you later. ☐ If you don't see what you want, please ask (for it). ☐ Long time no see. ☐ not able to see the forest for the trees ☐ Not if I see you sooner. ☐ see eye to eye (about something) ☐ See if I care! ☐ see someone off ☐ see something through ☐ see the (hand)writing on the wall ☐ see the light (at the end of the tunnel) ☐ see the light (of day) ☐ see through someone or something ☐ see to someone or something ☐ See ya! ☐ See ya, bye-bye. ☐ See you around. ☐ See you later, alligator. ☐ They must have seen you coming. ☐ wait-and-see attitude ☐ Will I see you again? ☐ You (just) wait (and see)! ☐ You ain't seen nothing yet!

SEED
run to seed

SEEP
seep in(to something) □ seep out (of something) □ seep through something

SEIZE
seize (up)on something □ seize onto someone or something □ seize up

SELL
sell like hot cakes □ sell out (to someone) □ sell someone a bill of goods □ sell someone or something out □ sell someone or something short □ sell something off

SEND
send away (for something) □ send for someone or something □ send off for something □ send one about one's business □ send out (for someone or something) □ send someone in for someone □ send someone in (to something) □ send someone off (to something) □ send someone out (for someone or something) □ send someone over ((to) some place) □ send someone packing □ send someone to the showers □ send something by something □ send something off (to someone or something)

SENSE
come to one's senses

SEPARATE
separate something out (of something) □ separate the men from the boys □ separate the sheep from the goats

SERVE
Dinner is served. □ First come, first served. □ serve as a guinea pig □ serve someone right □ serve something up □ serve under someone or something

SERVICE
out of service

SET
have one's heart set on something □ not set foot somewhere □ one's heart is set on something □ set foot somewhere □ set great store by someone or something □ set in □ set off (for something) □ set off on something □ set one (back) on one's feet □ set one back on one's heels □ set one's heart on something □ set one's sights on something □ set out (on something) □ set out to do something □ set someone down (on(to) something) □ set someone off □ set someone or something up □ set someone or something up (for something) □ set someone's teeth on edge □ set something (up)on something □ set something down (on something) □ set something down to something □ set something in(to something) □ set something off □ set the world on fire

SETTLE
settle down □ settle down somewhere □ settle in(to something) □ settle someone down

SEVEN
at sixes and sevens □ in seventh heaven

SEW
get something sewed up

SHADOW
afraid of one's own shadow

SHAG
shag (off)

SHAKE
in two shakes of a lamb's tail □ Let's shake on it. □ shake in one's boots □ Shake it (up)! □ shake some-

thing out □ shake something up □
What's shakin' (bacon)?

SHAME
For shame! □ put someone to shame
□ Shame on you! □ The shame of
it (all)!

SHANK
shank it

SHAPE
in bad shape □ in good shape □
shape someone up □ shape up □
Shape up or ship out.

SHAVE
have a close shave

SHED
shed crocodile tears

SHEEP
black sheep of the family □ separate
the sheep from the goats □ wolf in
sheep's clothing

SHIFT
shift out of something

SHINE
Make hay while the sun is shining.
□ rain or shine □ shine out □
shine something (up)on someone or
something □ shine something up □
shine through (something) □ shine
up to someone

SHIP
desert a sinking ship □ Don't give
up the ship! □ run a tight ship □
Shape up or ship out.

SHIRT
give someone the shirt off one's back

SHOCK
get the shock of one's life

SHOE
(as) comfortable as an old shoe □
drop the other shoe □ fill someone's
shoes □ have the shoe on the other

foot □ If the shoe fits, wear it. □
The shoe is on the other foot.

SHOESTRING
get along (on a shoestring)

SHOOT
shoot from the hip □ shoot in(to
something) □ shoot one's cookies □
shoot out □ shoot the bull □ shoot
up □ Shoot! □ Sure as shooting!

SHOP
bull in a china shop □ talk shop

SHORT
caught short □ cut someone or
something (off) short □ fall short
(of something) □ get the short end
of the stick □ in short order □ in
short supply □ make a long story
short □ make short work of someone or something □ over the short
haul □ sell someone or something
short □ short out

SHOT
Not by a long shot. □ shot down □
shot in the arm

SHOTGUN
ride shotgun

SHOULDER
carry the weight of the world on
one's shoulders □ have a chip on
one's shoulder □ have a good head
on one's shoulders □ head and
shoulders above someone or something □ on someone's shoulders □
put one's shoulder to the wheel □
straight from the shoulder

SHOUT
all over but the shouting □ shout
someone down

SHOVE
(I) have to shove off. □ shove off
(for something)

SHOW

(It) just goes to show (you) (something). □ make a great show of something □ not show one's face □ show off (to someone) □ show one's (true) colors □ show someone around (something) □ show someone or something off (to someone) □ show someone out (of something) □ show someone the ropes □ show someone through (something)

SHOWER

send someone to the showers

SHRINK

shrink up

SHRIVEL

shrivel up

SHRUG

shrug something off

SHUT

shut off □ shut someone or something down □ shut someone up □ shut up □ Shut up about it. □ Shut your face!

SHY

shy away (from someone or something)

SICK

(as) sick as a dog □ I was up all night with a sick friend.

SIDE

be a thorn in someone's side □ choose up sides □ come over (to our side) □ drop by the wayside □ get up on the wrong side of the bed □ laugh out of the other side of one's mouth □ other side of the tracks

SIFT

sift something out (of something)

SIGHT

buy something sight unseen □ love at first sight □ lower one's sights □ Out of sight, out of mind. □ raise one's sights □ set one's sights on something

SIGN

sign in □ sign off □ sign off on something □ sign on □ sign on the dotted line □ sign one's own death warrant □ sign out □ sign someone or something in □ sign someone or something out (of some place) □ sign someone up (for something) □ sign someone up (with someone or something) □ sign something away □ sign something over (to someone) □ sign up (for something) □ signed, sealed, and delivered

SILK

make a silk purse out of a sow's ear

SILVER

born with a silver spoon in one's mouth □ Every cloud has a silver lining.

SINCE

Since when?

SING

sing out □ sing something out

SINGLE

single someone or something out (for something)

SINK

desert a sinking ship □ everything but the kitchen sink □ sink back (into something) □ sink down □ sink in (to someone or something) □ sink one's teeth into something □ sink or swim □ sink something in ((to) someone or something)

SIPHON

siphon something off (from something)

SIREE

No siree(, Bob)! □ Yes siree(, Bob)!

SIT

Come in and sit a spell. □ Do sit down. □ like a sitting duck □ sit (something) out □ sit around □ sit back □ sit down □ sit in (for someone) □ sit in (on something) □ sit on its hands □ sit on one's hands □ sit out □ sit through something □ sit tight □ sit up □ sit up and take notice □ sit up with someone □ sitting on a powder keg

SIX

at sixes and sevens □ six of one and half a dozen of the other

SIZE

size someone or something up □ That's about the size of it.

SKATE

skate on thin ice

SKELETON

skeleton in the closet

SKIM

skim through something

SKIN

(That's) no skin off my nose. □ Beauty is only skin deep. □ by the skin of one's teeth □ get under someone's skin □ jump out of one's skin □ no skin off someone's teeth □ nothing but skin and bones □ Skin me! □ There's more than one way to skin a cat.

SKIP

Skip it! □ skip over someone or something

SKULL

get something through someone's thick skull

SKY

out of a clear blue sky □ pie in the sky

SLACK

slack off

SLAM

slam some beers

SLAP

slap something on □ slap something on(to someone or something) □ slap something together

SLATE

start (off) with a clean slate

SLEEP

(I've) got to go home and get my beauty sleep. □ doze off (to sleep) □ Let sleeping dogs lie. □ not sleep a wink □ put someone or something to sleep □ sleep in □ sleep like a log □ sleep on something □ sleep something off □ sleep through something

SLEEVE

laugh up one's sleeve

SLICE

slice in(to something) □ slice something off □ slice through something

SLIDE

let something slide □ slide out of something □ slide something in(to something) □ slide something out (of something)

SLIM

slim down □ slim someone down

SLIP

let something slip by □ let the chance slip by □ slip in(to something) □ slip of the tongue □ slip off ((of) someone or something) □ slip off (to some place) □ slip one's mind □ slip out (of something) □ slip someone five □ slip something off □ slip something on □ slip through someone's fingers □ slip up

SLIPPERY
(as) slippery as an eel

SLOUCH
slouch down □ slouch over

SLOW
Slow and steady wins the race. □ slow down □ slow someone or something down □ slow up

SLUMP
slump over

SLY
(as) sly as a fox

SMACK
smack-dab in the middle

SMALL
big frog in a small pond

SMASH
smash into something □ smash out of something □ smash something in □ smash something up □ smash through something

SMILE
crack a smile □ Smile when you say that.

SMOKE
Where there's smoke there's fire.

SMOOTH
smooth something down □ smooth something out

SNAG
hit a snag

SNAIL
at a snail's pace

SNAP
snap back (after something) □ snap back (at someone) □ Snap it up! □ snap one's cookies □ Snap to it!

SNAPPY
Make it snappy!

SNEAK
sneak in(to some place) □ sneak out

(of some place) □ sneak up on someone or something

SNIT
in a snit

SNOOP
snoop around (something)

SNOW
(as) white as the driven snow □ snow someone or something in

SNUFF
snuff it

SNUG
(as) snug as a bug in a rug

SO
(Are you) leaving so soon? □ (I'm) afraid so. □ (I) hope so. □ (So) what else is new? □ Don't stay away so long. □ I guess (so). □ I've heard so much about you. □ Is that so? □ on someone's say-so □ So (what)? □ So do I. □ So much for that. □ so still you could hear a pin drop □ What makes you think so?

SOAK
soak in(to something) □ soak something off ((of) something) □ soak something out (of something) □ soak through something

SOAP
soap someone or something down

SOBER
(as) sober as a judge □ sober someone up □ sober up

SOCIETY
pay one's debt (to society)

SOCK
Stuff a sock in it!

SOFT
(as) soft as a baby's bottom □ have a soft spot in one's heart for someone or something

539

SOMEHOW
end up somehow

SONG
buy something for a song □ go into one's song and dance about something

SOON
(Are you) leaving so soon? □ (as) soon as possible □ (I'll) see you (real) soon. □ (I'll) talk to you soon. □ A fool and his money are soon parted. □ Don't speak too soon. □ I spoke too soon. □ Not if I see you sooner. □ Sooner than you think. □ The sooner the better. □ Yesterday wouldn't be too soon.

SORRY
(Are you) sorry you asked? □ (I'm) sorry to hear that. □ (I'm) sorry you asked (that). □ (I'm) sorry. □ Sorry (that) I asked. □ You'll be sorry you asked.

SORT
in bad sorts □ out of sorts □ Sort of. □ sort something out

SOUL
Don't tell a soul. □ every living soul □ with all one's heart and soul

SOUND
I don't want to sound like a busybody, but □ safe and sound □ sound off □ sound off (about something)

SOUP
(as) easy as duck soup □ (as) thick as pea soup □ everything from soup to nuts □ Soup's on!

SOUR
strike a sour note

SOW
make a silk purse out of a sow's ear □ sow one's wild oats

SPACE
space someone out □ spaced (out)

SPADE
call a spade a spade

SPARE
have something to spare □ in one's spare time

SPAZ
have a spaz □ spaz around □ spaz out

SPEAK
(speaking) (quite) frankly □ Actions speak louder than words. □ as we speak □ Could I speak to someone? □ Don't speak too soon. □ I'd like to speak to someone(, please). □ Speak of the devil. □ speak out □ speak out (about someone or something) □ speak out (against someone or something) □ speak up □ speak up for someone or something □ speaking (quite) candidly □ With whom do you wish to speak?

SPEAR
take the spear (in one's chest)

SPEECHLESS
I'm speechless.

SPEED
speed someone or something up □ speed up

SPELL
Come in and sit a spell. □ Do I have to spell it out (for you)?

SPEND
Don't spend it all in one place.

SPICE
spice something up □ Variety is the spice of life.

SPIFFED
spiffed out □ spiffed up

SPILL
cry over spilled milk

SPIN
go into a tailspin □ spin off

SPIT
be the spit and image of someone

SPITE
cut off one's nose to spite one's face

SPLASH
splash down

SPLIT
(I've) got to split. □ split off (from something) □ split people up □ split someone or something up (into something) □ split something off ((of) something) □ split the difference

SPOIL
To the victors belong the spoils. □ Too many cooks spoil the stew.

SPOKE
I spoke out of turn. □ I spoke too soon.

SPONGE
sponge someone or something down □ sponge something away

SPOON
born with a silver spoon in one's mouth

SPOT
have a soft spot in one's heart for someone or something □ hit the spot □ in a (tight) spot □ Johnny-on-the-spot □ on the spot □ spot someone (something) □ X marks the spot

SPOTLIGHT
steal the spotlight

SPREAD
spread like wildfire □ spread oneself too thin □ spread out □ spread something on(to something) □ spread something out

SPRING
no spring chicken □ spring for something □ spring up

SPRUCE
spruce someone or something up

SPUR
on the spur of the moment

SQUARE
square peg in a round hole

SQUASH
squash something down

SQUEAK
squeak by (someone or something) □ squeak something through □ squeak through (something)

SQUEEZE
squeeze (themselves) up □ squeeze someone or something up

SQUIFF
squiff out

SQUIRM
squirm out (of something)

STAB
stab someone in the back

STACK
stack something up □ stack up

STAG
go stag

STAGE
at this stage (of the game)

STAKE
burn someone at the stake □ pull up stakes □ stake someone out (on someone) □ stake something off

STALK
stalk in(to some place) □ stalk out of some place

STALL
stall someone or something off

STAMMER

stammer something out

STAMPEDE

stampede out of some place

STAND

Don't stand on ceremony. □ make someone's hair stand on end □ not have a leg to stand on □ stand around □ stand aside □ stand back (from someone or something) □ stand by □ stand down □ stand in (for someone) □ stand on one's own two feet □ stand one's ground □ stand out (from someone or something) □ stand up □ stand up against someone or something □ stand up and be counted □ take the stand

STANDSTILL

come to a standstill

STAR

get stars in one's eyes □ thank one's lucky stars

STARE

stare someone down

START

from start to finish □ jump start □ off to a running start □ start (off) with a clean slate □ start from scratch □ start off □ start off (by doing something) □ start off (on something) □ start out □ start out as something □ start over □ start someone off (on something) □ start something up □ start up

STATION

(as) busy as Grand Central Station

STAY

Come back when you can stay longer. □ Don't stay away so long. □ stay away (from someone or something) □ stay back (from some-

thing) □ stay out (of something) □ stay up (for something)

STEADY

Slow and steady wins the race.

STEAL

steal a base □ steal a march (on someone) □ steal away □ steal someone's thunder □ steal the spotlight

STEAM

let off steam □ steam someone's beam □ steam something off ((of) something) □ steam something out (of something) □ steam something up □ steam up □ steamed (up) □ under one's own steam

STEM

from stem to stern

STEP

(Do) you want to step outside? □ at someone's doorstep □ fall in(to step) □ step aside □ step back (from someone or something) □ step off the curb □ step on someone's toes □ step on the gas □ step out (of something) □ step out (on someone) □ step out into something □ step out of line □ step outside □ step over (to) some place □ step right up □ step something up □ step up □ step up to something

STERN

from stem to stern

STEW

stew in one's own juice □ Too many cooks spoil the stew.

STICK

get the short end of the stick □ have one's words stick in one's throat □ one's words stick in one's throat □ stick around □ stick one's neck out □ stick one's nose in(to something)

☐ stick out ☐ stick out (from someone or something) ☐ stick out (of someone or something) ☐ stick someone or something up ☐ stick something down ☐ stick something in(to someone or something) ☐ stick something out ☐ stick to one's guns ☐ stick together ☐ Stick with it.

STILL

(Someone had) better keep still about it. ☐ so still you could hear a pin drop ☐ Still waters run deep.

STINK

stink on ice

STIR

stir someone or something up ☐ stir up a hornet's nest

STITCH

stitch something up

STOCK

have something in stock ☐ in stock ☐ lock, stock, and barrel ☐ stock up (on something)

STOKE

stoked (on someone or something) ☐ stoked out

STOMACH

have eyes bigger than one's stomach ☐ one's eyes are bigger than one's stomach ☐ turn someone's stomach

STONE

A rolling stone gathers no moss. ☐ a stone's throw away ☐ cast the first stone ☐ have a heart of stone ☐ leave no stone unturned ☐ millstone about one's neck ☐ run into a stone wall ☐ stoned (out)

STOOD

should have stood in bed

STOOP

stoop down ☐ stoop over

STOP

I'll put a stop to that. ☐ stop by (some place) ☐ stop in (some place) ☐ stop over (some place) ☐ stop something up (with something) ☐ Stop the music! ☐ stop up

STORE

set great store by someone or something

STORM

storm in(to some place) ☐ storm out (of some place) ☐ take someone or something by storm

STORY

cock-and-bull story ☐ make a long story short

STRAIGHT

get something straight ☐ straight from the horse's mouth ☐ straight from the shoulder ☐ vote a straight ticket

STRAIGHTEN

straighten out ☐ straighten someone or something out ☐ straighten something up ☐ straighten up

STRAW

That's the last straw.

STREAK

talk a blue streak

STREAM

change horses in midstream ☐ stream down (on someone or something) ☐ stream in(to something)

STREET

put something on the street

STRESS

no stress

STRETCH

stretch out ☐ stretch someone or

something out □ stretch something out (to someone or something)

STRIDE
take something in stride

STRIKE
be out (on strike) □ get two strikes against one □ go (out) on strike □ it strikes me that □ strike a happy medium □ strike a match □ strike a sour note □ strike back (at someone or something) □ strike for something □ strike it rich □ strike out □ strike out (at someone or something) □ strike someone funny □ strike someone's fancy □ strike something down □ strike up a friendship □ strike while the iron is hot

STRING
control the purse strings □ string someone along □ tied to one's mother's apron strings □ with no strings attached

STRIP
strip down

STRONG
(as) strong as an ox

STRUGGLE
struggle through (something)

STUBBORN
(as) stubborn as a mule

STUFF
Stuff a sock in it! □ stuff and nonsense □ stuff the ballot box □ That's the stuff!

STUMBLE
stumble through something

STUMP
(You've) got me stumped.

STYLE
cramp someone's style

SUBJECT
Drop the subject!

SUBSIST
subsist on something

SUCCUMB
succumb to something

SUCH
(I) never heard of such a thing. □ as such

SUCK
suck something up

SUDS
in the suds

SUIT
(It) suits me (fine). □ in one's birthday suit □ suit someone to a T □ Suit yourself. □ This doesn't quite suit me.

SUITCASE
live out of a suitcase

SUITE
Tout suite!

SUM
sum something up □ sum up

SUN
Make hay while the sun is shining.

SUNDAYS
(I) haven't seen you in a month of Sundays.

SUPPLY
in short supply

SUPPOSE
(It's) not supposed to. □ (Someone or something is) supposed to. □ Suppose I do? □ Suppose I don't? □ supposing

SURE
(I) can't say for sure. □ Charmed (, I'm sure). □ Don't be too sure. □ For sure. □ Likewise(, I'm sure).

□ Oh, sure (someone or something will)! □ Sure as shooting! □ Sure thing. □ Sure. □ What do you know for sure?

SURFACE
scratch the surface

SURGE
surge in(to something) □ surge out (of something) □ surge up

SURPRISE
I'm not surprised.

SUSPICION
under a cloud (of suspicion)

SWALLOW
look like the cat that swallowed the canary □ swallow someone or something up □ swallow something down

SWEAR
swear at someone or something □ swear by someone or something □ swear someone in (as something)

SWEAT
break out in a cold sweat □ by the sweat of one's brow □ Don't sweat it! □ no sweat

SWEEP
sweep something off ((of) something) □ sweep something out □ sweep something up □ sweep up

SWEET
have a sweet tooth □ lay some sweet lines on someone □ take the bitter with the sweet □ You bet your (sweet) life!

SWELL
swell up

SWIM
make someone's head swim □ sink or swim □ swim against the tide

SWINE
cast (one's) pearls before swine

SWING
get into the swing of things □ in full swing

SWISH
swish something off ((of) someone or something)

SWITCH
asleep at the switch □ switch back (to something) □ switch off □ switch someone or something off □ switch something back (to something) □ switch something on

SWOOP
at one fell swoop □ swoop down (up)on someone or something

SWORD
cross swords (with someone)

SYSTEM
All systems are go.

TAB
pick up the tab

TABLE
clear the table □ put one's cards on the table □ under the table

TACK
get down to brass tacks

TAIL
can't make heads or tails (out) of someone or something □ Get off my tail! □ have one's tail between one's legs □ in two shakes of a lamb's tail □ one's tail is between one's legs □ tail wagging the dog

TAILSPIN
go into a tailspin

TAKE
(I've) got to take off. □ (Is) this (seat) taken? □ (just) taking care of business □ (You) can't take it with you. □ (You) took the words right out of my mouth. □ as a duck takes to water □ Could I take a message?

□ Could I take your order (now)? □ Give one an inch, and one will take a mile. □ sit up and take notice □ take a backseat (to someone) □ take a dirt nap □ take a hike □ take a leaf out of someone's book □ Take care (of yourself). □ take five □ take forty winks □ Take it easy. □ take it or leave it □ take liberties with someone or something □ Take my word for it. □ take names □ take off □ take off from something □ take one's medicine □ take out after someone or something □ take over (from someone) □ take someone in □ take someone or something away □ take someone or something by storm □ take someone or something for granted □ take someone or something off (something) □ take someone or something on □ take someone or something out □ take someone or something out (of something) □ take someone under one's wing(s) □ take someone's breath away □ take something apart □ take something at face value □ take something down (in something) □ take something in □ take something in stride □ take something lying down □ take something off □ take something on faith □ take something on the chin □ take something over □ take something up □ take something with a pinch of salt □ take the bitter with the sweet □ take the bull by the horns □ take the law into one's own hands □ take the spear (in one's chest) □ take the stand □ take the words out of one's mouth □ take to one's heels □ take too much on □ take up one's abode somewhere □ taking care of business □ That takes care of that. □ That takes the cake!

TALE
tell tales out of school

TALK
(I'll) talk to you soon. □ (It's been) good talking to you. □ Let's talk (about it). □ Look who's talking! □ money talks □ Now you're talking! □ talk a blue streak □ talk around something □ talk back (to someone) □ talk down to someone □ talk in circles □ talk on the big white phone □ talk oneself out □ talk shop □ talk someone into something □ talk something out □ talk something up □ talk through one's hat □ talk until one is blue in the face □ We need to talk about something. □ We were just talking about you. □ Who do you think you're talking to? □ Who do you want (to talk to)?

TALL
tall in the saddle □ walk tall

TALLY
tally something up

TAP
tap dance like mad □ tap out □ What's on tap for today?

TAPER
taper off

TARGET
on target

TASTE
in bad taste □ leave a bad taste in someone's mouth □ There's no accounting for taste.

TAT
give someone tit for tat

TEA
not someone's cup of tea

TEACH
That'll teach someone! □ You can't teach an old dog new tricks.

TEACHER
be the teacher's pet

TEAM
team up (with someone) □ team up against someone or something

TEAPOT
tempest in a teapot

TEAR
blink back one's tears □ break (out) into tears □ shed crocodile tears □ tear (oneself) away (from someone or something) □ tear away (from someone or something) □ tear down something □ tear off (from someone or something) □ tear one's hair □ tear out (of some place) □ tear someone or something down □ tear someone or something up □ tear something away (from someone or something) □ tear something off ((of) someone or something) □ tear something out (of something) □ That tears it!

TEE
tee someone off

TEETH
(as) scarce as hens' teeth □ armed to the teeth □ by the skin of one's teeth □ get one's teeth into something □ grit one's teeth □ lie through one's teeth □ no skin off someone's teeth □ pull someone's or something's teeth □ set someone's teeth on edge □ sink one's teeth into something

TELL
(There's) no way to tell. □ a little bird told me □ Could I tell someone who's calling? □ Do tell. □ Don't tell a soul. □ Don't tell me what to do! □ How many times do I have to tell you? □ if I've told you once, I've told you a thousand times □ Tell me

another (one)! □ tell one to one's face □ tell someone where to get off □ tell tales out of school □ What can I tell you? □ You're telling me!

TEMPER
lose one's temper

TEMPEST
tempest in a teapot

TENSE
tense up (for something)

TEST
put someone to the test □ test out (of something) □ test something out

THAN
(It's) better than nothing. □ Actions speak louder than words. □ Better late than never. □ bite off more than one can chew □ Half a loaf is better than none. □ have eyes bigger than one's stomach □ in less than no time □ more than you('ll ever) know □ No more than I have to. □ One's bark is worse than one's bite. □ one's eyes are bigger than one's stomach □ Sooner than you think. □ There's more than one way to skin a cat. □ wear more than one hat

THANK
(I) can't thank you enough. □ I'll thank you to keep your opinions to yourself. □ I'll thank you to mind your own business. □ no thanks to you □ No, thank you. □ Not right now, thanks. □ Nothing for me, thanks. □ Thank goodness! □ thank one's lucky stars □ Thank you for a lovely evening. □ Thank you for a lovely time. □ Thank you for calling. □ Thank you for inviting me. □ Thank you very much. □ Thank you. □ Thanks (a lot). □ Thanks a million. □ Thanks awfully. □ Thanks

for the ride. □ Thanks loads. □ Thanks, but no thanks.

THAW
thaw out □ thaw someone or something out

THICK
(as) thick as pea soup □ (as) thick as thieves □ get something through someone's thick skull □ lay it on thick □ through thick and thin

THIEF
(as) thick as thieves

THIN
on thin ice □ out of thin air □ skate on thin ice □ spread oneself too thin □ thin down □ thin out □ thin something out □ through thick and thin □ vanish into thin air

THING
(Are) things getting you down? □ (I've) (got) better things to do. □ (I) never heard of such a thing. □ (Things) could be better. □ (Things) could be worse. □ A little knowledge is a dangerous thing. □ amount to the same thing (as something) □ Don't worry about a thing. □ first thing (in the morning) □ first things first □ get into the swing of things □ How're things (with you)? □ How're things going? □ How's every little thing? □ I have to wash a few things out. □ narrow something down (to people or things) □ Sure thing. □ Things will work out (all right).

THINK
(I'm) (just) thinking out loud. □ (I) never thought I'd see you here! □ come to think of it □ Don't even think about (doing) it. □ Don't even think about it (happening). □ How dumb do you think I am? □

put on one's thinking cap □ Sooner than you think. □ think back (on someone or something) □ think back (to something) □ Think nothing of it. □ think on one's feet □ think something out □ think something over □ think something through □ think something up □ What do you think of that? □ What do you think of this weather? □ What do you think you are doing here? □ What do you think? □ What makes you think so? □ Who do you think you are? □ Who do you think you're kidding? □ Who do you think you're talking to? □ who would have thought? □ You've got another think coming.

THORN
be a thorn in someone's side

THOUGHT
(I) never thought I'd see you here! □ food for thought □ get second thoughts about someone or something □ lose one's train of thought □ lost in thought □ on second thought □ Perish the thought. □ who would have thought?

THOUSAND
if I've told you once, I've told you a thousand times □ No, no, a thousand times no! □ Not in a thousand years! □ one in a thousand

THRASH
thrash something out

THREE
like a three-ring circus

THROAT
cut one's (own) throat □ get a lump in one's throat □ have one's words stick in one's throat □ one's words stick in one's throat

THRONG

throng in(to something) □ throng out (of something)

THROW

a stone's throw away □ throw a map □ throw a monkey wrench in the works □ throw caution to the wind □ throw down the gauntlet □ throw good money after bad □ throw in the towel □ throw one's toenails up □ throw one's voice □ throw oneself at someone's feet □ throw oneself on the mercy of the court □ throw someone a curve □ throw someone for a loop □ throw someone over (for someone else) □ throw someone to the wolves □ throw something back □ throw something into the bargain □ throw something off □ throw something together □ throw something up □ throw up

THRUST

thrust out □ thrust someone or something back

THUMB

all thumbs □ have a green thumb □ thumb a ride □ thumb one's nose at someone or something □ twiddle one's thumbs

THUNDER

steal someone's thunder

TICK

(as) full as a tick □ make someone or something tick □ ticked (off) □ what makes someone tick

TICKET

That's the ticket! □ vote a straight ticket

TICKLE

tickle someone's fancy

TIDE

swim against the tide □ tide someone over (until something) □ turn the tide

TIDY

tidy something up □ tidy up

TIE

have one's hands tied □ tie in (with someone or something) □ tie in(to something) □ tie someone down (to someone or something) □ tie someone in knots □ tie someone or something down □ tie someone or something in(to something) □ tie someone or something up □ tie someone's hands □ tie something back □ tie something off □ tie something up □ tie the knot □ tied to one's mother's apron strings □ with one hand tied behind one's back

TIGHT

(as) tight as Dick's hatband □ in a (tight) spot □ run a tight ship □ sit tight

TIGHTEN

tighten one's belt □ tighten something up □ tighten up

TIGHTROPE

walk a tightrope

TILL

have one's hand in the till

TILT

tilt at windmills

TIME

(I'll) try to catch you some other time. □ (I'm) having a wonderful time; wish you were here. □ (I'm) having the time of my life. □ (I) had a nice time. □ (I) haven't seen you in a long time. □ (It's) time for a change. □ (It's) time to go. □ (It's) time to hit the road. □ (It's) time to run. □ (My,) how time flies. □ at the present time □ Better luck next time. □ Don't waste my time. □ Don't waste your time. □ get time to catch one's breath □ hardly have time to breathe □ Have a good time. □ have the time of one's life □ How many times do I have to tell you? □ I don't have time to catch my breath. □ I had a lovely time. □ I'm having quite a time □ I've had a lovely time. □ if I've told you once, I've told you a thousand times □ in due time □ in less than no time □ in one's spare time □ in the interest of saving time □ in the nick of time □ It's time we should be going. □ Long time no see. □ make up for lost time □ Maybe some other time. □ No, no, a thousand times no! □ run out of time □ Thank you for a lovely time. □ Time hangs heavy on someone's hands. □ time in □ Time is money. □ time out □ time someone in □ time someone out □ Time to call it a day. □ Time to call it a night. □ time to cruise □ Times are changing. □ when the time is ripe □ You're (just) wasting my time.

TINKER
tinker (around) (with something)

TIP
have something at one's fingertips □ on the tip of one's tongue □ tip someone off (about someone or something) □ tip something over □ tip the scales at something

TIPTOE
on tiptoe

TIRE
tire out □ tire someone out

TIT
give someone tit for tat

TODAY
What's on tap for today?

TOE
on one's toes □ step on someone's toes □ toe the mark □ turn up one's toes

TOENAIL
throw one's toenails up

TOGETHER
band together (against someone or something) □ Birds of a feather flock together. □ crowd together □ draw people together □ flock together □ hang together □ have it all together □ huddle (up) (together) □ Let's get together (sometime). □ mesh together □ patch something together (with something) □ piece something together □ put two and two together □ room together □ slap something together □ stick together □ throw something together □ toss something together

TOKEN
by the same token

TOMORROW
(I'll) see you tomorrow.

TON
hit (someone) like a ton of bricks

TONE
tone something down

TONG
fight someone or something hammer and tongs

TONGUE
bite one's tongue □ Bite your tongue! □ cause (some) tongues to wag □ hold one's tongue □ Hold your tongue! □ on the tip of one's tongue □ slip of the tongue □ tongue-in-cheek □ Watch your tongue!

TOODLE

Toodle-oo.

TOOL

tool around □ tool something up □ tool up

TOOT

toot one's own horn □ You're dern tootin'!

TOOTH

(as) scarce as hens' teeth □ An eye for an eye, a tooth for a tooth. □ armed to the teeth □ by the skin of one's teeth □ get one's teeth into something □ go over something with a fine-tooth comb □ grit one's teeth □ have a sweet tooth □ lie through one's teeth □ no skin off someone's teeth □ pull someone's or something's teeth □ set someone's teeth on edge □ sink one's teeth into something

TOP

(right) off the top of one's head □ at the top of one's voice □ from top to bottom □ off the top of one's head □ on top □ on top of the world □ over the top □ top something off (with something)

TOPPLE

topple over

TORCH

carry a torch (for someone) □ carry the torch

TOSS

toss one's cookies □ toss one's hat into the ring □ toss something off □ toss something together

TOTAL

total something up

TOTEM

high man on the totem pole □ low man on the totem pole

TOUCH

touch (up)on something □ touch down □ touch someone or something off □ touch something up

TOUGH

tough act to follow □ tough row to hoe □ tough something out

TOUGHEN

toughen someone or something up □ toughen up

TOUT

Tout suite!

TOW

tow someone or something away □ tow someone or something in(to something) □ tow someone or something out (of some place)

TOWEL

throw in the towel

TOWER

live in an ivory tower

TOWN

go to town □ I'll look you up when I'm in town. □ Look me up when you're in town. □ out on the town □ paint the town red

TRACK

drop in one's tracks □ get the inside track □ jump the track □ on the wrong track □ other side of the tracks □ track someone or something down □ track something in(to some place) □ track something up

TRADE

trade something in (for something) □ trade something off

TRAIN

lose one's train of thought □ ride the gravy train

TREAT

get the red-carpet treatment □ give

out ☐ turn someone's stomach ☐ turn something on ☐ turn something to one's advantage ☐ turn the other cheek ☐ turn the tide ☐ turn to ☐ turn turtle ☐ turn up ☐ turn up (somewhere) ☐ turn up one's toes ☐ Whatever turns you on.

TURTLE
turn turtle

TWIDDLE
twiddle one's thumbs

TWINKLE
in the twinkling of an eye

TWIST
twist someone around one's little finger ☐ twist someone's arm

TWIT
in a twit

TWO
A bird in the hand is worth two in the bush. ☐ get two strikes against one ☐ in two shakes of a lamb's tail ☐ Make it two. ☐ put in one's two cents (worth) ☐ put two and two together ☐ stand on one's own two feet

TYPE
type something up

UNDERSTAND
I don't understand (it).

UNITE
unite against someone or something ☐ unite someone against someone or something

UNSAID
better left unsaid

UNSEEN
buy something sight unseen

UNTIMELY
come to an untimely end

UNTO
law unto oneself

UNTURNED
leave no stone unturned

UPGRADE
upgrade someone or something to something

UPPER
get the upper hand (on someone)

UPROAR
Don't get your bowels in an uproar!

UPSET
upset the apple cart

UPTAKE
quick on the uptake

USE
Could I use your powder room? ☐ use every trick in the book ☐ use something up ☐ Use your head!

USHER
usher someone or something in(to some place) ☐ usher someone or something out (of some place)

VACATION
on vacation

VACUUM
vacuum something up (from something)

VALUE
take something at face value

VANISH
vanish into thin air

VARIETY
Variety is the spice of life.

VEG
veg (out)

VENTURE
Nothing ventured, nothing gained.

VERDICT
bring a verdict in

from someone or something □ warn someone off

WARRANT
sign one's own death warrant

WASH
come out in the wash □ I have to wash a few things out. □ wash away □ wash off ((of) someone or something) □ wash one's hands of someone or something □ wash someone or something away □ wash someone or something off □ wash something off ((of) someone or something) □ Where can I wash up?

WASTE
Don't waste my time. □ Don't waste your breath. □ Don't waste your time. □ Haste makes waste. □ lay something to waste □ waste one's breath □ You're (just) wasting my time.

WATCH
(You) (just) watch! □ A watched pot never boils. □ bear watching □ Watch it! □ watch out (for someone or something) □ Watch your tongue!

WATER
as a duck takes to water □ get one's head above water □ in deep water □ like a fish out of water □ like water off a duck's back □ make someone's mouth water □ not hold water □ of the first water □ pour cold water on something □ pour oil on troubled water □ Still waters run deep. □ water under the bridge

WAVE
make waves

WAX
whole ball of wax

WAY
(Are you) going my way? □ (That's the) way to go! □ (There's) no way to tell. □ Anything new down your way? □ argue one's way out (of something) □ buy one's way out (of something) □ by the way □ Clear the way! □ elbow (one's way) through something □ fight (one's way) back to something □ fight (one's way) through something □ fight one's way out of something □ find one's or something's way somewhere □ get something under way □ Have it your way. □ have the right-of-way □ look the other way □ No way! □ No way, José! □ one way or another □ rub someone's fur the wrong way □ That ain't the way I heard it. □ That's the way it goes. □ That's the way the cookie crumbles. □ the way it plays □ There's more than one way to skin a cat. □ to put it another way □ Where there's a will there's a way.

WAYSIDE
drop by the wayside

WEAK
(as) weak as a kitten □ have a weakness for someone or something

WEALTH
Early to bed, early to rise(, makes a man healthy, wealthy, and wise).

WEAR
Don't let the bastards wear you down. □ I don't want to wear out my welcome. □ If the shoe fits, wear it. □ none the worse for wear □ wear (up)on someone □ wear more than one hat □ wear off □ wear out □ wear out one's welcome □ wear someone or something down □ wear someone or something out

WEATHER

(I've) been under the weather. □ fair-weather friend □ How do you like this weather? □ lovely weather for ducks □ Nice weather we're having. □ under the weather □ What do you think of this weather?

WEEP

Finders keepers(, losers weepers).

WEIGHT

carry the weight of the world on one's shoulders □ carry weight (with someone) □ worth its weight in gold

WEIRD

weird out

WELCOME

I don't want to wear out my welcome. □ wear out one's welcome □ Welcome to our house. □ Welcome. □ You're welcome.

WELL

(Well,) I never! □ (Well,) what do you know! □ All's well that ends well. □ hail-fellow-well-met □ might as well □ Well done! □ Well said. □ well-heeled □ well-to-do

WET

(as) mad as a wet hen □ all wet □ get one's feet wet □ wet behind the ears

WHATEVER

Whatever turns you on.

WHEEL

put one's shoulder to the wheel

WHEN

Come back when you can stay longer. □ cross a bridge when one comes to it □ I'll look you up when I'm in town. □ Look me up when you're in town. □ Say when. □ Since when? □ Smile when you say that. □ Some people (just) don't know when to quit. □ When do we eat? □ when I'm good and ready □ When in Rome, do as the Romans do. □ When the cat's away the mice will play. □ when the time is ripe □ when you get a minute

WHILE

(I'll) see you in a little while. □ After while(, crocodile). □ Make hay while the sun is shining. □ strike while the iron is hot

WHISTLE

blow the whistle (on someone)

WHITE

(as) white as the driven snow □ in black and white □ talk on the big white phone

WHOLE

make something up out of whole cloth □ whole ball of wax

WHOM

With whom do you wish to speak?

WHY

why don't you? □ Why not?

WIDE

give someone or something a wide berth □ wide of the mark

WIFE

How's the wife?

WILCO

Roger (wilco).

WILD

sow one's wild oats □ wild-goose chase

WILDFIRE

spread like wildfire

WIMP

wimp out (of something)

WIN

(You) can't win them all. □ Slow and steady wins the race. □ Win a few, lose a few. □ win by a nose □ win someone over (to something)

WIND

get one's second wind □ get wind of something □ in the wind □ throw caution to the wind □ wind down □ wind something on(to something) □ wind something up □ wind up (by) doing something

WINDMILLS

tilt at windmills

WING

clip someone's wings □ take someone under one's wing(s) □ try one's wings (out) □ wing it

WINK

(as) quick as a wink □ not sleep a wink □ take forty winks

WIPE

wipe someone or something off □ wipe something off ((of) someone or something) □ wipe something up

WIRE

down to the wire □ Hold the wire(, please). □ under the wire □ wired into someone or something

WISE

(as) wise as an owl □ Early to bed, early to rise(, makes a man healthy, wealthy, and wise). □ penny-wise and pound-foolish

WISH

(Don't) you wish! □ (I'm) having a wonderful time; wish you were here. □ I wish I'd said that. □ With whom do you wish to speak?

WIT

at one's wit's end □ live by one's wits

WITHER

wither on the vine

WOLF

cry wolf □ throw someone to the wolves □ wolf in sheep's clothing

WONDER

(I was) just wondering. □ (I'm) having a wonderful time; wish you were here. □ (I) wonder if

WOODS

babe in the woods □ out of the woods

WOOL

pull the wool over someone's eyes

WORD

(I) won't breathe a word (of it). □ (You) took the words right out of my mouth. □ Actions speak louder than words. □ by word of mouth □ Don't breathe a word of this to anyone. □ eat one's words □ from the word go □ get a word in edgewise □ get the last word □ get the word □ go back on one's word □ hang on someone's every word □ have one's words stick in one's throat □ I'd like (to have) a word with you. □ in other words □ one final word □ one's words stick in one's throat □ or words to that effect □ put in a good word (for someone) □ put words into someone's mouth □ Take my word for it. □ take the words out of one's mouth □ The word is mum. □ true to one's word □ What's the good word?

WORK

(as) regular as clockwork □ (It) works for me. □ all in a day's work □ All work and no play makes Jack a dull boy. □ Does it work for you? □ Don't work too hard. □ get down to work □ get worked up (over someone or something) □ go like clockwork □ I've got work to do. □ make short work of someone or something ☐ Things will work out (all right). ☐ throw a monkey wrench in the works ☐ work (up)on something ☐ work away (at something) ☐ work like a horse ☐ work on someone ☐ work one's fingers to the bone ☐ work out ☐ work out for the best ☐ work something in(to something) ☐ work something off ☐ work something up ☐ work up to something

WORLD
carry the weight of the world on one's shoulders ☐ come down in the world ☐ come up in the world ☐ dead to the world ☐ How's the world (been) treating you? ☐ in a world of one's own ☐ move up (in the world) ☐ not long for this world ☐ on top of the world ☐ out of this world ☐ set the world on fire

WORM
open a can of worms ☐ The early bird gets the worm.

WORRY
Don't worry about a thing. ☐ Don't worry. ☐ Not to worry.

WORSE
(I've) seen worse. ☐ (Things) could be worse. ☐ none the worse for wear ☐ One's bark is worse than one's bite.

WORSHIP
worship the porcelain god

WORST
if worst comes to worst

WORTH
A bird in the hand is worth two in the bush. ☐ An ounce of prevention is worth a pound of cure. ☐ for what it's worth ☐ It isn't worth it. ☐ It isn't worth the trouble. ☐ put in

one's two cents (worth) ☐ worth its weight in gold ☐ worth one's salt

WRAP
wrap something up

WRENCH
throw a monkey wrench in the works

WRINGER
put someone through the wringer

WRITE
Remember to write. ☐ write away ☐ write away for something ☐ write off (to someone) (for something) ☐ write someone in (on something) ☐ write someone or something off (as a something) ☐ write someone or something up ☐ write something back to someone ☐ write something down ☐ write something in(to something) ☐ write something off (on something) ☐ write something out

WRITING
see the (hand)writing on the wall

WRONG
bark up the wrong tree ☐ get up on the wrong side of the bed ☐ in the wrong ☐ on the wrong track ☐ rub someone's fur the wrong way ☐ What's wrong?

X
X marks the spot ☐ x someone or something out

YA
See ya! ☐ See ya, bye-bye.

YANK
yank someone around ☐ yank someone's chain

YEAR
(I'll) see you next year. ☐ Not in a

thousand years! □ ring in the New Year □ year in, year out

YELL
yell out

YES
Yes siree(, Bob)!

YESTERDAY
I need it yesterday. □ not born yesterday □ Yesterday wouldn't be too soon.

YET
You ain't seen nothing yet! □ You'll be the death of me (yet).

YIELD
yield something to someone

ZERO
zero in (on someone or something)

ZIP
Zip (up) your lip! □ zip something up

ZONK
zonk out □ zonked (out)

ZOOM
zoom in (on someone or something) □ zoom off □ zoom through (something) □ zoom up

NTC'S LANGUAGE DICTIONARIES

The Best, By Definition

Spanish/English
Vox New College (Thumb-index & Plain-edge)
Vox Modern
Vox Compact
Vox Everyday
Vox Traveler's
Vox Super-Mini
Cervantes-Walls

Spanish/Spanish
Diccionario Básico Norteamericano
Vox Diccionario Escolar de la lengua española
El Diccionario del español chicano

French/English
NTC's New College French and English
NTC's Dictionary of *Faux Amis*
NTC's Dictionary of Canadian French

German/English
Schöffler-Weis
Klett's Modern (New Edition)
Klett's Super-Mini
NTC's Dictionary of German False Cognates

Italian/English
Zanichelli New College Italian and English
Zanichelli Super-Mini

Greek/English
NTC's New College Greek and English

Chinese/English
Easy Chinese Phrasebook and Dictionary

For Juveniles
Let's Learn English Picture Dictionary
Let's Learn French Picture Dictionary
Let's Learn German Picture Dictionary
Let's Learn Italian Picture Dictionary
Let's Learn Spanish Picture Dictionary
English Picture Dictionary
French Picture Dictionary
German Picture Dictionary
Spanish Picture Dictionary

English for Nonnative Speakers
Everyday American English Dictionary
Beginner's Dictionary of American English Usage

Electronic Dictionaries
Languages of the World on CD-ROM
NTC's Dictionary of American Idioms, Slang, and
Colloquial Expressions (Electronic Book)

Other Reference Books
Robin Hyman's Dictionary of Quotations
British/American Language Dictionary
NTC's American Idioms Dictionary
NTC's Dictionary of American Slang and
Colloquial Expressions
Forbidden American English
Essential American Idioms
Contemporary American Slang
NTC's Dictionary of Grammar Terminology
Complete Multilingual Dictionary of Computer
Terminology
Complete Multilingual Dictionary of Aviation &
Aeronautical Terminology
Complete Multilingual Dictionary of Advertising,
Marketing & Communications
NTC's Dictionary of American Spelling
NTC's Classical Dictionary
NTC's Dictionary of Debate
NTC's Mass Media Dictionary
NTC's Dictionary of Word Origins
NTC's Dictionary of Literary Terms
Dictionary of Trade Name Origins
Dictionary of Advertising
Dictionary of Broadcast Communications
Dictionary of Changes in Meaning
Dictionary of Confusing Words and Meanings
NTC's Dictionary of English Idioms
NTC's Dictionary of Proverbs and Clichés
Dictionary of Acronyms and Abbreviations
NTC's Dictionary of American English
Pronunciation
NTC's Dictionary of Phrasal Verbs and Other
Idiomatic Verbal Phrases
Common American Phrases

Polish/English
The Wiedza Powszechna Compact Polish and
English Dictionary

For further information or a current catalog, write:
National Textbook Company
a division of *NTC Publishing Group*
4255 West Touhy Avenue
Lincolnwood, Illinois 60646-1975 U.S.A.